A NEW WORLD

A New World

An Epic of Colonial America

from the Founding of Jamestown

to the Fall of Quebec

Arthur Quinn

Faber and Faber

BOSTON • LONDON

Library of Congress Cataloging-in-Publication Data

Quinn, Arthur.
    A new world : an epic of colonial America from the founding of Jamestown to the fall of Quebec / by Arthur Quinn.
      p. cm.
    ISBN 0-571-19837-6 (cloth)
    1. United States—History—Colonial period, ca. 1600–1775.
    2. Canada—History—To 1763 (New France)   I. Title.
    E188.Q56   1994
    973.2—dc20   93–46455
                                                               CIP

Jacket design by Paul Perlow
Printed in the United States of America

Perhaps someday looking back upon
even this will be joyous.
                              —Virgil

Contents

PREFACE

L ONGFELLOW, IT HAS BEEN SAID by way of dismissal, could not look at the world except through the windows of literature; he did not create poetry so much as compose it.

I do not know if this is a legitimate characterization of Longfellow's poetry, but I do think it would be a fair analysis of the prose that comprises this narrative. It is, by intention, not so much an original creation as an allusive compendium of older eloquence. This may seem a fundamental limitation, but it is one that I have embraced from the beginning.

I started this project intending only to work up a few episodes from colonial American history that, taken together, might evoke the whole. My plan was to tell each episode from the perspective of the contemporary writer who seemed most appropriate—Champlain as a character out of Corneille, for instance. I intended this to constitute an implicit critique of the Romantic interpretation of history that sees the past as culminating in the present.

The chief problem I had initially in the actual writing was not so much with this technique as with my ambition to evoke the whole. I kept doing more and more episodes until I realized that I needed an overarching literary model or myth, a Zeus to smooth out the differences among the squabbling local deities. Virgil's *Aeneid* seemed the obvious choice, since this was the great civilized epic for the period about which I was writing, the epic in terms of which educated Europeans of the seventeenth and eighteenth centuries would have understood and measured their own achievements. John Dryden's translation of Virgil, itself made at almost the exact middle of my period, constituted an ideal guide to how they would have understood him.

Of course, my use of Virgil would reflect not just their understanding of him but also my own. Early modern readers tended to take the *Aeneid* as a cel-

ebration of the Roman Empire as the greatest historical achievement of the
human race. Twentieth-century interpreters and translators of Virgil, at least
those I find most persuasive, have not so much disputed this as given it a pessimistic twist.

Virgil did see Rome as the greatest achievement of the human spirit, but
also as one that he could not morally justify. It was a Pyrrhic victory for the
human spirit. So his great Latin epic begins with Virgil celebrating Aeneas's
founding of Rome but ends abruptly with Aeneas's gratuitous killing of a
prostrate enemy. Aeneas plants his colony in Italy and plants his sword in
Turnus—and Virgil uses the same verb, *condere*, to indicate both actions. The
good and the evil of history seem inseparable to him.

So Virgil will rewrite passages or even episodes from Homer to reflect his
own ambivalent attitude toward Rome's achievement. Readers have long been
amazed at how a few changes introduced by Virgil could transform Homeric
brightness into Virgilian twilight. This profoundly effective technique
seemed to suggest incidentally a possible answer to an important question
about my own project that had much troubled me.

What was to be my use of the great nineteenth-century interpreters of the
colonial American experience? I had initially tried to ignore them, although
implicitly my narrative was largely being written against them. Yet the genius
of Parkman, Longfellow, Cooper, and the rest, especially their descriptive
genius, I found irresistible if ultimately unsatisfying. Working on my own
narrative, I kept having passages from their works coming unbidden to my
mind. Virgil, in his own use of Homer as well as other literary predecessors
such as Apollonius, showed me how to incorporate these Romantic giants
while still remaining true to my own task. I would use my predecessors as he
had used his.

If Virgil wrote a secondary epic, then I was writing a tertiary or worse. The
composing process as a result became for me primarily an exercise in literary
counterpoint, with the contemporary writers vying for control against the
universalizing voice of Virgil. Yet at times the nineteenth-century writers
would offer an equally strong, if not quite as consistent, perspective on the
events.

In the end my narrative became, at least in aspiration, a true polyphony.
To reach this understanding of my project was a very long struggle—yet, in
retrospect, the difficulty of it seems silly to me, since I was predisposed to just
such an approach to writing by my admiration for Czeslaw Milosz. As
Dostoevsky developed polyphony in the novel, Milosz, among others, has for
poetry—and I, I guess, have ended up trying to do the same within history.

(Perhaps it is significant that the closest precedent I can find for my work within historical writing itself is a poet's essay on early America, William Carlos Williams's "In the American Grain.")

Henry Adams once wrote a telling letter to the scholar Henry Osborne Taylor in which he tried to distinguish what he was doing with history from what scholars like Taylor tried to do. Adams said that to him accuracy was a relatively secondary concern; his primary concern was that his ensemble be in scale. When I started this project more than a decade ago, that was all I hoped for it. Now it is finished. And, although still hoping that it is in scale, I also feel inclined to invoke the concluding lines of Milosz's "Ars Poetica?".

There he describes how difficult it is for a writer to remain just one person; his mind is like a house without locks on its doors, a house where "invisible guests come in and out at will." Writers aware of this are left "only with the hope/that good spirits, not evil ones, choose us for their instruments."

Chapter I

SMITH'S VIRGINIA

I WRITE OF PEOPLES and of a struggle. Of peoples whose fate or relentless longings made them exiles from their homelands and drove them to North American shores. And of a struggle, their struggle to make a new life for themselves here, here of themselves to make a new people. This struggle compelled them and their leaders to endure many crises and trials, at times with a courage and steadfastness that all but defies our belief. And compelled them too, or so they thought, to dispossess the native peoples they found already here, and then to fight amongst themselves over the spoils.

Did they think rightly? Does history require such viciousness for so noble an end? If so, then the forces that govern it are perverse. And the free and prosperous American republic that would eventually emerge from this tumultuous process of colonization was itself little more than a Pyrrhic victory for the human spirit. And we, we might well ask with the prophets of old, where can the righteous rest, for the earth lies under evil?

Of course, questions such as these are beyond the ken of history as we now conceive it. To ask them with the hope of an answer, I should be a singer of tales who can invoke Clio, muse of history, daughter of Divine Memory, guardian angel of the backward look, to inspire me and thereby to help preserve me from cynicism and despair and indifference. But we have treated this sacred spirit of history so long as a consoling fiction, an invigorating delusion, that she has now abandoned us altogether. So I cannot sing, and must seek merely human help.

And I find myself turning to pious Virgil, Virgil who sang of the mythic origins of his own republic, Virgil who himself fought against hopeless sadness and intolerable disgust to celebrate the empire that was at once the fruit and death of that republic, Virgil who sought the meaning of history amidst the slavery and innocent blood of ancient Rome, Virgil who died his task uncompleted, Virgil who as he died bid his wondrous work be committed to the flames.

To this Virgil I turn for help. He can guide us, if anyone can, through the mythic, wilderness time of American history. He can guide us as he once guided Dante through a more daunting course. Virgil, Dante's master, mother, and muse.

As we try to navigate our way through the now dim colonial past wondering whether it is an earthly inferno or purgatorio we are witnessing (it is certainly no paradiso), Virgil must help us attend to these shades from time gone, some demanding our attention, some reluctant to have it, some long thwarted into abject silence (their voices now faint as if hoarse from lack of use), yet all there somehow, geniuses of a certain time and a certain place, and all strangely requiring only a little of our own blood to return to fleeting life, to speak to and through us. For they do wait for us, you know, not as the faint spoor of long-vanished existences, but as real persons, real yet speechless until some questioning voice dissolves the spell of their silence.

In those precious moments their fleeting lives and ours will become one. And if they should by chance pause in telling us of their times to ask of ours, what do we say? So prodigiously far have the changes in the land they began progressed, telling would not be enough; we would have to show them, if we could. But what? Should we proudly show them the grand monuments of Washington, hoping they would not notice the squalid slums adjacent? Or perhaps in whimsy we should show them descendants of Iroquois braves working the high steel of Manhattan skyscrapers. More likely, we should just let them take in the nightscape of a great city near where once they had been engaged in a close struggle for mere subsistence. But, of course, they would no longer recognize the place. And, if we stubbornly insisted they look carefully at the dark contours of the coast to see a familiar outline at least, they would probably still insist that this was an earth, but not theirs; somewhat like theirs, but not theirs. And we can imagine them then turning their eyes to the sky, to see if there was a new heaven to go with this new earth. Only then to explain to us that the stars over their earth were much brighter, a veritable canopy of light.

No, let us not waste our time with futile gestures. If they should ask, we will show them nothing (it is a kindness), saying only that the earth has changed much, and the sky not at all. They will understand that, and it is enough. They knew as well as we do the humbling, almost oppressive beauty of the night sky. And they knew better than we do how to ponder this beauty beyond our earth.

Compared to human beings, the stars have been given permanence. They seem to float forever in the quiet fullness of their unconscious life and know not age, while we despite ourselves fragment their great joyous harmonies into multiple melodies, a jarring cacophony of desire. We unquiet hearts who live under the moon are forced to seek perfection in mutability, in the very instability of human things, the instability that pious Virgil equates with tears.

The earth has changed much, the sky not at all, and we live under the moon. Would that all the conflicting voices crying out to us from the past could constellate themselves into wholes to be contemplated in peace, into epochs of perfect stillness living beyond time, beyond words, when all is joyously understood. Come then, Virgil, and help us as we begin our narrative journey. For we begin it as you began yours so long ago—with a great fleet and a providential storm.

✛

The year to end all years would be 1588. So had predicted the necromancer Regiomontanus who could read the future like an open scroll. That year would unleash the primordial forces of chaos that at the beginning of time God had imprisoned when He had separated the dry land from the deep, had shaped the heavens with a firmament, had unmixed the daylight from the darkness He called night. The chains that ordered creation would be removed. The heavenly firmament would be rent, the sun darkened with spots; the earth would be uprooted from its foundations and then would dissolve into the air. And as all the world that humans knew and cherished was being hurried into the cosmic abyss, there would be blood on the moon.

All this would begin in the year 1588. Or so Regiomontanus and others after him had predicted. These were firm decrees of fate that no human counsels could change or delay. It would all begin in 1588 and take an aeon to complete. Regiomontanus wrote that we would know it was all beginning when we observed disruptions in the heavens, and on earth empires topsy turvy hurled.

As 1588 approached, a blazing star suddenly appeared in the sky, so large it could withstand the sun in the day and bring to the night an unwholesome radiance. There it stayed for months, brandishing what looked to some like crystal tresses. Even in ordinary times such a comet would have been taken as a portent of kingly deaths that would soon be mourned in black and blood.

Then, in 1588 itself, there was an eclipse of the sun, soon followed by two of the moon. Those who had initially scoffed at Regiomontanus as a pagan were now reminded of Jesus' apocalyptic words, "And there shall be signs in the sun and in the moon and in the stars; and on earth trouble among nations, with perplexity." And then in July of 1588, the invincible Armada sailed from Spain for England.

The Spanish monarch, Philip the Prudent, believed that the chaos had already been unleashed upon the human world long before 1588. First the Italians had revived paganism and made man the measure of all things. Then Germans had made the individual the measure of religion, and rejected both tradition and hierarchy. The infections of the Renaissance and Reformation, as they had spread throughout Europe, had striven to subvert all the foundations of human order, had sought to engender an earthly chaos in which Satan himself could exult.

This was a spiritual not a physical chaos. Men were no longer seeking the true God, the Lord of History and the Creator and Sustainer of the World. They were no longer interested in the God to whom the universe gives its unending hymn of praise, as the heavens, the planets, the earth itself observe priority and place. These rebellious men disdained to add their own voices through Holy Mother the Church.

Rather they were turning to the empty, inner regions of their own human pride. Self-consciousness, the fool says, is the native realm of truth; and in that idolatrous kingdom he thinks we will be at home. But the effect is to lose the true center of our existence; and so we can see all about us human life breaking asunder into innumerable fragments, as if it were recoiling from itself. In the end we are each alone, our own identity fragmenting within, a succession of passing moods.

How can such rootless individuals perceive the infinite, transcendent ground of all existence? Ask them of Being, and they will talk of universal dissolution, of the flux of all that has been. Being itself had become for them a fluent substance of pure motion, an enduring negation, a dark void.

Yet Providence itself was equal to this pitiful human challenge. The day was at hand for us to lay aside the works of darkness and put on the armor of light. And Spain had been chosen to be the instrument of restoration, and Philip the Prudent its architect.

The Old Spider of the Escorial really thought he could encompass the whole of Western Europe in a vast medieval web, to begin a holy age of suspended animation.

And why should he not have? He already controlled more of the earth's surface than had any other ruler in history. Spain had long since been unified under his line, and Portugal had recently been bloodlessly added. In Italy he controlled the two Kingdoms of Sicily, the Duchy of Milan, and various Tuscan strongholds. He had recently broken Turkish naval power at the battle of Lepanto, and had added the Barbary coast to his list of kingdoms. The commercial center of Europe, the Netherlands, was mostly his. With Portugal he had gained its slaving colonies on the coast of Africa as well as its outposts in the Indian subcontinent. Spanish power was also being felt throughout the archipelagoes and coastlines of Asia, where the Philippines had recently been named in his honor. Proud Romans used to boast that the Mediterranean was their private lake; the private lake of the new Spanish Empire was the Pacific Ocean. The western side of that lake provided much of the gold and silver out of which Philip would spin his web. Spain already had transformed Mexico and Peru and Brazil and the larger Caribbean islands; it was now probing into Florida, Texas, and lower California. This was the first empire the world had ever known on which the sun could literally never set; and it was still growing. As the great nineteenth-century American historian John Lothrop Motley put it, "The Papuan islander, the Calabrian peasant, the Amsterdam merchant, the semi-civilized Aztec, the Moor of Barbary, the Castillian grandee, the roving Comanche, the Guinea negro, the Indian Brahmin, found themselves— could they but have known it—fellow citizens of one commonwealth."

They might not have known it, but Philip most assuredly did. Compared to his, the Roman Empire had been a paltry thing. And Philip endeavored to control it all with his pen; he would rule the world with a sheaf of papers. His care for detail was legendary; no less a scholar than Leopold von Ranke said Philip knew more about the Europe of his day than any scholar of later days ever would. His loyal subjects were not always pleased by this. One pleaded, "God did not send your Majesty and all the other kings, his viceroys on earth, to waste their time in reading or writing, nor yet in meditation and prayer." But he was wrong. The world could be ruled by pure intelligence.

So each year Spanish fleets from the New World and elsewhere would stuff Philip's treasury with a golden fleece; each year Philip would use it in God's service, to expand and to reunite Christendom; each year Spanish power would increase.

England, the Netherlands, and France—these were the barking dogs that Philip had now to bring to heel. With judicious Spanish help, France had already become a jarring discord of factions, each trying to shoulder the other out of the way, all contributing to ruin and confusion. The Dutch, their leader William the Silent permanently silenced by a Spanish assassin, were now struggling against a Spanish invasion. As for the English, Queen Elizabeth could only harass the Spanish fleet with pirates and provide half-hearted assistance for the Dutch to keep alive a lingering war at little cost and thereby to distract Spanish ambitions.

Philip, however, was not one to be distracted. Elizabeth had already judicially murdered the chief Catholic claimant to her throne, and this had played into Philip's hands. Mary Stuart, before her execution, had named Philip as her legitimate successor. Now those English who regarded Elizabeth as a bastard, heretic, and usurper owed loyalty to the Spanish king as their own. So Philip began to plan what he called "The Enterprise of England."

Philip put the full resources of the Spanish Empire behind the building of a great fleet, a fleet even greater than that which had recently broken Turkish power in the Mediterranean. This new Armada would swamp in its wake all resistance to Spanish hegemony throughout Western Europe.

The Armada, a fleet of 131 ships carrying a force of soldiers and sailors of more than 20,000, would first sail into the English Channel and defeat any naval forces the English could send against it. When in control of the seaways, it would link up with the Spanish forces in Flanders and ferry this army, along with its own, across for the invasion of England. Once England had fallen, the Dutch could not hold out for long. Then would be the moment for the Spanish faction in France to seize power in that wretched country. And then the pax Hispanica could begin, thanks to God's Providence and Philip's prudence.

So the most happy, utterly invincible Armada sailed, the largest fleet ever seen to that day. Its banner was *Exurge domine et vindica causam tuam* (Lord, send and vindicate your cause). After another battle of Lepanto, the Atlantic would become a Spanish lake as the Pacific already was.

Despite Spanish propaganda and English fears, victory was far from assured. The small English ships were faster than the Spanish galleons, and their guns better at long range. The Spanish fleet needed to keep in close order, endure the harassment of English bombardment, and make certain that any decisive naval battle would be fought on Spanish terms—namely, at close quarters. And there was always the inherent uncertainty of the sea itself to be worried over.

A storm on its voyage to the channel reduced the Armada significantly. Nonetheless, the fleet kept its fearsome crescent-shaped formation fully intact during the early encounters with the English fleet. Then, at Gravesline during the night of August 8, 1588, in an enterprise of venturous desperation, the

English fired eight of their own ships and sent them drifting into the anchored Spanish fleet.

These "hellburners," as they were called, broke the Spanish order as the English guns could not. The Spanish cut their cables and ran into the night chaotically before the infernal ships. At dawn the English attacked the disordered Armada, and for the next four days the English ravaged the Spanish ships. The Spaniards fought with valor worthy of crusaders, but to no avail.

All hope of invasion or even naval victory now gone, the remnants of the fleet fled north and circled back along the west coast of Ireland to salvage what they could from their disaster. Whatever our opinion of the merits of their cause, we must pity them now, struggling to preserve themselves, in spent ships and spent bodies, against the sea.

We can pity, but the elements west of Ireland seemed controlled by a deity full of resentment and spite who fed on human woe. The remnant fleet, lifting prayers to heaven against the terror of the winds and waves, now encountered storms as merciless as goaded furies. Soon the sea was tossing liquid mountains against the unhappy wandering train, and ship after swamped ship was being sacrificed on altars of rock.

One of the Spanish survivors, one of the few, left a poignant account of the last moments of many of his comrades in arms. Some Spanish just go down with the ships, screaming out to their God; others cast themselves into the water, immediately to sink out of sight for good; a few bob up and cling to anything floating. Sailors fight over a piece of timber or a few barrel staves; noblemen struggle to throw to the sea their chains with jeweled crucifixes and their pouches full of crown pieces, once-cherished wealth now having become hated encumbrances—and all the while the waves sweep over them, washing away now this one, now that one. On the shore hundreds of wild Irish do a jig of delight at these misfortunes, and then like fiends finish the work of the sea on those whom the surf spares. This last brutality is clearly visible between the waves to those still trying to survive amidst the battered wrecks, and still troubling a deaf heaven with their bootless cries.

Philip, when he learned the full extent of the disaster, is supposed to have said, "I sent my ships to fight against men and not against the winds and waves of God." This pious prince resisted despairing thoughts and refused to bewail his fate. "Even kings," he said, "must submit to being used by God's will without knowing what it is." Perhaps someday, or in the future life, remembering even this would make him glad. For now Philip could only sigh and submit to the unfathomable but ultimately adorable Divine Will.

During the debacle of the Armada, Philip had in one of his prisons a maimed veteran of the battle of Lepanto who had been accused of fiscal malfeasance during the preparations for the Armada. Miguel de Cervantes had used his enforced leisure to begin a mock epic that in its own cruel way remains a commentary on the pretenses of the Armada. In *Don Quixote* Cervantes exposes the irrelevance of heroic ideals in our new world. Anyone who tries to act consistently on these ideals will seem to all a fool and a madman, and in the end will bring only pain and grief to himself and those he tries to help. As time went on, Philip's aspirations would, in their futility, more and more resemble those of the Knight of the Sorrowful Countenance.

Philip did continue to work for the union of western Europe, to tilt against the windmills of growing French, Dutch, and British power. But he would continue to fail, and would reluctantly realize in a few years that his own great empire had already reached its apogee and now was in a slow but irretrievable descent. The finest hour of the Spanish Empire was ending with the sixteenth century.

Philip himself retreated more and more into the incense-shrouded recesses of his monkish palace, the Escorial. There, listening to the daily chants (the Eternal breaking into sound), he could feel aloof from the suspicions, the conjectures, the ignorance and snares that were politics. There wisdom itself seemed not a call to action but a splendid object of pure contemplation.

Christendom was obviously entering a dark and bitter wood, with no golden bough to seek. Its citizens were not to be envied. The lion would stalk them by day, the she-wolf would despoil them by night—and day and night the leopard would crouch over their habitations. In that spiritual wilderness no one—no, not one—shall be spared. Transgressions will multiply, rebellions strengthen, and all the nations of the earth shall drink deeply of immorality until the whole world is aflame with the glint of the red horse. Then will dawn the day of the angel's trumpet and the second death. And on that day the blessed in their glory will have no pity for the eternally damned generations.

As if his failure in life were not enough, Philip in death would become one of the most vilified figures in all world history. Historians of later centuries have outdone even the worst that his enemies and adversaries could say about him. Let John Lothrop Motley speak for the prosecution: "It seems like mere railing to specify his crimes. Their very magnitude and unbroken continuity, together with their impunity, give them almost the appearance of inevitable phenomena. The horrible monotony of his career stupefies the mind until it is ready to accept the principle of evil as the fundamental law of the world."

The principle of evil as the fundamental law of the world. Philip was even charged with crimes which were not his. He did use the *auto-da-fe* as an instrument of rule, but he did not invent it. And there is no evidence that for reasons of state he ordered the murder of his own son. One historian, having followed the normal black legend of Philip as Motley did, realized belatedly that it was unconvincing; no one could be pure evil. So he tried to make his portrait more persuasive by finding some redeeming traits in Philip; he could find but two: his genuine affection for his daughters and his instinctive dislike of the paintings of El Greco.

Yet it is hard to hate so unhappy a man, whose personal life seems to have been a uniform dismalness broken only by an occasional brief period of surpassing gloom. It has been left to the twentieth century to try to recast Philip as one of its own hollow men, a banally competent bureaucrat whose reasonable policies have been misconstrued because of their inadvertent consequences.

This modernist trivialization of Philip, expressive as it is of our own culture, constitutes perhaps the unkindest cut of all. Nonetheless, it fails to explain why Philip held such a fascination for earlier generations of Americans, why his great palace, the Escorial, continually drew American travelers. Here was a monument to what would have killed our new society before it had ever begun its life, aborted it in the womb of Europe—and to what, in some unspeakable way, still haunted that new life and needed to be exorcised from it.

Let us follow one such traveler, John Hay, former private secretary to Abraham Lincoln, who visited the Escorial after his captain was dead but the American republic, that last best hope of mankind, preserved—albeit at a horrific cost.

Who knows why Hay, a dear friend of Henry Adams, was drawn here. Perhaps just to distance himself from a devastated America. Certainly not consciously to confront the ghost of Philip, a ghost that if evoked would certainly have told him that its own worst fears about modernity had been borne out. Hay had come to the Old World to regain his nerve, not to shake it further.

The Escorial, Hay quickly realized, was not the usual opulent palace he expected but a stark monastery, purposely built out of sight of Madrid and its worldly distractions. The first impression was all of sheer size and barrenness. The Escorial was a "stupendous mass of granite," he wrote, "the most cheerless monument in existence." It represented both the stupendous empire and its cheerless king.

Then there was the land around, more cheerless still. This was less a landscape than the corpse of a dead world. It was lashed by glacial gales in the winter, blasted by a vertical sun in the summer, and cursed in all seasons with the curse of barrenness. It was an environment of Lent without Easter, Good Friday without the Resurrection. It was Abraham Lincoln in the darkest nights of his soul that none knew about except Hay and a few others.

Philip had loved this place, preferred it to all others. And Hay in disgust could understand why. Philip, living in a world that was changing all about him, wanted to believe that time could be stopped, or rather that time itself was a passing illusion—that beneath it somehow was a secure center for our existence, a sacred core that we could reach in moments of pure contemplation; time as the moving surface of eternity. Philip, to assure himself of this that his age seemed bent upon denying, wanted to look out on a landscape of uniformity from a fixed, unchanging point. That at least, Hay thought, he had achieved—"the stricken waste, the shaggy horror of the mountains, the fixt plain wrinkled like a frozen sea, and in the center of the picture the vast chill bulk of that granite pile, rising cold, colorless, and stupendous."

This was the sight that strengthened Philip in his sense of his calling, the God-given task to arrest change, to foreclose history, to return Christendom to the regular rhythms of the sacred year, to retrieve for it a sense of Aristotelian wholeness and symmetry, the eternal recurrence of the same, everything moving in its own closed path except the unmoved mover who animates the whole. All this seemed obvious to Philip as he looked out upon the world with his basilisk gaze from his colossal hermitage in the flinty heart of the mountains of Castile. All seemed obvious, until of course the Armada. Or so Hay thought as he himself looked out on the same scene centuries later. And perhaps just for a shuddering moment wondered if a world without history would not be better, as in his mind the images of the thwarted Philip and the dead Lincoln blurred into one.

The defeat of the Armada, of course, took on a completely different aspect when viewed from that sceptered isle, that little world called England. There Divine Providence seemed quite scrutable, at least for the moment. While Philip knelt and bent his head to Dies Irae, Elizabethans could sing madrigals and brightly dance. A victory medal was struck with the inscription *Flavit Jehovah et disipati sunt* (God breathed and they were dispersed).

Shakespeare wrote his own lines of celebration, but he chose to focus them on the dour predictions for 1588:

> The Mortal Moon hath her eclipse endured.
> And the sad Augurs mock their own presage.

The Armada's crescent had proven a mortal moon, and was now fully eclipsed. Yet the prophets of doom did not have to mock themselves; in this, Shakespeare's patriotic exuberance had misled him. The earth may not yet have been driven into the cosmic abyss, but 1588 did mark the beginning of human empires topsy turvy hurled. Spain was in decline, and who was to rise in its place?

Philip's use of the riches of the New World to restore placidity to the Old had proven in the assay fool's gold, like pleasing dreams that leave you upon waking only with the regret of ever having believed in them. The forces of the new—England, France, the Netherlands—were now bravely unleashed upon the world, with consequences that no one could foresee. And those who persisted in trying to read the future could choose between the lusty exuberance of Shakespeare and the mocking sorrow of Cervantes. In such a world, at such a time, the North American colonies were begun.

The man who was to emerge as the most prominent leader of the first successful colonizing expedition to North America was a perfect specimen of lusty Elizabethan exuberance. The son of a ne'er-do-well English yeoman, John Smith had decided to risk all as a soldier of fortune. His chief assets were his daring, his cunning, and his luck. The authors who had provided him with what little bookish education he had were Niccolò Machiavelli, the Florentine diplomat who in his *Prince* and historical reflections described the ruthless world of Renaissance politics and war, and Marcus Aurelius, the Roman emperor whose meditations showed how to retain a stoic detachment in the midst of such a ruthless world. The modern diplomat and ancient emperor agreed that a human life could be a work of art if everything an individual did was shaped by a single end. Where they differed was largely in the choice of worthy ends, and Machiavelli was for Smith the more persuasive teacher. To the Italian, at least as Smith read him, the general claims of truth and virtue were but externally imposed inhibitions that could impede the individual from fully exerting his will. What Machiavelli taught, John Smith had already felt in his blood. Soft-hearted visionaries might sigh longingly for their peaceful millennium. Smith did not belong to this dreamy class of men. For him life from minnows to men was incessant war.

This cast of mind makes the accurate reconstruction of Smith's early life almost impossible. To be sure, Smith had by the end of his life left ample published accounts of his early adventures. He loved to spin a yarn. In fact, he spun so many so well that people from that day to this have not been able to distinguish the truth from the embroidery from the fiction whole cloth. If a quarter of what he claimed about his earlier life was true, he did not need the embroidery. But for Smith, a true Elizabethan, verbal embroidery was a way of life. Or, as one nineteenth-century admirer put it, Smith "did not always consult the convenience of the historians of a later age."

John Smith had been, by his own account (a good bit of which can be corroborated), a soldier of fortune, a vagabond, a castaway, a pirate, a consort with papists in Rome, a slave who murdered his Muslim master, a celebrated guest in far Muscovy. His greatest glory in the Old World, however, was service beginning in 1600 to the Hungarians in their wars against the infidel Turks. First he helped the outnumbered Christian forces to a series of victories by providing them with contrivances and ruses he had learned from a careful study of Machiavelli's *Art of War.* Then the Turkish commander, out of frustration, challenged the Europeans to provide a champion to fight his own best warrior to the death before the collected troops. On three successive days John Smith—who else?—met a Turkish foe, and each day returned with a Turkish head thrust aloft as his trophy of victory. The Hungarians honored Smith with a pension and a coat of arms dominated by three infidel heads with Smith's motto beneath: *Vivere est vincere* (to live is to conquer).

The motto of the now-Captain Smith was the marrow of what he had learned in facing the Turks. He had discovered a mad freedom in risking his own life in trials by death. To stake his life in a struggle was to face voluntarily what could well be the vanishing moment of his own existence. Strangely, this was invigorating, almost intoxicating. Fear of death, he realized, had been his sovereign master and was no more. He was now completely free, and the fulfillment of this freedom was to seek to become the sovereign master of others. His most exquisite pleasure was to make others fear for their lives as he no longer did for his.

Of course, opportunities for such an exalted pleasure did not routinely present themselves in civilized company. In such circumstances Smith would have to content himself with simply asserting his own superiority at every occasion. He found the most effective way to do this was to tell stories of his past adventures. And to hear him tell of those adventures, you would have thought he was Odysseus and Achilles all in one.

And don't forget the ladies he courted. Throughout his adventures, beautiful ladies were transfixed by the mere sight of him, and then were pleased by his eloquence and ravished by his grace; they came to admire his achievements but admired still more the man. One lady after another risked her position, and perhaps lost her virtue, to help Smith make his way in the world. Odysseus and Achilles, and for good measure Paris as well.

When Smith returned to England in 1604 full of brag and confidence, he was still only twenty-four years old. Seeking for himself further opportunity to display his worth, he had soon worked his way into a circle of men intent on establishing English colonies overseas. This in itself was a feat to be admired, since Smith could contribute neither money nor respectability to the enterprise.

A noisy little knot of men in England had long advocated such overseas expansion, well before the Armada. For these advocates the brutal Elizabethan suppression of Ireland provided perfect schooling for broader projects of colonization. Elizabeth in her usual cautious way permitted a few tentative efforts, and then withdrew her support when these ended in disaster.

Sir Humphrey Gilbert led one of the first of these efforts. He had qualified himself by his service in Ireland; during that campaign he located his tent at the end of a lane lined on each side by the heads of executed rebels. His expeditions to the New World were undertaken in a similar spirit. The objective of colonization was little more than a pretext for plunder—"a cloak to hide a dagger," as one contemporary observer put it.

In his expedition of 1583, Gilbert made his way to Newfoundland where dozens of vessels—French, Portuguese, and Spanish as well as English—were peacefully fishing. He claimed the best drying grounds for fish as the site of his ostensible colony, hundreds of miles of coastland, and then rented them back to the grumbling fishermen. If they did not like the arrangement, they could fight. Gilbert was a man after Smith's heart.

But the New World soon started to charge its own rent. Soon so many men were sick, so many others on the verge of mutiny, that Gilbert sent one ship back to England. Then his largest ship went aground and was destroyed, with as many as eighty of its hundred-man crew lost. Finally Gilbert was forced to return to England with his last two ships. One night in high seas the ship that was carrying Gilbert and his young son disappeared without a trace.

His enterprise was taken up by his half-brother Walter Raleigh. Raleigh's colony was to be placed far to the south of Newfoundland, and much closer to Spanish territory. This commodious region of the New World he called, with his queen's approval, Virginia. A small colony was established on the island of Roanoke in the 1580s. Then it was temporarily abandoned except for a well-provisioned force of five, which promptly disappeared, either overrun or absorbed by the Indians. A second colony was established at Roanoke. Not long after, in 1588, Elizabeth had to recall a relief expedition to it because of the war with Spain. When relief was finally sent, this larger colony too had disappeared, men, women, and children, all gone. The wilderness had swallowed Roanoke as completely as the sea had Gilbert, his son, and his crew. In the New World, not to conquer was not to live.

However discouraging the news from Roanoke, the promoters of empire used the victory over the Armada to renew their call upon their countrymen to arise from their sluggish security and take their place in the broader world. For instance, Richard Hakluyt's *Principal Navigations . . . of the English Nation,* published the year after the Armada, was calculated propaganda, a lengthy rallying cry for the English to become an imperial people. There was a divine promise to Britannia like that to Rome of old, the promise of an empire without bounds or necessary end.

Grand visions of empire had little impact on the aging Elizabeth. She was intent on preserving what she had already gained. For decades England had been little more than a bone between two dogs. At first the snarling between Spain and France had permitted it an uneasy independence. Then, when France began to destroy itself in civil war, Spain sought to seize England but somehow failed. Elizabeth would rest content in that. To try more was to risk a descent into the funnel of hell.

Others were impatient with her tepid policies. England for them was like a horse repeatedly shying away from a jump it would have to make, sooner or later. In 1596 Walter Raleigh sought to force Elizabeth's hand by mounting his own expedition to establish an English colony on the north coast of South America; he would boldly strike at the heart of the Spanish empire and watch it crumble. So he struck, and it did not crumble; but Elizabeth was pleased because Raleigh the colonizer had incidentally turned a profit as a pirate. Raleigh was back in favor, but Elizabeth had also been reconfirmed in her suspicion of colonies. So grand imperial designs, whatever the merits of the case, remained in limbo.

When Elizabeth was succeeded by her Scottish cousin James, at first the prospects for colonies seemed even dimmer. He wished peaceful relations with Spain for the newly united Great Britain. He suspected the loyalty of Raleigh, the aspiring Lancelot to the old queen who had killed his mother. In 1603 Raleigh was arrested, condemned to death, and sent to the tower of London until it pleased the king to have the sentence carried out, if ever. For someone so fixed on the affairs of the world and so restless by nature, even the enforced leisure would be a severe punishment, particularly when prolonged.

The fate of Raleigh should have chilled Smith's ardor for high politics and colonizing adventure, were it not that Smith looked at things the other way around. Raleigh had had a wonderful run at the top, his name was on everyone's lips and would likely live forever. What more could a man aspire to in life? Moreover, Raleigh was not dead yet.

There was an important difference between the plans Smith now saw being made and the earlier ones of Raleigh. Raleigh's had been essentially individual enterprises. Now merchants, especially in London, were beginning to think that profits could be made, perhaps extraordinary profits, by expeditions to the New World. Of course, the risks were great. Nonetheless, a joint-stock company could spread the expenses among a number of wealthy investors. Pressure could be brought by them upon the court for recognition with a minimum of interference. A few adventurers like John Smith would be eager to lead. The main body of colonists would be recruited with the fantastic promises of a paradise on earth—or at least an escape from the hardships of poverty and toil. Such propaganda was so successful that Virginia was soon the subject of satire on the Jacobean stage from no less a pen than Ben Jonson.

A lesser pen but one soon to be named poet laureate, Michael Drayton, offered a patriotic assessment. His poem celebrating the new Virginia expedition began:

> You brave heroic minds,
> Worthy your country's name,
>> That honour still pursue,
>> Go and subdue,
> Whilst loitering hinds
> Lurk here at home with shame.

Those who loitered behind with shame were going to regret their decision, for fame and wealth awaited the aspiring Virginians who were going to a land still in the golden age.

> And cheerfully at sea
> Success you still entice,
>> To get the pearl and gold,
>> And ours to hold
> Virginia,
> Earth's only paradise!

Some organizers of the expedition apparently took this pleasing nonsense seriously; among the initial colonists were two refiners, two goldsmiths, and a jeweler, this out of a total of not more than one hundred fifty.

The expedition sailed from London in three ships on Friday, December

16, 1606. The 120-ton *Susan Constant* was the flagship, commanded by Captain Christopher Newport. It was followed by the forty-ton *Godspeed* and the smaller pinnace *Discovery*. The first discovery the three ships made was that they were not going to proceed with godspeed, or even with constancy.

The voyage, to put it bluntly, began badly. Through all of January, the ships were pitching on the English coast, simply trying to hold anchor. For Smith, who had ridden the main on Turkish galleys, the high seas were only a regrettable delay, partly compensated for by the amusement of watching others making wild vomits over the side. Such lack of sympathy for sufferers, as well as an unwillingness to find a Providential hand behind a meteorological disturbance, may have led to the dark complaint of a most pious and seasick member of the company that some few among them were "little better than atheists." More than a few were little better than landlubbers.

The voyage itself, once truly begun, was like a transition into a mythic realm. They were not far off England when a blazing star appeared to guide their way—or perhaps to warn them off. As they proceeded, they saw many wonderful things. A battle between a whale and a swordfish was not the least of these. The most striking sights, however, were on islands; first the Canaries, then, after making their dash across the open Atlantic, various Caribbean islands on which they tried to refresh themselves before heading north.

On one island they found natives wholly naked except for the red paint with which they covered themselves as a protection against mosquitoes. They saw a smoking volcano and cooked some meat in a scalding pond nearby. The flora and fauna produced their own surprises. Some men were almost driven mad with pain and swelling just from having touched a dew that collected on an apparently innocent type of wild fig. On one island the colonists feasted on wild boar and iguana. On another, they could fill their skiffs with eggs left unprotected and unhidden by birds ignorant of predators until now. On one of these islands they left behind the last remains of a gentleman, Edward Brookes, "whose fat melted within him, by the great heat and drought of the country." They also almost left behind the remains of John Smith, but in his case the land was not to blame.

Early in the voyage, the colonists decided that they had among themselves a potential tyrant. It began when, perhaps to kill time, the passengers told each other of previous adventures, and then listened with growing exasperation as the twenty-eight-year-old Smith told of his.

What had Smith done to arouse their suspicions? After listening to the others (if he did even manage to let them finish), he could not be expected to remain silent about his own merits that made him obviously preeminent among the prospective colonists. They should all know that he was valiant and virtuous, full of haughty courage, not fearing of death nor shrinking from distress but always resolute in extremities, a man acquainted with peril and accustomed to command. Smith would outstare the sternest eyes that look, outbrave the most daring heart on earth. And so, understandably, he could not tolerate those who usurped the sacred name of knight by inheriting it rather than earning it through noble deeds of war. Why, one time in Hungary, he himself whom—but, finally, his shipmates had enough. They decided that this Achilles/Odysseus/Paris was plotting to be Agamemnon too. As they were leaving the Canary Islands, Smith was seized by them and accused of intending to "usurp the government, murder the Council, and make himself king." Well, let the self-crowned king of hot air boast and bluster to an empty cell.

Smith, of course, dismissed the charges as the envy of his repute by lesser men. He apparently refused to be cowed by the charges or the incarceration. This was mere tribute paid to the potency and incisiveness of his character. Weak men do not call forth such belligerency. Realizing now that he was incorrigible, the other colonists decided to be done with him for good. On one island they began to construct a gallows for him. But, as he put it in his memoirs, "Captain Smith, for whom they were intended, could not be persuaded to use them."

Actually, the captain of the ship, Christopher Newport, seems to have been the one whose failure to be persuaded made the difference. Smith still had friends back in London, and the captain did not want to have to explain how being a boasting windbag had become a capital offense; besides, there was no evidence that Smith seriously intended to become king of Virginia. So the captain soothed the angry mood, kept Smith apart, and finally deflected the desire for blood.

Nonetheless, what his shipmates sensed was true. Smith intended to rule in Virginia, and eventually would. Although his shipmates did not prevent that, they at least saw to it that he would arrive at his future kingdom in chains.

The expedition finally reached the New World after four months of arduous voyaging. The secret instructions could now be opened. The colonists were to seek out the largest river they could find, and follow it into the interior as far as possible in large ships. There, perhaps as much as one hundred miles from the coast, they should establish themselves. In such a location they would not have to worry about raids from Spanish patrols along the coast. Even if the Spanish sent out an expedition to destroy the new colony, they would hardly be able to find it.

The expedition followed the instructions but not quite to the letter. They sailed into a great bay. This was a region where for centuries the hungry kingdom of the ocean had been slowly and persistently making advances against the kingdom of the shore, and they were sailing on a past battlefield of that never ending conflict. The Chesapeake Bay was really a drowned river valley. The victory of the sea here had left the old tributaries of this once-great river as independent rivers that divided the west side of the old river valley into a series of thick peninsulas protected from the sea by the east side of the old river valley, now a thumb of land that would be called Accomack. Coastal Virginia was a place that the salt sea had been forcibly taking back from the land for centuries, a place where estuaries, marshes, and swamps had been slowly expanding so that now in the summer the tributary rivers became plugged by the tidewater and could not empty fresh water into the sea. On the plains to the south of the Chesapeake River were pine barrens that collapsed into what came to be aptly called the Great Dismal Swamp.

This all looked less like a new world than the portals of a haggard, old continent where hope had long since died. If Virginia was the earth's only paradise, then the earth was a creation of irony, and Virginia a throne for fools. Perhaps God had shaped it not during the first week of creation but after the fall, as an expression of His displeasure.

The relative barrenness of the coast may have been a surprise. Out at sea, trees had been smelled days before land was sighted; this was the vast inland forests' invisible benediction on the air. Now the three ships began to make their way up the southernmost of the rivers emptying into the Chesapeake, the river they called after their monarch, the James. They explored up this river until it began to narrow. Although this happened far closer to the mouth than the hundred miles the investors sitting in London had suggested, they found nearby a peninsula jutting into the river, a peninsula at once accessible to large ships and defensible from Indian attacks by land. There they began to build Jamestown. Even John Smith, who was not feeling very friendly toward his fellow colonists at this point, had to admit that the peninsula was "a very fit place for erecting a great city." This was one of the last decisions made by the colonists that Smith would approve of.

The collection of shacks that aspired to be a great city had to have a government. The colonists were to be assured, according to the charter, of all the rights of British subjects. However, power was to be placed in the hands of an oligarchy of councillors named from London. The list of councillors was among the secret instructions to be read only after landfall. These councillors in turn were to elect from among their number a president who would serve at their pleasure and be the chief administrative officer for the whole colony.

The list was read aloud, and the colonists discovered to their shock that on it was the name of the man whom shortly before they had been trying to persuade to use a gallows. Smith, however, had little time to gloat. The council convened, and selected as president the man who had distinguished himself by having led the attacks on Smith, Edward Maria Wingfield. Lest that be thought an accident, the council as its second act then voted not quite unanimously to expel John Smith from its number. Allowing Smith to serve as a councillor had never even been considered as a possibility, for they had refused to allow him to take the oath of office.

To say that Smith was furious at his treatment would be the most faint and faded of understatements. For Smith this was no time or place for stoic meditations. There was more at stake here than the scoffs and scorns and contumelious taunts he had now to endure. The settling of petty scores with him by the council was but a symptom of a broader malaise he saw endangering the whole colony. The colony, Smith concluded, was dominated by an invincible alliance between anarchic self-interest and moralistic sentimentality.

Most of the colonists were blinded by their desire for immediate wealth. As Smith put it, "There was no talk, no hope, no work, but dig gold, wash gold, refine gold, load gold." What Christopher Marlowe had called "the wind that bloweth all the world, the desire for gold" was blowing through Virginia at full gale. As near as Smith could tell, the colonists did not seem to realize that their unbridled pursuit of private wealth would doom the colony. Instead of cooperating to strengthen their fledgling society, they were obsessed with gaining every imagined advantage over their fellow colonists in the pursuit of what Smith contemptuously dismissed as "gilded dirt." As a result, the life of the colony was one of rancorous spite, furious raging broils. They addressed one another with envious carping tongues, and responded to the admonitions of their leaders in vile and ignominious terms.

Or so Smith thought. And the leaders, for their part, seemed at a loss to find an appropriate response to such willful insubordination on the part of the colonists. They did not seem to realize that such insolence was like a weed that if not plucked immediately will overgrow a garden and choke it to death. However, from all appearances, the leaders did not care about their position of leadership except insofar as it gave them an advantage in the pursuit of private gain. They, like the rest, chirped only, "I, I, I." They had, in short, no understanding of the world as it really was. Wealth was ephemeral; it did not provide permanent fame. Only successful leadership left to posterity an imperishable monument to your name, such as the ages would never obliterate. Yet Wingfield and the other councillors, having excluded Smith from leadership, refused to lead themselves.

Moreover, even if wealth were the only objective for this colony, the particular circumstances in which it was pursued here could not be ignored. Yet the colonists were oblivious to the obvious—namely, that they were seeking their fortunes amidst a fickle, wavering nation of savages who had already destroyed one English colony. The colonists looked out from Jamestown and saw only what they wanted to see—potential riches for themselves. Smith saw something different. He saw a colony hemmed about with grim destruction. And self-delusion about such a harsh reality was for him an immodest, clamorous outrage.

But delude themselves about the Indians they did. One could forgive the London directors of the company for entertaining pious hopes about the Indians. From such a safe distance, they could talk as if they saw clearly a protecting hand of Divine Providence guiding this expedition. They could sentimentally imagine, if they wished, an angel specially sent to the Indians to instruct them that they should receive the English in love and friendship. However, such pious reveries, if believed for a second, were dangerous in the extreme, at least to those living in the wilderness.

Smith had fought many battles for Christendom, and he knew that piety had won none of them. He was as religious as the next man. But in the world of politics and war Machiavelli, not the Bible, rules. Any man of experience knows that reality is almost never in harmony with one's hopes—and so hope can only be attained through the brutal imposition of one's will. Such an imposition was the measure of a man. By such a measure Smith judged his fellow Virginians to be puny creatures indeed.

Their failure to measure up was nowhere more apparent than in the simple matter of defenses. Like any outpost, the colony needed, as quickly as possible, effective battlements. The Indians skulking about had to learn as soon as possible that in seeking to harm the colony they would only be courting their own destruction.

Yet what did the wonderful leaders of Virginia do? Nothing. They professed sanctimoniously that they did not want to offend the Indians by appearing to mistrust them. Smith suspected another unspoken reason for this enthusiastic embrace of folly. To have defenses built they would have to give orders. The colonists as a group were not used to obeying orders, and did not take kindly to them; in fact, they would be inclined to refuse any work that did not promise private gain.

So nothing was done, and the grumbling Smith waited for the worst to happen. He did not have to wait long. Within a few weeks of their arrival, an Indian attack overran the whole colony with little difficulty. One colonist was killed, numerous others wounded. Only cannon fire from the remaining ship repelled the attack, more by sound than effect. If the Indians had only waited a little longer until the ship had sailed for England to replenish supplies and get more colonists, Virginia would have joined Roanoke in the annals of lost colonies. Belatedly, a meager fort was built.

Never one to sit and fret and bite his tongue, Smith now began to find more of an audience for his complaints. He suggested that a tempered breast-plate is a better defense against arrows than a pure heart. And that Indian aggression against the colonists was like a little fire that can be quickly trodden out but that, if suffered without retaliation, rivers cannot quench. Smith somehow could not persuade himself that he should die cheerfully for some-one else's misplaced kindness or mindless greed. He had not come to Virginia to end up lying at the feet of Indians, a stinking fly-blown corpse. Others now started to agree, however much they still might dislike the swaggering Smith.

Much of this had to do with the simple physical condition of the colonists. Newport, shortly after the Indian attack, had left to return to England for new supplies and colonists. Rations had to be reduced to a pint of wheat or barley a day. But as one colonist put it, this grain "having fried for some 26 weeks in the ship's hold, contained as many worms as grains." He added with forced good cheer, "Had we been as free from all sins as gluttony and drunkenness we might have been canonized for saints."

Certainly they had begun to suffer a kind of slow martyrdom. During the hot Virginia summer their only drink was water taken from the James. But the salt water was then pushing back the fresh. At high tide, the James was an estuary—and at low, its water was, as one put it, "full of slime and filth which was the destruction of many of our men." All the infections that the summer sun could suck up from the bogs and swamps and marshes of the tidewater seemed to descend on the colony until it had been transformed by inch-meal into a single great suffering disease. Let one survivor describe the hell they all endured:

"Thus we lived for the space of five months in this miserable distress, not having five able men to man our bulwarks upon any occasion. If it had not pleased God to have put terror in the savages' hearts, we had all perished by those wild and cruel pagans, being in that weak state as we were; our men night and day groaning in every corner of the fort most pitiful to hear. If there were any conscience in men, it would make their hearts to bleed to hear the pitiful murmurings and outcries of our sick men for relief, every night and day for the space of six weeks: some departing out of the World, many times three or four in a night; in the morning their bodies being trailed out of their cabins like dogs, to be buried."

After a while, so many were dying they had to be buried at night, lest the Indians realize how weakened the colony was. Of course, every catastrophe is an opportunity for someone. Not surprisingly, in this case it was Captain John Smith.

Smith used the misfortunes of the colony to try to undermine the authority of the president. Smith caught him providing supplies from the company stores to a very sick friend. The food was not his to give. Wingfield apparently rose to the bait. He was not going to have his character questioned by a man who had once wandered Ireland as a beggar. Smith responded in kind, a duel of insults. Soon he was saying that Wingfield was so lowly bred if they were both back in England Smith would not allow his valet to associate with him. (Smith, of course, had never had a valet.)

Such rancorous exchanges must have provided some distraction from the day-to-day suffering, but not enough. By the end of the first year, of the approximately 150 original colonists who started, there were only 38 left. Then, to make matters worse, almost the whole colony burned down: clothes, books, many of the remaining provisions were destroyed—burnt offerings to the spirit that wanted the English gone from this place. Only three shacks remained to shelter the survivors.

The year was over but not their sorrows. Only a year, and they were already worn with toils, spent with woes, tainted with fear. Smith, himself ascendant, now could try to allay the common grief with cheerful words that he himself could hardly believe. He could exhort them to resume their former courage and dismiss their present cares. If they could only endure the purgatory of these depressing hardships, they would live to see great things. To such encouragement the likely response was that the greatest thing any of them could hope to live to see was England once again, and that hope each day seemed dimmer.

If at this moment someone could have foretold to these first Virginians the destiny of this enterprise in history's grand design, if someone had imagined for them a great republic stretching across the continent, a nation larger in extent than western Europe, all under the single rule of law, of an independent republic preeminent in power both economically and militarily in the whole world, hundreds of millions of people under a single constitution, governed from an artificial city constructed on another swamp just to the north of

Jamestown—if someone with divine foreknowledge could have sketched this future for the colonists, they would only have dismissed the prophecy as incredible, a macabre, unfeeling joke at their own expense. This was a time when even the small words of encouragement they might offer one another could not have been heartfelt. Virginia had become an aristocracy of wretchedness.

Common misery, needless to say, scarcely strengthened the fragile bonds of this community. Wingfield was deposed when he was caught hoarding supplies for himself and a few cronies. Another leader of the colony was executed by firing squad after it was discovered that he intended to make off with the colony's pinnace to betray its location to the Spanish, and thereby perhaps salvage some reward for himself. A few colonists had even slipped away, fled to the savages for succor: Better red than dead.

Throughout it all, Smith continued his boasting. The key to the colony's survival was getting the Indians, however unwilling, to provide supplies. And Smith was certain he knew precisely how to deal with the Indians. You must be proud, bold, pleasant, resolute, and now and then stab as occasion serves. The leadership of Jamestown happily permitted Smith to lead expeditions of a few men into Indian territory for food. If he got food, good; but if the Indians soon found Smith insufferable (as likely they would), the loss of Smith would be a gain.

At first Smith came back from his forays laden with food and full of boasting. Then an expedition went out and did not return. Weeks later, Smith himself showed up back at the settlement, alone. They had been ambushed. All of his men had been killed. Smith alone had been taken captive.

But he had, as always, a great tale to tell. He was no longer having to deal with local chieftains. He had seen the great Indian emperor of Virginia, Powhatan. He had been to Powhatan's great bark-covered house, more than one hundred feet long, an aboriginal palace. To gain audience one had to make his way through the court that attended the emperor, many body guards and many wives. (Powhatan was as prodigiously polygamous as a Turk.) All the attendants were elegantly decked out; his wives had faces painted bright red, and each had a lovely chain of white beads about her neck. Powhatan, when finally reached, looked the part of a monarch. He sat on what Smith took to be a bed, but his position was elevated by numerous mats and a pillow of leather embroidered with pearls and beads. This was a great man with whom John Smith could deal as an equal.

The starving colonists, however, were uninterested in listening to more of Smith's yarn spinning. Smith had been responsible for getting some good men killed—and then did not have the good grace to be killed himself. And then he returned as if he expected to be congratulated for his success. The only congratulation he was going to receive was an Old Testament sort—an eye for an eye. Once again, the colonists attempted to persuade Captain Smith to use a gallows; for a second time he assured them he found their reasoning unconvincing. Then, as if by magic, Newport's ship appeared, and amidst the joy of his return Newport managed to save Smith again.

Smith, for his part, seems to have been daunted not at all by these brushes with death, first from the Indians, then from his colleagues. He had come out of these encounters only stronger, at least in his own mind. In forgoing his execution, the Jamestown settlers had tacitly acknowledged, however reluctantly, that he was becoming more and more essential to their survival. His release from Indian captivity, on the other hand, had occurred because he had found in the depths of the forest a true kindred spirit.

With the help of his brother Opechancanough, Powhatan had spent his long life in pursuit of empire. In this pursuit he had shown a shrewdness and courage that any disciple of Machiavelli would have to admire. As many as thirty previously independent tribes and more than ten thousand Indians now accepted his sovereignty. They now called themselves, after him, the Powhatans. He had more titles than James I; and Powhatan, unlike James, had earned most of his. In looking at Powhatan, John Smith could see an older, Indian version of what he himself wished to be.

Of course, the English were an unwelcome intrusion on Powhatan's rule. He wanted them gone, much as the Roanoke colonists were now gone. Rumor had it that Powhatan had personally ordered the execution of the survivors of the earlier colony, but this was the kind of act he would have others do at a distance so that he would be free to disavow it, if need be.

Nor would he admit that he wanted Jamestown to disappear. The English could cause him trouble by allying themselves with the few tribes that still resisted him. So he tried to avoid confronting the English in open battle. As time went on, whenever he was pressed (usually by Smith), Powhatan would make great public shows of friendship. Privately, of course, he would encourage the tribes nearest Jamestown to pick off as many colonists as possible. Smith and his fellow colonists also suspected him of arranging attempted massacres, but Powhatan would insist that these were always the result of local Indians acting on their own, against his explicit wishes.

Powhatan and John Smith eventually seem to have come almost to relish their face-to-face encounters. From the first they lied to one another repeatedly and without the slightest compunction. In his initial meeting with

Powhatan, for instance, Smith assured him that the English had come to Virginia to escape Spanish patrols and would leave as soon as it was safe. And from the first they understood each other's lies for what they were. Powhatan in great earnest would regularly provide Smith with the most reliable recent information on the whereabouts of the Roanoke survivors. Gestures of friendship were regarded by both as stratagems to catch the other off guard. They suspected one another even when bearing gifts, most when bearing gifts. Smith, for his part, did not seem to have taken even the occasional assassination attempt amiss, as long as it did not publicly challenge his courage or authority.

Of course, Smith fully expected Powhatan to test these as well. Once, for instance, he had arranged to meet Powhatan's brother Opechancanough to trade for food. The meeting had no sooner begun than Smith realized he and his men were badly outnumbered, virtually at the mercy of the Indians. He immediately challenged Opechancanough to a fight to the death, hand-to-hand or with whatever weapon he chose. When the startled Indian declined the challenge, Smith pushed his way through the chief's body guard, grabbed him by the hair, struck a pistol in his ribs, and demanded complete submission. Once the Indians had thrown down all their weapons, Smith delivered a violent harangue. If one drop of English blood was shed, he, John Smith, would personally see to it that every man, woman, and child of Opechancanough's people would be exterminated off the earth so completely that not even their name would be spoken among men. Smith got his way that day like most others.

In short, Powhatan and Smith understood each other quite well. As a result, Smith now had even less patience with those English who did not understand how things stood. For instance, orders had come from the Virginia Company with Newport as to what the colonists should do next. They should find either a passage to the Pacific Ocean or survivors from Roanoke or gold. Was it not nice that the company officials respected local initiative by letting them choose from three preposterous tasks? Then, just for good measure, the company secretary added that the colonists should also go through a formal coronation of Powhatan as king of the Indians and vassal to James.

Upon hearing this Smith warmly expressed his disapproval of the orders, so warmly that he seems to have shocked the ordinarily tolerant Newport. The company was run by a collection of fools all right, fools steadfastly consistent in their foolishness, to be admired as fools by principle. Smith's actual choice of words was mercifully left unrecorded. Nonetheless, he would have agreed with the nineteenth-century historian John Fiske who concluded that the order to coronate Powhatan, in particular, was "grotesque enough to have emanated from the teeming brain of James I after a mickle noggin of his native Glenlivet."

By this time Smith had become, almost by default, not only the chief Indian trader for the colony but also its chief explorer. He welcomed any reason to be away from the ill-led colonists, themselves as full of chatter as magpies in May and not as intelligent. So he made two lengthy explorations of Chesapeake Bay. He worked his way up the Potomac River, past the lowlands that would one day be the site for the greatest monuments of the American republic. He fought or traded with the local Indians as the occasion seemed to demand.

There were dangers enough without fighting the Indians. Once as much out of caprice as out of need, he went spearfishing with his sword. The fish he speared was a stingray, which in its death throes slashed him badly on the arm. Soon the whole arm seemed infected, and the feverish Smith thought he had finally exhausted his store of luck. Determined to be obeyed beyond his life, he selected the site for his grave and gave orders for his funeral. Then the swelling stopped, the pain eased, and by nightfall Smith insisted on eating some of the creature that had caused him such a fright. He had faced death and overcome it once again. No fish or other lower creature, however well armed, was going to separate Captain John Smith from his destiny.

Then, on September 10, 1608, it happened. Smith was elected president of the colony. His undeniable achievements together with his incredible luck (and the apparent lack of other plausible candidates) had put him in power.

His enemies could console themselves that the council, which included some of his enemies, would hold him in check. Then the council disappeared. First, some on the council decided to return to England. Shortly afterward, accidents and disease took the lives of the others. President Smith was now the sole remaining member of the council. John Smith had become the legally constituted dictator of Virginia. Anyone who knew him knew he would brook no challenge to his authority. Smith would deal with the Indians and the settlers as he saw fit. And he saw everything, as always, very clearly.

The Indians were enemies but at least temporarily indispensable. Smith admired the Spanish, who had reduced their Indians to slaves who did all the drudgery and left the Spanish to live as soldiers off the fruits of their labors. That, for the time being, was not feasible in Virginia. Perhaps the day would come when gangs of Indian laborers would be building English roads, towns, forts, and churches, be tending English fields and flocks, be laboring in

English mines and industries. Happy the Virginians who would see that day, but it was far off.

The Indians who controlled this coast did so because of good fortune and shrewdness and strength. Like most men, all men, they always desired more power and wealth than they had, and would use any stratagem, commit any cruelty to gain it—and then would make up some tale, some novel pretense to justify their wickedness. Smith had known that about the Indians before he ever met them because he knew human nature. The tedious annals of human history, that train of woe, would reveal this dire truth to even the most desultory student.

If God did bless this enterprise, He would bless it through the strength and shrewdness of the English, not their simplicity or kindliness. His blessing would seem cruel and unkind and unfair to the Indians because they would then become vassals to the English throne. For the English to prosper the Indians must decline. In the nature of things the interests of the two parties were at odds. But that did not make temporary alliances impossible or unprofitable.

At present the Virginia colony could not survive without the Indians. Thanks to reinforcements, the colony now had hundreds of mouths to feed. Just to avoid famine, the colony needed three bushels of corn a day, three bushels it was scarcely capable of producing itself. The Indians around them could provide that. Yet getting them to, Smith had already learned, was a delicate matter. Too much force and you would scare them away; not enough, and they would not provide you with the necessary sustenance.

The colonists of tender heart disapproved of his indelicate methods. He would respond that these very colonists who thought the Indians saints and Smith the oppressor still ate the corn he extorted and stole. And the colonists did find it hard to argue with his results. A gun is missing, but the most likely culprit has slipped away. Smith simply grabs an Indian at hand, a friend of the accused—and he announces that unless the gun is returned by the next morning the captured friend will be strangled on a gallows. Nobody, English or Indian, doubts that Smith will be true to his word. The gun is returned the next morning. To whatever ails the colony, the sovereign remedy is action.

He dealt with the colonists almost as firmly. The reason that the colony had to depend on the Indians for food, he thought, was the simple laziness of the colonists, especially those who prided themselves on their noble blood. Well, in John Smith's hive there would be no lazy, yawning drones. We would soon find out who dreaded punishment less than they feared labor.

High-born colonists might think it unseemly to take orders from someone they thought fit only to kiss their rings and hold their stirrups. But Smith reminded them that it was not altogether impossible for gentlemen like themselves to die at the hand of a knave such as himself. In fact, he could guarantee that any mouth that quibbled at his authority would soon enough be preaching obedience, wordlessly, from the top of a pike. With such sweet talk, John Smith steadfastly invited his betters forth to labor in the sun, lest they shortly be shorter by a head. The choice, as Smith framed it, was between blisters and death. Soon each colonist was working six hours a day for the commonwealth.

The results from this were striking. By the first of April twenty houses had been built so that everyone was decently sheltered, and Jamestown itself began to look like a real village. A deep well had been dug, and so the colonists would no longer be dependent upon the foul James, especially in the summer. The colony now had dozens of pigs and hundreds of chickens. The colonists were beginning to set out fields for agriculture, and they had begun to fish systematically with nets and weirs in the neighboring waters. The colony, quite simply, was rapidly moving toward self-sufficiency, and a new fort was going up so that it could stand its ground against the Indians in any crisis. Smith turned even setbacks to his own advantage, to strengthen his control. When the corn stores were ruined by rats, he organized the whole colony as a military company, with himself as commander in chief. During Smith's two-year term, the colony prospered. It was not yet self-sufficient, but had improved remarkably. The colonists, nonetheless, chafed under his autocratic rule, and the brutal threats through which he gained his way with Englishman and Indian alike. They did not like being told they were the kind of jades who needed to have their necks broken to learn to bend their heads, or that kindness toward the Indians would make cowards of us all, cowards and then corpses.

Finally, after the most successful year the colony had yet known, Smith's enemies had their chance. Food had been running low while they waited for the arrival of new settlers and supplies. Smith ordered that Jamestown disperse into self-sufficient units. Each group would forage for itself in its own locale. In such small groups the opportunity for freeloading would be lessened.

Smith had been visiting one of the groups. It had been a rancorous visit. He had not liked where they had placed their camp. They had not liked his interference. He had not liked their impudence. (A gallows was the way to choke a jibing spirit.) And they had not liked his threats. A typical happy day in Virginia, that earthly paradise.

Then, as he was making his way back to Jamestown by water, Smith's run of luck abruptly ended. His powder bag was suddenly ignited by a stray spark, from someone's pipe perhaps. On fire, he jumped into the water; he was pulled out half-drowned and severely burned. Back at Jamestown, bedridden but still giving orders, he soon faced a mutiny. The mutineers first wanted to kill him, but on reflection contented themselves with removing him as president for being "an ambitious, unworthy and vainglorious fellow."

A healthy Smith would have challenged them all to fight to the death, one at a time. From his bed, however, Smith could only preserve his life by retreat; lest they try to kill him again, he took a returning supply ship back to England, vexed by this grievous usage but still thinking how passing brave it had been to be a king. Ruling other men was the ripest fruit of all, a perfect human bliss for all the warring elements within our breast.

Back in England, Smith set about promoting himself through a book, *A Map of Virginia*. In it he explicitly described this promising new land, on which he was himself the greatest living authority. He soon found his way back to North America as the leader of a modest two-ship expedition that was supposed to make a good return on the investment by whaling. However, the crew proved unable to learn this difficult skill on the job. This was fine by Smith. He could recoup the investment by trading for furs along the coast, and in the process have the opportunity for some exploring.

Both his trading and his explorations were successful. He decided that this whole northern region should be called New England. He also recorded names for its locales that have lasted from that day to this. Sometimes he accepted the Indian names, such as Massachusetts, for a particularly inviting portion of the coast. Sometimes he would apply an English name; on the cape that jutted out from Massachusetts was a harbor that the Indians called Pawtuxet, but that reminded Smith of Plymouth.

His names stuck, and the furs he brought back assured him of backing for another voyage. This time he carried a sufficient number of colonists to establish a base in his New England. His luck, however, started to turn all bad. The ship was run down by pirates. Although Smith was determined to fight to the end, his officers were not so doughty. Imagine the shock to all when the pirates finally boarded under a truce, and a number of them recognized Captain Smith as their commander from an earlier, less respectable period of his life. They thought well of him, so well they wanted him to lead them once again. He declined, but his ship was allowed to go its way, only to be captured shortly after by French men-of-war. So Smith had to work his way back to England from French captivity.

With Smith gone, Powhatan set about ending the Virginia colony once and for all, but in his own indirect fashion. Suddenly no Indian tribe had any corn to provide the English. Parties sent out to trade for food simply disappeared. When Jamestown inquired as to their fates, Powhatan would assure them that none of his subjects would have done them harm. Perhaps they had met up with the remnants of the Roanoke colony, and could not pull themselves away from their convivial company.

Of the eighty-six men sent out on three such expeditions, only fourteen made it back. Without provisions, Virginia entered into what came to be called "the starving time." Compared to this, the original hardships of the colony had been a luxury vacation. First, all the pigs and chickens were eaten; then cats and dogs; then what rats and snakes could be caught; finally, anything that would fill the stomach and temporarily ease the pain. One colonist was executed for digging up the graveyard for the decaying corpses. Another murdered his pregnant wife, dismembered her, and salted the pieces he did not eat immediately; after his grisly cache was discovered, he was first tortured, then burned to death. Of the five hundred who began that starving time only about sixty survived to see a relief ship come, with hundreds more colonists and with provisions for a year.

Imagine the faces of the new colonists as they realized what they had come to. They had fed their spirits on images of a virgin land somehow exempt from suffering, and now they confronted the grievous reality, a wretchedness greater than any human being could think to endure—all sighs and groans and helpless hands and lifeless friends, a miserable distillation of all the tears in human things.

Renewed in strength, the colony now sought revenge on the Powhatans. Smith's threats were to be made good by others. The English took the killing to the Indian villages. Parties were sent out with no other objectives but death and destruction. When one such returned after a particularly successful massacre, they were admonished for having brought back alive the chief's wife and two children. To remedy the situation, the children were thrown into the river and their brains shot out; as for the mother, the president insisted they should burn her, for strangling on a gallows was too good. But those who had borne the brunt of the killing had seen enough for one day, so she was quickly dispatched with a sword.

They were certainly doing nothing that Smith had not threatened. But Smith's threats were intended to achieve other ends. Smith would never have destroyed Indian corn fields out of simple spite, when the colony needed desperately to trade for Indian corn. The colonists and the Indians starving together could scarcely be considered a victory for either. Too much force and too little force were equally ineffective. Jamestown had survived its starving time only to act with suicidal malice.

The new president had decided that a state of total war existed between the peoples. That was terrible news for colonists who found themselves attracted to the Indian way of life. Faced with the unrelenting hardships of Jamestown, many colonists, especially those who had nothing to return to in England, preferred to live among the Indians as Indians. They slipped away from Jamestown and got themselves adopted by local tribes. Such new "Indians" could have been seen as a remarkable opportunity for the colony. In the short run, the drain on supplies would be lessened. In the long run, those Europeans of the bush, living now with Indian wives and Indian children, could provide a bond between the two peoples. The new president did not see it that way. Those who slipped away to the Indians were racial traitors pure and simple. Their betrayal of their European origins threatened the very identity of the colony. They had to be punished most severely. Trade with the Indians during truces had to be conditioned on their return. He pursued this policy with the utmost consistency and rigor.

Some of the new Indians from Jamestown he hanged, some he burned at the stake, some he had simply shot; a few were exquisitely broken on the wheel. As for those who had stolen supplies from the common stores for their voyage, he would mutilate their tongues so they could not swallow any food—and then have them chained to a tree where all could watch them starve to death. If the Indian life had such great attractions to his common run of Jamestown settler, then the president had to assure their continued loyalty through calculated terror.

Despite the terror, the struggling colony seemed to be on the verge of dissolving into the wilderness. It could not stand the hostility of the Virginia Indians much longer and survive. Then the president hit upon a tactic that had been much favored by Smith: the taking of children as hostages. Smith had found that the Powhatans loved their children inordinately and nothing would make them more cooperative than placing their darling children at risk. If this kidnapping had worked for Smith, then it should still work. Since they now needed the cooperation of Powhatan himself, they would take as hostage his favorite daughter, Pocahontas.

However shrewd, there was something particularly ungracious about making Pocahontas a hostage. If a heavenly messenger had been sent to predispose the Powhatans to the English, it had been sent to this girl, and to her alone. From the first the little Pocahontas had hung about the colony, entertaining

with her cartwheels. "Little Wanton," the English called her. What she wanted most was for the English to stay, and at times she would betray her father's
secret plans, to help them survive. This princess with flowing hair and loose-
fitting clothes, who once arranged for the young women of her village to
dance for Smith and the English naked, now was herself of marriageable age
and hence particularly valuable to her father. So the English seized her, and
offered to trade her back for concessions from Powhatan. The ransom negotiations progressed very slowly, with the usual delays and threats and jockeying
until finally Pocahontas was brought into the presence of the Indian delegation, two full years after she had been abducted. Perhaps now for the first time
the English saw her behave fully like a princess. She acknowledged the existence of only the leaders of the delegation, and them barely. But then she
made a startling declaration: she wished to remain among the English, who
loved her.

The English could scarcely have expected what happened next. Powhatan,
on learning of his daughter's request, agreed to it. The English would get their
concessions and his daughter too. They would now be friends, and his daughter the bond of that friendship. Powhatan, now in his old age, had apparently
reconciled himself finally to the permanent existence of Jamestown, if that
would mean peace for himself and his people. Never had the prospects for the
colony looked more hopeful than in that spring of 1614.

Pocahontas's insistence on remaining with the English who loved her is
indirectly explained by a letter written about this time by one of the colonists,
John Rolfe. Rolfe himself had paid heavily for his efforts as a colonist. He had
lost first an infant child and then his wife. In a letter to the president of the
colony he describes how he has recently struggled with what has begun "to
root itself within the secret bosom of my heart." To his wonder and surprise,
he is charmed by the very sight of Pocahontas. He wants to believe his feelings
for her are not simply "the unbridled desire of carnal affection." Although he
knows all the injunctions in the Old Testament against the Jews taking wives
from other peoples, he does not think that they apply to the Christian dispensation, especially if the husband means to bring his wife to God. So John
Rolfe concludes his letter by asking the permission of the president to marry
Pocahontas, "to whom my dear and best thoughts are and have been a long
time so entangled and enthralled in so intricate a labyrinth that I was even
wearied to unwind myself thereof." In their growing love he thought he saw
the very hand of God, leading him and perhaps the colony along the safest
paths to tread.

On April 5, 1614, Pocahontas and John Rolfe were married in Jamestown.

Those present saw it as a solemn confirmation of the peaceful era that was beginning between the two peoples. Supporters of the colony thought this could be best dramatized for the benefit of the colony by having the Indian princess visit England. This was the news that greeted Smith when he returned from France.

Nothing could have pleased Smith more. His propaganda on behalf of Virginia had been received well, but had not gotten him the desired reappointment. He was honored, but then ignored. Now the trip of Pocahontas gave him a whole new chance. Of course, he would have dismissed the idea of a permanent peace with the Indians as another of those pious delusions that had so vexed the colony. The colony was an invasion of the Indians' land and its final objective could be nothing other than their conquest and enslavement.

Even so, there was no need to emphasize such hard truths on so sentimental an occasion, especially if playing on its sentimentality might help him dramatize his unique success as the leader of Virginia. He wanted to return to Virginia, preferably in power. Perhaps Pocahontas's visit would provide the way. Many times before Smith had found himself rescued from a dangerous situation by the good graces of a fair lady. Now he would return to the New World on Pocahontas's deerskin skirt.

How could he exploit this opportunity? He decided to write a public letter describing her many services to the colony, and urging that as soon as she arrived she should be honored, received at court perhaps. To whom should he address the letter? The queen, yes, Queen Anne. Of course, in recounting Pocahontas's many services he had to allude to his own. But how could he dramatize their combined contributions so that they would be forever associated?

He hit on relating to the queen a story about his own captivity and first encounter with Pocahontas. It is an episode he never mentioned before, although he had opportunities in his other writings—and none of the other earliest accounts of Virginia mentioned it. But if it never really happened as Smith recounts it, it should have.

After first being taken captive amidst the corpses of his men, he was brought back to the village of Powhatan himself. For six weeks he was treated very well, fattened up in fact. Only after he was fully restored to his strength and health would he be a suitable human sacrifice. So the village collected to watch his execution, presumably an offering to the demonic powers. The death would not be a pleasant one; he was to have his brains beaten out, his head crushed between large rocks. Yet suddenly a young girl interposed herself between Smith and the executioners. It was Pocahontas, the king's favorite daughter. Smith was spared. So Pocahontas's good heart first saved John Smith, then through many intelligences helped preserve the colony, and now led her to embrace Christianity and fair England.

When Pocahontas did arrive, she was invited to court. Her stay in England was in fact a triumph for everyone involved. She could now speak English well; she and Rolfe had a son. Her pension from the Virginia Company permitted her to live and dress like a lady (no deerskin skirt for her in England), and she comported herself well.

Pocahontas, long attracted to the trinkets of civilization, now could be dazzled by civilization in its full force, compared to which Jamestown was a collection of huts fit only for lowly farmers and shepherds. All was before her: stately towering buildings, the great gates and streets, the noise and throng of the marketplace. Here she could see the parliament, there a cathedral, everywhere elegant palaces decorated by paintings and sculptures. She even attended a masque in the presence of the court and listened to the poetry of Ben Jonson while wearing elegant clothes worthy of a lady-in-waiting, clothes she could not even have imagined a few months before.

Pocahontas's stay in England was a triumph for everyone involved—except John Smith. If he had once seemed important to her, he now seemed very small. Her husband and the officials of the Virginia Company had certainly disabused her of any illusions about him. Perhaps they told her about his Pocahontas story, and that offended her. At any rate, he was a commoner, and she was moving among the nobility with ease.

Smith did not get to see her until well into her visit. Then at first, when he came into her presence, she refused to talk to him. What they did finally exchange was not recorded. It could not have been encouraging, for Smith did not try to see her again. He had played his chance, his trump card, and still lost.

If Pocahontas thought she was better than Smith, she soon learned differently. The Virginia Company that had paid for her trip decided that she and her husband had served their purpose, and they were to return to the colony. She did not want to go, but that made no difference. Perhaps Rolfe in trying to persuade her predicted that all this one day would be found in Virginia. If so, she could have responded, "Happy the people whose walls have already risen." But, as it happened, she was not to return to her homeland. On the way to the ship she suddenly sickened and died.

Smith must have been bitterly amused at the sentimentalists who had her dying of a broken heart. He knew better. Her death was just another instance of the horrific mortality consequent to contact between worlds old and new.

Indians died from European contagions as quickly as Virginians died from their first contact with the swamps and hardships of the Chesapeake. Deaths ordained by nature far exceeded deaths willed by men. A strange conquest, this—with no honor. England could keep sending wave after wave of settlers, like troops charging a defensive position. The defenders, for all their superiority, had one weakness. They, unlike the attackers, could not replenish their numbers. So they were destined, sooner or later, to be completely overwhelmed.

John Smith realized that John Rolfe had inadvertently contributed to making this almost certain, but not by his marriage to Pocahontas. Why would wave after wave of colonists come to Virginia, especially after the dangers and hardships became well known? The first colonists had expected to become wealthy from gold, silver, and jewels. But Virginia apparently had none, nor wealthy Indian empires to plunder. There was no golden fleece here, equivalent to what the Spanish had discovered in Mexico and Peru. For Virginia to continue to draw colonists another road to wealth had to be found. And the person who inadvertently found it was none other than John Rolfe.

In 1611, long before he had left with Pocahontas for England, Rolfe had planted some tobacco seeds, just to satisfy his own habit. Tobacco then was a virtual monopoly of the Spanish colonies and very expensive. Rolfe found that tobacco thrived in Virginia soil, and by 1613 Rolfe was growing enough to export some back to England. Within two years the colony was sending back 2,000 pounds; two years later 20,000 pounds; two years later 60,000 pounds. Tobacco established itself as the quick road to riches that the Virginia colonists had long sought in gold. One man, working with six servants, could become wealthy in a single growing season. By 1620 laws had to be passed against too conspicuous a display of the new wealth. How far Virginia had come from the starving time! How strange that its prosperity would be built on the addictive smoke sucked from the embers of a burnt weed!

Of course, a society built on smoke was far from ideal. Nevertheless, efforts to curb tobacco production and promote other crops, such as corn, failed. So did the opposition of King James himself to smoking. (He wrote in his "Counter Blaste To Tobacco" that it was "a custom loathsome to the eye, hateful to the nose, harmful to the brain, dangerous to the lungs, and in the black stinking fume thereof, nearest resembling the horrible Stygian smoke of the pit that is bottomless.") Tobacco farms spread throughout the Chesapeake, wherever good soil could be found. Immigration increased. In the three years from 1619 to 1622, 3,750 new colonists arrived in Virginia, mostly indentured servants. This scarcely was sufficient to double the population to 1,240, for the death rate for new arrivals continued to be shockingly high. But even those who lasted less than a year could make their small contribution to the expansion of tobacco cultivation.

The new prosperity of the colony permitted the idealists to try to make the present harmony with the Powhatans permanent. An endowment was established to raise Indian children with English families. Whole Indian families were invited to live on the prosperous farms so that they could become more familiar with European modes of life. Ten thousand acres were set aside to support an Indian college. Smith, far away in exile, could only smile and shake his head.

He knew that such gestures and plans did little to change the underlying logic of the situation. Most who came to Virginia considered themselves transients. They wanted to survive only long enough to return to England rich. They preferred to live in shacks, like prospectors beside a stream that might soon play out. Their maltreatment of their indentured servants became proverbial.

That was all fine as far as Smith was concerned. Greatness had to be built on the backs of the laborers. His great disappointment was that the Indians could not be persuaded to join in the labor. They were, according to all reports, no good at working on the tobacco plantations, and their villages were in the way of further expansion of tobacco. Hence they were regarded by most colonists as indigenous pests, like the mosquito. Even one Virginian who worked hard for harmony between the two peoples, George Thorpe, admitted what Smith could have predicted ahead of time: "There is scarce any man among us that does so much as afford them a good thought in his heart and most men with their mouths give them nothing but maledictions and bitter execrations."

Smith had hoped there would be a role for the Indians in the new society, a servile one. Unfortunately, they had none, and that was disastrous for them and dangerous for the colony. But no one was listening to Smith these days. The Indians, after all, seemed docile enough. The peace established under Powhatan was assumed to be permanent; and tobacco farms were established far from one another with no eye to mutual defense. Although Powhatan had died shortly after Pocahontas, he was succeeded by his brother Opechancanough who assured the English that the sky would fall before the peace between these two peoples would end. George Thorpe, the leading advocate of Indians among the colonists, assured the colonists he had had long talks with Opechancanough on religion, and thought him remarkably close to conversion. All this fine talk could have served to make any disciple of Machiavelli worried and wary. The interests of these two peoples remained directly at odds.

By 1621 there was a steady flow of reports describing the lasting friendship established between the two peoples, or rather an Indian docility interpreted as friendship. English houses were open to Indians, who frequently dined with the colonists and even slept in their bedrooms. "Temperance and Justice kissed each other," one advocate of the colony wrote, "and seemed to bless the cohabitations of English and Indians in Virginia."

However, Opechancanough, as Smith who had offered to fight him to the death knew, was neither a fool nor a coward. He could see the results of the long peace of Pocahontas and Powhatan. More and more English arrived. The tobacco took more and more of the Indian lands. Despite the protestations of friendship, the concessions of the Indians would never end, until they had finally ceased to exist as a people altogether. The longer Opechancanough waited, the stronger the English got. The time for patience and friendship was over. So it was that on March 22, 1622, the sky fell on Virginia.

Simultaneously, throughout Virginia, unarmed Indians laden with food and other trading goods presented themselves to the colonists they knew best. Then, at an apparently prearranged time, they all fell on their hosts, killing the English with their own weapons and tools, afterward mutilating the corpses horribly so that those survivors who found them might lose heart and leave. Women and children were not spared, for they were as much invaders as the men, living off a land that was not theirs. In fact, the women and children, if anything, were worse than the men; for they showed the promise of Smith years ago to be a lie. The English were never going to leave of their own will. To be rid of them, the Indians would have to plant them in the ground.

Three hundred forty-seven colonists, including George Thorpe, were killed, about a third of the whole colony. (John Rolfe also died that year, whether in the massacre or not is not known.) Plantation after plantation was looted and destroyed. Heirs of the dead would find little worth inheriting, except land that now seemed too dangerous to cultivate. The very existence of Virginia was at risk. As one colonist wrote back to England, "The last massacre killed all our country; beside them they killed, they burst the heart of all the rest." All their hope had turned to a hell of grief.

Nonetheless, not everyone was in despair. John Smith saw this disaster as yet another opportunity to promote himself. Rebuffed during the happy time of Pocahontas's visit, he now felt in his element, the war god's rich livery of blood. He would come to the rescue of Virginia, first with his pen, then with his sword. This, this was his kind of fight.

How strange Lady Fortune was! Smith had been given one last chance to mount an expedition to New England a few years before. His small fleet, however, had been kept in harbor by persistently perverse winds until the expedition was abandoned. He was now marked as a man knowledgeable but unlucky. Then, just when he seemed to have no further hope, fortune glanced his way again. His old adversary Opechancanough had given John Smith one last chance. He immediately set to work to explain what had gone wrong, and to reassert his philosophy of colonization; *The General History of Virginia* (1624) was another of John Smith's advertisements for himself.

The problem with the colony from the very beginning had been kindliness, he wrote. Its transgression was too much clemency. The colonists and their supporters in England had persisted in thinking of the Indians as their friends, not their adversaries. Smith, while he was in Virginia, had tried to show the foolishness of this. Time and again, his aggressive policies had benefitted the colony and had kept the peace. But the colonists would not learn, either from Smith's example or their own sad experience. In Smith's words, "Yet were the hearts of the English ever stupid and averted from believing anything that might weaken their hopes to win them [the Indians] by kind usage to Christianity."

But the massacre of 1622 should change all that. The Indians had shown what kind of men, what monsters, what an inhuman race they truly were. So Smith could draw on the traditional images of slaughter to transform grief into fury—young infants swimming in their parents' blood; headless carcasses horribly piled up in heaps; young virgins dragged by their hair to be violated on pikes; an old man with a sword through his aged side kneeling for mercy to an Indian brave, only to have his brains dashed out with an axe. The mutilations to George Thorpe's body, in particular, were too horrible to relate to civilized ears; but, Smith did not need to say, do-gooders like Thorpe deserved to be the first to die.

Now the English had to respond with the mouth of Mars and the tongue of Achilles. Smith should not have to remind his readers (but did anyway), "Rome grew by oppression and rose upon the back of her enemies." The English must now crush the people who conspired the fall of Virginia. They must find within themselves, as the Romans did and the Spanish have, the will to reduce their adversaries to slavery. Only after such sternness will peace come to Virginia. Only then will the Indian be sincerely receptive to civility and Christianity.

And John Smith was just the man to undertake this stern task, to be the scourge and wrath of God. "The wars in Europe, Asia and Africa taught me how to subdue the wild savages in Virginia." He could have done this sixteen years ago if he as governor had been given the proper support. Perhaps he should be unwilling to serve now because of his earlier mistreatment. But no, now was Virginia's time of woe, and how could he, its loving father, bear to be absent from it? They need but ask him to rise and conquer. He would need only one hundred experienced fighting men. With fire and sword he would make the Indians flee, wondering where they might go in their grief and baleful discontent. And, never slack or pitying, he would pursue, giving them no rest until finally they would beg for peace and "give all they had to be relieved of their hourly misery." They would cede us everything. The ground would be ours that gives them sustenance, the air they breathe, the water, fire, all that they have, their lands, their goods, their lives. As for Opechancanough, Smith would drink his dying blood. Then all would know that England had begun to take its rightful place in Christendom, that it had become "as great as any monarchy that ever was since the world began." Indeed, one day the British monarchy would be renowned as not even the Roman emperors had been, renowned as the chosen vessel of Christian civilization.

Despite his eloquence, Smith never did get his hundred men; nor did he ever return to the New World. His *History of Virginia,* however, was a success, one of those few books rightly credited with having helped shape the future.

Certainly, the harsh policies toward the Powhatans after the massacre were all he could have wished. Too much money was to be made from tobacco to let the Indians enjoy their victory, or to tolerate their broader claims. Smith must have been pleased with this belated wisdom, however frustrated that he could not implement it with his own hands.

A governor now would write, "Our first work is expulsion of the savages." The council declared a "perpetual war without peace and truce" against the Indians, and exhorted colonists to set aside the rules of justice when dealing with so perfidious an enemy. The company in London, itself no longer on the side of mildness, now advocated "rooting them out" from "the face of the earth." Even propagandists for the colony tried to turn the massacre to advantage; before the massacre, the colonists as good Christians had been obliged to treat the savages with gentleness and fair usage, but now after the outrage they could by right of war take the Indians' cultivated fields from them and reduce them to bondage. Had Smith lived to see all this implemented, he would have had much occasion to boast about his vindication. But, then again, his

History of Virginia does endure as just such a boast. In fact, the writings of John Smith may in the final analysis be his greatest achievement.

Smith would have shuddered at this judgment. He was a man of action, not of words; a maker of war, not of phrases—or so he liked to think. He had little interest in enduring in memory as an "author." He wrote for the future only to make sure that his actions were not forgotten, that they were not appropriated by other selves as insatiable and unscrupulous as John Smith. His final defense of his achievement would be with a palisade of language.

His will to succeed in this world was so fierce and unslaked, it is not hard to imagine Smith's spirit lingering here to follow the development of his Virginia in the decades after his death. That singular development, as other European colonies were established along the North American coast, was enough to make any human being shudder, except perhaps a John Smith, and maybe even him. Virginia, eldest of the colonies, seemed alone worthy to be called permanently a land of the dead.

The successful planting of any colony along this coast required that the ground be repeatedly fertilized with the bodies of would-be settlers, but in Virginia alone that requirement threatened to be a perennial levy. In the others there would be much death for a year or two or three. But finally the colony would take root, and the yearly sacrifice of human innocents could end—and the death rate would decline to that of an ordinary European village or town. The frontier would still contain its own hazards, and the presence of the European settlers would continue to extract a horrifying human cost from neighboring Indian groups. But in the settled parts of the colony, away from the frontier, life could go on with a normal round of expectation and routine, contentment and disappointment. Or so it was throughout most of eastern North America. But to go from New France or New England or New Netherlands to Virginia in the mid-seventeenth century was like leaving this world for the nether regions.

Here in Virginia every year was like the first planting, when the land itself seemed to be revolting against the alien intruders. Every summer new pestilences would sweep out of the tidewater swamp lands into the colony, killing many and breaking the health of many more. Mosquitoes, bad water, a scurvy diet—no one today can be certain of the principal cause, if there was only one. It is better to see Virginia with seventeenth-century eyes, a new Egypt under the permanent judgment of God, or perhaps just one of those cursed places of the earth where doomed souls collected before crossing the river Styx.

Much of the death, not surprisingly, occurred among those in their first year as colonists. When the ships brought new arrivals, the Virginians would have lively discussions about how many of them were likely to survive their "seasoning," as it was called. They would likely have made the subject of grand bets had there been reliable numbers.

Bringing the arriving colonists in had its own dangers for the ship's crew, for they had to face their own brief version of "seasoning." One captain reported that when he arrived in Virginia one summer, he counted thirty-six other ships at anchor. By the time he left (which was quickly since he knew Virginia) fifteen of the other captains had already become a permanent part of Virginia topsoil. This was a place where you were quick or dead.

Not that those who survived their initial seasoning were to be envied. Their health was just broken down at a more leisurely pace. The few women in Virginia—one for every three men—seemed to stand up a little better. An enduring female could become quite wealthy by marrying a succession of husbands. After planting one husband, a widow would usually wait as much as a month before taking another, but sometimes as little as a week. (It has been estimated for one Virginia county that less than 10 percent of the families had both natural parents caring for the children.)

A stay in mid-seventeenth-century Virginia was an education in the cheapness of human life, the valuelessness of the individual in the sum total of things. As William Fitzhugh, who grew to maturity in seventeenth-century Virginia, wrote, "Before I was ten years old . . . I looked upon this life here as but going to an inn, no permanent being." This was harsh experience, not religious piety, speaking.

Slavery had yet to become pervasive, but that was only an accident. The Indians never did make good slaves; about this Smith had been mistaken, trusting too much the example of the Spanish in enslaving the Indians of the Caribbean, Mexico, and Peru. Even treated with the utmost harshness, the Virginia Indians would not provide the labor necessary for the expanding tobacco plantations. (By 1629, more than one and a half million pounds of tobacco were exported every year by Virginia.) The Indians simply did not work well outside their tribal setting, and would run away into the wilderness when mistreated.

The obvious answer to this need for labor was the importation of slaves from Africa, much as the Spanish were doing now that the Indian population in their American colonies had collapsed. Virginia, however, was so unhealthy that even the importation of slaves was not particularly profitable. A slave might cost 2,000 pounds of tobacco, perhaps 3,000 if skilled. (Pounds tobacco, not pounds sterling, was the currency of seventeenth-century Virginia.) However, an indentured servant with an obligation of four to five years would cost only 1,000 pounds of tobacco. If a servant did not survive his seasoning, you would not have lost as much as you would have on a slave. And almost all laborers who survived their seasoning would then be worked to death within three or four years.

In general, Virginia planters cared for their laborers in about the same spirit that John Smith cared for Turks. Medical treatment, for instance, was expensive in Virginia; a thousand pounds for the treatment of a serious disease. As a result, planters would not bother with medical treatment for any servants stricken ill or hurt in an accident. It was better to let them just die and buy new ones. Given the state of seventeenth-century medicine, this is probably the only factor that favored the servant over his master; when the servant felt poorly, he would not be bled.

A few principled sea captains, once they became familiar with Virginia, refused to carry indentured servants there, for much the same reason they refused to carry slaves. The question remains, who would willingly come as an indentured servant to such a place? The answer is simple enough. Only someone with no other choice, and therefore with nothing to lose.

In the first days of the seventeenth century, when English colonies were still plans and speculations, Francis Bacon had written, "It is a shameful and unblessed thing to take the scum of the people and the wicked and condemned men to be the people with whom you plant." If so, then Virginia itself was assuredly a shameful and unblessed thing. As one early Virginian put it in disgust, the colony was being used as a "sink to drain England of her filth and scum."

This might have revolted even John Smith himself. Not even he, we would hope, could take pride in having been the heroic founder of a drain for filth and scum. So let us have his spirit lingering on this earth, feeling more and more alienated from his once virgin, now-wanton land, until finally he is reconciled to thinking of his life as one fulfilled primarily through language. Finally he realizes that his activity as a leader was only a piece of cleverness, a paltry effort that mattered only within a pathetically limited range, too limited to satisfy his still burning ambition. This ambition prodding him on, he realizes that as an author alone he can aspire to having a universal power over a whole world. If John Smith was still John Smith, this realization would have made him more Smith still. Let us imagine him, expansively, if belatedly, declaring that cities, empires, conspiracies, wars, havoc, and desolation are ordained by Providence only as food for historians such as himself.

Yes, that is what Smith would tell us. And his literary achievement was considerable. No one, not even Christopher Marlowe, expressed better the grasping, insatiable spirit of the Renaissance. Smith's undying achievement is himself, captured for us forever in his words, forever in the amber of language, like some huge predatory insect frozen hideously at the moment of the pounce, mandibles eternally agape.

Chapter II

CHAMPLAIN AT QUEBEC

"HE WAS THE AENEAS OF A DESTINED PEOPLE." So the greatest nineteenth-century historian of colonial America, Francis Parkman, described Samuel de Champlain, founder of Quebec. Champlain was a man as ambitious and courageous as John Smith. Yet there was about him more the quiet sadness of Aeneas or Cervantes than the voluble exuberance of Smith or Marlowe.

While Smith's early adventures had taught him that fortune smiled only on those who seize her with daring, Champlain's early life had left him haunted by the eerie feeling that a demonic destructiveness always lurked nearby, ready to sweep away in a moment whatever human beings had built. Like a good stoic, he seems always to have felt himself on the edge of an abyss. Whereas Smith appears on the stage of the New World as the swaggering warrior king of Virginia, Champlain is rather the father of New France, the frowning, worried father. The famous lines of Corneille's *Cid:*

> Never do we taste of perfect joy.
> Our happiest success is still tinctured with sorrow.
> Always, as things work out,
> Some worry mars the purity of our content

could have been easily written about Champlain, as if the tragic dilemmas being grandly acted out on the classical French stage were also being lived by that small portion of France trying to establish itself on the Saint Lawrence River under the leadership of Samuel de Champlain.

Champlain was someone long familiar with human tragedy. While the youthful Smith was fecklessly seeking his fortune in the broad world, Champlain was growing up in a France torn by civil war. The civil war between Puritan and Anglo-Catholic that would disrupt English life in the mid-seventeenth century was prefigured in murderous fights between Catholics and Protestants in sixteenth-century France. In this French civil war, Champlain's hometown of Brouage was dangerously positioned.

Brouage was the second greatest port of France, and was reputed to have the safest harbor in all Europe. Brouage, incidentally, was only about twenty miles from La Rochelle, the greatest port of France and also the greatest Protestant stronghold. This proximity of La Rochelle and Brouage was the decisive factor in the unhappy history of Brouage during much of the civil war, for both sides regarded control of its harbor as crucial and continually fought over it as a prize, the Catholics to have at least one major sea port in Brittany, the Protestants to assure their complete dominance at sea there.

When Champlain was born, Brouage was controlled by the Protestants. Perhaps Champlain's family was at that time Protestant as well; Champlain, a devout Catholic his whole adult life, was named not after a Catholic saint but, in Protestant fashion, after an Old Testament prophet. In 1570, when he was perhaps three, the Catholics succeeded in taking Brouage after a siege during which the Protestants defended bravely, their dead estimated at twelve hundred.

A few years later Brouage was once again Protestant, and in 1576 it feted the most famous leader of the French Protestants, Henry of Navarre. The nine- or ten-year-old Champlain had more sights to remember, especially the naval battle staged in Henry's honor in Brouage harbor, a fight to the death between some captive Moors on one vessel and Christians on four others. The burning of the Moorish vessel amidst the cheering of a whole city was a triumphant conclusion to a great celebration. The next year starvation replaced celebration in Brouage, as it once again came under siege from the Catholic forces. This time Brouage capitulated for good, to be henceforth steadfastly Catholic and Royalist.

Such apostasy the Protestants of La Rochelle could scarcely be expected to forget or forgive, especially from a lesser city that was also a commercial rival. And so Brouage was repeatedly attacked by Protestant forces. The closest it came to falling was in 1585, when it was besieged from land and assaulted from the sea. Champlain, who had already begun his career as a seaman, could well have been on the ships that defended the Brouage harbor against the La Rochelle fleet. Although the siege was a failure, the Protestants did manage to enter the harbor, and there sank twenty ships that they had brought loaded with sand and rock. Twenty old ships was a small price to pay to ruin a religious and commercial rival. Brouage harbor overnight became one of the most treacherous in all Europe. Brouage's days of prosperity were over; never again would the Protestants and Catholics bother to contest over the languishing town and its faithless bay.

The story of Brouage was the story of many communities in the French civil war, communities caught in between and destroyed out of spite. In the world of power politics and military tactics their loss was a commonplace expedient, part and parcel of the process of history. However, for this to be the fate of your community was not a commonplace, but a tale of unutterable grief too terrible for tongues. Champlain grew up amidst such vicissitudes and such grief.

As he reached maturity, he could see this grief on a national scale. In the aftermath of the Armada, Philip II did not give up his designs on France. Henry III, who had tried to mediate between France's Protestant and Catholic factions, was assassinated by a Catholic fanatic. This left two claimants to the throne: one Henry of Orleans from the Catholic league (supported by Philip), the other Henry of Navarre.

Navarre was clearly the legitimate successor, were it not for his Protestantism. His Protestantism, however, was lightly held. He soon converted back to Catholicism. As he put it, "Paris is well worth a mass." The sincerity of this conversion was, needless to say, questioned. Philip, to assist his candidate, invaded France. Champlain's Brittany was the initial objective of this invasion. Although he had an uncle who had gone over to serve as a pilot for Philip's forces, Champlain fought for Henry of Navarre, now Henry IV.

During this campaign Champlain's education in the human capacity for depravity and destructiveness was completed. The treatment of noncombatants by his army was bad even by the standards of the day. It left a path of looting and rape through the very communities it was supposed to be defending. On one day alone Champlain's commander had to execute twenty-eight of his own men for crimes against civilians. Even without the kind ministrations of the army, the suffering of the civilians was extreme. Wolves of the region had become man-eaters, and some were so bold as to run down prey within villages.

If the suffering of the French people was extreme, Champlain also had occasion to pity the invading Spanish troops, who after all were only doing their duty. Four hundred of the best Spanish soldiers found themselves trapped on a small peninsula. Asked to surrender, they decided to fight to the last man, which they almost did. Of the eleven Spaniards who survived the assault, all but two were severely wounded. Yet the dead had sold their lives dearly; French casualties were said to number in the thousands.

By 1598 Brittany and its Spanish invaders had, in Champlain's phrase, "been reduced to obedience." Now Catholic France and Catholic Spain professed only friendship for one another; Henry IV could for the time being feel secure on his throne (at least if he did not think about his predecessor). Perhaps the French could now work together to build something. Champlain, for himself, had certainly learned enough about human destructiveness, enough about depravity and death.

This lesson of destruction was empty wisdom, and he sought no more of it. Let others try to affix blame for past wrongs. Let others flatter themselves by predicting the future. Such inquisitiveness had become for him nothing but disguised sloth. All he wished to learn was how to act, how to build something. To build something human that, with good fortune, might withstand the vagaries of time—of time and human greed, of stupidity and weakness. He thought the Spanish might teach him how.

The Spanish had shown him how to die futilely on what had come to be called the Pointe des Espagnola. But he also knew they had built whole societies in the New World, and *that* was living productively. France had never succeeded in such an enterprise. Perhaps this was one explanation for the continuing destruction raining on France, for the persistent rancors that were like moths fretting her fabric. Mother France had become obstinate in her misery. She must look outside herself for her salvation.

Champlain wanted to see the Spanish colonies at first hand. He visited the Spanish troops still in France, and there he found the uncle who had gone over to the Spanish side, now a prisoner of war awaiting transport to his newly adopted country. Through the good offices of his uncle, Champlain shipped out first to Spain and then to the New World. When Champlain finally reached New Spain, he was dazzled:

"A more beautiful country could not be seen or desired than the kingdom of New Spain, which is three hundred leagues in length and two hundred in breadth. On this journey to Mexico, I admired the fine forests that are encountered, filled with the most beautiful trees that one could wish, such as palms, cedars, laurels, orange and lemon trees, cabbage palms, guavas, avocadoes, ebony, Brazil and Campeachy wood, which are all common trees in that country, with an infinity of other kinds that I cannot name on account of the variety of them, which gives the greatest possible satisfaction to the eyes; together with the quantities of birds of diverse plumage that are seen in the forests. Next, one comes upon great plains stretching as far as the eye can reach, covered with immense droves of cattle, such as horses, mules, oxen, cows, sheep, and goats, which have pastures always fresh in every season, there

48 A NEW WORLD

being no winter, but a very temperate atmosphere, neither hot nor cold. It only rains twice in the year, but the dews at night are so heavy that the plants are thereby sufficiently watered and nourished. Moreover, this whole country is adorned with very fine rivers and streams, which traverse almost the whole extent of the kingdom, and the greater part of which are navigable for boats. The soil is very fertile, producing corn twice in the year, and in as great abundance as one could desire, and, whatever season it may be, there is always very good fresh fruit on the trees; for when one fruit arrives at maturity, others are coming on and thus succeed one another; and the trees are never bare of fruit and are always green. If the king of Spain would permit vines to be planted in the said kingdom, they would fructify like the corn; for I have seen grapes produced from a stock which someone had planted for his pleasure, every grape of which was as large as a plum, half a thumb in length, and much better than those of Spain. But all the contentment I felt at the sight of things so pleasing was but little in regard to what I experienced when I beheld that beautiful city of Mexico, which I had not supposed to be so superbly constructed of splendid temples, palaces and fine houses."

Champlain could not find enough superlatives to describe what the Spanish had achieved in little more than a lifetime. This was an enterprise with which any man worthy of life could be satisfied. Nonetheless, he was not uncritical. He envisioned possible material improvements for New Spain—a canal, for instance, across the isthmus of Panama. (The passage to the Pacific that others were seeking in the north could be built right here at the middle latitudes.) He also thought that the conquering spirit in which the Spanish usually approached the new Indian groups was itself mistaken. The lessons they had learned against the Aztecs and Incas were misplaced when applied to others. A new colony should seek friends and allies amidst the indigenous peoples.

A new colony, a French colony—this clearly was what Champlain was thinking about, one that would learn from the Spanish example and improve upon it. Yet, for all his enthusiasm, he could not forget the lesson of his youth. He could not forget the vulnerability of all human enterprises, the instability of human things. Colonies could pass away as quickly as they sprang up, and the cause of their passing could just as easily be the malicious jealousy of others as any intrinsic failure.

If he had been inclined to forget this sad truth, it had been brought home to him by his visit to Puerto Rico, once one of the most prosperous of the Spanish colonies, now the victim of a capricious fate. The harbor was a good one, much as Brouage once had been; but now the place was desolate, the once populous town deserted. Puerto Rico had recently been pillaged by the English. Most of the houses had been burned, and almost all the population had been carried away or had run off. To those with ears to hear, deserted Puerto Rico had become a kingdom of lament. He saw before him a Puerto Rico strewn with the husks and formless ruins of past promise.

So on his first trip to the New World Champlain discovered his vocation: to establish a French colony there. He knew his vocation then, but he also knew the risk. He could spend a lifetime building such a colony and a passing cloud could sweep it all away, like the uncertain glory of an April day. A squadron of English ships (or Spanish or Dutch) could reduce it in a single day to the desolation he had seen in Puerto Rico. All the shrewdness in the world is useless when heaven withdraws its aid. Fortune, fate, providence, or whatever name you give it, is more important than all a human being can do. But we must each still have our try, and Champlain would have his.

Champlain's chance, unlike John Smith's, was more than a calculated gamble at self-aggrandizement. Having confronted the aimless fickleness of history, the porcelain brittleness of human achievements, the giddy whirl of what seemed a perpetually self-creating disorder, he instinctively realized that he need not be entirely of it; he could be other than it if he chose. He could be outwardly involved and inwardly detached—*pace inter media arma*. Constant, grim, persevering, he forged for himself an identity by choosing an enduring shape for his desires, a permanent purpose for his fleeting life. With such a purpose he could be free—whether on a throne or in fetters, whether an emperor or a slave, whatever the final results of his actions—free and not disquieted by what cannot be comprehended.

So about Champlain the mature man there is a studied stubbornness that he himself regarded as the tranquility of a well-ordered mind, a stolid singleness, somehow independent of any of his particular words or experiences or actions, sitting unmovably behind them. This finally renders Champlain the man boring in his constancy, his personality having faded into a wearisome blandness, a quiet vacant composure, thoroughly admirable in its way but largely devoid of the living warmth of personality except in its deeply hidden fears. And fears there always remained in his depths. He could not deny the flux flowing around all that he would have secure and determinant in this world, flowing around and under until finally decomposing all into glistening infinitesimal fragments. Champlain was not going to pour his own soul out onto the sand of this unstable world. Himself he would always keep in reserve, or so he seems to have resolved.

We should not set a high price on anything hurrying by, into or out of existence. That is like falling in love with a sparrow as it flies by. We no sooner make it an object of our affection than it has disappeared for good. Even if—God forbid—the universe is a chaos huddled together, even if our lives are but meaningless instants in a purposeless succession, we can still follow the enduring inner voice of principle, follow it with dignity and perseverance, with fidelity and modesty and justice and truth. It has to be enough to attend to this purpose within. Whatever his fears, Champlain's life would be a succession of solid achievements, a life eventful and exciting and yet at its core colorless, taking on whatever hues it had from all that happened around him. Of course, he rarely perceived this. His world, as he wished to see it, was all gray on gray. When the outside world occasionally broke through the pallid haze with which he purposefully surrounded himself, he could be temporarily dazzled by its beauty, blinking like an owl forced into daylight. But soon his protective instincts would take charge and he would regain his composure, never quite forgetting that the beauty of the world was inexplicably allied to his deepest fears of its insufficiency. When Champlain returned to France in 1601 after a two-year absence, he quickly published an account of his travels—*A Brief Discourse . . . on the West Indies*—and was soon recruited by a group to help them establish a trading colony just south of the mouth of the Saint Lawrence River, a place they would call Port Royal; there perhaps France could establish its first permanent outpost in North America. To this end, they had gained a monopoly from Henry IV for fur trading with the Indians. Soon Champlain was once again on his way to the New World.

There was, however, an inherent weakness in this project of which Champlain was now a junior member. For decades fishermen and whalers from many nations had been harvesting the rich waters of this region. Some of these had discovered how lucrative trading with the natives along the coast for furs could be as a supplement to their ordinary catch. These fishermen could not be expected to respect a monopoly given by the French king; even the French among them would try to defy it, and would use whatever influence they had at the fickle court of Henry IV to get it rescinded. So the monopoly that was to provide the economic foundation for the trading post was neither secure nor really enforceable.

There was an obvious remedy to this weakness. The colony could have a *de facto* monopoly if it established a post well inland, far beyond the range of fishermen. Champlain set out to explore up the Saint Lawrence, also with the faint hope that a passage to the Pacific might be found:

"We came to anchor at Quebec, which is a narrow part of the said river of Canada, some three hundred paces broad. At these narrows on the north side is a very high mountain, which slopes down on both sides: all the rest is level and beautiful country, where there is good land covered with trees such as oaks, cypresses, birches, fir-trees and aspens, and also wild fruitbearing trees, and vines; so that in my opinion, if this soil were tilled, it would be as good as ours."

So Samuel de Champlain blandly described the site where he would found the capital of New France. But he would do no founding on that day in June 1603. The purpose of the expedition was only to discover how far European ships could travel along this waterway into the heart of the continent. The Indians told of ferocious rapids some days beyond the narrows they called Quebec. These rapids were so dangerous, they said, that not even a canoe could pass them. The French decided to travel there in skiffs, to see for themselves.

Champlain, nonetheless, was obviously observing the terrain with an eye to possible future settlement. He found the country that lay beyond the natural fortress of Quebec, if anything, even more inviting. This land was also obviously very fertile. Champlain duly tasted the many indigenous fruits and pronounced them delicious. He even found a root that tasted to him like truffles, a gourmet in the wilderness. While Quebec would be the ideal location to place a fort to defend the upper river, a confluence of the rivers farther along Champlain thought would serve well as a trading post. He could imagine Indian canoes laden with furs arriving from each of the three rivers. Such pleasant reveries of the future, however, were interrupted when the explorers reached the rapids about which the Indians had warned them.

They heard the rapids before they saw them, like the mumbling of distant thunder. When they saw them, they realized the Indians had told the truth, had even understated it. What they saw was so dreadful and beautiful it would have taken a Fenimore Cooper to capture in words. It was as if the water itself was intent upon revealing its full perversity, its defiance of all order or shape or proportion. It seemed to move by no rule at all, sometimes leaping, sometimes tumbling, here skipping, there shooting, in one place as white as snow, in another as green as grass, here rumbling like a deep drum, there singing in sweet ripples like a brook, deadly whirlpools and lazy currents side by side. And all to what purpose, except to obstruct or to confuse?

But if the water had no purpose, Champlain did, and was immediately making assessments, not one to be beguiled by beauty. These rapids would be impossible to pass through, even in the smallest boat. Portage around the rapids too would be extremely difficult. Champlain and the others could see how well suited for this land were the Indians' light birchbark canoes. To travel past the rapids Europeans would have to accustom themselves to traveling by canoe. The expedition had no time for this now, but the Indian guides, whose incredible stories about the rapids had proven true, were asked what lay beyond them.

Fifteen leagues of easy river, they said, then five small rapids in quick succession, then a lake fifteen or sixteen leagues long, then two more leagues of river, then a smaller lake, then thirty leagues of river with five more rapids, then a huge lake perhaps eighty leagues long with many islands and brackish water, then a waterfall as large as a mountain, then another large lake from which there was a strait which if followed would lead to the greatest lake of all, so vast no man had ever ventured across it—and its water was very salty, like the sea.

Champlain hoped that this greatest lake, of whose existence he had been told by other native informants, was the Pacific Ocean. Whether it was or no, the Saint Lawrence, with its intricate, almost devious, system of lakes, rapids, and falls, presented an irresistible challenge. Traversing this you would have ample opportunity to show whatever courage, patience, and endurance you had within you. Indeed, to look out onto this uncharted expanse of wilderness, to look out across rapids of unprecedented size and power, to imagine the European society that one day might flourish there—this could make a man, the right man, feel that any other purpose for his life was paltry.

Tully had taught that a man was born primarily for his kinsmen and country; only a very small part of his soul was for himself alone, and this was largely fulfilled through friendship—for Tully, this friendship was with Atticus. Champlain never found his Atticus, if he ever had looked. New France would soon become both Rome and Atticus to him. And the personal part of his soul, never large or strong, would begin to shrink toward nothingness.

Champlain's account of his first trip up the Saint Lawrence, however brief, is pregnant with future happenings. For instance, Champlain proposed settlements not only at Quebec and Three Rivers, but at the rapids—and eventually, seven years after Champlain's death, Montreal would begin to flourish there, as he had predicted. But for all the future achievements that are somehow carried within Champlain's sparse narrative, even more striking is an omission: Champlain's failure to mention Jacques Cartier, who had explored the Saint Lawrence a few decades earlier and whose own accounts were available to Champlain and his fellows. (The very name "Saint Lawrence" derives from him.) Some of the sites Champlain described as suitable for settlement Cartier had himself described earlier. Cartier had mapped many of the same land formations, had found the same fertile soil and tasted the same fruits, and had marveled at the same forests and streams full of game—but Cartier did not have to argue, as Champlain did, that these sites were suitable for human habitation. Cartier had found the banks of the Saint Lawrence already teeming with indigenous human life. Two distinct Indian nations were then flourishing there. When Champlain returned less than a human lifetime later, the land was the same but the people had vanished.

Many explanations have been offered, from Champlain's day to our own, for this startling change. These two nations were attacked from the north, perhaps by the Algonquin, and moved to the south to become part of the Iroquois Confederacy. Or they were attacked from the south and dispersed to the north—or was it to the west or the east? Or they overtilled their fields and the ground became temporarily infertile, and they freely moved away, somewhere. Or they died of European diseases that were introduced by Cartier but only became virulent after he left. Or perhaps they destroyed one another in a ferocious war that made the Saint Lawrence a scene of bloody havoc, death alone triumphant.

What actually had happened Champlain did not know. All he knew was that the banks of the Saint Lawrence were deserted and invited colonization—and his informants could not tell him when they were deserted, or why, or where the descendants of these once flourishing peoples now lived. Perhaps at the narrows called Quebec there had been a glorious conflict, noble deeds and exploits, an Iliad of the New World. An Iliad that the wilderness had watched with an indifferent silence, as it watched Champlain now.

Not that Champlain, at least in his public reports, was given to such melancholy meditations. Champlain, the man who wished to lead new endeavors in this land, was all fearlessness and optimism as he recounted his voyage up the Saint Lawrence to the scenes of his own future triumphs. Yet at the end of his account, he could not resist including an image of demonic destructiveness; he retailed uncritically (and unstoically) some Indian lore. "They told me he had the form of a woman, but most hideous, and of such a size that according to them the tops of the masts of our vessel would not reach to his waist, so large do they represent him; and they say he often devoured and still devours many savages; these he puts, when he can catch them, into a great pocket, and afterwards eats them; and those who had escaped the danger of this ill-omened beast said that his pocket was so large that he could put our vessel into it. This monster, which the savages call Gougou, makes horrible noises in that island, and when they speak of him, it is with unutterably strange terror, and many have assured me that they have seen him."

To understand why Champlain took this fantastic report seriously is to understand a good deal about the man. He had found his vocation on his first trip to the New World—and now on his second he saw Quebec. He could imagine the shores of the Saint Lawrence teeming with human settlement, a new France of which he would be the father. A lifetime of rewarding labor spread before him. Yet as he assented to this future, the Indians broke into his reveries with tales of the Gougou. Champlain could not help but to be much moved and then to recount the tales, despite himself, with a shudder.

For this credulity he was mocked in France. He was one of those who went to the New World just to lose their reason. The Indians had only given a shape, a local habitation, and a name to an airy nothing of fear. Or so one critic contended:

"The truth is that these tribes who live at constant war and are never out of danger—bearing with them this curse for they are forgotten of God—often have dreams and vain imaginings that the enemy is at the gate; and the reason that they are thus full of foreboding is that they have no walled towns, wherefore they find themselves often, indeed usually surprised and overcome; which being so, one must not wonder that from time to time they have panic terrors and imaginations . . . Such is the nature and humor of many savages; for their whole life is sullied by a mutual bloodshed, more especially with that of their enemies in war, and thus they have great fears, and invent for themselves a Gougou, who is the torturer of their consciences; even as Cain, after the murder of his brother Abel, had the wrath of God ever at his heels and could nowhere find ease of soul, thinking ever that he had this Gougou before his eyes."

This sensible ridicule seems to have chastened Champlain; at least he became more guarded in his public reports. In all his later writings, where he recounts the building of his own walled town on the deserted Saint Lawrence, and recounts too his leading of native allies in surprise attacks against villages of their enemies, he never again mentioned the Gougou. But neither, one senses, did he ever doubt that the Indian tales held profound human truths that few would wish to confront directly.

On his return to Europe, Champlain had reason to shudder about French society as well. At the time Smith was insinuating himself into the group organizing an expedition to Virginia, Champlain was publishing his account of his second voyage to the New World, an account he called simply *The Savages*. He now knew the ideal place for his colony. Yet he could find no equivalent to the London merchants who were funding the Virginia expedition. He would have to wait five years, until 1608, before he would be able to colonize

Quebec. By the time he arrived at Quebec the second time, John Smith was already the governor of Virginia.

In the intervening four years Champlain had tried to keep active with the paltry French efforts. In 1604 he returned to spend a winter at the French outpost near the mouth of the Saint Lawrence. The voyage over served as a reminder of the divisions still tormenting his country. Theological discussions among the passengers, who included a priest and minister, soon became rancorous debates that quickly degenerated into fisticuffs. Champlain was disgusted by the exhibition, for what it told about the old and for what it portended for the new.

So was the rest of the company, it seems. When the priest and the minister sickened and died upon landing, the crew, with nondenominational good humor, put them both in the same grave to see if they could finally reach peace with one another there.

After having endured a winter in which scurvy took many of his fellows, Champlain set out to explore toward the south, along the coast where Smith would place the names New England, Massachusetts, Plymouth. Champlain gave these places names as well, French names that did not endure. Neither did Champlain's interest in the southerly coast. The Indians there seemed numerous and hostile. Both times he explored he took significant casualties; Quebec was empty and friendly in comparison. Then, in 1607, word came that Port Royal had to be abandoned because the monopoly on the fur trade had been revoked.

Once again Champlain returned to the court and the arts of the courtier, and at last he received authorization to establish his own colony at Quebec. It would be a meagerly supported expedition. Two ships, one for colonization, one for fur trading; a monopoly of a single year to support the colony. The trading ship was ready early, so Champlain sent it ahead. Then on April 12, 1608, he himself sailed for the New World. But even in his great happiness Champlain still feared a great reverse—the mistake of a moment could deny him his destiny.

Such a moment almost occurred shortly after he arrived in the New World. When he boarded his other ship to check on its trading, he discovered to his shock that one of the ship's crew had been shot to death, and three others, including the captain, were nursing serious wounds. They had arrived to discover another vessel already there, a Basque whaler that was doing a little trading on the side. Henry IV's decree was quite explicit. Champlain and his lieutenants were "to seize, apprehend, and arrest all those violating our present injunction and ordinance as well as their vessels, merchandise, arms, provisions and victuals."

When the Basques had been informed of this, they replied that the king of France was but a man, and like other men made mistakes. The king could grant as many monopolies for New France as he liked, so long as he stayed in France and left the Basques to do as they pleased. Champlain now saw the results of his captain's attempt to chastise these Basques for their impudence. The fool had forgotten that one must always navigate between the dangerous shores of will and judgment, caution and desire.

His men obviously expected him, with superior armament, to bludgeon the Basques into submission in the name of his king and his expedition. He knew what pride allegedly demanded when so outraged, but he was not seeking an opportunity to display his honor. To do further battle was to risk the expedition. He might win, and probably would, but perhaps at the cost of forgoing his settlement of Quebec. The whole carefully planned enterprise could end up in fragments at his feet, and for what?

After gaining assurances from the Basques that they would cause no more trouble if left to their business in peace, Champlain and his ships simply continued on, lest (as he put it) "a good cause should now become a poor one and thus all be ruined." Some of his men concluded they had a coward for a captain.

The navigation to Quebec occurred without incident, but negotiating places with names like Devils' Point or Whirlpool River required not just skill and experience but good fortune for safe passage. On July 3 Champlain and his men arrived at Quebec and began to build the edifice that would enable them to command the river at this point. The compound was to consist of three main buildings two stories high; his first buildings were particularly attentive to the needs of defense, unlike the shacks initially thrown up in Jamestown.

"Each building was three fathoms long and two and a half wide. The storehouse was six long and three wide, with a fine cellar six feet high. All the way round the buildings I had a gallery made, outside the second story, which was a very convenient thing. There were also ditches fifteen feet wide and six deep, and outside these I made several salients which enclosed a part of the buildings, and there is an open space four fathoms wide and six or seven long, which abuts upon the river's bank. Round about the buildings are very good gardens, and an open place on the north side of a hundred or a hundred and twenty yards long and fifty or sixty wide."

Along a nearby river his men discovered the remnants of a chimney, some worm-eaten boards, and a few cannon balls. "All these things show clearly that this was a settlement which was founded by Christians." Champlain concluded that these were the relics of Cartier's Saint Croix. It had quietly crumbled in the solitude of the wilderness, neglected and largely forgotten, like the now-departed circumstances and men that had called it into being.

Champlain did not need relics from Saint Croix to remind him how perilous were his own efforts. While the compound at Quebec was being built, he faced a plot on his very life. One of his men had apparently been much impressed by the Basques. These were courageous and unscrupulous men, men who would snub a king at a distance, and a Champlain to his face, if a sufficient profit were involved. Such businessmen would pay handsomely for the fort that was being built by Champlain. The first step in making such a deal would be to kill Champlain and take over the fort.

This subversive recruited three others as leaders of his conspiracy, and they in turn pressured a number of others into at least acquiescing to their plan. One of these, however, the more he thought about it, found that he disliked the conspirators even more than he did Champlain—he especially feared the prospect of being at their mercy once the conspiracy had succeeded. He confessed the whole mutiny.

Champlain took the news calmly, losing neither his temper nor his grip. The art of life, the Stoics taught, was more like a wrestler's than a dancer's—it was always having just the right response to the unexpected onslaught. Through a second party he made some wine, plenty of wine, available to the conspirators, at a place of his choosing. Only after they had sufficiently imbibed did he spring an ambush and take them captive without a fight.

Champlain did not permit himself a satisfying vengeance on those who had planned to take his life. The best way to avenge oneself is not to become like the wrongdoer. With the exception of the four chief conspirators, a miscreant had only to repent and testify against the leaders to get full pardon. Of the four remaining, three were simply sent back to France to face justice there. Only on the instigator of the plot did Champlain demand that the full fury of the law fall. Perhaps the men did now pity him as he sobbed out his heart in repentance, all sighs and tears; they could not see beyond the immediate moment. This was the man whose selfishness, stupidity, and ill-weaved ambition had threatened the whole group. Had they ever really believed in his vain plans? Did it ever occur to them that Champlain's death would do nothing to make the dangers hemming them all about disappear? He could predict for them the sequence of their demise had he been killed: first would come the doubtful thoughts and petty dissensions; then would come shuddering fears and violent fright; and finally all would rashly embrace a premature despair.

The chief conspirator was executed, and his head displayed on the highest part of the fort so he could watch the progress he had plotted to thwart—and the men as they worked could sneak a glance at him, and check the progress of the birds with him, a jeering warning against further treachery. Let no one else babble treason.

Champlain's handling of this incident was not motivated by clemency, but by hard calculation. He knew what the winters were like this far north. So he knew that what winter would bring, to guilty and innocent alike, was a punishment far worse than any deserved. By the time the exposed head had become a pure white grin, death would be wandering the colony in sundry shapes.

Champlain, in his account of the trial in his *Voyages* (1613), expressed his annoyance that it delayed the completion of the storehouse. As a result, the provisions "had been left unprotected by all these scoundrels, who husbanded nothing, never considering where they were to find more when these failed." They saw for themselves only a short-term advantage in getting rid of him. They made no careful plans for their survival afterward, nor (as the informer realized) for the basis on which they were to conduct their affairs once he was gone.

Perhaps those who had not spent a winter in New France (as Champlain had) did not realize how grave a concern food would become. Winters were hideous, barrenness everywhere for months on end. "While the carpenters, sawyers, and the other workmen were busy at our quarters, I set all the rest to work clearing the land about our settlement in order to make gardens in which to sow grain and seed, for the purpose of seeing how the whole thing would succeed, particularly since the soil seemed to be very good." If Quebec was to survive many winters, it had to produce its own food, for supplies from France could be cut off by enemies some day and could be delayed by circumstance anytime.

The first frost was on the ground that year on October 3. On November 18 there was a heavy snowfall blown by gale winds, a blizzard. That month also witnessed the first two deaths, one of them the informant, both from dysentery caused by eating bad food. Snow and ice would remain on the ground until April. By February starving Indians had begun to appear from the north; their food having long since run out, they hoped the French would give them succor. Champlain described one group that dramatized the general desperation:

"On the twentieth of the month some Indians made their appearance on the other side of the river, and shouted to us to go to their aid, but this was out of our power, on account of the large amount of ice which was flowing down the river. So hungry were these poor wretches, that being at their wits' end, they, men, women and children, resolved to die or to cross the river, in the hope that I would succor them in their dire need. Accordingly having taken this resolution, the men and women seized their children and got into their canoes, thinking they would reach our shore by an opening in the ice which the wind had made; but no sooner were they in the middle of the river, than their canoes were caught between the ice floes and broken into a thousand pieces. They maneuvered so well that they jumped with their children, whom the women were carrying on their backs, upon a large block of ice. While they were upon it, we could hear them screaming so much that it was pitiful; for they expected nothing less than death. But fortune favored these poor wretches so much that a large ice floe struck the side of the one upon which they stood with such force that it threw them upon the land. They, seeing such a favorable turn of events, went ashore with as great joy as they ever experienced in spite of the famine they had endured. They came to our settlement so thin and emaciated that they looked like skeletons, most of them being unable to stand."

The French did provide them with what little food they could spare. It was not enough, and the Indians then discovered the carrion that the French had put out to trap varmints. The smell of the Indians cooking a two-week-old dog head was a nauseating reminder of the plight that was never remote, even from the most prosperous people (as the French had been before the civil war).

Even with proper leadership, this New World, of course, took its toll. While the Indians starved, eighteen of the French suffered from scurvy; eleven of these died, including the doctor. There were three more deaths from dysentery after those first two in November. Of the twenty-eight men Champlain had with him that first winter in Quebec, he lost twenty to the Gougou.

Champlain realized that their diet had something to do with disease (he was particularly suspicious of the salted dried meat, which seemed good primarily for toughening teeth); he also realized that the extreme cold weakened the resistance of his men. But he thought more than these two factors were at work. He thought clearing the land itself worked its own vengeance on those responsible: "From the earth, when it is exposed, there come forth certain vapors trapped therein and these infect the air. This has been seen in the experience of people who have been in other settlements the first year the sun shines on what had been cleared." Polluted air, Champlain thought, was the revenge nature takes on those who clear its land.

Once this first, horrific winter had passed, Champlain wished to explore more fully the region around the Saint Lawrence. But there was a complication. Between the tribes who lived to the north of the Saint Lawrence—the Montaignes, the Algonquin, the Huron—and the Iroquois Confederacy that dominated the south there existed a traditional feud. For as long as anyone could remember, young men of the North and South proved their bravery, their worthiness as men, in raids. Not much life was lost in these raids; wooden shields and armor had made most arrow wounds minor. Nonetheless, any warrior taken alive by the enemy was likely to be brutally tortured to death. Other than that, the continual feuding had more the air of a blood sport than a war. This was the dueling of the New World. Even the torture of a captive, so hideous to European eyes, provided him with the perfect occasion to display his courage to the fullest. This, unlike a summary execution, was a death without shame. While these feuds were not wars of conquest, they did serve to make certain areas no-man's-lands. The feuding tribes instinctively drew back from one another and left the region in between, however otherwise attractive for hunting or settlement, as a land one entered only at his own risk. Anyone found there was fair game, and was himself likely looking for trouble.

Champlain had no doubt how best to exploit this situation to his own advantage and to that of his colony. He wished his colony to live in friendship with the local peoples. The French would trade European goods for American fur, but true friendship had to be based on more than mutual profits. Champlain had to show the native peoples that he would make sacrifices for them, risk his life for their well-being. If they wished to war against their enemies, then he would march with them. Of course, they would be marching together through land no European had yet trod. So Champlain could use the war path as a road to exploration and discovery. Champlain did not realize that in participating in these raids he was sowing dragon's teeth for his colony, the harvest of which would last generations.

He and a few of his men were soon traveling with an Indian raiding party not by canoe but on foot through the pathless forest itself. This was a strange experience for a European, like moving through a single room of vastness, its vaulted arches supported by thousands of high columns, its ceiling a trembling canopy of leaves, a continuous cloud cover of foliage—an apparently limitless cathedral of pleasing gloom broken only by occasional oases of light, bright islands that the traveler came to long for, as a bedouin did for a little shade.

The forest was a place of beauty and of ambush, the clearing one of refreshment and exposure. It was hard to keep both perspectives in view at the same time. The aesthetic novelty of the forest should be as nothing compared to the task at hand, especially as Champlain began to notice that the number of Indians on this raiding party was constantly dwindling.

Champlain had made the mistake of giving generous presents to his new friends before they had begun, and they were now deciding, one by one, that they would rather take them home than risk losing them to the enemy. As the Indians started to melt into the forest, the French volunteers who were accompanying Champlain began to talk more and more about the attractions of Quebec. Why should they fight a war the Indians themselves did not take seriously?

This was a crisis to which Champlain felt fully equal. He welcomed the opportunity to establish that he, whatever the quailing of his native allies or his fellow French, would do what he promised. He, the Indians had to know, would keep his word to them even if that meant he went without them to face the Iroquois alone. He would do his duty as a man of honor; and in doing his duty, he would teach them theirs.

He would not even deign to force his own men to take the risk with him. He allowed any French who wished to turn back: no need to have men with you whose noses bled at the first sign of danger. Only two chose to stay with him. But the Indians were impressed with Champlain himself, and the remaining warriors continued with him into no-man's-land.

Champlain was rewarded for his unyielding persistence almost immediately. They came to an extraordinarily beautiful lake. Champlain was the first European to see it. So beautiful was the lake with its many islands and the rivers that fed it, the many fine trees on its shore, and its numerous wild fowl and beaver dams on the rivers and other animals all around—the vines alone were among the finest he had ever seen—that Champlain decided he would call this one place after himself, Lake Champlain. And when the reddening sun threw a broad sheet of splendor across his lake, the scene was of such exquisite loveliness as to capture any painter's fancy and elude his paints.

At the lake Champlain saw for the first time one of the most successful predators of New World lakes and rivers. At full growth larger than a man, with a two-foot-long snout, a double row of teeth, scales so strong he could not pierce it with his dagger, "this fish makes war on all the other fish which are in these lakes and rivers." It even lay in ambush for unsuspecting birds. Champlain preserved a head of the monster, a gar, to take back to France with him. No one would be able to say that this monster was imaginary.

In the morning Lake Champlain (for so he thought of it now) reflected the surrounding forest like a radiant smile. At night a breeze ruffled the surface just enough to set a thousand mimic stars dancing, joyous glimmerings of the heavens mocked only by the shrill, tremulous night cries of the loons nearby and the distant bayings of wolves. At moments like these it was hard to believe that this was a place where men for countless generations had come to risk and gain scalps.

But they had, and Champlain's party was just a recent participant in this bloody tradition. So they moved on in search of unsuspecting Iroquois. They soon found Iroquois, but they were far from unsuspecting. Now both groups drew back, realizing any chance for ambush was gone. They camped within sight of each other; that night emissaries were sent to the Iroquois to ask if they wanted to fight. They replied that they had no other desire, but did prefer to wait for good light so they knew whom they were killing. The rest of the night both sides spent in dances and songs as well as in hurling insults and boasts at one another across the darkness. The Iroquois could not have realized that one of the routine boasts they heard would prove literally true: "You will see such deeds of arms as you have never seen before."

The preliminaries of the skirmish that next day were traditional enough. Hot for battle, both sides approached one another in close order, brandishing their wooden shields. Within a few years these shields would be entirely discarded. By that time, due to trade with the Europeans, the tactics of the skirmish would have changed, mobility being the best defense against the devastating new European weapons that could give mortal wounds through the old armor. And the Iroquois themselves would prove to be the great masters of the new tactics. But that was in the future.

On this day the Iroquois could not know that anything had changed in their beloved, deadly game—that is, until their opponents, upon reaching almost within arrow shot, separated and revealed from within their midst a white man carrying a strangely shaped object that he pointed at their headmen, who were proudly distinguished from the rest by the large feathers sticking up from their hair. The Iroquois and their leaders stopped at this safe distance, this distance that had always been safe before—stopped and gaped at the unexpected.

Then a loud clap, and three of the chiefs fell, two of them instantly dead, the third dying. The Iroquois were so closely packed together (the shields worked best in such formation) that three were hit with one discharge from Champlain's gun. Stunned as they were, the shame of defeat without a struggle steeled the Iroquois. They mended their disorder, moved within range to use their own weapons. But then from some trees off to the side (where Champlain had placed two brothers in arms) came another report, and another warrior fell dead, apparently killed by nothing more than a malevolent sound in the air, a sound which somehow tore straight through his armament and flesh. Finally the Iroquois realized that this combat was truly unequal. Whoever stood and fought would only find death.

"They lost courage and took to flight, abandoning the field and their fort, and fleeing into the depth of the forest, whither I pursued them and laid low still more of them. Our Indians also killed several and took ten or twelve prisoners. The remainder fled with the wounded. Of our Indians fifteen or sixteen were wounded with arrows, but these were quickly healed."

Strange were the differences between the Old and New Worlds for Champlain. His allies, for all of their brutal threats before the battle, had been content with the victory of a mere skirmish. Champlain, trained in Europe, was disappointed because his allies had not allowed him to place them so that a full battle would have inevitably been engaged. The Iroquois force could have been annihilated, rather than being permitted to retreat largely intact to fight another day. The allies seemed content with trophies and a few captives rather than with complete victory.

This might have been interpreted as mercy, had it not been for the treatment of the prisoners. Champlain could not bear watching the cruelties, worse than the reveries of demons, now practiced on these helpless men. He was prudent enough to realize that he could not altogether forbid what were obviously traditional pleasures, pleasures that had been refined through generations of trial and error. He did express his disapproval to his uncomprehending brothers in arms, and insisted on ending the particularly gruesome agonies of one prisoner with his gun. It was all so strangely mixed, the good and bad together, even in his dreams that night: "I dreamt I saw in the lake near a mountain our enemies, the Iroquois, drowning before our eyes. I wanted to succor them, but our Indian allies said to me that we should let them all perish; for they were bad men."

Still, Champlain had kept his promise, and his allies had had their victory. And Champlain himself had seen his own lake, its serene beauty and the monster that hunted its depths, its surface first playfully reflecting the crisp light of the stars and then being flailed nightmarishly by drowning men.

The second winter at Quebec passed without loss of life; in fact, with scarcely any illness at all. Both the food supply and the air were better. Champlain's men found, he reported, that "their greatest trouble had been to amuse themselves." Champlain was satisfied that, once the ground clearing was over, one could be as healthy in the New as in the Old France.

That spring he again set out with his allies in their search for Iroquois to kill. The allies once again had promised to show him new lands, and he once again brought guns. This time there was no open battle. The Iroquois had sufficient warning so that they had fortified their position with a barricade. After the allies were repulsed in their first assault, Champlain assumed something like command. While the French guns pinned down the Iroquois defenders, the attackers under Champlain's direction fastened ropes to some posts that supported the barricade and pulled them away. Once they had penetrated the fort, the massacre began: "We took some fifteen prisoners, the rest having been killed by arquebuses, arrows, and swords." This was victory in the European mode.

Early in the attack Champlain himself was wounded. An arrow split his ear and lodged in his neck. Champlain pulled it out, and continued his business. As he put it, "My wound did not hinder me, however, from doing my duty." From this day forward Champlain's courage did not need to plead its cause; for his native allies his mutilated ear and badly scarred neck were its most effective spokesmen.

Before he left his allies to return to Quebec, Champlain asked the Hurons a favor. Would they take one of his young men home with them to let him winter with them and learn their language thoroughly? (His name was Étienne Brulé.) The allies were hesitant. Wouldn't Champlain be angry if the change of diet, or just some accident, hurt the young Frenchman? "I answered them that as to the life they led and the food they ate, the lad could well adapt himself to these, and that if from sickness or the fortune of war, any harm should happen to him, this would not prevent me from being kindly disposed to them; for we were all liable to accidents which we ought to bear patiently."

They were reassured and agreed, but with the condition that Champlain take one of their braves back with him to France. Champlain agreed to reciprocate. "This gave an additional reason for the better treatment of my lad." Indeed, the Hurons seemed to be offering their brave just to give additional reassurance.

Sauvignon, as the brave was called, did return to France with Champlain that fall, and did see many wonders. On the crossing to France the ship passed over the tail of a sleeping whale. In France he was particularly astonished by the carriages drawn by antlerless deer, the clocks that tolled the hour, and especially by the fancily dressed men who would insult one another but not fight. And the trip back to the New World was for Champlain as well as

Sauvignon a wonder; it was the worst of more than thirty crossings Champlain would make in his life. They found themselves sailing among icebergs, some two hundred feet high. Once, Champlain himself thought all was lost. And even after the danger had passed, "each one's blood cooled down slowly from the fright we had had."

Sauvignon, when he returned to his people, reported that he had been treated well, and told of the wondrous sights he had seen. Although now a celebrity, Sauvignon was apprehensive about returning to village life. Champlain reported that "he went away regretfully." A missionary who came across Sauvignon in his village ten years later found him very melancholy. No one any longer believed his stories about France and his sea trips; he had become an object of ridicule among his people, dismissed as a fabricator and a dreamer. He asked the missionary if another trip to France could be arranged for him; this time he would stay. He had collected a large number of beaver robes so that he could afford a wife once he got there, which he never did.

Whatever the personal unhappiness caused to Sauvignon by his voyage, for Champlain it served a greater public good; he had demonstrated once again his reliability. Champlain would do what he said he would do. Champlain used the happy occasion of Sauvignon's safe return to inquire of the headmen about the geography of the North American interior: "They spoke to me of these things in detail, showing me by drawings all the places they had visited, taking pleasure in telling me about them. And as for myself, I was not weary of listening to them, because things were cleared up about which I had been in doubt until they enlightened me about them."

Over the next few years as the colony at Quebec grew slowly, Champlain continued to show his friendship for native groups north of the Saint Lawrence by participating in raids against the Iroquois. Such raids were not all successful, but Champlain had ample opportunity to show his friends that he was willing to risk his life for them. On one occasion Champlain endured the worst agony of his whole life while being carried with a severe arrow wound in his knee; as a result he spent the winter recuperating in a Huron village, returning to Quebec the next spring, long after he had been given up for lost.

In exchange for his military help, he asked only that he be shown more and more of the New World. At times, for the new and marvelous he was willing to risk all, only later to rebuke himself for his irrational behavior. Once he lost contact with his party because he wandered off in pursuit of an extraordinary bird. At least his description of it is extraordinary, for no one has ever seen such a bird in an eastern woodland since. Like an uncanny creature from a fairy tale, it always stayed just out of reach, leading him deeper and deeper into the forest, only then to disappear. And only then, its spell over him broken, did he come to his senses. He realized he was completely lost and his chances of survival trifling. The forest, it seemed, was going to swallow him up, its high arches serving for his tomb. After wandering for days, he stumbled back into camp, where his friends had already given him up. He could then, in safety, berate himself for having behaved like a child, for having succumbed to the bait of novelty. He had actually almost wasted his life in pursuit of pretty plumage, a humbling realization.

In 1610 Champlain was in France lobbying for support of his colony. He had an audience with Henry IV and presented him with some tokens of the New World, such as the head of the monster fish. (He refrained from presenting the Iroquois head that his allies had given him as an even more fitting gift for his king.) Having impressed the king himself, Champlain felt that support for his colony was as secure as it could be. Within a few months, however, Henry IV was dead.

François Ravaillac, a Parisian madman, had seen visions that gave him a divine commission to kill the king, and the Great God Hap agreed. The king's carriage happened to stall in traffic near where Ravaillac stalked Henry, and on that day Henry happened to have left his bodyguards behind for some reason. Ravaillac leapt into the carriage and stabbed the king, as it happened mortally, before any of the noblemen with him realized the danger. An isolated act by an obscure and obviously deranged individual changed the course of a nation, so unstable are the foundations on which even a great king builds.

Apparently, no one else was involved in the preparations for Ravaillac's act, but many thousands were involved in its aftermath, including a Frenchman who was spending his adult life trying to establish a permanent French presence thousands of miles away, on an obscure North American river. Louis XIII now ascended the throne as a young boy. The administration of his regency was, not unexpectedly, the occasion of a power struggle among the highest nobility.

Champlain could not help but get involved. He had to seek a patron in the court to serve as viceroy of New France. To keep abreast of the political vicissitudes, Champlain was making the long journey each year between France and his colony. At first he thought he had an influential viceroy for the colony in the Prince de Condé. But then the prince decided he should share the regency of Louis XIII with the Queen Mother, and was arrested for his presumption. Champlain moaned, "Our enviers will not be long in spewing forth their venom."

In this instance, at least, he was unduly worrying. Condé was replaced by a friend of the queen. New France and Champlain were too unimportant to be held responsible for the indiscretions of the prince. Condé had gotten 1,000 livres a year for his troubles over New France; the new viceroy would take 1,500, and all would be forgiven. Champlain had many better ways to spend livres on his colony, but under the circumstances he must have felt he had gotten off easily.

Although Champlain himself appeared safe for the time, the tumult of the new administration, the jockeying of factions, and the rising and falling of favorites made consistent support for New France unlikely in the near future. Champlain had to worry that in their preoccupation to defend the regency, the queen and her allies would have little time or resources for a remote colony. He had to worry that his colony might be allowed to wither into nonexistence by mere inattention. Such worries could not have been far from his mind when he wrote his first report on New France during the reign of Louis XIII, a report desperate in its exaggerations.

Champlain promised soon to discover "the means of easily reaching to the Kingdom of China and East Indies, whence great riches could be drawn." These explorations, moreover, would make the king "Lord and master of a country nearly 1,800 leagues in length, watered by the fairest rivers in the world and by the greatest and most numerous lakes, the richest and most abundant in all varieties of fish that exist, and full also of the greatest meadows, fields, and forests." Living along these rivers and lakes are an "infinite number of souls" whose conversion would only require the presence of missionaries. Moreover, the center of New France was destined to become a major city, as large perhaps as Saint-Denis—and because of the destined greatness of this city, Champlain proposed to change its name from Quebec to Ludovica, after Louis himself. The English and Dutch, Champlain assured his readers, were so fearfully aware of the potential of the French colony that they were looking for an opportunity, any opportunity, to drive the French entirely from the Saint Lawrence, something they probably would do soon unless Champlain was given more military support. And how much potential commerce would the kingdom be losing if New France fell? Champlain's own careful calculations showed that the commerce would be—using, of course, conservative estimates—5,400,000 livres.

The advisers to the king received Champlain's report politely. Perhaps they were not sufficiently familiar with his project to ask how a population of a few dozen was to produce commerce of a few million. In principle they were in favor of such grand projects as Champlain's. And they would pass it on to the king with their tepid approval. So the report was passed on, and that was the last of it. Champlain's hyperboles went unchallenged, and his report went unattended. All he had achieved for his efforts in France was to retain his command. In the circumstances, that was something.

He obviously needed some dramatic breakthrough to bring his colony effectively to the attention of those powerful during the regency. In 1612 he thought he had found it, thanks to Nicholas Vignau. Vignau was one of the young Frenchmen Champlain had placed with his Indian allies after the success with Brulé. Vignau had wintered with the Ottawa Algonquin along the Ottawa River. Returning to France, Vignau briefed Champlain on what he had learned. He told Champlain he had seen the great northern sea, and on its shore the wreck of an English ship. Champlain had heard independently of Henry Hudson's expedition to the huge bay that would be named after him. The threat of being flanked to the north was just the kind of thing to mobilize the court. With much ado, he set about returning to New France with Vignau to confirm this discovery. Upon arriving at Quebec he made plans for a trip first to the villages of Algonquin and then beyond.

The initial stage of the trip was arduous enough, just by itself. At one point Champlain (who never did learn how to swim) almost drowned. While he was pulling his canoe through some rapids because the banks were too dense for portage, the canoe was sucked into a whirlpool, dragging Champlain in after. At the last moment he became partially lodged between two rocks. For a few moments Scylla and Charybdis warred over him. Then a sudden eddy from the whirlpool sent the wayward canoe back to him. He judged it a miracle, a sign of divine favor for his expedition. He was wrong, as he soon realized.

When Champlain and Vignau finally reached the Algonquin territory, they arranged a meeting with the wily Algonquin headman, Tessouat. After many orations and much tobacco, Champlain proposed that the Algonquin lead Champlain, their friend and ally, so that he too could see the great north sea as Vignau had. Tessouat responded with outrage. If Vignau had ever seen such a sea, he had done so in his dreams. Tessouat and his people had not taken their ungrateful guest to any sea. Vignau deserved death for lying, and Tessouat would happily save Champlain the bother. Champlain turned on Vignau, furious at the graceless traitor. Vignau, for his part, was speechless before this unexpected fury.

The substance of Vignau's geography was true. He, however, could not hope to lead Champlain to Hudson Bay without the help of the very Algonquin who were asserting him to be a liar. Perhaps Vignau had never actually been to Hudson Bay himself, but had only overheard Algonquin geographical secrets and decided to exaggerate his own experience. He certainly did not realize that the Algonquin, when confronted with the enthusiastic Champlain, would regret having ever told or shown him anything. And he knew how the Algonquin killed enemies left in their power—very slowly. Faced with this, young Vignau became mute, while his gaze—we might imagine—darted all over the place like a small fish startled in a rock pond.

In his exasperation Champlain presented Vignau with a choice. If he persisted in his story, Champlain would act on it; but if they then failed to reach Hudson Bay, Champlain would personally see to it he was killed. If, on the other hand, he admitted he had lied, Champlain would not punish him, nor would he let the Algonquin have their way with him. Vignau tearfully chose to confess, and Champlain kept his word.

The disgraced Vignau did not return with Champlain to Quebec. Champlain writes tersely, "As for our liar, none of the Indians would have him, in spite of my request, and we left him in God's keeping." Nothing more was ever heard of him. Alone, shunned by the Algonquin, with few supplies, he could not have lasted long.

This episode points to a serious limitation in Champlain as a leader. A person of simple and largely unexamined motives, Champlain could not fathom complexity in others. Confronted with Tessouat's voluble accusations and Vignau's failure to contradict, Champlain concluded that Vignau was a liar. He could not even suspect that a young man first caught in what was at worst a well-intentioned half-truth, then threatened with a horrible death, might act guilty.

Worse still, Champlain did not reflect on the motives of Tessouat, who was someone not much disquieted about the difference between truth and falsehood. Throughout his dealings with his allies, Champlain had chosen to regard them as more like himself than like, say, the Prince de Condé. He did not see clearly enough the tensions between his allies. Tessouat had only recently moved his people to the banks of the Ottawa River. Tessouat had started to charge tolls to any Indian traders who passed through his territory to the French, and perhaps also intended that his people serve as middlemen in any trade between the French and the people who lived near Hudson Bay. But all this presumed that Tessouat and his people could minimize direct contact between the French and those other peoples. The Algonquin along the Ottawa intended to prosper as they had never prospered before—and this prosperity required that the French be prevented from establishing trading posts beyond them. The French would eventually learn that Tessouat and the other headmen of Ottawa Algonquin were willing to engage in any mischief to retard French penetration either to the north or west. But they would learn it too late for Vignau.

Champlain's life now seemed a continual round of frustration; his troubles came in battalions. Trade with the Indians alone made the colony profitable for those who were supporting it in France. Yet the Indians did not seem to understand this, so when Champlain was unavailable they would trade their furs with whoever happened by. More and more of those European traders who coasted off North America were discovering the advantages of working up the Saint Lawrence as well. If the Indians would ask these traders of Champlain, they would be told he was dead. Then the dead man would appear, wanting to make new discoveries but also needing furs, only to find that others who had risked nothing on their behalf against the Iroquois had been given all. When he complained, the Indians told him exactly what he wanted to hear: they had been forced to trade; they had been told he was dead; they regarded him as a father; they wished in the future to trade only with him, or with Frenchmen under his leadership; they never wished to harm their special friendship; please do not be angry; they could give him no furs this year but could tell him of new lands. With such words Champlain could be mollified.

Champlain would still complain that those outsiders who were profiting from the trade had sacrificed nothing for the colony, whereas he who had sacrificed greatly was often left empty handed. When Champlain spoke of his sacrifices for his colony, he was speaking of more than just the dangers he had faced. His own private life had been stunted. Champlain was fully forty years old when he contracted marriage with a young girl from a respectable French family, Hélène Bollé. Of his motivations in contracting this marriage—his hopes for it, his feelings toward her, hers toward him, their courtship, their initial living together—nothing is said in Champlain's many writings. Nonetheless, his public actions—especially his repeated absences from her, for ever longer periods—do say a great deal. Whatever he told her or himself, this marriage was a dalliance from his duty, and his duty he held dearer than anything else. So he allowed the public side of his life to entomb the private.

He did once try to bring his wife to live in Quebec, but she did not stay there long. Champlain might be proud of the permanent buildings that were replacing wooden shacks, but she would not think that a wood shack was much of a measure. He could brag that the gardens were now "wonderfully beautiful, some with peas, beans, and other vegetables, squash, several kinds of excellent roots, cabbage, white beets and other necessary herbs." She could then counter that "necessary" in that context meant "necessary to survive without scurvy." He might envision the great city he thought Quebec would certainly one day become, but she would be more impressed with the present reality, a settlement so meager that barely fifty souls lived there year round.

After Champlain's wife hastily returned to France, she announced she wished to enter a convent, and be done with her husband entirely. She relented only after he formally promised that in the future they would live their brief times together as brother and sister (or father and daughter). Perhaps they had always lived so, for they had no children except the colony that he was fathering in the New World, a stepchild she had ample reason to hate.

This child itself seemed more and more stunted in growth. In the early 1620s, when the population of Virginia was approaching two thousand, the residents of New France numbered scarcely one hundred. Champlain had done his best to show the fertility of the soil. Grain seemed to flourish in it. He had himself a small garden where he cultivated different vegetables. He even tried his hand at roses. The soil was good, but Champlain could not get the distracted government to invest sufficiently in his colony.

Champlain knew he had to be patient, and suffer with his colony until the head was sufficiently well to attend the needs of the members. This occurred only after the regency ended, when Louis XIII had achieved his majority and Cardinal Richelieu had emerged as his chief minister. A sign of hope was Richelieu's appointment of a new viceroy for New France, a man who took the position more for piety than profit. This viceroy, rather than being a drain on the budget, was going to have missionaries sent to the various Indian allies. Moreover, Richelieu had soon reorganized the administration of New France, with his usual efficiency.

The reforms were designed to ensure that secular projects also had sufficient support. The colony would be run by a company of one hundred associates, each one of which would be assessed a substantial sum. New France was never to be undersupplied again. Moreover, the company, to keep its trading privileges, had to contract to bring at least two hundred new settlers to New France each year. A decade or two of such colonization and New France would begin to rival the English colony of Virginia in size.

Richelieu also meant to challenge the English. He wanted to challenge them in the New World, and he wanted to challenge them in the Old. But that meant that he had to challenge them on the seas. How could he do this when the greatest French port, La Rochelle, behaved as if it were an independent city-state, and could never be trusted in any test with Protestant powers?

So not too long before he sent off the first supply ships that Champlain expected would begin a new age of prosperity for New France, Richelieu had also begun the siege of La Rochelle. The English understood that the attack on La Rochelle was the beginning of a challenge to their own interests, so they sent a fleet to relieve La Rochelle, and a squadron to attack New France.

In Quebec, Champlain was waiting for the beginning of the new era that finally would put his colony beyond danger. The uncertainties were past; the foundations for New France that Champlain had so carefully laid during Henry IV's reign were now going to be built upon. The past winter had been difficult, and the few dozen colonists with him had suffered much; but this would probably be the last of such suffering. Now the ships with supplies were on their way, as they would be every year under the efficient care of Richelieu. Each year there would be not just supplies, but hundreds of colonists to spread along the Saint Lawrence into the heart of the continent. Champlain even had a family now, three little Indian girls who had been given to him as a sign of friendship. Faith, Hope, and Charity, Champlain had named them. With them, he could shine with a quiet joy that Epictetus could not have understood with his short-winged reasonings alone: this was a sweetness that if not tasted could not be understood. As his colony would grow and prosper, so would the girls. And as the French settlements grew, as the Indians became converted to Christianity and civilized, the French of the New World and their Indian allies would become a single people. Or so Champlain did at times believe, hope, and dream, lulled uncharacteristically by a seductive sense of security. But he was soon brought back to his old suspicion of the world.

The report reached Quebec that the big-bellied sails of six ships had been sighted at the mouth of the Saint Lawrence. This should have been cause for rejoicing. Champlain, however, at least as he remembered it, was only somewhat cheered. Six ships were too many. A Captain Michel from Dieppe was said to be in command. But Champlain knew of Michel, and he was "not the kind of person for so important a command." The Indian who brought the story, moreover, could not keep it straight under questioning. Champlain was wary. He sent someone disguised as an Indian to spy. One could not be too careful. Everything could go wrong at the last minute. At the very gate of Heaven, it was said, was a by-way to the Pit.

Champlain soon learned that his worst fears were to be realized. The ships were British, and they had already intercepted the two French supply ships. They now intended to conquer New France, as a letter delivered to Champlain made clear. The British captain wanted Champlain to surrender, but also announced that if Champlain refused, he would not attack immediately. He would simply blockade the colony and wait for the next winter to do his work of conquest for him. So Captain David Kirke put the issue as he understood it to Champlain: "Wherefore now consider what you wish to do: whether you are willing to surrender the settlement or not; for, sooner or later, with God's help, I must have it, and I should desire for your sake that it might be rather with a good grace than on compulsion, so as to avoid the bloodshed that might occur upon both sides. If you surrender the place with courtesy, you may rest assured of receiving good treatment in every respect, both as regards your persons and your goods, which later, on my faith and on my hope of paradise, I shall preserve as carefully as if they were my own, without diminishing them by the smallest possible portion."

Champlain realized immediately that all the advantage was with the British. Without new supplies he had not remotely the provisions necessary to hold out. Nonetheless, there was no reason to surrender prematurely. He would present to Kirke an unperturbed face (as he would to his own men), even prevaricate a little about the supplies, and hope to have some extraordinary stroke of luck. Kirke was not before Quebec yet; perhaps on his way up the Saint Lawrence the Gougou would swallow Kirke and his ships whole. So Champlain responded:

"It is true that the better a fortified place is provisioned, the better it holds out against the storms of time; nevertheless the place can make good its defence upon slender supplies when good order is maintained in it. That is the reason why, having still grain, Indian corn, peas, and beans, not to mention what this country produces, a diet that the soldiers of this place can content themselves with as well as they could with the finest kinds of flour in the world; and knowing well that, were we to surrender a fort and a settlement conditioned as we now are, we should not be worthy of the name of men in the presence of our King, but rather reprehensible and merit chastisement in the sight of God and men, honor demands that we fight to the death. For these reasons I know that you will think more highly of our courage if we firmly await the arrival of yourself and your forces than if, in a cowardly fashion, we abandoned something that is so dear to us without first making proof of your cannon, your approaches, entrenchments, and battery against a place which I am confident, when you see and reconnoitre it, you will not judge to be so easy of access as perhaps you have been led to believe, nor its defenders to be persons destitute of courage to defend it, seeing they are men who have tried the hazards of fortune in many different places. Then if the issue is favorable to you, you will have more cause, having vanquished us, to bestow your offers of kind treatment, than if we put you without a struggle in possession of a place the preservation of which is enjoined upon us by the strongest considerations of duty that can be imagined. We are now waiting from hour to hour to receive you, and resist, if we can, the claims you are making to these places, exempt from which I shall remain, Sir, Your affectionate servant, CHAM-PLAIN."

As Kirke and the English waited at the mouth of the Saint Lawrence for winter to come to do their work of conquest for them (the English had ample supplies, thanks in part to the French ships), Champlain tried to muster his resources. He traded beaver pelts back to the Indians for dried eels, and was saddened at the exorbitant rate they charged him in his time of need. He had the Quebec crops carefully tended, realizing all the while that they would be woefully inadequate. He even considered a desperate plan to lead a raid on Iroquois villages, just to steal from their corn caches.

The colony did manage to survive that winter, but only with much suffering. Champlain had sent one of his girls back to her people to spare her this, but Hope and Charity remained with him, steadfast. The English ships did not reappear in the spring, and so spirits revived. Perhaps they had had to end the blockade of the Saint Lawrence, and perhaps French supply ships were on their way to relieve Quebec.

Then in January 1629, after a full year of waiting, three British ships appeared before Quebec and demanded surrender. The rest of their fleet was still guarding the entrance of the Saint Lawrence, but these three would be enough because they had together twenty cannon.

The traders in Quebec wanted Champlain to fight. They were, of course, worrying about their goods. Champlain in surrendering would be giving up much more, his life work. Yet he knew all about sieges. He knew what he was sparing his people when he surrendered. There was, after all, a distinction to be made between heroism and absurdity.

But this was not much consolation for a sixty-year-old man whose work had apparently come to nothing. His hopes for Quebec seemed now like an empty dream at the break of day, inconsequential, insubstantial, evanescent. He could try to think stoical thoughts—how his colony had never truly been his, hence it had not been taken from him. He had known all this from the beginning, for he had seen Puerto Rico. He could also think about what would be left of his life without New France—could brood about his failed marriage, to which he was now returning.

What he most certainly did was pray. He made a vow to the Virgin Mary. *Salve Regina*, our life, our sweetness, and our hope. If Quebec was somehow recovered by the French in his lifetime, he would build a church to her there.

Notre Dame de la Recouverance, he would name it, Our Lady of the Restoration. O clement, O loving, O sweet Virgin Mary.

Beyond his prayer for eventual recovery, Champlain's only consolation was in his two girls; Kirke had agreed that he could take them back to France with him. Then even this consolation was deprived him. An enemy of Champlain, who had gone over to the English in order to stay in Quebec, told Kirke that the Indians demanded the girls' return. Champlain was certain he lied, but Kirke could not afford to take the chance. He was new to this country and he could not risk offending the natives. The girls had to stay; he was sorry; there was nothing else he could do. By this decision Champlain seems to have been left at first stunned; then he became like a mourner who, though not insensitive to the kindness of those around him, yearns only to be left alone with his grief. There was little of the stoic left in Champlain now.

When Kirke and Champlain reached England, they learned that La Rochelle had fallen; moreover, after the fall, a truce had been declared between France and England. It was dated three full months before Champlain's surrender. Kirke had been just a little too careful. Because seizure of territory during the truce was a violation of it, New France would probably be returned to France in any peace settlement. Champlain could sail for France full of thanks to the Virgin for her intercession. He had eluded the Gougou once again, and his composure was restored.

Of course, the return of New France was, if likely, not certain. The French could bargain their right to it away at the peace table. So Champlain, when he reached France, had to lobby on behalf of his colony. He wrote his usual exaggerated descriptions of the colony's prospects, even still speaking of the imminent discovery of a passage to China. He personally met with the king, Richelieu, and anyone else of influence who might be able to help. "I made them listen, and hear all about my voyages, about what they should do in respect to the well-being of New France." And then he waited. If his pleas were not taken seriously, he would be left in Old France to drag out a lingering life, bereft of comfort or of hope, a shuffling sunset for a long and faithful career of service.

While he waited he could attend to the business involved in having published his *Treatise on Seamanship* (1632), which was his final testament of advice to those who would lead as he had led, an exhortation to clear the clouds from their minds. Good seamanship, as Champlain described it, requires a cup of technical expertise, a barrel of courage and experience, and then finally a whole ocean of worrisome care. The good seaman, no matter how expert, courageous, or experienced, can never be truly at rest while at sea, knowing as he does how in this devious, almost perverse world, a Gougou can appear when and where least expected. The leader must nurse the anxious thought:

"The wise and cautious mariner ought not to trust too fully to his own judgment, when the pressing need is to take some important step or to deviate from a dangerous course. Let him take counsel with those whom he recognizes as the most sagacious, and particularly with the old navigators who have had most experience of disasters at sea and have escaped from dangers and perils, and let him weigh well the reasons they may advance; for it is not often that one head holds everything, and, as the saying is, experience is better than knowledge. He should be wary and hold back rather than run too many risks, whether in sighting land, particularly in foggy weather when he will bring the vessel to or stand off and on according to the position of the ship, inasmuch as in this fog or in the dark no one is a pilot. He must not carry too much sail with the idea of forging ahead; this often splits the sails and dismasts the ship, or, if she heels over easily and is not as well ballasted as she should be, it makes her turn bottom up. He should make the day his night and be awake the greater part of the night, always sleep in his clothes, so as to be promptly on hand for accidents that may happen, have his own private compass, often refer to it to know if course is being properly kept, and see that every member of the watch is doing his duty."

However full of worry and care he is within himself, the commander must never let it show in his demeanor. If he blanches, his crew might panic. He must instill hope and daring when he feels none himself. He must seem to be everywhere, to see everything, to anticipate every contingency—but, of course, the contingencies are infinite. The ship must be kept clean, lest the filth breed pestilence. No smoking between decks, for "a mere spark is enough to set all on fire." The commander must accustom his body to bad food, lest danger strike when he is indisposed. He must be abstemious with wine. His sleep must always be as light, as fitful, as easily scared away as a small bird hopping on a twig. He must make certain the timbers under his guns are strong enough to hold them, and that his gunners can aim, and his doctors know something of medicine, and the charts are accurate, and that the bottom is good wherever he casts anchor, and a thousand, thousand other things. Above all, he must know that despite all his care, all his worry, he will frequently be left at the mercy of inhuman might—and so, above all else, he should be "a God-fearing man, not allowing God's holy name to be blasphemed on his ship, for fear (since he is often in danger) that the Divine Majesty chastise him."

Champlain was still his old sententious self, almost slothful in his bland-ness. Even so, as the negotiations for the return of New France progressed, he must have had a few moments of worry, even panic, that the Divine Majesty might just take this occasion to chastise Samuel de Champlain for his lack of fervor. The return, which had seemed so certain, at one point became very doubtful. How worthless and contemptible and sordid and perishable and already dead are the things of this world. King Charles of England used the negotiations as an occasion to complain that hundreds of thousands of crowns had not been paid on the dowry of his queen, Henrietta of France. Charles would prefer the money; but if France refused, then he could keep the colony on the Saint Lawrence as the rest of her dowry. The negotiations seemed caught in a deadly eddy when Louis XIII and Richelieu took the matter under advisement. How much was New France worth? Perhaps Champlain's exag-gerations finally did some good, for the French government decided to pay the money. New France was returned officially to France in the Treaty of St. Germain-en-Laye, which was signed March 29, 1632.

Champlain could now make preparations for his return to the colony. He intended it to be his last. He was old. He did not expect to make any more trips across the Atlantic. In his *Treatise on Seamanship* he had written, "The advice I give to all adventurers is to seek a place where they may sleep in safe-ty." In New France Champlain had found the place where he wished to sleep. Before leaving France for the last time, he settled all his property there on his wife.

So Champlain returned to his colony, to discover that it was now little more than a disordered heap of ruins, a headless carcass ready for a nameless grave. The English, suspecting that their tenure was to be brief, did nothing to arrest decay; had negotiations continued much longer, Quebec would have been little better than Saint Croix. As it was, Champlain could find little from his earlier labors that would help the new. His own house he had to have razed and built over again to make it habitable. And, true to his word, he began work as soon as possible on Notre Dame de la Recouverance.

Beginning again, he was once again beset with woes on every side. His colony seemed to live in a permanent mist of trouble. At least his limbs were not yet useless with age. There was no better way to spend his remaining strength than to rebuild the colony that he loved, and that would be his life beyond his life.

He strove to renew his friendship with his old allies, the Algonquin and the Huron. This proved unexpectedly delicate and demanding because the English, for quick profit and with no heed of consequences, had introduced the Indians to the joys of alcohol. Champlain had no interest in substituting French *eau de vie* for English rum, but he had to proceed carefully. He did not want the Indians to seek to continue British trade.

Of course, some of the British who had profited from the Canadian conquest were likely to be far from respectful of the new treaty. In fact, when Champlain was returning to Quebec, he saw some British ships illegally trading. He had every right to seize them, but they would certainly have resisted—and in a battle he was not sure he would prevail. He simply passed by. The Basques, all over again. Nothing really changes.

While Champlain was rebuilding his colony, he did not feel he could risk confrontations with the British. When some traders established an illegal post down the Saint Lawrence from Quebec, he did not attack them, but rather established his own post a little way from them, and barred any of his Indian allies from passing it laden with furs. He was being, like a good mariner, perpetually wary, fully realizing how much at the mercy of circumstances he and his colony remained.

This was brought home to him with particular poignancy when he inquired after his surrogate family, Charity and Hope. During the English occupation they had been carried back into wilderness by their people. Champlain's inquiries were to no avail; he would never see them again, nor even have the sad enjoyment of second-hand news. They had vanished to European eyes, had been restored to the wilderness from whence they had come on loan to him.

There were other disappointments. Richelieu was now so preoccupied with the continual warring in Europe that his promising plan for increased colonization was not being implemented. Richelieu would spare no troops for the campaign against the Iroquois that Champlain advocated. Champlain pleaded that after such a campaign he would be able to dictate a peace that would assure the prosperity of New France by cementing its alliance with the Huron and Algonquin, while removing a potential military threat. Richelieu had more immediate needs for seasoned troops, and Champlain's case was not helped by the fact that one of his strongest supporters in court had been recently executed for plotting against Richelieu and the king. Another Prince de Condé.

So France was not convinced, and Champlain had to content himself with strengthening the colony's defenses and watching it grow slowly, too slowly, but continuously. He was the esteemed leader of New France, his body now worn by toils, his mind by cares. The colonists could imagine how each line of his brow told of some great deed of former days, his scars of wounds he had suffered for their future.

In October 1635, Samuel de Champlain suffered a stroke that left him partly paralyzed. A new governor, unbeknownst to anyone in Quebec, was already on his way from France. Champlain could be grateful that the stroke had granted him this brief interlude in which there was little for him to do except review his life. Lying there, looking at his Saint Lawrence, surrounded by those he had so long led, he could but bless the work he had chosen for his life. Alone, late at night in the friendly stillness of the silent moon, drowsing on the borders of sleep and wakefulness, he could conclude that he would do it again, if he had it to do. He had been brave; for New France to survive others would have to be brave tomorrow. He could rest content, but he would not have been himself if he had been entirely free of cares, if he had not occasionally let his mind wander to his old, persistent worries—the Iroquois, the British, the Gougou.

He had only one final act through which he might do just a little more, one final gesture against the abyss that threatens all. He would write a will. In it he would distribute the little property he had with him carefully, each piece to wherever it might best serve the colony. Most of his property he gave to his church, Notre Dame de la Recouverance—perhaps her intercession would be needed again one day. But there were other, more specific bequests. He had, for instance, a few articles of women's clothing, mementoes of his young wife, remnants of her unhappy visit to the place with whose charm she could not compete. These clothes he would give to a worthy widow he knew who had sacrificed much to raise a family here.

Typical of Champlain's thoughtfulness was a relatively large bequest of money to an Abraham Martin, to be spent in clearing his land. Land around Quebec needed to be cleared of forest for New France to be strong, and Martin apparently used Champlain's bequest for its assigned purpose. Martin cleared one piece of land near Quebec so thoroughly that it was henceforth named after him—the Plains of Abraham.

Chapter III

PILGRIM SEPARATISTS

A
S SAMUEL DE CHAMPLAIN lay on his deathbed in Quebec, another man well on in years, two hundred miles to the southeast, was reviewing his own travels and tribulations in far bleaker terms. His colony had survived, and prospered in a material way. But this was not enough for him, for he viewed this prosperity as a tide of worldly principles encroaching. So his reflections were dominated by a sense of failure and humiliation, with memories crowding his mind like gravestones in a church-yard:

"O sacred bond, whilst inviolably preserved! How sweet and precious were the fruits that flowed from the same! But when this fidelity decayed, then their ruin approached. O that these ancient members had not died or been dissipated (if it had been the will of God) or else that this holy care and con-stant faithfulness had still lived, and remained with those that survived, and were in times afterwards added unto them. But (alas) that subtle serpent hath slyly wound in himself under fair pretenses of necessity and the like, to untwist these sacred bonds and ties, and as it were insensibly by degrees to dis-solve, or in a great measure to weaken the same. I have been happy, in my first times, to see, and with much comfort to enjoy, the blessed fruits of this sweet communion, but it is now a part of my misery in old age, to find and feel the decay and want thereof (in a great measure) and with grief and sorrow of heart to lament and bewail the same. And for others' warning and admonition, and my own humiliation, do I here note the same."

So William Bradford, in the weak hand of his old age, added to the manu-script that recounted the labors of a lifetime. For two decades and more he had tried to record the memorable events of the Plymouth colony, which he had served as governor for almost all of that time. Now he searched his history for the worm of his failure.

He had intended these pages to show how God had led a guiltless people, His people separated lovingly from the rest of mankind, through the fields of exile to a distant and deserted land. There God had led them; there they planted their colony; there they preserved themselves as a company of saints, unspotted by the world.

Yet something had gone wrong, when and how Bradford could not quite say, although it was all before him on these pages. He now found himself listless when the time came to record the annual events. Was anything important happening in his colony any more? At the end of 1647, when he sat down to his task, he wrote "anno 1647" and found he had nothing he wanted to record. He did not even add the "domini" to make it a year of the Lord. A year later he simply added "And Anno 1648" and nothing more. After that, he gave up the pretense that he had anything left to record. The events of the present mattered to him not at all.

Rather he would go back through his manuscript again and again, again and again reliving the wandering pilgrimage of his people. With such purity of intention, where had it gone wrong? He could certainly find great sins, especially in the latter days of the colony, a recent past he hated. Despite the diligence with which he and the other leaders guarded against uncleanness, and despite the severity with which it was punished when discovered (iniquity had to be searched out and punished in the sight of the people), the colony was somehow never fully free of the world. There was incontinence not only between the unmarried; there was also adultery, even sodomy and buggery (things fearful to name). There was avarice, pride, covetous envy, ambition— all the sins in the calendar.

Of course, this only showed how profoundly corrupt our human nature is. There is enough poison in each man's heart to supply a brood of vipers. If we were all judged according to our deserts, who would escape the pit? Paul had said repeatedly, and Calvin never tired of amplifying, that we could never be saved by the works of our own hands but only by the irresistible grace of God's spirit. An so even within a chosen community like Plymouth, amidst a people who had given up everything to follow God's will in everything, even there we should not be surprised to find, on occasion, the unmistakable stench of the old Adam. And so it will forever be, until Christ comes again and this forlorn world, this sterile promontory passes away.

Yet Bradford thought he understood a more specific reason why he and his fellow Pilgrims seemed peculiarly bedeviled by these sins. "Bedeviled" was the word. The Devil, perverse king of this polluted creation, has a special interest in those few communities that strive to preserve the purity of God's law. Satan wants nothing more than to cast a blemish or stain on these pure few. The more watchful the community, the more devious and concerted the arch-tempter's efforts to find a way. So even here we should expect to find evil acts in the fraudulent service of the demonic.

This all made good theological sense. Bradford had worked through it before, especially when he wrote about the horrible year of 1642, in which that youth Thomas Granger had to be executed for bestiality. The law of Leviticus was explicit. First the animals he had polluted had to be killed before his eyes; then he himself dispatched. Bradford as governor had officiated at this sad spectacle, which none there had seen before. None there would wish to see it again, and all there would pray to be freed of its memory, a memory that lingered and had occasionally to be put out of mind at once, by force if necessary, as the insidious whisperings of fallen angels. How weary, stale, flat, and unprofitable seemed to him now the uses of this New World.

They had certainly lived up to the stern demands of God's law on that day. So where had they made their mistake? Was it in their decision to come to this New World as a mixed multitude? Was this what eventually stole from them the pith and substance of whatever can be a joy and nutriment to the soul? Like the Chosen People leaving the Egypt of old, they had allowed others to join with them. When they had talked to John Smith, he had impressed upon them the need for men of action like himself among their numbers. They knew enough not to let him lead them, as he clearly wanted and expected. But they had not entirely ignored his advice. Simple as a dove but as wise as a serpent, Jesus had said. So they had selected Captain Miles Standish to attend to their military needs. Should they have rather abandoned themselves to Divine Providence completely? Should they have wandered in the wilderness naked like the savages, without a thought of the morrow? That could not have been God's wish for them. Where then did they betray their vocation? Why did they deserve to have their pilgrimage reduced, like Zion of old, to moral desolation, a warning for others and a humiliation for themselves?

Bradford brooded over his manuscript again and again, but he could never quite find the place it had gone wrong. He could find lessons that needed to be drawn out more plainly, but no mistake that doomed the colony's soul. At times the contrast between the hopes the Pilgrims had entertained and the reality of what the colony had become was excruciating for him, as it was that day when Bradford was re-reading his account of the preparations he and his fellow Pilgrims were making for their "weighty voyage" to the New World. Opposite the passage, Bradford wrote in his manuscript an expostulation that began "O sacred bond whilst inviolably preserved!" All his hopes these days turned out, upon reflection, to be disguised memories misconstrued.

At the time of their preparations for this voyage no one could deny that this small group had preserved their bond with God, at least as they understood it, no matter what the cost. The cost they had already paid was very high—so high that many in their native England thought them plain fools.

When Heaven overturned Philip II's design to reunite western Christendom under the papal tiara and the Spanish throne, opportunists like John Smith and patriots like Samuel de Champlain were not the only ones invigorated. So too were religious enthusiasts in England, especially the party called the Puritans, those who, William Carlos Williams later thought, were the "seed of Tudor England's lusty blossoming." ("The flamboyant force of that zenith, spent, became in them hard and little.")

The Church of England represented to the Puritans a belated Protestantism of the most compromised and compromising sort. The episcopal hierarchies, for instance, had been preserved almost completely intact, except that now they owed their allegiance to the king. These mitred prelates had, not surprisingly, kept much of the liturgical trappings of Catholicism. With the external threat from Spain now passed, England had to deal with the devil within; the true work of religious reformation had to begin in earnest, or so the English Puritans believed. The scanty virtue of the present Church of England was not for them.

The taint of history had long ago reached the vitals of Christianity. Centuries upon centuries had progressively obscured the eternal light of revelation until Luther and Calvin had begun to retrieve it in its original purity so that it could once again bear witness against the pretensions and corruptions of mankind. Yet the hierarchy of England was singularly uninterested in being instructed concerning its own pretensions and corruptions, particularly by those "proud without learning, presumptuous without authority, zealous without knowledge, especially holy without religion" (as one of the Anglican polemicists put it). Preachers who persisted in crying out for the purification of Christianity found themselves on occasion suffering under the full weight of the state, for they, no less than plotting Jesuits, were challenging the established order.

With Puritans being generally harassed and their leaders imprisoned and occasionally executed, some among them despaired of a reformation of the whole. They no longer believed that the wholesale conversion of England would spring from ground watered by their martyrs' blood. Such martyrdom only displayed the irredeemable wickedness of the English church. Martyrdom was futile, and there remained the danger of spiritual pollution from simply living in so corrupt a country. Since they could not reform England, they should not risk tainting themselves in the trying, or being swallowed up in a deluge of persecution.

An alternative course was for pious groups to seek hallowed seclusion, to separate from the greedy, struggling, self-seeking world, to live in their own artificial circle of exclusion from ordinary human society. This would be, as one of its earliest advocates had put it, a reformation without tarrying for any. Christendom was like a city of destruction that had already fallen to the enemy and was being engulfed in hellish flames. For those with a vantage to see, there was nothing left to do but band together in small groups, feeble remnants of the once-strong whole, to save themselves in hope that God had some plan for them elsewhere. If He did, this would not be the first time God's highest design would be fulfilled by a pilgrim people.

Bradford and the small separatist community from Scrooby in rural Nottinghamshire resolved to fly this city of destruction called England, to fly with all due haste and not to look behind them. As they left, some among those worldlings left behind would mock, others would threaten, others would cry after to return. But Bradford—then only twenty years old—and his fellow pilgrims knew they were a people of a double ancestry, and their affection for their English countryside was a subtle snare to prevent them from getting their true inheritance, an inheritance that was incorruptible and undefiled, and that would never fade away. They knew, as they should always have known, that they would be nowhere at home in the wilderness of this world. They were on a pilgrimage and were only passing through this unstable and polluted place. God alone knew the paths they would take, the places they would pause—and in Him alone they would trust.

As they traveled, and when they paused, they must still stand apart. They were seeking the house of God their Father, which is not in this world, or will not be until Christ descends upon the Mount of Olives and God Himself sits in judgment of the nations in the Valley of Jehoshaphat. While they are in this world, and on this journey, they would receive what succor they could from their Holy Mother the Church. Yet this Mother was not to be found in the splendor of the popes or bishops, nor in the power of kings, nor even in the beauty of nature—no, She was only to be found in the small, still voice that is sometimes heard within a congregation of saints, the believers who have separated themselves from all evil and thereby preserved their gracious bond with God.

Separation from this world is no small task. And perhaps a people driven by such convictions would inevitably seek their rest in lands as distant and desolate as North America seemed to be. Initially, however, separating themselves from England was trial enough. The Pilgrims concluded, amidst sighs and tears, bound together by friendship almost as much as religion, but weighed down by doubt and dread, that England was a land of cruelty and iniquity from which they must flee to preserve themselves as a people apart. So in 1608, the year Champlain founded Quebec and the year John Smith finally became governor of Virginia, they embarked on their pilgrimage, uncertain where God wished them to travel, yet determined to trust the Almighty Pity to stretch forth His strong right hand and guide them safely to the right harbor.

Initially the Pilgrims took the most likely route; they crossed the English Channel to the Netherlands. Other Englishmen in the seventeenth century might dismiss these lowlands as the "undigested vomit of the sea" or as nothing more than a quagmire; but this diked and drained land was a bastion not only against the chaos of the sea, but also against the advancement of Philip II. England may have retained its independence against Philip's collected forces, but the Dutch had gained theirs, and then preserved it despite continual threats of Spanish inundation.

As northern Europe's dike against Catholicism, the Netherlands was not inclined to a Protestantism of a compromised sort. Officially their society was Calvinist, a Calvinism at the forefront of the Reformation. The Dutch in their propaganda compared themselves to the Hebrews of old; as the Dutch had to free themselves from the yoke of the Spanish, so the Hebrews had escaped the Egyptians. And the Dutch, like the Hebrews, had not freed themselves solely by their own efforts. They were predestined to be freed because they were a people specially covenanted with God. Amidst such a people, the Pilgrims thought they would find a place for themselves, if they would find such a place anywhere.

Those who doubted that God had a hand in Dutch independence had only to look upon the gifts He showered upon His people once He had delivered them from their enemy. With independence, the Netherlands had quickly become a land flowing not just with milk and honey, but with all the riches of the world. It had become, with breathtaking suddenness, the great *entrepôt* and manufacturing center of all Europe. In its vast warehouses could be found Polish grain, Venezuelan cocoa, Swedish copper, timber from all the Baltic,

Virginian tobacco, English tin, Scottish coal, Austrian mercury, French wine. Armies of skilled workers, many from persecuted religious sects, descended on the Netherlands to work in its manufactures. All were welcome, so long as they brought marketable skills. Even an atheistic Jew like Spinoza could find work, polishing lenses. And an independent Catholic philosopher like Descartes could find peace of mind.

With the goods came the financiers, some Dutch, some not. They could speculate on future prices, chase monopolies, create joint ventures. Capital would come with them, its masters seeking safe haven in Dutch banks. The agents of kings and princes would come as well, for the Dutch were also the arms merchants of Europe. They had long had eminence as ship builders; now they took the lead in powder, cannon, and other instruments of death. They would soon excel in the African slave trade, supplying to the world both cannon and human fodder.

All this had happened so swiftly, and with so little conscious planning, that the Dutch could be forgiven if they saw in it the predestined choice of God, God giving his people material preeminence so that even worldlings would have to acknowledge their superiority. One piously smug Dutchman express-ed the sentiments of many countrymen when he wrote, "The whole world stands amazed at its riches, from east and west, north and south they come to behold it. The Great and Almighty Lord has raised this city above all others."

"This city" was the Jerusalem of the Dutch Israel, Amsterdam. A town of a mere 30,000 in 1567, it was approaching 100,000 in 1600, and would be doubling again not long after mid-century. And it was to this pulsing center of mercantile vitality that the Pilgrims came to find God's plan for themselves. God had created the world, the current joke went, so that the Dutch might trade in it—and God saw the trade, that it was good.

The first sight of Amsterdam always awed the seventeenth-century travel-er, even those used to London or Paris. And the Pilgrims were from the coun-tryside of England, where a few thousand inhabitants constituted a proper town. As travelers struggled to describe their first sight of Amsterdam harbor, one phrase was repeated again and again: a forest of masts. It was as if the city was separated from the open sea not by a harbor but by a strange forest of dead and denuded trees, hung with cloth.

So the Pilgrims watched as their ship made its way through this interna-tional forest of ships that were the foundation of Dutch prosperity. Then, as they disembarked, they were brought, unwillingly, face to face with the other side of Dutch prosperity, the side not mentioned in the patriotic broadsides about Dutch prosperity as God's reward to His Chosen People. The area around the docks was a human slough, where the scum and filth of the city collected to live off the vices of sailors, or just to live in the most abject poverty. A sidelong glimpse at this moral sewerage of Amsterdam was enough to fill the virtuous Pilgrim with fear and apprehension. What was a prosperity purchased at such a price? The prostitution alone here was so extensive and varied that later in the century a guidebook of sorts was written, *Amsterdam Whoredom*. To those prudes who might object to his candor, the author responded frankly, "The world cannot be governed Bible in hand."

But could Amsterdam be lived in, Bible in hand? That was what the Pilgrims had to decide. The Pilgrims could see the effects of an overflow of riches on a people covenanted to God. Dutch souls had soon become smothered in the goods of this world, junk in a marsh of materialism. Private houses exceeded public buildings in their opulence, and worldlings were praising Amsterdam over that older epitome of material decadence, Venice. Gluttony was commonplace among the prosperous, while women and children from the lower orders went without bread. Intemperance of all kinds was cultivated, as if an art. There were five hundred alehouses in Amsterdam alone, more than two hundred breweries. Instead of the alehouse, connoisseurs paid to spend time in the Great Tun, a huge cask in which thirty-two people at a time could sit to be inebriated by its fumes. Huge amounts of money were spent in the most frivolous ways. An exotic flower from Turkey, the tulip, was to become the rage, and before the fad was over, individual bulbs would fetch thousands of guilders, while the ministers preached the gospel and the poor died, broken by their poverty.

For the Pilgrims, to see Amsterdam was not to be reminded of the Hebrews of the Exodus. It was to be reminded of the Hebrews against whom the prophets bore witness: prophets like Hosea, who compared the Hebrews to a beloved wife who has sold herself into whoredom; or Amos, who denounced a dazzling wealth that was merciless to the poor as the surest path to destruction.

The Pilgrims were a virtuous people who wanted to work hard and did not expect wealth. As they had sailed across the Channel, they could meditate on the gulls, those little citizens of the sea who drew such continual noisy pleasure from toil for mere subsistence. As little as the Pilgrims did expect, they were soon challenged to compete in a society where competition was everything. They quickly found themselves confronting an enemy who temporarily distracted them from broader judgments about Amsterdam; it was, in Bradford's phrase, "the grim and grisly face of poverty coming upon them like an armed man."

For months the Pilgrims struggled with him. And while they never fully overcame him, neither did he overcome them. The threat was constant, but within a few months they had managed to live with it. And in those months they discovered a more serious threat to their purity as a people, a spiritual pollution that threatened them.

The Pilgrims knew that they would be free from religious persecution in the Netherlands. They would also be free from being taken seriously. Critics of Dutch toleration jibed that every sect in Christendom croaked and spawned in the Dutch marshlands; these sects presented to the world the same interminable variety that the Dutch warehouses provided in material goods. A variety of goods or a variety of opinions, truth was irrelevant where price was all. To the Dutch, the Pilgrims fancied their beliefs as would the tulip enthusiast fancy his bulbs. Both could be permitted to croak and spawn, and to speculate on the future. To speculate on the black tulip or the original sin, the preference was a matter of taste.

As persecution refined and hardened sects, so this watery tolerance dissolved them. Having nothing to fight on the outside (save the armed man of poverty), they would take to fighting within, and in the process they slowly melted into the indistinguishable mass of humankind.

Bradford and his fellows could see this from the example of the Ancient Brethren who had preceded them here to Amsterdam. These separatists had escaped England in 1593 when their leaders had been imprisoned and executed. The visage that the Ancient Brethren now, after thirteen years of exile, presented to the Pilgrims must have frightened them more than the grim and grisly face of poverty. This was a brotherhood armed and fighting against itself. They would fight over almost any issue, always ready to denounce the other side as impure. Women's clothing was one such issue. Was starch really the Devil's liquor? While they uncharitably questioned one another's motives, the general morality of the group became less and less distinguishable from that of the world around them. Soon their church would become nothing more then a convenient roost for any passing unclean bird. The Brethren, despite the spiritual heroism of their origins, had become, as one polemicist put it, "Amsterdamnified by their brainless opinions."

The Pilgrims left Amsterdam little more than a year after they had arrived. They had no sooner established themselves and evaluated their new surroundings than they had decided that this was but a brief way station in their pilgrimage; they were not going to stay to get Amsterdamnified by the pollution of this place. They had to flee this port of cruelty, this city of avarice and indifference, avarice for gold and indifference to the spirit. The Ancient Brethren had been as good as killed here; the Pilgrims could only flee.

They had not yet given up on the Netherlands, just on Amsterdam. They moved away from that thickening center of worldly commerce to Leiden. The choice was a measure of their prudence. Leiden was a much smaller, more manageable city, much like the Amsterdam of old. Its commerce centered on the cloth trade, which would provide the industrious Pilgrims with opportunities for apprenticeships. Moreover, the University of Leiden was the best in the Netherlands, and among the most respected in Europe. Its influence should offset the worldliness of the commercial class.

All this was well and prudently reasoned. The Pilgrims did live in Leiden for a decade, almost as long as the Ancient Brethren had lived in Amsterdam when the Pilgrims had first seen them. William Bradford, writing decades later, would remember this time as one in which the community grew in knowledge and other gifts and graces of the Spirit of God, and lived together in peace and love and holiness.

There was truth in this recollection. Their revered leader during this period, John Robinson, had written, "We ought to be firmly persuaded in our hearts of the truth, and goodness of the religion, which we embrace in all things; yet as knowing ourselves to be men, whose property it is to err and to be deceived in many things; and accordingly both to converse with men in that modesty of mind, as always to desire to learn something better, or further, by them, if may be."

This was the ideal to which the Pilgrims aspired, a humble firmness between dogmatism and dissolution, an openness that would permit growth while on guard against backsliding. Yes, there was truth in this recollection of Bradford, but not the whole truth. The same threats that had driven them from Amsterdam came upon them here—but slowly, gradually, insidiously, so the Pilgrims hardly recognized the threats for what they were.

Poverty no longer confronted them like an armed man. They now had learned all manner of trades. The Pilgrims labored that their earthly masters might satisfy their insatiable whirlpool hunger for pernicious gold. (All the gold beneath the moon, that ever was, could not give rest to a single soul.) However, as they labored from dawn to night year after year, the community was slowly ground down. The elders of the community, who had to come to Leiden in the prime of life, were now beginning to face old age; the cheerfulness and courage with which they had born their unrelenting hardships now began to be eroded by apprehension and fear. These fears were increased by the children. They had to be put to work young to help their parents, and now

the toll of this premature labor was visibly being paid. Their youthful vigor
was being consumed in the bud, and they were becoming decrepit before their
time. Not surprisingly, some were rebelling against this yoke, and were seeking their fortunes within a Dutch world, to the dishonor of God and the grief
of their parents. The community, despite the peace and love and holiness
within, was being slowly dissolved by the world. Their burden, they came to
realize sadly, was laying too hard upon them.

A theological debate contributed to the sense of unease. The tolerance of
divergent religious opinions within Holland meant the toleration not just of
Separatists but also of those who denied central truths of Christianity. The
most famous of these was a late professor at the University of Leiden, Jacobus
Arminius. Arminius denied that God had chosen a special and separate people for himself predestined for salvation. He asserted Jesus was the instrument
of salvation for all human beings, Christians and non-Christians alike.
Providence did not settle who would be saved; individuals did that for themselves, in their freedom. Some, like believing Christians, had advantages in
working out their salvation; but this advantage was only relative, not absolute.

John Robinson, firmly of the opinion that this was not an opinion his
humble flock could even entertain as good Christians, was drawn into a dispute with followers of Arminius. With tact and charity and great learning (or
so his Pilgrims proudly thought), he showed that in asserting human freedom
they were denying God as the lord of history. Providence is nothing more than
a word if it depends upon human choice. The Arminians, whatever their
intentions, are instruments of the dissolution of Christianity itself. All the
righteousness that Arminius praised is as filthy rags. Civility is not sufficient
to salvation. By the works of law and reason, the work of our own wills, no
man is justified. All our efforts are unprofitable to ourselves. The wisdom of
Arminius is the wisdom of the world, and is ignorance. That which is in high
esteem among men is counted as an abomination before God, as less than
nothing. In accepting this philosophy, the Dutch were being launched into a
gulf of misery. Without grace they will perish everlastingly in their own
deceiving. The soul of an Arminian was as empty of religion as the white of an
egg was of savor. Arminius's doctrine true Christians must abhor.

The Pilgrims were proud of their pastor, and believed he had won a great
victory as a champion of the Truth, vanquishing enemy after enemy in single
combat. Even so, there was a deeper logic working here, and the Pilgrims
sensed it. The individualistic rationalism of Arminius was closer to the heart
of the Dutch social system than Calvinism, no matter how widely the latter
was professed. The dissolution of Christianity that Arminianism represented

to the Pilgrims in the realm of ideas was happening all around them in the realm of social fact. It was happening within the Pilgrim community itself as it struggled to preserve its values from one generation to the next.

A crisis had slowly snuck upon them. They had to reassert their faith in themselves as a separate people, and thereby to reaffirm their belief in God's Providence. God had chosen them as a people, and He had destined them to be a part of a great work. Of course, Mr. Worldly Wiseman would tell them that they had traveled enough for their beliefs, sacrificed enough, and should now attend to their own soft comfort. They were too weakened as a people to endure another relocation. But they knew it is with the weak that God chooses to confound the wise and powerful.

If they left Leiden, where would they go? No other European country offered the religious toleration they needed. The alternative seemed to be leaving Europe altogether, a complete separation. Yet when the New World was proposed as the new way station in their pilgrimage, even the bravest found their bowels grating within them with fear, and the weak simply quaked and trembled. Then they tried to talk themselves through the problem, as they had so often before talked themselves through lesser problems.

If they allowed their lives to be governed by worldly prudence, they would be no better than the Arminians who thought themselves in control of their own lives. As Pilgrims, they placed their lives in God's hands. Given the sincerity and high religious purpose of their enterprise, and given all that they had already suffered uncomplainingly for the purity of His Gospel, they could expect God's special blessing on their enterprise. And even if this enterprise proved a failure in the world's eyes, the Pilgrims could be sure of a good death, the needful repose that would restore their weary souls. They had to remember that all that men labored for by their own hands—all the mighty wealth of the Netherlands, for instance—was, when weighed against the will of God, so much smoke. They would once again abandon themselves to Him, and let Him do with them as He would.

They would not fret at the powers and terrors of what is yet unseen. They might be cut in pieces and burned in flames by Indians, or devoured by wild beasts, or drowned in the seas before they even arrived. But even the sea will give up its dead at the angel's trumpet. And on the last day they would all be made whole and then clothed in the garment of immortality. Why then fear? Against the passions of this world, they must have the patience of the world to come. Christian Pilgrims would always seem an outlandish people to those whose primary trade and traffic was not heaven.

Nevertheless, to have a chance of success, the enterprise required trade and traffic of a worldly sort as well. The Pilgrims were prepared to commit their accumulated wealth to founding their colony. But more than a decade of labor had left them with far less than they would require. They needed to form a company with a group of investors who would risk capital on the success of the colony.

Their piety was a marketable commodity amongst those wishing to invest in the New World. Their exaggerated faith in God, however ridiculous it might seem in polite society, meant that they would not be discouraged by even great suffering and losses. The setbacks that would cause a self-seeker to quit would be regarded by these people as the bites and blows sent by God to remind them that their race of creatures was still under the penalty of the old Adam. They would make the best of whatever came. They were scrupulous in their morals, industrious in their work, and frugal in their habits. They would not be yearning to return home, for they had already been, as Bradford put it, "well weaned from the milk of the mother country." A people who regarded the whole world as an allegorical wilderness in which they would never be at home should be in their element facing a wilderness *per se*.

There was no lack of Dutch investors interested in supporting them. Dutch merchants had long been sending ships on trading voyages to the New World. That was not because the Dutch had any particular interest in the New World; it was just that the Dutch in the seventeenth century were sending ships on trading voyages everywhere in the world that a profit might be turned. They had little interest in colonization, but they would be delighted to have someone else establish a permanent trading post for them. And the investors interested knew just the place. Between the Saint Lawrence River and Chesapeake Bay, between the areas of French and English control, a major river had been discovered by an explorer in Dutch employ, Henry Hudson. At the mouth of the Hudson River was an island, Manhattan, that would provide the ideal site from which to control trade along that river. The Pilgrims could plant the Dutch flag there, to the profit of all.

But the Pilgrims did not want to leave the Netherlands in order to become little Dutchmen abroad. They did not wish to become agents of Dutch economic expansion. If they were successful, what would happen? Their colony would be transformed by the Dutch into a new Amsterdam, the epitome of all they had fled. The Pilgrims sought profit in the New World, but not the kind that would register on Dutch ledgers.

So they felt themselves blessed by God when they happened on Thomas Weston, a British merchant who was willing to put together a group of English backers for their colony. Although not a Puritan himself, he was so effusively admiring of their community that they felt him a brother. The Pilgrims began to take irretrievable steps toward leaving Leiden, with a generous agreement all but signed with Weston and his associates. Their colonizing expedition was to be led by Pilgrim father John Carver, and a council that included the thirty-three-year-old Bradford.

Only too late did Carver, Bradford, and the rest conclude that Weston was no true friend of theirs. He and the other investors were harpies determined to feast off the Pilgrims and unconcerned if the little they left behind was spoiled by their greed. In the world of business in which the Pilgrims were now moving, a tender conscience was counted an unmanly thing, and Weston's conscience was far from tender.

Weston and his colleagues waited until they were certain that the Pilgrims could not back out, and then refused to sign the agreement of support unless further concessions were granted. The earlier contract had specified that after its seven-year term, all the accumulated wealth of the colony would be divided equally between the colonists and the investors. Only a colonist's house and garden would be exempted from this general division. The investors now insisted that this property be included.

What was the justification for the change? The investors said they were afraid that the colonists would save their best labor for their own property and let the commonwealth languish at its expense. But this proposed change in the agreement implicitly questioned the honesty of the Pilgrims, or so they thought. It treated them as if they were thieves looking for their first chance to swindle their benefactors. Bradford and the rest offered to extend the length of the contract, even double its length, if only this odious calumny be replaced by the old terms. They did not want to leave with an official agreement which implicitly impugned their integrity.

The investors, however, were not interested in integrity; they were interested in shrewd bargaining. And they had the colonists at their mercy. Why not squeeze out a little more potential profit? Weston and the other investors, all pleasing faces and foulness within, knew they only had to remain firm to get their way. So the Pilgrims had finally to agree to sail under the degrading agreement.

With much uncharacteristic bitterness and complaining, the Pilgrims realized they had been too trusting in their arrangements. They were so full of the divine purpose of their enterprise that they had forgotten the lessons they had learned from more than a decade in a commercial center. Weston and the investors were not the only ones to take advantage of their trust.

Weston and his partners provided the *Mayflower* to transport them. The

Pilgrims bought with meager savings a smaller ship, the *Speedwell*, to accompany it. The *Speedwell* was to remain in the New World and help the colonists with fishing and the like. Only belatedly did they realize they had been swindled: the *Speedwell* proved unseaworthy. Then it was the ship repairers' turn to profit. Expensive repairs were made, dwindling their resources further. Nonetheless, the *Speedwell* remained useless to them, and had to be abandoned.

Now they had to make a humiliating appeal to Weston. They were selling provisions to pay their bills. They realized they no longer had enough to last them the first winter. Would he not advance them further funds? Of course he would not. Weston had become a man of few words, most of them abusive. What were a few Pilgrims more or less to him? And in his walnut-hearted refusal they could read a prophecy of famine for themselves.

Throughout this time of tumult, they exhorted each other not to be polluted by these dealings with the world. Amidst the hubbub of avarice, all this worry and flurry, they must suffer what was cast upon them with meekness and patience. In retrospect, this experience would prove a caution and an example. After all, this was why they were leaving. Selfishness was as contagious as the plague. Whatever jostling they were suffering now, whatever hardships awaited them in the New World, this was a voyage God meant for them. If they thought they were going to be lost, they must remember the story of Jonah who had tried to shirk an apparently impossible mission God had chosen him for. God would bring forth a great fish, if need be, to get them to their appointed place. The souls of the just are in the hands of God and the torment of death shall not touch them.

Such godly wisdom, however sincerely and deeply believed, paled before an ugly fact. With every setback the number of Pilgrims going to the New World diminished. From the beginning, not all had planned to go, at least on the first voyage. The very hardships at Leiden that contributed to the decision to leave had made many of the community unfit for the rigors of initial settlement. The old, the weak, and some of the young (including Bradford's only child) would remain behind. So would—and this was the most difficult to bear—the beloved pastor of the Pilgrims, John Robinson.

When the *Speedwell* was given up, another group had to be left behind. So God continued His inscrutable sifting of His people. Then individuals, frightened by the increased difficulties, began to drop out, with plausible excuses and promises to come when they could. The tension between piety and fear was epitomized in a single joking sentence by one of the Pilgrim leaders: "Poor William Ring and myself do strive who shall be first meat for the fishes; but we look for a glorious resurrection."

By the time the *Mayflower* finally left in 1620, with the sea moaning and tossing like an awakened conscience, only about forty of approximately one hundred passengers were "Saints"; the rest were "Strangers," recruited primarily in England. The Pilgrims would begin as a minority even within their own colony. That could be rectified when the rest of the Saints found their way to the New World, if they ever did. This uncertainty added poignancy to the parting in Leiden. The scene remained vivid in the memory of William Bradford years later.

Most of the community had come on board, to be together for a last time. They all knew the dangers in store for those leaving, the difficulties those who chose to follow would face in arranging passage, and the grinding poverty in which those who remained behind for good would live. This was their last time together in this world. And what they had shared in their wanderings were the only things that made this world worth living in at all, the jewel whose splendor dimmed all earthly things. Yet belief in another life beyond this proved almost insufficient before the immediate prospect of wholesale bereavement, or so Bradford wrote.

"Truly doleful was the sight of that sad and mournful parting, to see what sighs and sobs and prayers did sound amongst them, what tears did gush from every eye, and pithy speeches pierced each heart; that sundry of the Dutch strangers that stood on the quay as spectators could not refrain from tears. Yet comfortable and sweet it was to see such lively and true expressions of dear and unfeigned love. But the tide, which stays calm for no man, calling them away that were thus loath to depart, their reverend pastor falling down on his knees (and they all with him) with watery cheeks commended them with most fervent prayers to the Lord and His Blessing. And then with mutual embraces and many tears they took their leaves one of another, which proved to be the last leave to many of them."

And we can imagine those left behind standing at the dock for a long time, first shouting and waving, then watching the sails flit and fade like moths in the distance, then just staring out at the steel-blue rim of the sea.

So with a prosperous wind the aspiring colonists left behind first the cities of the Netherlands and then the shores of England, hoping for clear answers to doubtful prayers. Bradford, as he thought back on this sad and portentous embarkation, was reminded of a passage from the Epistle to the Hebrews. They had just left, he wrote, a "goodly city that had been their resting place for twelve years, but they knew they were Pilgrims, and looked not on those things but lift up their eyes to the heavens, their dearest country, and quieted their spirits."

So they sailed off in their crowded ship, which was also laden with their insufficient supplies, and as well with a ghostlier freight, the first consignment of the New England conscience. What was this conscience? It was a contrite consciousness forever dividing itself against itself, its only true enjoyment in its own unhappiness. In this house divided whatever was good came from God as an undeserved grace, whatever was evil came from its own fallen self, an accurate expression of our worthlessness. The fuller the soul with God's grace, the more excruciating the sense of guilt it felt for the remaining taint of corruption. Satisfaction was an accurate gauge of sinfulness. The height of sanctity, therefore, was a dark night of the soul for which few if any could sincerely wish, an ordeal of unimaginable psychic torment.

If the Pilgrims had wished for a material image of this torment, they had only to look at their tiny island called the *Mayflower* as it struggled across the Atlantic. It was soon hit by such storms that the captain had to pull in the sails and let the ship drift at the mercy of waves and winds until the tumult passed. The modern church as Jesus asleep in the bark of Peter.

Apart from the storm, the voyage was uneventful, except for two "special providences," as Bradford called them. A young crewman who repeatedly taunted and blasphemed the Pilgrims soon sickened and died, thereby becoming the first food for the fishes. (Blasphemy, they had to remember, was a tormented soul's perverse call for the return of faith.) Then a young Pilgrim was swept off deck in heavy seas, and was nonetheless retrieved from the water against all odds. So even in the most desolate of regions God does as He pleases, and those who are seeking Divine instruction can find it.

When the ship sighted land on November 19, 1620, the Pilgrims learned more of God's pleasure. They soon realized that they were far to the north of where they wished to be, a dreary stretch of coast dominated by smashed boulders, such as might have emerged after the first sinning when the ground was cursed. They had hoped to seek settlement on the Hudson River near the island of Manhattan, but they had actually arrived at Cape Cod, and an attempt to turn the *Mayflower* south was beaten back after half a day by dangerous shoals and roaring breakers. God was speaking to them again, out of the elements of the sea; and so they sought their place on Cape Cod. They found it in a small inlet called alternatively on British maps Thievish Harbor and (from John Smith) Plymouth. The first was perhaps the more appropriate, for the colonists had been treated like thieves by their merchant backers, but after crossing the English Channel they had set out from England from the port of Plymouth. So this colony should be a new Plymouth, a place far from the merchant thieves of the old world, far from the pomp that beats high upon that doomed shore.

They could thank God for preserving them from the vast ocean, and piloting them through their earlier sea of troubles. But this was no land of milk and honey to which He had brought His separate people. He had placed them, with their weary limbs in much need of ease, at the edge of what Bradford saw as a "hideous and desolate wilderness." This truly was a country for Pilgrims, for it offered no external object on which to feed hope. For hope they had to look to heaven and cry to the Lord that He might hear their voice and look on their adversity. Now they needed their courage, now if ever a stout heart.

The Pilgrims, who were always looking for God's special providence, could find in this hideous wilderness one sign of His favor: its human emptiness. Despite all the frightening stories of Indians, the Pilgrims could scarcely find any human beings at all. During the first few months, there were only a few sightings, and one inconsequential skirmish. People had lived here before, that was certain. The Pilgrims found large caches of corn to which they helped themselves freely. Human bones were also evident. Not just the occasional skeleton, but larger collections—as if this had been a battlefield where the corpses had been left to rot.

There were so many skulls the place could have been renamed New Golgotha. The Pilgrims could not help feeling that they saw God's hand in all this. He had brought them here, and forced them back when they tried to go south, because He had already cleared this land for them of other human beings while having left them food for survival, to recompense them for the stores swindled away from them over the *Speedwell.* God had arranged that they would face no enemy here but winter and rough weather and their own weakness; but that would be enemy enough. They had survived a wintry crossing to arrive at this desolate shore between the merciless surge of the ocean and the howling wilderness, a land of sand and skulls and sorrows, themselves so lonely and wretched, huddling in sad, sunless, makeshift shelters, trying to still the whisper from within, "But I, why did I come here?"

The first to break seems to have been William Bradford's own wife, Dorothy. In January 1621, only six weeks after arrival, Dorothy Bradford drowned over the side of the *Mayflower.* How did she fall in such calm weather? Why did she not call for help, with so many of her friends nearby? Bradford and the other Pilgrim fathers, usually so assiduous at finding meaning in human tragedies, could find none in this one, and passed over it briefly, as if Dorothy had scarcely existed. Apart from one scant mention, she is written out of their histories. Had she, after seeing the place to which her husband and her God had brought her, despaired and thrown herself, mute with grief, over the side? There were certain destinies by which the pious must pass in silence, as Bradford did by that of his beloved wife.

Within a month of Dorothy's death, she seemed in her despair, if despair it was, to have been a true prophet who, like Cassandra of old, went all unheeded. Weakened by the months of anxious preparation, and then by the arduous voyage, and then by the labors needed to establish themselves at least in shacks and shanties, the Pilgrim colonists were suffering what they could only describe as a "general sickness," since it combined the symptoms of a legion of diseases. Soon death had spread its wings over the colony, which in response started to sprout a garden of graves. And the Pilgrims, amidst unutterable misery, struggled to walk in the strength of the Lord. Any not completely prostrated by the sickness—and occasionally these were as few as six or seven—had to minister to the rest, dividing their duties between the graves of the dead and the beds of the dying, until they too became invalids and others less sick had to take their place. All the while, the winds blew as if to wake the dead, and persistent cold probed the surviving hapless Pilgrims with doubts like devils' claws. "I, why did I come here?"

Before the sickness had passed almost half the colony was dead, including Governor John Carver. The women had borne the brunt, for they had spent themselves to save their children. Thirteen of the eighteen wives were dead. Their efforts did not go unrewarded, though, for seventeen of the twenty children did survive. Bradford was elected to replace Carver as governor.

Months would pass before the colony fully regained its strength. Some members never did. Captain Jones of the *Mayflower*, seeing the straitened circumstances of these good people, stayed the winter against his orders and generously shared of his stores. He was a seaman to the salt in his blood, and knew his duty. After standing by the colony through its ordeal and enduring it with them, he returned to England, his own health now broken. He died in old Plymouth less than a year after his return.

The Pilgrims endured what God had sent them, and without audible complaint. The Strangers, living intimately with them, endured without complaint as well. The patience on their part was encouraging.

Worldlings would say that they had only survived by luck. Without the corn caches, or if they had been pressed by hostile Indians, none would have survived, man, woman, or child. So the worldlings, such as the Arminians, would reason; but the Pilgrims knew better. God, if He wished, could make the stones speak or rain bread from heaven. Whatever had happened, had happened because it was His pleasure, and His Will be done. This Will the Pilgrims did not claim to understand in all its particulars. In those incomprehensible particulars the world may well have seemed to be governed by accident. But general patterns were observable, especially to those deeply read in Scripture. God's people would be severely tested repeatedly, but these tests would then lead to a greater awareness of His gracious kindness, His tender mercies.

After the ordeal of the general sickness the Pilgrims enjoyed a special illumination from God. The instrument of this illumination was an Indian warrior who, during that first winter, happened to wander into the colony, naked but fully armed. Fear was suddenly transformed into amazement when the Indian said in clear English, "Welcome," and then asked for a beer. They eagerly supplied him with a drink (of hard liquor, for they had no beer at hand), and gave him a coat to cover his nakedness, and then served him a good meal, at least good compared to what they had become accustomed to.

Samoset, as he called himself, told his hosts about his region. Four years before, the tribe of Plymouth had been wiped from the earth by a mysterious plague. All the tribes of the region, including his own Abenakis in Maine, had suffered from this disease, but the Pawtuxet here were singled out for special suffering by the illness and did not endure. With the Pawtuxet gone, the nearest great chief was Massasoit, with whom Samoset was staying. Massasoit lived approximately forty miles to the southwest, on a large bay called by the Indians Narragansett.

Through the good offices of Samoset, the colony began to establish friendly relations with this great chief. Unlike Powhatan, Massasoit did not regard the Pilgrims as invaders; and unlike Champlain's Hurons, he did not expect military favors in exchange for his friendship. He did expect to be entertained, however—both himself and his retinue. Although the Pilgrims eventually had to complain to him that his braves were taking advantage of their hospitality, this was a small matter, especially compared to what the Pilgrims had been led to fear from the blood-curdling tales of New World savagery that they had been told in the Netherlands.

Remarkable as all this was, worldlings might still explain it away as a remarkable run of good luck. However, one additional occurrence put this all clearly beyond simple luck into the realm of a special providence. Within the retinue of Massasoit was the sole surviving member of the Pawtuxet, Squanto. No one could doubt that he had been chosen by God for the Pilgrim colony.

Years before, Squanto had been kidnapped by an unscrupulous European trader coasting in North America, probably by Smith's exploring expedition here. Smith's second-in-command had freelanced in the slave trade, against his orders. He had separated from Smith to have a free hand, and eventually made his way to Spain to sell his cargo of Indians for private profit. Squanto apparently was one of those he had lured on board and then carried back to Spain. For Squanto that only began a series of adventures worthy of John Smith, but without the blood. He escaped from his Spanish owners and went to England, where he became fully conversant in English and the English way of life. He eventually talked himself into passage back to the New World, and had then made his way slowly to Cape Cod, arriving six months before the *Mayflower*. His return, which should have been the occasion of joyful celebrations, was rather met with silence. No one was left alive to greet him. Instead of a village, he found a desolation. So he drifted into the service of Massasoit, his life having become purposeless.

But he saw now a new people at the site of the old Pawtuxet village, as if sprung up from their dry bones. The Pilgrims provided a purpose for his own earlier wanderings. He understood their language, and something of their customs and the ways of their old land. He could now teach them the customs of this land, of this place. He could teach them how to plant corn and fertilize the fields to ensure its growth, how and where and when to catch the fishes and the eel and the clam and the lobster, where and when to gather the wild fruits, to hunt game. He would do all this, and serve as their interpreter with the neighboring tribes. And they would be his new people, providing him with what he had lost while he was away, struggling to free himself from the slavery of their world.

With Squanto at their side, the success of the Pilgrims' colony seemed assured, thanks be to God. God had sorely tested them, but only to share more fully with them His wondrous bounty. When the first crops were harvested that next October, they formally gave thanks in a harvest festival that some of them remembered from youth in rural England, a faded memory to be re-enacted in this new place. They invited Massasoit and his Indians, and so many came that they sent them back out to get enough venison for the three-day feast.

They had so much to be thankful for. While the crops were ripening, another gift had been given to them so that their cup runneth over. In a shallop they had been exploring to the north, and had come to the harbor that came to be called Boston. At first they were struck with a tinge of envy. This place seemed so much better for planting a colony than Plymouth, why had God not led them here? Squanto, however, warned them that the Indians here, the Massachusetts, were traditional enemies of his people and quite jealous of their land. Even as far away as Plymouth was, the colony was still in danger from this aggressive people.

When the colonists saw their first group of Massachusetts, Squanto's warnings were quickly ignored. The women were wearing beaver robes. Such furs were extremely valuable trade items. As Champlain had already learned, a steady beaver trade could support a whole colony; beaver was the tobacco of the northern colonies. And here they had before them a possible source.

Squanto tried to dissuade them. If they had to have the beaver robes, they should just simply take them by force, for the Massachusetts would never trade peaceably. For once, the colonists decided to ignore his advice. He was speaking out of old tribal hatreds—and colonists wanted steady trade, not just raids between themselves and the Massachusetts. They offered the women beads and other trinkets for the robes; the women were, if anything, too eager. They immediately stripped themselves of all their furs, and were left only with hastily constructed skirts of brush to hide their nakedness.

So when the Pilgrims sat with Massasoit to give thanks for the successful planting of their colony, they were thankful not just for the friendship of Massasoit and the help of Squanto that assured its survival. They could be thankful too for the prospect of a beaver trade that could make the colony modestly prosperous, and hence help them fulfill their outstanding legal obligations. Worldlings like Thomas Weston and his Merchant Adventurers would be impressed by that.

That the Merchant Adventurers would be pleased, however, should have been a warning of sorts. The events of this world were not always as they seemed. Suffering and other "bad luck" could be the most needed good of a soul, making it realize that its true end is not of this world. Prosperity and good fortune, in contrast, could do great harm to a soul, for a soul could thereby be lulled into a smug satisfaction with the things of this world. As the most severe suffering could be an expression of God's loving kindness, so the most joyful prosperity could be a vicious snare of the devil. The sober Pilgrim had to discipline himself to see the events of his life from this higher perspective, which worldlings could never imagine. He had to realize that from the depths of his soul would constantly rise, like exhalations, the misty phantoms of pride and covetousness, delusions of Lucifer that seemed like angels of light.

Such thoughts were foremost in the mind of Robert Cushman when he was asked to give a sermon to the collected colony less than a month after the harvest celebration. He called it "The Danger of Self Love." The colonists must not think that they had somehow deserved or earned the bounty that

God had bestowed upon them. If they thought that even for a moment, they were starting the slide away from Christianity into the abyss of the Arminianism that they had left behind in Leiden, a smugness that was satisfied with the froth of fleeting joy instead of the rock of salvation.

Once they fell in love with the achievements of their own hands, they would then, out of their pride, start to jostle among one another for precedence. Their little commonwealth would become an arena of competition over who was better, who was best. This competition would center on the accumulation of worldly goods. Then their colony would be no better than the societies they had left, and their pilgrimage would have ended in failure.

Good Deacon Cushman exhorted them that as Christians they should not try "to live better than thy neighbor." Self-love is a one-eyed monster that sees everything only from the perspective of me. Was it not Satan that introduced this "particularizing" into the world when he "was not content to keep that equal state with his fellows, but would set his throne above the stars"? Such satanic particularizing now dominates the world; yet in this world a saint can still give the contrary witness that this world is not all. No such witness is more effective than that of communities united by true love. Nothing in this fallen world of ours "doth more resemble heavenly happiness than for men to live as one, being of one heart and one soul; nor does anything more resemble hellish horror than for every man to shift for himself."

Cushman's vision of heaven and hell was much admired by the leaders of the Pilgrim colony, and was soon published in Old England itself. Cushman also contributed an essay to a tract promoting the new colony. In it he adapted the arguments of his sermon in order to exhort true Christians to join the colony. Christians had to realize that the very structure of English society made a Christian life virtually impossible; merely surviving in this society polluted the heart.

"Each man is fain to pluck his means, as it were, out of his neighbor's throat. There is such pressing and oppressing in town and country about farms, trades, traffic, etc., so as a man can hardly set up a trade but he shall pull down two of his neighbors." A Christian, however saintly, cannot hope to reform this living hell; he can only separate himself from it, and thereby retain the purity of his heart. He might even find for himself a foretaste of heaven "in a spacious land the way to which is through the sea."

Cushman in his eager eloquence had overlooked a disturbing possibility. Some settlers might come to Plymouth for a taste of heaven, but others might bring hell with them. And the first new settlers to arrive in Plymouth after Cushman's essay was published definitely brought hell with them. They were unwelcome guests stealing in to disturb the feast, men of the fallen and world-worn race that hates the way of humility and submission like a torture.

The new settlers were sent by the Pilgrims' old false friend, Thomas Weston. The bickering over profits had become so bad among the investors that the company itself was dissolving, or so he said. As far as Weston was concerned, the Pilgrims, as leaders of the colony, were themselves to blame; they should have taken greater care to make sure that the investors had gotten a better return. Too many sermons and not enough beaver. It was now everyone for himself, he announced all blithe and bonny. The settlers who were arriving were his and his alone. They were to establish their own colony, *his* colony, on Boston bay. Until this could be done, would the Pilgrims please supply these new colonists with food, drink, and lodging? His colonists would pay in good hard cash.

This request placed the Pilgrims in a quandary. They had barely enough supplies for themselves, and now Weston had dumped on them sixty new mouths. His cash was not going to see them through the crisis. Yet they could not leave the new colonists to fend for themselves when that meant exposure, starvation, and death.

The crisis was partly allayed when a British trading ship happened into their harbor. The captain, however, once he realized the plight of the colony, exploited their need to make a huge profit for himself. He would trade supplies only for beaver pelts, and for these he would trade at about one seventh of the going rate. How unlike this Captain Jones from the Captain Jones of the *Mayflower*, but how like the Thomas Weston who had put the colony in this predicament!

Weston had recruited colonists after his own heart. Their low character threatened the moral integrity of the colony; yet charity still demanded that the Pilgrims take these lowlifes into their own homes, and thereby expose the young to the contagions of their wily viciousness. As a group, they were "not fit for an honest man's company," as Bradford bluntly put it. But now the Pilgrims could only expose their inmost family life to a ridiculing ingratitude, and hope that the colony would emerge without irremediable pollution. So the Pilgrims, out of Christian duty, had to nurse a serpent in their bosom.

When Weston's colonists finally left a few months later, they presented a whole new set of problems. They did establish themselves successfully on Boston harbor, the site the Plymouth colonists had long coveted. They now cut off the Pilgrims' beaver trade with the Massachusetts. Moreover, they were so eager to trade that they were offering the Indians far more for the skins than the Pilgrims had established as a fair price.

These worries were bad enough, but then Squanto sickened and died. He had taught them what they needed to know, but they lost him when they most needed his diplomatic skills. This was especially true when news reached them of the Virginia massacre of 1622. According to the account they heard, the Virginia Indians had long lived in friendship with the colonists until they rose up as one to massacre the whole colony. Could a similar conspiracy be afoot here? The colonists concentrated their communal efforts to build a fort to protect them against come what might. Or rather they fortified the largest building of the colony, their church.

In 1623 they began to hear that Weston's men had badly mismanaged their affairs at Boston. The Indians were refusing to trade with the colonists. Weston's men had been reduced to working for the Indians or to stealing from them just to survive. So the Pilgrims might sing with the psalmist, the ungodly are trapped in the work of their own hand, the wicked make for themselves a hell.

But the situation was not so simple. The Indians were treating Weston's men with contempt. This contempt the Pilgrims would see in the faces of those Indians with whom they traded. In such a short time Weston's men had polluted respectful relations the Pilgrims had spent years developing. And the Pilgrims were the ones most likely to reap what these worldlings had sowed. Then in the midst of all these worries, an Indian friend (who probably had as much love for the Massachusetts as Squanto) told the Pilgrims that the Massachusetts were planning to massacre first Weston's colony, and then their own. Now at night their fears could feed upon themselves. They could hear the whoops of unseen savages in every fitful gust of wind that issued from the surrounding forest. And fearful as they were of noise, they were more fearful still when the night became oddly quiet. As the little colony squatted there near the scowling surf and its grim boulders, with the wet mass of fog eddying all about, as they imagined Indian chiefs like so many princes of darkness plotting out there somewhere to make the Pilgrim people a prey to their obscene appetites, the Pilgrim fathers decided to strike the first blow, preemptively.

In reaching this decision they were led by their military expert Miles Standish. As Bradford had emerged as the most prominent Saint of the Plymouth colony, so Standish was easily the most prominent Stranger. He had been with the colony from the first, and respected the religious discipline of its Saints. He had stood with them whenever their authority over the colony was questioned by the Strangers. And they had relied upon him for military leadership, much as they had depended upon Squanto to teach them wilderness ways.

Standish did not question the friendship the Pilgrims had established with their neighbors, but he was always ready to provide visiting Indians with a formidable display of European arms, just as a precaution against the day when friendship needed to be buttressed by fear. If friendship failed, Standish would defend the Pilgrim state by force of arms. Or rather *when* it failed, for Standish believed that the only tongue a savage could understand was the tongue of fire that speaks from the mouth of a cannon, a pagan Pentecost.

Bradford and the other Pilgrim leaders were grateful to have among the Strangers so useful a supporter. They only regretted his extreme irascibility. Tiny in stature, Standish was always on alert against possible slights. He was their little chimney, they joked, and heated hot in a moment. He also did his best to keep the colony collectively on alert as well against possible slights.

Now, with the horrifying news of the Virginia massacre, with Squanto dead and rumors about Weston's colony rife, the Standish interpretation of events became far more persuasive than did Pilgrim pieties about God as the shield and weapon of His people, their fire and their sweetness. The decision was made to send a relief expedition to Weston's colony under the leadership of Captain Standish, a relief expedition that was really an unprovoked attack on the Massachusetts.

When the expedition arrived there, some of its members must have been surprised that Weston's men did not think they needed military help. To Standish's offer of protection, they replied (as Standish reported their words), "We fear not the Indians, but live with them and suffer them to lodge with us, not having sword, gun or needing the same."

For Standish this response was only further evidence of how deluded and unfit these men were. Standish sternly took command of the whole colony. He kept everyone on high military alert so that any attack could be repulsed. He also sought to lure the Massachusetts into an ambush. His plan seemed to be working when Wituwamat, the chief of the Massachusetts, arrived at the colony along with another brave and a young boy. Wituwamat soon made it plain that the Indians understood fully Standish's intentions. Wituwamat had come to the colony to show that he and his people were unafraid, and also to express his own personal contempt for the puny Captain Shrimp. Standish, turning pinker by the moment, finally lost his composure and ordered these Indians put to the sword. The fight that ensued was ferocious, although the Indians were hopelessly outmanned.

Standish himself had to admit later that he would never have believed that a man could receive as many wounds as Wituwamat had and still continue to fight. Not once did Wituwamat or his brave cry out or ask for mercy. The young boy they captured alive, and summarily executed. The name Miles Standish, like those of the Hebrew Judges of old, was going to strike fear in the heathen nations.

So Standish and his men marched out to eliminate the Massachusetts from the face of the earth. However, Wituwamat, in giving up his life, had forced the colonists to reveal their true intentions. He died knowing that he had at least saved his people from being lured into a massacre, and perhaps that had been his intention all along. Wituwamat had died to warn his people. So the Massachusetts now simply retreated before the superior force of the colonists, and then consolidated themselves in an unassailable position within a swamp.

Realizing that he had failed in his objectives, the infuriated Standish challenged to a fight a champion of the Massachusetts before their assembled troops, hand-to-hand, to the death. But, however much Standish might have resembled a shrunken John Smith, the Massachusetts refused to play the Turks that day. Standish's challenge was answered only with obscene taunts.

Standish did get his trophy, though. He returned to Weston's colony to get the head of Wituwamat. He also put to Weston's men a question. Did they wish to stay any longer in their dangerously exposed position? Of course, if their position had not been dangerous before, Standish in his purblind self-righteousness had certainly made it so now. Indians were no longer going to lodge there without sword and gun. And the Plymouth colony had showed a side of itself they had scarcely expected. Weston's men prudently decided to abandon the colony and to return to England by the quickest route possible.

Standish himself returned to Plymouth a hero. The head of Wituwamat was stuck on a high point on their fort, a suitable ornament for the steeple of their cathedral to self-defense. No longer at the mercy of the world, they were tasting the first fruit of being an autonomous people. Giddy at their success, proud of their hero Standish, they had one of their number publish an account of their great victory in England as "Good News from New England." The account was published so that God could be given "that honor, glory and praise which belongeth to Him."

"Good News from New England" was read eagerly in Leiden where the remnants of the Pilgrim community still awaited their opportunity to come to the New World. Chief among those who waited was the kindly pastor, John Robinson. When he read the "Good News," he felt obligated to write Bradford and the others from his flock to rebuke them for the blood they had shed. He did not think this massacre had anything to do with honor, glory, or praise of God. Nor was it good news, except the kind of good news that governs this Satanic world that will one day pass away to fire and judgment. It was not the good news of Christ Jesus, Lamb of God, Prince of Peace.

There was almost sarcasm to be heard when Robinson wrote, "Oh! how happy a thing it had been if you had converted some before you killed any." He did not dispute their contention that the Indians were plotting evil; he was in no position to question their facts. But even assuming that there was a plot, and that the Pilgrims had reliable auguries of these ruthless intentions, who were the Pilgrims to judge that the Indians had not been sufficiently provoked by Weston's "heathenish Christians"? Weston's men embodied just the kind of hypocrisy that the Pilgrims had left first England and then the Netherlands to avoid, lest they be polluted by commerce with it. Now, Robinson gently implied, the Pilgrims were being polluted far more grievously than they would have been had they never left. In Leiden there were at least no opportunities for Pilgrims to kill in the name of God.

Could these be the same people he prayed with on the deck of the *Mayflower?* How could they be? These people killed without remorse or regret. Circumstances alone restrained their homicidal rage from taking more lives. Even if the punishment was justified, punishment of the leaders would have been enough. But clearly they had intended to massacre, and massacre satisfies not justice but blood lust.

He did not question their admiration for Captain Standish. He knew that they considered him a special gift sent by God to help them in trying and unfamiliar circumstances. Of course, his joining the Pilgrims was a part of God's providential order, predestined from the beginning of all time. Within that order he could well be a gift to the Pilgrims, but every gift is also a test. We must use God's gifts rightly. From this distance Robinson cannot question Standish's virtue as someone meek and humble whose ordinary life fits well into the virtuous company of the Saints. But Robinson must suggest that Standish seems to lack the tenderness that is becoming in someone who professes to believe every human being to be made in God's image. And Robinson has to remind his old flock, "It is a thing more glorious in men's eyes than pleasing in God's . . . to be a terror to poor barbarous people." Was that so difficult a thing to realize in the New World? It would not be in the New Jerusalem.

This was the last communication the Pilgrims would ever receive from John Robinson. He would never be reunited with his flock in the New World as they had all hoped. He would die in 1625, a year after the publication of "Good News from New England." Bradford, for his part, wrote that although the Pilgrims had always revered Robinson, it was only after they lost his help that they realized "to the grief of their hearts and wounding of their souls his true worth."

Nonetheless, far from being chastened by Robinson's rebuke, the Pilgrim colony seemed invigorated by the attempted massacre, regenerated by the violence. The Indians now treated them with a new respect, or so they imagined. Some Indians groups, in fear of the newly aggressive Pilgrims, removed their villages to a greater distance, retreating permanently into the swamplands where their people sickened and died in great numbers, retreating and leaving behind good land for colonial expansion.

Bradford himself began a reorganization of the colony that emphasized both its autonomy from the English investors and the self-reliance of the colonists themselves. No longer would all work together for the commonwealth. This was an ancient vanity of Plato and other pagan thinkers, as if they knew better than God. God had made some stronger and more fit than others. Those who were stronger and more fit did rightfully object that they should "spend their time and strength to work for other men's wives and children without any recompense." To think that all should share equally was to ignore the natural hierarchy God had established amongst His people. To share all was an indignity to those who did the most, and undermined the respect that the successful deserved. Bradford insisted that this principle was not a sign of man's natural corruption; it was a wisdom to which God had led them.

Their new self-assurance was further bolstered by a beggar who showed up at their doorstep. It was their false friend, Thomas Weston, not so blithe and bonny now. He had found passage on a fishing boat, and expected to make a triumphal arrival at his flourishing Boston colony, which in fact no longer existed. First, he was almost drowned in a storm on the coast, and upon landing was pillaged of everything, including his clothes, by unsympathetic Indians. Finally realizing that his colony had vanished, he somehow made his way to the Plymouth colony where he was treated with a smug kindliness appropriate to an object lesson.

Here was the kind of man who mistakes sweating lust for love, who prefers forged lies to honest truth, who measures the grace of God in coin. He had sought the froth of fleeting joy, the mirth of a minute. So he had trusted the cursed fickle dame of fortune; and predictably he had lost his way among the thorns and dangers of this world as he tried to forget that we have immortal longings that cannot be satisfied by purse or power. Now he had learned that the judgment of God could be as pitiless and unforgiving as a New England winter. He who once had flourished in ungodly pride now was reduced to beggardom, so uncertain are the mutable things of this unstable world. God had cast him up upon this shore that we Pilgrims might take caution from his misery, and be strengthened in our virtue by his suffering.

Of course, Weston could not but think that the Pilgrim fathers, where his colony was concerned, had assisted mutability and instability as best they could. The fact that they piously helped him now when all the world failed him only embittered him against them more. He left Plymouth with nothing but bad to say of the colony, but at least they were now finished with this worldling.

The world, nonetheless, continued to intrude. No intrusion was more exasperating than Thomas Morton. Morton was a well-educated aristocrat who had practiced law for a time. He was also a *bon vivant* and a wit who had caroused with Ben Jonson, and like a character from Jonson he had fleeced a widow by wooing her. Now his humor was to become a colonist, a humor much enhanced by some close questioning of his sharp legal practices back in England: it was better to make acquaintance with New Plymouth than with Old Bailey. And for Providence to place a man like Thomas Morton amidst the Pilgrims was a ribald joke worthy of Jonson.

Morton seems to have first come to the New World with Weston's aborted colony. He then joined a trading expedition. When it did not go well, he persuaded some of its number to settle with him rather than continue on from Plymouth to Virginia. He established his colony just to the north of Plymouth. His was, not surprisingly, the antinomy of theirs. While the Pilgrims had sought to separate themselves from the corruptions of civilization, Morton seemed intent on escaping its restraints. He called his colony Merry Mount. Actually he spelled it Mare Mount—to make a Latin pun, the mount by the sea. Soon reports were reaching the Pilgrims that Morton and his men were merrily mounting Indian maids. Mare Mount—could there be a pun about bestiality in the name?—was less a colony than a drunken country fair. Morton had a maypole set up at its center, for pagan rites. About this flower-bedecked abomination the colonists and Indians could be found "dancing and frisking together like so many fairies, or furies rather." That was Bradford's disgusted description. Morton for his part celebrated his return to the pure prodigality of nature in Rabelaisian doggerel that, in the Pilgrims' judgment, was not fit for decent folk to hear. (It would later be published in his account of his colonial experience.)

To support his frisking about the maypole, the Lord of Misrule, as the Pilgrims now called him, traded with the Indians. Without a thought for the morrow, he traded to them whatever they wanted—and what they most wanted were guns and ammunition. Then, as a further sign of his friendship, he began to teach his Indian brothers how to shoot, for which they soon showed a natural if disconcerting aptitude.

This last development was more than the Pilgrims could tolerate. They sent a delegation to remonstrate him solemnly. For their efforts they were rewarded only with insolent witticisms. These pious little men were so amusing in their earnestness. Finally, Miles Standish was given command of an expedition to settle the matter once and for all. The Lord of Misrule was about to meet Captain Shrimp. It was to be no contest.

By Morton's account he surrendered because to resist would have meant shedding blood. The Pilgrim version was somewhat different. The inhabitants of Mare Mount had every intention of resisting, but they were so drunk that they had a hard time lifting their weapons, let alone aiming them. So the only casualty was a Mare Mounter who lurched into a sword with his nose. Standish, for his part, would have liked to introduce them all to the Christian maypole, the whipping post.

The Plymouth colony sent their captive, Thomas Morton, back to England to be prosecuted for his high crimes and merry misdemeanors. They sent with him a colonist to assure that he was prosecuted to the full extent of the law. In England Morton, however, was now back in his element. He talked his way out of everything, and then took his verbal revenge on Captain Shrimp and all the rest.

Morton's *New English Canaan,* published in London in 1637, mocks the Pilgrims bitterly and skillfully as an assembly of sad-eyed hypocrites who continually thanked God that they were not like other men. For all his malice, Morton understood the politics of the Pilgrims and their vulnerability. Anyone who deviated from their precepts would find himself ostracized within the community. Against the contaminating touch of such a person everyone had to be put on guard. Soon the offender would find himself transformed by mere words into a spotted leper to be forced out of the colony lest he pollute the land and those that are clean.

Whatever the exaggeration, Morton had pointed to the heart of a virtue that sought to preserve itself by separation from the world, a community of Pilgrims who sought reformation without tarrying for any. Yet, as the example of Morton himself showed, the world was not going to permit such a separation. The process might take longer than it would have at Leiden, and much longer than at the Vanity Fair called Amsterdam, but the community of Saints would be surrounded and dissolved by a world from which it could never fully escape. Never was this clearer than when the very Dutch from whom they had separated themselves arrived in the New World. The Dutch had finally organized an expedition to occupy the long-coveted Manhattan and the Hudson River.

Some said that when the Pilgrims had accepted English backing for their colonial effort, the rejected Dutch suitors had bribed Captain Jones to plant them as far away from the Hudson as possible. Rumor in this case had no foundation in evidence, but did have a firm and deep foundation in the seventeenth-century reputation of the Dutch as unscrupulous commercial schemers. If something happened apparently by accident but to Dutch profit, the natural assumption of envious competitors was that someone somewhere somehow had been paid off in guilders. God Himself, it seemed at times, was on the Dutch take.

So Dutch colonists were finally planted on Manhattan and at the earliest convenient moment formally purchased the whole island from the Indians for a modest price, yet another exemplification of the famous seventeenth-century couplet:

> In matters of commerce the fault of the Dutch
> Is giving too little and asking too much.

The Dutch meant to control the whole Indian trade between Virginia and Plymouth. They established one trading post, Fort Orange, far up the Hudson to control the trade of the river. They meant to establish another outpost on the Delaware, the major river between the Hudson and Chesapeake Bay—and yet another on the Connecticut, the major river between the Hudson and Cape Cod. Unlike New France or Plymouth, where trade was to provide the basis for colonization, in the New Netherlands and its capital New Amsterdam colonization was to provide the means for the pursuit of trade.

At first the Dutch, eager to make up for lost time, moved too quickly. Fort Orange became involved in local Indian wars, lost some of its best men, and finally was almost overrun. As a result, the Connecticut River had to be abandoned to consolidate the Dutch position along the Hudson.

The Pilgrims were understandably distressed at the coming of the Dutch. They had been content with their plantation on the rocky ground of Plymouth rather than the more fertile land to the south because they could then keep their distance from the corrupt and self-seeking colonists of Virginia. Now, it seems, they had exchanged the Virginians for the far more efficient worldlings from Amsterdam.

With their own outpost on the Connecticut abandoned, the Dutch wanted the Pilgrims to serve as middlemen for trade with Indians farther north than the Dutch could now reach on their own. In 1627 an official of New Netherlands, Isaack de Rasieres, wrote to Bradford to broach this possibility. He used the occasion of a new alliance between the Netherlands and Great Britain to suggest economic cooperation in the New World as well. Bradford was amused and pleased, but also worried by de Rasieres' letter.

He was amused at the piling on of titles and praise for him and his fellow colonists. The Dutch never changed. Always buttering up when they wanted something. Perfectly harmless as long as you did not take it seriously and think that you could count on them when their self-interest was no longer involved.

Bradford was pleased at the offer of trade. New Amsterdam could be useful as an alternative market for Plymouth furs. The Dutch would drive a hard bargain, but the Pilgrims would no longer be at the mercy of English traders. Bradford could even piously hope that in their dealings the Dutch and the Pilgrims could give an example of neighborliness to a world much in need of it.

He could hope that, but he knew better, and hence his worry. Plymouth was a British colony as far as international politics was concerned. However remote the Pilgrims felt from the claims the British monarchy made on them, they were, as far as the world was concerned, British subjects. So they had to render to a different Caesar from the Dutch.

As a British subject, and as a governor who was worried about the eventual designs of the Dutch on the commerce of the whole region, Bradford had to point out to the officials of New Netherlands that according to the British view they had no right to be on Manhattan at all. The British crown claimed the whole of the North American coast from Virginia to Massachusetts. Bradford assured the Dutch that they did not have to worry about any trouble from Plymouth; nonetheless, particularly in light of the kindness his people had enjoyed in Leiden, Bradford felt he should warn them that trouble might come from other sources. He did not need to point out that Virginians would be far more jealous of British imperial rights than would mere Pilgrims who regarded themselves as true citizens of a kingdom not of this world.

Bradford's amusement and worry were, in the end, both dwarfed by the pleasurable prospect of Dutch trade. This would remove from the Pilgrims the risk of transport. Recently a ship that a number of colonists had taken back to England loaded with trade goods had been attacked by pirates; the goods were all lost, and—worse—the passengers were sold into slavery, never to be heard from again. The news of this reversal was almost too great for the colony to bear. Some even complained that God's hand lay too heavily on the colony. To this Job-like lament, Bradford could respond, as Paul had in Romans, that "God's judgements are unsearchable." He would also add that this event bore a lesson: "it shows us the uncertainty of all human things and what little cause there is of enjoying them or trusting to them." But now with the Dutch on the Hudson the Pilgrims could let others expose themselves to the full uncertainty of transatlantic commerce. Bradford, nonetheless, knowing the Dutch, asked for specific information about how much they would be giving for pelts and how much they would be marking up trade goods. He knew this had to be established with them before even considering trade.

The correspondence between Bradford and New Amsterdam continued for a year. The Dutch plied Bradford with flattery, sugar, and cheese. Plymouth traded with them when it could, and apologized when it had nothing to offer. Bradford continued to warn them that Virginia was likely "to make a prize of you, if they can." But the Dutch firmly insisted on their own rights to this region they had spent so much money exploring.

To solidify their friendship with Bradford, they were eager to have him visit. He respectfully declined; he had not left the old Netherlands to be tainted by direct contact with the new. So the Dutch finally sent an official emissary to him.

Once again, they did their best to impress the unimpressible Bradford. They had their emissary accompanied by a suitable retinue, including some trumpeters to blast fanfare at his approach. The trumpets were less significant than another item they brought with them: wampum. These strings of shells served as the gold or money of Indian trade along the east coast. The Dutch, who seemed to find money of any kind by a sixth sense, had stumbled on a major source of these shells on Long Island. They had transformed this site into the North American equivalent of a mint. De Rasieres brought with him full fifty fathoms of wampum.

Eyeing covetously a recent Pilgrim crop of tobacco, he assured the Pilgrims that trading wampum with the Indians would increase Pilgrim profits many times over. The Pilgrims, knowing the Dutch as they did, could not help but think that they were somehow being set up for a swindle. How would they live with themselves if these clam shells turned out at some future date to be as worthless as tulip bulbs? Fear the Dutch, especially when bearing goods.

Still, the wampum was too inviting an investment opportunity to pass up. They bought the wampum with their tobacco, and seem to have been somewhat surprised when all the Dutch had promised turned out to be true. With wampum, trade became both easier and far more profitable. The Pilgrims and the Dutch could see eye to eye at least on the Indian trade. For years the

Pilgrims' colony would supply the Dutch with their nicotine, until New Netherlands had a large enough smoking population for Virginians to take notice.

That was not to say they agreed on other things, especially on how Europeans ought to comport themselves in this new world. Thomas Morton and his ilk would have found New Amsterdam a far more hospitable environment than New Plymouth. This was suggested by the account of de Rasieres of his visit to New Plymouth. He begins not with a description of New Plymouth but of the Dutch colony and its environs.

He seems particularly interested in the Indians of New Netherlands, especially Indian women, especially their loose sexual habits. These women are "fine looking, of middle stature, well proportioned, and with finely cut features." (Alas, they do smell bad.) Usually a gift of a salmon is sufficient to make them "lascivious." They are "very libidinous" and "very unfaithful." Turning to Plymouth, de Rasieres recounts his shock on learning that the Pilgrims have "stringent laws and ordinances upon the subject of fornication and adultery." The laws do not in themselves surprise him so much, since the Dutch had similar laws. But the Pilgrims enforce theirs "very strictly." More surprising still was that the Pilgrims interpreted these laws as applying to Indian women.

How de Rasieres gained this knowledge of the Pilgrim penal system can only be imagined. Perhaps after trading his wampum, and after the pleasures of a hearty dinner, de Rasieres began to make discreet inquiries of his distinguished host. What are the laws? Yes, but surely they cannot be strictly enforced. Yes, but not for relations with Indian women.

All that is known for certain is that at some time during his visit de Rasieres was upbraided by Bradford for the lewdness of the Dutch at New Netherlands. "They speak very angrily when they hear from the savages that we live so barbarously in these respects, and without punishment." If de Rasieres shrugged that a man must take his pleasures (like his profits) where he can, Bradford could only have sighed that the Dutch in the New World were no different from the Dutch of the Old.

The Pilgrims were the ones changing in the New World. Their colony was becoming just one among a number seeking their share of the Indian trade, jostling with one another for their full place in the sun. They tried to establish a trading post in Maine, only to be run off by the French. They were soon to be clashing with the Dutch along the Connecticut for the best trading locations. Greed was making its inroads among the Pilgrim leadership. One of Bradford's most trusted assistants almost bankrupted the whole colony by misappropriating public funds for his own use and then losing them through bad investments. Other scandals occurred with depressing regularity. A papist was even discovered living in the colony, living with his pretty young niece who was not his niece. Attempts to enforce public morality became more difficult as more Strangers settled among the Saints. The Saints themselves, profiting mightily by selling supplies to the newcomers, were frequently inclined to wink at the moral dangers these Strangers presented. By the late 1630s these old families had begun to disperse to found other villages where they could more profitably pursue their farming, and also increase their holdings inland. The Church of Plymouth itself then began to separate into fragments and the old sense of community—that foretaste of heaven—was diluted, if not lost.

All this was reflected in Bradford's annual history, which became more and more episodic as the hand of Divine Providence became harder for him to see. This was the last and most difficult trial of Bradford's long journey. He and his people had somehow wandered back into the land from which they thought they had escaped. The one-eyed monster of self-love had devoured them as a separate people, special to God. They had lost the guiding hand of their Father, the care of all their cares, the solace of all their pain.

Without the feeling of the eternal breath within, Bradford's own life was becoming like a dreary tenantless mansion haunted by vain regrets and pallid sorrowful faces. He tried to console himself: It was the will of God and His mercy endureth forever. But it was no good. The cistern had cracked, the golden bowl had broken.

We can imagine the elderly Governor Bradford, grown grim and gray in the harness, walking the bluffs above Plymouth, aided by a gnarled stick and chilled by the east wind, occasionally stopping to stare out onto the familiar harbor below, himself as full of grief as of age and wretched in both, his chief companion the calm despair that yields to no second spring of hope.

The Pilgrim spirit had fled, hard as it was to believe. The same waves rolled in the bay as when the *Mayflower* first moored here. The same mists still brooded on the tide, and the same rocks yet kept their watch nearby. But the Pilgrim spirit had fled. The morning's flame looked no different on the hillside, nor the moon's cold light on the surf. But the Pilgrim spirit had fled. Like the wing of an angel that breaks a cloud and is as quickly withdrawn. Like a sunbeam that dances on a wave, and then disappears as it crashes. Hard as it was to believe, the Pilgrim spirit had fled.

When he gave up seeking some ill-recognized vestige of that earlier light, Bradford found he could no longer write in his history, nor did he wish to see it published or read. The abandoned manuscript would only be discovered and published in the nineteenth century. So he made an end of it with a blank page instead of a conclusion. He was an old man with nothing left to say and no one left to listen. The darkness and horror that were now descending upon him would have to be faced alone, with even his remembrance of those sweet refreshments he had enjoyed on his pilgrimage fading from his mind. This was a night without a morning to wait for, at least in this life. So he made an end to his story, ceased, and was silent.

Chapter IV

GODLY COVENANT

WILLIAM BRADFORD'S CONSUMING SENSE of failure would not have surprised the man who led the next major colonizing effort, John Winthrop. The cruel anguish that Bradford suffered was sadly predictable to any Puritan with a shrewdness to match his piety. And John Winthrop, most assuredly, had a shrewdness to match his piety.

Winthrop was of those Puritans who had tried to steer a middle course between the separatism of the Pilgrims and the Anglo-Catholicism of the Established Church. He knew that a pilgrimage of separation was not the true course of reformation, even if it were possible. And any man with the slightest common sense could tell you it was not possible. Attempt to separate yourself from the world, and the world will only overtake you unawares—as it had the Pilgrims, to Bradford's grief. One either rules the iniquity of this world or is ruled by it.

The world will not leave the people of God in peace; so the world must be confronted, and made to conform to God's will for it. For an Englishman that meant the Church of England must be reformed and British society reordered.

As Calvin had made plain, the saint should expect a hard, toilsome, and unquiet life, crammed with numerous and various challenges. In this life we are to seek and hope for nothing but struggle. The ideal of an earthly tranquility is a diabolical snare, a cunning stratagem to gain our acquiescence to our fallen state. So it is the weak who are concerned to find a quiet life. Those who are most like God are those who strive to be of profit to all, even at the cost of their own deep hurt.

This was powerful Wisdom that the Bible so lovingly described, not the false wisdom of monks retiring into silent contemplation. Biblical Wisdom was more active than all active things; it could reach and touch everywhere, for it was an exhalation of the power of God, a pure emanation of the glory of the Almighty, an unspoiled mirror of the Divine Majesty. It was also a Wisdom for the chosen few.

John Winthrop had no illusions about the common run of mankind. They were hopelessly corrupt and predestined to eternal damnation. There is nothing consistent about our cursed nature except its inclination to villainy. It was understandable that the redeemed should want to separate themselves from the commonality, understandable but mistaken. The virtuous had an obligation to control the rest, for the glory of God and their own security.

This was clear if one had a proper understanding of God's covenant with His people, who are the salt that gives the whole earth its savor. God, unknowable and unfathomable in Himself, had condescended to enter into a contract with His People. We can comprehend God no more than a cockleshell can encompass the ocean; His Glory is like the luster of the sun, so great that we can behold it only indirectly, in reflections suitable to our limited understandings. One such reflection that we *can* comprehend is the covenant between God and His people that is revealed in the Bible. This we can understand, and hence have no excuse for not fulfilling.

Our part in the covenant has both an individual and a social dimension. We must, of course, order our individual lives according to His Will. We must also, however, order the lives of those who are around us, as the father orders the life of his family. We must make the common run of men, however unwilling, conform to God's law in their actions; we must do so knowing full well that they will never receive His grace into their souls. We must, nonetheless, make the word of God bear on every aspect of every human life.

But why should we care how the unregenerate act? Because if we fail His punishment will be visited upon us all. The Bible shows that whole societies are punished for tolerating the wickedness of some: *All* the firstborn of Egypt were killed for the enslavement of the Hebrews, and all the mighty army that chased them into the wilderness was swept away in the Red Sea. Therefore, to try to separate oneself from a wicked society is only a self-deluding form of worldly toleration. For such deluded toleration God permits a special punishment. He will allow you to be surrounded, subverted, and overwhelmed by the very world you sought to deny without controlling. You will be left, as Bradford had been, wondering where it had all gone wrong. Bradford, dear brother Bradford, it had gone wrong from the very beginning.

In such terms John Winthrop and other reforming Puritans would have understood the inevitable failure of the separating Puritanism of the Pilgrims.

Winthrop's reformation, far from refusing to tarry for any, was obliged to shepherd as many as possible along. Shepherd them in good order toward what would be for most damnation at the Last Judgment, and that second death that Scripture tells us will be so far worse than the first, the eternal slaughterhouse of hell.

Winthrop's was a Christianity of the narrow gate, a cheerless view of the divine economy that was more a witness to human depravity than a hymn to life. Yet it suffused the life of Winthrop with the irresistible vigor of unquestioned self-assurance. It would never occur to Winthrop that he was not born to be a leader of any social group of which he found himself a member.

Nonetheless, at about the same time the Pilgrims were being wooed with fathoms of Dutch wampum, Winthrop and an influential group of fellow Puritans were reluctantly considering a belated separation from England. They insisted that such a decision to establish a colony of their own in Massachusetts would not represent an abandonment of their earlier commitment to the complete reformation of Britain. They still aimed for that end, but circumstances prevented their reaching it by the most direct route. Winds were roaring directly across their destined course; they must trim their sails and seek a safe haven until the storm had passed.

The storm had to be severe indeed for John Winthrop to consider leaving England. He, unlike the obscure Pilgrims, had too much materially at stake in Old England. His estate had been in his family since Henry VIII had distributed it as part of the booty from dissolving the monasteries. Winthrop, like his father and grandfather before him, had become a prominent leader in county Suffolk. From such a base in normal times he could reasonably have aspired to political influence. In fact, he had so aspired.

He had first been justice of the peace for his county. From there he had gained a lucrative London position within the king's legal bureaucracy. In London he followed the parliament closely, preparing himself for the day when he, as a staunch member of the country party, would be one of those whose sleeves were plucked in the corridors of Westminster. There was much to do in his England, and Winthrop felt himself called by God to do much.

But Charles succeeded James to the throne, and suddenly England had a monarch far less tolerant of opposition to his centralized authority than James had been. Moreover, Winthrop's own prospects dissolved like the mist, giving him ample occasion to reflect on the insubstantiality of worldly things. He lost his government position—and had no means of getting another one, for Charles dissolved the parliament and vowed to rule without it in the future.

All this had happened at the worst possible time for Winthrop personally.

His county was in economic decline, and income from his property falling. Moreover, as he approached forty, he had three sons entering their maturity who had to be launched into the world. Without influence any longer in government, he had to establish them out of his own substance. He watched his land holdings shrink to less than half of what they once had been. He could see the day coming soon when he would be able to support only seven or perhaps at most eight servants in his household, and would lack the wealth even to be a suitable candidate for justice of the peace.

He could have reconciled himself to his own decline as God's punishment for his innumerable sins. He had only recently given up hunting as frivolous and unprofitable, and still he struggled with his addiction to tobacco. He could reconcile himself to being thwarted in his worldly ambitions, did this not seem part of a general pattern.

The countryside to which he returned was being corrupted by the values of the city and court, or so it seemed to him. Competition was replacing the traditional cooperation that had made the life of the countryside harmonious and tranquil for rich and poor alike. Human life was no longer valued as an end in itself, something to be cherished as the bearer of God's image in this world. The poor were treated as lamentable burdens on the land; friends, family, even one's own children were viewed with suspicion, as drains upon the individual. Once the community had been regarded as an extended family; now the family was regarded as just another field, a particularly small one, where individuals vied with one another for personal advantage. He had not returned to the countryside to preside over the funeral games for his father's and grandfather's way of life. Yet that was the most the countryside seemed to offer him.

Besides, he could not expect to be left in peace to worship as he saw fit. Charles's centralizing of power was touching all. He disbanded Parliament when it tried to check his power. He was replacing the voluntary local militia with a professional standing army, the better to pursue his follies abroad. And he undertook to eliminate what had been the growing autonomy of local churches.

Charles's chief instrument in this last outrage was Archbishop Laud, who would soon be installed at Canterbury as the head of the whole English Church. As near as Winthrop could tell, Laud was nothing more than an Arminian with a weakness for the ceremonial trappings of popery. Yet Laud, with Charles's approval, was energetically transforming the English hierarchy with men of like mind. Soon a bitter joke was making the rounds: "What does Arminianism hold? Every good living in England."

What Arminianism held theologically was to Winthrop sheer blasphemy. It proudly exalted human freedom, and vainly demoted God from Lord of History to its mere Conscience. History became a chaos produced by the collisions of our individual freedom, and God Himself a weak spectator exhorting the good.

Yet Winthrop knew better. He knew that this freedom, this chaos is only the surface of history, and that in the depths God's Providence controls all. The races on which men spend themselves in their pride are predestined at His pleasure. We win and lose not out of our own merit, but out of God's choice.

So Winthrop had to ask himself hard questions. Why did God let his estate decline? Why was God permitting the virtuous country life to pass away? Why was He letting Laud have power over the Church of England? And there was a harder question: Why was He letting the Reformation be defeated on all fronts?

That the Reformation was being defeated on all fronts, and not just in England, could no longer be denied. Cardinal Richelieu had recently destroyed the Protestant stronghold at La Rochelle, and now the Protestants of France were at his mercy and Huguenot refugees streamed into England. In Germany Protestant forces had suffered similar defeats; the religious war that was beginning there seemed to favor the Catholics. The Netherlands had been ruined by prosperity, and now was Amsterdamnifying the rest of the world with its avarice and attendant Arminianism.

What was God's intention in all this? The more Winthrop thought about it, the more convinced he became that these lamentable events were but the first signs of a general wrath to come. God was obviously preparing massive punishments, perhaps on an apocalyptic scale, because of Christendom's continued toleration of popery, freethinking, and licentiousness. These first signs were to serve as a warning that only God's people could understand. God's people were to seek for themselves a shelter and a hiding place until the awful storm of His wrath had passed.

A group of Puritan leaders who had reached similar conclusions were already planning a new colony for Massachusetts Bay. They approached the respected Winthrop to join them. After some hesitation, he yielded to their logic and importuning. He then committed himself fully by selling all his lands. A Puritan colony, he was convinced, could serve as a bulwark against the rising tide of superstition and disbelief. In later times it could also serve as a model for the restructuring of England and of Europe itself into a true

Christian commonwealth. Winthrop felt within himself an irresistible rousing of the spirit that disposed him to the extraordinary course of emigration.

But pure motives, as Winthrop well knew, did not free him from the necessity for shrewd calculation. In certain respects the devil had to be beaten at
his own game. The rules of that game of power Winthrop had learned in government without ever having read the devil's disciple, Niccolò Machiavelli.

Winthrop knew perfectly well that the organizers of the colony, however
pure their religious professions, would have mixed motives in their support.
London merchants of Puritan sympathies were still London merchants, forever on the prowl for a profit. They could not be permitted to exercise undue
influence on the course of the colony, as investors in Plymouth had tried to
exercise over the Pilgrims. And God showed Winthrop how to prevent it.

The colonists first needed a charter from the king for the company that
would control the colony. Everything they did was to be of irreproachable
legality. But that meant getting the king's signature without their enterprise
being scrutinized too closely, for this was to be a Puritan colony. If Charles
understood what their colony represented, he almost certainly would not sign
the company charter.

The matter was so delicate that we do not even know the name of the official who managed to slip it past the king. He must have been someone whose
loyalty to the king was unquestionable to all but those who knew him most
well. And the charter he did get signed had within it a bonanza, a subtle but
probably calculated omission. Nowhere was it specified where the meetings of
the company officers would be held. With London investors prominent
among the supporters of the colony, London, of course, would be the expected site.

However, Winthrop and a few others seized on this with an instructive
rapidity. They wanted the company directors to meet only in Massachusetts.
In other words, investors who did not share in the hardships of colonization
would have no say in how the company and its colony were run. There must
have been considerable resistance to this unexpected proposal, because
Winthrop and his supporters made its passage a condition of their own continued commitment to go on the expedition. The choice for the merchants
was between giving Winthrop his way or having the whole enterprise dissolve
before their eyes. Of course, Winthrop won the test of strength, the very kind
of test that Pilgrims would always lose. (Compared to Winthrop, Bradford
seems like some untutored youth, with his mother's milk scarce out of him,
still unlearned in the world's false subtleties.) Investors, or for that matter
king's ministers, who wanted to interfere with the internal affairs of the

Massachusetts Bay Colony would have to cross the Atlantic to do so. And when the directors held their first (and last) meeting in London, they quickly elected as governor of their colony John Winthrop.

The colonial leaders were careful to blow a little more smoke in the direction of the government before they left. Since the expedition was clearly a repudiation of the Church of England under Laud, its leaders issued an open letter from the very decks of their departing ships to proclaim their continued loyalty and affection for the Church of England, their Mother. Such hope as they had for eternal salvation they had received from Her bosom and nursed from Her breasts. They would continue to have Her foremost in their prayers. They would pray too that they would never be mistaken for those misguided visionaries who repudiate established institutions because they think they can achieve perfection in this world. With such well-oiled phrases the Puritans bid a fond adieu to an institution they thought was continuing to prostitute itself before images and kings.

Of course, there was a sense in which these phrases were true. Governor Winthrop and the other Puritan leaders did not intend to separate themselves from ordinary human society as the Pilgrims had. For the Pilgrims, the mixture of Strangers with the Saints was an imperfection in their colonizing; the Saints would have come by themselves and excluded all others if they could have. Winthrop wanted no such premature separation of the sheep from the goats. Until the end of time there would always be a mixture of the saved and the damned. And the saved would usually be in a clear minority, as they were on this colonizing expedition. The challenge of God's covenant was for this minority to control the majority according to His law. This was no longer possible in the England of Charles and Laud. Court and city had so perverted the natural order that the worst elements in society now lorded it over all the rest. In the New World the proper order could be reestablished.

During the passage to the New World, John Winthrop delivered a carefully considered lay sermon that would eventually be published in England as a manifesto for the whole enterprise. "A Model of Christian Charity," as it was called, begins resolutely: "God Almighty in His most holy and wise Providence has so disposed the condition of mankind, as in all times some must be rich, some poor, some high and eminent in power and dignity, others mean and in subjection."

To question this natural hierarchy within society was to doubt God's ruling providence, to become little better than an Arminian. God has produced and ordered a diversity within mankind, much as He had produced a diversity and ordered it within the animal kingdom. All men are obliged to preserve and strengthen the providentially ordained hierarchy among men. Therefore the high and mighty must use their power and dignity to moderate and restrain the wicked.

The rich must be satisfied with the wealth they have, and use it to benefit the poor and not to oppress them. The poor and lowly, for their part, must never rise up against their superiors and try to shake off the yoke that God in His wisdom has placed upon them. Society as a whole must restrain, even punish, those who envy and resent those whom God has raised by His favor—and must also rein in wandering thoughts and overreaching curiosity, which can only sow suspicion and increase woe. In the properly ordered society every man has need of the other, and is conscious of this need. This dependence is the ground for loving thy neighbor as thyself. As God loves His creatures as an image of Himself, as the mother loves the child as an image of herself, so the citizen sees a reflection of himself in his neighbor, and loves him for it. Such a love, based upon mutual dependence, provides the sinews and ligaments that hold together the hierarchical body of society.

Such a society, Winthrop wanted his fellow colonists to understand, they were about to found in Massachusetts. Their leaders had sealed a covenant with God on its behalf. In this society we are not to succumb to carnal temptation, or to seek great things for ourselves as individuals. Rather we must follow the counsels of the prophets:

"We must be knit together in this work as one man; we must entertain each other in brotherly affection; we must be willing to abridge ourselves of our superfluities; for the supply of other necessities, we must uphold a familiar commerce together in all meekness, gentleness, patience and liberality; we must delight in each other, make others' conditions our own, rejoice together, mourn together, labor and suffer together."

If we do all this, we will always have the unity of the spirit, the bond of peace. Ten of us will be able to resist a thousand of the enemy. And New England will be as a city upon a hill, the eyes of all people upon us.

The Puritan expedition that arrived in Massachusetts in June 1630 surpassed all its predecessors in North America both in its size and in the care with which it was planned. Before, squadrons had carried settlers to the New World; now a whole fleet was required for the thousand well-equipped colonists. The advance party that had established itself the year before at a place they called Salem was larger than the whole of many earlier efforts. The Puritan colony in Massachusetts from the very beginning dwarfed the much older colonies of Quebec and Plymouth. And while the colony of Virginia seemed to reflect or even exaggerate the social disorder of seventeenth-century England, Massachusetts from the start appeared to transcend it. The Puritans made the earlier colonists look like amateurs.

In charge of it all was Winthrop. And he led as much by example as by law. So he not only commanded the servants and others of the laboring class to begin immediately to build permanent settlements around the bay, he also labored from dawn to dusk himself, much as the lord of the manor might work in bringing in the harvest to inspire his peasants. Seeing the governor at work with his own hands, who could remain idle in good conscience? Soon after arrival, despite the natural lethargy that might set in after a long voyage, there was not an idle person in the colony. Massachusetts was a model of Christian charity and mutual dependence. Or so it was reported back to England.

Winthrop had other matters to look after, beyond the building of the settlements. They had brought ample provisions, but he was taking no chances. As soon as possible, he sent his best ship back to England for further supplies. Another he sent down the coast to trade with Indians for corn.

There was hardship that first winter. Winthrop had many another occasion to exhort the settlers to recollect the precepts of resignation and endurance that piety had taught them long before there was a need. An estimated two hundred of the thousand died, a small number given the experience of other colonies. There was hunger but no starvation, illness but no general sickness. Some of the losses were saddening. Winthrop lost a son in a drowning accident. He also lost eleven of his servants, a serious blow in a colony where manpower would be a valuable commodity. Moreover, Lady Arbella, after whom his ship had been named, died that first winter, soon to be followed by her husband. This loss in a way was significant. Massachusetts was to supposed to replicate the social patterns of rural England; however, in this peculiar county there would be almost no nobility, and so gentry such as Winthrop would become the peers of this realm.

Winthrop assumed his role eagerly. He gained for himself six hundred acres of good land. His surviving servants began the next spring to plant the land and to build him a manor house of stone. There were also many details for Winthrop to attend to as governor: His colony was not going to be at the mercy of others for trade. Instead of the gold refiners and jewelers that had burdened the original Virginia settlement, Winthrop had brought shipwrights, including one reputed to be the best in all of England. They immediately set about their craft. By the first July they had built a thirty-ton vessel; by the next year a sixty tonner. The Massachusetts Bay Colony had become already a significant presence in the fur trade.

With hundreds of colonists spreading around the bay to establish small towns, Winthrop had to decide on a seat of government. He had first decided on a peninsula they called Charlestown, where he also intended to live. However, the water supply soon proved unreliable, so Winthrop had the frame of his town house taken down and moved to another peninsula jutting into the bay. They named this peninsula and its settlement after a prominent coastal village of Lincolnshire: Boston.

He meant for his colony to prosper, but he and the other leaders did not intend for economic motives to dominate colonial transactions, as they so often did in London. Skilled labor was at a premium in the early days of the colony, as were supplies from England. The governor and his assistants set wages and profits, lest artisans or merchants succumb to temptation and undermine the spirit of charity that should be the sinews of a Christian society covenanted to God. Winthrop could take pride in the energetic leadership that he and his assistants provided in the early days of the colony. However, he could see clearly the Hand of God contributing to the success of the colony more than anything he did.

The land was well suited for the colonists to reproduce their virtuous country life. The climate, although somewhat more severe, was suited to the same crops that they had cultivated in England. And unlike the Pilgrims, who had been city dwellers for more than a decade, the Puritans were well acquainted with the land and needed to add only corn cultivation to their agrarian skills. They did not need to experiment with exotic crops like tobacco that were better suited to plantations, nor did they have to become as dependent on the fur trade as had Quebec. Just good English farms were all Massachusetts needed for ample prosperity, and English towns.

The earlier destruction of the Indian population by disease had made the Pilgrim colony possible. Given the large numbers of Puritans arriving at Massachusetts, the Indians presented no problem at all for Winthrop. For self-defense the Puritans needed no specialists like Miles Standish. The few they had were continually frustrated by local militia, which selected their own commanders, the very military structure that Charles had endeavored to suppress in the name of efficiency. New England was all that Old England once had been, and should one day become again. Or so its proud advocates thought.

Winthrop's most delicate task was to assure that New England did not go the way the Old had. This meant that a stable government had to be developed out of the company charter they had carried with them. In this charter the king had granted Winthrop and the few other company members who were colonists "to make, ordain, and establish all manner of wholesome and reasonable orders, laws, statutes, and ordinances, directions, and instructions, not contrary to the laws of this our realm of England, as well for settling of the forms and ceremonies of government and magistracy fit and necessary for the said plantation, and the inhabitants there, and for naming and styling of all sorts of officers, both superior and inferior, which they shall find needful for that government and plantation, and the distinguishing and setting forth of the several duties, powers, and limits of every such office and place." It was the kind of power John Smith would have killed for.

Nonetheless, Winthrop had not been in Massachusetts long before he had agreed to relinquish some of the power that the charter concentrated in the hands of the company. The members of the company were called "freemen" in the charter. These men were to meet four times a year as "the General Court." The court would in future elect the governor, his deputy, and assistants once a year and have all legislative responsibilities for the colony. According to a strict interpretation of the charter, all the power of the colony would be concentrated in the company members who were present in Massachusetts, a number that would vary from ten to twenty.

Such an exclusive government by the few violated Winthrop's sense of natural hierarchies. An orderly hierarchy requires a sequence of steps. In the great chain of nature, plants were higher than rocks, animals than plants, and men than animals. So it was with social orders—the wife submits to the husband, the children to her, and the younger children to the elder. King Charles's mistake had been to try to concentrate all power on himself, and thereby to eliminate the middle ranks between his court and the country as a whole.

A colony of a thousand or more that was ruled only by a governor, his deputy, and a few assistants could scarcely be stable without further discriminations among the people. So Winthrop and his assistants extended the definition of "freeman" in the company charter to include all adult males who were not servants. So over one hundred freemen, almost all Puritans, met for the first General Court.

Yet this was not intended to be a democracy. Democracy for Winthrop was the worst form of government. Democracy was government by the mean and poor, which would soon degenerate into an aristocracy of orators, an oligarchy of demagogues. Winthrop wanted an aristocracy in the strict sense, a rule by the best who had the interests of the whole at heart.

In light of this, an adjustment was made in the liberal definition of "freeman." Future male colonists would be accepted as freemen only after they had been accepted for membership in a Puritan congregation. This would assure that the godly would never be swamped by the ungodly. Unbelievers were welcome to the Puritan colony so long as they conducted their lives according to the Puritan precepts; however, even if they did, they could not expect to participate in the governance of the colony until they could convince a Puritan congregation that they were regenerate—that is, that their moral life was not just expedience or social conformity but sprang from a genuine conversion experience.

There was a further constraint that Winthrop and the assistants placed on the freemen. The charter had been explicit that the General Court of freemen had the power of legislation in the colony. This was going too far in the direction of democracy for Winthrop and his assistants. They would yield to the freemen the power to select the assistants, but that was all. The assistants would select the governor and his deputy from their own number, and they all together would then legislate. In this way a delicate balance could be preserved; the freemen could participate in government without being permitted a degree of power that was clearly beyond their capacity to exercise responsibly.

In Winthrop's eyes, neither the selection of the assistants nor that of the governor and his deputy was an election in the strict sense. Within a human community covenanted to God, an important matter such as the selection of a governor is not made by men, whatever the appearances. Anyone who thought the assistants chose the governor was falling into the heresy of Arminianism. God chose the governor; the assistants simply had the opportunity to confirm His choice by discovering it within their own hearts. As for Winthrop, within his own heart, he had heard God's call to be governor, and to God alone he felt he had to answer for his exercise of power.

For a few years the improvised system worked smoothly. Each year the General Court of freemen would meet; each year they would select the same assistants; each year these assistants would select the same governor and deputy. And each year Winthrop would rule as he thought God wanted: But he would try to get his way through persuasions and discretion. He demonstrated his skills in a variety of minor incidents.

A minister in the warm gush of a new idea suggested that since the Puritans had kept in communion with the Church of England (corrupt as it was) they might as well also stay in communion with the Roman Catholic Church (corrupt as it was). His congregation was persuaded by his arguments, and the rest of the colony was appalled. Winthrop rode off to Watertown to persuade them of their error.

A man was sentenced to banishment from the colony; after the judgment was delivered, the winter turned bad. To banish him now would be a death sentence, certainly not what the court had intended. Winthrop, on his own authority, permitted the man to winter in the colony.

Watertown now was short of food, and the independent Plymouth colony short of powder and shot. Winthrop permitted Watertown to fish with a weir out of season; he sent shot to Plymouth. A dispute erupted in the Boston church: Does the New Testament require women to wear veils in church? The congregation was divided. The governor intervened to suggest there were more important matters to argue about. So the matter was postponed.

John Endicott, who had led the advance party in 1629 to establish Salem, suddenly developed scruples about the red cross on the colonial flag. It was a symbol of paganism, prelacy, and persecution; he wanted it cut out of every flag flying in Massachusetts. Many found his argument persuasive, including perhaps a few who were earlier eager to share communion with Catholics. Winthrop had to persuade them otherwise, being careful not to mention the main reason—such symbolic acts of defiance would be likely to bring upon Massachusetts the scrutiny of the central government, the last thing the colony needed. (He never did persuade Endicott, in whose mind the red cross was fixed, like the nail in Sisera's brain.)

Thomas Dudley, his deputy governor, remained angry that Winthrop decided to move the capital of Massachusetts to Boston. Dudley had already built himself a fine house in Charlestown, the original choice, and now his neighbors were deserting him for Boston. Winthrop convinced a newly arrived group of colonists to repeople Dudley's town. Dudley appeared mollified—but in fact the knot of anger remained tight within him. Winthrop now had a determined enemy.

The harbor needed fortifications against a possible French or Dutch raid. When the assistants neglected to act, Winthrop funded them out of his own pocket. Then when they did vote to fortify one of the towns, another town resented the preference and refused to contribute its share. Winthrop had to convince them that the decision of the assistants had a binding force. Nonetheless, he saw their point. The assistants were chosen from the colony as a whole, and hence individual towns could feel they were not represented. Within a year Winthrop had sponsored a law that provided that representatives from each town must be consulted on matters of taxation.

Some of his loyal assistants were furious that the power and dignity of their office was being eroded by such concessions to the ordinary people. One resigned his assistantship in disgust, but Winthrop refused to accept the resignation. And he persuaded his other assistants to accept this concession to local interests.

The first four years of Winthrop's administration contained an extraordinary string of victories, a political decathlon in which he met every challenge. He seemed to know when to insist, when to persuade, and when to plead; also when to engage in honest sleight of hand. He defused the theological disputes that could divide so opinionated a collection of colonists as his. He worked toward material independence from England while avoiding any provocation. He balanced the needs of the colony as a whole against those of local towns, and the needs of his elite against those of the common people, always seeking compromise between genuine interests, even if that meant a change in the structure of government itself. Most of what he achieved was by example and persuasion.

The prosperity of the colony was undeniable. Large as the colony was at its founding, within a few years its population had tripled. Towns founded at what seemed ample distances from each other were now pressing against one another. The original colonists were becoming wealthy just from providing the newer ones with livestock and other supplies. Farms had already made Massachusetts virtually self-sufficient with food. Boston had already developed its own small merchant class, who lived by trade without working the land.

No one could deny Winthrop's decisive role in this success, but criticism of him was growing. Chief among his critics was his deputy governor, Thomas Dudley. Dudley was older than Winthrop, and had been more experienced in administrative matters, so he may well have resented the choice of Winthrop over him as governor. If not, he certainly had ample cause to resent him anyway. Winthrop had not only moved the capital away from Dudley, but also publicly criticized him for building a house too ostentatious for a beginning colony. The rich were not to lord it over the poor; they were to serve the commonwealth in a spirit of charity. Dudley was unimpressed with Winthrop's criticism. Even as a manager of an estate in England, the older man had been known for striking hard bargains. Now in Massachusetts he had corn when many were in dire need of seed; he had made an extremely profitable contract with several poor farmers—the first perhaps of many—only to find himself being charged with usury by the governor. The poor farmers got their corn at a reasonable rate, but Dudley became an open enemy.

He first sought support among the assistants. He charged Winthrop with overstepping his authority, and listed eight occasions on which he had countermanded explicit decisions of assistants, or at least had taken upon himself decisions that were rightfully theirs. Winthrop defended himself heatedly and effectively against the charges. He did concede that he had on occasion been too lenient in dealing with individual cases, but the hardships of founding a colony dictated leniency. A strict and unyielding enforcement of God's law was suitable only for a settled society.

Winthrop survived the carefully orchestrated attack, but Dudley was making some progress with the assistants who were jealous of their prerogatives and inflexible in their religious zeal. Then Winthrop outmaneuvered Dudley, as perhaps he had been doing since they were both candidates for the governorship. He learned that the freemen were going to propose that the General Court allow them to elect the governor and deputy governor directly. Before they could do so, Winthrop himself persuaded the assistants to agree to this diminution of their power. Winthrop's calmness carried the day against Dudley's outrage.

To get Winthrop removed, Dudley now had to appeal to the democratic sentiments of the freemen, rather than to the oligarchic sentiments of the assistants. So Dudley began to raise questions about the company charter. What exactly did the company charter specify concerning the relative powers of the governor, assistants, and freemen? For Dudley this was a move of unusual subtlety.

While preparing for the General Court of 1634, a committee of freemen asked Governor Winthrop to see the charter, a request he could scarcely deny. Then they discovered what Winthrop and Dudley knew they would: the charter specified the freemen, and not the assistants, would have the chief legislative responsibility for the colony. They demanded an explanation from the governor. He explained as best he could. The definition of freeman had been so expanded that the legislative powers were judged to be better placed with the assistants.

The freemen seem to have accepted Winthrop's explanation, more or less. The prudence of the original decision could not be disputed given the extraordinary success of the colony. No one could question that Winthrop had acted in the best interests of the colony as he saw them. Nonetheless, the freemen could not be expected to forgo the power that the charter granted them. And a governor who deceived the freemen should not expect to go unchastened. So the General Court of 1634 elected Thomas Dudley as governor; John Winthrop could continue to offer his advice to the colony as an assistant to Governor Dudley.

If Dudley wanted to gloat over his victory, the demeanor of the defeated Winthrop gave him no cause. He accepted his demotion without protest or complaint or the least sign of resentment. Others might have thought that he had lost an election, but he did not. He was no Arminian. This decision had not been made by men, despite all of Thomas Dudley's machinations. It had been made by God. He also knew that patience was the truest fortitude, and freed one from the apparent tyranny of happenstance. God had provided him with an opportunity to reflect on the fickle state of human affairs, on our ever-failing trust in mortal strength. What in man is not deceivable and vain?

Winthrop still felt strongly his vocation to be a leader of God's people and to administer His covenant with them. However, God did not want him to lead now: he would wait quietly until He did. It would be three years before Winthrop was returned to power. During that time the colony would be tested by a series of crises during which his discretion and leniency were much missed.

The first of these was the selection by the Salem congregation of its new minister. Roger Williams was already well known to Winthrop. When he had arrived in Massachusetts, the young minister so impressed Winthrop and other members of his congregation in Boston that they asked him to join as an assistant to their minister. He refused on principle, because they as a congregation had kept in communion with the Church of England. Williams was a strict separatist; he was a strict everything he was.

This, in itself, was no great problem. Each congregation in Massachusetts was autonomous. Some, like that of Salem, inclined more to extremes than did Boston's. Each was allowed to pursue its own course of conscience so long as it was done in a way that did not harm the well-being of the colony as a whole. One could be a separatist, as long as one was a quiet separatist. Noisy separatists would attract unwanted attention from Archbishop Laud and his minions in England.

Williams, alas, was the farthest that could be imagined from being quiet, about his separatism or anything else that might stir the pot. Salem had been quietly separatist until Williams joined the congregation as an assistant minister to stir them up, with the strong support of old John Endicott of the red cross and the iron frown.

Winthrop had managed to parry the initial trouble from Salem when Endicott, with Williams's eloquent support, had declared against the papist cross in any flag. Winthrop must have thought that Williams had found his true place when he left Massachusetts for Plymouth. However, Williams soon returned because he found the Pilgrims not pure enough for him.

He returned to Massachusetts while Winthrop was still governor. And with sweetness and sanctity and a consummate lack of good sense he set about preaching to all who would listen about how this colony should purify itself in the eyes of God. His prescription for purity was to the eyes of prudence little less than the happy suicide of the colony. Williams would sanctify the colony by placing it on its funeral pyre and striking a match.

Williams had decided that the very charter from King Charles was blasphemous. He had no right to grant the lands of Massachusetts. The lands, if they were owned, were owned by the Indians. Yet Charles claimed to grant the lands in the name of God. Using God's name to enhance a lie was simple blasphemy. For the Massachusetts settlers to live under this charter was to participate in this sin of blasphemy, and to be no better than Charles himself. The colonists should send the charter back to Charles, and with all charity instruct him of his sin. They could also indicate the changes required in the charter before they as Christians could accept it.

John Winthrop had no sense of humor at all, but this pious foolishness must have caused even him to smile. The Puritans had few friends and many enemies in Charles's court. Some of the latter were trying on their own to get the Massachusetts charter revoked and to have Charles send a royal governor to bring the colony under the direct control of the Crown. That would mean the end of everything Winthrop and the others had been trying to build here. The only way to avoid this catastrophe was to mollify and mislead the court as much as possible. Somehow they had managed to do this, at least so far.

And here comes Roger Williams, good, noble, pious, sincere, sweet-tempered Roger Williams, the holy fool. He now convinces a number of the colonists that they would be blasphemers if they do not throw Charles's charter back in his face. Yes, and they might preach at Charles the way Williams preaches to his flock. They could quote Revelations to show that the English court was the whore of Babylon and Charles—or was it Laud?—was the Antichrist. Declare that to Charles, and he would soon start acting like the Antichrist. To protect the colony from Charles, Winthrop would have to save it from Williams.

The irony was obvious, even for Winthrop, who did not have irony in his usual verbal armory. Men like Williams were the leaven of the colony. They epitomized what distinguished this Christian commonwealth from a mere pagan community like the ancient Roman republic. Nonetheless, they had to be tempered by conditions. They had to allow themselves to be led by men like Winthrop who shared their enthusiasm but also had a little of the Roman senator about them. By the end of his governorship, Winthrop had managed to deflect Williams's scruples about the charter; but the matter was not really settled, only quieted for a time.

Then Salem selected Roger Williams to be its full minister. Soon Williams was at it again, but this time Thomas Dudley was governor. Now Williams was preoccupied with the oath of allegiance that citizens were to swear to the colony. This pledge had seemed a simple matter to the General Court when it was voted upon: It was just a formal ceremony to emphasize the obligations that new colonists had assumed by joining this society. Williams as usual saw things differently and ominously.

Not all the colonists who were swearing allegiance were regenerate. There were sinful men, non-church-goers, who were being required to take this oath. Such people were taking the name of God in vain when they swore such an oath. And the government, rather than preventing such blasphemy, was requiring it. Therefore, the government of Massachusetts was a government of and by and for blasphemy. All good Christians had an obligation to oppose it. So Williams preached holy revolution as sweetly and cheerfully as could be.

Ministers from other churches tried to reason with Williams, but got nowhere. Exhort Williams that the Lord wanted us to walk on an even footing between two extremes, and Williams was sure to respond that even-footed walking was damnable when the extremes were Christ and Antichrist. Was not the Lord in the last days going to spit the lukewarm from His mouth? Would any serious Christian wish to risk, in the name of prudence, the scorpion's torment?

It was now Thomas Dudley and his administration who had to deal with the recalcitrant Williams and his loving congregation. First the loving congregation had to be taken care of. Boston, of course, could not interfere with the internal affairs of the Salem congregation. Salem town was another matter. The town, like many of the towns, was feeling cramped by new settlers, and asked for an allocation of more land to help it grow. Boston decided that no land would be allocated to a town whose minister declared the colonial government to be a government of blasphemy.

Support for Williams in Salem suddenly began to wane, as more and more Salemites began to weigh good land against high scruples. Williams, with his characteristic instinct for doing just the wrong thing, then demanded that his congregation declare all other Massachusetts congregations ungodly assemblies because they had not supported him in his godly struggle. His support in Salem now in full ebb, Williams was brought before the General Court and sentenced to banishment for sedition. He received a reprieve until the winter passed, but was admonished to stop spreading his errors. They might as well have asked him to stop breathing.

Although Winthrop did not disapprove of what the General Court had decided, he lamented the confrontations that made the decision necessary. Yet Dudley, no less than Williams, regarded confrontation as the true test of a man's mettle. So when Williams continued to preach his errors (as everyone should have expected), and when he began once again to attract followers (as no one who had heard him should have doubted), the government decided that Williams had broken the terms of his reprieve. Roger Williams was to be seized and sent back to England under guard on the first available ship.

John Winthrop could refrain from acting no longer. Williams, despite his obstinacy and garrulousness, was a sincere and holy man. He was admirable and simple-minded all at once. He should not be spirited away like a common criminal. Such ruthlessness had no place within a Christian community that aspired to be a model of Christian charity.

So John Winthrop violated the secrecy of the government, and warned Williams of the plan. He suggested that Williams flee immediately, although that meant he would have to travel through winter storms. Winthrop recommended that he go south to the as yet uncolonized Narragansett Bay, where the Indians were likely to receive him in friendship. There he could draw his few remaining followers to himself, and found his own colony.

Williams did as Winthrop suggested, and his colony would come to be called Rhode Island. He never forgot the kindness that Winthrop had done him in his time of need, and wrote of it warmly late in life. Winthrop for his part never mentioned it, not even in his own journal. The decision to help must have been a painful one for him. He had long believed that charity and hierarchy were inseparable within a Christian commonwealth. Yet in this case they had been at odds, and Winthrop had been forced to choose between his responsibilities as a member of the Massachusetts hierarchy and the charity he owed a fellow Christian.

Williams and Winthrop remained in friendly communication for a number of years after Williams's banishment, each trying to influence the other. Winthrop asked Williams to reflect on what he had achieved through his inflexible adherence to his principles. Had it not been only great grief, his own and that of many others? Williams in response exhorted Winthrop to reflect on how little he was achieving through compromise and casuistry, and how great the dangers to his soul. "Abstract yourself with a holy violence," Williams wrote to his friend, "from the dung heap of this earth."

The next crisis for the Massachusetts colony had much to do with holy violence, and much with dung heaps of earth. The request of Williams's Salem for more land was not an unusual one. As the colony grew in size beyond anyone's expectation, towns had to expand, and new ones to be founded. The General Court would grant new land to a town, and a town commission would then distribute tracts among settlers.

This distribution was itself a source of tension among the settlers. For Winthrop, land distribution was a chief means of strengthening the natural social hierarchy of the colony. So, for instance, when Winthrop's Boston was distributing land along Muddy River, twenty-one men received ten acres or less; four high-office holders (including Winthrop) received between fifty and two hundred acres; and the town minister, John Cotton, received a grant of two hundred fifty acres.

Not all freemen in Boston were satisfied with this arrangement. On one occasion the ordinary freemen rebelled against the local leadership and elected a land commission representing their interests. Significantly, Winthrop himself was the only member of the ruling elite elected to this slate. No one accused Winthrop of avariciousness. He would so neglect his private affairs that he would be almost bankrupt by 1640, despite grants totaling thousands of acres. However, for every Winthrop in the colony there were half a dozen Thomas Dudleys, willing to use their position to grind the poor.

Nonetheless, Winthrop regarded the egalitarianism of the new commission as a threat to the good order of society. He refused to serve on the commission. Then the town minister preached to the freemen about God's providence and the natural hierarchy within society. They relented, and in a new election selected a commission that distributed the land according to social position.

Winthrop might be able to control land distribution in Boston by the force of his own character, but other towns were not so admiring of their leadership. Charlestown, for instance, had a number of citizens who thought that a hierarchy culminating in Dudley could scarcely be a model of Christian charity. His grasping might have been overlooked by his neighbors if there had been ample land nearby for everyone—but there was not. The town was now squeezed between two others. So a group decided to seek ample land for themselves, as well as more autonomy, by moving their settlement beyond the boundaries of Massachusetts into the Connecticut Valley.

Winthrop did his best to dissuade them, at least to keep them within Massachusetts. But of course he was no longer governor, and their complaints were reasonable. So he tried to keep control over the proposed Connecticut settlements indirectly. He knew that a group of Puritan investors had been given a charter for the Connecticut Valley. He had also, while governor, negotiated a treaty with the Pequot Indians who controlled the valley. (The Pequots had become fed up with the grasping Dutch who "love us only with beaver!") Using his remaining connections in England, he arranged to have his son, John Junior, named as the first governor of the Connecticut colony, and to command the valley from a fort at the mouth of the Connecticut River.

The new settlers seemed to have been outmaneuvered by the sly ex-governor. They were settling on land that was opened for the English by a treaty negotiated by John Winthrop Senior and was now governed by a charter administered by John Junior. The Connecticut Valley would remain under the effective control of Massachusetts. Or so it seemed.

The settlers, however, were not without their own resources. They simply established their settlements far up river, and ignored Junior's fort. They would conduct their own diplomacy with the local Indians—without any influence from Boston, thank you. Massachusetts, however, refused to leave well enough alone. Connecticut had to be brought to heel. So Massachusetts sent officials to the Connecticut fort to continue negotiation with the Pequots. One of these officials, a particularly irascible colonist named Oldham, was found murdered on his ship. The Indians caught with his body were killed immediately, without any serious effort to find out what really happened. But that did not end matters.

Massachusetts had been looking for an opportunity to demonstrate its control over Connecticut, and here it was. A punitive expedition was sent out, led by a man noted for his rigidity and harshness, John Endicott. (It was said of Endicott that when he reached heaven he was not going to go in but rather was going to patrol its gates to repulse those who reached there by any other path but his.) Endicott now tried to bring the red cross to Connecticut.

He first attacked the tribe apparently responsible for Oldham's death, the Niantics. They simply ran away, however; so he contented himself with burning all villages and crops he could find. Then, on the excuse that the Niantics were dependent upon the Pequots, he marched against them. This time he tried to be subtler by drawing them into ambush, but subtlety was not in his line. He was another Captain Shrimp who received for his efforts only taunts. Once again, he destroyed villages and crops, as well as a few pet dogs. Finally in frustration he returned to Massachusetts, not exactly in triumph.

Nonetheless, the Pequots had been hurt. They needed their crops to get through the winter. As far as they could see, the attack had been entirely unprovoked, so they began to attack the English whenever convenient. They were better at marauding than the Puritans, and soon were picking off both soldiers from the fort and colonists from the upriver settlements with alarming efficiency. The soldiers could stay in their fort and get their supplies by sea. The colonists, in contrast, to survive had to work their fields. In one incident alone eight colonists were killed and two young women carried off.

The settlers now faced the choice between returning to the control of Massachusetts and seeing to their own safety. Returning to Massachusetts was unthinkable, for the arrogance of Massachusetts had been the cause of the Indian trouble. Massachusetts had stirred up the wasps; now Connecticut would have to deal with them.

The Connecticut settlers put together an armed force led by a commander experienced in the European wars of religion. They got auxiliaries from Indian rivals of the Pequots, long resentful of their preeminence. Rather than march directly on the Pequots, the commander decided to ship his troops up the coast in order to come at them from behind. Thereby he caught one of their major villages by surprise, at a place the Europeans called Mystic.

The Puritans fought their way into the stockaded village, set it on fire, and then retreated in good order. Most of the Indians simply burned to death in the conflagration—men, women, and children, old and young, all alike in the flames. Some large family groups were led out of the village by their men, in hope of surrendering to their Indian enemies. Custom would have submissive prisoners treated well. A few of the warriors might be tortured to death, but the women, children, and the rest of the men would be adopted into the victorious tribe.

The Puritans, however, had formed a circle between their allies and the stockade. Pleas for mercy were answered by the vigorous wrath of the God of the Hebrews. The slaughter was systematic; no prisoners were taken. One participant boasted that "there were about four hundred souls in this fort, and not above five of them escaped out of our hands."

The Indian allies who had come to see the Pequots humbled were appalled. They pleaded, "This is evil, this is evil, too furious, too many killed." But they were ignored, or even laughed at. When later another group of Pequots, two hundred of them, did manage to surrender to the allies, the Puritans separated all the men, bound them, took them out into the bay and dropped them for the fishes. One Puritan apologist dubbed the ship that was used in this action "Charon's ferryboat."

The Pequots had taken revenge against the English for hurt done to them without apparent provocation. For this they faced not revenge, but extermination. The Puritans were now running them down like wolves. The Connecticut settlers also put a bounty on Pequot heads, and scarcely a day passed for many months without at least one Indian ally appearing to collect. Within a year of the massacre at Mystic, the Pequot had been entirely destroyed. What had been a thriving people was now only the emptiness of a name (that would fittingly survive on the side of Ahab's ship). So the Connecticut settlement had established its independence from Massachusetts. They needed no help from Massachusetts; what few Indians remained in their valley of death cowered in their presence.

John Winthrop, for his part, regretted the independence of Connecticut, but not the death of the Pequot, although he had played no direct role in the latter. The uncircumcised were ultimately the enemies of the people of God. The rage and envy of the gentiles is an eternal tempest that will not be quieted even by the end of time. But those who plot evil always contrive their own ruin. Sooner or later, but inevitably, the Pequots would have to feel the full force of an impartial, severe, inexorable Puritan rage. Now all the Indians, so brave and boastful with their tongues, could learn from this open combat whose god was God.

Winthrop was not one of the dreamy race of men who thought that perfection was possible in this world. In that sense the world is a dung heap. Extraordinary effort is required just to make it a habitable place for saints. And sometimes that effort requires holy violence.

A realist must know that most within a Christian society are predestined to damnation, *and* that all outside it are. We must be a model of Christian charity within our society; all who behave according to God's covenant must be treated as if they were saved, although we know from scripture that many will not be. To God alone is the abyss of the human soul naked. Nonetheless, we do know that outside of Christian society all are damned, mere creatures of the devil, and we must treat them as such. They are outside the covenant, beyond the pale.

Did not God through the prophet Samuel order King Saul to smite all the Amelkites "both man and woman, infant and suckling, ox and sheep, camel and ass"? Did not Joshua in the valley of Achor destroy by fire as a holocaust to the Lord Jehovah not only Achan but "his sons and his daughters and his oxen and his asses and his sheep and his tent and all that he had"? Did not David in one of his songs to the Lord bless the Hebrew who takes the baby of his enemy and smashes its head against a rock? One cannot escape this evil world, but one can with holy violence keep at bay that part of it one cannot directly control.

So John Winthrop approved the slaughter of the Pequots at the place called Mystic, as well as their subsequent extermination as human vermin. He was troubled not at all by it, for he had no illusions about the brutality of this world outside the covenant of grace. In contrast, he was much troubled by events in his town of Boston where the covenant of grace was in the process of being perverted. These events seemed for a time to represent the end of John

Winthrop as an influential leader of the Massachusetts colony—yet they had
the final effect of bringing him back into power as governor. So inscrutable are
the ways of God to human calculation.

The Boston church, due to the influence of its minister, John Cotton, had
long been among the most rigorous in the demands it made upon prospective
members. In general, congregations required that a prospective member be
leading an exemplary moral life. However, all realized that such works were
not sufficient to ensure the salvation of a candidate. Salvation came from faith,
not works. Someone could lead a blameless life not out of God-given conviction but from worldly motives, such as qualifying for full citizenship in the
colony. An unregenerate person, in fact, might be himself entirely unable to
discriminate between these motivations, having never experienced the former.

John Cotton, nonetheless, felt the Boston congregation should try to
make this difficult discrimination. He required of candidates that they
recount their conversion experience. The congregation could then decide
whether this conversion was of a divine or worldly origin. This added requirement improved the selection process but did not perfect it. The unregenerate
could qualify by telling the congregation what it wanted to hear; the unregenerate could also still delude themselves as to their own inner state.

None of this particularly bothered John Winthrop. He was satisfied with
improvement, not perfection. For Massachusetts or the Boston congregation
to function effectively as human societies, such imperfections, or "leniencies,"
had to be tolerated. God would make the final and infallible separation
between the sheep and the goats. In the meantime, His people were expected
only to do the best they could, given their limitations.

Not all in Winthrop's congregation shared his spiritual pragmatism. One
who did not was Mrs. Anne Hutchinson, an admired midwife who lived on
the same street in Boston as Winthrop. She and her husband had emigrated to
the New World in 1634 largely in order to remain parishioners of the
Reverend Cotton. Anne Hutchinson had known no other minister who was
able to follow out the logic of salvation more convincingly than Cotton.

This logic Hutchinson herself sought to explicate. Works were no evidence
of justification. Neither was profession of religious orthodoxy. Neither in the
end was profession of a conversion experience. How could the saved be infallibly recognized? For Hutchinson this was not difficult. The Spirit of God dwelt
in the saved; their human personality had virtually ceased to exist. They were
one with God. Therefore, the sacred could intuitively recognize each other.
The divine spark in the breast of the saved would dance at the sight of others.

(Needless to say, a dance of sparks within human hearts bore little resemblance to the stern covenant with which Winthrop disciplined his inner life.)

Soon an exclusive group, from some of the best families in Boston, had formed around Anne Hutchinson. They listened as Hutchinson in the privacy of her home explained the implications of Cotton's sermons. As the group became larger and Hutchinson grew more confident, she also began to contrast the pure doctrine of Cotton with the confused, even erroneous teachings of other ministers in the colony, including the senior minister of Boston, Reverend Wilson. Eventually she began to speak plainly. Hutchinson, and through her others, knew who was saved. Unfortunately many of those who were pillars of the community were not really saved—this included almost all the ministers, except of course John Cotton. All these people priding themselves on their virtuous lives were no better than the Pequots, an abomination in the sight of the Lord. They were worse; they were the Pharisees who had persecuted our Lord, and would persecute Him again if they had the chance.

The result was intolerable for Winthrop, a female usurpation of rightful authority. This woman was creating a faction within Boston, and was undermining the authority of a duly constituted official of the Church. Yet who could complain when she put her opinions in Cotton's mouth and did so only privately? Winthrop had to wait for a public test of strength, but it was not easy as her audience grew and colonists began to travel into Boston to hear her teaching. Was the whole colony going to live uxorious to her will, in perfect thralldom? Was she herself so shameless as to be insensible to the impropriety of displaying her naked mind to the gaze of the world?

Finally Hutchinson's faction made a move that Winthrop could challenge. They proposed that Boston accept a third minister, Reverend Wheelwright, who also happened to be Hutchinson's brother-in-law. Winthrop opposed this with all his vigor. He now could question before the whole congregation gathered in the church the suspect opinions that Hutchinson had been fostering. The debate was acrimonious. The Hutchinson case was weakened by the simple fact that Boston did not need a third minister. Choosing one was simply a way to repudiate Wilson. Winthrop did in the end carry the vote, but barely. And he was subsequently treated by many of his neighbors as someone who was himself an instrument of evil, who had revealed in the moment of truth his cloven hoof.

As if this were not bad enough, among the strongest supporters of Anne Hutchinson and Wheelwright was the new governor of Massachusetts, Henry Vane. Everyone, including Winthrop, had been infatuated with the twenty-year-old Vane when he arrived in Massachusetts in 1635. The charming and graceful young convert to Puritanism was the son of Sir Henry Vane, among the most powerful peers of England and a trusted councilor of Charles. Vane, having given up everything for religion, became an instant celebrity upon his arrival in Massachusetts, and in 1636 he was elected governor. He was also drawn to the uncompromising Christianity of Anne Hutchinson.

Against such support, Winthrop could do nothing except bide his time and wait for his enemies to make a mistake. At one point he wrote a tract attacking the Hutchinsonians for leading the colony into the quicksands of heresy. Before publishing it, he showed it to a minister friend, and learned to his chagrin that he had fallen into worse heresies than those of which he had accused Wheelwright and Hutchinson. For instance, in defending leniency, in insisting on good works as a sign of sanctity, he had fallen into Arminianism. Shaken, he destroyed the tract.

Winthrop did have support outside of Boston, especially among clergy and elders who did not wish to face a similar rebellion against their authority. They did not want some charismatic woman deciding whether they were among the saved. When the General Court began to make pointed inquiries of Governor Vane about his role in the Boston disputes, Vane did not help the cause by bursting into tears and resigning. And then withdrawing his resignation shortly after, the impetuous behavior of a boy whose angel of judgment was but half fledged.

John Cotton had remained infuriatingly aloof throughout the controversy. He basked in the adulation of Hutchinson and her followers, and yet refused to embrace them against the pragmatism of Winthrop. It was perhaps to force Cotton to take sides publicly that Wheelwright rose before the Boston congregation after a sermon by Cotton. Wheelwright sought to draw the radical conclusions that Cotton in his discretion had left implicit. Good works were not evidence of salvation. Those who thought they were, as evidently did most of the ministers of Massachusetts and a former governor, had thereby declared themselves as enemies of God. The more virtuous their personal lives—Wheelwright could have paused at this moment to look at Winthrop—"the greater enemies they are to Christ." Such holy hypocrites, such whitened sepulchers, such servants of Satan, we must "kill with the word of the Lord." They preach the adder's wisdom, which is death to the Spirit of God.

There was no explaining away this proclamation. It was an open challenge to the authority of magistrates, however lawfully and virtuously they fulfilled their responsibilities. If Wheelwright was taken seriously (one can almost hear Winthrop thinking), the whole moral foundation of Massachusetts would be undermined in the name of theological purity. Winthrop had exactly what he wanted: for someone in the Boston congregation, remaining cool amidst the excitement, had jotted down Wheelwright's exact words, and had then made them available to the General Court as evidence of heresy.

The next meeting of the General Court was the tensest moment in the whole early history of the colony. As Winthrop put it, "There was great danger of tumult that day, and some laid hands on others." Vane wanted the charges against Wheelwright decided immediately, with himself in the chair. Over his strenuous objections the freemen decided that first the governor for next year should be chosen. Vane was turned out; in his place was selected, by the freemen and God, John Winthrop. The General Court was done with innovations, both political and theological.

With Winthrop now in the chair, Wheelwright, of course, was condemned. Winthrop then delayed sentencing; he knew he needed to proceed carefully. He wanted to separate as many people as possible from Wheelwright before the sentencing. John Cotton would be crucial here. He had to be persuaded to distinguish his views from those of this fanatic. Then others would have good reason to come to their senses and remain with the colony, rather than following Wheelwright into his inevitable exile.

Dealing with Anne Hutchinson herself, Winthrop seems to have thought, would be a relatively easy matter. She was a woman after all; and in argument with a man, a woman will always get the worse, although not for lack of words or breath. In a series of private meetings with qualified ministers Hutchinson was to be questioned, solicited, commanded, threatened, urged, and adjured by all the bonds of civic duty and revealed religion. Finally she would be led to repent her rash and unfortunate misdeed with becoming submission to masculine authority. She would repent or she would be gone.

Yet here Winthrop miscalculated. The ministers got nowhere with her. She neither repented nor confessed, and she certainly did not betray any womanly frailty in her argumentation. Winthrop was indignant at her circling wiles, her feigned piety, her smooth hypocrisy; he was indignant most of all at her imperturbable intelligence and confident learning. She seemed so calm and self-assured. Whenever her inquisitors became particularly aggressive, she would simply roll up into an impenetrable ball, and wait for the yappers to test her quills.

Despite having made no progress with her, Winthrop had this disturber of Israel brought up before the General Court the next year in hopes of a better result. One look at that collection of petrified physiognomies sitting in judgment (including sweet John Endicott) and Hutchinson should have known:

Woe to the wretch that sought mercy here. Hutchinson, standing before these patriarchs, would not be cowed. She was no wretch, and she had not come to ask for mercy. She was a very skillful theological dialectician, and, it turned out, a canny lawyer as well.

The Court asks her to provide scriptural justification for her unauthorized classes. She does. The court insists that these do not apply. She insists, with all due respect, that they do. The Court repeats its insistence; she demurely repeats hers. One judge senses weakness and presses the matter further, only to be asked sarcastically, "Must I show my name written therein?" A quill has found its mark, and a Puritan elder is left rubbing his nose.

Others then tried to get her to expound her unorthodox opinions, but she consistently refused to take the bait. She had never spoken in public as Wheelwright had. She had only spoken amidst the privacy of her followers. To the allegations of the court against her, she simply replied, "Prove it." Then the court called John Cotton, who had finally come to the side of orthodoxy against Wheelwright. But Cotton would not turn against Mrs. Hutchinson. He denied she had held the unorthodox opinions attributed to her.

The situation had become desperate; the case against her was simply collapsing. Winthrop knew what the Court had to do, and was determined to do. Yet the decision to exile Hutchinson could not be an exercise of naked power. It had to be publicly justified. Nonetheless, Hutchinson had outwitted them at every turn, disputing when she had a good defense, dissembling when she did not. Their inability to handle this serpentine woman only increased their conviction that she must be gone. What was to be done? The specious monster had vanquished authority with a peal of words. Then the merciful and covenant-keeping God answered their unspoken prayers.

Suddenly Hutchinson was speaking out of turn. "If you please to give me leave, I shall give you the ground of what I know to be true." Winthrop did not give her leave, and tried to quiet her. But she was exultant in her victory. So she continued. While still in England, she received consolations from above, sweet and secret refreshments that enabled her to distinguish true ministries from false, churches of Christ from those of the Antichrist. Then, she fell silent, and looked for the first time distant and distracted. Something weird was happening.

One of the judges decided to follow this up; they might as well, given the new and strange tone to her voice. So she was asked how she knew this gift of discernment was truly from God. Her response was the theological equivalent of self-immolation.

She knew the same way that Abraham had known that it was God who had bid him to kill his son. By an immediate revelation. The voice of God's spirit spoke directly to her in her soul. These commands took precedence over all His formal commandments, as His command to Abraham took precedence over His sixth commandment; the laws of God do not constrain those who hear His voice. Moreover, know this: God had told her that she was to be afflicted for her gifts and also assured her He would deliver her of her afflictions. Beware, any who persecuted her would be cursed on her behalf, they and their children and their children's children, down through the generations. Thus spake the Lord through His servant Anne.

So Mrs. Hutchinson claimed to be a prophet. Her inner light freed her of any external restraints. The Spirit of God had descended upon her. She could kill and curse as she saw fit. Finally, she had unburdened herself, this Delilah who would have sapped God's people of their strength. Winthrop could at least agree that the Lord had spoken through Anne Hutchinson; He had said as clearly as He could through this warped instrument that Anne Hutchinson and her followers must be condemned. Praise be to God for the sudden cure of this lingering disease.

Everyone on the Court understood the implications of what Hutchinson had insisted upon saying. The bright day had finally brought out this viper to sun itself on a rock. Endicott and Dudley now tried to ferret out the viper's brood. They turned on John Cotton and began to question his beliefs. If he thought Hutchinson orthodox, then his own understanding of orthodoxy was heretical if not a species of pious fraud. Under close questioning Cotton began to blink with bewilderment, like an owl forced into daylight. His normal tone of studied meekness quickly began to slide toward something close to a whining cringe. Pathetic as this was, Winthrop permitted it to continue for a few minutes until the learned Reverend John Cotton had been thoroughly frightened. Cotton had discomfited the court; let him be a little discomfited as well. Then, just when Endicott and Dudley were smelling blood, Winthrop cut the questioning off.

Hutchinson and Wheelwright would be exiled. As many of their followers as possible had to be retained for the colony. And John Cotton was too distinguished a minister to lose for Massachusetts. This was the kind of pragmatism that neither Hutchinson nor Vane would ever understand, nor Dudley nor Endicott. Extremism in the pursuit of anything, even religious purity, was a vice.

The damage that this crisis had caused the colony was already considerable. Winthrop himself was treated contemptuously in Boston even after he was elected governor; the town refused to supply the honors usually given to a governor. This must have been extremely painful for Winthrop, although he likely did not admit it to himself. He cared not for fame, the admiration of the distant, unknown many; but he did need the respect if not the love of those immediately around him.

One who no longer either loved or respected him, Henry Vane, had soon returned to England in bitterness and disappointment. All the advantages Massachusetts had hoped to gain from his presence in the colony now turned against them as Vane recounted to influential Puritans and others the un-Christian ways of the colonial government.

As for Winthrop's congregation in Boston, it was a spiritual ruin; for years after no new members presented themselves to be accepted as regenerate. Whenever Winthrop even thought of Hutchinson, a breath of indignation seemed to sweep across his frame.

Hutchinson's free testimony against herself was a special providence on behalf of the colony. But Winthrop, with a bitter hatred and withering scorn that kept his own wounds green, took care to record other special providences that showed beyond question he and the Court were doing God's will. He discovered a scandal that Hutchinson had kept private during the crisis. One of Hutchinson's closest disciples, with her in attendance as midwife, had given birth to a monster. When this rumor reached him, Winthrop had the baby exhumed so that this Divine judgment against the Hutchinsonians could be empirically confirmed. Moreover, after the trial Hutchinson herself was found to be pregnant. Her exile was delayed so that she could give birth. Her baby too was a monster. Blessed be God. Then years later word came that Hutchinson, who had finally settled in Dutch territory, had been tomahawked to death in a general Indian uprising. So ended the life of a strumpet of Satan, and yet one senses that this tale of human pride and frailty was never given a decent burial within Winthrop's mind.

In the eleven years left of his life after Hutchinson's exile, Winthrop would never quite be forgiven in Boston for his role. His popularity in the colony as a whole, in contrast, was unassailable. Of those eleven years Winthrop would be chosen governor in all but two. In 1640 and 1641 Winthrop lost close elections, and even those losses show the esteem in which he was held. Those who were opposing his reelection came to him in a delegation. They professed admiration for him personally. They just feared that having anyone continue so long in an office might make its tenure seem for life, and its transfer hereditary. Winthrop had become so identified with the governorship of Massachusetts that some, even among his admirers, feared the development of a monarchy. So in 1640 Dudley tried his hand at governor again, doing no better this time; he was succeeded by Richard Bellingham in 1641. Then in 1642 John Winthrop was returned to what he and many others had come to regard as his rightful place.

The dates of these changes are significant because they correspond to momentous events in Britain that would confront Massachusetts with its last great crisis of Winthrop's lifetime. In 1640 Charles finally had to call for a parliament, after having tried to rule Britain without one for more than a decade. In that year the General Court of Massachusetts decided to show that ultimate power of colonial government resided in itself by replacing the man who was the closest to a king that the colony had, John Winthrop.

The British parliament, to the shock of many, soon began to move in the same direction. The House of Commons defied the king's authority at every turn. They executed some of Charles's most hated instruments, including Laud who had tried for so long to teach Dissenters the full meaning of persecution. By 1642 the House of Commons, the Puritans, and much of the Country party were in open rebellion against Charles and his court. Civil war was imminent.

The implications of this for Massachusetts were impossible to fathom. So in 1642 the General Court prudently recalled its most experienced pilot to chart its course through these threatening seas. Old Winthrop could only pray, "A little onward lend thy guiding hand to these dark steps, a little further on."

To many, especially among the young, the seas seemed not threatening at all. These were the events for which Massachusetts had waited, for which Massachusetts had prayed, for which Massachusetts should provide leadership. Dozens of the ablest young Puritans in the colony were returning to England, now no longer a servile house of grief, to play their role in the great events of history.

These young men could but envy Henry Vane, who had left years before and now was a spokesman for the rebels. He, not John Winthrop, seemed to be the voice of the future. Massachusetts had served its purpose as a nursery for new leaders of England, so had Winthrop and his generation. Now was not the time to tarry, not the time to use the stale excuse of habit.

Certainly there was no longer any reason for Puritans to emigrate to Massachusetts. Winthrop had been justified in his decision of 1630 because all reasonable hope for true reformation seemed gone. The very air of England had become too close and damp, too unwholesome; the Church of England itself a prison within a prison. But now it was Laud who was gone, executed by Parliament. Reformation, complete reformation, was at hand. Emigration under such circumstances would be little less than desertion.

Many reasoned so, and the migration to Massachusetts virtually ceased. Those few who did come could scarcely be regarded as committed Puritans. Without a continual influx of new colonists, the economy of Massachusetts went into a depression. The old colonists had profited mightily from outfitting the new. Now that income was gone, and at the very moment trade with England was being disrupted. For two full years prices in Massachusetts fell, until crops and livestock were worth from a half to a third of what they had been. The General Court had to adopt special measures for debtors and bankrupts so that they would be treated in Christian fashion.

As for the events in England, Winthrop's response was to respond as little as possible. God, not man, was directing these events. Human decisions counted for little. Massachusetts was to bide its time until the hand of God could be discerned. Winthrop did not dissent when in 1643 the General Court decided to remove reference to the king from its pledge of allegiance. And he agreed when the Court forbade open support for Royalists, either in word or deed.

Massachusetts was not for the king and the Royalists. Massachusetts was sympathetic to the parliament and its Puritans. Sympathy, however, was distinct from unqualified support. Massachusetts, Winthrop was the first to insist, was established to be an example for future English reform. Winthrop wanted to see how well England would follow the example. He could only hope that Henry Vane had matured.

Perhaps it was only his age speaking, or his weariness. But he felt that the joy of the revolutionaries like ebullient Henry Vane and eloquent John Milton was presumptuous and premature; the disruption of revolution sounded to him from a distance like a hideous noise. And the revolutionaries themselves might well be like so many Samsons, bringing down the polluted house of England but upon their own heads, a purification at the price of self-slaughter.

Just are the ways of God, and justifiable to man. Yet Winthrop knew, as Milton would learn to his sorrow, how various, one might even say contrarious, is His hand on those whom He specially elects to some great work for His Glory. Chosen by God, and adorned with the needed gifts and graces, they may yet suddenly, inexplicably be cast down and degraded, unseemly falls to human eyes. This was the loving complaint of the prophet Jeremiah, and the bitter fate of King Saul.

We might imagine Winthrop, on petty business, traveling between towns in western Massachusetts during the late autumn, pausing on high ground to view the colors, the yellows, the russets, the scarlets, so ravishing to the eye, every tree, every leaf bursting with a beauty that can be so easily mistaken for vitality. The New Englander knew better. This was only a final salute of the dying; the blaze of autumn colors would soon be dulled into a uniform, cheerless brown. And then would come the stern, pitiless New England winter, and this whole landscape would quickly become a world sheeted with slippery brightness, a frigid glory to drain the life out of an unlucky or imprudent man. The very roads on which Winthrop was traveling would be drifted with snow up to the armpits, impassable in places for weeks, if not months.

The revolutionaries in England, and those leaving Massachusetts to join them, thought that their revolution was the reformation finally matured into its full manly vigor, a vigor that would sweep all before it. One prayed they were right. But might it rather be the autumn of the reformation, a last dazzling display before a Christian winter in which revelation would have no more impact than the peal of church bells over a field of snow? Perhaps this was his age speaking, and his weariness. But there still might be a place in God's plan for a distant city on a hill, a role for those who stand and wait.

In 1645 many of Winthrop's worst fears about the revolution were confirmed in the person of Robert Child. Child was Henry Vane born again. In him, Winthrop could find all the weaknesses of Vane. Child was one of those young men who had left Massachusetts to participate in the revolution. Now that the firm hand of Oliver Cromwell held the reins of government, Child had come back to share with Massachusetts what he had learned. He had learned that Massachusetts had become a religious and social backwater. While once it might have been a city on a hill providing light for English reform, now it had fallen behind and needed outsiders to lead it.

Child gathered about himself a number of like-minded enthusiasts for reform. Together they produced a "remonstrance and humble petition" that skillfully appealed to all the dissident elements within the colony. Reading it, Winthrop the old fighter (who, if we believe Hawthorne, was soon to be measured for his burial robe by Hester Prynne) must have realized that he was going to have to take up his cudgels once again. He was not too old to be a spendthrift with his remaining strength.

The remonstrance was nothing if not smooth. It began by praising Winthrop and the rest of the Massachusetts leadership: "We cannot but with all thankfulness acknowledge your indefatigable pains, continual care and constant vigilance, which, by the blessing of the almighty, hath procured unto this wilderness the much desired fruits of peace and plenty." The remonstrance, however, went on quickly to point out that prosperity and even peace were now things of the past. Massachusetts was now in a depression that could only be regarded as God's judgment against the present leadership. Child even had the audacity to interpret a recent outbreak of syphilis as a sign of God's displeasure.

What would return peace and prosperity and God's blessings to the colony? Nothing less than a repudiation of fifteen years of prudence and experience, or so Child's proposals for reform seemed to Winthrop. For Child these proposals were simply a check to the "overgreedy spirit of arbitrary power" that now possessed leadership.

Massachusetts must bring itself entirely into conformity with the laws of England. (So much for the autonomy granted by the charter and carefully preserved against enemies at court.) Political franchise must be extended to all men, unregenerate and regenerate alike. (So much for the Christian commonwealth.) Church congregations should be open to all believers who wish to join. (So much for orthodoxy or moral order even within the walls of the church.) While he was at it, why did Child not suggest that the colony also change its name and move to Rhode Island?

If Child's reforms were accepted, Massachusetts would be no better than England. But that, of course, was precisely Child's point. England now provided the model for Massachusetts to follow. Moreover, if Winthrop and the others did not accede to the demands, Child and his fellow petitioners "shall be necessitated to apply our humble desires to the honorable houses of parliament, who we hope will take our sad conditions into their serious considerations."

This threat left little doubt that a fight to the finish was involved, but Winthrop resolved to proceed slowly. Child and his allies were inexperienced, and hence all impatience; Winthrop would take his time, and wait for God to provide him with the right opening. He was weary and old with service, but not yet out beyond his depth.

He first negotiated with the petitioners privately. They had to concede that Massachusetts was not an autocracy. After all, the leadership had shown itself willing to compromise in the direction of democracy. One of the first acts of government had been to broaden definition of "freeman" considerably; one of its most recent had been to permit nonchurch members limited participation in the internal affairs of towns. So Massachusetts was changing. Let Child be patient and hopeful, and withdraw his imprudent remonstrance.

Child saw no reason to be patient when he was confident that Parliament, once adequately informed about Massachusetts, would give him complete victory. Having failed with the preliminaries, Winthrop then turned his attention to the object of the petition, his assistants. The remonstrance, to be sure, was insulting. Winthrop as much as anyone else disliked to have his motives questioned. Nonetheless, the remonstrance would only have the importance that the Massachusetts government placed on it. Let it be dismissed as quietly as possible.

Winthrop must have known that his assistants were about as likely to follow his advice on this matter as were Child and his petitioners. So the former called the latter before them to convict them of their insolence and punish them for it. Led by Child, the petitioners were unrepentant; even in open court they were defiant. The only error they acknowledged was to have bothered with the Massachusetts oligarchy at all. They should have appealed directly to Parliament. This was enough for the court, which fined them both for their seditious original petition and for their subsequent contemptuous behavior.

They remained defiant. Parliament would make it all right. But they had underestimated old Winthrop, who had yet to strike his first blow. He waited until they were ready to leave for England. He then had them seized, and their belongings searched. He seems to have known just where to look for new petitions to Parliament asking for fundamental changes in Massachusetts. Apparently he had penetrated their circle with a spy; one did not have to love the poison of deception to use it, and to use it without remorse. So they were charged with sedition again.

Once again, they were to be brought to trial. Winthrop prepared the case with utmost slowness so that they would be detained in Massachusetts until the next spring. In the meantime, he had the Massachusetts government send its own agent to Parliament. (The agent's salary and expenses were covered by the earlier fines to Child and the others; they paid his way.) By the time Child finally reached England months later, he found that his grievances had already been presented for him, by Winthrop's agent. Parliament in its wisdom had decided against Child and in favor of a renewal of the Massachusetts charter. The case was closed.

When earlier discussions were being held among the Massachusetts leaders as to who should be sent to England to present their case to Parliament, all eyes turned to Winthrop himself. He, however, refused to consider the appointment. He had no interest in returning to England, and never would return. Even when news from the mother country was calm and clear, he found himself instinctively distrustful. It had become for him a foreign shore.

Chapter V

A SOCIETY OF JESUS

W HILE THE PURITANS WERE CLEARING the Connecticut Valley of Pequots, another mission to the Indians was under way far to the west, this one by the French. John Winthrop, had he known of this initiative, would have regarded it as far more threatening to the future of New England than either the Pequot War or the Hutchinsonian heresy. Here was the perversion of all that Massachusetts cherished.

The objects of this mission were the Huron, whose powerful confederacy occupied a substantial portion of the eastern shore of the Great Lakes. Although the center of this confederacy was estimated to be nine hundred miles from Quebec, Champlain had long realized that the Huron were the key to French penetration into the continent. Fortunately they, like the Algonquin near the French settlements, were also traditional enemies of the Iroquois; in aiding one of his allies militarily, Champlain had been really helping both.

The Huron, however, were far more powerful than the Algonquin. The Algonquin needed French protection, and hence quickly became clients of the French settlements—not altogether submissive, but clients nonetheless. The Huron, in contrast, stood as an independent people, fully capable of resisting pressure from the Seneca, the westernmost tribe of the Iroquois Confederacy.

Moreover, the Huron were the Dutch of aboriginal North America, the greatest trading people. They lived near the northern limit of successful corn production; the peoples to their north and west had largely remained hunters and gatherers whose survival was severely tested each winter. Long before the French were a significant presence in the New World, the Hurons had been trading their surplus corn and other food to these peoples. When the French came with their insatiable appetite for furs, the Hurons quickly used their already extensive trading network to prosper. French hatchets, cloths, metal arrowheads, kettles—all these were soon accumulating in Huronia, a previously undreamt of material wealth. The Hurons brought prosperity to Quebec as well. The arrival of the Huron canoes each year—a flotilla of a hundred, as many as two hundred canoes each laden with furs, and together carrying five or six hundred Huron traders—was a cause for a Mardi Gras. Even by itself, it was almost sufficient to make the colony profitable for the year; this was a Mardi Gras that meant there would be no commercial Lent.

The Algonquin did what they could to discourage closer ties between the Huron and the French. They would have preferred to play the middleman between them. However, they could do little to resist their two much stronger allies, beyond occupying the Ottawa River to the east of the French settlements and taking tolls from canoes that came through their territory. This, to Champlain and the Hurons, was little more than a temporary nuisance. Eventually the Ottawa Algonquin and their wily leader Tessouat would be squeezed into complete submission.

A few years before Quebec fell to the British, Champlain had established among the Huron a young Frenchman, Étienne Brulé, who was like a son to him. Soon Brulé had far exceeded Champlain's hopes for his becoming a reliable scout and translator. Brulé became fully a Huron. This caused some scandal in Quebec where it was rumored that Brulé used the promiscuous customs of the Hurons as unending pretexts for his own lusts. How could Champlain place any trust in a man who could not morally answer for himself?

Champlain, however, paid little attention to the complaints against Brulé. The alliance with the Huron was too important, and Brulé was too useful. But when the British seized Quebec, the moralists' prediction about Brulé was sadly verified. The British expulsion of the French meant for Brulé an exile from the only land he ever really knew, and from a life he had come to love. How could he return to France, to a society in which he no longer belonged? Brulé chose to remain with the Hurons the only way he could, by offering his services to the British conquerors.

For Champlain, Brulé's decision was treason pure and simple. Therefore, when Champlain returned to Quebec in 1632, he wanted both to establish close relations once again with the Hurons and to execute the scoundrel Brulé. Brulé himself knew perfectly well that an unpleasant death waited for him in Quebec. The Hurons would not have found Brulé's service to the British strange; prisoners of war were not infrequently adopted into the victorious tribe. But Brulé must have realized that European trade items had become so desired by the Hurons that he could not expect them to shield him for very long. Sooner or later, and probably sooner, he would be negotiated into the stern care of Samuel de Champlain.

Brulé was in danger and knew it—and he responded in character, with daring. He traveled to the Neutral Nation, that group uneasily residing between the Iroquois and Huron confederacies. Through these neutrals he tried to parley with the Iroquois. Perhaps he went to the Neutral Nation, as he told the Huron themselves, to begin negotiations for a treaty between the Iroquois and Hurons. (Certainly such a treaty would have provided Champlain an excuse to forget Brulé's recent indiscretion by dramatically demonstrating his continuing worth.) Or perhaps he went there to seek safe passage through Iroquoia to place himself at the disposal of the Dutch at Albany. Whatever the purpose, the Hurons did not care.

Brulé *was* a Huron now. And negotiating with an enemy on one's own, without the support of a consensus, was treason. Allegiances were too easily shifted by individuals from one group to another for this to be tolerated. Treason, like sorcery (and unlike murder), was for the Hurons a capital offense. When Brulé returned to Huronia from the Neutral Nation (whether in hope or despair we do not know), he was hatcheted to death—and, some said, his body was used as the centerpiece for a feast.

The Huron traders of 1633, the first since Champlain's return, had worried that the French would want revenge for this death. They actually sent a scout ahead to make certain that Champlain would at least parley with them. This scout, just for safety's sake, made his first inquiries not to Champlain, but to French who could approach him.

The response of the French and Champlain was encouraging, but also in its way perplexing. Champlain acted as if Brulé, for whom he had earlier professed affection, was worthless blood. The Huron were pleased to trade with the French as if nothing had happened, but they were also wary. The behavior of the French, they knew from experience, was entirely unpredictable—their apparent indifference about Brulé was just another example.

What they soon came to understand, if not entirely to believe, was that Champlain now had another plan to bind the two peoples together. He wanted the Hurons to take back to their country a group of missionaries. This is what would have horrified Winthrop, for these missionaries were Jesuits.

No group in all of Christendom was more feared and detested by Puritans like Winthrop than the Society of Jesus, the religious order founded by the Spaniard Ignatius of Loyola in the mid-sixteenth century. Compared to the

Society of Jesus, the Spanish Armada was a children's crusade against Protestantism and true religion.

The Society was based upon a model of military discipline that Ignatius himself had learned in his earlier career as a soldier. Ignatius provided a handbook, *The Spiritual Exercises*, to train his followers. The exercises were designed to eliminate any attachment the prospective Jesuit had to worldly things as ends in themselves. As Ignatius put it, "The true religious is he who is wholly free not only from the world but from himself as well."

The world, and even his own self, had ceased to exist for the true Jesuit, except as means—instruments whereby one might serve the greater glory of God. Again and again in his writings Ignatius repeated, "All for the greater glory of God." Everything had God in it in the sense that it could be used to serve His greater glory. The test for the Jesuit was to discover how each occasion could be seized as a divine opportunity. Holiness was not enough to make a true Jesuit. Ignatius had said that great shrewdness with ordinary holiness was preferable to great holiness and ordinary prudence. "Let your first rule of action be to trust in God as if success depended entirely on yourself and not on Him." You trust that there is always a way for you to serve God in any situation, but you act as if He has left it entirely to you to divine it. To a Puritan this sounded like an Arminianism camouflaged as orthodoxy, a Satanic sophistry.

The Society of Jesus had already achieved great successes in the religious politics of the late sixteenth and early seventeenth centuries. The order controlled the most impressive system of higher education in Europe, and Jesuit confessors and spiritual advisers flourished in the world of court informers, haunts, and royal spies. These successes were directly attributable to the pragmatism with which Ignatius insisted his followers be inculcated; to subvert the fixed foundations of a stubbornly sinful heart required the utmost guile.

"To gain men's goodwill in God's service we must become all things to all men. . . . If you want to bring anything to a successful conclusion, you must accommodate yourself to the task, not the task to yourself." Again and again, aspiring Jesuits would ponder Ignatian maxims that taught an instrumentalism as uncompromising as Machiavelli's. "To seek to bring all men to salvation by a single way is very dangerous. He who does so fails to understand how many and various are the gifts of the Holy Spirit."

This cast of mind also made Jesuits formidable missionaries. A Jesuit confronted with an alien culture would first be expected to assimilate as much as possible. In China Jesuit missionaries became mandarins; in India they worked within the caste system, one group becoming brahmins conversant with Sanskrit scripture, another living as untouchables. In the New World they tried to behave like Indian headmen.

Once they had assimilated, they sought to effect a marriage between the indigenous culture and Christianity. The indigenous culture, no less than the European, was but an instrument to be shaped to serve the greater glory of God. As western culture had achieved a marriage between Athens and Jerusalem in Catholicism, so Jesuits sought other marriages for Jerusalem so that the many and various gifts of the Holy Spirit would be fully revealed.

To the Puritan, the Jesuit "marriage" of cultures was but a calculated defilement of true religion, a specious name to veil a blasphemous crime, spiritual whoredom. Rather than demanding true conversion, a true repudiation of this world, the Jesuit used his priestly rites to bless the shame of natural man. Yet the Society of Jesus perpetrated this travesty repeatedly, self-consciously, and with the utmost determination. Jesuits were the true minions of the Antichrist, so mingling truth with lies it could scarcely be retrieved again. Collectively the Society of Jesus was for the Puritan a monstrous phantom, horrible and vast, spreading its shadows of perverted Christianity throughout the world. A good Puritan would rather kill a Jesuit than a Pequot.

For Samuel de Champlain, in contrast, the Society of Jesus was an extraordinary resource for his colony. Missionaries had been in New France almost since its foundation. However, the missionaries of other religious orders had dismissed the native allies of his colony as benighted savages who could scarcely understand enough for baptism. The Jesuits, on the other hand, could be expected to embrace the native culture enthusiastically. Moreover, they could pay their own way. The reports from their New World missions, published in their periodical *The Jesuit Relations,* brought generous support from pious benefactors.

In the 1630s, as dissident Puritans were beginning to plan to move into Connecticut, the Jesuits were organizing a major missionary effort into Huronia. This required the cooperation of the Hurons themselves. To reach Huronia from Quebec required a canoe voyage of one month and thirty-five portages (a more accurate measure than mere miles). The Jesuits would have to travel in the canoes of the Huron traders. At first the traders were reluctant, still fearing reprisals for the death of Brulé. The Algonquin were also doing their best to discourage both sides, telling the Jesuits that the Hurons meant to kill them as soon as they were out of sight of Quebec, and telling the Hurons that certain Algonquin had vowed a blood revenge against any canoes carrying Frenchmen through their territory. (An Algonquin was being held for murder in a French jail.)

The Jesuits, however, negotiated persistently. Their leader, Jean de Brébeuf, had before the fall of Quebec traveled to Huronia, begun a study of Huron customs, and was quickly becoming fluent in the Huron language. He could negotiate with them like a Huron, with the appropriate gifts, flattery, and admonishments; he made many speeches with them and smoked much tobacco. Brébeuf trusted in God, but acted as if all depended upon him. After more than a year of effort, he finally found a group of Huron traders who provided him and his men with passage.

Then began what the missionaries came to call "the long journey to the country of the Hurons." This long journey was to be itself used for the greater glory of God. From the beginning, Brébeuf was quite clear in his own mind how this could be done.

First, the journey was simply penitential. Any missionary who made the long voyage was going to suffer intensely and thereby could make himself worthy of the tasks ahead. The missionaries would be separated, one to a canoe, for the canoes were neither stable enough nor large enough to contain the person and baggage of more than one inexperienced European. Each canoe went at its own rate, each missionary being left to make out as best he could with his own crew. The birchbark canoe itself was to the European neophyte a trial. It was hard to be at ease when flying through rapids like a bird, seeing nothing but sheets of glancing foam, hearing nothing but the roar of waters obliterating every human sound, all the while only a finger's breadth of bark separating you from almost certain death. But the very lightness of the canoe enabled skilled paddlers to maneuver through waters that appeared impassable to the untrained eye. Of course, in a canoe so sensitive to shifts in weight, passengers had to sit perfectly still to let the paddlers do their work—and the Hurons would become impatient (or worse) with any passenger who fidgeted in the midst of rocks and white water. (One of Brébeuf's missionaries was almost marooned for misbehavior.) The Jesuit should remain still, and meditate on the rapids as an image of the human condition (although ordinarily in human affairs a Jesuit would make sure he was one of those with a paddle).

When the water and rocks became too dangerous for even Indian canoeists, the lightness of the canoe made the necessary portage easier. There were dozens of such portages on the long journey to Huronia. Since the Hurons regarded the amount of baggage Europeans required as ridiculously excessive, they felt no obligation to help carry it. So the missionary had to make numerous trips at every portage, while the Indians lounged and joked.

The Hurons themselves, apart from trade items, had hardly any baggage at all, and almost no food. Every second day they would fetch corn that they had hidden along the way. The broth they made from this—sagamite, their staple—most Europeans did not find an epicurean temptation, partly because the stones used to crush the corn were often dirty, and partly because the birchbark bowls in which it was served were also used as urinals in the canoes.

Hardship piled on hardship as the trip progressed. For instance, insects—notably mosquitoes, gnats, and midges—were a continual torture, biting any exposed skin. A missionary who did not protect his eyes would in a few days be blinded by swelling.

For Brébeuf all this suffering could be used to good purpose. During it the missionaries could meditate as Ignatius had taught them. They should form images in their minds that would strengthen them. For instance, they should imagine in detail—sight, sound, smell—the death of Brulé, until it became so real that they were there, not just watching, but in Brulé's place, suffering their own martyrdom, and in this last suffering still using all to praise God. If they could do this during the hardships and distractions of the long journey, they would be likely to behave well during a real martyrdom, should that be God's will for them.

The missionary should also use the journey to start to overcome his European prejudices. He must start to appreciate the coherence and suitability of the Huron way of life. He must admire the skill and endurance of the canoeists; he must try to learn how they find the apparently unmarked caches of corn. He must seek in their customs virtues on which the missionary could build—the generosity, for instance, with which everything is shared, without bickering or even reflection. The selfless sense of the group was not altogether unlike that of the Jesuit for his order. Within the Huron customs they must find sparks of Divine Love, the Voice within the voices.

Beyond that, the missionary must use the journey to start to establish himself as worthy for inclusion into the Huron people on their own terms. Here Brébeuf had a decisive advantage. Hurons were accustomed to ridiculing the French for being weak and puny. Jean de Brébeuf, however, was a bull of a man, who towered over even the tallest of the Hurons. Like a Huron, he displayed his strength with pride, and suffered discomfort without deigning even to notice it.

On this voyage back to Huronia Brébeuf took his turn as a paddler and carried all his own baggage at every portage, three to their one. He therefore arrived in Huronia with his reputation as a man of worth already established. He would later warn prospective missionaries that Huronia was a society in which first impressions were decisive. He who stumbled during the long voyage would find himself to be of little use to the mission afterward.

After enduring the long voyage, Brébeuf and the other missionaries tried initially to live amongst the Huron as unobtrusively as possible. They did retain their distinctive clerical garb, and hence were known to the Indians as the Blackrobes. They also retained their beards as protection against the insects, although this choice offended Indian taste. Nonetheless, they attempted to accommodate themselves to the Huron way of life.

Brébeuf quickly realized that the role he and the other missionaries had to play was that of a shaman. Much as a Jesuit had become the court astrologer for the Chinese emperor, so the Jesuits had to establish themselves as the foremost shamans in the Huron Confederacy. To do so, they had simply to wait, to listen, and to learn until an opportunity presented itself. It came the very first summer.

The crucial Huron corn crop was being destroyed by drought. The native shamans had tried in succession their various rain rites, but (as Brébeuf put it) "the Heavens were as brass to their foolishness." Then a particularly prestigious Huron, shamed by his own failure, announced he had discovered the cause of both the drought and the impotence of traditional remedies. The cross on the Jesuit chapel was bewitching the whole region. Suddenly the situation became dangerous. Crowds of Hurons surrounded the Jesuits and swirled about them shouting with hostility.

Far from being frightened, Brébeuf was elated. All now depended upon him. He shouted back at them like an Old Testament prophet confronting the worshippers of Baal. The cause of the drought was their own sinfulness. The gods the Hurons worshipped, if they were not just projections of their own imaginings, were demons. The Christian God made all, water, land, sky, and the demons as well. He controls the Heavens over Huronia as fully as He does over France. He is an awesome God who does not condescend to allow Himself to be controlled, dictated to, by paltry ceremonies of human invention. He shows His Glory when and where He wills, and if He decides to destroy a people, it is but play for His awful Hand.

Brébeuf had gained their attention, and he continued. The Blackrobes did not make false promises to the Huron people, as did their own shamans. They would not promise rain when they knew its coming was not certain. They would, however, help as best they could, if the Hurons themselves would cooperate. The Hurons had to repent their wickedness. If they did, the Blackrobes would lead them in a procession on each of nine successive days; the novena of processions would be the Hurons' outward sign of their inner repentance. Only such repentance might propitiate God's amply justified wrath against them.

The headmen agreed and the processions were held. On the ninth and last day gathering clouds obscured the sky, lightning forked in the distance, and thunder rolled. As they walked in procession, the downpour came. When the Jesuits retired to the dim interior of their chapel to sing a *Te Deum* of thanksgiving, the joyful cheers of the Huron still darted among them, like swallows at dusk. (This, like all the important episodes in their lives, the missionaries reported in *The Jesuit Relations*, which was published in France and distributed among the pious.)

Later the drought returned (presumably on the heels of renewed Huron sinfulness). Once again the Jesuits conducted their novena, and this time it broke the drought on the second day. Brébeuf and his Jesuit confreres had not been in Huronia a year, and already they had established themselves as the most powerful shamans in the whole confederacy. Their rituals had proven superior to the traditional ways, as French hatchets and kettles had proven to the works of traditional craftsmanship. Villages now vied with one another for the honor of having a Blackrobe live with them. Brébeuf gladly permitted his missionaries to disperse throughout the confederacy.

So esteemed were they now that the Blackrobes were invited in 1635 to participate in the Huron Feast of the Dead. This most solemn of Huron religious feasts, through which they strove to release the souls of the departed for a happy afterlife, took place only every ten to fifteen years. Blackrobes were invited because the headmen assumed that they, as honorable men, would want to assure the souls of their own dead—their few converts, Étienne Brulé—freedom to enter the afterlife.

Participation in such a pagan rite would have been unthinkable for a Puritan; for a Jesuit it was near the essence of his missionary vocation. Of course, Brébeuf saw the same difficulties that a Puritan would. Christian converts, strictly speaking, should be buried separately from non-Christians and in individual graves, which was far from the Huron intention. And what should be done about the remains of Brulé? Did he even deserve to be treated as a Christian and buried in consecrated ground?

Despite these difficulties, the invitation was an opportunity to be embraced for the greater glory of God. Once Jesuits fully understood the rite, they might find a way to baptize it, to incorporate it into a fully Huron Christianity. There were, after all, obvious parallels with Christian practice. This was a Huron All Souls' Day, except that here the souls in purgatory were being honored. So the intentions of the rite were laudable: this was the Huron way of praying for the souls of relatives.

Once the parallels were understood, then the differences between the two religions could be understood more precisely. The salvation the Jesuits preached was individualistic; individual souls were saved or damned because of what each did individually while on earth. The Jesuits had already discovered how difficult this was for a Huron to understand. To their argument that an individual should be baptized because thereby he would be placed on the path to salvation, they had come to expect what they called "the usual rebuttal of Savages"—namely, that he did not want salvation if that meant separation from all those loved ones who had died before. Salvation for the Huron was, like life itself, collective, communal, inconceivable apart from the family and tribe.

The Hurons believed that the souls of the dead remained trapped in their bones, and that this incarceration was a natural process having nothing to do with the moral worth of the individual. To free the souls the community must act in concert—and the length of time between feasts assured that virtually every family would have at least some cherished member to mourn. There would be an elaborate exchange of gifts in honor of the dead; thus families that had prospered during the past decade would, out of pride and love for their own departed members, distribute throughout the community much of the wealth they had accumulated. Death, the universal leveler, would give the Hurons an occasion to reduce the differences among the living.

The remains of those who had died since the last feast were gathered up from the graves by their families. Each family mourned its dead with such intensity the grief seemed fresh, as if all the Huron departed had died in a single recent catastrophe. The sight was at once moving and hideous. "The flesh of some was quite gone, and there was only a parchment over the bones. Some bodies looked as if they had been dried or smoked, and showed scarcely any signs of putrefaction. Others were all swarming with maggots."

During their mourning, the families seemed oblivious to the conditions of the bodies. Each family dressed its dead—both those who died in the fullness of years and those who died as children—in the finest of robes, and brought the corpses back to the longhouses for a final feast of farewell, with the corpse or corpses being propped up as if sitting in the place of honor.

Brébeuf had long ago become inured to the discomforts of the Huron longhouse—the heat and smoke, the dogs and vermin, the all but suffocating close quarters. Brébeuf did not have a sensitive nose—or if he did, he had long ago suppressed it. And yet, as he went from longhouse to longhouse to pay his respects, the stench of the corpses, added to all the rest, made each longhouse in turn almost unendurable, even for him.

Eventually, after the eating was over, the families would lovingly remove what skin, hair, and flesh remained on the corpse. Then the bones of all the dead would be placed together in a pit that was to become the common ossuary. There would be bonfires in the pit, tended by Hurons whose responsibility it was to stack the bones. The grief of those passing the bones into the pit was extreme, indecorous by European standards.

The pit, the fires, the bones being tossed, the people screaming—all this together might remind the Jesuits of the confusion that reigns among the damned. But they also could see it through the eyes of the Hurons as the most profound expression of communal solidarity—their griefs were one, their ancestors one, their future one. The remains of the dead were mingled together so that the spirits could begin their afterlife, begin it as they had lived this life, as one, together.

The Feast of the Dead was Huron culture as the Jesuits hoped to find it. The Feast could be admired, participated in, and built upon. Other aspects of Huron culture were not so easy. The pervasive sexual promiscuity that had so delighted Brulé was a continual source of exasperation. First the Jesuits had to convince the Hurons, particularly the young women, that they themselves were resolutely celibate. Then they sought ways to insinuate the ideal of stable marriages as the only legitimate outlet for sexual drive. This, they knew, would be a lengthy process of education. Essential to it would be to keep Huronia as isolated from the French settlements as possible. Let the Huron traders go each year to Quebec, but keep the French traders out of Huronia. Jesuits back in settlements were expected to use all of their guile to keep rowdy young Frenchmen at home. One Brulé was enough.

Sexual permissiveness was a problem for Jesuit missionaries that required a considerable measure of patience. There were other aspects of Huron culture, however, that could not be dealt with patiently or by compromise. These were purely demonic, and had to be confronted no matter what the consequences. Most notable was the abomination of the platform.

For as long as anyone could remember the Iroquois had been the enemy of the Huron. They feuded with one another constantly. Champlain himself had used the perennial feuds of the Huron and Algonquin against the Iroquois as a way of ingratiating himself and the French with their Indian allies. He tried to see these feuds in European terms as wars. The missionaries could see that they were not; they served much the same function as dueling did among the European aristocracy.

Young men in each group established their bravery and their worthiness of a desirable wife, and of one day perhaps becoming a headman themselves, not just in hunting and trading, but preeminently in forays against the enemy. To be a man you had to spill Iroquois blood at the risk of your own, knowing that to do so would be to incite the enemy to acts of vengeance against you and your people—acts that in turn would provide you with provocation to demonstrate your prowess further.

To all this the Jesuits could have easily accommodated as they had accommodated to the customs of the European ruling class. Nonetheless, accommodation had its limits, one of which was passed when they witnessed the treatment received by a captured Iroquois brave in 1636. He was initially treated with all the honor and respect that would be accorded a family corpse during the Feast of the Dead. He was dressed in a fine beaver robe, and given the place of honor at a feast. His hosts were solicitous about his hand, from which he had lost two fingers during the struggle with his captors. Only after he was fully comfortable and at his ease did the tortures begin.

All participated, men and women alike, all unremitting in their task. First each person burned the captive's body in a different place. When little skin was left uncharred, red hot hatchets were applied to the bottoms of his feet, and hung from about his neck to sear through the flesh of his chest and back. Burning sticks were forced into his ears and rectum. Especially shocking was the behavior of the old women. Crones, themselves as withered as age and hardship could make them, thrust themselves into the forefront of the torturers, as if inflicting pain was the one pleasure left to them—doting grandmothers suddenly transformed into vile witches, their welcoming smiles become screaming grimaces.

Throughout all this, the victim was expected to dance and sing continually, as if this really were a celebration in which he was the honored guest. Occasionally his strength failed, and then the Hurons would gently revive him with water and kind words until he was able to continue. Indeed, during his physical torments the captive was also the object of Huron irony. While the Hurons were doing their worst by him, they affectionately addressed him as uncle, and he, as best he could, responded in the same spirit of light banter.

Finally, somehow still able to walk, priding himself on his ability still to walk, he was led out of the longhouse to a platform in the center of the village. The torture had taken much of the night, and the finishing touches were made in honor of the dawning sun. With the captive secured to the platform, the pace of the torture quickened. First his eyes were gouged, then a foot chopped off, then one hand, then the other. Throughout he was still conscious, and yet his blood was pouring so freely that the bonfires around him could scarcely be kept lit. Finally there was nothing left to do but reluctantly end his misery by severing his head.

The true Huron feast then began: a celebration of their own superiority, of the pain they had inflicted, and of the worthiness of their enemy. Every possible feeling of cruelty in the village had been given the occasion to purge itself without shame, indeed to sate itself in exultation. The body of the Iroquois captive was butchered, and his choice parts cooked for the feast. After these festivities had finally concluded, as the now unattended fire began to collapse into embers, the Jesuits saw in its flickering light a Huron wandering back to his longhouse carrying a skewer on which was a half-roasted human hand.

From the first arrival of the Iroquois captive until his final death, the Jesuits, whatever their personal revulsion at the proceedings, felt obliged to remain near him in order to attempt to convert him during his few moments of respite. Surprisingly, once he realized that their concern for him was sincere and not ironic like his hosts', the Iroquois was receptive. Brébeuf explained to him that what he was about to endure was as nothing compared to the eternal torments suffered by the lost souls in hell. The Blackrobe assured him that if he took baptism he would only have to repeat, "Jesus, have mercy on me!" to receive special grace to strengthen him throughout his ordeal. The Iroquois consented, and they baptized him, and on the platform they could see his lips still forming that simple prayer long after he had ceased to be able to speak.

The Hurons approved of the Jesuits' action toward the Iroquois almost as little as the Jesuits did of their actions. This human sacrifice was intended to strengthen the Huron people at the expense of the Iroquois enemy. How could the very Blackrobes who behaved so civilly during the Feast of the Dead be so malicious here? How could they actually offer solace to the Iroquois? Why would anyone who was a friend of the Huron give an Iroquois warrior magical sayings to ease his suffering? Why would they offer to save him from the fires of hell? If there was hell, did not Iroquois above all others deserve to be sent to it?

The Jesuits, after the Hurons had time to reflect on their action during the torture death, found themselves being questioned closely about French customs. Yes, they had to admit, the French did in certain cases resort to the torture of their prisoners. Yes, they had also to admit, certain particularly heinous criminals—notably heretics and sorcerers—were in fact burned at the stake. Once they admitted this, they found it impossible to convince the Huron headmen that anything was wrong with their own traditional practices.

Neither could they convince them that offering spiritual solace to the very person being tortured by the community was anything other than hypocrisy. Nonetheless, despite strong opposition and considerable risk to themselves, the Jesuits persisted in fulfilling what they took to be their priestly duties toward all prisoners brought back to the villages for torture and death.

The danger that the missionaries faced during torture ceremonies was only occasional. Much more serious was the danger presented by the European contagions now sweeping through Huronia with alarming regularity. The Huron traders would return from Quebec each year, with French kettles and clothes and hatchets, sometimes with a few more missionaries, and frequently with the Angel of Death. The Hurons, unbeknownst to them, had already embarked on a long voyage for which their past life as a people could scarcely have prepared them.

From the first, both Huron and Jesuit alike realized that the contagions were somehow due to European–Huron contact. As usual, the Hurons sought help from their own shamans. Many of their religious rites were curing rituals. When seriously ill, they would commonly try one rite after another until they found one that worked. However, the European diseases seemed to resist all the native shamans' best efforts; so there quickly spread throughout Huronia the sickly, dry yellow of death.

As with the drought, the Hurons turned to the Jesuits. Hurons who earlier seemed indifferent to their offers of baptism now eagerly sought the French water cure. At first the Jesuits thought that suffering had occasioned widespread conversion. Only belatedly did they recognize what was really happening.

For instance, one Jesuit was shocked to find a promising recent convert participating in a particularly lewd communal curing rite. (Some of these rites did require public sexual acts.) When sternly challenged by his Jesuit mentor, the Huron replied with complete aplomb, "Shall we pray now?" The Jesuit's response to this polite inquiry was not, by Huron standards, civil.

So Brébeuf had to have his men withhold baptism. He was not about to allow baptism to become a new specific in the aboriginal pharmacopeia of magic. He realized this would seem unsocial, even traitorous, to a people accustomed to sharing everything. The Jesuits did offer the Hurons what medical help they could, including bleeding all who wanted it. But they performed their most precious rite of baptism only on those clearly dying.

This presented its own difficulty. The Hurons were not long in observing that the water rite had the opposite effect from what it was supposed to. If it was truly a curing rite and not sorcery, why did almost all those baptized die soon after? The Jesuits now found that the ordinarily tolerant and courteous Hurons were obstructing their approach to the ill. The very appearance of these "birds of death," as the Blackrobes were now called, was enough to throw an ill person, even one who had before listened with much sympathy to the priests, into a state of extreme agitation, often to be followed by the listless resignation of the doomed.

The headmen wanted the Jesuits to end the epidemic much as they earlier had ended the drought. The headmen promised complete cooperation. They would march in as many processions as the Jesuits required. They would build them a chapel to their specifications. They would recite any prayers the Jesuits wanted as many times as they wanted—they would even do it in the unseemly position of kneeling if that was what the Jesuits wanted. They would do anything, if only the Jesuits would make their God end the destruction of the Huron people. His angry Hand was too great for the Huron people to bear.

This presented Brébeuf with the opportunity to preach to the Huron headmen on the true nature of conversion. His God would not listen to the pleas of a people who served Him only with their lips and not with their hearts. As He was the God who made them all, so He demanded that all of their lives be given in service to Him. To do that they would have to admit what they would ordinarily shudder to admit: certain of their traditions were permeated with perversity and wickedness. They must rise up as a people, break off all the covenants with evil, root out iniquity from among themselves. That meant the establishment of permanent marriages, the end of sexual promiscuity, and no more listening to dreams or to shamans who led the gullible Hurons into shameful practices.

Aenons, the very headman commonly thought responsible for the death of Brulé, and responsible too for the trading party that brought the French missionaries to Huronia, made the formal reply to Brébeuf's proposal and accusations. The time had passed for the polite and inconsequential acquiescence that, to their frustration, the Jesuits had usually received when they challenged the Huron traditions. Aenons rebutted Brébeuf in frank terms (which were duly reported in *The Jesuit Relations*):

"I cannot dissemble, I express my sentiments frankly; I consider what you propose will prove a stumbling block. After all, we have our own way of doing things and you have yours, as do other nations. When you speak to us about obeying and acknowledging as our master Him whom you say has made heaven and earth, I imagine you are talking of overthrowing the country. Your ancestors assembled in earlier times, and held a council, where they resolved to take as their God Him whom you honor, and ordained all the ceremonies that you observe; as for us, we have learned others from our Fathers."

Brébeuf had seriously miscalculated. He thought that a bold challenge would be all that was required to effect the general conversion of Huronia.

Jesuits were not supposed to be such holy fools. His challenge the Hurons interpreted as an admission that the missionaries were responsible for the disease. Someone had to be responsible for so great an evil. Brulé's wounds late at night called to the Blackrobes for revenge. And Brébeuf was obviously defiant in his refusal of relief. So the Huron headmen were faced with a stark choice— either the Jesuits would die, or the Hurons would.

The headmen met and formally decided to execute them all for sorcery. The French in Quebec would become their enemies, but the choice seemed between extinction and French enmity. In the villages where they resided the Jesuits were now treated as if they were already dead men—and the Jesuits understood what this meant, and understood too that they could not escape from Huronia even if they wished.

Brébeuf wrote calmly to Quebec concerning the expected martyrdom. "We are, perhaps, upon the point of shedding our blood and sacrificing our lives in the service of our Good Master, Jesus Christ. It seems that His Goodness is willing to accept this sacrifice from me, for the expiation of my great and innumerable sins, and to crown, from this hour forward, the past services and the great and ardent desires of all our priests who are here."

In the face of death, Brébeuf regained his shrewd composure. He would use the death sentence to show that he was truly a Huron. Brébeuf gave a great feast, the kind of feast a Huron who knew himself to be dying would traditionally give, a funeral feast, a feast in anticipation of the Feast of the Dead when he would be brought back to sit among them as a corpse.

Brébeuf, with his fellow Jesuits around him, gave his feast. And those invited came, as politeness required. And, as politeness required, they remained silent during the feast while the dead man addressed them, according to tradition, about what most concerned him. Brébeuf spoke to them of nothing new, but he spoke to them as one who knew he was doomed and who, far from fearing death, welcomed the opportunity to give witness to the sincerity of his faith.

This was a bravery the Hurons had not expected from a Frenchman, even Brébeuf; this was a defiant bravery that welcomed the worst, a bravery worthy of a Huron warrior. Could such a man be a sorcerer? There was hesitation in carrying out the death sentence. Then the epidemic temporarily eased, and the sentence was withdrawn, although not entirely forgotten. The headmen had decided to reconsider, to postpone any final determination—but the Jesuits were far from exonerated.

This is also not to say that the Hurons went entirely without revenge. The most prominent Christian convert among the Hurons was Chiwatenha, whom the Jesuits baptized Joseph. He appears frequently in *The Jesuit Relations*, where supporters of the Jesuits' work could read of Chiwatenha's exemplary piety; even the deaths of his own children in the epidemic only increased the ardor of his faith. He seemed destined to become a patriarch among his people. Then in April 1640, Chiwatenha, while tending his fields, amidst the corn and beans and squash, was hatcheted to death. The headmen who held the inquest insisted that Iroquois marauders were responsible, but Chiwatenha's family knew better. His brother, who alone of the family had resisted conversion in part because of his prominence as a shaman, now presented himself for baptism and pointedly took the name Joseph.

The Jesuits responded to Chiwatenha's death prudently. They accepted the inquest decision without complaint. But they did use the death for good effect within his family. When Chiwatenha went out to his field the day of his death, he was accompanied by a niece, Thérèse Oionhaton. Although a niece, she was his true spiritual daughter. He knew it and had great hopes for her. He planned that she should be the first of the family to be educated in Quebec by the French. He was going to see to it that she should receive a complete Christian formation. Oionhaton had been with her uncle when he sensed the danger. He quickly sent her back to the safety of the village. Significantly, he did not raise an alarm, as he would have if he had suspected Iroquois. He just wished her out of harm's way while he faced his executioners. After his death, his family carried out his deepest wishes for Oionhaton: She was sent to the nuns of Quebec.

For them she was a pearl of great price, much as Chiwatenha had been for the Jesuits in the field. The nuns had known much disappointment in their attempts to educate Indian children, especially those brought in from long distances. Separated from their families and villages, forced to live in a convent setting that even many European girls found constricting, the Indian children too often would become melancholy and unresponsive. The meager results the nuns gained were hardly commensurate to the dangers the children faced in their continual exposure to European contagions.

But all this changed with Thérèse Oionhaton. She loved the nuns and their life. She learned her lessons easily, and soon amazed skeptical Europeans with her reading and writing. But above all was the enthusiasm with which she embraced the nuns' teaching about Christ. Under Thérèse's leadership, the children began to imitate the penitential rigors to which the nuns submitted themselves. When asked why they were doing this, the children are supposed to have replied that Jesus' "suffering inspired them with the desire to suffer for the salvation of their countrymen and for their own sins." The nun who reported this added, "Such sentiments do not grow in nature's garden without being well watered by grace." To such piety a Jesuit would only add that Ignatian prudence played a role as well.

The character of the Huron mission itself was changing in the late 1630s. Brébeuf was a heroic pioneer, but his daring had brought the mission close to disaster. He loved for himself and his missionaries to live the life of the Hurons, but in dispersing them to the various villages he increased risks. His superior in Quebec decided to replace Brébeuf in 1638 as head of the mission with Jerome Lallemant, an experienced administrator.

Huronia was a strange assignment for someone with Lallemant's disposition. He was appalled by the physical conditions of Huron life: "I do not doubt that many persons could be found who would prefer to receive at once a hatchet blow upon the head than spend their years enduring the life that one must every day lead here, working for the conversion of these barbarians." In contrast to Brébeuf, who could participate in the Feast of the Dead with aplomb, Lallemant found entering a longhouse under ordinary circumstances an ordeal. "Everything is in a cloud of dust, and, if you go within, you will not reach the end of the cabin before you are completely befouled with soot, filth, and dirt." And, he notes, "you must go there oftener than once a day, if you would perform your duty as you ought." So alien was the Huron tongue to him that Lallemant never developed more than a rudimentary knowledge of it.

Lallemant loved order, and he sought to regularize everything around him. He established certain times each day at which the Hurons would not be welcome at the Jesuits' longhouses, so that the fathers could be assured private times for prayers, uninterrupted. He arranged to have Huronia mapped, and a census taken. He sought to formalize relationships between the Society of Jesus and the various Frenchmen who were lay helpers of the Huron missions; contracts were signed in which the Society promised food and shelter, and the donnés, as they were called, vowed chastity, poverty, and obedience.

These smaller measures were but preparation for Lallemant's grand design to establish a large mission center for all of Huronia. No longer would missionaries live, helter-skelter, among the various villages. Now they would have their own village, a fort really, from which to spread the gospel. After a year of consulting the maps and the census, Lallemant decided on the best location for Sainte Marie, and plans were drawn up.

Through the early 1640s the building program proceeded apace. At Sainte Marie, Lallemant wanted Europeans to be able to live, as much as possible, as Europeans. Indeed, he had Sainte Marie divided into two compounds, one for the Hurons, one for the Europeans. Non-Christian Hurons were not even permitted to enter the European section. There were also two houses of worship—a church for public worship, and a private chapel for Jesuit devotions.

Whatever the limitations of Lallemant personally, no one could deny the great material advantages of his reorganization. There was now a hospital for Huron and European alike. The mission was growing its own crops and importing farm animals from New France; dairy products were to be found in Huronia for the first time. The mission was becoming economically self-sufficient. Largely thanks to Lallemant, the mission could now support a population of more than forty Jesuits and laymen devoted to spreading the gospel among the barbarians. By 1640 they were also baptizing about one hundred Huron each year.

These times were a trial for Brébeuf. His vow of obedience required him to accept his superior's decisions as if from the mouth of God. Nonetheless, it is hard not to hear disapproval in his description of the new orderliness introduced by Lallemant: "Religious discipline is not only as successfully observed as in colleges, but the exact observance of all rules is increased from day to day."

Brébeuf received permission to do what he did best—to start a new mission, with all the attendant hardships and challenges. He went to the Neutrals, the Indians who lived uneasily between the Huron and Iroquois confederacies. He hoped they might provide a gateway to the long-desired mission to the Iroquois themselves.

The Hurons apparently understood his ultimate objective as well. They did their best to frighten the Neutrals away from Brébeuf. He could learn their customs, quickly gain a reasonable knowledge of the language, and roughly map out the country and the distribution of villages. Nonetheless, he could make no progress against the fear that the Hurons had planted. He was treated as a dreadful sorcerer, too powerful to kill, too malevolent to trust.

After four months of futility, Brébeuf returned to Huronia. Now he faced the same charges that had killed Brulé. He was a traitor who had tried to parley with the Iroquois. He must have known that his new mission, if a failure, would put him at risk among his beloved Hurons. Now the worst had happened.

The years since his funeral feast had been grueling for him—the death of Joseph, his own replacement by Lallemant, the failure with the Neutrals. Yet Ignatius had said, "God's habit of goodness is to defend most skillfully what the devil attacks most bitterly." And Brébeuf had been given a special consolation during this dark night of his soul.

He had, of course, continued to meditate in Ignatian fashion. He would meditate using an imaginative recreation of biblical and other scenes. Not just the words, but the very looks of Jesus should be imprinted in the Jesuit heart. One skilled at the techniques of Loyola's spiritual exercises could make the imaginative scene as real to himself as his own surroundings. Occasionally the meditative image could take on a life of its own—and that had begun to happen to Brébeuf.

He would suddenly find himself confronted with a vision of something he had not intended but of compelling reality. It might be a throng of demons coming toward him, to devour him—a vision that, strangely, filled him with complete confidence in God. It might be of a mountain covered with saints, and with Mary at its peak—then he could look among the saints for those he knew who had gone before. Or it might be, as it was after Chiwatenha's burial, something more specific—a vision of Joseph's grave from which a tent rose toward heaven. So God drew the soul of his servant Joseph to Himself from the hollow grave and restored light to eyes closed by death.

Despite such spiritual gifts, Brébeuf still must have found being treated as a traitor by his beloved Hurons a difficult cross to bear. But he could understand why even the hint of interest in the Iroquois was now regarded as completely traitorous. The traditional feud between the Hurons and Iroquois had been transformed by the pressures of European trade into a full-scale war.

Both the Iroquois and the Huron had become increasingly dependent upon European trade goods. The epidemics of the 1630s, which affected both peoples, made this dependence even greater because the old who were traditionally the craftsmen of a village had been especially vulnerable to the diseases. Many villages could no longer do without European goods, even if they had wanted to. So both the Iroquois and the Huron wanted more beaver pelts to trade, but the beaver within their own territories, especially the Iroquois', were starting to be hunted out.

For the Huron this was not a problem. They would spend less time gathering their own furs and more extending their trading network. The Iroquois had no such options. All their neighbors, such as the Huron and the Algonquin, had economies virtually identical to theirs. They were bordered by no semi-nomadic hunters eager to trade furs for corn. When the Iroquois needed more furs than their hunting grounds could provide, they had to get them not by trade but by force. What trade was to a Huron, war was to an Iroquois. And the very geography that so favored the Huron in trade, favored the Iroquois in war.

The Iroquois usually traded with the Dutch in Fort Orange. For the

Mohawks, the easternmost Iroquois nation, this required a voyage of only forty or fifty miles. And while the voyage of the westernmost Iroquois nation, the Seneca, was considerably longer, it was made through the lands of the Iroquois confederacy. The Huron, in contrast, were almost five hundred miles away from the French settlements. And their month-long voyage had to follow relatively well-defined water routes through Algonquin territory, and within easy striking distance of the Iroquois.

There was another geographical advantage for the Iroquois. The Hurons, in practice, could trade only with the French—unless they wanted to trade with the Iroquois for Dutch goods. The Iroquois had ready access to the Dutch, the French, and then the English once they had established themselves in Connecticut and exterminated the Pequots. This last source proved to be crucial. All the European colonies were officially opposed to supplying Indians with guns. They all realized that to arm Indian allies in this way was to jeopardize the very continued existence of the colonies themselves, for guns were the decisive advantage that the Europeans had in any test of strength between themselves and the natives. However, some of the English, trying to break into a new market in Connecticut by offering new services, had no such scruples, at least once the Pequots were dead. The Dutch merchants were then faced with a choice between losing the Mohawks' trade and arming them. Efforts of Dutch officials to enforce a ban on the gun trade understandably failed in these circumstances. If the Mohawks were going to have sufficient arms to destroy Fort Orange, they should at least be beholden to Fort Orange for supplying them.

The more arms the Mohawks received, the more furs they could pirate; and the more furs they pirated, the more arms they could get. The transformation occurred very quickly. In 1641 a war party of about three hundred fifty, which earlier might have had two or three guns, now had more than thirty; in 1643 a similar war party had three hundred. The same transformation was occurring in the western Iroquois, only more slowly. And when all the Iroquois Confederacy was fully armed, a total war against the Huron Confederacy was possible. If successful, such a war could result in the absorption of the Huron Confederacy into the Iroquois—and the population of the Iroquois would be back close to what it was before the epidemics. Moreover, the Iroquois could then inherit the Huron trading networks.

The Mohawks did not enter into their war against the northern tribes without first trying to neutralize the French. They tried to negotiate a peace with the French. To show their good faith, they returned unharmed two French prisoners they had recently taken. The French were now expected to give the Mohawks some presents (notably a few dozen guns), to show their good faith.

The French, however, did not underestimate the shrewdness of these Iroquois. "Their danger was to make a patched-up peace with us, so as to be free from the dread they have of our arms, and to massacre, without fear, our confederates. . . . Such is their conduct, which lacks indeed the true Spirit of the children of God, but not the Spirit of the children of this world."

With these negotiations going nowhere, the French tried to consolidate their position in Huronia. Brébeuf, who had been temporarily assigned to the settlements, was sent back with the first available canoes in September 1644. They made it, but only after some desperate paddling while being chased by an Iroquois war party.

Then it was decided that Thérèse Oionhaton should return as well. Her success in Quebec had made her an object of stories from returning traders who had spoken with her. As one put it, "She is so steadfast, so well taught, so beloved, so fervent in the Faith that on seeing her, one would not take her for a Huron. She will be the greatest mind among the Hurons when she shall return."

When she shall return—the nuns could be forgiven if they quietly hoped that she should never return, that their little Thérèse would have the grace to become the first of her people, of any of the peoples of the region, to take religious vows. This was a life in which she had flourished, for which she seemed preternaturally suited—as a cloistered nun she could bear witness to the great missionary enterprise, and perhaps become, in time, with God's continued grace, the first true saint of this New World.

But such pious reveries were impractical. Thérèse remained an important Huron, and even Christian Hurons had not progressed far enough in their Christianity to understand celibacy as an option for themselves. Monogamy was problem enough. And the Jesuits were eminently practical men. They had the task of converting Huronia, the whole people, not just isolated individuals like Chiwatenha and Thérèse.

The Jesuits, as soldiers of Christ, knew that individuals had to be placed where they could save their souls to the greatest advantage of Christendom. For young Thérèse that meant returning to Huronia to give witness among her own people. A Christian woman, a Christian marriage, a Christian family—these were examples much needed in Huronia, especially during this Iroquois crisis, which Huron traditionalists blamed on the French. Thérèse's family and the Jesuits agreed: she was to return to make a good marriage.

The decision was met with grief and resignation at the convent. As she waited to embark, Thérèse sent back to her mother superior a brief note: "My good Mother, I am about to leave. I thank you for having taken such care of me, and having taught me to serve God well. Do I thank thee for a small thing? I shall never forget it." Receipt of this small thing must have been the occasion of more tears, more resignation.

Because of the danger involved in the trip, the canoes were going to travel in a convoy. In it were not only some of Thérèse's relatives, but a Jesuit missionary, Isaac Jogues, who eventually recounted the subsequent events, and two young laymen who were coming to assist at the mission. Most important for the safety of the group was the presence of Ahatsistari, probably the greatest of the Huron warriors and certainly the greatest who had converted to Christianity.

Just the last year Ahatsistari had led a band of Hurons that routed Iroquois although outnumbered six to one. After that he was with a group of canoes that encountered a superior Iroquois force. Ahatsistari headed straight for a canoe full of Iroquois, jumped into it, killed one paddler, capsized the canoe, and swam around killing all the others he could catch. The Iroquois were so unnerved by this outrageous bravery that they fled. A Jesuit wrote, "This man's life is but a series of combats, and from his childhood his only thoughts have been of war and it was through this that God made him a Christian." Ahatsistari judged that if he was assured of salvation he would be even more reckless in battle. It is hard to imagine him and Thérèse in the same canoe.

As the convoy progressed, signs were observed of a raiding party in the area. Some of the Huron warriors tried to steady themselves by arguing that the party was clearly Algonquin. Ahatsistari assured his passengers that even if it was Iroquois, the convoy had more than enough defenders to repulse them. Of course, Ahatsistari had his own way of calculating odds.

The raiders were Iroquois, and they caught the Hurons by surprise. Perhaps they would have been repulsed if another Iroquois party had not been attracted by the sounds of the fighting. As it was, the Hurons were overwhelmed. Twenty-two were taken captive, including Ahatsistari, Thérèse, and the Frenchmen.

Thérèse as a young girl had undoubtedly witnessed Huron torture of Iroquois, although when her family converted they may well have tried to shield her from this aspect of traditional life. Now she was, after years in the convent, scarcely a Huron; her sensibilities had been continually softened. Her penance now would not be fasting or vigils, but witnessing the brutality of traditional life at its worst.

The preliminary treatment of the male prisoners on the trip back and immediately after arrival in Iroquois villages was bad, even by Iroquois standards. The priest Jogues himself lost a thumb, and had a number of fingers crushed by Iroquois teeth. Needless to say, the worst was saved for Ahatsistari, who by his honor as a warrior did his very best to provoke it. He had both thumbs severed, and the Iroquois took turns seeing how far they could poke sharpened sticks up the sockets. After a number of trials they managed to reach the elbows.

The women received nothing more than a casual roughing up, but they were expected to witness the torture, even encouraged to participate. Jogues's thumb, for instance, seems to have been severed by a captive woman singled out for the task because she was known to be a Christian. For all that, the lives of the women were not in danger. Thérèse, in particular, as a pubescent girl (she was about fourteen at the time) was certain to be adopted.

After the preliminary tortures on arrival at the villages, the Iroquois headmen decided that only three of the captives would be executed. Iroquoia had been as brutally treated by the epidemics as Huronia. Surrounded as they were by enemies, the Iroquois needed to replenish their numbers quickly. Raids like this one were a chief means to do so, especially when they brought back suitable young women.

The joy in being able to torture Ahatsistari to death more than compensated for the lack of numbers condemned to the platform. Ahatsistari, who knew he was doomed from the beginning, confronted his hideous death with a courage and composure that Europeans expected only from saints whose lives had been much watered by God's grace. When the tortures on the platform had become particularly gruesome, Ahatsistari still had enough awareness to notice through the smoke and blood that Jogues (who had been made to attend) had begun to sob. Such a display could compromise the Jesuit's adoption, and could also indirectly reflect ill on Huron courage. Ahatsistari shouted above the din that he was weeping not from fear of the Iroquois, but for love of him. Ahatsistari kept his composure until the end. With almost his very last breath he shouted for himself and the other two already dead next to him, "Arise, someone from our bones as avengers." Noble, but not what Jogues or Thérèse would have wished him to say.

Once the torture deaths were over, the captives were separated into their respective adopting families. They would have only occasional glimpses, perhaps at most a few stolen moments of communication with one another. Although they were adopted, they were still in danger; any behavior strange to Iroquois eyes could be judged sorcery and result in immediate death. One of the pious laymen who had been captured was playing with a child of his long-

house, and as a natural expression of his affection for the child made the sign
of the cross over it. He was immediately hatcheted to death for hexing, by a
grandfather who had had his suspicions all along.

Shortly after this, Thérèse herself was sent to a separate village, away from
the other captives. Subsequently, whenever negotiations took place between
the French and the Iroquois, her name was brought up by the French as a captive who should be returned to them. But she was never among the prisoners
exchanged during truces. The Iroquois could understand why the French
wanted to take back their own people; they could even be sympathetic when
the French wanted to exchange Iroquois headmen for headmen of their allies
captured by the Iroquois. All this made sense in traditional terms. But the
exchange of a woman, a young woman who had now been given in marriage
to an Iroquois warrior, this request made no sense at all, and the Iroquois just
ignored it. The French could not insist; more important things were at stake
than the fate of one girl.

As the aggressiveness of the Iroquois increased, the French dispatches back
to superiors in Paris soon showed signs of panic. If the Iroquois captured you
alive, you were destined "to be the sport of flames and of their rage, and to be
the food for their wretched stomachs. Such is the funeral, and such is the
tomb that awaits us, if we ever happen to die by the claws of these tigers, and
in the fury of these Demons."

The Algonquin were now continually suffering from the Iroquois raids. In
1642 the Algonquin living along the Saint Lawrence concluded that their
position was indefensible. They moved up to Ottawa to merge with the
Algonquin there. This, however, did not deter the Mohawks. A war party simply followed them, and overwhelmed a large village. The captives were herded
back toward Iroquoia. Those too old or too young to endure the hardships of
the trip were killed along the way—three suckling babies were torn from their
mothers and roasted alive for food. These Algonquin women, these Trojan
women of the New World, would soon have Iroquois babies to suckle.

After the capture of Thérèse, contact between Huronia and Quebec was
extremely difficult. Few parties could get through the Mohawk raiders that
patrolled the trade routes. At the same time, the western Iroquois, the Seneca
and Onondaga, threatened Huronia itself. They attacked not canoes but villages. The traditional blood feud had, thanks to European guns, become on
the Iroquois side a war of extinction.

One frontier village had been overwhelmed as early as 1640, another in
1641. The Hurons responded by sending their own raiding parties, but the
Iroquois were often waiting for them in ambush. In 1642 almost a hundred

Huron warriors were lost in an ambush, and from 1643 on the Hurons seemed at the mercy of the raiders (who had never been noted for their mercy). The Iroquois were particularly successful at kidnapping groups of women as they worked the fields. With the fields so dangerous, food production dropped, and the Hurons began to suffer famine. A Jesuit wrote in 1643, "The scourge of war, which has recently carried off such a large number of these people, has continued so savagely for the last year that one may say that this land is but one scene of massacre."

Lallemant had been doing his best to turn the war to the Jesuits' advantage. Clearly the French could not long resist the pressure to arm the Hurons. Guns were now a simple matter of survival. So the French had begun to trade guns for beaver. However, at the insistence of the missionaries, guns were given only to *baptized* traders. As Lallemant put it dryly, "It seems that our Lord intends to use this means to render Christianity acceptable to these regions." Conversion or turning the other cheek was now the choice faced by Huron warriors.

Brébeuf upon his return to his beloved Huronia almost immediately had one of his visions: "In the chapel of Sainte Marie of the Hurons, during evening prayers before supper, I seemed to see bloodstains, or purple spots on the clothes of all our Fathers, and on my own, too. This filled me with surprise, but then there came to mind that saying of Isaiah (64:6) that 'all our righteousnesses are like dirty clothes!'"

Brébeuf found consolation in this quotation. We are soiled, therefore we are righteous—this seemed to be his interpretive reasoning. Brébeuf, however, was misremembering his Scripture. This verse when placed in its context is far from a consolation: "But we are all as an unclean thing, and all our righteousnesses are as dirty clothes; and we all do fade as a leaf; and our iniquities, like the wind, have taken us away. And there is none that calleth upon thy name, that stirreth up himself to take hold of thee; for thou hast hid thy face from us, and has consumed us, because of our iniquities. But now, O Lord, thou art our Father: we are the clay, and thou our potter; and we all are the work of thy hand. Be not wroth very sore, O Lord, neither remember iniquity for ever; behold, see, we beseech thee, we are all thy people. The holy cities are a wilderness, Jerusalem a desolation. Our holy and our beautiful house, where our fathers praised thee is burned up with fire: and all our pleasant things laid waste. Wilt thou refrain thyself for these things, O God: Will thou hold thy peace, and afflict us very sore?"

If this had been pointed out to Brébeuf at the time, he undoubtedly would have brushed it aside, as he brushed aside the increasing danger to the Huron

Confederacy. Brébeuf had too much to be joyous about, too much to be grateful for, to allow himself to be distracted by the questionable interpretations of
visions. First, he could now see that Lallemant had been right about the need
for a mission center. Sainte Marie was not just a church; it was a veritable
Zion, a walled city (a city at least by Huron standards), the greatest fort in all
Huronia. Certainly it was easier to attract laymen now, easier too to survive
isolation from Quebec during the Iroquois war. The Huron mission might
not have survived had the Jesuits persisted in Brébeuf's approach.

And yet his approach had also persisted in a way. Brébeuf thought that the
missionaries should live in individual villages, adapting as much as possible
to Huron customs, going about the business of conversion as unobtrusively
as possible. This approach and Lallemant's had seemed mutually exclusive,
but now Brébeuf could see they were not, and could only marvel at God's
providence.

Lallemant's plan had failed in one respect. He had underestimated the
hold of the traditional village on the Huron. The Jesuits had found they could
not persuade Huron converts to leave their traditional villages to come to live
permanently at Sainte Marie. Therefore, while the missionaries spent some
time each year at Sainte Marie, those responsible for the converts' care had to
live for much of the year in their villages. What had evolved was a synthesis of
the two approaches that no single missionary had foreseen.

Moreover, the Superior in Quebec had judged that Lallemant had
achieved what he could in Huronia and had recalled him. His replacement,
Father Ragenau, although possessed of much of Lallemant's administrative
talent, had also learned the practicalities of life among the Hurons from
Brébeuf. Everything, it seemed, had worked out for the best—and, best of all,
Brébeuf would now be nothing more than a simple missionary, residing in his
own village, a short distance from Sainte Marie, toward the Iroquois frontier.
He could now simply live among his beloved Huron and do God's pleasure.

If all that were not enough, the Christian Hurons now comprised a
significant minority in almost all the major villages. Brébeuf reported a conversation between a Christian convert and a prominent traditionalist. The
traditionalist said that the new faith had imperceptibly gotten the upper hand
over the customs of the forefathers and now needed to be opposed. The convert responded simply: "That would have answered at the beginning, but,
now that matters are so advanced, such an undertaking would be completely
beyond human strength. It will be easier for us to convert those who still
remain infidels, than for you to make us abandon our resolution and give up
the faith."

There was a profound truth to this observation because the Huron religion required for its effectiveness that it be an expression of communal solidarity. Hurons walking through their traditional villages with rosary beads about their necks were a far more effective refutation of the old religion than any Jesuit eloquence. If the Huron religion could not hold the Huron people together, then it *was* false.

Brébeuf realized that the battle for Huronia was almost won, and his enthusiasm made him all the more impatient. In his private journal he pleaded with God like the Psalmist: "O God why are You not known? Why is this barbarous country not all converted to You? Yes, my God, if all the torments which the captives can endure here in the cruelty of the tortures were to fall on me, I offer myself thereto with all my heart, and I alone will suffer them."

The Iroquois war was playing its own part in the Huron conversion. The traditionalists would use this war as an argument against Christianity: "You tell us that God is full of goodness; and then when we give ourselves up to him, he massacres us. The Iroquois, our mortal enemies, do not believe in God, they do not love the prayers, they are more wicked than Demons—and yet they prosper; and since we have forsaken the usages of our ancestors, they kill us, they massacre us, they burn us, they exterminate us, root and branch. What profit can there come to us from lending ear to the Gospel, since death and the faith nearly always march together?"

But these traditionalists knew as well as the Jesuits that the Iroquois attacks were in fact driving Hurons toward the new religion, especially now that the warriors needed guns and ammunition from the French. And Sainte Marie *was* the best defended village in all Huronia. Whenever an Iroquois raiding party was rumored in the region, hundreds of frightened refugees would seek temporary shelter at Sainte Marie, the Christians to be confirmed in their religion, the non-believers to be solicited in their time of need. The superior estimated that in the year from April 1647 to April 1648 approximately three thousand Hurons at one time or another sought shelter at Sainte Marie. In that year there were more baptisms than there were Huron Christians in 1645.

The traditionalists must have realized that they had only one hope: to seek peace with the Iroquois. In 1647 they took their chance. An Iroquois raiding party was captured with a very prominent Onondaga headman; he alone of the group was spared from the platform so that he could go back to his nation to begin negotiations for a truce and the exchange of prisoners. Iroquois representatives then came to Huronia, bringing with them Huron captives to return as a sign of good faith. Despite the promising beginning, the Hurons had the same difficulty in negotiating a peace with the Iroquois Confederacy the French had had a few years before. The Iroquois nations were acting independently from one another on matters of diplomacy, with the Onondaga and Mohawks vying for wartime supremacy. The Hurons had successfully negotiated peace with the Onondaga Iroquois. The Mohawks intercepted the Huron diplomatic mission on its way home from the Onondaga and massacred it. A prominent Onondaga headman who had been left in Huronia as a hostage to assure safe passage slipped away and killed himself after he heard of the massacre.

To renew negotiations with the Iroquois, the Huron needed some dramatic action that would convince even the Mohawks of their sincerity. A crisis had to be provoked in which the French would be expelled. The Hurons then would submit to the Iroquois and receive the required European supplies from the Iroquois as middlemen. That such a gamble would be undertaken shows how desperate the traditionalist leaders had become.

They directed two young warriors to kill the first Frenchman they happened upon. They happened upon a young French workman, and hatcheted him to death. Now the Hurons would offer the usual reparations; the French would refuse and insist that the murderers be punished in the European manner; and the traditionalists would have the crisis they needed. Or so they thought.

Actually, they misjudged the shrewdness of the new superior. As the annual baptisms reached more than a thousand, Father Ragenau could afford to be more compromising toward many traditional Huron practices that his predecessors had condemned: "It is easy to call irreligion what is merely stupidity." To be sure, he preferred that the Huron converts not engage in such practices, but to expect a Huron to do so was to ask of him heroic virtue. While heroism was necessary for the first converts in their apostolic purity, now that Christianity was becoming the common religion of whole villages the Jesuits should remember that "the King of Heaven has crowns of different value, and the Church cannot be equally holy in all its members."

When the traditionalists offered compensation for the murder, Ragenau simply accepted it. He knew that many in France would be shocked that he had accepted beaver robes and wampum belts as a blood price for a pious young Frenchman. In *The Jesuit Relations* he explained that this Christian martyr was now enjoying his eternal reward, and that "every country has its customs, which are in accordance with the diverse nature of each nation." He also pointed out that he had forced the Hurons to pay an unprecedentedly large compensation. Ragenau's shrewdness broke the final resistance of the traditionalists. The spokesman for the headmen in the reparation negotiations admitted as much, in terms that should have given the ghost of Brulé more than a little satisfaction:

"This country is now but a dried skeleton without flesh, without veins, without sinews, without arteries—like bones that hold together only by a delicate thread. . . . My brother, have pity on this country. Thou alone can restore life to it; it is for thee to collect all those scattered bones, for thee to close up the mouth of the abyss that seeks to swallow us."

For this submission the Jesuits could thank their God, and His four horsemen. In the two years after the murder of the French worker, three thousand baptisms were recorded. The baptized in Huronia were now close to outnumbering the unbaptized. But while the Jesuits prepared the individual Hurons for their salvation, Huronia itself moved inexorably ever closer to the abyss. As the superior himself put it, "God peoples these poor desolate tribes with excellent Christians; and He is pleased to establish his Holy Name in the midst of their ruins."

The first major catastrophe occurred in 1648, when the Iroquois destroyed the largest Huron village near their frontier. In that attack the Hurons lost approximately seven hundred people, a full tenth of their dwindling population. Many from the village were able to escape for refuge to Sainte Marie. The Jesuit Antoine Daniel chose to remain behind baptizing and giving absolution where he could. He was killed and his body first abused and then tossed into the burning church. The Jesuits, going through the ruins later, could find not so much as a fragment of bone.

When in the troubled aftermath of the catastrophe, a Jesuit had a vision of Father Daniel, the only question he thought to ask him was "how Divine Goodness could suffer the body of his servant to be so shamefully treated after death,—disfigured as if by disgraceful wounds,—and to be so consumed by fire that nothing, not even a handful of ashes, was left to us." He then heard the reply, "Great is the Lord and most worthy of Praise. He beheld this reproach of his servant; and, to compensate for this in Divine fashion, he granted me many souls from purgatory, to accompany my triumph in heaven."

That same year the Jesuit mission was threatened from an unexpected source: Quebec. A new governor had decreed that all Frenchmen had the right to travel to Indian villages to trade. This meant that the Jesuits might have to contend with laymen whose interest in the Hurons was entirely commercial. A few Frenchmen in Huronia with the morality of a Brulé would do much damage to the Jesuits' work. This change of policy would have caused grave worry in Sainte Marie, had not a graver worry taken precedence.

On the morning of March 16, 1649, those at Sainte Marie saw a portent of disastrous news; they noticed smoke on the eastern horizon, toward the village of Saint Louis where Jean Brébeuf was the chief missionary. Soon refugees began to arrive. Their story was worse than anyone had feared. Not one, but two major Huron villages had been taken by a large Iroquois war party that was now moving toward Sainte Marie itself.

A force of a few hundred Huron warriors went out from Sainte Marie to meet them. The battle lasted into the night, and in the fading light they looked like swarming ants to those watching anxiously from Sainte Marie. The Iroquois eventually retired, but the Huron force itself had taken frightful losses. In one day Huronia had lost two of its major villages and many of its best warriors. No longer were the Iroquois attacking at the frontiers. They had shown they could bring a large force unharassed into the very heart of the Huron Confederacy.

Word came that Brébeuf, unlike Father Daniel, had been captured alive. When the Iroquois had rung the walls and began to mine them, there was nothing for a man of God to do but lift his hands in prayer and the forgiveness of sins—to prepare to die and help his people die. With Brébeuf, the Iroquois, encouraged by adopted Hurons who held him responsible for their people's travail, were unremitting in the torturer's task; with him they had their hideous triumph. All this the French knew before they sent out a party to the village of Saint Ignace, where Brébeuf had been captured. Still, the ruins reduced their stern purpose to sighs, groans, and tears.

They found the stockade strewn deep with slaughtered Huron Christians. They found too the mangled members of Brébeuf's corpse. After his death the Iroquois had honored his courage on the platform by eating his heart and drinking his blood. Knowing what the wounds in the corpse signified, they were sickened by its sight. Nonetheless, all was for the greater Glory of God. So one of the Jesuits, after the body was brought back to Sainte Marie, was ordered by Ragenau to examine it closely to verify the details of the martyrdom to facilitate possible future canonization procedures.

"Father Brébeuf had his legs, thighs and arms stripped of flesh to the very bone. I saw and touched a large number of great blisters, which he had on several places on his body, from the boiling water which these barbarians had poured over him in mockery of Holy Baptism. I saw and touched the wounds from a belt of bark, full of pitch and resin, which roasted his whole body. I saw and touched the marks of burns from the collars of hatchets placed on his shoulders and stomach. I saw and touched his two lips, which they had cut off because he constantly spoke of God while they made him suffer. I saw and touched all parts of his body, which had received more than two hundred blows from cudgels. I saw and touched the top of his scalped head. I saw and touched the opening which these barbarians had made to tear out his heart. In sum, I saw and touched all the wounds of his body, as the savages had told and declared to us."

The bones of Jean Brébeuf were destined not to remain long in their grave. Within a month his body had been disinterred, dismembered, boiled in lye, the remaining flesh scraped away, the skull and bones first dried in the sun, then baked in an oven, finally wrapped in silk and placed in a chest. The Jesuits were leaving Huronia and they were not going to leave behind these precious relics.

The Hurons, now a broken people determined to fly from a struggle they could not win, could reach no consensus about where they should seek haven; the confederacy itself was breaking apart, each group going its own way. Some would seek refuge with the Neutrals. Others intended to travel into Iroquoia itself to throw themselves at the mercy of the enemy; at least there, if they survived, they would be with their many relatives who had been taken captive. All were fearful of winter and future wants.

The Jesuits hoped that the Christian Hurons and any others who now looked to the French for leadership would move to a large island to the north, in Algonquin territory, where they would be beyond the range of Iroquois raiders. But the remaining Huron headmen rejected this plan because to move that far north meant giving up corn as a staple and item for trade—it meant living like Algonquin hunters. The headmen had an alternative plan.

The westernmost portion of Huronia was a peninsula, jutting out into a large bay of what is now called Lake Huron. Off that peninsula was an island large enough to support the remnant of the Huron Confederacy. They would be able to grow their corn there, and the water would serve as a moat against the Iroquois. Would the Jesuits lead them there?

Ragenau could not deny this request. The Hurons who remained around them were converting *en masse*. Ragenau wrote, "We count over three thousand baptisms, during the year, but the dead outnumber those who survive the ruin of their native land."

Ragenau knew better than to question the economy of Divine Providence. But such questions arose, nonetheless, if only to be dismissed. "Whatever happens, it must be enough for us that He derive His glory from it; and if it pleases Him to augment the faith of these people by multiplying His crosses upon both them and upon us, our hearts are prepared for it and we shall embrace it with joy." If God required more blood and martyred corpses, He would find them freely offered. Yet the Hurons were now bereft of honor and exposed to shame. Could God not bring Himself to pity the fortunes of a falling race? God shall never despise a broken, contrite heart.

Most difficult for Ragenau and his fellow Jesuits was to abandon Sainte Marie. They not only had to leave it, they had to destroy it, lest the Iroquois use it as a fort. Ragenau watched what he would rather have died than see. "We ourselves set fire to it, and beheld it burn before our eyes in less than one hour, our work of nine or ten years." It had been, he said, "our home of innocent delights." Their holy city in the wilderness was now a desolation. So the Jesuits and the relics of Brébeuf led the precious remnant of Huronia into exile, all the while looking back with yearning on their old life together.

The retreat to Christian Island, as it was called, proved a gruesome miscalculation. The tragic story refused to end. The Hurons had almost no food to take with them because of the Iroquois disruption of their agriculture. Although the land of Christian Island was fertile and they reached it amidst the outgushing life of spring, the land had be to be cleared of trees before planting, and this proved too much of a task for a spent people. Then the weather turned against them, and novenas did no good. So Christian Island quickly became an island of woe and cruel torment, a final bitter fruit from a sweet seed.

The Jesuits brought their food reserves from Sainte Marie with them, but this was less than a fraction of what the hundreds of families that followed them needed even for subsistence. The Jesuits tried to ration the food fairly, but soon the Hurons were facing starvation. Now the Hurons were crossing their moat to hunt, and to risk being picked off by the Iroquois who had free run of what once had been Huronia. The people left on the island ate roots and acorns, but soon these were exhausted as well. They sought to ease their starvation by picking through excrement and animal carcasses. Then finally Ragenau observed an ultimate horror.

"Necessity had no longer law; and famished teeth ceased to discern the nature of what they ate. Mothers fed upon children; brothers on their brothers; while children recognized no longer, in a corpse, him who, while he lived, they had called their Father."

A delegation of headmen appeared before Ragenau and one of them spoke: "Brother, your eyes deceive you when you look at us; you think that you see living men, and we are nothing but ghosts, and souls of the dead. This land you tread is not solid; it will open very soon and swallow us, and to put us among the dead, among whom we therefore already count ourselves. This night in a secret council, it has been resolved to abandon it before it opens.

Some retreat to the woods, accounting themselves more secure among the wild beasts than when exposed to the Iroquois; others are going away, 6 days journey to the North, upon the rocks of the fresh-water sea, in company with the Algonquins; others to New Sweden, 500 miles distant. Still others openly say that they themselves will take their wives and children to the country of the enemies, where they will find many of their captive kinsmen, who exhort them to flight unless they will utterly perish. And what will you do alone, forsaken by all, in this island? Have you come here for the cultivation of the earth, or of souls? Will you preach the faith to these oaks or these pines? Have perhaps these lakes and these rivers ears to listen to thee, or sense to understand thee? Where will you go? Who will you follow? Can you really follow a people which scatters itself into so many countries? Most of these fugitives will find death, where they think to find life; but though you had a hundred bodies, to divide yourself in a hundred places, you could not do so without being heavy and burdensome to them, and, soon, even an object of hatred. Hunger will attend them everywhere, and they will not be exempted from the scourge of war. What is the remedy? Have courage and we will show it to you; look toward Quebec, and you will see it. Undertake it ardently, and you will achieve it successfully. You must save the remains of this ruined country. Take us in your hands, you who say you bear us in your hearts. You have seen more than ten thousand of us dead at your feet; if you wait longer, not one of us will be left to you; and vainly you will grieve for not having saved at least what you could. It is not necessary to deliberate any longer; it is necessary to depart, and to convey these remains of the Huron Church to the shadow of the fort of Quebec—and that as soon as possible, now that everyone is fleeing in order not to await the arrival of the enemy. There our Faith will not only not be in danger, but, on the contrary, it will revive by seeing the examples of the Algonquins and the French; and their charities will help us. But even if they could not or would not, and if we must die there, we would at least have this consolation, of dying not abandoned in the woods, but near one who may encourage us in that trying passage, without prejudice to our Faith, which we esteem more than life."

Obviously the Hurons could not survive another winter on Christian Island. Not all wished to follow the Jesuits back to Quebec, however. Some again went to the Neutral Nation; some again went to beg mercy of the Iroquois; a few decided to take their chances where they were (promising that they would eventually follow the Jesuits to Quebec). And so the Jesuits led only a remnant of a remnant back to become wards of the French. Of the tens of thousands Brébeuf set out to convert in 1634, a few hundred were in the convoy carrying his bones back in 1650.

Somehow the canoes managed to elude the Iroquois. They reached the Ottawa River without serious incident. Then occurred, at least according to one account, a final indignity. The Ottawa Algonquin had been disdained for decades by the affluent Hurons. They could not even exploit effectively their position between the Huron Confederacy and the French. And the Iroquois were now raiding them too almost at will.

Nonetheless, however weak a people they had been, however grim their own future looked, they now, for the moment, surpassed the broken Hurons. Their cohesion as a society could be strengthened by dramatizing that fact. They would enjoy their advantage, as the Hurons had enjoyed theirs. The Hurons were now, as all could see, a people inferior to the Algonquin; the Hurons should act as became their new station. They should be submissive.

The Algonquin stopped the convoy and demanded a stiff toll for traveling on their river, for passing through their territory. Ragenau, who had been through so much, who had witnessed the Hurons endure so much, seems at this point to have lost control of himself. He responded with fury. He was a Frenchman, he was a man of God, he was a leader of his people. They were not going to Quebec laden with furs to trade; they were going with what little remained to them in this world—they were going with what little was left of their guttering life to beg the French for subsistence, mere survival. Ragenau was not going to permit the Algonquin to take anything from the Hurons, let alone extort the amount asked.

The Blackrobe was not being civil. The Algonquin showed the good father what happened to someone who was uncivil and weak. They took Ragenau captive, tied him up, and hung him from a tree. He was released when his mighty friends the Hurons had paid their toll, in full.

On July 28, 1650, the Huron canoes were sighted from Quebec ending their last long voyage. But even after the Huron people had entered the end-less night (their fatal course finished), Thérèse Oionhaton refused to follow. Rather, she haunts *The Jesuit Relations* like a ghost, appearing suddenly, unex-pectedly, and then as suddenly dissolving back into obscurity. One missionary sees her for a few moments. She assures him she is remaining true to her Christianity; she says the rosary using rocks; she looks "exceedingly sad"; she says to him, "Alas, if the virgin sisters could see me in this condition among these wicked Iroquois who know not God, how they would pity me." Later, another sees her, and she now has a baby. Does she want it baptized? No, she has taken care of that herself. She had recited over the baby, "Jesus, take pity on this child, I baptize thee, my little one, that thou mayest be blessed in heaven." This is not exactly the prescribed form, but the Jesuit is sure it will do.

Finally, in 1655, well into her second decade of captivity, Thérèse Oionhaton disappears from the pages of *The Jesuit Relations* altogether. The apparitions stop. This one struggling soul is finally loosed from history, and dissolved in the air for good. Just as well.

Chapter VI

DIRECTOR GENERAL
OF BABEL

OF ALL THE CONTAGIONS that spread from the Old World to the New, none was more virulent than the worship of riches. Riches, the dumb god, makes all men eloquent. It does nothing itself, but drives men to do all things. So riches, left to its own, would quickly become for men a greater good than the wisdoms of tradition and nature. This contagion the Indians had insensibly imbibed from the colonists. And now they were fervently destroying one another, while the European colonies became more and more firmly established. What a rare punishment was avarice to itself.

One Jesuit had the opportunity to reflect on all this as he traveled through New Netherlands late in 1643, the colony most responsible for arming the Iroquois and destroying the Huron. Isaac Jogues had been taken captive with the canoe convoy that also carried Thérèse Oionhaton. His hands had been mutilated by Iroquois teeth but he had been spared the platform. The Dutch came to know of his survival through their traders, and eventually managed to help him escape, first to Fort Orange (their northernmost trading post) and then down the Hudson to New Amsterdam.

The Dutch, Jogues learned, had no illusions about the Iroquois. They knew the Iroquois were using their military preeminence to behave like the very devil. Yet the Dutch, in North America as elsewhere, were prepared to do business with the devil himself if the profits were sufficient. Anyway, if the Dutch did not give the Iroquois guns, the English in Connecticut would. So the Dutch traded unscrupulously with the Iroquois and soothed their consciences with such small acts of kindness as helping Jogues escape.

The Dutch had only one complaint against the Iroquois: they were too much like the Dutch. In the early days of Fort Orange, which the English later called Albany, the Iroquois had tried to monopolize trade with the Dutch by driving away the Mohicans, the local Algonquin tribe, much as the Dutch would have liked to drive away the English traders from the Connecticut River. The Dutch leaders sided with their own interests, which meant they sided with the Mohicans. These leaders did not survive the subsequent Iroquois displeasure long enough to reflect on their mistake. However, those Dutch who had the responsibility for rebuilding the ruins of Fort Orange had learned the lesson well. Trade would take place on Iroquois terms or not at all. So the Dutch did as the Iroquois pleased, and had to content themselves with bringing to heel the Esopus Indians who lived along the Hudson between Fort Orange and New Amsterdam. They could treat the Esopus as they would have liked to treat the Iroquois. And they would listen patiently when the Iroquois proudly asserted, as they did on almost every occasion, that Iroquois, unlike other Indians, were not dogs to fawn on a master and to lick or bite whatever hand he bid them to.

Much of this Jogues knew before he traveled through New Netherlands from Fort Orange to New Amsterdam. What most intrigued him was his glimpse of what he took to be a society completely devoted to private gain. He was used to shaping all he witnessed to moral or spiritual purposes. Here was a pure moral fable, an earthly comedy of social disintegration, a human society being speedily dissolved by the natural incongruity of its parts.

The New Netherlands, as he described it, was a babel ridiculously on the edge of chaos. New Amsterdam, for instance, the capital of the colony, was scarcely a Dutch city. Among the four or five hundred inhabitants as many as eighteen different languages were spoken. The buildings were as incoherent as the speech, scattered here or there, with no sense of order or community, just individual structures jostling one another for advantage, an image of the inhabitants themselves. Even the most elementary communal needs were neglected. The Fort of New Amsterdam was a fort in name only, a laughable shambles that offered free access to any who wished it, and from all four sides.

The trading posts Jogues had seen up the Hudson were no better. Fort Orange, which should have had formidable defenses, was a miserable little effort, composed of logs and defended by a few ancient cannon which were as likely to explode as to fire in an emergency. The houses nearby were little better than huts. As near as Jogues could tell, an invincible alliance between avarice and individualism undermined even the effective pursuit of wealth. The Dutch were so anarchically competing with one another for Indian trade that they scarcely made enough profit to sustain themselves. And anyone who succeeded soon found himself being undercut by his neighbors and reverting to the communal level of poverty.

As a result, the Dutch were unable to respond effectively to intrusions into their territory by other European powers. Although the Connecticut River was supposed to be the boundary with New England to the north, the English now effectively controlled the whole valley. To the south of the Dutch colony was the Delaware Valley, where the Dutch had also established trading posts. But so had the Swedes, and their settlement was at the mouth of the river and hence potentially controlled access from the sea. Particularly galling and revealing was that New Sweden had originally been promoted by a former governor of New Netherlands and funded by Amsterdam merchants. The Swedish flag, at least initially, was but a cover for the Dutch to compete among themselves, and against their common interest.

If the Dutch were disloyal to their own national cause when profits intervened, how could settlers of other nationalities be expected to behave any differently? Much of Long Island had been settled by British who had fled the restraints of the Puritans, including Anne Hutchinson. However, rather than being loyal to their hosts, they repeatedly played New Amsterdam off against Hartford and Boston to get concessions for themselves. As near as Jogues could see, the whole of New Netherlands was a living argument for original sin, and against all vaunted freedoms of the modern world.

Jogues, it must be said, was no neutral observer, and did see the Dutch colony at its nadir—after it had been demoralized by its failure to settle accounts even with the Esopus. No Iroquois, the Esopus still proved resourceful and resilient. The Dutch had waged their own Pequot War, with comparable brutality but without comparable success. A colony that could not sustain a single fort in its capital had too many divisions within itself to mount an effective punitive campaign. Once a truce had finally been negotiated, the colonists had bickered among themselves more bitterly than ever, now over responsibility for the losses suffered during the war. These unyielding recriminations did have one effect. The director general, as the Dutch governor was called, had to be relieved of his duties. In 1647, shortly after Jogues's unflattering portrait of New Netherlands was published in France, the new director general arrived in New Amsterdam.

There is no evidence that Peter Stuyvesant ever read Jogues on New Netherlands. Evidently he did not need to: He was an experienced colonial administrator, and quickly reached the same conclusions. But for him this was not some moral fable from which he could extract a pleasing lesson and then leave with it neatly filed away for future sermons. This was his world from which there was no leaving, except with a promotion or in disgrace.

Avarice ruled this world, and anyone who sought to lead its men had to command avarice first. In Stuyvesant's deeply held opinion, the Dutch government was successful because it understood this. It had turned all responsibility for the administration of its empire over to corporations—in the New World, the West India Company. This company was given not only the monopoly on Dutch trade, but exclusive political power as well. The company established trading colonies and ruled them on behalf of the Dutch government. Of course, a Dutch citizen who thought he was being treated arbitrarily could appeal to the Dutch government, but in practice the company ruled. So Stuyvesant, although with the powers of a governor, was officially a company director.

This arrangement expressed well the Dutch conviction that colonization was but a means to business. And therefore colonies should be organized like businesses. Rather than having numerous independent traders and settlers competing with one another for the Dutch portion of the trade in a particular part of the world, all should be ordered on a center so that profit would be collectively maximized for the good of all and of the nation. This system had worked brilliantly in other parts of the world; and the commercial innovations of the Dutch were imitated by other European nations envious of Dutch wealth. Peter Stuyvesant had committed his life to making this system work in the New World as well. The motto of the company was "Unity makes Strength." Stuyvesant sought to be the personification of that unity.

Just as Stuyvesant saw the prospects for a Dutch sea-born empire in the New World, he also saw that the Dutch could be their own worst enemies. He had seen painfully and in detail how greed would lead the Dutch to act against the interests of their own colonial administration. What had happened on the Delaware would have been no surprise to him, for in the West Indies he had seen Dutch serve the enemies of their own country whenever prospects for individual profit were good enough, and sometimes when they were not (greed being so frequently the half-brother of stupidity).

The Dutch world was for Stuyvesant divided into two groups, the patriots and the parasites. The struggle of this world was for the former to control the latter, for the good of them both. The parasites could never win, for they could only succeed in destroying the society of which they were part. But that does not mean that the patriots invariably prevailed.

This was brought home to Stuyvesant in the most wrenching episode of his West Indian time. In 1644 Stuyvesant, at once businessman and military commander, had led an attack to recapture Saint Martin's island from the Spanish. The advantage of this for the Dutch empire all his colonists, even the most selfish and cowardly, could understand. And in a military conflict none could contest his right to command.

In the very first assault one of Stuyvesant's legs was shattered by a cannon-ball. He insisted that the attack be continued, although what little chance for survival he had required immediate withdrawal. But without him in the fore-front his forces hesitated, and retreated. He unexpectedly survived the subse-quent ordeal of amputation, and now walked on a peg leg, a permanent reminder of his bravery and failure.

On his return to the Netherlands one of his friends tried to write a poem in celebration of his heroism. What came out was somewhat different than intended, as the title indicates: "On the shot-off leg of the valiant Seigneur P. Stuyvesant." In his own poem Stuyvesant is upstaged by his lost leg. All his courage and determination is rendered risible by his maiming. This was unfair, but then humor is always unfair, even cruel. And the fate of valiant P. Stuyvesant was to be, if anything, unfair and cruel.

Stuyvesant was a man of considerable ability and ambition, with enough ruthlessness for good measure. He had every reason to expect that his return to the New World would be the beginning of great things. He would be a cen-tral figure in the heroic drama of the Dutch maritime empire. And so he should have been. Instead, alas, he would find himself cast as the lead in a provincial farce. All of his sense of purpose, of his own dignity and worth, only increases our merriment at his expense. He works himself up into a divine fury and we, half-embarrassed, cannot help but laugh the harder as he stumps about.[*]

---

[*]Jogues's fate was different. On his return from France he found to his horror that he had become a celebrity. Letters he had slipped out to his superiors during his captivity had been published in France as they were received. This living martyr then suddenly and unannounced appeared in France in the flesh. He was a sensation, and members of polite society vied to honor him. The queen herself, recently a widow and now rumored to be the mistress of a car-dinal, received Father Jogues in one of her palaces that she might weep over his mutilated hands. Jogues wanted only to return to preach the faith of high cathedrals under a forest canopy, and finally he did prevail over his reluctant superiors. In New France he was at first used on diplomatic missions to the Iroquois, since he knew them better than anyone else did. Finally, during a truce, he was permitted to return to Iroquoia as a missionary. What happened on this brief mission was subsequently learned only in the barest of outlines from captives of the Iroquois sympathetic to the French. Jogues and his young assistant had no sooner arrived than the truce dissolved; they were stripped and beaten, and then Jogues himself was hatcheted to death. Late that night his assistant slipped away from his captors to go to the body, probably to get a relic of the martyrdom—but he was discovered. His head joined Jogues's on the Mohawk palisade.

Nonetheless, let us at least try to be fair. Let us permit Peter Stuyvesant a few moments of dignity before the debacle. We might start by seeing Stuyvesant as he wished to be seen, Stuyvesant as he had himself presented in a formal portrait. I will not try this description myself, lest I succumb to the temptation of humor, but will let the greatest historian of Stuyvesant and his reign describe him for us. Here is Peter Stuyvesant as envisioned by the man who devoted his life to securing his reputation, one Diedrich Knickerbocker, in his noted chapter, "Portrait of the Great Peter":

"Methinks I at this moment behold him in my imagination—or rather I behold his goodly portrait, which still hangs up in the family mansion of the Stuyvesants—arrayed in all the terrors of a true Dutch general. His regimental coat of German blue, gorgeously decorated with a goodly shew of large brass buttons, reaching from his waistband to his chin. The voluminous skirts turned up at the corners and separating gallantly behind, so as to display the seat of a sumptuous pair of brimstone coloured trunk breeches—a graceful style still prevalent among the warriors of our day, and which is in conformity to the custom of ancient heroes, who scorned to defend themselves in rear.— His face rendered exceeding terrible and warlike by a pair of black mustachios; his hair strutting out on each side in stiffly pomatumed earlocks and descending in a rat tail queue below his waist; a shining stock of black leather supporting his chin, and a little, but fierce cocked hat stuck with a gallant and fiery air, over his left eye. Such was the chivalric port of Peter the Headstrong; and when he made a sudden halt, planted himself firmly on his solid supporter, with his wooden leg, inlaid with silver, a little in advance, in order to strengthen his position; his right hand stuck a-kimbo, his left resting upon the pummel of his brass hilted sword; his head dressing spiritedly to the right, with a most appalling and hard favored frown upon his brow—he presented altogether one of the most commanding, bitter looking, and soldierlike figures, that ever strutted upon canvass."

Great Peter, as he sized up his colony, was less concerned by the "confusion of tongues" that had so impressed Jogues about this babel of the New World than by the simple fact that these tongues were usually slurred with drink. One out of four buildings in New Amsterdam was a tavern. Neither the minister of the colonial church nor former director Kieft could have been expected to control this continual debauch since they were by common account sober themselves infrequently.

This domination of the colony by alcohol was just a specific instance of a more general lack of discipline, as Stuyvesant saw it. Trade with the Indians was still largely uncontrolled. Even attempts to control the trade of arms or alcohol to Indians were circumvented by individuals, with characteristic indifference to the threat this trade might present to their neighbors or the colony as a whole. Moreover, the sexual promiscuity of the Dutch colonists with Indian women was notorious throughout eastern North America. In fact, in the recent Esopus war, one chief had used as evidence of his tribe's friendship for the Dutch, "we have given them our daughters to sleep with." And many an Indian child had unmistakable signs of Dutch blood.

This general lack of discipline had been revealed most painfully during the Indian war that brought a disgraceful end to Kieft's disgraceful administration. The war had been started without adequate preparations or warnings or objectives. Some claimed that the governor had ordered the initial attacks while in a drunken rage. Not surprisingly, nothing had been gained from this war except the destruction of many outlying Dutch homesteads. The defenses of New Amsterdam itself were still a disgrace; Fort Amsterdam was "more a molehill than a fortress," Stuyvesant wrote.

Needless to say, no coherent policy had been developed toward either the English incursions on the Connecticut or the Swedish competition on the Delaware. Life in the colony was so disordered that there was not even a regular market day in New Amsterdam. No wonder this community still could not produce the meagerest profit for the West India Company. It was in such disarray the surprise was that it still existed at all. If the colony were a man, we might speak of its gaping mouth and drooping eyelids, a freezing numbness in its limbs and a slow dull pulse—and wonder whether there was still time to call a physician. Well, a physician had been called. And his name was Peter Stuyvesant. And he had brought with him the most sovereign and approved remedy, although some would find it more lamentable than the death it would prevent. He would deliver doses of medicine to cure their tumorous pride. He was going to cleanse the foul body of the infected colony—and the colonists were going to receive his medicine patiently, whether they liked its taste or not.

The colony wanted only stern discipline. To be sure, all the elements for a thriving life were here: a perfect location, natives eager to trade, an ample and diverse population of colonists, the support of a prosperous homeland. Only lacking was a disciplining leadership to bring all these elements harmoniously together, and that specific Stuyvesant meant to supply. Without much discipline and soon, this colony was going to be a fruit rotten before it was ripe.

He first attacked the problem of alcohol. He restricted the hours during which the taverns could legally sell drink, and made the penalty for those who defied it a stiff fine and loss of license. He placed a tax on imported drink, and specified that the funds collected would be used on public works, such as the fort. The tax was a particular instance of the general lesson he sought to teach: private vices, if tolerated at all, would be used for the public good.

He offered stern discouragement to those who illegally provided Indians with drink. He substantially increased the fine, and then added liability for any damage done by the drunken Indian. So serious did the problem remain, he observed, "It may every day be plainly perceived that Indians are running drunk along Manhattan." But he knew that such pleas were most effective if made whip in hand; so he added corporal punishment to the list of penalties for those who sought profit by inebriating Indians.

He tried to organize the town as well. He established a market day, and set aside an area for both the weekly market and an annual fair. He issued an elementary building code—no privies on the street, for instance, and fences around property where billy goats were kept. He tried to control fires by outlawing wooden chimneys and appointing fire wardens.

He closed the taverns on Sunday, to encourage his people to become more godly. To reduce their excuses for not attending services, he ordered ministers to provide two sermons each Sunday, and ostentatiously attended both himself. He prohibited any business transactions on the Sabbath, even on the ships in the harbor. One colonist wrote back to a friend in Europe, "Stuyvesant is starting a whole reformation here." Although this might have seemed at times a reformation made in the name of God, its insistent objective was the service of mammon. And woe to all who endangered prosperity.

All this Stuyvesant did in a magnanimously autocratic fashion. He was the boss, and the colonists were his employees. If they did not approve of the way he was serving them, they could look for work elsewhere. Nonetheless, Stuyvesant did not claim omniscience. He realized he should consult the opinions of at least the respectable portion of his population, if only for the sake of appearances. (As for the rest, left to themselves, they were lazier than if sloth were their sister.) He had a Great Council that advised him on affairs affecting the colony as a whole. He also established a Board of Nine to consult for matters concerning New Amsterdam. The way this latter group was chosen shows that Stuyvesant expected to control it: Eighteen candidates would be elected, from whom Stuyvesant would personally select the final nine.

When the colonists first began to call Stuyvesant "Hard-headed Pete" is not altogether clear, but the name was probably occasioned by his early differences with these advisory bodies. Within a few months Stuyvesant, who never had been touched by the angel of humility, decided that they had been a mistake, and showed he was quite prepared to go against their wishes when he thought they were acting like cracked-brain simpletons. The result was series of crises, the first of which concerned his failed predecessor, former director Kieft.

Two settlers, Joachim Kuyter and Cornelius Melyn, were not content with Kieft's dismissal. They had lost everything due to his mishandling of Indian affairs, and sought redress, or rather revenge. As far as Stuyvesant was concerned, however, this was milk spilt by somebody else. He was content to let his superiors in Amsterdam affix responsibility. Melyn and Kuyter, after all, had decided themselves to establish their farms far from the colonial defenses, weak as they were. Kieft may have been rash or incompetent in his attack on the Esopus, but Kuyter and Melyn should have realized the risks attendant to establishing a remote homestead. So Stuyvesant sought to keep the peace by hiding beneath a carapace of equivocation.

Kuyter and Melyn, however, to his annoyance, would have none of it. They had been wronged; Kieft was at fault; those closest at hand should render the judgment. Now Kieft got into the act. Since Stuyvesant had arrived, he had made a study of his successor, and had done his best to ingratiate himself. It had taken a good deal of patient work to overcome the initial bad impression at the dock. Kieft had then sought to say a few formal words of greeting to Stuyvesant. His welcome, however, was instantaneously met with an outcry against himself, at once sportive, contemptuous, indignant, and loud—so loud he could scarcely make himself heard by Stuyvesant above the din. Nonetheless, even in the midst of this humiliating debacle, he realized that Stuyvesant detested the mob more than he did the object of its deserved derision. Knowing his man and the choler of his own opponents, Kieft decided that he would counterattack later, when briefing Stuyvesant on the colony.

After all, as much as half the truth was on his side. The lack of strength in the colony was due not to a failure of leadership by the director but to a lack of unity among the colonists. They crusted their badness over with the name of liberty, but it remained badness, especially when that liberty entailed uncontrolled trade with the Indians. If he had made a mistake, it was in behaving too generously to the likes of Kuyter and Melyn, men who like the winter winds sounded the lament for the very desolation they brought upon us. Kieft, having warmed to his own defense, was beginning to wax eloquent:

"This liberty then which in every respect should have been most gratefully received, of which use should have been made as a precious gift, was very soon perverted to a great abuse. For everyone who thought that now the time had come to make his fortune, withdrew himself from his comrade, as if holding him suspect and the enemy of his gains, and sought communication with the Indians from whom it appeared his profit was to be derived."

Kieft came close to claiming that those whose homesteads had been destroyed had gotten their just desserts. They were the ones who for their own profit had supplied the Indians with the means of war. They were also the ones whose behavior had led the Indians to regard all Dutch with contempt. Now they sought to complete their destructive work, again out of pure selfishness, by attacking the one institution capable of rebuilding the colony: the office of director general. These were most excellent varlets with a rare ingenious knavery. Kieft pleaded, nay, demanded that they be found guilty of sedition and banished from the colony forever. Their pestilential individualism had to be purged from the colony once and for all if the colony was ever to flourish.

Had Kieft approached his responsibilities as director with half the attention and energy he showed now when looking out for his own skin, he would have been one of the great leaders of colonial America. He had certainly demonstrated himself a shrewd judge of Stuyvesant. Stuyvesant's demeanor toward Melyn and Kuyter began to change with instructive rapidity. But Melyn and Kuyter were not to be instructed. All they saw was that they were in the kind of fight they wanted. They responded with relish.

The only arguments Kieft could present were arguments in words, mere words twisted one way and then another. They had better arguments, arguments that could not be refuted, arguments that could be seen and touched and even smelled. Their arguments were ashes and bones, the ashes from burned barns and houses and barracks, and the charred bones of livestock and settlers, sometimes too far destroyed to be distinguished. Did not this destruction argue most eloquently against the verbal weaseling of former director general Kieft? In this fashion Melyn and Kuyter continued, on and on, at times with a sarcasm almost withering.

It was a most impressive performance, too impressive for their own good by half. The more eloquent they were, and the more impassioned, the more Stuyvesant came to agree with Kieft that, whatever the merits of the case at hand, these were dangerous fellows. He said simply, "These churls may hereafter endeavor to throw me down also, but I will manage it so that they will have their bellies full for the future."

Actually Stuyvesant sought to fill their bellies by stretching their necks. Going beyond what Kieft had asked, Stuyvesant demanded that at least one of these impudent, misbegotten little men end up dead, as an object lesson to all the other glib tongues in the colony that might be tempted to rash and insub-

ordinate words. His stunned council worked hard to dissuade him from such
harsh punishment. The members finally convinced him that *misericordia*
demanded a punishment of only perpetual banishment.

In the meantime, Melyn and Kuyter had become meekly if uncharacteristically tongue tied. But once they were out of the shadow of the gallows, they
reverted to type. That is, they began to talk excitedly and pointedly, and with
abuse. Stuyvesant was no better than Kieft. The fool of a soul in the body of a
hermaphrodite would not have been more of a monstrosity than peg-legged
Pete Stuyvesant. You would be more likely to find a blue toad with bat's wings
than get fairness from a man with a head of solid bone. This balding, beetle-
browed, wall-eyed, hook-nosed, slack-jawed, doughy-chested, pot-bellied,
shuffling-gaited, pigeon-toed, would-be tyrant. His mother must have had
wormwood in her spent dugs to have suckled so curdled a being. And the
psalmist must have had the grown Stuyvesant in mind when he sang, "I am a
worm, and not a man." Well, Melyn and Kuyter were going straight back to
Amsterdam, and were going to bring to their knees both Kieft the elder and
Kieft the younger.

Stuyvesant raged at the indignities he was suffering; this ill-natured merriment was galling to himself and destructive of his office. Melyn and Kuyter
and their sympathizers in turn baited him with glee. Confronting one of them
he shouted that he wished he could save his superiors the trouble by having
him "hanged immediately from the highest tree in New Netherlands." He
wished he was an Iroquois who could hatchet his enemy on sight, and then
pay the family off with a few beaver robes.

Stuyvesant *needed* a hatchet. He was helpless under the law to change his
punishment—and for that he could thank his wonderful council, whose
advice had proven as trustworthy as Simon's. The damage was done. Melyn
and Kuyter, the horned snakes, had made his authority an object of fun, the
butt of gibes and sneers. The others now regarded him as a governor in jest,
only to fill out the scene. All of the petty hostility over his efforts to discipline
the colony was now released in a general mocking of Hard-headed Pete, and
unfairly fused with the hatred of Kieft.

When Melyn and Kuyter, along with Kieft, sailed off to Amsterdam to
present their cases, Stuyvesant was left to repair his own administration and to
continue to endure the smiles full of mockery and malice. He decided that the
time was now for New Netherlands to show a clear profit for the first time.
That would demonstrate to his superiors the true mettle of Peter Stuyvesant,
Director General, especially if they were at all tempted to believe the fabricat-
ed calumnies of Melyn and Kuyter. Profit was the best argument with the

company, and the only one its little thistle patch of bookkeepers always understood, since theirs was a knowledge of the New World gotten from a map and a ledger.

Stuyvesant settled on a means to turn a profit that was tinged with revenge against those settlers who had chuckled with Melyn and Kuyter. Stuyvesant decided to call in all the outstanding debts to the company. Most notable of these were the loans given out to settlers to soften the effects of the Esopus war. The intent was obvious: The settlers who owed the company the most were the very ones most likely to have sympathized with Melyn and Kuyter's complaints against Kieft. Stuyvesant would save them from hypocrisy by withdrawing the hand that they were biting.

If Stuyvesant thought that this measure was going to be accepted meekly, he had learned nothing from his encounter with Melyn and Kuyter. Or rather he had learned exactly the wrong things. His council now stood up to Stuyvesant without fear. Far from cajoling him, they insisted that he put off indefinitely this disastrous collection of loans outstanding. Stuyvesant had no idea of the effect such a measure would have on ordinary struggling settlers, or he would never have even considered it. He had demonstrated how far out of touch he was with their needs. Faced with an adamant council, Stuyvesant acquiesced—not, one might imagine, without some muttering unfit for polite society, or one of his famous *ex tempore* rages. Now the Board of Nine turned on Stuyvesant. The council having blocked an increase of revenue for the company for the sake of outlying settlers, the board then sought to decrease company levies on New Amsterdam merchants.

Control of the board had been effectively seized from Stuyvesant by a respected and able young settler, Adriaen Van der Donck. Van der Donck had earlier distinguished himself by helping negotiate the end of Kieft's disastrous war. He now made the enormously popular proposal that the Company forgo some of its customs on goods coming into the colony. It was enormously popular with everyone in New Amsterdam—everyone, that is, except for one particularly thick-headed individual who perversely would not somehow see the light. And kept repeating over and over that peculiar word "deficit."

What happened next passed belief. Van der Donck and his cronies announced that they had discovered why the colony was in such a weakened state, why it was not flourishing like New England. The comparison with New England was the key. English colonies could be directly chartered by the British government, and hence were at liberty (there was that word again) to pursue their interests within the broad limits set by their charters and the laws of Britain. They had no company between them and their government, no company skimming off their profits and thwarting local initiatives. To flour-ish, New Netherlands had only to be freed from the stultifying grasp of the West India Company.

This argument was so preposterous that Stuyvesant had much ado to con-trol himself. He had set up this board, and personally had chosen its members. He had encouraged it to offer advice and sought its help in solving the finan-cial problems of the colony. He did not even mind if individual members sent back complaints to the Netherlands about the administration of the colony, so long as he saw them beforehand and could then answer them if he thought need be.

How had they repaid him for this magnanimity? They had attacked the very foundation of his authority. Was there no one in this colony except him who did not have anarchistic designs? These envious, ungrateful miscreants could term the company a parasite and the director general a parasite on a par-asite. But if his leadership and the support of the company were withdrawn, this same envious crowd would be exposed as a collection of eunuchs and fools. At least the situation was clear. These harpies could delude him no more. The Board of Nine were his implacable enemies.

The Nine, for their part, agreed that they and Stuyvesant were enemies, but with professed reluctance. By February 1649, they had set Van der Donck to work on a petition attacking the administration of New Amsterdam, espe-cially Director General Peter Stuyvesant. In Van der Donck's account, he and his colleagues had made only some modest proposals for the improvement of the colony. Stuyvesant's response had been so irrational as to be perhaps symp-tomatic of an incipient stage of dementia, or so Van der Donck wrote.

"This excited in him a bitter and unconquerable hatred against them all, but principally against those whom he supposed to be its chief authors; and although these persons had been good and dear friends with him always, and he shortly before had regarded them as the most honorable, able, intelligent and pious men of the country, yet as soon as they did not follow him, they were this and that, some of them rascals, liars, rebels, usurers and spendthrifts, in a word, hanging was almost too good for them."

No one who had witnessed Stuyvesant's conduct of the Melyn-Kuyter case should have been surprised that Stuyvesant would use the full range of his authority to crush those who now challenged it outright. So Stuyvesant wait-ed until Van der Donck was well along in his seditious tract, then seized all his materials, placed him under arrest, and began to proceed against him and the conspirators. He brought his charges to the larger council of the colony, on whose loyalty or at least acquiescence he thought he could still count.

However, while Stuyvesant was trying to put the Nine in its place, he suffered a piece of monstrous luck. Melyn returned from the Netherlands.

The ship on which Kieft, Melyn, and Kuyter had been traveling back to the Netherlands had been shipwrecked on the coast of Wales and plundered by the Welsh like some latter-day Armada. Kieft had gone down with the ship, but Melyn and Kuyter somehow had survived, although Melyn lost a son in the process. Perhaps out of sympathy for what they had gone through, but more likely because no one was there to present the prosecution's case, the Dutch government tentatively decided in their favor and against Stuyvesant.

Melyn returned to New Netherlands in triumph. While the Board of Nine was beginning to take the offensive, Stuyvesant had to suffer the additional indignity of restoring to Melyn all his property and then allowing this avowed enemy the full freedom of the colony from which he had been banished. Knowing Melyn, we can scarcely expect that he exercised this freedom quietly.

Now Stuyvesant had to face the most recent challenge to his authority at a time when everyone was abuzz over his superiors' failure to support his handling of the last challenge. Still Stuyvesant did not back off. The authority was his and he would continue to exercise it as he saw fit. He proceeded with the meeting of the Great Council in which he would demand the condemnation of Van der Donck and the rest of the conspirators against the best interests of the colony.

In this decision he had underestimated Melyn. Perhaps the death of his son had made Melyn more wily in his pursuit of revenge. Never one to forgo vindictive pleasures, now Melyn showed himself to be a true epicure in that line. On his return trip to New Netherlands he obviously had brooded over the various wrongs he had suffered, and had decided to serve Stuyvesant his humiliation in doses. He had saved the bitterest draught until it would best serve his pleasure. The meeting of the Great Council, with all the leaders of the colony present, was the most delicious time imaginable.

Melyn showed the enemies of Stuyvesant a legal writ which he had yet to show Stuyvesant. It ordered Stuyvesant, or a representative, to return to the Netherlands forthwith to give a thorough accounting of his handling of the Melyn-Kuyter affair, presumably a preliminary to a formal dismissal. Stuyvesant had no sooner convened his meeting of the Great Council, with much of New Amsterdam present as an audience in tingling anticipation, when one of the disloyal Nine rose from his place and began a public reading of the document, the audience responding with unwonted jollity.

It took Stuyvesant a few moments to realize what was happening. At first he must have thought that this was just another of their insubordinate proclamations. Their amusement, however, was too great. Then he realized that this purported to be an official document from the Netherlands. It had to be a cheap forgery.

Stuyvesant stomped over to the reader in such rage it looked as if he might burst. His demeanor was so intense that both the reading and the amusement it was promoting immediately ceased. He demanded to see the document. When the reader momentarily hesitated, Stuyvesant grabbed it from his hands with such sudden force that the official seal was partly torn from it. Seeing the seal, Stuyvesant could not doubt its authenticity.

There was nothing to be done. He returned the document, hobbled back to his place, and listened impassively as the reading was completed. Then he said slowly and in a flat voice: "I honor the States General and their commission and I will obey their commands. I will send an agent to maintain the judgment. It was well and legally pronounced."

This was not the defiant explosion for which his enemies had hoped. Immediately they were on their feet demanding that Stuyvesant put his submission in writing. Stuyvesant was not to be provoked, however. He said, with only a slight edge in his voice, that he would submit in writing when he received the writ in writing.

With this as prologue, the prosecution against Van der Donck was an anticlimax. Stuyvesant did get his conviction of Van der Donck, but there could be no thought now of a serious punishment, satisfying as that might be. Stuyvesant, who only a few hours before had probably intended to hang Van der Donck from the highest tree in New Netherlands, now meekly agreed that he should be punished by being removed prematurely from the Board of Nine. That was all.

Everyone now regarded Stuyvesant as a ruined man, and began to treat him as such—that is, they went out of their way to give him an extra kick. One of his most trusted members on the Great Council deserted him with great fanfare, explaining that he had only voted to convict Melyn and Kuyter because Stuyvesant misled him. However, he would no longer support someone who deemed chains as fit garb for free born Dutchmen.

Kicking Hard-headed Pete around seemed to have become a chief recreation of the colony. The pastor whom Stuyvesant had appointed and strongly supported also began to trim with the wind. His sermons denouncing tyranny were quite popular, especially with the tyrant himself sitting in the first pew, an instance of the very flesh and blood of putrid pride. So insults and gibes, like little fiery flakes, snowed down on Pete Stuyvesant, who did his best to acknowledge what was happening to him only with disdain and scowls.

People were treating Stuyvesant as if he had already been recalled. The very excess of their abuse was one of the few factors that could be worked in Stuyvesant's favor. When he sent his own account of his administration with a representative back to the Netherlands, he emphasized the "mutinous and insulting" way the writ had been served him. He would rather have never been honored with his high office of director general than to be, just because of a simple petition, so disparaged by his neighbors and subjected to "the degradation of justice, authority, and our granted commission."

Enemies of Stuyvesant, certain of victory, fed their calumnies to enemies of the West India Company in the Netherlands; and so Stuyvesant became a name on which to hang their general attacks, a seventeenth-century Dutch equivalent of Colonel Blimp. In one such attack Stuyvesant is described as hypocritical, fickle, dishonest, and irresolute; he whines like a dog and is as ravenous as a wolf. "To say all in a word, this man has so many particular qualities, of which not one is serviceable in a desirable republic, that he is not fit to rule over Turkish slaves in the galleys, much less over free Christians."

Stuyvesant's enemies were enjoying themselves so much that they overplayed their hand. As long as Stuyvesant was just a bad or ineffective governor, then he could be dismissed at the pleasure of the company. Now, however, pamphlets had made him the personification of the company. Remove him and opponents of the company would regard this as an admission of guilt and of weakness. They would then turn to have the monopoly of the company itself withdrawn by the government. When the situation was understood in this way, the company had to regard the recall of Stuyvesant as a last resort.

The colonists did not seem to understand this; they thought they only had to assure the Dutch government that Pete was still as headstrong as ever, and it would force the company to remove him. One wrote that to expect him to change was "to wash a black moor." He continued, "Our great Duke of Muscovy goes on as usual, with something of the wolf; the older he gets, the more inclined he is to bite. He proceeds no longer by words or writings, but by arrests and stripes."

Stuyvesant was far more complicated than such polemics would allow. As his handling of both the Melyn and the Van der Donck cases showed, he had a very clear idea of the limits of his authority. He knew when to fight and when to retreat. He would growl a great deal, but as often as not his growls were a bluff that preceded a retreat. He knew very well when to play the fox, and when the wolf. Even his well-documented rages seemed to be called up for effect. Nowhere was this clearer than in his dealings with New England, which took almost as much of his energy as his troubles with his own colonists.

With New England, Stuyvesant knew from the start he was dealing from decided weakness. Just in population these colonies outnumbered that of New Netherlands by as much as ten to one. Moreover, John Winthrop in his last years had formed a loose confederation that allowed them to act in concert. In any pure test of strength, the New Netherlands would soon be at their mercy.

Stuyvesant did his best to play the New England colonies off one against the other. Massachusetts valued trade with New Amsterdam; to this colony Stuyvesant was all friendship and kind words. His letters to the governors of Massachusetts usually were amply seasoned with obsequious grace. Connecticut, on the other hand, was composed of aggressive frontier communities, hardened by the Pequot War and eager to expand at the expense of the Dutch. With Connecticut Stuyvesant was as querulous as a weasel.

Early in his governorship he had learned of a Dutch vessel trading in Connecticut without permission of the West India Company, an illegal but common circumvention of the rights granted the company by the Dutch government. Stuyvesant mounted a clandestine naval raid that seized the vessel while at anchor at New Haven, on a pleasant Sunday while the good Puritans were at church. When the governor of the violated colony complained, Stuyvesant disputed the right of Connecticut even to exist, let alone complain, since it had been largely founded on territory that rightfully belonged to the Dutch. He then grandly offered asylum for any refugees from the upstart government of Connecticut. And for a short while the governor of Connecticut and Hard-headed Pete exchanged snarling insults by messenger.

About the time Stuyvesant was settling his affairs, however unsatisfactorily, with the Nine, he was also negotiating with New England over the disputed southern border with New Netherlands. In 1650 he traveled to Hartford, Connecticut, to work out the details of a formal treaty. He established his debating position from the start. After he had arrived at Hartford, he sent a preliminary note to the British representatives from "Hartford, the New Netherlands." This was his sly way of asserting that Hartford had been taken forcibly from the Dutch—a point at once true and irrelevant, as the ruins in Hartford of the Dutch Fort Good Hope ambivalently attested. But, of course, the British quickly protested in correspondence that this peevish discrimination threatened the whole negotiation. Stuyvesant, as quickly, apologized for his slip of the pen. This first exchange was, in a way, the negotiation in microcosm. Any Dutch contentions soon crumbled before British pressure. Both sides tacitly acknowledged the disparity in their relative strengths, as would any treaty worth its parchment. The brute fact was that to get any treaty New Netherlands was going to have to cede to the British colonies significant tracts of territory. This the Dutch negotiators did.

The treaty reflected the *de facto* distribution of population. Almost all of Connecticut went to the British. The British acknowledged Dutch rights to Fort Good Hope by making it a Dutch enclave within their territory. But this was an empty concession since the useless fort would soon be sold to the British. The terms for the division of Long Island were even more painful.

Here the Dutch negotiated away their rights to some of Long Island just to get the British to acknowledge their rights to the rest. The Dutch gave up the wampum works that had so impressed the Pilgrim fathers in order to secure the portion of Long Island that protected the entrance to the Hudson.

No matter how severe the terms, the treaty represented the relative strengths of the British and Dutch colonies. In fact, bad as the terms might have seemed, they were good for the Dutch. The British were having far greater success attracting settlers than were the Dutch. The imbalance in population, and hence the English pressure on Dutch territory, was only going to increase for the foreseeable future. The Dutch were simply conceding what they had already lost or soon would. In so doing, however, they were establishing legal rights to territory that British settlers were soon going to covet.

Of course, this was a reasoning that no leader, especially one as beleaguered as Stuyvesant, would want to acknowledge—especially to incomprehending superiors who would then only conclude that he had given up territory rightfully belonging to the Netherlands. So Stuyvesant, pleading ignorance of English, had left the room and let others negotiate the terms of the treaty. Then, when the final terms were presented to him, he howled betrayal. His negotiators were met with poetic fury and histrionic storms. According to one account of the scene, he had to be restrained from physically attacking them. They must have been a bit perplexed when he then composed himself and meekly signed the treaty.

Stuyvesant did his best to keep the terms of the Treaty of Hartford secret. Time and again, his superiors would ask for a copy. Time and again, he would forget or procrastinate. Of course, sooner or later they would read the document. But he calculated that the later they read it, the better his terms would look. If they read it too soon and sought to chastise him, he could howl betrayal once again, and bring forth witnesses that the treaty had been signed by him over his outraged protests.

Would to heaven that a spate of words over a few signatures could assure the territorial integrity of his colony. But Stuyvesant knew that the wax would still be warm and the ink not yet dry when pressure would begin to build again in Connecticut for further British expansion. Everyone knew that the vault of heaven would not crack if someday soon Connecticut chose to ignore the treaty altogether. Nonetheless, he had gained one concession to which he could expect the British to remain true, at least for a while. The leaders of Connecticut had agreed to give up plans to flank New Netherlands by establishing a colony on the south river, the Delaware.

The New Netherlands could attempt to fight a holding action, or at least to conduct a slow retreat, against the expanding British colonies to its immediate north. However, also to be faced with an expanding British colony to its immediate south was a sure recipe for a slow death by squeezing. The Treaty of Hartford could be expected at least to spare Stuyvesant this unhappy prospect. That meant Stuyvesant, having played the fox to his north, could now turn his attention south and begin to play the wolf.

For decades the Dutch had shared the Delaware with the Swedes, thanks initially to disloyal Dutch money and a disgruntled former director general. Sweden had subsequently supported the colony like an illegitimate child sired by a father she would as soon forget. In New Sweden Stuyvesant had a colony to which he could justly condescend. New Netherlands was at the middle of a spectrum of power in which New England and New Sweden occupied the opposite ends.

While Stuyvesant was distracted at home and to the north, affairs continued on the Delaware as uneventfully as usual. The Swedish fort was on the west bank, the Dutch on the east. Neither would imperil the other, directly or by intercepting ships reaching it from the Atlantic—not that many ships cared to.

The Swedish governor, Johan Printz, who was as noted for his ample girth as Stuyvesant for his missing leg, understood that the roughly two hundred souls under his care were permitted to stay on the Delaware only by Dutch sufferance. Repeatedly, he tried to impress on the Swedish authorities back home that his people were at the mercy of the Dutch. A decision in New Amsterdam could overnight doom his small colony. He thought that little was required to secure a permanent Swedish foothold in the New World. Printz needed only sufficient reinforcements to drive the Dutch from the Delaware and to defend the river against all comers.

In response to his pleas, he was told to stay friends with his Dutch neighbors, and to use force only in answer to force. For Printz this was like waiting for your execution. Nonetheless, during the inept term of Kieft in New

Netherlands, this oily policy of peace seemed to be working, at least when mixed with as much vinegar as Printz could rationalize within the letter of his orders.

Printz did build two new forts, placed to cut off access to the Dutch Fort Nassau from the Atlantic. It was not that Printz was going to prevent any Dutch ship from reaching the fort. He was just going to insist that such ships acknowledge Swedish sovereignty over the lower river before they could proceed farther. This way he could start building a case for Swedish sovereignty over the most desirable portion of the Delaware, as well as establishing workable boundaries with the Dutch outpost upriver. The Dutch should not regard this situation as threatening, since they could always reinforce their fort overland, assuming the Indians in between would let them pass.

This was all an elaborate bluff since Printz did not have enough men to staff adequately more than one fort. Printz could only hope that his initiative would rouse Sweden to action before New Netherlands recovered from its disastrous war against the Esopus. It didn't. And in Stuyvesant, Printz found an adversary who enjoyed playing chicken.

Early in his administration, before he was in any position to take effective action, Stuyvesant decided to probe Swedish weakness, much as New England was continually probing Dutch weakness. To dramatize Dutch claims to the whole Delaware, he established a fort on the west bank of the river, between the two Swedish forts closest to the mouth. This calculated provocation drew a measured retaliation. The Swedes did not directly attack the fort, but they did destroy any fortifications the Dutch tried to throw up around it; they also denied access to any ship trying to reach it. Printz did not want to take responsibility for attacking the fort, but he was going to do all he could to help it dry up and blow away.

When Stuyvesant signed the Treaty of Hartford, he was free to up the ante in the smaller game. He marched 120 men from New Amsterdam to Fort Nassau. At the same time he sent eleven large Dutch ships up the Delaware.

The Swedes in the first fort were supposed to use their cannon to stop the progress of these alien intruders on their river. They could also count, however. And it did not escape their notice that the Swedish *soldiers* were outnumbered by the Dutch *ships*, two to one. Members of the garrison of Fort Elfsborg, therefore, prudently decided not to draw any unnecessary attention to themselves. So the Dutch squad sailed past without a shot being fired.

Stuyvesant must have had a good laugh over this, for he was running a bluff of his own. All but four of his ships were entirely unarmed. He continued the charade when the ships reached Fort Nassau and met up with the other portion of the expedition. Rather than turning against the trembling Swedish establishments, they conducted practice exercises. Stuyvesant was not engaged in conquest; he was simply communicating nonverbally with Printz.

The message was not very complicated: Act in a manner becoming in someone so weak; on the Delaware the Dutch do as they will; forget this, and we come again, in earnest. To test whether or not Printz had gotten the message, Stuyvesant then built a new fort, this one near the mouth on the west side; now any ship that wanted to progress very far would have to acknowledge Dutch sovereignty. To navigate the whole of the river, a foreigner would have to be a chameleon, changing colors back and forth at every bend.

The local Indians seem to have entered perfectly into the spirit of the drama. Fort Casimir, as the new Dutch fort was called, was on land that the Indians had already sold to the Swedes. If someone offered you a good price for something no one could own, why not sell? Anyway, here came Stuyvesant wanting earnestly to buy the land again. The headman, while seeming to enjoy the attention, also could see the potential for trouble. There was obviously going to be trouble between the Dutch and the Swedes in which he and his people had no interest in becoming involved. Neither did he want either of them mad at him. With an inspiration worthy of the whole episode, he responded to Stuyvesant's grandeur grandly. He announced that he so valued his newfound friend that he would take nothing for the land. The Dutch could regard it as a gift. If Stuyvesant had somehow managed to use this headman in Hartford as his negotiator, the Dutch might still have owned the wampum works on Long Island.

Whatever his setbacks in dealing with his own colonists, Stuyvesant had achieved as much as he could have hoped with the bordering colonies. He had put New Sweden in its proper place, right next to the abyss; and he had made unavoidable territorial concessions to New England to get recognition of boundaries that would permit New Netherlands to survive.

This was all well and good within its limits. But, of course, there was no reason to believe that the world was going to respect the limits as Stuyvesant wanted to define them. The British, for instance, might still cause trouble from the south. In the late 1620s, King James had permitted a prominent Catholic family, the Calverts, to try their hand at colonizing. They had initially established the colony of Avalon on the island of Newfoundland. Newfoundland had been described in the travel literature as an island paradise, which it turned out to be—in the spring. George Calvert, Lord Baltimore, however, soon learned that it was not always spring in Avalon. He fled to winter on the Chesapeake, and the king had soon granted him the border lands there between Virginia and New Sweden, which Baltimore named Maryland.

Maryland was scarcely without problems in Stuyvesant's day. The Calverts were attacked by extreme Protestants for practicing religious toleration; they seem to have reasoned pragmatically that the only way Catholics would have freedom of worship was if Anglicans and Puritans had it too. Puritans fulminated against this sly popery—and Anglicans in Virginia also complained that Stuart England seemed to prefer this young Rachel over her older and more fruitful sister.

Stuyvesant cared not at all about these rivalries between the British colonies, except to be slightly cheered by them. But he could see that the weakness of the Swedes and Dutch on the Delaware could be regarded as an invitation to Maryland to make the Delaware a three-handed game. This was a remote worry, however, compared to others. No worry was greater than his over the very survival of New Netherlands.

Stuyvesant knew as well as anyone that this survival was ultimately dependent on the place of the Netherlands in the larger world. In the early seventeenth century, when Stuyvesant had decided to enter the colonial service, the position could scarcely have been more promising. The Netherlands and Amsterdam of the early seventeenth century, which had so awed the Pilgrims, was a brave new economic world, apparently unprecedented in European history. The Netherlands, small and unimposing as it was physically, had become the major economic power in Europe without having to develop comparable military strength. It had achieved its preeminence solely through commerce and manufacturing. Others supplied the raw materials; the Dutch transported them by ship to the Netherlands, and there transformed them into finished goods.

As the century moved into its second half, however, the Dutch experiment began to reveal limitations and vulnerabilities. Ironically, this was largely due to the decline of the Spanish threat. The Netherlands, Britain, and France had all successfully resisted the Spanish effort to establish hegemony over them. With Spain in decline, they no longer needed to stand together, and they could pursue their individual interests. In Britain these interests were increasingly being understood as directly opposed to Dutch prosperity, since this prosperity was based on the Dutch ability to fish in other people's waters, both literally and figuratively.

For instance, 20 percent of Dutch workers derived their livelihood from herring fisheries. And nowhere did the Dutch do better fishing for herring than in waters around Great Britain. British patriots had begun to ask why its government was allowing a foreign people to appropriate this precious resource of Great Britain. They also had hard questions to ask about British wool. The Dutch traders would take British wool and half-finished cloth back home, finish it, and then prosper as the chief cloth merchants in all of Europe. Why did not British manufacturers transform British wool into British cloth to the benefit of all Britain? Moreover, Baltic timber, coal, ore, and other raw materials came to Britain primarily on Dutch ships. Why were not British ships, or for that matter Swedish ships, carrying the commerce between the two nations? Why were the Dutch being permitted to interpose their greedy hands? Why was so much British treasure ending up on Dutch laps?

So in 1650 the British government promulgated a Navigation Act, a shrewd attempt to pluck all British feathers from Dutch plumage. The terms of the act were as simple as they were effective. Foreign goods being imported into Britain must arrive on British ships or ships of the country of origin. Moreover, no fish or fish products were to be imported or exported except on British ships. The British were going to be in control of their own trade. If other countries followed suit, the Netherlands would soon return to its fitting role as a backward watery bog.

The Dutch tried to coax the British out of their hostile stance. But the British were adamant, and relations between the two countries deteriorated until in 1652 there was a state of war. War was just what the British leadership wanted. The Dutch economy, and hence the Netherlands itself, depended upon the free passage of its ships through the English Channel, and the Dutch did not have sufficient navy to protect in convoy all of these slow trading vessels. The British navy could simply destroy Dutch shipping at will, without ever venturing very far from the safe haven of British ports. In such a naval war, as the Dutch leaders realized long before it ever began, the Netherlands had everything to lose and nothing to gain. As one leader put it, "The English are about to attack a mountain of gold, but we are about to attack a mountain of iron."

The declaration of war by Britain against the Netherlands was met with jubilation in Connecticut. The Treaty of Hartford could be set aside, and the conquest of New Netherlands begun in earnest. Of course, the populace had to be whipped up. Rumors were spread that the Dutch were conspiring with the Indians to overrun the British colonies. A pamphlet was published with the subtitle "a Faithful Account of a Bloody, Treacherous, and Cruel Plot of the Dutch in America, Purporting the Total Ruin and Murder of all English Colonists in New England." The argument was that the Dutch had done such a thing thirty years before in the East Indies, and therefore were going to do it here, now.

It was necessary to have the American Indians be part of this Dutch plot since the Dutch colony was obviously so weak it could present no serious threat to the British. And certainly the Connecticut settlers still had in their minds a bloody, treacherous, and cruel plot that resulted in murder and total ruin, their plot against the Pequot Indians.

Stuyvesant himself was clearly shaken by the news of likely war. He immediately sent a messenger to Massachusetts, the colony he had always counted on to moderate more aggressive Connecticut. European troubles did not have to be theirs, he insisted. "For my own part I do not only desire but shall unfailingly endeavor that all love, friendship and neighborly compliance may be duly observed betwixt us." As a sign of this, he suggested a treaty against the Indians. For their mutual defense the colonies could present a common front. When a little later he received formal notification of the war declaration from the Netherlands, he wrote again proposing a "loving neutrality." But all he received in response was an accusation that the Dutch were arming hostile Indians against the British settlements.

If that were not bad enough, Stuyvesant also now faced opposition within his own colony from an unexpected source. Throughout his earlier troubles with the colonists, his staunchest supporters had been the English settlers on the Dutch portion of Long Island, who had suspected that liberty for Dutch merchants in New Amsterdam would be liberty to exploit them. So they had written on his behalf to Amsterdam during his struggles with the Nine. He, for his part, had defended their loyalty to the company when it had worried about nursing snakes within the bosom of the Dutch colony.

The snakes then, in gratitude, chose this moment of crisis to present a "Humble Remonstrance and Petition" to request more autonomy for their villages. Officers and magistrates should not be appointed without their consent; neither should Director Stuyvesant issue laws or orders affecting them without submitting said edicts at least to their elected representatives for approval. To do otherwise was to treat them as a conquered and subjugated population.

From Stuyvesant's point of view there could be no stronger argument against democracy than the example of it he saw before him. In such a form of government everyone would seek their own individual interests with no concern for the whole. The thief and the smuggler would buy their own representatives so they could commit their felonies with that much more freedom.

This petition was typical since it attempted to exploit this precarious time for individual gain.

Although there was anger, there was also simple weariness in Stuyvesant's response to the humble remonstrance. He, of course, dismissed the demands, but did nothing against the demanders. For this leniency he eventually found himself being castigated by his superiors. "We think that you should have proceeded rigorously against the ringleaders of this work and not have meddled with it so far as to answer protests with counter-protests and then let it pass without further notice."

As the war progressed in the English Channel with the Dutch taking most of the losses (as earlier in peace they had taken most of the profits), Cromwell made a daring proposal for peace. Cromwell would concede the Dutch a monopoly in East Indian trade if the Dutch would concede the British a monopoly on the Atlantic trade. To show their sincerity, the Dutch were to assist the British for seven years in campaigning against the Spanish in the West Indies. The proposal was daring, and preposterous. Dutch trade needed peace; it did not need a peace that entailed another war.

Cromwell, apparently miffed at the rejection of his bright idea, decided to proceed on his own to consolidate Atlantic trade in British hands. The first step would be the seizure of the New Netherlands. An expedition left England for the New World in the spring of 1654; but before it could get the necessary troops from New England and begin its mission of extirpating the Dutch from North America, the Dutch sued for peace in Europe.

That peace was a relief, but no cause for joy in New Amsterdam. Stuyvesant had no illusions about the weakness of his colony in comparison with his British neighbors to the north. He also had no illusions about these neighbors themselves. These second-generation Puritans had shown themselves, repeatedly, to be masters of the sanctified lie. Without support from Europe, the Treaty of Hartford was worthless, except as marking a temporary pause in British aggression. All that he knew. What he had not known, and what must have come as a stunning revelation to him and many of his Dutch contemporaries, was how weak the Netherlands was in the European game of power. Its economic empire was vulnerable to any determined naval challenge. Cromwell, moreover, had sensed the position to which the Dutch might have to retreat to preserve any of their maritime empire—namely, to concede the New World in order to preserve a position in the East India trade.

Stuyvesant's whole career, it seemed, and those of many others, had been based on a miscalculation. They had seen Dutch economic power stretching further and further out into the non-European world. They thought the next region to be yoked to Dutch prosperity would be the New World. They had not realized that Dutch power would prove ephemeral, and had already reached its zenith. The New World, once the most promising theater for Dutch expansion, now was its most vulnerable and expendable outpost. The Dutch imperial enterprise in the New World had started to wind down almost before it had truly begun. Those, like Stuyvesant, who had committed their lives to it had been given by the recent war a glimpse at an unwanted future; far from being lords in this New World, they were probably going to be left behind in a Dutch retreat, to peck for carrion in order to survive.

The irony was that this same war had also saved Stuyvesant's career. Van der Donck had returned to the Netherlands, and had doggedly persisted for two and a half years in prosecuting the claims of the Nine against Stuyvesant's administration. He finally won the case, and an order was issued for Stuyvesant's recall. Then came for him villainous luck: The war between the Netherlands and Great Britain was begun. The recall of Stuyvesant was itself recalled, for war was no time to remove a strong leader of a vulnerable colony. In fact, war made Stuyvesant's autocratic tendencies look like virtues. So Stuyvesant, whatever his long-term pessimism, could take satisfaction in the fact that the war had inadvertently defeated his ablest adversary. Van der Donck would return to New Netherlands with nothing to show for five years of struggle against Stuyvesant except a broken spirit; he would die in 1655, at the age of thirty-five.

That other adversary of Stuyvesant, Johan Printz, the governor of New Sweden, was despairing as well. He had not had any supplies, reinforcements, or even instructions from Sweden since 1647. He had asked to be relieved, but had received only silence for a reply. Finally in 1653 he tired of waiting. He, his family, and twenty-five disillusioned settlers set sail for Sweden.

The joke was on him. Just at this moment Queen Christina of Sweden had authorized the very relief expedition for which he had so long pleaded, an expedition of three hundred colonists with ample supplies. Moreover, its leader, Johan Rising, had explicit instructions that he was to attempt to seize control of Delaware from the Dutch by any means short of open war. One would like to think that when Printz learned of all this upon returning to Sweden he had a good hearty laugh. However, from what we know of his temperament, it is more likely that he turned purple and then systematically destroyed every object smaller than himself that was within reach, including perhaps the newsbearer.

The sea quickly took care of whatever enthusiasm Rising brought to his task. The crossing was particularly ghastly. One third of the colonists were lost to disease. A survivor wrote, "The person who cannot pray to God, let him be sent on such a long and dangerous voyage and he shall surely learn to pray." He would also learn how frequently prayers were answered in the negative.

The expedition finally reached the first Swedish fort up the Delaware, only to find it deserted. And the fort offered them relief not at all, for immense clouds of mosquitoes made the fort unendurable. The colonists who had survived the crossing now became so swollen with bites and stings that they appeared to be suffering from some horrible plague. All that Rising could do was allow his colonists to change the name of Fort Elfsborg to Fort Myggenborgh, Fort Mosquito—and then permit them to leave the place to its new namesakes.

The next fort the expedition reached was Stuyvesant's Fort Casimir. The Dutch sent out a greeting party, and Rising responded with great show of friendship by giving them a party on his ship. He offered them entertainment for the entire evening, much of it liquid. Late in the evening, but early enough that most of his guests still had their speech, Rising, just by way of conversation, made inquiries about the Dutch fort. Perhaps he had held forth on the dilapidated condition of Fort Mosquito, and listened in sympathy while the Dutch soldiers explained that theirs was little better. With all the troubles to the north, their fort had been allowed to fall into disrepair; there were only nine soldiers left to hold it; and they had virtually run out of powder. As the Dutch soldiers were pushing off after the shipboard party, Rising asked for a slight favor from the commander of his new friends. Would he please surrender the fort forthwith, without a fight?

Of course, Rising himself could not fight without violating his explicit instructions. Of course, his own company had been severely weakened by the crossing and the stay with the mosquitoes. But sometimes a pair of deuces is enough to win a hand. The Dutch commander, once he realized what his voluble soldiers had told the Swede, surrendered without even the pretence of resistance. Rising, despite all the difficulties his expedition had endured up to now, must have found it hard to believe his luck. What he had neglected to consider was that he was going to have to play the rest of the game with this same pair of deuces.

Perhaps he hoped his own position would be strengthened when he made contact with the Swedish forts farther upriver. If so, he was severely disappointed. This territory he found was an "empty country, partly disturbed by despondency, partly by mutiny and desertion." So Rising had written on July 13, 1654. On July 16, 1654, Stuyvesant received formal notice that peace had been reached between the Netherlands and Britain. This freed him to attend to the Delaware. Rising's leadership of New Sweden was to be short lived.

Rising was nothing if not jaunty. Once he had taken Fort Casimir, he had blithely written to Stuyvesant as if to thank him for the gift. He noted that the fort had been voluntarily surrendered without a shot being fired, like a transfer between friends. He certainly regarded New Netherlands as his friend and ally, much as Sweden and the Netherlands were friends and allies in Europe. The whole episode he tried to present as a *fait accompli*, hardly worth the notice.

Stuyvesant noticed. He had also noticed, during the expedition that established Fort Casimir, how easy a conquest of New Sweden would be. And then he would no longer have to worry about his southern flank. When you faced a British lion, you did not need to be vexed by Swedish mosquitoes biting your behind. Rising had made things even easier. Stuyvesant had only to report this open act of Swedish aggression. The order from Amsterdam was immediately returned: Retake Fort Casimir and then drive the Swedes from the Delaware "as they did us." This was the kind of "do unto others" that Peter Stuyvesant understood. His invasion force was between seven and eight hundred men carried by seven ships, all seven armed.

The attack did not start until the summer of 1655. This gave the Dutch time to provide armaments, notably the warship *Wagh* (*The Scales*) with thirty-five cannon on board to help tip the balance of justice in the Dutch direction. The delay also gave the Swedish government time to reinforce Rising, which it did not. Sweden was entering into war against Poland, for reasons no one on the Delaware (and, to be frank, few people in Europe) could comprehend. But one consequence was plain enough: New Sweden would have to fend for itself.

Rising had divided his forces between Fort Casimir and Fort Christina farther up the river, and positioned himself at Fort Christina. He seems to have thought that a truce might still be worked out between him and Stuyvesant. He might have to give back Fort Casimir. On the other hand, Stuyvesant, faced with a long siege, might be willing to compromise. None of this was unreasonable; it just all turned out to be wrong.

As Stuyvesant sailed past Fort Mosquito (now with a handful of soldiers to hold it), he cannoned the banks of the river, just to make certain they did not give in to heroic impulses and decide to try to annoy the stately procession of his fleet. They did not; they sat quietly in their prudence, swatting insects.

When Fort Casimir was reached, Stuyvesant sailed past until out of range of its guns. Stuyvesant had built this fort. He knew that its effective defenses faced the river; so he landed his forces and approached it from land. Once in position, he demanded immediate surrender. The commander asked permission to consult by messenger with Rising in Fort Christina; permission denied. Stuyvesant had already placed troops on the route to Christina; and a relief party from there had been intercepted and captured. The commander was once again invited to avoid bloodshed and other grief by surrendering the Dutch fort that he now occupied. The next morning the Swedish commander proposed to transfer the fort to Dutch control on the condition that he and his troops be allowed to leave it with full military honors; proposal accepted.

After the fort had been effectively transferred to Dutch control, Stuyvesant innocently inquired where the Swedish commander now intended to go. He replied that he intended to lead his troops to Fort Christina. Then Stuyvesant graciously pointed out to his brother officer that the articles of surrender just signed did not stipulate the right of the Swedish forces to retire wherever they pleased. Full military honors did not entail complete freedom of movement. And it did not please Peter Stuyvesant that they should retire to Fort Christina, because that happened to be the next stop on his own itinerary. So Rising faced the full Dutch invasion force without the forces from Fort Casimir and further weakened by the loss of the relief column he had just sent there.

Rising, nonetheless, refused to capitulate. Stuyvesant in response busied himself with destroying any Swedish homesteads nearby, while he waited for the Swedish provisions to run out. That was enough for Rising, and he folded his hand. Unknown to Rising, Stuyvesant had just received word of an Indian uprising back near New Amsterdam. If Rising had held out just a little longer, Stuyvesant would have had to withdraw. Now that Rising had surrendered, Stuyvesant was going to have to withdraw anyway. Stuyvesant's own hand was busted, so he made Rising an astonishing proposition.

He offered him Fort Christina back. Rising had only to agree to a permanent alliance between the two colonies, an alliance that would respect Dutch rights to Fort Casimir. Rising and his men, however, had seen enough to develop a mortal aversion to frontier life. They voted unanimously to make Stuyvesant keep the terms of their surrender, and send them back to Sweden. They had found an honorable exit to this emptiness broken only by despondency, mutiny, and desertion. On reflection, they counted themselves lucky to be out of the game. You've got to know when to fold for good. So ended what Diedrich Knickerbocker, the perfect historian for this episode, called "the most horrible battle ever recorded in poetry or prose."

With the southern boundaries now ridiculously secured, Stuyvesant could hope to address the more difficult threat from the north, a glummer task. The

West India Company hoped that the peace negotiations between Great Britain and the Netherlands would result in a formal ratification of the Treaty of Hartford by both governments. There were unmistakable signs that this was not going to be nearly as easy as they thought, for the British knew who had won the war and seemed to be strongly of the opinion that this ugly fact should figure prominently in the negotiations. This was very crude of them, but there it was.

A London pamphlet of 1656 reviewed what it called "English Rights to the Northern Parts of North America," and it concluded forthrightly that the Hudson and Delaware had been illegally seized by the Dutch. In 1657 a letter to all English settlers on Long Island was intercepted by the Dutch authorities; it exhorted them to rise up against Dutch tyranny. In 1659 Boston merchants claimed that the Massachusetts charter entitled them to establish trading posts on the Hudson, and had the gall to request free passage from New Amsterdam so that they could do so. The omens on the Hudson were all bad.

West India Company officials in Amsterdam could delude themselves about a new era of good feelings between Britain and the Netherlands. Peter Stuyvesant had to deal with more concrete realities, such as a Boston ship impudently trying to bluff its way past Manhattan so that it could establish a post that would cut off a large portion of the trade on which Manhattan depended for its economic survival. To permit this would be to allow the Hudson to go the way that the Connecticut already had. Stuyvesant told the offending ship that he was as likely to permit free trade on the Hudson as the British were to permit it up the Thames. The ship could withdraw or be seized.

Despite the continual testing of the Dutch resolve in North America, the West India Company thought it had good grounds for hoping that a final accommodation would be reached. These derived from changes in the British government itself. Oliver Cromwell, the Puritan dictator, died in 1658. After an uneasy period of transition, Charles was invited back to England as its restored monarch.

Cromwell the ardent Puritan should have been the friend of the Dutch who stood with him against Spain. But economics and politics had taken precedence over religious solidarity. Anyway, the easygoing toleration practiced by the Dutch did not look like Protestantism to Puritans. Now the Dutch, especially those in North America, could look to Charles as a possible friend. The West India Company reasoned that my enemy's enemy is my friend.

The colonies of New England, whatever the reservations of a careful leader like John Winthrop, had been firmly on the Puritan side of the English civil war. It had even provided a political schooling for some of its prominent leaders, such as Henry Vane. With the Restoration these same men became public enemies; Vane, for instance, was himself executed for his role in the execution of Charles I. When Charles II looked to the New World, therefore, he saw New England as a place where his authority needed to be established. Only the meek Pilgrims of Plymouth had unequivocally recognized his restoration as monarch. Two of the regicides Charles wanted executed were thought to be hiding somewhere in Massachusetts or Connecticut, and the local authorities were being far from completely candid or cooperative in responding to royal demands that they be given up.

The West India Company judged that in Charles they had the best possible audience for their complaints about the unjust usurpation of Dutch territory by these rapacious Puritans. So confident were they of his sympathy, they even suggested to his representatives that the Treaty of Hartford was unjust. (They had read it by now, with considerable displeasure.) Their weak governor Peter Stuyvesant had allowed portions of Connecticut and Long Island to be bargained away. Fortunately, neither the Dutch nor British government had formally confirmed this treaty, so that Charles in friendship and generosity might choose to restore to the Netherlands territory taken away from their colony by his British enemies.

Stuyvesant did not share their purblind optimism. Whatever the professions of friendship of the new British king for the Netherlands, there were deeper forces at work here, against which friendship weighed like a feather. The rule of history was that the strong do what they will, the weak what they must. In North America Britain was strong, the Netherlands weak. To think that boundaries would be set as if the Netherlands were dictating the terms was mindless idiocy. Even to think that they would be set as if between equals was folly. New Netherlands should enjoy the peaceful lull and prepare for the worst.

The lull was short. The Netherlands soon learned that the vulture Cromwell may have died but he had been replaced by a ravenous old raven. Charles intended to establish firm central control over his colonies. Crucial to this for him was enforcement of the navigation acts that gave Britain absolute priority in trade with its colonies. Such enforcement was made extremely difficult, if not outright impossible, by the existence of a Dutch colony right in the midst of an otherwise continuous British coastline.

Stuyvesant realized the problem, if his superiors in Amsterdam did not yet.

He might have taken some wan pleasure when, only two years after the Restoration, Charles took unmistakable steps against New Netherlands. He might have if he had not ample reason to accuse himself for having been insultingly, shamefully, disgracefully deceived by the sanctimonious Puritans. How could he have forgotten that a face that smiles when there is no occasion and a tongue out of measure smooth are infallible evidence for insincerity of purpose?

Stuyvesant knew he needed a friend in Connecticut, and he thought he had found one in John Winthrop Jr., son of the founder of Massachusetts and himself still governor of Connecticut. Winthrop's problem was that New Haven refused to acknowledge his authority and behaved as if an autonomous colony. He needed to slip back to Britain as soon as possible to get a charter confirmed by the new monarch, a charter that would put New Haven squarely under Governor Winthrop's thumb.

Stuyvesant seized on this as an opportunity to establish a bond with Winthrop. He arranged passage for Winthrop and entertained him royally during his brief stay in New Amsterdam. It had all seemed so promising. Only too late had Stuyvesant realized how much more full of danger was an enemy who could beguile under the cover of friendship. That was what Winthrop had been doing during his stay with Stuyvesant, feigning friendship and milking hopes, all taffeta phrases and silken tones, while planning to serve up a most delicious poison. Amidst all his soft words, there was a hidden pair of fangs.

Winthrop got his charter in London. Who could doubt that he would? The man could prevaricate his way out of his own skin. And he did get official control over New Haven. But that was not all that he got with his huckster's patter. He had gotten King Charles to grant Connecticut all the North American coastlands from the Connecticut to the Delaware. On paper at least, the governor of Connecticut with that signature had become the most important British official in the New World, and Peter Stuyvesant had become his subject.

Connecticut responded with characteristic energy to the news. Captain John Young was immediately dispatched to the English towns on Long Island that were still under Dutch control (as confirmed by the Treaty of Hartford). He delivered letters advising the towns that they were now under Connecticut control, and were obligated as loyal Englishmen to obey the directives of their king. Stuyvesant, of course, protested to Hartford; the reply he received was worse than even he could have anticipated.

New Netherlands? The officials at Hartford knew of no such colony.

Would Mr. Stuyvesant be so good as to acquaint them with this new colony so that they can be sure it was not a figment of his imagination? A charter or patent from the British king would be sufficient to establish it as a reality in Connecticut eyes.

Stuyvesant wrote to his superiors in Amsterdam pleading with them to recognize the danger. Boston had already made specious claims on the Hudson, and now Connecticut, not satisfied with swallowing Dutch land on their own river and Long Island, was claiming the whole coast to Delaware. If Amsterdam did not act quickly, they would find that New Netherlands had become a figment of *their* imagination because not a square foot of land would be left to the colony. Couldn't they see that the colony was being slowly dismembered for the crime of being led from Amsterdam by the gullible and irresolute?

He might as well have tried to make his case to a bevy of quail whistling in the meadow. Amsterdam chose to regard all this as a simple misunderstanding. Sometimes the left hand does not know what the right hand is doing. When coherence was achieved in British policy, Stuyvesant would find his fretting had been needless. And Stuyvesant should stop being so irascible. He need only approach the Connecticut governor in the right spirit and certainly an acceptable accommodation would be reached. John Winthrop was his name, wasn't it? A most estimable fellow.

Stuyvesant could almost wish that the life of New Netherlands was over. Certainly, there was no point in replying to blatant inanities. Good lord, what a job it was to be a servant to superiors enveloped in a waking dream. He might give them the best possible advice, but if they chose to act otherwise, he was forced to share responsibility for the subsequent calamity. All he could hope was that Connecticut would soon show its intentions so clearly they could be seen three thousand miles away. Approach Winthrop with the right spirit! The right spirit in this case would be a bodyguard and a drawn sword. He could at least count on Connecticut not being sly in pressing its advantage soon. He could count on Connecticut at least for that.

In 1663, not content with stirring up trouble on Long Island, Connecticut started to move toward the Hudson. The town of Westchester, clearly given to the Dutch by the Treaty of Hartford, was blithely annexed by Hartford. This was Stuyvesant's chance to bring matters to a resolution, not in North America but in Amsterdam. He immediately traveled to Boston to present his grievances before the collected representatives of New England, including his dear friend John Winthrop Jr.

Stuyvesant began by simply asking for a clarification. Was the Treaty of

Hartford still in effect or not? Rather than respond with a simple answer to a simple question, the representatives initially decided that, since Stuyvesant's quarrel was with Hartford, the Connecticut representatives should respond and the rest remain silent. For their part, Winthrop and the other representatives from his colony were deeply grieved that they did not feel able to respond either. They had been given insufficient notice of Stuyvesant's unexpected complaints, and hence had not received explicit instructions on how to respond to questions about the Treaty of Hartford. And they did not want to go beyond their commissions. They knew that Stuyvesant would understand. (Veins starting to protrude from his forehead likely showed he understood quite well.) There was going to be another meeting next year in Hartford. Perhaps if Stuyvesant would be so good as to attend that meeting there would be time to instruct the representatives properly.

Of course, both Stuyvesant and Winthrop knew that the treaty was no longer in force, if it ever had been. Connecticut's new charter and subsequent intrusion could not have made this more obvious. Nonetheless, if Stuyvesant for his purposes somehow needed a simple "no" to his question, then Winthrop for his own would try to delay as long as possible before obliging.

Stuyvesant, it must be said, kept his composure. He was going to play out this scene without shouting. After all, if he did tell Winthrop what he thought of him and what he would like to do to him (slowly), he would have to sit there and listen while Winthrop declared himself the most unhappy innocent person ever accused of his own goodness. Then he most assuredly would lose his temper.

To continue talking with Winthrop was pointless. Stuyvesant may have thought he could find some common ground, as he had so often in the past, with Massachusetts. Its leaders could scarcely be happy at the move by slimy Winthrop to make Connecticut the most powerful colony in New England. He turned to plead with the Massachusetts representatives, but their worried looks made it plain that they were preoccupied with their own problems. They had a suspicious, even hostile king to deal with.

Asked about the Treaty of Hartford and forced to reply by Stuyvesant's persistence, the Massachusetts representatives walked around the question at a distance as if it were an infectious disease. They finally settled on a response that pleased them, since it meant they never really had to touch the question with an answer. They said that the treaty was binding on the British colonies except insofar as it conflicted with their heartfelt performance of their duties to their new king. That seemed to mean that the treaty was binding except when it wasn't. Apparently Massachusetts, so recently filling the air with huzzahs for regicide, now was going to use every occasion to show that it still remembered all the words to "God Save the King."

The representatives of Plymouth colony did try to mediate for Stuyvesant. They seemed still to remember fondly the safe haven the Dutch had provided the Pilgrims before they finally emigrated to the New World. But New Netherlands had no need of powerless friends, and Plymouth was no longer of any consequence in the politics of New England. It would itself soon be absorbed into Massachusetts as quietly as New Haven had been into Connecticut. In this increasingly predatory colonial world, the autonomy of Plymouth was a quaint anachronism that could be dispensed with at the earliest convenient moment. Its representatives could indulge themselves in earnest respect for Dutch territorial rights because these rights were as paper-thin as the integrity of Plymouth itself.

Stuyvesant was nothing if not persistent. He realized that the responses he had gotten from Connecticut and Massachusetts were empty, plausible words without the marrow of truth; the efforts of Plymouth only underlined the naught. As he would write back to Amsterdam, he knew Winthrop's invitation to come to Hartford the next year "as clear as the sun that shines at noon to be but frivolous." He also realized ruefully the sun shone very infrequently in the lowland minds running the West India Company. (Perhaps the imbeciles were thinking with their broad Dutch bottoms.) So he took one final step to do his best to clear any remaining possible clouds.

Obsequiously, he offered to the New England representatives a series of agreements that could not possibly be controversial: a mutual defense pact, for instance, against hostile Indians. Who could be against that? The answer to that question of course was, as he well knew, anyone who questioned the right of New Netherlands to exist. Such a person would want to avoid making any agreements with Stuyvesant, no matter how beneficial, because to do so might be interpreted as acknowledging this right. So his proposals, once again, were politely postponed for consideration until next year, or a week after doomsday, whichever came later.

Returning from Boston empty-handed, he should have felt he had done enough to convince even the slowest of slow learners in Amsterdam that the very existence of his colony was at risk. However, he knew that his superiors frequently exceeded his most pessimistic estimates. He could almost hear them wondering why he had not followed up good John Winthrop's friendly suggestion to come to Hartford to negotiate next year.

He was past wasting his own time on such a fool's errand, but the next year he did send three representatives with the meekest of new proposals. He would temporarily cede to Connecticut the town of Westchester until the matter could be settled in Europe. This one town should not be allowed to disturb the long history of friendship between Connecticut and New Netherlands, and the personal bond between Winthrop and Stuyvesant that had so enriched both their lives. All that Stuyvesant asked in return was that Hartford agree to leave alone the Dutch portion of Long Island.

Winthrop could not have been more pleased at the opportunity to entertain the representatives of so esteemed a friend as Peter Stuyvesant. Nor could he have been happier with the proposal of that august leader. These were the kinds of initiatives that could assure that this new world of ours would be free from all the rivalries and pettiness of the old. Winthrop could not say how much he regretted that a few unavoidable technicalities prevented Hartford from acting on this initiative immediately. But perhaps in a little while . . .

For their trouble, the representatives got to bring back the message in a letter addressed to "Peter Stuyvesant, director general at Manhattan." Well, at least Connecticut had decided who Stuyvesant was. He was a director general (of somewhere unspecified) who happened to be living for the moment on the island of Manhattan. Winthrop's way of expressing friendship was passing strange.

Finally Stuyvesant could write to his superiors concerning all his efforts to achieve an understanding with New England, efforts which had obviously come to absolutely nothing (unless the accumulation of slights and insults was counted as something). With sarcastic exasperation, Stuyvesant pointed out that you did not have to be the oracle of Delphi to foretell the future: "Bloodshed, and with bloodshed—which they only seem to wish—the loss of all we possess."

If Amsterdam still doubted this, they had only to attend to recent British activity. Stuyvesant—wearily, oh so wearily—had to remind his superiors that, if the British were allowed to filch Long Island, New Amsterdam and the rest of the colony would likely fall, or at best be rendered worthless.

The instigator of the new troubles on Long Island was an opportunist named John Scott. Scott had judged that Long Island was soon to become British, and that whoever got himself out in front of this inevitability would make his own fortune.

Scott had actually gone to London about the same time as Winthrop. He had tried to get a new and separate charter for Long Island, only to be outmaneuvered by the better-connected and more dexterous Connecticut governor. With nothing to lose, Scott had hung around after Winthrop left with his new charter; in doing so, Scott discovered something that made Winthrop's victory far less secure than it seemed, but that made Stuyvesant's defeat even more likely.

Charles's brother, James Duke of York and Albany, was casting around for some great military adventure to underwrite. He had settled on action against the Netherlands, in particular the conquest of New Netherlands. Moreover, the king had belatedly promised him this colony as his very own. In light of this, the recent Connecticut charter was worth little more than the Treaty of Hartford. Scott, learning this at court, resolved to return to North America to be John the Baptist to this new dispensation.

He returned to Long Island by way of Connecticut. During his stopover he could not resist having a little fun at the expense of his rivals. He ostentatiously mended fences with Governor Winthrop by telling him news from the court, all the news except the most important. Winthrop was so impressed that he had Scott appointed a Connecticut magistrate for Long Island. In receiving the appointment, Scott must have had difficulty not laughing. The duplicity was scrumptious, worthy of Winthrop himself.

When Scott arrived in Long Island, he quickly gathered about himself a troop of 170 men, and declared the island an independent colony, loyal only to King Charles and his brother the Duke of York. Until the duke personally took charge of his colony, Scott would rule on his behalf. He then toured the Dutch towns of his realm, and sent a letter to Peter Stuyvesant, "governor of the Dutch on Manhattan," to explain to him the situation.

The perplexed Stuyvesant had finally found a British leader eager to negotiate with him, albeit one he'd never heard of before. Scott wanted to be recognized formally for what he had become. And Stuyvesant wanted to negotiate with Scott—or so he said. He, however, just could not spare the time to meet outside Manhattan. He bid Scott come to New Amsterdam to enjoy his Dutch hospitality. Scott realized perfectly well that this Dutch hospitality would include a room with a view obscured by bars, and that the only negotiations would be between his neck and a rope, and he couldn't imagine his neck getting any satisfactory concessions from the rope. So Scott contented himself with marching around Long Island threatening, as was reported back to Stuyvesant, to "stick my rapier in the guts of any man who says this is not the King's land."

Stuyvesant for his part did not know what to make of Scott. To be born a fool is a disease incurable, but no one could be so stupid to undertake such an uprising entirely on his own authority. (As was said, Stuyvesant did not know Scott.) Stuyvesant reasoned that Scott must have private assurances from Winthrop at the least. In fact, this was just the kind of spidery trap one should expect from Winthrop. Stuyvesant takes any action against Scott, and Winthrop uses this as an excuse to conquer Long Island, ostensibly to protect the innocent British settlers there.

Stuyvesant in the end sent emissaries to Scott to propose a settlement so he could put his rapier away. There would be a year-long truce during which Scott would be granted *de facto* control of all predominantly British towns, including some specifically guaranteed to the Dutch in the Treaty of Hartford. Scott, in return, would respect the integrity of the Dutch towns that would be governed from New Amsterdam. During the truce, a settlement of the dispute could be reached by the representatives of the two national governments. (Or at least the idiots at the West India Company would finally realize that Stuyvesant needed substantial reinforcements if he was not to end up governor of the island of Manhattan only.)

Scott then made the mistake of repairing to Hartford to enjoy his victory. He there discovered to his sorrow that John Winthrop did not take kindly to those who did unto him as he did unto others. Scott was promptly arrested for "heinous crimes and practices seditious." After all, Scott had usurped Connecticut's legal sovereignty over Long Island and had thereby violated King Charles's charter. On the other hand, Winthrop was quite happy to accept Stuyvesant's gracious concessions on Long Island, as if they had been made to him. With Scott safely in chains at Hartford, Winthrop traveled to the new Connecticut towns on Long Island and installed officials loyal to the governor of Connecticut—and offered the point of *his* rapier to any Scott loyalists who felt inclined to complain. None did.

Of course, Stuyvesant protested. But even he must have felt himself to be acting out a role for the sake of form. It was a role he once had relished; but now that it had become detached from the substance of any real power, it was a role that any man would have found a tiresome charade, all wind and smoke. At least it was a charade that could not last for much longer. At least the troublesome fool Scott was being reasoned with by irons; Stuyvesant only regretted they were not Dutch irons.

In March 1664, King Charles formally granted his brother James not only Long Island but all the Hudson and Delaware valleys as well. James then quickly organized an expedition under Colonel Richard Nicolls to seize what was now rightfully his.

Early in July Stuyvesant received intelligence that an invasion fleet had arrived in Boston, to pick up supplies and more men on its way to New Netherlands. While Stuyvesant was preparing the defenses of New Amsterdam for the attack, he received a letter from the West India Company with its usual cheerful interpretation of baleful events. The arrival of the fleet in Boston, Stuyvesant would be happy to learn, was really good news. Charles was at last going to bring the unruly Puritan colonies to heel. Stuyvesant could start dusting off his copy of the Treaty of Hartford, for the boundary questions were soon to be settled once and for all, and to the advantage of the Dutch.

Stuyvesant, who also expected that the boundary questions were soon to be settled once and for all, replied with tact concealing rage. He will not discuss, much less contradict, the interpretation offered by the company of the newly posted British fleet. (To discuss it at all would be to contradict it.) He prays that it is correct. (Prayers alone could save the colony now.) He will only communicate what on the best intelligence are the plans of the fleet, as he is warned daily, both orally and in writing, from the most reliable sources. (They are going to conquer us!)

There was an air of resignation to Stuyvesant's letter. He had been anticipating the worst for so long now. New Netherlands should have fallen so long ago. Yet it still survived. Perhaps there was a deeper logic here that Stuyvesant did not understand, or perhaps logic had nothing to do with history, even in the long run. It was all a roll of the dice, and flukes could carry the day. Perhaps you really could set clouds to catch the wind.

History is a prankster, and it was now determined to have a little more fun with Pete Stuyvesant, as if it hadn't already had enough. So first it gave him tangible hope. He received a message from his best spy in New England, the one who had been first to warn him of the invasion. Everything had changed; the invasion had been called off. Stuyvesant, who had prepared himself for furious action, now acted anyway; he hurried off to Fort Orange, soon to be renamed Albany, to settle an Indian dispute there.

Near the end of August 1664 he arrived back in New Amsterdam, soon to be New York. Everything now had changed back. The invasion fleet was on its way to New Amsterdam, and in fact was sighted from Dutch territory the very next day.

Stuyvesant's situation was hopeless, but he still knew how to play out a losing hand. Nothing could help now but forthright impudence. He sent a messenger challenging Nicolls to declare his intentions. Nicolls responded bluntly: He wanted the surrender of all Manhattan. If it was forthcoming, he would guarantee every citizen of the Dutch colony his life, his security, and his wealth. This was followed by a letter from Winthrop exhorting Stuyvesant to avoid bloodshed by submitting to the inevitable; Winthrop pleaded with him on the basis of their long-standing friendship to behave sensibly.

There was some consolation in being reminded of the duplicitous Winthrop at this point. Stuyvesant might be losing everything, but Winthrop and Connecticut were not winning. The successor to New Netherlands, with the support of the king's brother, would be more than the equal of upstart Connecticut. The Connecticut snake was not to grow fat on swallowing New Netherlands whole. Of course, Winthrop unfortunately was smart enough not to fight against the inevitable. Still, there was some satisfaction to be gained from imagining Winthrop's private disappointment.

Stuyvesant tried to keep the letters from Nicolls and Winthrop secret because he knew the moment the merchants of New Amsterdam realized that their property was safe they would immediately become in their hearts the loyal subjects of the Duke of York. He made a blustery show of eagerness to engage the enemy. At one point, when he was being pressed to release the terms offered, he tore up the letter, and according to one account tried to eat it. He postured that he would be carried out of New Amsterdam in his coffin rather than be the one who surrendered her. It was all high drama, his last good scene—and perhaps he really believed it. The performance was unquestionably convincing. The leading citizens, terrified by his histrionics, now meekly prostrated themselves before him in supplication, as he had always wanted them to. "We, your sorrowful community and subjects, beg to represent, with all humility, that we cannot conscientiously foresee that anything else is to be expected for this fort and city of Manhattan (as your Honor must be convinced) than misery, sorrow, conflagration, the dishonor of women, murder of children in their cradles, and, in a word, the absolute ruin and destruction of about fifteen hundred innocent souls, only two hundred and fifty of whom are capable of bearing arms, unless you will be pleased to adjust matters according to the conjuncture of the time."

This was a triumph of sorts for Stuyvesant. They actually seemed to believe that he could, single-handedly, right at the end of the last act, somehow transform Gilbert and Sullivan into Wagner. This was a delectable morsel for his memory.

Oh, by the way, talks for surrender began in earnest the very next day. When they were finished, and they were quickly, Hard-headed Pete Stuyvesant sailed for the Netherlands, in disgrace.

Chapter VII

BACON'S VIRGINIA

THE FALL OF HURONIA was tragedy, the fall of New Netherlands farce; taken in sequence, they pointed toward a descent from hope into darkness and the grotesque.

The New World had failed to provide a refuge from the absurdities of history. By stripping away some traditional inhibitions, it had only revealed these absurdities more nakedly. Who could have thought that the meek Pilgrims, whatever the exigencies, would have turned to massacre? Had Bradford's wife been given a vision of all this before she threw herself over the side of the *Mayflower?*

No escape was left except hers. It was no use in seeking a newer, still-pristine place; to go farther west, or north, or south would be only to replicate what had already happened here: the same contagions, the same results, a dark and bloody ground.

Needed was a new vision, not a new place—or at least an old vision newly understood, a saving vision to help preserve seekers after a new world from bitterness and disgust. But a new vision was what few, if any, European colonists were looking for. They looked for land, for fields to plant and forests to fell, for the game that hid in these forests and the fish and beaver that crowded the waters; even for valuable ores lying quietly within the mountains. For all this they looked, and more—but not for a new understanding of themselves or of their world.

Yet there was such a vision for them to find here. The very hardness of this place, its steadfast resistance to individual desire, could on rare occasions do wondrous things to a human soul, drawing from it hidden, previously unknown seeds of fire that, as they escaped, would momentarily illumine the world in an unearthly light. All would then be, for that precious moment in which time stopped, clear and simple and right, a joy.

About the time the Europeans were first imagining colonies along the North American coast, about the time Philip the Prudent was dreaming imprudently of a Europe united under the Spanish crown, such a vision was granted to an obscure North American named Deganawida. But do not expect to learn much for certain about him or it. The story of Deganawida and his vision survives for us not as history but as myth. His life has been absorbed into his vision and is now no longer separable from it (if it ever was). Even as myth it is garbled, surviving in disparate versions and conflicting interpretations. The epistemologically fastidious among us will insist that it is impossible to disengage from this myth a single incontestable particle of truth. To learn of Deganawida we must therefore retell his story for ourselves, and hope that his spirit will somehow guide our lips.

Deganawida was the child of an outcast Huron woman. She had no men left in her family to protect her, and she had lost any chance for a husband by becoming pregnant without marriage. Her own mother, or perhaps her adopted mother, now turned against her, and beat her unmercifully. When the baby was finally born, the grandmother tried to kill it by throwing it through the ice of a frozen lake. But the baby Deganawida survived the ordeal, and his now-frightened grandmother realized that the powers protecting him were too great for her. She still despised him and his mother, but did nothing against them anymore.

So the mother and child were left entirely alone, without any family or clan to help them, ostracized to the edge of their village—outcasts really, their only human sustenance one another. Despite the hardships, Deganawida grew to be a comely man, tall and strong, who nonetheless was ridiculed as soon as he spoke, for he had an uncontrollable stammer. The torture of saying his own name was enough to make him prefer silence and solitude, or the company of his mother with whom no speech was necessary.

Without friends, Deganawida had much time for brooding thoughts little different from daydreams. He would for hours on end give his mind free play, letting it wander wherever it would in search of pleasing things. But his mind, however free he made it, would always return to images of families—large and boisterous families, husbands and wives, many of them, living together, per-haps the wives all sisters, lots of children, sons and daughters all playing, and loving elders, grandparents and uncles and aunts. All human beings should be united into a single great family from which no one would be excluded. He turned this idea over and over in his mind, like a pebble gradually being made smooth and shiny by a stream. Finally all that he thought and felt was contained for him in a single lapidary phrase: The Sisterhood of Humanity. Not brotherhood, for brothers came together in war. Tradition taught that war was the province of the man, the family the province of the woman. If tradition was right—and who should not respect it?—then let there be a single sisterhood of all humanity, encompassing all tribes and all divisions in one motherly embrace. Then the whole world might become a single longhouse, a great fireside around which we could all find a place warm and near the light, in peace and contentment and unspoken acceptance. Then the land itself would become attentive to our needs and the waters would have no more waves, and you could go anywhere without fear. And men would not have to learn war anymore.

These were his private, obsessive broodings, which he preferred to the world around him. These were the sustenance of his solitude. Into these placid mists of pure contemplation he would also escape, when villagers would mockingly stutter out his name ("de-de-de-degagaganaweeeeeda") as he walked through the village, oblivious and smiling, like an idiot. Best of all, his broodings were pure sustenance for him, and made no demands upon him. Until, that is, he had his vision.

He saw a tree, a fir tree it was, suddenly begin to grow up out of the ground near him; a silver-tipped spruce it seemed to be, but no spruce had ever grown so quickly, so magnificently. Soon it had reached the heavens, brushing the cheeks of both our elderly brother the sun and our silent great-grandmother the moon. The branches too stretched out as no branches had ever before, out to the horizon and beyond.

Deganawida knew he was standing at the base of the great tree, so close he could reach out and finger the roughness of its bark. However extraordinary, this was a real tree. He was at its base, and yet he could also somehow see its crest as if it too were next to him. And there was a darkness on that crest that he only gradually realized was a tremendous eagle, an eagle as large as a man, its purplish body unmoving, but its great white head alert and ferocious.

The sight of the eagle so frightened him he fell to the ground, lest he be seen and attacked. Now he noticed something else strange. There were no shadows under the canopy of the great tree; light was everywhere, a flickering light that seemed to caress his body, and to give his eyes peace just in the seeing of it. He then realized that the ground under the tree had turned a pearl white, and seemed to be giving off its own soft, lustrous light from within. He could sense the great roots of the tree—he did not know how—spreading beneath the earth, and every secret and hidden thing they touched turned white, and was at peace.

Strangely, Deganawida could now no longer distinguish himself from the great tree. Where it was, he seemed to be, many places at once. He knew from within himself that the tree was still growing, its vitality still pulsing out through him. He finally realized that the tree would continue to grow until nothing within the earth, or upon it, or in the heavens remained untouched by its whiteness. Only then—everything seemed so clear to him now—only then would its eagle finally close its eyes in rest, like a child in its mother's arms.

When Deganawida awoke from his vision, he found he could no longer remain silent about the Sisterhood of Humanity. He felt compelled, although he did not know quite why, to speak at every opportunity of the family of humanity and the great tree of peace. The Hurons must have been amused at this change, at least initially. But soon his obsessive preaching became an annoyance. The stammering, unmanly bastard would not hold his tongue. Deganawida responded, with what eventually became characteristic if unseemly vehemence, that they, not he, were the ones with crooked tongues. Finally the Crooked Tongues (as he now called the Hurons) drove him out of their lands. And they laughed when his hateful grandmother reluctantly prophesied that the expulsion of the Idiot Deganawida would be the destruction of the Huron people.

Now Deganawida began his period of wandering, without even his mother to console him. How long he wandered is unknown even to the mythic accounts that profess to know all else. Let us imagine him wandering for a long time, going from tribe to tribe, at considerable danger to himself, explaining to all as best he could the Sisterhood of Humanity and the Tree of Peace—explaining in stammers to all but converting none. Eventually we find him in an Iroquois longhouse with one woman listening to him attentively. She seems sympathetic. The Iroquois have been brutally fighting among themselves; there is little life left for an Iroquois outside these endless feuds. Everyone's hands, she admits, have become slimy with blood. To emphasize her point, she tells him of one man, once much admired as a warrior and speaker, who had his whole family, wife and seven children, slaughtered by a rival headman. Now the bereaved man has gone beyond revenge, and has repudiated all humanity, and makes war upon all indiscriminately, hunting human beings for pleasure and food. Deganawida knew immediately that this cannibal needed to know about the Sisterhood of Humanity and the Tree of Peace.

Deganawida sneaked to the lodgings of Hayowentha (that was the cannibal's name) and climbed onto the roof to hide. Soon Hayowentha returned
with the body of a man to eat for supper. As Deganawida watched through the
smoke hole in the ceiling, Hayowentha butchered the body into small pieces
and threw them into his pot, which he then filled with water and began to
heat. Suddenly Hayowentha recoiled from the pot in horror. He had looked
into it while he waited for it to boil, and in the still water he saw the image of
a face looking back at him in sorrow and forgiveness. This was the reflection
of Deganawida, but Hayowentha thought it was his own inner self. So he
jumped back from the pot, and then he stared at it for a long time. Finally he
carried the pot outside and emptied it, loudly vowing never to taste human
flesh again. When he turned to go back to his house, he saw Deganawida
standing there at its entrance, a man with the face from the pot, but now the
face was smiling, ready to greet him.

So Deganawida explained to Hayowentha about the Sisterhood of
Humanity and the Tree of Peace, and told him that he was to become the
spokesman for Deganawida and was to preach of the Great Tree to all peoples.

In Hayowentha Deganawida had found his Aaron and his Paul. Hayowentha's pleas for repentance and peace, unlike those of Deganawida, were so
eloquent and moving that soon all five nations of the Iroquois had converted
to the vision of Deganawida. Hayowentha's appeals seem to have been personal, each listener thinking he was speaking to him or her alone.

Hayowentha carried with him a string of shells. This first wampum was
not money, a medium for commercial exchange. Rather, Hayowentha used
these beads as he spoke, to remind him of his own sorrows, those sorrows that
had driven him to murder and cannibalism. It is said that when Hayowentha
preached the sorrows that had almost destroyed him as a human being the
people listening thought of their own deepest sorrows. And when they did,
their sorrows and Hayowentha's become one in the shells. And once this happened, Hayowentha's listeners realized they were now sitting under the Great
Tree, surrounded by whiteness and forgiveness and peace.

One striking image is recorded of this conversion process. Deganawida
had sent Hayowentha for his first mission to Tadodaho, the killer of his family, the one man Hayowentha could justifiably hate, the one man he would
wish to remain beyond the canopy of the Great Tree of Peace. Of Hayowentha's initial reluctance, of Deganawida's insistence, of the dangers in
Hayowentha's approach to his enemy, of Tadodaho's hostility and suspicion,
of Hayowentha's words of forgiveness—of all this about which we should so
like to know—the surviving versions of the myth remain silent, as if mocking

our idle curiosity about the inessential. Nothing is recorded except an image: Tadodaho lying with his head on Hayowentha's bosom and Hayowentha carefully combing the snakes out of Tadodaho's hair.

As Hayowentha brought his eloquence to the service of Deganawida, so Tadodaho brought his political and even military acumen. If all the nations of the earth were to be united, and if the hatchet of war was to be thrown permanently beneath the earth, then a certain shrewdness needed to be exercised in the interim. Tadodaho's own nation, the Onondaga, could serve as the capital for the new empire of peace. The Iroquois collectively would be the parents of the new confederacy—other nations would address them as befitting a father. When new nations were invited into the confederacy, it had to be made clear to them that although peace existed under the Great Tree, only war existed outside it. In fact, to decline inclusion was to insult, to attack the Great Tree. Everyone should know that its Eagle was swift and merciless in defense of the Great Tree.

The threats of punishment did not assist the conversion process. No matter how eloquently Hayowentha preached, no matter how swiftly Tadodaho the eagle of Deganawida punished, Indians around the Iroquois did not wish to be part of a confederacy with the Onondaga as its capital and the Iroquois as its fathers. Such a conversion did not seem to them sufficiently different from conquest, no matter how beautiful the vision of Deganawida. So they resisted. The internal peace of the Iroquois, so admirable in itself, became the foundation for an external ferocity that the Europeans would come to fear and admire, a ferocity that would eventually doom the Hurons altogether.

This transformation of Deganawida's spiritual vision into an imperial ideology seems to have occurred during his own lifetime. Deganawida himself seems to have realized, belatedly, that Hayowentha had not combed all the snakes from the medusa head of Tadodaho, but had rather himself become infected by their poison. But about all this the stammering Deganawida found he could do nothing, especially in the face of repeated Iroquois victories and a general external prosperity.

So Deganawida called his followers together at the edge of the lake that Champlain was soon to name after himself, the lake of inexpressible beauty with horrors in its depths. From a canoe he told them, haltingly, that he would return if they ever needed him, and then paddled off into the mists, never to be seen again.

When New Netherlands fell to the British (not more than a full human lifetime after Deganawida's departure), the most prominent headman among the Iroquois was considered by many to be a true follower of Deganawida's vision. Garacontié was a headman of the Onondaga and the greatest Iroquois orator of his generation. He had the lineage of Tadodaho and the skills of Hayowentha, but his policies were those of Deganawida. Garacontié was an apostle of peace.

The Iroquois had now destroyed Deganawida's own people. Perhaps when Garacontié as a young man had listened to the elders' stories, he came to see the contradiction between this great victory and the vision of the Great Tree of Peace. Perhaps he came into contact with captive or adopted Hurons who now lived out their lives as Iroquois. But it is too much to think he might have spoken to an elderly Thérèse Oionhaton.

Whatever the reason, Garacontié pursued a consistent policy of peace, particularly with the neighboring European colonies. The Iroquois should now bury the hatchet with the French, and bring them as well as the British, as equal partners, under the Great Tree of Peace. His policy was clear, both clear and clearly dictated by the vision of Deganawida. Following it, however, was not easy.

The French were understandably suspicious, even when he offered to exchange prominent prisoners. If he then managed to convince them, or most of them, of his sincerity, they still doubted that he could guarantee the conduct of the other Iroquois; and they doubted correctly. The Mohawks were especially hostile to a peace with the French, for during any French war the western Iroquois would have to trade through the Mohawks with the British in Albany.

Garacontié as a result was forced to play a double game in his pursuit of a French peace. More than once, Garacontié had to save a fragile truce by warning the French of impending Mohawk attacks. Through such acts, that from another perspective might have been regarded as treasonous to his own people, Garacontié slowly built trust between the two traditionally hostile people. He invited the Jesuits to come to preach Christianity; he saw no contradiction between the traditional beliefs of the two peoples, and would himself eventually be baptized.

Nonetheless, he steadfastly resisted French efforts to make the Iroquois Confederacy a mere tool of French policy. New friendship with France was his chief aim, but this did not entail a repudiation of the older alliance with Albany. There was room under the Great Tree of Peace for all. When the officials at Albany would rebuke him for his friendship with the dastardly French, he would preach to them and do his best to comb the snakes out of their hair.

Garacontié eventually went to his death in 1677 revered by most and respected by all. One would like to say that his life showed the relevance of Deganawida's ideals to our world, that in Garacontié Deganawida had returned, now eloquent and able to act. So one would wish. Nonetheless, the sad truth seems to be that the renewal led by Garacontié had the same effect as the original foundation of the Iroquois Confederacy: strength and prosperity for those within the covenant, death and destruction for those outside. In this case it would be the native groups to the east and south of the Iroquois Confederacy that would suffer.

In early 1675 Connecticut, through its continual expansion, finally began to reap a whirlwind for all New England. The Algonquin groups, intermingled with the ever-multiplying British settlements, had found a leader in Metacomet, called by the Puritans "King Philip." Amazingly, he seems to have been able to forge an alliance among most Indian groups along this New England frontier. So when war began, settlements were attacked from Rhode Island to Massachusetts, and by raiding parties now long accustomed to using European arms. So New England settlers could exhort each other to be like the stout old worthies of the founding generation who prayed to the Lord of Mercy and gave no quarter. Nonetheless, all military advantage seemed at first to be Metacomet's. Twelve towns were completely destroyed, and fully half of the rest severely damaged. By the end of the war at least one out of ten European adult males in New England had been killed or wounded—and numerous women and children had been taken captive, many never to be seen again. Throughout New England, the British were being pushed back to a narrow ribbon of settlements near the coast, and in their panic were turning against even those Indians who tried to remain neutral. For instance, one hundred fifty Narragansett Indians, the same group that had welcomed Roger Williams to Rhode Island, surrendered themselves to remain out of the fighting, only to be quickly sold—every one of them, man, woman, and child— into West Indian slavery. Other neutrals, understandably, then rallied to Metacomet's standard.

All was going as Metacomet must have hoped, but then the Mohawks intervened. The Mohawks were free to do as they wished precisely because of Garacontié's successful pursuit of peace. Not having to worry about the French, they could strike with full force to the east, against the emerging native confederacy of Metacomet. Rather than allow their traditional rivals to get strong, they could break them once and for all, by forcing Metacomet to fight a two-front war. And Puritan divines could preach that the kingdom of Satan divided against itself could not stand.

The Governor of New York, Edmund Andros, also was delighted, but for different reasons. As the forces of Philip were pushed back toward the coast by Mohawks, loyal New York troops could quietly follow at a distance, gobbling as much territory for New York as they could. Perhaps soon the Connecticut River would once again serve as a boundary marker for New York.

The Mohawks were all too happy to play their bloody part in this scheme. They penetrated far into New England, their faces smeared with bright yellow so that they would not be mistaken for the indigenous Indians who had become fair game for Mohawk and colonist alike. Once the Mohawks attacked Metacomet in earnest, his alliances began to dissolve. Eventually Metacomet, his cause lost, would retire to his peninsula fortress on Narragansett Bay, called Mount Hope by the British. He would be assassinated there by an Indian in the pay of the whites, the killer afterward touring New England to exhibit Metacomet's famous left hand that all knew had been long ago maimed in an explosion. On Metacomet's peninsula would be established the town of Bristol, which alone of the New England port towns would specialize in the slave trade. Around the bay of Narragansett would be the only plantation economy of New England. It was as if the blood of Metacomet still cried from the ground and cursed the place.

As the Iroquois peace of Garacontié freed the Mohawks to move against Metacomet, so it also freed the Seneca to probe to the south, with equally disastrous consequences for another native people.

While the Huron Confederacy had been the great enemy of Iroquoia on its northwest marchlands, the Susquehanna Confederacy was its great enemy to its southwest. The Seneca in the 1670s began new southern raids in earnest into the valley of the Susquehanna. Reports reached New France in 1675 that the Susquehannas had been overrun and utterly destroyed, as the Hurons had. These reports, although exaggerated, contained a grain of truth.

The Susquehanna Confederacy was not destroyed; nonetheless, its leaders seem to have decided that the continuation of this war with the Seneca would be self-destructive, and they were unwilling to submit to Iroquois domination, the only condition for being included under the Great Tree. So they abandoned their traditional valley, and moved themselves out of the way of Iroquois raids. They seem to have done so in the spirit of peace, as if *they* were the true followers of Deganawida. They wanted no trouble with anybody. They petitioned the British to be allowed to resettle between Maryland and Virginia, near the Potomac River, near where now we have our national monuments. The petition was granted—and so this story of the peaceful but strong Susquehannas should end, if the world were as Deganawida or even Garacontié had envisioned.

But it is not, and soon the Susquehannas were innocently caught up in a sequence of events as disastrous as those being acted out in New England. Here as in New England interracial war would lead to an intraracial civil war, but in this case the civil war would not be one of Indians killing Indian neighbors but of British killing British neighbors. Nonetheless, this frenzy of mutual destruction would not be, at least in retrospect, a complete loss. Out of it, albeit perversely, would come an ideal. Nothing as lofty as that professed by Iroquois or Christians; rather a much tainted ideal, one much weighted down with this world, perhaps just enough to be realizable within its confines. Be forewarned, the story of its origins is not pretty to contemplate—but at least it offers the pleasures of a convoluted tale, with many unexpected turns.

The Susquehannas moved near the Potomac Valley where outlying Virginia planters lived in a state of continual feud with the small local tribe, the Doegs. The Susquehannas innocently got involved in this feud when a raiding party of colonists killed fourteen of them before the Virginians realized they were not Doegs. At this point the Susquehannas had every right to reprisals against the Virginia settlements; it was a measure of their pacific intent that they did not take them. They had not ended their war with the Iroquois to engage the British in new hostilities.

The Seneca, however, not having the Susquehannas to fight, had simply extended their raids farther south, and themselves began to destroy western Virginia plantations. The Virginians, moreover, were about as good at distinguishing Iroquois from Susquehannas as they were Susquehannas from Doegs. Virginia and Maryland sent out a joint expedition to find and punish those responsible. The Susquehannas were the chief suspects precisely because they had good grounds for punitive raids against Virginia.

Led by John Washington and Thomas Truman, the thousand-man force surrounded a palisaded Susquehanna village, and demanded satisfaction. The Susquehannas sent out five or six headmen to parley—in particular, to explain that the Iroquois were responsible for the raids. When Washington became threatening, one of the headmen showed him a medal of friendship given him by the Maryland governor. Washington and Truman were not concerned about such niceties. Settlers had been killed, and Indians were going to pay. The first to pay were these headmen, who were summarily executed for the crime of professing friendship and peace. There would be no racial neutrality in this war.

Truman and Washington, it turned out, were as incompetent as soldiers as they were despicable as human beings. They tried to mount a siege of the village, but the Susquehannas snuck off one night, with women and children in tow, killing seven sleeping guards to clear the way.

The Virginia governor was livid when he received the news. It was hard to imagine how Washington and Truman could have done worse. The murder of the envoys, in particular, was unthinkable. It assured a war that would be difficult to stop. How could Virginia ever again expect the Susquehannas to negotiate peace with Virginia after this? The governor said, "If they had killed my grandfather and grandmother, my father and mother and all my friends, yet if they had come to treat peace, they ought to have gone in peace."

The Susquehannas themselves, in fact, still seem to have wanted peace; but first they had to honor the great men whom the colonists had so treacherously killed. Ten colonists for each great man, that was their blood price.

So the Susquehannas swept through the outlying Virginia plantations perpetrating the very crimes for which they had been punished in advance. As the eastern Iroquois were ending King Philip's War, the western Iroquois were incidentally instigating its Chesapeake equivalent. In January 1676 alone, thirty-six settlers were killed in various raids.

The war on the Chesapeake, however, took an unexpected turn. The colonists did not effectively unite against the Indians, but rather behaved like the Indians of the northeast—and soon were inflicting the worst damage on one another, until Jamestown itself lay in ruins. To understand how this could have happened, we must pause for a moment to see how Virginia had changed since we left it in the 1630s.

Virginia was no longer a shameful and unblessed thing, at least in the eyes of the restored Stuart monarchy and the Virginian planters who supported it. Virginia had become almost exclusively a tobacco colony. Although this meant a recurring cycle of boom and bust, in general supply had a difficult time keeping up with demand, as addiction to the golden leaf spread throughout the populations of Europe.

For the Stuarts tobacco was a boon, for they fueled a significant portion of their administration with nicotine fumes. Stuarts got tuppence for every pound of tobacco sold, no matter what it sold for. And it sold for between four and two-and-a-half pence. There were ways of lessening this duty, but the simple fact was that the monarchy was making at least as much off the tobacco as the producer. As a result Virginia tobacco provided one-twentieth of James's and Charles's total income. Compared to this, the long-term prosperity of Virginia was weighed like so much smoke.

That did not sit well with the old planters of Virginia, but they had found another way to produce wealth for themselves: the colonial government. They got themselves into positions of preferment, and made those positions pay handsomely. So the average Virginian paid not only for his distant kings, but for his local lords and ladies as well.

At the time the Stuarts took over, something else was happening that was revolutionary for Virginia: People were starting to live longer. Between 1625 and 1640 there had been more than fifteen thousand immigrants, but a net increase of less than six thousand persons in the colony—a true measure of the horrific death rate. However, between 1640 and 1660, with the immigration not significantly increased, the population had more than tripled.

The older planters understood that this growth in population meant an ever-increasing demand for land. They began to accumulate legal rights to as much good land as possible. These patents cost as little as forty pounds of tobacco for fifty acres of land. To establish legal title the prospective owner, once he paid the patent fee, had only to "use" the land. That meant clearing a small portion, building a shack (to be called a "house"), and planting a single crop. The owner could then, after this meager effort, let the land revert to wilderness, but the title was his permanently.

Between 1650 and 1675 the established planters gained title to vast tracts of land as a speculation on the future. Total land holdings of more than ten thousand acres were not unusual. In one area, one hundred thousand acres had been patented by only thirty owners; and it was common for large land holders to have holdings in different areas—five thousand acres on one river, three thousand on another, six thousand more upstream. What was unusual was a large land holder who was cultivating more than a small fraction of his real estate. In this manner, between 1650 and 1675, well over two million acres of Virginia land were distributed. As one observer put it, "Everyone covets so much and there is such vast extent of land that they spread so far they cannot manage well a hundredth part of what they have."

As a result of this, indentured servants who reached the term of their contract found that the economic opportunity which led them to the New World was now largely denied them. What security there was could be gained from becoming a sharecropper for one of the landed magnates. You would develop his land for him, and pay him a certain rent in crops. You could scrape by while you and dozens like you made him wealthier. Your house and all the other improvements were his. And if you failed in payments, he could use your debts to force you into servitude for another term.

For many of the freedmen, becoming a sharecropper was little better than remaining a servant. Some of these sought to retain their independence by living by their wits in the Virginia towns or even in the forests. (These towns were themselves too small to provide much chance of employment.) This choice was not regarded as "respectable" by the ladies and gentlemen of planter society, who railed against these homeless wastrels. Laws were passed to bring them back into the good societal order, where they would be of use. For instance, the killing of a feral pig in the forest carried a fine of two thousand pounds of tobacco. The pig, or one of its ancestors, had obviously belonged to some respectable person sometime in the past—and hence deserved a better fate than to satisfy the hunger of a homeless vagrant. Of course, the pig killer would not have two thousand pounds of tobacco handy—if he had, he could have bought a hundred pigs of his own. Therefore, it was back to indentured servitude for him.

But there was another option for the new freedman who insisted on both independence and responsibility. He could get his own plantation farm. Of course, he would have to go far up one of the Virginia rivers, past thousands of acres of unused but patented land. He would have to go to the frontier to eke out a living. The government seemed intent on making life even more difficult for the freedmen: It supported itself by a poll tax rather than a property tax. That enabled the magnates to keep their vast holdings at no cost, while bringing a disproportionate burden on the small planter.

So there they sat, this growing group of freedmen, struggling on the frontier, fiercely independent, deeply aggrieved and very, very angry. The individual for whom they as a group held the most anger was the governor himself, Sir William Berkeley.

Berkeley, born in England about the time Virginia was founded by John Smith, had become governor of the colony in 1641. He had had a glimpse of that earlier time, for the Powhatan Confederacy was still led by Powhatan's brother, Opechancanough, when Berkeley arrived in Virginia. Opechancanough, so old he had to have an attendant to lift his eyelids when he wished to see, had tried in 1644 to lead one final uprising to push the unwanted colonists back into the sea. In this unequal contest young Governor Berkeley had distinguished himself, and then in an act of youthful hubris exhibited the captive Opechancanough for all to see.

Berkeley had remained a determined Royalist during the English Civil War. He drove more than one thousand Puritans from his colony and gave their places to Royalists fleeing Cromwell's England, including the Washington family. His Old Dominion was to be an aristocracy with him as governor at the top.

During Cromwell's government, Berkeley was removed from power. He and the other Virginia cavaliers were, needless to say, enthusiastic supporters of the Restoration, which restored Berkeley himself as governor. It was not true that Virginia recognized Charles II a year before England itself, but the fact that the story gained currency dramatized the loyalty of the Virginia planters to the monarchy. The motto of Virginia had become "And Virginia gives the fifth." Virginia was His Majesty's fifth domain, after England, Scotland, Ireland, and France. (News of the outcome of the Hundred Years War had apparently yet to reach Virginia.)

The aristocracy of Virginia was committed to living in manorial splendor, and with manorial indifference to the suffering of the lower and middling classes. Duke, or rather Governor, William Berkeley held to this unswervingly. Anyone who questioned his arrogant ostentation would be met with anger and contempt. One can scarcely improve on the description of Berkeley by the late nineteenth-century historian of the American colonial experience, John Fiske: "Sir William was an aristocrat to the ends of his fingers, a man of velvet and gold lace, a brave soldier, a devoted husband, a chivalrous friend, and withal as narrow and bigoted and stubborn a creature as one could find anywhere. He had no sympathy for the common people nor any clear sense of duty." For Fiske, Berkeley was strong in his opinions, and usually wrong.

From this description two essential items are left out. First is Berkeley's extraordinary estate of Green Fields. Its scale can be judged by the fact that its orchards contained between 1,500 to 2,000 trees, and the hall of the great house could easily be used to meet the Virginia Assembly. Large as was Green Fields, it was dwarfed by the second item omitted in Fiske's description—Berkeley's temper.

One newcomer to Virginia complained that he had been treated by Berkeley in a "brittle and peevish" manner. His friend then asked him if the governor had called him a dog, rogue, and the like. No. "Then you took him in his best humor, these being his usual terms when he is angry." The implication being that the governor was angry most of the time.

The common people might complain that he and his friends ran Virginia to their own convenience and profit with no thought of anyone else. Berkeley would assure them that he did think of them. He thought of them as an ignorant, superstitious collection of beggars unfit for polite society, and particularly unfit for rule. The growth of the number of freedmen eligible to vote in elections to the assembly was an awkward fact of Virginian life; but Governor Berkeley would not be worthy of his position as the king's representative if he could not deal with awkward facts. The freedmen might be eligible to vote, but only if elections were held; the law did not specify how often elections should be held. And Berkeley held them never. The same congenial assembly had been meeting for twenty-five years, legislating wisely the interests of the wealthy.

A measure of the imbecility of the ordinary people was the tumult among them over the "omens" of 1675. First, a comet, rising from earthly vapors, shone in the sky with a tail that resembled a horse's, pointing to the northwest. What prodigious horsey thing was going to descend upon the colony from the northwest? Then hordes of bugs, each one about the size of a finger joint, arose from the ground, millions upon millions of them. They covered trees, blighting all new growth—and then after a few months disappeared as suddenly and inexplicably as they had come. And no one knew quite how to interpret this apparent war between the overarching trees and these lowly creatures of the earth.

Most unnerving of all, however, were the pigeons. Once a year, during their migrations, passenger pigeons became a staple of the diet of the American colonist. Some planters and small farmers actually kept two or three blinded pigeons which they would stake in their fields; their cooing would then draw passing pigeons down to roost where they could be killed. But no such cruel deception was required in 1675. In that year all the pigeons of the world seemed to descend simultaneously upon Virginia, like the souls of the dead of all ages past. They roosted in such numbers on the trees that the smaller branches cracked and broke. After firing into such flocks, the huntsman needed only pick up the fatter birds, and leave the rest for his hogs. All the vultures and eagles and wolves and other predators seemed drawn by the abundance from their wilderness homes to the edge of the settlements—and no one, this once, begrudged them their fill of these dainty morsels.

Everyone took their fill of the birds equally, but some Virginians did so with a worried eye. Once before in living memory, barely in living memory, had Virginia been covered with pigeons beyond number. That was in the year 1644, right before the last great Indian attack. It was not hard to imagine what the chatterers were making of this. The aged Opechancanough had cursed the young Governor Berkeley for showing him off as a freak. Now that Berkeley himself was an old man, the curse was to be fulfilled. The long-moldering corpse of Opechancanough would rise up from its grave to lead invincible Indian hosts against the helpless colony. It was a good ghost story, the kind you could almost believe, late in the evening, after a few pulls on the jug, when the wind was blowing through the trees and the moon was new. The people, of course, could believe any stories they wanted, as long as they did not expect their silly caprices to influence Berkeley's policies.

Then Berkeley had some real trouble on the frontier, and he sent out trusted John Washington, along with misnamed Truman, who together made a thorough botch of it. The Indians were the injured party and the frontiersmen wanted further innocent blood. That was the way of these fools. They demanded that Berkeley do something.

But what could he do? The Susquehannas were justifiably, more than justifiably, aggrieved, and seemed to be working out justice in their own way. They were masters of this wilderness fighting, and he certainly could not expect a force of Virginians to find, let alone defeat them under such circumstances, especially when the Virginians were led by a noble warrior like John Washington. (He himself was long past tramping in the wilderness.) So Berkeley went through the motions of a response, but in fact did nothing. He had little sympathy for the frontier planters, anyway. If they wanted to strike out on their own away from the supervision of their betters, then let them take their risks. Berkeley did build some forts at the heads of rivers where plantations were vulnerable. But everyone knew that these would be useless in protecting plantations from the skulking approach of Indians. (They were, on the other hand, little engines of profit for Berkeley and his friends.) Berkeley ordered a cessation of trading with the Indians. But everyone knew, or thought they knew, that Berkeley's cronies were continuing to trade on the sly, even guns. As usual, the sufferings of the struggling frontiersmen only served to increase the profits of the wealthy of Jamestown.

Berkeley, for his part, cared not a fig what people thought of him. The resentment was real, but he had only to ride out this awkward time. The Susquehannas would eventually be sated, and would then sue for peace. The frontier would return to its uneasy simmering state. And so it might have, had not colonial resentment found its leader. His name was Nathaniel Bacon.

Nathaniel Bacon was an unlikely rebel. He was a well-born young man who could claim Sir Francis Bacon himself as part of his lineage. He had been well educated at Cambridge, and seems to have taken the Grand Tour with John Ray, the foremost naturalist of his day. Bacon had come to Virginia in 1674 with the best possible connections; his childless uncle of the same name was one of the wealthiest members of the Virginian aristocracy and a member of Berkeley's council. Young Bacon was in fact exactly the kind of person who could expect preferment from the aging governor, and within a year of his arrival he too had been appointed to Berkeley's council of inner advisers, at twenty-seven by far its youngest member. Perhaps the elder Bacon was not the only Virginian who regarded Nathaniel as his heir. Berkeley himself could see in young Bacon the fair and gusty April of his own prime. Nathaniel seemed only to need patience for Virginia to fall in his lap, like a ripe fruit.

Yet there was another side to Bacon, quite different from the public person who could effortlessly charm the old governor. People were disturbed by what was called in one late memoir his "delight in solitude and mystic employments." While engaged in such employments, he was said to be "ominous, pensive, aloof." Occasionally these reveries would be interrupted by shocking statements—or as one scandalized Virginian put it, "logical discourse tending to atheism."

The Virginian probably did not understand. Bacon's tutor, John Ray, was a pillar of Anglican orthodoxy, but nonetheless held many specific opinions that, out of context, could shock. For instance, he dismissed what he called "the generally received opinion that man is the end of creation as if there were no other end of any creature but some way or other to be serviceable to man." In later works Ray would bid his readers to observe the vital force that animates the whole of the living world. Each piece of this world seemed engaged in an incessant struggle to express this living force. The slips from a plant try to regenerate, every acorn struggles to become a great oak, the insect can regenerate its lost limb, the salmon must destroy itself to deposit its eggs in the hereditary stream: all pulse with the business of living, nature itself as the sum of these conflicting efforts to fulfill instinctual duties that none can understand, except perhaps man, who can meditate on this all as the earthly reflection of a single transcendent force called God.

The wilderness certainly gave Nathaniel Bacon a suitable environment in which to meditate on the theme that nature had its own ends to accomplish without prevision of human service or even witness. The history of Virginia gave much opportunity to think of the human costs, extracted primarily from the weak and unwilling, of imposing human ends upon other, more ancient wisdoms. And then there were the strange dead forests of Virginia.

The new tobacco planter, in order to get a crop as soon as possible, would refrain from the arduous labor of clearing the elm, oak, chestnut, hickory, and walnut trees that crowded the best Virginian soil and raised their limbs high and broad to try to gather for themselves all the life-sustaining light. These aristocrats of the wilderness were too many and too strong for the planter to challenge directly. But cunning sufficed where strength was lacking. The planter simply girdled the trees, stripping the bark in a complete circle around each trunk, to allow the vital force of the tree to seep out before ever reaching its leaves. The tobacco farmer would then plow and plant among the doomed trees, for he knew that by the time the tobacco plants had broken the soil to seek the sun, no leaves, no buds would be on the old rulers to deprive the lower plants of light. Such a field in the spring was an eerie sight, especially for someone by temperament or training inclined to meditate on natural things. New life was bursting from the ground amidst a forest of skeletons, bare ruined choirs where birds would perch but not nest. During the next few years, the planter could harvest the wood for his fire at his leisure, until finally the great but now rotten stumps could be removed at last, tottering reminders of the older order. Traveling upriver from the older plantations to the newer, the attentive observer could note all stages of this patient revolution made by the persistent hands of men. And a few of the great trees would be left intact around the plantation house to provide shade for their new masters, a fitting expression of their newly subservient condition.

Bacon seems to have had the meditative disposition to make the most of such scenes, but only intermittently. When he felt his own sap rising, he could not contain or resist its impulses. He, like all the beings he saw around him, was driven by this force pulsing within. Ray sensed this about him; he wrote of Bacon's "quick wit" but added that he was "impatient of labor." In fact, Bacon's quickness and impatience were the reason he was in Virginia.

He had left Cambridge under a cloud because of some unspecified "extravagances." Back in his native Suffolk, he then quickly wooed a local heiress, and married her before getting parental consent; as a result, she was disinherited. He had an ample income himself but could not seem to live within it. Finally he became peripherally and perhaps innocently involved in a scheme to swindle another young man out of his inheritance. Bacon's father finally decided that the boy had simply too much uncontrolled energy for a fully civilized society. So he sent him with considerable funds to the frontier of Virginia where, with the help of his uncle, he might have sufficient scope and freedom of action.

At first all seemed to be going well. Not only did his uncle take to him and the governor himself accept him in his inner circle, he was able with his uncle's help to purchase a suitable twelve-hundred-acre plantation. The plantation was in two portions. This was not unusual; what was surprising is how close both portions were to the frontier. One was only about twenty or thirty miles from the frontier directly west of Jamestown; the other was right at the falls that marked the frontier itself.

Perhaps Bacon's uncle was surprised that his nephew had chosen to live so far from the polite society of Jamestown. But to Berkeley the decision must have seemed a boon. He could now have a trusted, respectable young man living amidst the unruly frontiersmen of Henrico County. As a sign of his pleasure, Berkeley awarded Bacon a much-coveted patent to trade with the Indians of the area. Of course, the grant of the patent was not entirely selfless;

for the privilege Bacon was to give Berkeley six hundred pounds' worth of beaver each year. But, then again, everything that happened in Virginia somehow rebounded to Berkeley's profit.

So Nathaniel Bacon settled into the life of a Virginia planter on the frontier. His local village was Varina, and he could hear there the legends of early Virginia. (He was only a bend in the river away from the house to which John Rolfe brought Pocahontas.) Away from the great centers of Europe, removed even from the pretenses of little Jamestown, he could be amused with what passed for important events in this isolated place. Varina, for instance, was abuzz over the fine given to Sam Mathews for saying that Reverend Ball was "fitter to make a hangman than a minister."

Into this life Bacon settled, or rather he could have if the frontier had been peaceful and Bacon suited for calm. But the frontier was soon aflame, and Bacon the kind of man who steered into storms.

As the storm was later reconstructed from the reports of witnesses, one afternoon Bacon and three of his fellow planters were sitting around "making the sadness of their times their discourse, and the fear they all lived in." Bacon's own outer plantation had recently been raided, and his foreman killed; moreover, his license to trade with the Indians had been withdrawn for the duration of the trouble. About the sadness of the times and their own angers and sadnesses Bacon and his fellows waxed with increasing eloquence as the afternoon progressed, thanks to repeated lubrications with rum.

Toasts apparently were raised to the two hundred volunteers who had come together at nearby Jordan's Point, against Berkeley's wishes, to protect the plantations as the governor would not. Toasts were not good enough for such men; they should be given the rum themselves. So off Bacon and others went to Jordan's Point with large quantities of rum, which were consumed quickly and gratefully. And the men then began to chant in gratitude, "A Bacon! A Bacon!" He was being urged to assume the role of commander of these irregulars.

This adulation was a kind of intoxication Bacon had never felt before, and he discovered in himself an immediate addiction to it. Some would later say that Bacon, an inexperienced and well-intentioned young man given to the impetuous gesture, was himself misled, impassioned by the flattery of the few and blinded by the adulation of the many. Some would even single out a shrewd planter named Lawrence who saw in Bacon a means for himself to exercise power without the risk. In that scenario Lawrence had played Achitophel to Bacon's Absalom, with Berkeley as the aging David—and

Lawrence, in particular, deserved to be rent from mouth to crotch for his wicked instigation.

There was a certain plausibility to this. Bacon could be told that when fortune chooses us for some great act we must seize the moment and not count the cost or odds, lest she glide away like the wind leaving us to repent forever our foolish hesitance. And his friends could repeatedly urge him to act when they should have been reminding him that the support of the people is not true loyalty but just a passing humor. So young, most promising Nathaniel Bacon was debauched by praise.

This is plausible, and perhaps true as far as it goes. But it neglects what was perhaps most important to Bacon, the surging vitality he felt as he stood before the cheering troops. This might have been dismissed as an insignificant rum-soaked pleasure, but over the next few weeks he discovered he could have it at will whenever he used his prodigious gift of eloquence to give these frontiersmen a voice.

Bacon somehow realized that more than a commander, they needed to be provided with a language of public complaint. And he could do this, for he had the power of utterance; he now knew how naming something brought it into view, how words could be sparks that kindled the consciousness of a people.

The government of Virginia had become a chain of bondage used to suppress the rightful aspirations of ordinary Virginians. What did the frontiersmen aspire to? Only to live out their lives in peace, and to enjoy the fruits of their own labor. Berkeley had given them peace all right, a peace with the Indians, that alien race, a peace that was really a war in masquerade, a war in which the skulking Indians possessed all the advantage. Good Virginians would pay for this phony peace with their own blood, and Berkeley and his cronies would reap the dividend in coaches and silks. Well, this traitorous tribe of God Almighty gentlemen had had its way too long. Power and wealth are not the substance of society, but good and bad. A government without the consent of the people will always become a lifeless instrument of oppression, its soul of legitimacy long fled. Rebellion may be thought a crime, but self-defence is nature's oldest law. Cicero himself had said, "The safety of the people is the highest law." Therefore let thoughts of liberty reign solely in the hearts of every man, liberty and revenge.

So he, Nathaniel Bacon, in bold defiance, would raise up the buckler of the people's cause. He would end the shameless rapacity of the Jamestown parasites. He, as a guardian angel of the frontier, would break the Indians' resolve and drive them from this fair land of which they were so unworthy.

Then Virginia would flourish, like God's only paradise. Every man could sit under his proverbial vine and fig tree; he could sit there in contentment and without fear, and know that he as much as the God Almighty governor was truly a man, and master of his own earth and his own freedom.

So it was that the twenty-eight-year-old Nathaniel Bacon, after little more than two years in Virginia, discovered his true vocation as a demagogue. He found that there came almost unbidden to his lips just the right words to rouse the people, to make them believe in themselves and in him, to make them dream with him of true liberty. When he spoke, the words at their moment of utterance seemed to have the power to make whatever they said be so. This was a godlike gift to be exercised to its fullest extent, whatever the risks. If he trusted his star, he could not fail to reach a glorious port. Trust it he would.

Of course, this realization came to him in bits and pieces, as did his recognition that he could extend his influence to those beyond the sound of his own voice by issuing proclamations to be carried to the far corners of the colony by loyal subordinates.

At first Berkeley thought he could manage the crisis. Bacon could not take seriously the adulation he was receiving from an unquestioning herd who thought too little and listened too much. Bacon had to realize that Berkeley as governor could not become a slave to the ill-considered whims of those whom he ruled. What little truth there was in their complaints was seasoned with lies and brewed in stupidity. Bacon, as an educated young man, had to realize all this, and realize too the dire consequences for society when the lower classes begin to overrun the established channels. The opinion of the common man was a giddy, unsure foundation for power, about as fixed as a feather in the wind. Why then was Bacon filling the people's ears with jealousies and fear?

Of course, this ill-considered mutiny against his authority was a scurvy requital for all the preferment that Berkeley had given the young man. One could hope this was just a fit of youthful temper that would soon purge itself by boiling over. And if Berkeley wanted to take revenge for this impudence and effrontery, now was not the time, not now when Bacon had become the darling of the headstrong, moody, murmuring dregs of Virginia, people as unfixed in principles as in place.

So Berkeley sent to Bacon a series of messages to try to return him to his senses before there would be nothing left for him but dire disgrace. If Bacon would only come to Jamestown (under the smiling promise of safe passage, of course), the two of them could quickly resolve their misunderstanding, for that was all that stood between them, misunderstanding. He was sure that

Bacon wished as much as he only to stop honorably what had begun by accident, lest circumstance transform a mistake into tragedy.

So Berkeley did, amazingly, keep his own temper for a time—and was all soothing words and forgiving gestures, whatever he was thinking. But there was no stopping. It was already too late to end this public lunacy. As Berkeley put it in retrospect, it was as if a train of powder lay along the whole Chesapeake frontier, and Nathaniel Bacon happened to be a man with a firebrand for a mouth.

Not that Bacon defied Berkeley immediately. His response to Berkeley did not breathe flames. But neither did it comply with the old man's request. Bacon assured the good governor he was no mutineer, and had only the deepest respect for his office and loyalty to his person. He could not, however, spare time for a conference in Jamestown when the frontier and the settlers there lay naked to attack. He owned as how he would be willing, in all due humility and respect, to accept a commission as head of the volunteers. Indeed, this was his only request: "entrust me with the country's safety." If Berkeley did accede to this request, then Bacon would permit him to decide which Indians should be killed first, and which spared for the time being. But he was not going to be deterred from his calling by teacup flattery.

This patronizing response pushed Berkeley's admittedly limited patience well beyond breaking. Nonetheless, Bacon may well have thought he was making a substantial concession to the governor by allowing him to specify suitable objects for the frontiersmen's racial rage. Bacon was constantly growing in his knowledge of his people, not in his mind but in his pulse. He allowed their fears and exasperations to animate him, almost without reflection. Only after identifying with his people in this way could he help them understand themselves, understand the force that pulsed through them, and what this force required of them that they collectively might rise and flourish.

He knew that condemnation of the "unworthy favorites and juggling parasites" (as he indelicately described Berkeley's inner circle) would get cheers. But the true hatred, hatred that could generate effective actions by the frontiersmen, was of the Indians. This was not a subject on which the people had patience; they especially had no patience with distinctions that were impossible to apply in practice, such as the distinction Berkeley insisted upon between friendly and unfriendly Indians. Bacon found he got his most rousing support when he advocated a completely coherent and universally intelligible Indian policy: they should all be killed. He ridiculed those who still fed themselves on the dainty food of reconciliation between the races. The Indians love us not, though cunning often restrains their hands. Could these red devils work their will, trees would soon be growing again in the ploughed fields of Virginia and the woods would be whitened with Christian bones. Let the Christian fields of Virginia continue to spread and flourish. This was the gist of Bacon's first proclamation, which he issued in April 1676: "The Humble Appeal of the Volunteers to all Well-minded and Charitable People."

One person who did not feel at all well-minded or charitable toward the volunteers and especially toward Mr. Nathaniel Bacon was, of course, Governor William Berkeley. Didn't Bacon have the eyes to see the whole plain truth of the situation? Had someone sewn them shut? Nobody—not Berkeley, not Bacon—was going to change the water of these poor freedmen into wine. The loaves and fishes of a human society do not multiply miraculously when they are shared. For the few to be wealthy, the many had to be poor, and deserved to be.

Well, Mr. Nathaniel Bacon was going to learn that old age in a man like William Berkeley was tough and green. To assist him in delivering the lesson, Berkeley quickly assembled a force of three hundred men and rode out to Henrico "to call Mr. Bacon to account," as he put it. However, Berkeley only got for his trouble another infuriating note from Bacon, this one informing him that he and his volunteers were off on maneuvers, looking for "a more agreeable destiny than you are pleased to design me." So Berkeley was reduced to declaring Bacon and two of his subordinates rebels; those three ringleaders, when captured, would be given a fair trial. (The promise was ominous since apparently needless.) As for their followers, they were given to the end of May to come to their senses; if they did by then, all would be forgiven.

Berkeley tacitly admitted responsibility for the present situation. Not for his pacific Indian policy; on that he insisted he was right and the murderous frontiersmen wrong. But for holding the reins of power too tightly, too long. He ordered a new election to the assembly; in the next session, therefore, the new representatives of the people would have ample opportunity to air the grievances of their constituents. If Berkeley himself turned out to be the greatest grievance (as was not altogether impossible), he promised he would "most gladly join with them in a petition to his Most Sacred Majesty to appoint a new governor of Virginia."

Berkeley thought all should now agree that he had done everything which could be reasonably expected of him—and more—to remedy the situation. This certainly seemed to be the case, if his promises were sincere. But we will never know whether they were sincere, for he made them too late. Bacon had already discovered a most agreeable destiny for himself, and the present maneuvers would confirm it by giving him a taste of blood. Berkeley's promises would be as nothing weighed against the churning resentment of Bacon's followers and the incendiary eloquence of Bacon himself.

A group of friendly Indians, the Occancechee, had reported to Bacon that a group of Susquehannas had taken up residence near them, and were trying to force them to join in their attacks on the settlers. Bacon and his men had arrived at the Occancechee village, after a forced march, in little condition to fight. Seeing their exhaustion, the Occancechee, as a further gesture of good faith, then attacked the Susquehannas for them, and enjoyed a complete victory. Bacon and his men, now revived, could then sit and watch the celebrations, including the torture death of some Susquehannas.

This seemed only to sour Bacon's men on their successful allies. The Occancechee were flourishing; by rough estimate this single village had one thousand pounds' worth of beaver pelts. Here Bacon and his men were, good respectable Englishmen, having to rely on the charity of these savages just to have enough supplies to get back to their struggling plantations, with nothing to show for it except a first-hand witnessing of the exquisite tortures that these monsters could just as easily be practicing on Virginian women and children.

About the details of what happened next, the sources are confused and understandably so. No justification for the atrocity was possible. One says that the Occancechees refused to give the English enough supplies for the return trip. Another, that the English in general, and Bacon in particular, had meditated too long on what the Occancechees' beaver skins could mean back home. Another, that Bacon had demanded the Indian slaves the Occancechees had freed from the Susquehannas, and the demand had been refused because the slaves had earned their freedom by helping in the attack; in the resultant tension a shot was fired, and an Englishman killed.

Whatever the events that led up to it, the result was in keeping with Bacon's coherent Indian policy. The Occancechees, having proven their friendship and loyalty beyond question, were as a reward surprised at night by Bacon and his men in an attack that allowed them to penetrate within the palisades of the village. Then followed fierce fighting that lasted into the next day. When it was over, all the Occancechees were dead. Bacon returned to Henrico loaded with beaver and expansive tales of his glorious victory. Governor Berkeley, it seemed, was not to be the only man who cast his lengthened shadow over Virginia.

Berkeley, when he heard of it, was incredulous, as incredulous as he was worried. "That very action where he so much boasts was rashly, foolishly and (as I am informed) treacherously carried out to the dishonor of the English nation. Yet he lost more men than I did in three years war." Didn't the fools realize it was a victory for no one? It removed Indians who were no threat and in fact quite useful as spies on truly dangerous Indians. Did Bacon think any other Indians would now help him find other hostile raiding parties?

The disgusted Berkeley formally declared Bacon a rebel against his authority. He ordered all government officials to help in bringing him to justice. Berkeley also wrote to London informing the ministers of this crisis; two days later, June 3, 1676, he sent his wife back to England. He also pleaded with London "on my knees" to be himself recalled. Had he already heard that the representative from Henrico to the new assembly was to be none other than Nathaniel Bacon himself?

When the assembly was about to convene in June, Berkeley's predicament seemed hopeless. The assembly itself was composed predominantly of recently freed servants, just the kind of men Bacon could do with as he wished. Berkeley's own estimate was that at most eight of the forty assemblymen could be counted upon not to be dazzled by the fiery furnace of Bacon. Bacon himself had sailed down the James in a sloop with an entourage, or rather bodyguard, of fifty well-armed volunteers.

Berkeley knew he needed bold measures, and he did his best. He took Bacon by surprise on his sloop and had him brought before him. The whole of Jamestown, or so it seemed, now rose up in the defense of the young hero of the frontier; perhaps as many as two thousand were in the crowd determined to prevent any harm coming to the gallant young man.

Bacon made his usual professions of loyalty; whatever his misdeeds in the past, if any, he promised he would do them no more. Then Berkeley himself seized the moment with the timing of a trained actor. "God forgive you, I forgive you." (Pause.) "God forgive you, I forgive you." (Pause.) "God forgive you, I forgive you." The last repetition apparently made the absolution complete. The assembly formally requested that Bacon be pardoned, the council concurred, and Berkeley not only pardoned him but with a suitable flourish had him restored to his seat on the council. With that, the crisis had passed, or so Berkeley mistakenly hoped.

Berkeley then set about educating and shaming his new assembly into good sense. His means was a quiet but firm insistence on the law. He did promise to grant Bacon his frontier commission, but he got the assembly to support an order that all such commissions would "prohibit the falling upon or injuring in any sort any Indians who are and continue in friendship with us." There were to be no more massacres of allies, no matter how satisfying to blood lust. Berkeley was in his lordly element now, and Bacon in a growing agony of hesitation, and the assembly increasingly cowed.

Did the distinguished members of the assembly doubt that Virginia still had friends among the Indians if she wanted them? Berkeley made a show of bringing before the assembly the successor to Opechancanough, the old queen of the surviving fragment of the once-great Powhatan Confederacy, the Pamunkeys. (She is called in the Virginia records only "the Queen of the Pamunkeys.") He asked her for help in the impending war against the foreign Indians, such as the Susquehannas. The old queen, however, rather than agreeing, began to complain. Her husband had been killed leading an attack on behalf of Virginia; she had lost her husband for Virginia and was still waiting for the promised compensation from the ungrateful colonists. She was majestic and queenly in her bearing; even in complaint, her face showed not so much as a momentary ebullition of feeling.

There was nothing to say in response, as the recorder of this incident admits, for she was right. Virginia had proven a poor friend to the Pamunkeys. But she had been called to prove that the local Indians would be true to Virginia, despite past mistreatment. So perhaps this was just as well. She was pressed as to how many scouts she would supply, but she refused to acknowledge the question. She was asked again, and then again, more firmly. Finally she said simply, "Six." Then she was asked again, and said, "Twelve." At this she got up and walked out, with a cold dignity that should have shamed them all.

Berkeley must have been pleased with this little drama. (Shame, it must be said, had likely never once cast the faintest shadow across his conscience.) He did seem thoroughly the master of the situation now, a skillful if aging animal trainer on the verge of making his growling Baconite assembly jump through hoops. Berkeley's advisors, however, were not so sanguine. Bacon and his closest supporters, while outmaneuvered in the assembly, now were fully aware how much support they had in Jamestown. Virginia was Bacon's, no matter what words were formulated in the assembly or proclaimed by Berkeley. Virginia was Bacon's.

Philip Ludwell was one of those of Berkeley's circle who saw the growing confidence of Bacon and guessed what it portended. For all Berkeley's temporary success, Ludwell had begun to write of an "approaching conflagration." His judgment of Bacon's great victory was as scathing as Berkeley's, but having seen Bacon in Jamestown he wrote, "The Indians are now our least care, though we hardly know (or deserve to know) a friendly Indian round our borders. Judge our Condition." Berkeley's lordly manner was no match for Bacon's fidgety vehemence.

Then one morning startling news spread through Jamestown like fire, until the whole town was a single conflagration of excitement: "Bacon is fled, Bacon is fled." At first this seemed all to the good. The assembly was now entirely Berkeley's—or, as one Berkeley supporter put it, the assembly had been "mastered by some gentlemen of reason." With Bacon gone, the assembly even set about formulating a glowing tribute to Berkeley that pleaded with London to permit Virginia's good, wise, gracious, loving, and just governor to continue in his office. Before it could be sent, however, Bacon had reappeared, surrounding the State House with six hundred followers, armed and ready for a fight.

Once again, Berkeley and Bacon confronted one another before a large audience. Bacon was no longer the meek suppliant. "God damn my blood, I came for a commission, and a commission I will have before I go." Bacon wanted to be a general, general of the volunteers—no, general of all the forces in Virginia against the Indians.

Berkeley was no longer playing the forgiving father confessor. If Bacon was defiant of his authority, he could be defiant of Bacon's superior strength. He tore open his shirt, and bared his graying sunken chest. "Here! Shoot me, foregod, fair mark, shoot." (Pause.) "Here! Shoot me, foregod, fair mark, shoot." (Pause.) And so forth.

Repetitions did not seem to do the trick this time. So Berkeley turned to walk back into the building, exclaiming that he would have his hands cut off, both of them, before giving in to Bacon. Bacon walked close behind, so full of barely contained energy that every motion seemed an unnatural spasm; his hand jerked back and forth between his hat and sword, as if the arm had become autonomous and yet couldn't decide whether to doff the hat to the old governor or to run him through. A detachment of armed men followed Bacon to make sure he or his arm could do whatever the occasion demanded. Among the crowd of spectators that had gathered the air was so heavy with expectation that some were have a hard time getting their breath.

The governor tried another dramatic turn: "For the prevention of the effusion of Christian blood, let you and I decide this controversy by our swords, come along with me." Bacon was scornful. His business was not duelling with grandfathers. He came to demand for the people their rights.

Now Bacon's followers began to lose patience. They pointed their weapons at the legislators watching the drama from the windows of the State House. They began to chant at them, "We will have it, we will have it." And Bacon began to curse anew. Damn his blood but he would kill the governor, the council, the whole assembly and all the rest if he did not get his commission. No one could doubt that this possessed man meant what he said. A member of the assembly, thoroughly terrified, began to wave a white handkerchief and shout, "You shall have it, you shall have it." With this Berkeley's defiance crumbled; he quickly agreed to give Bacon whatever he wished.

Bacon and his men marched out of Jamestown triumphant, cheered on all sides. Berkeley, for his part, felt as if a thief had forcibly taken from him his purse and then had the gall to "make me own I gave it him freely." Perhaps now he did experience the faintest shadow of shame. He had certainly been most despitefully used. And it was obvious that the worst of this storm was yet to be seen.

Bacon had begun to develop his own hierarchy, within his irregulars—the beginning of a shadow government to supplant the legitimate one. Berkeley wrote in a letter to Thomas Ludwell, "Everything here is now deplorable, and three young men that have not been two years in the country absolutely govern it: Mr. Bacon, Mr. Bland, and Mr. Ingram." Berkeley was correctly informed. Joseph Ingram and Giles Bland had emerged as Bacon's chief and most enthusiastic lieutenants.

Berkeley, still governor in name but defeated (and with only the madness of an unlikely revenge to comfort him), retreated to his extensive estate of Green Fields. One historian imagines him there looking out over his fields, meditating at length on how much more governable plants were than men. Their desires were so much more predictable, so much more rational than the phantoms that the brain conjured up. If Berkeley indeed was given to such reveries, they were soon interrupted.

Bacon had been marching north, requisitioning arms and horses as he went. One group of planters petitioned Berkeley in protest. There was obviously going to be a major Indian war, red against white, with no quarter given. Bacon was going to make sure of that. Yet now he was taking all means of self-defense from some plantations that were likely to soon be exposed to the conflict. They pleaded with the governor for protection.

Berkeley thought this provided him with an opportunity to act as governor again. He marched off in Bacon's wake, trying, he said, to raise troops for defense. But no one believed him. Berkeley was, the rumor running ahead of him said, going to raise a large force to come at Bacon from his rear. One of Berkeley's recruiters reported in disgust, "We are accused of raising forces against him, though we never designed anything but against the Indians and to have power to balance his, at the end of the Indian war if God gave us success, but in this we were so unhappy that few of the vulgar would follow us, saying we would not fight Bacon."

In this private complaint the cat is let out of the bag. Berkeley earnestly assured the people that he wanted to collect defensive forces. What he did not say, but what his recruiter admitted, was that this defense had two stages. First he wanted to defend the plantations against the Indians riled up by Bacon. Then he wanted to defend the plantations, or at least Jamestown, from Bacon himself. The sight of Bacon marching to the State House with a force of six hundred was still vivid in Berkeley's mind; he could easily imagine him marching again with a thousand, two thousand troops hardened by repeated Indian massacres.

When Bacon heard of Berkeley's efforts, he too concluded that Berkeley was coming after him. So he simply turned his troops directly around and started marching toward Berkeley. Better to face him now before the governor had collected a full army. Of course, Berkeley had barely collected a body-guard. Now it was Berkeley's turn to perform an about-face. He began a retreat that was really a flight, but to where? He certainly could not hold Jamestown, and a ship to England would look too much like desertion before the enemy. He settled on the peninsula of Accomack, which faced the mouths of the James and York rivers across the Chesapeake.

Only four planters and a few servants accompanied Berkeley. And on Accomack itself no more than half the population supported him. None-theless, there he could make his last stand, if need be. So it was that on July 29, 1676, Nathaniel Bacon became *de facto* ruler of all Virginia, except its east shore. On the next day he did what any new ruler might do, and what Bacon in particular liked to do. He issued a proclamation.

"If virtue be a sin, if piety be guilt, all the principles of morality, goodness and justice be perversity, we must confess that those who are now called rebels may be in danger of those high imputations, those loud and several bulls would affright innocents and render the defense of our brethren and the enquiry into our sad and heavy oppressions, treason. But if there be, as sure there is, a just God to appeal to, if religion and justice be a sanctuary here, if to plead the cause of the oppressed, if sincerely to aim at His Majesty's honour and the public good without any reservation or by interest, if to stand in the gap after so much blood of our dear brethren bought and sold, if after the loss of a great part of His Majesty's colony deserted and dispeopled, freely with our lives and estates to endeavor to save the remainders be treason, God Almighty judge and let guilty die. But since we cannot in our hearts find one single spot of rebellion or treason or that we have in any manner aimed at subverting the settled government or attempting of the person of any either magistrate or pri-vate man—not withstanding the several reproaches and threats of some who, for sinister ends, were disaffected to us and censured our innocent and honest designs—and since all people in all places where we have yet been can attest our civil, quiet, peaceable behavior far different from that of rebellion and tumultuous persons, let truth be bold and all the world know the real foundations of pretended guilt. We appeal to the country itself what and of what nature their oppressions have been or by what cabal and mystery the designs of many of those whom we call 'great men' have been transacted and carried on. But let us trace these men in authority and favor to whose hands the dispensation of the country's wealth has been committed; let us observe the sudden rise of their estates compared with the quality in which they first entered this country or the reputation they have held here amongst wise and discerning men. And let us see whether their extractions and education have not been vile, and by what pretence of learning and virtue they could so soon into employments of so great trust and consequence; let us consider their sudden advancement and let us also consider whether any public work for our safety and defense or for the advancement and propagation of trade, liberal arts or sciences is here extant in anyway adequate to our vast charge; now let us compare these things together and see what sponges have sucked up the public treasure, and whether it hath not been privately contrived away by unworthy favorites and juggling parasites whose tottering fortunes have been repaired and supported at the public charge—now if it be so, judge what greater guilt can be than to offer to pry into these and to unriddle the mysterious wiles of a powerful cabal; let all people judge what can be of more dangerous import than to suspect the so long safe proceedings of some of our grandees and whether people may with safety open their eyes in so nice a concern."

Bacon continued on, to refute the other articles of guilt against him and his followers. He admits, for instance, "open and manifest aversion of all, not only foreign but also the protected and darling Indians." He admits that he regards all Indians as outlaws in fact and that they should in principle be placed outside the benefit and protection of the law. But these admissions are not articles of true guilt; they are rather conclusions that would be reached by any disinterested person. The governor unfortunately is not disinterested because of his trade with the Indians; he is indifferent only to complaints against his darling Indians. Having dismissed the charges against himself, Bacon then can conclude with a rousing peroration that has reminded many a reader of Jefferson's Declaration of Independence:

"Judge therefore all wise and unprejudiced men who may or can faithfully or truly with an honest heart attempt the country's good, their vindication and liberty without the aspersion of traitor and rebel, since as so doing they must of necessity gall such tender and dear concerns. But to manifest sincerity and loyalty to the world, and how much we abhor those bitter names, may all the world know that we do unanimously desire to represent our sad and heavy grievances to his most sacred Majesty as our refuge and sanctuary, where we do well know that all our causes will be impartially heard and equal justice administered to all men."

Bacon was triumphant. He seized the ships on the James River, and dispatched an expedition to take Berkeley on Accomack. He ordered a meeting of all the great planters at the estate of one of them. There, after the appearance of an open discussion of the situation, Bacon produced a document to which they were to swear. It was an oath of allegiance to Bacon. It seemed almost innocuous, except for two clauses, which according to one source Bacon added at the last moment as if on impulse.

The first of these clauses stated that the signers would be willing to fight against Berkeley if need be. This was bad enough, but the second clause was worse still. They would also be willing to fight against any troops sent from England to support Berkeley, until at last the rebels' cause could be explained to the king. This was madness, or at least treason. Bacon controlled the uproar by allowing individuals to express orally their reservations when subscribing to the articles. As one source puts it, "many by threats, force, and fear were feign to subscribe." But he had their signatures; if the rebellion failed, they would now likely go down with him.

The closest supporters of Bacon seem to have realized that they had gone from being rebels against Governor Berkeley to being something very close to revolutionaries against King Charles. Most of them were undeterred. One named Drummond said, "I am in over shoes, I had as well be in over boots."

All, however, were not sanguine about this new turn in events. A conversation is reported between Bacon and a Henrico supporter, John Goode, that indicates as much. Bacon tells Goode that Berkeley is rumored to be getting two thousand reinforcements from England, but he thinks that five hundred Virginians could defeat them by using Indian tactics of ambush and hit-and-run. Goode responds that five hundred redcoats could destroy Virginia by controlling the waterways. He also points out that the planters, when their wealth is at stake, will quickly side with the English. Bacon insists that he can take care of the planters. But what of the colony?, Goode continues. Poor as much of it is already, how can it survive without support from England? Bacon counters that republics have existed quite nicely without the charity of kings—France and the Netherlands will be pleased to provide supplies for ample amounts of Virginia tobacco. Goode responds that this is a recipe for utter ruin and destruction, and he wishes to be excused from having any part of it. Bacon abruptly denounces Goode as a coward, but soon regaining his composure then adds almost by way of apology: "What should a gentleman do in my situation? You as good as tell me I must flee or hang."

With the planters having sworn their oath of allegiance and with his naval forces, led by Giles Bland, off to capture Berkeley, Bacon set out to do what he thought he did best after speechifying: kill innocent Indians.

He chose the objective he thought most easily at hand, the long-loyal and long-suffering Pamunkeys, whose queen had promised scouts to Berkeley and the assembly. The queen, however, seems to have received warning of Bacon's intentions. And she knew the English well enough not to consider standing and fighting. Even if she and her people repulsed this unwarranted attack by Virginia irregulars, she knew any English blood shed would be held against her and her people as if they were the treacherous aggressors. So she had her people retreat into the Great Dragon Swamp, to hide until the insanity passed.

It was a measure of her desperation that she led her people into this dismal place, one of the most fearsome in all seventeenth-century Virginia, to be approached like the land of the dead. The swamp was a large body of mire and nastiness that was thought to infect the air for miles around, killing many people nearby each year and leaving the rest looking like ghosts at cockcrow. The swamp was harmful to human beings by the sheer abundance of its living energy, as if we cannot stand coming into contact with too much vitality. Even in winter the swamp was fully green, the water itself a vast green reptilian ooze, an oppressive green only broken occasionally, by the skeletal form of a whooping crane shrieking in flight, or a copperhead silently wiling amidst the moss like a metallic vein come alive, or a tanager flitting from branch to branch like the torch of a mad incendiary. With ivy hanging everywhere and exuding a blistering poison, swarms of biting insects as dense as a dust storm, the air so fetid it felt like mold in the lungs—this swamp seemed to Indian and Virginian alike a place beyond imagination and hope.

It was a measure of the queen's desperation that she led her people into the swamp, and a measure of Bacon's exuberance that he followed her without hesitation into this *malebolge*. The sensible decision would have been for Bacon to leave the terrified Indians cowering in the swamp. If they ever had been a threat, they would not be now, especially after a few weeks of living inside the dragon. Nonetheless, Bacon realized that his own support had to continue to grow or it would start to erode. He needed another victory, or what would pass as a victory, to remind the people that they truly needed him. His defense of the country was real, not pretended; his intention was service

to the people, not the enhancement of his own power. The threat of the
Indians was real, not a cloak for his own ambition.

To all this protestation of sincerity Berkeley would only have responded
with a sneer. Perhaps Bacon was finally learning the simplest of all lessons
about democracy: it was a swamp in which the unchecked passions of the people would finally overwhelm the aspiring democrat, exhaust and consume
him, without a nod of gratitude or a blink of remorse.

Amazingly, after much weary struggling through the swamp, Bacon and
his men came upon the Pamunkey encampment. Perhaps the queen herself
could not believe that Bacon would be so foolish as to follow her even here,
especially when they both knew the Pamunkeys were no threat, so perhaps she
did not have her people hide their trail as well as they might have. Now having been discovered, she still instructed her people not to resist; they were only
to fly, if they could, more deeply into the hideous swamp.

So there was no battle to speak of. But Bacon's men, nonetheless, would
speak of it as a battle until the Great Swamp Fight became among the most
ferocious ever witnessed by the Virginian wilderness. Despite the hundreds of
ferocious warriors killed in the various tellings, apparently only eight fleeing
Indians were killed in the encounter, presumably shot in the back. Forty-five
more meekly surrendered, providing Bacon with the props he needed for a triumphal march through Virginia with these barbarian captives in tow, proof of
his selfless heroism.

The queen herself, a latter-day Pocahontas hunted and dispossessed of her
people by her John Smith, managed to escape during the attack into the deep
recesses of the swamp, unexplored even by the Indians. There she wandered
alone, lost for weeks, until she finally emerged, looking more like a corpse
than a human being, a fitting bride for the moldering Opechancanough.
Bacon, in contrast, emerged from his weeks in the swamp unscathed—or so it
appeared, if one viewed him from a distance. Up close, however, one could
not help but notice the change in him. He was suffering now from sweats and
fits of shivering; and the lice and other parasites from which all the men suffered seemed to multiply with unnatural swiftness on his body, the warm
moistness of the swamp having transformed them into a vast mob that could
be opposed, but now unleashed never truly brought under control.

Whatever his health, he had lost none of his eloquence, and his ambition
continued to expand as if feeding on itself. He took the capture of Berkeley as
a foregone conclusion. With all Virginia his, he now began to project himself
as the leader of a general American revolution against the British. All the
American colonies could join together, to stand for liberty and justice against

the worn-out, tottering older world. Though his own physical constitution was starting to fail, his mind was running far ahead, oblivious to his frailty.

Unexpected news brought him up short: Giles Bland had been taken captive with all his ships. The victory, the final victory over Berkeley, should have been achieved easily, but Bland in his overconfidence had trusted a ship captain who had betrayed him and all his forces. Berkeley knew how lucky he had been—a "great and miraculous mercy," he called it.

Berkeley gathered his forces and moved on Jamestown once again. Rumors circulated that his soldiers had been promised the plantations of those who had sworn allegiance to Bacon. As one of Berkeley's supporters put it, this promise was a "pack of untruths" that nonetheless produced the desired effect in people's minds. The armed force Bacon had prudently left behind in Jamestown when he marched off to the swamp outnumbered Berkeley's troops two to one, but nonetheless fled back to their leader without a fight. So Berkeley reoccupied Jamestown on September 7, 1676. Upon first placing his feet on the peninsula again, he immediately fell to his knees to give God suitable thanksgiving. Knowing him, we must believe he held the pose until all about him appreciated its aptness for a heroic painting.

If Berkeley was full of thanksgiving, Bacon was equally of hellfire and brimstone. Learning of the craven desertion of Jamestown, he made oaths upon his own blood that he would execute any man who disappointed him again. Then he had an inspiration. Virginia was destined to be a society of freedom. Having men in Virginia either indentured or enslaved was inconsistent with this destiny. All slaves and indentured servants who joined Bacon's forces, therefore, would be immediately freed from all further obligations to their masters. This emancipation proclamation had the desired effect of swelling Bacon's ranks for the campaign to retake Jamestown.

So Bacon marched on Jamestown for the second time—or was it the third? Berkeley thought he was ready. He had enforced the town's defenses, and was content to sit behind his superior position without giving Bacon the satisfaction of battle.

Bacon then set about a siege. He first needed to set up his defenses; knowing the unreliability of the morale of his own troops, he wanted to dig in without his men being fired upon. Berkeley was unlikely to oblige him in this, except that Bacon came up with a perfect cover. He ordered that his men round up all the wives of Berkeley's supporters that could be found on nearby plantations. He set these flowers of Virginia society up on the ramparts as an apron of defense for his men. Included among the women now trembling between the two armies was Bacon's own aunt. Bacon also put up the Indian captives from his recent fight in the swamp, gargoyles amidst the fair matrons. If the matrons showed he was willing to breach all decorum to win, the gargoyles showed that Bacon was a true Virginian still defending the interests of the colony against the inhuman monsters of the frontier.

Berkeley understood his own military position quite clearly: He had only to do nothing to win. Nonetheless, his officers did not seem to understand this as clearly, or at least could not communicate this understanding to their men. There began again much familiar talk about the bravery of vigorous Bacon and the cowardice of decrepit Berkeley. It became clear that the battle of Jamestown had devolved into a battle of gestures, and as usual Bacon was winning. Militarily Berkeley's position was unassailable. However, if he did not do something, his men were going to desert or mutiny.

Berkeley reluctantly decided that he had to give Bacon battle. Unfortunately the very men who were questioning his courage turned out to have little themselves. As one contemporary account put it, the loyalist forces "like scholars going to school, went out with heavy hearts, but returned home with light heels." Worse than that, they did not even stay for all the first lesson. With the first volley from the rebels, the attackers began to scramble for cover. The promise of a plantation was not enough, if all it provided was a burial site.

Berkeley's officers then reasoned that since they could not overrun Bacon's position they therefore could no longer defend their own. Berkeley responded that this conclusion said little about their position, and a good deal about their competence, loyalty, and courage—in short, about their manhood itself. Theirs was the logic of cowardice. Nonetheless, on his officers' insistence, Berkeley fled for Accomack once again. Jamestown was Bacon's once again.

This time Bacon did not want it. His place was on the frontier, and there he would soon have to go again to finish his extermination of the Virginian Indians and to await the British. From there he would have to resist the British troops who would soon come to attempt to place the tyrant Berkeley back in power. The frontier was Bacon's, but Jamestown would provide the forces of repression with a convenient base for operations. For Bacon to try to stay and hold it would be to doom his cause. He could not hold it, nor should he permit Berkeley or the British to retake it. The logic was simple and unavoidable. Jamestown should cease to exist. Like Neptune's Troy it should smoke from the ground. So on the night of September 19, 1676, with Berkeley and his forces looking on from the safety of their ships, Jamestown on the order of Nathaniel Bacon was put to the torch.

The Jamestown peninsula would thereby become the permanent monument to Bacon's Rebellion, a monument of emptiness and desolation. From this destruction, even after the rebellion was long passed, Jamestown would never revive. The administration of Virginia would shift to nearby Williamsburg. In the mid-nineteenth century Jamestown would become an agreeable place for Americans in search of patriotic ruins. They could punt over from the mainland (Jamestown was an island by then). Perhaps they would sit on the hollow trunk of a reclining and much-decayed old sycamore, and meditate on the few broken monuments left as the last tangible records of the first planting of an English colony on American shores. There were a few crumbling walls, half buried in earth, half covered in ivy, largely obscured by the high grass all around. In the midst of these was the old church tower, or rather the irregularly broken and ivy-topped lower portion of it. That was all, a few walls and a broken tower that stood like an aged mourner in the midst of a dead city, trying to remember what it had been like, but recalling only fragments that served to intensify the sense of failure and futility.

But the patriotic visitor could recover from these melancholy reflections, could remind himself that this was the old cradle of an infant world in which an empire lay, this was the birthplace of the glowing westward movement, this was the towering eagle's abandoned nest, sublime in its present obscurity.

Yet, when all was said and done, this was a place Nathaniel Bacon had made his own permanently by leveling its pretensions. In a sense he knew it at the time. There were tactics to justify this willfully destructive act; there always are. But it was the destruction Bacon wanted. Of all the nineteenth-century descriptions of the pathetic little island only one inadvertently evoked this sense of absence. This visitor was trying to describe the peculiar shape of Jamestown island. It was, he decided, the shape an Indian moccasin might leave on the sand, a moccasin print made a good while ago, so now crumbling at the edges.

Bacon had deluded others throughout much of his rebellion, but had he deluded himself? Marching out into the wilderness to kill Indians who did not really fight. Marching back to Jamestown to confront Berkeley, and to watch his histrionics. And yet nothing finally was settled, nothing substantively gained. How could he break the circle? Was the final choice to flee or to be hanged?

The alternative was to destroy, to destroy once and for all, to clear the ground in the hope that the life that would spring up here or elsewhere would be better. Let Virginia not live in Jamestown's shade. So destroy Jamestown he did, as he began to feel weaker and weaker with swamp fever, and as the tiny parasites multiplied on his body. He still tried to consolidate what he named his most recent victory. He composed a new oath of allegiance. He wrote an appeal to the people of Accomack to turn against the returned Berkeley, that "abominable juggler." But most of all he destroyed, or rather his troops destroyed in his name, while Bacon tried to pretend that the razing of Jamestown was only an exception to the orderly conduct of his men. Let one reluctant planter, a Colonel Edward Hill who had the misfortune to quarter Bacon's troops, describe what happened to his estate:

"My house was plundered of all I had, my sheep all destroyed, wheat, barley, oats and Indian grain, to the quantity of seven, or eight hundred bushels, and to complete their jollity draw my brandy, butts of wine, and cider by pails full, and to every health instead of burning their powder, burnt my writings, bills, bonds, accounts to the true value of forty thousand pounds of tobacco and to finish their barbarism, take my wife big with child prisoner, beat her with my cane, tear her bed-linen out of her hands, and with her lead away my children where they must live on corn and water and lie on the ground, had it not been for the charity of good people."

Perhaps it was the addition of servants and slaves, perhaps it was the gleeful destruction of Jamestown, perhaps it was Bacon's own failing energy as commander. But his forces, never gentle or orderly, now became like vermin that have arisen out the unclean earth and march to destroy everything in their path, with no purpose.

Nathaniel Bacon had become the king of vermin, and he looked as though he had been made up for the role. He was now ravaged by the lice that swarmed over his body in such numbers that he could wear a shirt but once and then would have it burned. To those around him it looked as if the lice were being bred within his body, for lice could be found even in his bloody, watery stools.

There is despair in Bacon's last orders. He bemoans his troops' "insolences" that are so great now the people of Virginia are finding them intolerable, especially because his followers no longer made "due distinction" between friend and foe. His troops had begun to treat Virginia as they had always treated the Indians.

Then finally Bacon was dead. And Berkeley's glee was entirely in keeping with the whole disgusting episode. He said that Bacon had so often said, "God damn my blood," God had finally obliged him. The good governor then offered an epitaph:

Bacon is dead; I am sorry at my heart
That lice and flux should take the hangman's part.

But this was not to be Bacon's epitaph. It was provided in a long anony-
mous poem that bears the mark of Bacon's own impassioned eloquence, as if
he wrote it when he knew he was dying. It begins:

Death, why so cruel? What! no other way
To manifest thy spleen, but thus to slay
Our hopes of safety, liberty, our all.

And it ends:

Here let him rest; while we this truth report,
He's gone from hence to a higher Court
To plead his cause, where he by this doth know
Whether to Caesar he was friend or foe.

Bacon's body was not given a proper grave. His followers worried that
Berkeley would find it and have the body exhumed to be hung from a gibbet.
His followers did not know how Bacon's spirit was now faring with the Caesar
of the higher court, but they expected no humanity from the black-hearted
Caesar of this lower court called Virginia. So they hid Bacon's body where no
one could find it, probably deep within a Virginia swamp, one would like to
think in the heart of the Great Dragon.

There was a sense of despair about this decision. Bacon was their commanding tongue; he was the spirit that nerved them. Only months before he
had shouted, "Come on, my hearts of gold, he that dies in the field lies in the
bed of honors." Now, with Bacon at peace in an honorless grave, Berkeley was
going to lord it over them as he had lorded it before. His rogues would rule
Virginia, his darling Indians would be free to ruin the frontier, and the honest
men who had answered Bacon's call, these honest men would swing.

So Bacon's rebellion collapsed. One of his lieutenants, Joseph Ingram,
tried to assume his command, but without effect. The quip went, "The Lion
had no sooner made his exit, but the ape (by indubitable right) steps up upon
the stage." Some slaves and indentured servants did fight on as if they did not
have anything to lose, which in large measure they did not. But most of
Bacon's men tried to save themselves by making suitable professions of allegiance to Berkeley.

So Berkeley could return to unquestioned authority. He could survey the ruins of Jamestown and the ruins of his own Green Fields. Bacon had revealed himself for what he was, a pure negation. Bacon was simply against—against form, against order, against society. Left to himself unopposed, he could build nothing, he could only destroy. Whatever the sufferings of his followers, the changes he wrought had only made them suffer worse. He purposed to mend the part and ruined the whole, to help the bee by destroying the hive.

Berkeley thought he had done his admirable best in the midst of this public lunacy so suited to the traitorous temper of the times, this pestiferous era beneath contempt. He had endured the spite of the vulgar. He had tried to stare them down with manly steadfastness, even dissembled admiration for Bacon when that was called for. But he had remained stiff in his opinion, and in the right.

Now he had tolerated the wrongs done to authority long enough, long enough had he delayed just revenge. The rebels would now learn the truth of the aphorism, "Beware the fury of the patient man." His lurid wrath might be difficult to kindle—but once aroused, as difficult to quench. He had counted the censure of this rabble as fame, its mocking as praise. He had withstood the onset of their brutal rage. Now the lawful power, although it had been driven back, had finally stood its ground. This rebellion would end, as all rebellions did, in a triumph of obedience.

Berkeley largely ignored the rank and file of the rebels as long as they submitted promptly and repented profusely. This seemed less out of mercy than out of a sense that they were beneath notice. However, with anyone who could be counted among those responsible for spreading this political plague across the frontier he was as merciful as he would have been with a mad dog.

Approximately twenty-three were executed, and five or six others escaped certain death by plunging into the wilderness, to take their chances with the Indians. But it would have taken the tongue of Bacon to explain to any Virginia Indians why they should not do Berkeley's work for him. As for Berkeley, he was greedy for vengeance, and relished every instance of it.

Berkeley's handling of the cases brought before him can be judged from his treatment of Mr. Drummond, who had thought he might as well be up to his boots. When he appeared, Berkeley made a sarcastic bow and said, "Mr. Drummond, you are very welcome. I am more glad to see you than any man in Virginia. Mr. Drummond, you shall be hanged in half an hour." And he was, with willful disregard of English law (it was later decided). Berkeley was trying to have as many executions as quickly as possible.

In fact, the number of executions may well have been far less than Berkeley intended. A member of the assembly during this difficult time said, "If we had let him alone, he would have hanged half the country." Perhaps he simply hanged as many as he could before the British government could interfere.

In January 1677, the same month that four rebels were hanged near Yorktown where General Washington about a century later would accept the surrender of Lord Cornwallis, a commission arrived from England to investigate what had gone wrong in Virginia and what needed to be done to get the tobacco revenues flowing back into the king's treasury.

The commissioners got off to a bad start with Berkeley, and their relations only got worse. From the start, they thought that one could reason from the disorder of the sheep to the unfitness of the shepherd. And this particular shepherd, they saw to their shock, was now emphatically perpetuating the same small-minded administration that had led to the disorder in the first place. In their final report they had little good to say about Bacon, but little good to say about Berkeley either. Clearly they had decided that he was an old man who had long outlived his usefulness to the crown. His errors in judgment had led the colony into a labyrinth of ruin that was costing England dearly. The commissioners repeatedly clashed with him over the harshness of his treatment of accused rebels, and particularly their families.

Drummond, for instance, may well have deserved to be executed, but not without due process—and should his whole plantation have been confiscated, and his wife and five children thrown out into the street to live as paupers? In general, the commissioners were opposed to having loyalists try to regain their wealth at the expense of the few plantations that stood intact. So many had sworn to one or another of Bacon's oaths, frequently under duress or having been deceived, how could any clear determination be made in most cases between loyalist and rebel?

Berkeley did his best to stymie the commission, but finally decided he had to return to England to present his own case. In a final gesture of what seemed friendship he bid the commissioners come to visit him before he left, as a social call. It appeared to go well. The commissioners and Berkeley would still disagree over what was best for Virginia, but at least they could disagree without anger or spite, like gentlemen. As they were leaving and about to enter the coach Berkeley had provided for them, the commissioners realized that they were still dealing with the old Berkeley, a man who had come to live on his hard feelings. Berkeley had arranged for them to be driven through the colony, back to their residences, by the common hangman. They walked. Berkeley, of course, assured them that he was "innocent in this as the Blessed Angels." And the commissioners responded with a Baconite rage. Perhaps one even said, "Damn my blood."

Berkeley's departure from Virginia was saluted with bonfires and cannon-ades. And he never did get to justify himself to the king. "That old fool," King Charles said, "has hanged more men in that naked country than I did for the murder of my father." Berkeley was dead within a few months, perhaps going into the afterlife to plead the prosecution's case against Bacon in the higher court. It would have been in character for him to pursue his enemy beyond the grave. In fact, one would like to think of them together, Bacon and Berkeley, in the same circle of hell, perhaps in the circle of the wrathful where they might gnaw on one another for all eternity.

Bacon's rebellion did nonetheless, in its own perverse way, promote liberty in Virginia, although even sketching how it did, how 1676 led to 1776, is almost as melancholy a task as recounting the course of the rebellion itself.

The rebellion of Bacon and the indentured servants and recently freed men dramatized how unsatisfactory was a system of labor based on inden-tured servitude. Servants were now living longer, gaining their freedom, and collecting in impoverished groups that were nothing but trouble. Let a fire-brand like Bacon appear amongst them, and this human kindling would ignite to threaten to sweep away all that respectable Virginians had accumu-lated through a lifetime of careful husbanding. It had happened once, and it would continue to happen at regular intervals as long as this unstable class remained in Virginia. That was the deep logic to the situation.

The solution to this problem was to replace the indentured servants with slaves. A slave did cost twice what an indentured servant did; but now that sea-soning was taking fewer and fewer newcomers, that would likely be a good in-vestment. And a slave population, properly managed, might reproduce itself.

So Virginia in the late seventeenth century began its slow but inexorable transition to a plantation society based upon slave labor. James, Duke of York, played a role by promoting British entry into the slave trade. A decline in sugar prices played its role by inhibiting West Indian demand for slaves. But the crucial role was played by Nathaniel Bacon, who inadvertently convinced the wealthy of Virginia that slaves were preferable to indentured servants. And then at a certain point the institution of slavery took root and took on a demonic life of its own. By 1700 there were perhaps ten to fifteen thousand slaves in Virginia; by 1750, one hundred thousand.

As this change was effected, Virginia became increasingly attractive for the wealthy immigrant. It was estimated that a man with three hundred pounds to invest could buy a fine plantation, staff it with eight or nine slaves, and be guaranteed with a comfortable income of over one hundred pounds a year for the indefinite future.

Of course, laws had to be instituted suitable to this new social system. The lawmakers of Virginia were fully equal to the task. "About the casual killing of slaves": the owner could not be tried for a felony "since it cannot be presumed that prepensed malice (which alone makes murder felony) should induce any man to destroy his own estate." Runaway slaves were pure outlaws, and could be killed by "any person or persons whatsoever . . . by such ways and means as he, she, or they shall think fit, without accusation or impeachment of any crime for the same." Impudent slaves could be beaten, or, in more severe cases, "dismembered" a little, by (say) clipping off a toe or two.

The line between slave and free had to be drawn clearly, with none of the old ambiguity of that old "middle class" of indentured servants. The older practice of allowing a slave, like an indentured servant, to own certain of his own possessions was no longer permitted. Children of slave mothers were declared slaves for life, no matter what the status of the father. Careful laws were also needed to prevent "that abominable mixture and spurious issue which hereafter may increase in this dominion." Any colonist, man or woman, who tried to marry a black, a mulatto, or an Indian was to be immediately banished. Virginia was no longer a colony in which the likes of John Rolfe and Pocahontas were welcome.

Of course, Nathaniel Bacon would not have been sorry to learn that the Indians were no longer welcome as free persons. When the line was drawn between slave and free, Indians were placed with the slaves. With the demand for slaves increasing, Indians were forcibly enslaved, especially those from the Carolinas to the south. Laws had to be passed to make sure that an Indian's conversion to Christianity no longer entitled him to become a full member of the colonial society. Reading through these discussions, one imagines the ghost of Opechancanough nodding with grim satisfaction; he had lost, but he had judged correctly.

Bacon had judged correctly too, in a sense. He had used a racist demagoguery to try to improve the lot of the poor white freedman. In Virginia in the late seventeenth and early eighteenth centuries a racism institutionalized as slavery did improve the material lot of the average Virginia freedman. The magnates could now afford to treat the poorer freedmen with more generosity. In the first half of the eighteenth century, the number of landowners in Virginia increased by two-thirds while the size of the average plantation declined by one-third. There was, it seemed, prosperity enough for all whites, once blacks and the remaining Indians were enslaved. Even the poor could be grateful that their skin placed them on the right side of the great chasm between free and slave.

In such a divided society one could scarcely help but reflect on what a precious thing liberty was. One would rather die than to let another exercise over oneself the tyranny that the slave owner routinely exercised over his slave. A whole generation of planter children grew up contemplating this self-evident truth and its corollaries. The more educated among them began to think of themselves as latter-day Greeks. The Greeks, after all, had rejected the confused degrees of freedom that had characterized ancient Near Eastern civilization. They rather had split their society clearly between the free and the enslaved, and then contemplated the importance of freedom to be truly human. And one might have to go as far as ancient Athens to find as distinguished a collection of citizens as the one produced on eighteenth-century Virginia plantations.

Let us have these great Virginians pass before us, like the great heroes of the ancient world, to remind us of the achievement of Virginia after Bacon.

First comes, like the crier to prepare us for the rest, the greatest orator of the American Revolution, Patrick Henry, scorn on his brows and sour disdain, a son of thunder prepared to defy earth or heaven with his torrents of sublime eloquence. He shouts in a commanding voice, "Is life so dear or peace so sweet, as to be purchased at the price of chains and slavery?" He glares at us all, as if wondering whether we Americans are still worthy of his presence—and then answers his own question, in a tone as uncompromising as his meaning, "As for me, give me liberty or give me death." His performance over, he passes on.

Next comes the godlike Washington, apart in lonely grandeur, seeming more a monument than a man, towering above his contemporaries (either in fact or perception) as his monument towers above all others in the city named after him. Father of his country, a man of regal bearing who declined the opportunity to become a king. A new Cincinnatus who wished only to repose under his own vine and fig tree and yet who quit his peaceful abode for an ocean of difficulties, even the evening of his life being largely consumed in public cares. So it could be said that while England's greatest contribution to the world is the works of Shakespeare, America's is the character of Washington. By the character of Washington even the easy cynicism of Byron was quieted:

> George Washington had thanks and naught beside
> Except the all-cloudless glory (which few men's is)
> To free his country.

Following Washington, as if in his train but at a distance, is the least of this galaxy of Virginians, Light-Horse Harry Lee, Washington's comrade-in-arms, the most dashing cavalry officer of the rebels, who steadfastly refused promotion so that he might always remain at the forefront of battle and who then in peace served three times as governor of Virginia. Lee represented the best of Virginian provincialism. "Virginia is my country," he said, a lesson his more famous son learned too well. Yet now he follows Washington, reciting the enduring words from his congressional eulogy for his greater compatriot, "First in war, first in peace, first in the hearts of his countrymen."

Next comes the lanky, shambling figure of Thomas Jefferson, freckle faced and sandy haired, his appearance unkempt as befits a true democrat. Perhaps we should imagine him in those shocking crimson breeches he wore as secretary of state to protest the aristocratic pretensions of Alexander Hamilton and others, including (must we admit?) Washington himself. Dreamy but unyielding Tom Jefferson, our most illustrious apostle of freedom to the world. Long before the Revolution he had insisted that our rights do not derive from precedent or tradition but are intrinsic to our nature and inalienable. Long after the Revolution the ringing words of his Declaration of Independence would continue to inspire others to risk their all against the slavery of unjust institutions. If Washington was the father of his country, Jefferson was its young, idealistic uncle.

Modest James Madison comes next, looking more like a dissenting minister than a president. He it was who, despite his temperament, had to lead the republic through its second war, a war that many thought might reverse the results of the first. Yet Madison's greatest contributions came earlier, in framing the Constitution. "Mankind has grown tired of keeping the ship of state afloat by standing constantly at the pump. Let the leaks which have endangered her be stopped." And then he, together with Alexander Hamilton and John Jay, composed the immortal essays of the *Federalist* to defend the new frame of government against those who preferred confederacy to union. Modest James Madison, with so much to be immodest about.

Then comes a pair, like twins in their exotic buckskins, yoked forever by history as well, Lewis and Clark, sons of Virginia soil who ranged far in the service of their growing nation. Lewis and Clark—whom Jefferson commissioned after the Louisiana Purchase to explore beyond the Mississippi, across the vast emptiness of the prairies (airy undulations without limit in high rank grass), over the continental divide, along the Missouri, the Yellowstone, the Columbia rivers, until they reached the roaring coast of the Pacific. This they did and then returned as they came—and during the whole unprecedented trek lost but a single man. Lewis and Clark, first citizens of the greater American republic, not the narrow strip of aspiring civilization that was Washington's America, nor the ramshackle, thriving America of Jefferson, but the continental America of Sam Houston, Manifest Destiny, and the locomotive.

After these exotic, boisterous explorers comes a figure almost as grave and aloof as Washington himself. No wonder he reminds of Washington: Washington was John Marshall's paragon; he had served under him during the Revolution, with admiration and without criticism even at Valley Forge, that Gethsemane of the Continental Army. Although the staunchest of federalists, Marshall had repeatedly declined federal office, declined even Washington's offer to appoint him attorney general—but then John Adams persuaded him to become chief justice. (The greatest achievement of Adams's presidency, one ungracious Virginian said.) Here Marshall found the place for which he was preternaturally suited. Marshall, the saying went, was born to be chief justice of any country in which he lived. Not true, he would insist. He was born to be chief justice of this one, born to put steel in the words of the Constitution by making the Supreme Court their final guarantor. And we can imagine that steel in his posture and step as he walks past, head high, eyes looking neither right nor left but only far into the distance ahead.

Finally, almost as an afterthought, is James Monroe, a man who would dominate almost any other collection of distinguished Americans, but here he brings up the rear. He was a governor of Virginia, represented it both in the House and Senate, represented the nation as a whole to three of the major powers of Europe, served as both secretary of state and secretary of war, and then for two terms as president. Of the major elective offices of the republic he never served only as vice president, yet another indication of his good sense and good fortune. James Monroe—of all his many services to the republic, two stand out above the others. He was the special envoy that Jefferson sent to negotiate the Louisiana Purchase, a transaction that Napoleon himself knew could transform the young republic into a world power. And then President James Monroe declared that the transformation had occurred. In his Doctrine he addressed the European powers as equals, and informed them that they would no longer be permitted to intrude on the development of the western hemisphere. The age of European colonization of the New World was over; henceforth the United States of America would be the principal arbiter of freedom and bondage here.

This is the extraordinary procession of Virginian patriots, a collection of men who, viewed in retrospect, seem composed more of marble than of flesh.

We might say of them collectively as a contemporary said of the greatest of them, "Had he lived in the days of idolatry, he had been worshipped as a god."

These are the human gods produced by Virginia and its slavery, much as Athens and its had produced Pericles, Socrates, Demosthenes, and all the rest so admired by these Virginians. Yet behind this stately procession of respectable Virginians, almost invisible in the shadows but there if you look, stands the glaring titanic presence of Nathaniel Bacon, the real guardian spirit of Virginia, John Smith returned with eloquence and chains, an Alcibiades of the New World—Nathaniel Bacon who tainted everything he touched, including the chaste form of Liberty herself.

Chapter VIII

SUN KING OF THE
WILDERNESS

"L ITTLE PROPERTY AND ABUNDANT CHARM"—so Duc de Saint-
Simon described in his memoirs Louis de Buade, Comte de Frontenac,
the most imposing presence in New France during the reign of Louis
XIV, and the man who benefitted most from the disruptions of King Philip's
War and Bacon's Rebellion. Memoirs by courtiers, of course, are notoriously
unreliable guides to the characters of their fellows. Too often, they are a
thwarted vanity's last attempt to settle scores. What better way to settle a score
than fix a personality for all time with a condescending phrase? Fairness in
such a case is out of the question if it might dull a witticism. Nonetheless,
Saint-Simon's phrase captures an essential tension that governed Frontenac's
life. This is especially true if "charm" is broadened to "gallantry."

Frontenac had the bearing and the charm that came from an unassailable
social position. He had been named Louis after his godfather, Louis XIII. But
Frontenac would not have regarded himself as worthy of his name if he had
distinguished himself only at court. "In France the only nobility that is recognized is the nobility of the sword. It is a warlike nation and one that glorifies
the profession of arms." So wrote one of Frontenac's contemporaries, and
Frontenac himself would not have disagreed.

His distant ancestors had won their nobility by military feats in time
immemorial. He owed the distinction bestowed upon him at his baptism by
the king to the continued military service of his immediate forebears. If he did
not distinguish himself on the field of battle, the glory of his ancestors would
only illumine his own lack of worth. His lineage would become his shame.

The Thirty Years' War was a more brutal war than any his ancestors had
seen. Provinces were ravaged repeatedly until cannibalism became commonplace, families having to place guards at the graves of their newly dead to pre-

vent the corpses being stolen for the pot. But this same war was a boon for Frontenac. He fought in the forefront against the Italian city of Orbetello, and had a wounded right arm as a reminder of his noble exertions. He had demonstrated he was a true Frontenac, worthy to carry the surname of a king.[1]

Later Frontenac would participate in a less glorious campaign with the Venetians in Crete against the infidel Turks. The intent was noble, more noble even than attacking the impudent Protestants. The Turks were a threat against the very existence of Christendom, and any knight of the realm should be willing to lay down his life to prevent another inch of soil to come under the barbarous sway of the minaret. Yet the campaign was lost, and the unseemly bickering between the Venetians and the French may well have contributed. The Venetian commander, in particular, charged Frontenac with placing the interests of France over those of the campaign; Frontenac countered by questioning the military competence of his superior (only in rank). A hearing before the doge himself resulted in Frontenac's dismissal from Venetian service without pay. Frontenac returned to France with no more money to feed his noble appetites, but with his sense of honor intact and with many a whispering tale for the ears of fair ladies. Many stories but no money—from one perspective, this was his life in a nutshell.

Of course, a strong sense of gallantry without an ample source of money is a social disease, the very disease for which Frontenac spent much of his adult life seeking a cure. And Frontenac, be assured, was one of those who by birth, training, and temper was prepared to reap where others had sowed. His most promising attempt at such a harvest was the wooing of his wife. She would come to be called one of the "Divinities" of the French court, and would have her portrait, as Minerva, hung at Versailles. Saint-Simon remembered (not entirely out of kindness) that like a divinity she demanded constant incense and usually received it.

When Frontenac first spied her, she was not quite a divinity yet, just the beautiful heiress to a huge bourgeois fortune. She found the dashing Louis de Buade, Comte de Frontenac, hero of battles, godson of a king, as irresistible as

---

[1]Twentieth-century scholars, with characteristic lack of grace (such peevish fellows could scarcely be proper men), have questioned this distinction. They point out that Frontenac alone among the senior officers is not mentioned in the dispatch sent back to the French court. They also point out that the wounded right arm might have been used as an excuse to avoid a duel, whereas his handwriting—strangely—shows no change. Frontenac would likely have said in response—if he deigned to respond at all—that the historian's task is to celebrate greatness, not to cheapen it. Other than that, history had no more significance than the endless chattering of a tiresome old fool.

he found himself. Unfortunately for them both, her father had a more mercantile way of estimating worth: It was better to immure his only child in a convent than allow the fortune of a lifetime's work be dissipated by a noble roué.

This called for derring-do. Frontenac was prepared to force even the sacred obstacle of the convent for the sake of his love. Presumably Frontenac told her this, and how he loved her dearly and that she was the most beautiful girl in the world. They were secretly married, and the father presented with a *fait accompli*. But noble impetuosity was not on this occasion rewarded by bourgeois acquiescence. After failing to get the marriage annulled, the father, a widower, hastily remarried in order to sire another heir (and did so—but only after his new wife complained that his constant attentions were nearly killing her). Neither lawsuits nor attempts at reconciliation achieved their purpose. Frontenac ended up with a wife much like himself, little property and abundant charm. He had won the war and lost Crete.

The bejeweled, artificial world of elegance in which these two now made their way together has been best evoked in miniature in the prose of Francis Parkman, the greatest of America's Romantic historians:

"Versailles was like a vast and gorgeous theatre, where all were actors and spectators at once; and all played their parts to perfection. Here swarmed by thousands this silken nobility, whose ancestors rode cast in iron. Pageant followed pageant. A picture of the time preserves for us an evening in the great hall of the Château, where the King, with piles of louis d'or before him, sits at a large oval green table, throwing the dice, among princes and princesses, dukes and duchesses, ambassadors, marshals of France, and a vast throng of courtiers, like an animated bed of tulips; for men and women alike wear bright and varied colors. Above are the frescoes of Le Brun; around are the walls of sculptured and inlaid marbles, with mirrors that reflect the restless splendors of the scene and the blaze of chandeliers, sparkling with crystal pendants. Pomp, magnificence, profusion, were a business and duty at the Court. Versailles was a gulf into which the labor of France poured its earnings; and it was never full."

This pomp, magnificence, profusion (which Parkman almost despite himself found so beguiling) was the very world against which Molière had his misanthrope complain: "There is nothing I hate more than the contortions of these protestation mongers, these affable exchangers of fatuous greeting, polite mouthers of meaningless speeches." In particular, Molière's Alceste hated the hypocrisy he saw at the heart of a courtier's charm, a charm that always amuses to the profit of self, and usually at the expense of those not present. "Stick to it friends, like the true courtiers that you are! You spare no one. Everyone suffers in turn but let any one of them appear on the scene and you would all rush to meet him, offer him your hands in fulsome greeting, and protest your eternal devotion."[2]

A well-connected habitué of the French court, Mademoiselle de Montpensier, who felt betrayed by Frontenac and his wife in just this way, sought revenge in her memoirs. "He kept open table, and acted as if everybody owed duty to him. . . . He praised everything that belonged to himself, and never came to sup and dine with me without speaking of some ragout or some new sweetmeat that had been served up on his table, ascribing it all to the excellence of the officers of his kitchen. The very meat that he ate, according to him, had a different taste on his board than on any other." Mademoiselle de Montpensier continued in like vein, systematically mocking one thing after another in his household, until finally she reached the stables: "All who wished his good graces were forced to admire his horses, which were very indifferent." What Montpensier does not mention is that Frontenac's possession of even indifferent horses is remarkable because he had no money.

Frontenac, like so many noble Frenchmen of the time, was attempting to lord it over his fellows on credit. Any courtier worthy of his place had to be able to lead men, seduce women, and gull creditors. And Frontenac's creditors, in particular, had far more substantial grounds for bitterness than did the Mademoiselle from Montpensier.

By 1663 Frontenac admitted to debts of 343,408 livres. Nonetheless, he still managed to put off his creditors; in 1664 they agreed to a small interest rate to be paid annually until the day he could start to make good on the principal. By 1672 that day had not yet come; neither had the day when he would make his first payment of interest. As one creditor complained to the king at the time, "We have inconvenienced ourselves in order to accommodate him and to give him time to settle his affairs, and he has always broken his word in such a way that no one could trust him any longer."

This creditor had to wait while Frontenac went off to defend Christendom in Crete against the Turks. How could one foreclose on a crusader? But now he had returned, and with no more money. In 1672 legal proceedings were begun to seize the fifty-year-old Frontenac's remaining property. But the

---

[2]The Duc de La Rochefoucauld, another contemporary of Frontenac, would allow not even military gallantry to escape such souring analysis. "Love of fame, fear of disgrace, schemes for advancement, desire to make things comfortable and pleasant, and the urge to humiliate others are often at the root of the valor men hold in such high esteem."

aging swordsman still had an unexpected parry left. He got himself appointed governor of the distant colony of New France. Among the perquisites of his new office was an indefinite deferral of all legal obligations to pay past debts.

By this time Frontenac was no longer living with his wife. She would assist his interests at court whenever she could, but that was as far as her wifely duties went. They were social allies, but sought broader fields for amorous conquest. This domestic situation provided an alternative explanation for Frontenac's appointment to New France. Frontenac's name had been intimately linked with another distinguished beauty at court, Madame de Montespan. This was an awkward matter now that Montespan had become the favorite mistress of King Louis XIV. It was made more awkward still by a ditty that was being passed around among the courtiers.

> I'm delighted the King our sire
> Loves la Montespan.
> I, Frontenac, do split my sides
> Knowing what goes on.
> For now I'm no longer her beast,
> and
> You've got what was left from my feast.
> You,
> You've got what was left from my feast.

Louis de Buade, Comte de Frontenac, may well have both spent and charmed his way right out of France.

Frontenac, although he was of unassailable social position and although he had apparently shown himself worthy of it by his military exploits, found that to continue to live as a nobleman he had to become a servant—we will not say slave—of the crown. If Louis XIV had not chosen him for New France, Frontenac would likely have been reduced to penury; he would have been noble only in name. As Madame de Savignée wrote about Louis XIV, "It may happen that in paying court to him we may find ourselves dependent upon what he tosses us." Frontenac had already found himself so dependent, a well-bred lap dog. Whatever Frontenac's individual responsibility for being reduced to a royal dependent, the memoirs of Louis XIV make plain that he intended to reduce all the nobility in just this way. All were to be dependent upon the king, as Savignée realized:

"All eyes were fastened upon him alone; it was to him alone that all wishes were directed; he alone received all deference; he alone was the object of all expectation; one strove, one understood, and one achieved anything only through him. His good graces were regarded as the sole source of all posses-sions; one thought of raising oneself only to the extent that one might approach his person or rise in his esteem; all the rest was sterile."

This reduction of the old nobility to obedience was a process begun long before Louis XIV, during the ministry of Richelieu. To understand Fron-tenac's administration of New France, we must understand the rudiments of the new system of absolutism, of which Richelieu was the greatest architect and Louis XIV the greatest practitioner.

After Richelieu had subdued the Protestants, the nobility remained the chief obstacle to the monarchy's exercise of absolute power. Richelieu would write to his king that his nobility were wont to act "not as your subjects, but as independent chieftains." As governors of the provinces they were conducting local business "like so many local sovereigns." Richelieu set about correcting this situation, much to the annoyance of the nobility itself. Under the gover-nors, he placed his own "intendants," and then he concentrated on them all financial powers (with the noble governor left in charge only of the local troops). He counterpoised to the old noblemen of the sword, who had inher-ited their titles from the distant past, a nobility of the robe, who had earned their titles through their own service in administration. (Frontenac's unwill-ing father-in-law was a prominent nobleman of the robe.)

Needless to say, the noblemen of the sword opposed these developments as well as they could. They continuously complained, frequently plotted, and occasionally rebelled. As one orator during a particularly dangerous rebellion declared: "Thus it is that nobility, not of blood but of your heroic spirits, not buried in the tombs of your ancestors but living again through these your noble actions, that has inspired you to assemble to preserve your privi-leges. . . . It is that ancient glory . . . which could no longer suffer all the af-fairs of a State, which is military in its very foundation and of which you form the most powerful and illustrious part, to be decided without your consent."[3]

---

[3] Despite the seriousness of the ends of such rebellions, and despite the eloquence with which these ends were often expressed, the rebellions collectively do, in retrospect, take on the foolish charm of a farce. Alas, the very number and variety of ways the noble plotters found to fail assure this. The chief farceur during the time of Richelieu was the brother of the king, Gaston d'Orléans. Five times this prince of the blood plotted against His Majesty, five times he belatedly decided he lacked the stomach, five times he asked for forgiveness to leave allies to face the scaffold on his behalf. Other noble plots were little more dignified in their outcomes. Once two assassins had the unsuspecting Richelieu at their mercy, only to have the two noble-men who had entrusted them with the task fail to give the sign. (Either they lost their nerve or just forgot which one was to give the sign.) One of these noblemen, the distinguished Comte

By the time of Louis XIV's reign the failure of the old nobility to check the erosion of their power was bitterly evident to them. Saint-Simon referred to his administration as "the reign of the vile bourgeois." Louis himself admitted he had "no ministers, only men of business." He explained to his son the reason for this: "It is not in my interest to select subjects of a higher degree. It was important that they should not conceive hopes any higher than it pleased me to grant them."

Nonetheless, despite complaints from men like Saint-Simon, Louis XIV had no intention of destroying the military foundations of French society in favor of the vile bourgeoisie. Louis himself professed disdain for economic matters. He was one of those princes, he liked to say, for whom the questions of honor took precedence over everything else. "If the English . . . would be content to be the greatest merchants in Europe, and allow me for my share whatever I can conquer in a just war, nothing would be as convenient for us as to cooperate."

Louis's greatest man of business, his intendant of intendants, the noblest of the robe (and the man who would be Frontenac's immediate superior), Jean-Baptiste Colbert, understood all this perfectly. He declared as a "beautiful maxim [that] it is necessary to save five sou on inessential things to pour out millions when it is a question of your glory." For Colbert, Versailles would be the enduring monument to that maxim; over twenty-five years, innumerable inessential things, including human lives, were sacrificed so that Louis could spend more than a hundred million livres to build the most elegant set of palaces in Europe. And yet Colbert understood his king well enough to know that Louis would no more have this domestic feat be considered the essence of his glory than Frontenac would have wanted his charm with the ladies be taken as proof of his nobility.[4] Glory, honor, nobility—these could be truly found only in military triumphs.

---

de Soissons, subsequently did the only honorable thing by taking to the field against the king's troops. He won a decisive battle, and began his triumphant march toward Paris where the king was already preparing to give up Richelieu. As de Soissons was riding toward his place in French history, he felt hot under his knightly armor, and tried to push up his helmet visor with the only thing handy, a loaded pistol. Heaven, it seems, had decreed that Comte de Soissons, like his archenemy Richelieu, was to die unchallenged, at the height of his power.

[4]Colbert for his part knew he had to make himself agreeable to Louis only. There was no need to try to share in the social graces of a Frontenac. One of the court divinities, in the midst of trying to soften him with her charms, was supposed to have exclaimed in exasperation, "Monsieur, at least make me a sign that you are listening." Colbert was a courtier only to his king. To the wits at court he was the North—and when he died, they said the cause was a stone not in the kidneys (as the doctors claimed), but in the heart.

While Colbert and other men of business would provide their king with the sinews of war, the old military aristocracy would provide him with his actual victories. This nobility had to realize that their own honor and their service to the king were really the same thing. And so, for instance, dueling was forbidden, a daring prohibition because the French nobility had long since acquired a taste for one another's blood. (Without a war at hand, how else could a young blade prove himself worthy of his own title and other men's ladies?) But for Louis, as for Richelieu before him, a bravery that proved itself at the price of weakening the state, if only by a single man, was a bravery that did not understand its place in the higher order of things.

And so the old nobility, with respect to dueling and other traditional independences, had to be made to give way, if not to cower, before the king, however much that might seem a poison to their pride. Only then could they, united under his divinely ordained leadership, make all Europe cower, for Louis's own highest work was to duel with the other powers of Europe.

At the time Frontenac was appointed governor of New France, 1672, Louis was beginning a duel with the Dutch. He had been offended by their "ingratitude, bad faith, and insupportable vanity." (He was particularly incensed at a medal struck by the Dutch depicting him kissing daintily the ample rear of a Dutch burgher.) The war to correct them would prove a great drain on the French treasury, the resultant taxes a hardship for her people, its casualties would be numerous, and during it little territory would be gained. Nonetheless, Louis would be pleased by the results. "I made my enemies tremble, astonished my neighbors, and brought despair to my foes . . . France has demonstrated the difference between herself and other nations."

The pursuit of honor and glory, although Louis XIV (or for that matter Frontenac) would like to forget this, did cost money. New France was primarily important for the Sun King insofar as it contributed to his capacity to make war. Almost immediately, New France offered the homeland an apparently inexhaustible supply of furs. Here the cold weather, which worked against New France in other ways, helped; the beaver from Canadian forests usually had fur of remarkable richness. Moreover, the Indians, by wearing these furs, oiled them with their bodies. Such "greasy" Canadian furs became the standard against which all others were judged by European connoisseurs. Colbert attempted to control the fur trade as he attempted to control everything else that could contribute to Louis's glory. Eventually he settled on establishing a monopoly in the trade for Canadian furs; the price of this monopoly for its lucky owner would be as high as 500,000 livres a year. To protect the suppliers of furs, their price would be fixed by Colbert and his ministry. Nothing could have contributed more to the expansion of the fur trade, for the gatherers were assured of a good price irrespective of the vagaries of supply and demand. And Louis could be assured of 500,000 livres a year to do with as he pleased. Helpful as this was, it was as nothing compared to that for which Colbert hoped.

Colbert had written that "the principal and greater part of commerce consists in trade with overseas colonies." Colbert dreamed of a France that, thanks to its colonies, would be economically self-sufficient. He believed that the greatest immediate problem for France's economic growth was caused by foreign merchants who, acting as middlemen in international trade, were draining France of considerable portions of its great wealth. Their very profit came from taking more wealth out of France than they brought in. Thereby, in Colbert's words, they "produced both their own prosperity and the want of this kingdom, and, as an undeniable consequence, their power and our weakness." Colbert's mercantilism was in this respect little different from that implemented by the British navigation acts. Nonetheless, Colbert's had an objective quite different from a French version of Dutch prosperity. Colbert's sound mercantile policies were intended to provide the economic foundation for a French political and military domination of Europe. For Louis XIV to achieve what Philip II had unsuccessfully attempted, for him to become king of kings, all that was needed was present French military prowess yoked to a thriving imperial trading system.

New France had an important role to play in this system, as Colbert understood it. It would not only supply raw materials to Europe, but it would also provide a market for French manufactured goods. To be such a market, New France had to be populous. In 1667 a census conducted at Colbert's urging showed that the total French population in Canada was only 3,215. Louis himself expressed his "regret" at the small number of inhabitants; Colbert sought to remedy the situation.

Colbert exhorted the Canadians to marry early and have large families. "I pray you to commend it to the consideration of the whole people, that their prosperity, their subsistence, and all that is dear to them, depend on a general resolution, never to be departed from, to marry boys at eighteen and girls at fourteen and fifteen; since abundance can never come to them except through the abundance of men." But Colbert, as was usual with him, did far more than exhort. Parents whose children did not marry early were to be fined. Those who were fruitful and multiplied in service of the general good were to be rewarded; anyone with ten living children received a pension of 200 livres a year, anyone with twelve, 300. Indigent gentlewomen were provided with dowries to attract suitors. And 6,000 livres were spent between 1665 and 1668 alone to stake military officers who wished to marry and settle in New France. Anyone of the lower ranks who decided to stay on after his tour was also given a bonus.

Colbert also opened the French treasury to encourage emigration. He was particularly concerned about women, since the census of 1667 had shown men outnumbering women two to one. Healthy young women became a chief export to New France; Colbert in one of his dispatches announces he will be sending on the next ship "150 girls, geldings, stallions, and sheep." Girls who came this way were called the "King's daughters"; most were peasant girls, a few were ladies, many came from orphanages, all were to be married off within a few weeks of their arrival.

What happened if a few young ladies were left over? That unwanted contingency had been planned for. The remaining bachelors were forbidden to go into the woods, hunting or fishing, until all the daughters of the king had received acceptable proposals. The court records tell the story of a François Lenoir caught breaking this injunction. He pleaded guilty and was given a year's reprieve to marry a woman in the next batch; if he did not, he would be fined 300 livres. He married.

The results of this paternalistic campaign were impressive. Between 1665 and 1668 the population would almost double, to reach 6,282, and in the early 1670s it was to pass 10,000. The only problem was that the economic development of France and its colonies always had to take second place to Louis's pursuit of military glory. In 1672, the year Frontenac became governor, the subsidies for emigration largely ended because Louis needed money to pursue his war against the insolent Dutch. (In one battle in this war, the Battle of Senef, 8,000 French soldiers died—more than the entire male population of New France.)

Colbert himself favored the war against the Dutch. They had thousands of trading ships while the French had only hundreds. And to get the proper timbers for building more ships, the French had to trade across the Baltic largely through Dutch middlemen. So to improve French shipping the French had to trade with the impudent Dutch and make them richer—unless Louis could conquer the Netherlands, or unless another source of timber could be found.

Louis failed to conquer the Dutch despite a glorious campaign. The official court historian—no less a pen than Racine—wrote of one siege, "Never did a city put up so great a resistance, never was fire more cruel and terrible . . . but what could their force and industry do against an army of Frenchmen dominated by the presence of their King." The Dutch were saved when they flooded their land and Louis found he could not part the waters.

Louis had failed to conquer the Dutch, but Colbert thought he knew where suitable timber might be found within the realm. New France could produce a "great quantity of wood suitable for all sorts of uses," most notably "trees of the size and height necessary for masts." This exemplified the other advantage of a flourishing colony in New France. While the colony would be a market for goods from France and other French colonies, the colony would in return provide France with raw materials that would contribute to France's economic independence from the rest of Europe.

The man whom Colbert chose to begin to transform New France into an economically productive colony was Jean-Baptiste Talon. As the first intendant of New France (appointed in 1665), Talon initially tried to promote minor industries that would contribute to the daily comfort of Canadians and make New France a more attractive place to settle. By 1670 Canadians could dress themselves in Canadian leather, wool, and linen, and could even get drunk on Canadian beer. Talon, in the spirit of Colbert, was always seeking regulations that would make Canadians act for the greater good. Typical was the way he sought to make them produce more hemp for inexpensive cloth. He distributed hemp seed free, and then created a government monopoly in thread, an essential imported item. Talon then declared that the thread could be exchanged only for hemp. Produce hemp or go without thread. Hemp was produced.

This action demonstrates the extent to which the government controlled the economy. In 1664, for instance, the government established profit rates for imported items, both dry goods and wines. Merchants were not delighted. One complained, "I have always deemed that I had a right to the free disposal of my own, especially when I consider that I spend in the colony what I earn in the colony."

He was mistaken; in Colbert's view of things he did not. Colbert was no lover of merchants who thought themselves more important than they were. Their activity might provide the sinews of war, but that did not mean they were as a group always the best guide to policy. They were interested typically in their own individual profits, not in the wealth of the state as a whole. Hence they would happily trade with foreign merchants if the profits were high enough, although this trade might be draining their country of its wealth. The wrong free enterprise could easily contribute to a country's decline. A merchant who engaged in such trade was like a nobleman who dueled with a fellow Frenchman: They were each satisfying their individual desires at the expense of the whole. As the nobility should fight only in the French king's wars, so the merchants would engage only in trade that would strengthen him. Men like Colbert and Talon, men committed to the center, to the Sun King, were the best judges of what the merchants should do.

And those at the center should be rewarded proportionately for their service. One reason that the merchants resented Talon's interference in their affairs was that he was a competitor. Talon owned the first two ships built of Canadian timber, and with them he attempted to develop trade between New France and the French West Indies. Talon owned the first commercial brewery built in New France. And then there was his warehouse of merchandise. Talon had the best supplied warehouse in all of New France, with merchandise that could be made available to selected buyers at extraordinarily low prices, so low other merchants became suspicious. Talon as an officer of the crown had the right to use the king's ships to import items for his own personal use without paying either transportation or duties. The merchants were distressed to learn that Talon's appetite for certain consumables had grown to Rabelaisian proportions. If the 420 barrels of wine and brandy that Talon imported in 1669 were really for his personal use, then his liver should have been preserved for medical science.

The merchants complained to Colbert that Talon was competing against them with an unfair advantage—but to no avail. Colbert did remind Talon that he was intendant for the glory of the king, not his own personal profits. However, as Colbert understood and the merchants apparently did not, this truth did not bear directly on Talon's relation to the merchants. The profits of Talon did not infringe on the glory of the king. Should not a man responsible for the economic development of the whole colony also profit from that development to a degree commensurate to his service? Should not Talon become one of the wealthiest men in New France just as Colbert himself was becoming one of the wealthiest men in all of France?

New France, like France itself, had to be a hierarchy centered on the king. Just as the nobility, the second estate, had to realize that their position was dependent on their recognition of the superiority of the king, so too the bourgeois of the third estate had to recognize that their very prosperity depended upon their subordination to the mercantile servants of the king, such as Talon and Colbert. Only through such hierarchies could the centrifugal force of selfishness be counteracted, and the order of society sustained. To forget this was to risk a descent into barbarism and chaos.

The preoccupation with the preservation of hierarchy was evident even in the organization of settlement. The seigneurial system, as it has come to be called, was an attempt to adapt the old feudalism of France to the conditions of the New World. Large parcels of land were granted to individual seigneurs, or lords, who in turn would grant portions of it to *their* peasants or "habitants" (as they were called). For an adventuresome son of a French merchant or perhaps a younger son of a nobleman, this seemed to offer the opportunity to play the medieval lord. He would pay nothing to the French governor for awarding him a fiefdom of a thousand acres. To keep it he had only to develop it. As the feudal lords of old had retrieved civilization from the Dark Ages, so he would bring civilization to where it had never been before.

His habitants would gather around him, help him clear the land for their use, and build a palisade to defend their prospective village against the barbarians. Within the palisades he would cede each family a small lot, perhaps a third of an acre, for which he would receive a small annual rent, perhaps a few chickens. Not so much rent really as an acknowledgment of his lordship and their mutual obligations. Outside the palisades he would give each family a field of perhaps forty acres to work, once again for an annual rent. For himself, he would keep the best few hundred acres, where he would erect a manor house from which to oversee the welfare of his people.

He would build a church for his people. The bishop would appoint the first pastor, but thereafter he and his descendants would have the right of appointment. Naturally he and his family would have reserved for them the foremost pew, there to be the first sprinkled with holy water and the first to receive blessings and communion.

The lord would have the traditional right of a few days' labor each year from his subjects on projects that he judged beneficial to the common good. He would build a community oven and mill for his people, and they in gratitude would give to their lord a set portion of their flour and bread.

The lord would oversee his own local court to settle his people's petty disputes with one another. And while he ruled in benign patriarchy, he would look forward to the day when a patent of nobility would arrive from France. The king himself had taken notice of the labors of his humble servant, had formally recognized his contribution to the glory that was France. This lord had done his part to show the distinction between France and other countries.

To such aristocratic fantasies the seigneurial system was specifically designed to appeal. One official in New France wrote back to Colbert to remind him that granting nobility to a few more colonists would "fill the officers and richer *seigneurs* with a new zeal for the settlement of their lands in hope of being recompensed with titles as well." He added slyly that this form of reward would be "more economical" than any other. This slyness is a reminder that the seigneurial system was not medieval or feudal. It was rather the calculated policy of a newly centralized national government to keep control over a remote colony. To control this particular colony would prove to be one of Colbert's most elusive tasks.

The most obvious threat to the crown's control over New France was the office of governor itself. A noble governor placed in charge of a colony thousands of miles from France, a colony moreover isolated from any communication with France during the long winter months when the Saint Lawrence was frozen—such a governor had much temptation to act as if he were a king.

When Louis XIV took personal control over the government of France in 1661 (a decade before Frontenac's appointment), he found as governor of New France a man against whom such complaints had already been made. Governor D'Avaugour, it was claimed, acted, when it suited him, directly against the specific orders of his superiors; moreover, he outraged the locals by his arbitrary decisions, which went against the nascent traditions of New France. Colbert had no time in the early days of Louis's reign (as he would by Frontenac's day) to investigate such charges—he had other, more immediate problems. The suspicion of insubordination was enough; D'Avaugour was recalled. Colbert then established a sovereign council to act as a check against any governor's pretenses to grandeur.

However, this council became its own problem, for soon it was controlled by the bishop of Quebec. Bishop Laval effectively thwarted the new Governor Mésy's efforts to exercise his legitimate power. Mésy, in a fury of frustration during one council meeting, actually took out after a council member with his sword. For this less-than-Christian behavior Laval excommunicated him until he publicly repented. The continual aggravation of the governorship was apparently too much for Mésy; he was soon dying, with Laval at his bedside praying for the repose of his soul. Laval himself was becoming, quietly and largely behind the scenes, a saintly Canadian Richelieu.

The most persistent battle of wills between Laval and the secular authorities was over *eau de vie*, "the water of life," brandy. From a strictly economic point of view, brandy was a water of life for the French economy. Here was a French-manufactured item that could be traded in the New World for disproportionately large quantities of furs. At times Indians would trade as many furs for a single keg of brandy as they would for twenty-five blankets. French winemakers had a large new market; Indians were getting the drink they wanted; Canadians were prospering as middlemen; and Louis XIV was being provided with the sinews of war. What more could one ask for?

The "more" that Bishop Laval insisted upon had something to do with being one's brother's keeper, irrespective of profit margins. Laval had once admonished a pair of his missionaries who were going to Lake Ontario, "As the Devil on his side, 'as a roaring lion goeth about, seeking whom he may devour,' so it is necessary that we are watchful against his efforts with care, sweetness and love." Laval had now concluded that in New France brandy was a devouring demon; it was the water of death.

The reports from the missionaries were consistent. Kegs of brandy transformed a village temporarily into a prevision of hell. Let us content ourselves with one account (of many): "The village or the cabin in which the savages drink brandy is an image of hell: fire flies in all directions; blows with hatchets and knives make the blood flow on all sides; and all the place resounds with frightful yells and cries. They bite off each other's noses, and tear away their ears; wherever their teeth are fixed, they carry away the morsel. The father and mother throw their babies upon the hot coals or into the boiling kettles. They commit a thousand abominations—the mother with her sons, the father with his daughters, the brothers with their sisters. They roll about on the cinders and coals, and in blood. In this frightful condition they fall asleep among one another; the fumes of the brandy pass away, and the next morning they awake disfigured, dejected and bewildered at the disorder in which they find themselves." Under the influence of this devouring demon supplied by the French, "everything is permitted them for they give as an excuse that they are bereft of reason."

This seemed as true of the Indians living near French settlements as those in the distant woods. In the settlements a whole season of furs could be drunk in a single binge, leaving a family without clothes or provisions for the whole winter (with the Church left to provide if it could). The explorer Louis Joliet thought that anyone who sold brandy to the Indians should simply be hanged. Another disagreed with those who thought the bestiality of the drunken Indians surprising: brandy has the same effect on Indians, he said, as the prospect of beaver furs has on Europeans.

Laval was unyielding on the subject of brandy. He regarded the brandy trade as a signal proof of the wickedness of his generation. He found all arguments in its favor equally detestable. To legalize the brandy trade was to license scoundrels. He had fought with the secular officials, notably Talon, on the subject. When they legalized the trade, he had excommunicated anyone involved in it. When during times of prohibition they quietly tolerated a bootleg trade, he denounced their hypocrisy from the pulpit.

Laval was obviously willing to use whatever power he had to frustrate any government action that he thought harmful to the interests of the Church and the moral well-being of its flock. So he could transform a governor into an object of ridicule (as he did with Mésy)—and he could also undermine a provision of the seigneurial system that detracted from his authority.

Clearly the king and his minister wished a seigneur to have the right to name the pastor to the seigneurial church. The bishop could name the first pastor, but after that the right would be one of the perquisites of the lord. Laval had his own ideas about that.

Such a policy would make the ecclesiastical hierarchy subservient to the secular. The lowest members of the Second Estate—indeed, those who just aspired to be members of the Second Estate—would have more local power than the highest ranking ecclesiastic. This could not be tolerated, and yet the king could not be opposed. It was a measure of Laval's shrewdness that he still found a way to assert his will.

Churches were not going to be among the first structures built on the new seigneuries, and Laval would appoint the first pastors. So he had time. He did not oppose the seigneurial right; such an open fight would have meant certain defeat. Rather, every time he mentioned this right he added a word of his own. The seigneurs had the right to appoint pastors of the *stone* churches they had built. He repeated this qualification so many times that it eventually found its way into government documents originating from Versailles. The principle was established.

People built stone churches in Canada rarely. They were too expensive, and lumber too cheap. By 1680 only three seigneurs—these very wealthy, and hence the kind of people who would have had influence with the bishop anyway—had built stone churches. Laval had won a great victory without anyone else even knowing that a battle had been fought, a classic bureaucratic triumph.

That this aspect of the seigneurial system did not work as planned should not be surprising because almost none of it did. And the failure of the seigneurial system to shape Canadian society was a far greater threat to the plans of Colbert than any machinations of the good bishop. In New France, prospective inhabitants, not aspiring noblemen, were at a premium. To get settlers you had to give them low rents that subsequently you had no right to raise. You wanted them clustered together in your little village; they rather insisted upon building houses on their own farms, and insisted too that they have their own river frontage. You could not enforce your rights to a community oven because during the harsh winters the dough would freeze before reaching it; everyone had his own oven. The mill was another matter. Skilled labor was scarce. The expense of building the mill, keeping it repaired, and paying the miller, was far greater than any income you would get from it. Settlers frequently complained to Sovereign Council that their seigneurs were not fulfilling the obligation of a mill; and the seigneurs would have to explain that they could not afford it, and would offer the settlers further concessions by way of compensation—no nobility in that. Colbert and Louis would frequently complain that the seigneurs were not clearing enough of their grants of forest to deserve to retain them, and the officials in New France would have to explain they were doing the best that could be expected under the circumstances.

In short, the seigneur, far from being a feudal lord living a life of glory and ease, was himself usually little better off than his habitants. He was at best first among equals. This was still an attractive opportunity for someone who wished to improve his station through a life of hard, constant toil. But the seigneur had to reconcile himself to the fact that he was no aristocrat, and would not be treated like one by his settlers. Those noblemen visiting from Europe who expected the settlers to behave toward them like French peasants were left shocked by their experiences:

"The peasants there are at their ease. What, did I say 'peasant'? Honorable apologies to these gentlemen! That term, taken in its usual meaning, would put our Canadians into the fields. A Spaniard, if he should be called rustic, would not wince, nor twirl his mustache more proudly. These people are not wrong after all; they do not pay salt tax; they hunt and fish freely; in a word they are rich. Then how can you compare them with our wretched peasants?"

"They hunt and fish freely." This is the key to the freedom of the settler, and to the failure of the best-laid plans of Colbert to reproduce in New France the social hierarchies of France. The very Saint Lawrence River that in one direction led back to France, in the other direction led deep into the heart of the continent. Ships could reach only Montreal; beyond it were rapids and waterfalls that prevented the passage of these vessels of civilization. To travel beyond, one had to become like the Indians and use canoes, the construction of which they had perfected long before Europeans had dared venture out into the Atlantic. The birchbark canoe was the Canadians' instrument of freedom.

The river, a canoe, and freedom. Many settlers and seigneurs alike took to the woods to escape the monotonous hardships of farming. These were the *coureurs de bois*, the "forest rangers." The officials of New France had little but hard words for the way of life of these lawless adventurers. Talon described them in disgust as "without Christianity, without laws, without magistrates, sole masters of their own actions, and of the application of their wills."

Subsequent officials in New France would return again and again to the same subject. "These disorders are much greater in the families of those who are gentlemen or who want to be so, either because of indolence or vanity. Having no other means of subsistence but the forest, because they are not accustomed to hold the plow, the pick, or the ax, their only resource being the musket, they must spend their lives in the woods, where there are no priests to restrain them, no fathers, nor governors to control them. . . . I do not know, my Lord, how to describe to you the attraction that all the young men feel for the life of the savage, which is to do nothing, to be utterly free of constraint, to follow all the customs of the savages, and to place oneself beyond the possibility of correction."

One of the greatest forest rangers, Pierre Radisson, described the appeal of his chosen life with admirable simplicity: "We were Caesars, there being no one to contradict us." Caesars of the forest, Sun Kings of the wilderness. The forest offered the skillful ranger not only freedom and adventure, but also wealth. The rangers could gain for themselves a sizable portion of the fur trade. Why should Indian trappers undertake the long trip to Montreal to trade with the French when certain Frenchmen were willing to travel out to meet them?

Colbert did his best to curtail the forest rangers' involvement in the fur trade. At times they would be simply outlawed. At others, when the futility of such a policy was obvious, they would be given amnesty—and the governor would then try to issue a limited number of permits for such trade. But the profits were too great, the rewards of farming too small, for even this limited toleration to be an effective control.

Colbert himself could see that the fur trade, whatever its immediate advantages, posed a threat to the development of New France. He observed that if "Canada found itself deprived of this trade, the settlers would be obliged to engage in fishing, prospecting, and manufacturing, which would yield them far greater benefits." And again: "It is to be feared that by means of this trade, the settlers will remain idle a good part of the year, whereas if they were not allowed to engage in it, they would be obliged to apply themselves to cultivating their land."

The very able-bodied young men who were ranging about the forest in search of furs ought to be rather building a permanent monument to themselves with prospering farms in the Saint Lawrence Valley, and large families to carry on their names. Colbert wished New France to remain compact and easily defended, but he found himself, because of the bad example of these colonial Ishmaels, continually pressured to allow the French to extend their permanent presence beyond the rapids at Montreal. Colbert persistently refused to be convinced of the need for such an expansion, especially in light of the very danger such an expansion posed to the honor of France and Louis. "It would be better to restrict oneself to an amount of land that the colony will be able to sustain on its own, rather than to embrace too vast an area whereby one would perhaps one day be obliged to abandon a part with some reduction of the prestige of His Majesty and of the State."

The forest rangers did, in another way, contribute to a grave threat to both His Majesty's prestige and the very existence of New France. They did so in their competition with the Iroquois. The Iroquois were now as dependent upon European goods as the Hurons ever had been, and they were still surrounded by enemies. They had heavily hunted their own land for furs; any expansion in their trade required more fur pirating at the expense of their neighbors. The Huron Confederacy was now gone, but the Iroquois Nations continued to prey on the Algonquin to their north, the Mohicans to their east, the Susquehannas and Andastes to their south, and a variety of nations to their west. The Iroquois were particularly concerned about relations between these western nations and the French.

The British had no choice but to seek the western furs through the Iroquois because Iroquois ferocity had effectively kept their people on the far side of the Allegheny Mountains. The French, however, through the waterways of the Saint Lawrence, had the possibility of flanking the Iroquois, trading with the western tribes directly, and in the process arming them to resist more effectively the Iroquois intrusions. These western nations, along with the Algonquin and the Mission Indians of New France, would provide an effective alliance against the Iroquois Confederacy. The Iroquois saw clearly that expansion of the French trade would occur largely at their expense; and with forest rangers slipping through to seek that very expansion, a direct conflict between the two societies was virtually inevitable.

In the year of Governor Mésy's death this seemed imminent. Pierre Boucher wrote then, "The Iroquois . . . hem us in so close they prevent us availing ourselves of the country's resources; one cannot go hunting or fishing without fear of being killed or captured by those knaves; nor can one cultivate the land, still less harvest the grain, except in continual risk; for they wait in ambush on all sides."

The next year a regiment sent from France especially for the purpose attacked the Iroquois in their own country to impress upon them French strength. This would not have been sufficient to bring them to a treaty had they not been at the same time ravaged by smallpox, and had they not also been feeling particularly pressed by their Indian enemies to the south. So the Iroquois were forced to make a peace with the French, a peace that they intended to keep in about the same spirit as Louis kept his peace with the Netherlands.

The Netherlands was a continual threat to the well-being of France; and Louis would keep peace with it only while it was to his tactical advantage— but in the long term his glory required that he neutralize the Dutch completely. So too the Iroquois regarded their relationship with the growing settlements of New France. As more and more French arrived, as more and more forest rangers slipped off to the west in search of furs, the strategic goal of the Iroquois became ever clearer. To use the phrase of one of their headmen, they had to make the French so afraid they would "not be able to go across their door to piss."

New France was a sparsely populated, wintry land, thousands of miles and a perilous sea voyage from France, a land where Frenchmen imitated savages and peasants gave no respect—some of Frontenac's acquaintances at court considered his posting there, even as governor, little more than an exile. The wife of another hopeful, his own finances as desperate as Frontenac's, was consoled by her mother that to be governor of New France one would have to live "amongst a people whom one would be ashamed to associate with."

Frontenac, in contrast, esteemed his "exile" to New France as he esteemed everything else connected with his person. Molière would have his Alceste say, "There is precious little satisfaction in the most glorious reputation if one finds one has to share it with the whole universe. Esteem must be founded on some sort of preference." In New France Frontenac would be the most esteemed of King Louis's subjects; there he would have to share his rank with no man. He could hold court and people would owe him homage. He would be the very image of the Sun King for the New World; he would be a true Caesar of the wilderness—and perhaps he might even make a little money on the side. And, of course, his great deeds would be such that not even his enemies would keep their tongues silent in praise of them.

Frontenac was fortunate in the timing of his appointment. Not only were the Iroquois temporarily unable to trouble the new governor, neither was Bishop Laval. Laval was in the midst of an extended stay in France, attending to the financial affairs of his bishopric; Frontenac would not have to face the threat of excommunication until later. Moreover, Intendant Talon was retiring, a rich man needless to say; he would be taking the first ship back to France after Frontenac's arrival. And Colbert could find no one competent to succeed him. Colbert then apparently decided that a replacement was not needed, for a virtually bankrupt nobleman would be careful to do exactly as he was told. Even Colbert, it seems, was not infallible.

Frontenac was so exuberant as he left France for the New World that even being becalmed a little way out of harbor he found amusing. He wrote to a friend that at least for these few days the coast of France was safe from foreign harassment, and he conjured up the image of Dutch and English fleet admirals cowering at the very mention of the name "Frontenac." His first impression on arriving at Quebec confirmed in him his high sense of purpose. "I never saw anything more superb than the position of this town. It could not be better situated as the future capital of a great empire."

The position of the capital could not be better, according to Frontenac— nor could the French settlements. Rather than being scattered along the coast as were the British, the French had settled along a river that struck into the heart of the continent. Colbert might himself be prejudiced in favor of a compact colony, but the French geographical position, as any military man could see, had an inevitable logic of its own. All that was needed was a leader who understood this and could act upon it, someone of Frontenac's skill, experience, and vision to awaken the flower that slept within the seed. Then there would be glory enough for all. And the earth would be astonished, once again, at the difference between France and other nations.

That there was much to be done, Frontenac could see from the very layout of Quebec itself. The upper town was dominated by ecclesiastical establishments, an understandable situation given the past of the colony but betokening too strong a clerical influence for its destined imperial future. The lower town was just a collection of houses, built by individuals according to their particular caprices, no single plan, no consistent style, lacking the coherence that only comes from a strong center. A superb position, but the religious element too prominent and the secular not centralized enough—this was Quebec, and this was also Frontenac's understanding of New France.

Frontenac had to do for New France what Louis XIV had done for Old. Frontenac would bring the diverse elements of his society together in the service of his person. Frontenac would be arbiter of choice for his colony. The Canadians would not find such an assertion of his prerogative disagreeable, for Frontenac would only ask for the docility, the obedience, the humility, and the profound respect that any subject should show his king or governor.

The members of the Sovereign Council had a taste of their future under Frontenac when he announced to them at his first meeting that he would not answer to "monsieur the governor"—he was to be addressed at all times as "High and Mighty Lord." Frontenac wished to teach his Canadian subjects the importance of such formalities. Frontenac's contemporary, La Roche-foucauld, called pomp "a mystery of the body designed to conceal flaws of the mind"—but Frontenac had seen for himself how Louis had strengthened his personal rule through the careful observance of protocol. What kind of chair one was allowed to sit in at court, if one was allowed to sit at all, had become an important sign of preferment; noblemen vied with one another to perform for the king menial tasks that in their own households were the responsibility of servants. To spin the fabric of society tightly these nuances had to be brought to the New World. Frontenac realized that formal ceremonies can become immemorial customs, manners of address can become modes of thought.

Frontenac, seeking out occasions for ceremonies in which the High and Mighty Lord could display the dignity of his person to his subjects, discovered one in the traditional oath of loyalty to the governor and the king that was to be administered by each new governor. No one had ever thought of this oath-giving as anything more than a proscribed formality to be done quickly and unobtrusively. Frontenac saw the opportunity to do much more.

He ordered the convening of a States General for New France. A States General had never been held in New France before. The last one held in France itself had been in 1614, and that one had been so much trouble for the monarchy that neither Richelieu nor Louis XIV had called another. (Their judgment in this matter has been confirmed by subsequent history; the next States General was called in France in 1789 and marked the beginning of the French Revolution that would sweep away the old regime.)

But such prudence was far from Frontenac's aspiring mind. New France did not have sufficient sense of itself as a distinctly unified society. New France needed an assembling of the clerical, noble, and bourgeois classes; it needed to celebrate the unity and coherence for which it would strive under the leadership of Frontenac, representative in the New World of the Sun King himself. Each state was to be turned out in style, head to foot, everything as it should be.

Amidst such unprecedented formal display, Governor Frontenac, the High and Mighty Lord, administered the oath of fealty. But before he did, he delivered an oration that detailed the implications of the oath which they were about to take, to take both for themselves and for the state they represented. Frontenac, in particular, reminded them that "Holy Scriptures command us to obey our sovereign, and teach us that no pretext or reason can dispense us from obedience." No reason, no excuse, no pretext can dispense the members of that collected assembly from the obligation at once human and divine to "unite with one heart in laboring for the progress of Canada." Each was to contribute to Canada in the ways appropriate to his station; the unification of their efforts in a single heart would be Frontenac's responsibility as governor, a responsibility he embraced with enthusiasm. "As for me, it only remains to protest before you that I shall esteem myself happy in consecrating all my efforts, and, if need be, my life itself, to extending the empire of Jesus Christ throughout all this land, and the supremacy of our King over all the nations that dwell in it."

When the states then swore their fealty to the king, Frontenac was satisfied that they had sworn their fealty to him as well. This was a solemn oath that by their honor and their God they could never break. They had sworn, and now New France could dispense with obedience to Frontenac by neither pretext or reason. New France was now his, and through his mediation alone the king's.

Needless to say, Frontenac was more than pleased with his ceremony. When some native headmen visiting Quebec heard of it and expressed disappointment at their having missed so singular an event, Frontenac was delighted to run through the ceremony all over again, including presumably the speech. The savages, too, this lowest state in New France, had to be brought into fealty to the governor if the empire Frontenac envisioned was to be realized. All the nations were to be brought under the sovereignty of Louis XIV. Frontenac seized the opportunity presented by the curiosity of these chiefs to begin their initiation into the higher mysteries of European society. Frontenac would start with these chiefs, like a father, patient and generous with his children. It was all most satisfying.

Frontenac wrote to Colbert a rather smug account of his great success, even estimating the number who participated in it well beyond the physical capacity of the church in which it was held. Perhaps he should have been made hesitant by the wariness of Talon. The experienced intendant had with the profoundest disappointment found himself so physically indisposed that he could not attend Frontenac's striking institutional innovation—and yet somehow had been able to attend to routine business only a few days later. Why did he not contribute his presence? Did he anticipate the likely response to such an initiative from Versailles?

Alas, Colbert's response to Frontenac's achievement was perplexing. "Your assembling the inhabitants to take the oath of fidelity, and your division of them into three states, may have had a good effect for the moment; but it is well for you to observe that you are always to follow, in the government of Canada, the forms in use here; and since our kings have long regarded it as good for their service not to convoke the States General of the kingdom, in order, perhaps, to abolish insensibly this ancient usage, you, on your part, should very rarely, or, to speak more correctly, never give a corporate form to the inhabitants of Canada."

Never? Never convene another States General? Never take the initiative as a nobleman to adapt the practices of the homeland to this, his province? Surely Colbert could not seriously mean that. Frontenac had mentioned in his dispatch how he had concluded that he personally could settle legal disputes more expeditiously—and, to be candid, more equitably—than the local courts. And he described how he had begun to do this, with notable success. But, no, Colbert was telling him to stop this as well; Frontenac was to let the legal system work as he found it, as the king had established it.

Poor Colbert obviously just did not understand. How could he when he scarcely ever left his desk, and sallied forth into the world only vicariously through his memoranda? This little fussbudget of a man—his was the barren bookkeeper's theory of life. As a high and mighty lord, Frontenac could afford to be generous to such men of lesser vision. Let us just say that many things happen in a remote colony such as New France that cannot be understood in Paris no matter how intelligent you are.

Frontenac had sworn on his honor as a nobleman and on his faith as a Christian his fealty to the Most Supreme Majesty, Louis XIV. This required him to act in the best interests of New France and the Crown. He would do this, whatever the sacrifice, and whether or not his sovereign's bourgeois minister understood. He would take his satisfaction from the doing of his duty. He, Louis de Buade, Comte de Frontenac, High and Mighty Lord, had at last found a stage where he could fully reveal the qualities with which heaven had endowed him. He was not going to be judged by inferior breaths, nor impeded by carping fools.

In the summer of 1673 Governor Frontenac enjoyed a triumphal tour of his realm. He not only went to Montreal, but past it to the still-wild shores of Lake Ontario. He showed his entourage he was not afraid to travel the Saint Lawrence in a birchbark canoe. And Lake Ontario might have had something to show him. The gentle heavings of that lake (sounding like the concussions of a distant gun), its unbroken surface amber and yet still limpid, the surrounding eloquent repose and calm grandeur of the forest—all this scene might have spoken to a man less full of business and importance, might have spoken the language of wordless contemplation and earth-bound humility. But His High and Mighty Lord had important negotiations to conduct on the shores of Ontario. He had arranged to meet there with the representatives of the still-dangerous, but temporarily quiescent, Iroquois. He wished to impress all his subjects, even these the most uncivilized and least tractable, with the majesty of his person. Other governors had carefully addressed Iroquois headmen as brothers, as virtual equals. Frontenac would have none of this; he would behave as Louis did among his nobility. He would call them his children, they would call him father, or (in their own language) Onontio, which meant Great Mountain. Yes, he would even deign to refer to himself as Onontio, thereby dignifying this barbarous tongue. In this spirit Frontenac began his first address to the assembled chiefs of the five allied Iroquois Nations.

"Children! Mohawks, Oneidas, Onondagas, Cayugas, and Senecas. I am pleased to see you come hither, where I have had a fire lighted for you to smoke by, and for me to talk to you. O, 'tis well done, my children, to have obeyed the orders and commands of your Father. Take courage, then, my children; you will hear this word, which is full of peace and tenderness; a word which will fill your lodges with joy and happiness; for think not that war is the object of my voyage. My spirit is full of Peace, and she walks by my side. Courage, then, my children, and take rest."

The Iroquois representatives allowed Frontenac to flatter himself by condescending to them. Circumstances had forced them into a waiting game. For now they would play the role Frontenac had assigned to them. They accepted his gifts, flattery, and affection for what they were worth. Only on the fifth day of their parley did Frontenac finally come to his point, the point that they had been waiting to hear all along.

"Listen to me and trust my words. I am frank and sincere, and shall promise you nothing but what I will exactly perform, desiring that you on your side may do likewise. The dread I feel of disturbing the peace I promise prevents me from reproaching you with the various treacheries you formerly committed against my nephews. No, I will not dispel from your countenances that joy which I there behold. I content myself with telling you only to reflect on the past and on the present; consider well the greatness and power of Onontio. If Your Father can come so far, with so great a force, through such dangerous rapids, merely to make you a visit of pleasure and friendship, what would he do, if you should awaken his anger, and make it necessary for him to punish his disobedient children? He is the arbiter of peace and war. Beware how you offend him."

Frontenac reported to Colbert that the Iroquois' replies were everything the French could have desired. They were especially pleased, he said, that he had presumed to address them as children, and had thereby bound himself to act as their father; no other governor had used this "mark of authority." "The five deputies spoke, one after another, and each testified, in his harangue, the joy experienced at meeting a real Father in Onontio, whom they had desired to persuade that they too would be obedient children; that they well understood that all the suspicions which others sought to foment among them were but chimeras, since he had not proposed anything to them but what was for their advantage; that they thanked him for having especially exhorted them to become Christians, since it was the greatest advantage that could ever accrue to them."

The Iroquois knew full well, of course, that Frontenac's voyage was not one of pleasure and friendship (just as Frontenac knew full well that these Iroquois headmen were quite unlikely to start saying the rosary). If the Iroquois had any doubt about Frontenac's true intentions, they had only to watch what the French were doing at the very time they were listening like obedient children to their peaceful and merciful father: The French were building a fort.

A fort on Lake Ontario had long been requested by officials in Quebec, but Colbert would only respond that he wished to keep the French in an easily defended compact colony along the upper Saint Lawrence. Colbert wanted economic prosperity, not a military frontier. Frontenac, not surprisingly, embraced the plans for a new fort with enthusiasm; the idea of expanding the French colony along the path of imperial destiny in the very first year of his governorship was irresistible. He even had come up with a name for the new fort, a name that had a nice sound to it: Fort Frontenac.

The mellifluous name of the fort, he knew, was not going to convince the pebble-hearted Colbert. In describing to the king and Colbert the efforts made in founding the fort, Frontenac used every possible appeal to the regal pride of Louis. The priests had regarded his expedition as a manifestation of divine providence; even the laity thought his ability to manage the whole passage without a single casualty was simply "miraculous." In the process he had inflamed his men with such loyalty to his person and the cause of which he was but an instrument—who could describe it? "No one has ever seen troops or officers . . . do what I saw these men do." The Indians themselves were "so astonished by it that they still have not recovered their amazement." And almost certainly never will.

Frontenac knew, of course, that Colbert would be as likely swayed by tales of knightly glory as had Frontenac's prospective father-in-law. So he appealed to Colbert using the only language he could be certain Colbert would understand: the language of economics. Frontenac had founded his fort to preserve "a trade that was about to be lost."

The fur trade came into Montreal largely along the Ottawa River directly to its west. The chief carriers of the trade were now the Ottawa Algonquins. Lake Ontario stood to the south of the Ottawa, between it and the homelands of the Iroquois Nations. Frontenac began his account of Fort Frontenac by claiming he had received reliable intelligence that the Ottawas and Iroquois were about to conclude a treaty that would divert the furs from the Ottawas through the Iroquois to the English and Dutch. According to Frontenac, "The only means to traverse and upset this negotiation was, as had been frequently before proposed, to establish a fort on the lake, which would prevent communication of the Nations of the South with those of the North, and force the latter to bring us . . . all the pelts that usually came by the river."

Did such a threat to trade really exist? Well, it has to be said that in a pinch like this, Frontenac tended to regard truthfulness as a measly bourgeois scruple. Colbert had no way to refute Frontenac's claims, but the people in Montreal felt they did. They had been pressed into service by Frontenac to ferry goods and provide the labor for the new fort. Frontenac had been able to do this through the same right exercised by a seigneur over his settlers; Frontenac, however, had expanded this right extraordinarily. Frontenac had impressed them for a whole month on a distant and dangerous project. It *was* a miracle no one was killed. And with the unreliable Iroquois present, there was always the risk, treaty or no treaty, that this incursion into what had been previously conceded as Indian territory would provoke a massacre.

Frontenac replied to such grumbling that this extraordinary project had an extraordinary cause. Frontenac was attempting to preserve the very economic foundation of Montreal. Here again, however, there were those who took another, dimmer view. Fort Frontenac was going to be at best an inconvenience in the commerce between the Ottawas and the Iroquois, if they really did want to trade. Moreover, anyone who knew about their traditional hostility would doubt that such a trade agreement was likely. Fort Frontenac might serve to discourage Iroquois raiding parties that would occasionally try to disrupt the Ottawa trade, but the effort that was going to be required to sustain Fort Frontenac was disproportionate to the little support it would provide the Ottawas.

People in Montreal could be forgiven if they tried to think of a covert end that would justify such an enormous effort on the part of the governor. The simple desire for glory, of course, could not be discounted, Frontenac striking a fine figure before the barbarians and leaving his permanent mark on the land. Yet there was another, if not incompatible, explanation, and one that alarmed the people in Montreal.

The High and Mighty Lord was staffing his fort with forest rangers, men less noted for their military experience than for their trading savvy. The fort, whatever its limitations as a defensive establishment, was ideally suited as a trading post. The suspicion in Montreal (a suspicion that turned out to be far from incorrect) was that Frontenac, ostensibly to protect the Ottawa trade from being diverted to the Iroquois, was in fact planning to divert it to himself and the officials at Quebec. Fort Frontenac was being established by his High and Mighty Lordship to assert his authority, to enhance his glory, and to line his pocket.

This project was particularly galling to Montreal Governor Perrot, a nephew of Talon who had gained for himself an intendant's share of the fur trade. Perrot, for once allied with the Montreal merchants who had often complained about him in the past, began, soon after Frontenac had returned to Quebec, to harass agents of Frontenac whom he suspected of engaging in the fur trade. Frontenac, for his part, was incensed at these incursions against his authority as representative of the king. From a purely legal point of view Frontenac did seem to have the better of the argument. Nonetheless, with a show of magnanimity, Frontenac through a clerical emissary invited his fellow governor to Quebec so that they might settle their differences like true gentlemen. Perrot quickly agreed, for there certainly were more than enough furs for both of them.

In coming to Quebec, Perrot had misjudged Frontenac, who considered him no gentleman and hence not the kind of person to whom you could be bound by your word. Perrot no sooner arrived in Quebec than his High and Mighty Lordship had reconciled him with a cell in the Quebec jail.

All Frontenac needed was for the Sovereign Council to condemn Perrot for his illegal actions; he couldn't doubt that the council, having seen what happened to those who defied his might, would meekly concur, especially when the evidence was at least on the surface against Perrot. Frontenac's careful plan, however, was upset by a little aside in a dispatch from Colbert that had come in the meantime. Talon had obviously been doing his work at court, for Colbert, completely ignorant of what had been happening in Quebec and Montreal, had written, "His Majesty also orders me to recommend to you particularly the person and interest of the Sieur Perrot, governor of Montreal and nephew of Sieur Talon." Suddenly the members of the Sovereign Council began to see in the case before them previously unimagined legal intricacies; a mere provincial assembly, with its limited experience, could not possibly understand the profound principles at stake in such a jurisdictional conflict between two so distinguished servants of the Crown. They could only send

Governor Perrot back to France, submit the case that had been so vigorously prosecuted by Count Frontenac, and humbly await to hear His Majesty's pleasure.

After reading this prudent decision to the governor, the council had occasion to observe how Frontenac reacted when his will was thwarted by those he regarded as his social inferiors. (This spectacle was duly reported back to France.) At first his expression became firmly set, pure contempt and anger on his lips, disdain and scorn in his eyes—but then his whole face began to tremble with complete incredulity at the absolute impudence. The trembling continued until finally incredulity became belief, and then his whole body convulsed in a fit of wrath, and he literally foamed at the mouth. It would not be the last time they would see him take on the aspect of a mad dog.

When the case was finally presented to Colbert, he opted for preserving appearances. Perrot was given a few days in the Bastille to consider his sins. He was then sent back to New France to apologize personally to Governor Frontenac. But then he was reinstated as governor of Montreal without prejudice. Colbert in his explanation of his action made it clear that he had supported Frontenac only because Frontenac was the representative of the king's power and that was never to be questioned.

Other than that, Colbert's sympathies lay entirely with Perrot. He believed that Frontenac, once again, had overstepped his authority. As a result, he decided that Frontenac was no longer to be trusted as the sole head of government. Frontenac was behaving as if New France had been in his family's care for centuries. Colbert decided the time had come to appoint a successor to Talon as intendant.

This decision must have rankled in Frontenac, although he did not let it show at the time. The issue between himself and Perrot had been a matter of his honor (and the king's); and that honor had been preserved. Never again would a governor of Montreal presume to behave as an equal to the High and Mighty Lord in Quebec.

Perrot, for his part, was only interested in the kind of honor you can put in the bank. After he made the required obeisances, he and Frontenac quickly reached a working agreement. By the 1680s Perrot was raking in at least 40,000 livres a year in furs, and had re-established himself as the least popular man in all Montreal.

The only obvious casualty in the fight between Perrot and Frontenac was the clergyman Frontenac had duped into playing peacemaker. After Abbé Fénelon, to his shame, realized that Frontenac had only wanted to lure Perrot to Quebec to incarcerate him, he returned to Montreal to give an impassioned sermon in which he argued that subjects had an obligation to obey only just rulers. That Fénelon should discuss publicly a theology of civil disobedience was sufficient to ruin an otherwise promising ecclesiastical career. Colbert saw to that.

Colbert himself had no love for the clergy; he once explained the commercial prosperity of France's rivals by saying, "There are no monks in Holland and England." And he specifically excluded any children who had entered orders from the calculation of pensions for prolific parents in New France. Colbert and his king, moreover, knew that a bishop like Laval thought his power came from God through the Pope, not the king—and he thereby thought himself empowered to pass judgment on the actions of the king himself. For Colbert the First Estate of the clergy could be as disruptive to the monarchy, at least potentially, as the nobility.

Frontenac knew well of this anti-clericalism, and sought to use it to consolidate his own standing with his superiors. He reformed ceremonials so that in ecclesiastical processions the governor and Sovereign Council now walked *in front* of the church wardens. He revoked permission to say Mass in the Royal Magazine during the winter; as these parishioners now made the long walk up to their church in Quebec, they could meditate on the superiority of State to Church. Had Colbert warned Frontenac against attempts by the Jesuits "to carry ecclesiastical activity farther than it should extend"? Well, Frontenac had soon discovered a Jesuit plot to use the secrecy of the confessional to establish an "inquisition a thousand times worse than that of Italy and Spain." Moreover, during his difficulties with Perrot, Frontenac reported he had become convinced that the Jesuits were playing their accustomed role in this affair, but did it so well they left no traces. Frontenac suspected them on the grounds that he suspected them.

Frontenac could get away with such loose accusations because there was no strong ecclesiastical leader to oppose him—until, that is, 1675 when Laval returned. Frontenac would not beguile him with flattering speeches and a sugary smile, nor with angry threats and protestations of honor. Laval had already broken one governor, and was prepared to take on another if need be.

On his return from France, Laval found that new Governor Frontenac was a proponent of brandy more formidable than any he had faced before. Frontenac's reports to Colbert concerning brandy show him at his most skillful. Frontenac presented the brandy controversy as simply another example of the clergy attempting to dictate to the secular authority; the pious pose was really a play for power. He himself had met with Indians in the wilderness during the building of Fort Frontenac. He had seen them drink brandy, and he observed none of the outrages the missionaries report. To be sure, a few young braves got drunk, but the English and Dutch also like to get drunk on French brandy, and no one has ever suggested that we should stop trading it to them.

Of course, the French officials must make certain that their children, the Indians, are not exploited. Colbert will be pleased to learn that Frontenac has instituted serious penalties for those who use brandy to swindle Indians out of their pelts at unduly low prices—and also for those who trade it to the Indians for their necessities—blankets, weapons, and the like. But this is as much as the French government can be expected to do. The Indians now have a taste for spirits. No action by the French government is going to transform them into a race of teetotalers. If the French do not provide the Indians with brandy, they will simply turn to the Dutch and English for rum. If the Jesuits and their supporters were really interested in spreading the true religion, they would find a little drunkenness a small price to pay for preserving the Indians from exposure to Protestant heresies. Could it be that they really want to keep the brandy trade all to themselves? Are they more interested in converting Indians into Christians or beavers into pelts?

These arguments, to Laval's horror, had convinced Colbert of what he already wanted to believe: brandy trade was "necessary for commerce." Laval had to renew his fight against the water of life. Any such trade, and especially when conducted by the moral scum of New France and regulated by the very gentlemen who were becoming rich on its profits, had to be opposed by every means available. Once more Laval issued excommunications, and reserved for himself the right to absolve such mortal sins. This was his ultimate weapon; anyone who persisted in the brandy trade could count on eternal damnation.

In an attempt to resolve the issue, an assembly was convened in Quebec in 1678 by order of the king. With Colbert providing the guidelines and Frontenac choosing the participants, a vote in favor of a completely free brandy trade was a foregone conclusion. If Frontenac or Colbert thought that such a formality would quiet Laval, they were mistaken. When the ships left with a delegation to present the decision to the king for his final approval, Laval was on one of them as well, making the arduous trip back to plead his case personally.

The next year the king announced his final decision, which was to end all squabbling, including edicts of excommunication from the bishop. Free trade was to be allowed in the French settlements; however, French subjects were prohibited from engaging in brandy trade away from the settlements. Laval had managed at least a compromise.

Throughout the brandy controversy Laval had been steadfastly supported by the new intendant, Jacques Duchesnau. This was powerful support because Colbert, in his dissatisfaction over the Perrot affair, had reduced the governor to a mere ceremonial head of the Sovereign Council, with the intendant as the new presiding officer. Duchesnau was an able man. He might have lacked the avaricious energy of Talon, but he was a competent, reasonable administrator with much experience in the French provinces. He might have distinguished himself under any other governor. His governor, however, was Louis de Buade, Comte de Frontenac—and Frontenac's pretensions to grandeur caused in Duchesnau a visceral reaction he could not dissemble.

Frontenac was accustomed to acting as both governor and intendant—and he certainly found it unthinkable that someone other than himself should have charge of the council meetings. Frontenac earnestly regretted that the king through his minister had made a mistake so great that it threatened the well-being of the colony whose care had been placed in his hands. Shortly after Duchesnau arrived, Frontenac had sought to remedy the situation.

There was some land to be granted, and the regulations specified that grants had to be issued under the signatures of both the governor and the intendant. Duchesnau presented Frontenac with the documents already signed by himself; Frontenac explained to his less-experienced colleague that a governor could not allow his signature to appear on the same document as an intendant lest the dignity of his office as representative of the king be compromised. Two copies of such documents had to be issued, one for the Robe, the other for the Sword. Duchesnau knew better, but he also had dealt with such members of the old nobility before. One had to let these stubborn children have their tawdry little victories. Advice to them was as useless as eyes on a mole. Any criticism they willfully confounded with insubordination. So Duchesnau had second copies of the documents drawn up for Frontenac, and Duchesnau sent his own to France, assuming that Frontenac was going to do the same.

Although Duchesnau had dealt with the old nobility before, he obviously had never dealt with quite as remarkable a specimen as Frontenac. Frontenac had long since learned that the only honor to be found in dealing with social upstarts, whether they be creditors or intendants, was in the sweet malice of revenge.

When the next set of dispatches came from France, Duchesnau was shocked to find himself being reproached in the strongest possible language. Frontenac, it seemed, had not sent his copies of the document, but had rather complained about Duchesnau's abuse of his power. Duchesnau had chosen, for reasons best known to himself, to act as if he were governor. Why, he was even granting land on his own authority! This just showed the danger of a divided authority, and how preferable was the earlier system with one unquestioned head.

It took Duchesnau more than a year to sort the matter out with Colbert, and he could never be sure that Colbert completely believed his side, so guilelessly had he walked into the trap. It was unbelievable. Frontenac was prepared to do almost anything to gain a short-term advantage against a perceived enemy. Now Duchesnau at least knew what he was up against. When Frontenac and Laval disagreed over the effects of brandy on the Indians, Duchesnau knew whom he should believe. Time and again, he wrote to Colbert to explain that Frontenac's claim of a clerical plot was at best a delusion, and at worst a calculated deception. Time and again, Colbert, with obvious reluctance, would ask Duchesnau for documentation.

Once Frontenac had sent off the final report on the brandy trade (and also could look forward to being free of the impudent bishop for a while), he decided the time had come to settle the issue of who was the true embodiment of the king in this colony, himself or the disloyal, seditious intendant. A recent dispatch gave him his opening when it referred to him as "chief and President" of the Sovereign Council. An obvious slip of the pen he chose to regard as a command from his monarch to take back sole direction of the council.

Frontenac presented Duchesnau and the Sovereign Council with his claim, but they chose to be rude and hard of hearing. Frontenac persisted. He beseeched; he argued; he threatened. Nothing doing. He finally said that he should be treated at council meetings the way princes of the blood are treated in Royal Councils. At this, Duchesnau professed shock; at that, Frontenac professed rage.

The dispute went on for months. Frontenac would try to disrupt meetings, and Duchesnau would adjourn them. Frontenac tried to bully the council secretary into including his title secretly in the minutes, but Duchesnau found out and rejected them. Frontenac tried absenting himself from the meetings for a time, but on returning found to his sorrow that the council had not missed him at all and would still make "no distinction whatsoever between a governor whom the king had established chief and president of their company, and any other particular." Finally he exiled three of the most senior councillors from Quebec. When one of these, an old man whom Frontenac had harassed unmercifully, died, Frontenac's case was hardly helped. Then Duchesnau filled the new vacancy with the grieving son, and Frontenac could only fume and rage. Finally in 1680 the king spoke:

"M. le comte de Frontenac, I was astonished to learn of all the new disputes and new divisions that have occurred in my province of New France . . . all the more so since I gave you clearly and firmly to understand, both in your instructions and in all the letters that I have written you in past years, that your one main purpose must be to maintain unity and tranquility among all my subjects living in that country. But that which astonishes me even more is that in nearly all the strife that you have originated, there is very little justification for all that you have laid claim to. My edicts, decrees and proclamations have made my wishes so clear to you that I have all the more reason to be astonished that you, who must always see to it that no one whomsoever evades their execution, you have advanced claims that are completely contrary to them."

To this Colbert added in his own hand, "His Majesty sees clearly that you are quite incapable of adopting the spirit of concord and tolerance that is needed to obviate all the dissension which occurs in that country." Such was the gratitude Frontenac received for spending himself in the service of the king's honor! He finds himself accused, by the king himself, of betraying it. Apparently in this government of the bourgeois, it was a sin to cherish honor; well then he, the godson of a true king, must be the most offending soul alive. Frontenac withdrew himself into a dignified disdain. "I will have nothing more to do with the intendant, the bishop, or the Jesuits." In particular, he would have nothing more to do with the outrageous accusations of these ridiculous creatures.

Frontenac had one reason not to feel completely forsaken, other than the fact that the king had stopped just short of recalling him. Business was going well. Ever since Perrot had been reinstated as governor of Montreal, he and Frontenac had made common cause in the conversion of the beaver. As to the regulations on commerce, Perrot did as he pleased, and Frontenac looked the other way. Those who interfered with Perrot's brandy trade were themselves arrested; those who spoke out against him found their property mysteriously vandalized.

But now, with its power vindicated by the king, the Sovereign Council sought to take the offensive against Frontenac by investigating Perrot's activities in Montreal. Less than a year after Frontenac's rebuff by the king, the Sovereign Council had brought charges against Perrot for violating the very laws he was supposed to enforce. The attorney general who was pressing charges was the new council member who regarded Frontenac as responsible for his father's death.

Frontenac tried to stifle the proceedings, and the council countered by sending the whole dispute to the king. When the next dispatch brought a direct threat of dismissal, Frontenac wrote back in a hurt tone: "Your Majesty will plainly see that I have never had to endure more than when I have been made to appear violent and as a man who would disturb the officers in the duties of their office." Everyone now realized that Frontenac's recall was only a matter of time. As soon as a replacement could be found, Frontenac would be gone.

Frontenac made the best of his last few months; like the Roland of legend, he was a surrounded warrior who was going to inflict as much injury as possible on the enemy before he was overwhelmed. He discovers an apparent irregularity in the appointment of the attorney general who prosecuted Perrot, and so he sends him back to France to explain. He uses his own reports to rail continuously against the members of the council, who "persist in their affronts against me"; in particular, he complains that Duchesnau had usurped his powers as governor. When Frontenac catches a Canadian critical of him using a boat rather than a canoe in trading with the Indians, he has him imprisoned on this technical violation. Then Duchesnau's sixteen-year-old son commits an adolescent act of insolence; Frontenac has this little fry of treachery, this reed-voiced pipsqueak with his mother's milk scarce out of him imprisoned, terrorizing both son and father with threats of physical punishment. They would not soon forget Louis de Buade, Comte de Frontenac.

And there was one final satisfaction. The dispatch of dismissal, when it did finally arrive, recalled Duchesnau as well. Frontenac had brought down his chief enemy with him. Duchesnau's career in government was emphatically over. The honor of the king's representative can never be challenged with impunity. This was the noble principle to which Frontenac had sacrificed himself.

Unlike Duchesnau, Frontenac was too highly born and too well connected at court to disappear down the dim corridor of a quiet disgrace. With characteristic energy he went about setting the record straight. In his own eyes, needless to say, Frontenac had not been disgraced at all. His governorship had been a series of glorious achievements, marred only by the disloyalties of a local cabal of low birth. How could such a cabal have gotten the ear of His Majesty? Could Frontenac be blamed if he thought he saw the hand of the Jesuits in this?

Still, he had returned with many tales to charm the ladies, tales of nights he spent in the Canadian forests, surrounded by prowling animals and Indians ravenous for his flesh, tales none the worse for having a few scalps in them. For epic majesty there was the story of his founding of Fort Frontenac, a feat so great, so unprecedented that the Indians had probably still not recovered from their amazement. And for tragic sadness, there were the unseemly events that led to his recall, a story sadder even than the one of his dismissal from Crete. Virtue could but blush, and merit sigh. Still there was the memory he left behind him in the wilderness—Comte de Frontenac, *stupor mundi novi.*

The truth about Frontenac's governorship was buried in a series of reports that only Colbert had read, and so deeply buried that a Colbert was needed to find it. But not even Colbert understood it all, for Frontenac had managed to deceive Colbert himself completely in one important respect, and thereby laid the foundation for his eventual vindication.

In his report to the king after his return to France, Frontenac marked as the single outstanding achievement of his governorship his diplomacy with the Indians, particularly the Iroquois. The Iroquois now, thanks to Frontenac's years of effort, wanted to live as permanent friends with the French— indeed, not only with the French, but also with the Indian allies of the French, such as the Algonquin, the Miamis, the Illinois. As a result, New France had enjoyed peace with the Indians throughout Frontenac's governorship. This peace could be continued as long as his diplomatic initiatives were followed by his successors.

Nonetheless, Frontenac, as the humble servant of His Majesty, felt obliged to warn him of a grave threat to this peace. The very upstarts who had sought to circumscribe his authority as governor, who gratuitously and repeatedly insulted the honor of his person (and thereby the person of the king), were seeking to undo his work with the Iroquois, jealous as they were of his special friendship with them. These men, for reasons best known to themselves, pretended that the Iroquois were planning to attack the colony. These men had repeatedly tried to trick Frontenac in this regard, but he knew his Iroquois children too well. The Iroquois might be unruly at times, even violent. But these were passing moods. Frontenac did not believe for a moment that the Iroquois "had all the evil designs that were being trumpeted forth, because for the past ten years they had always shown their good will and been very compliant." If there was war, it would be caused by the maliciousness and incompetence of the French leaders in Quebec.

This report was of a piece with others Frontenac had written on Indian affairs as governor. Colbert seems to have taken it, like the others, at face value. Frontenac, whatever his limitations as a domestic administrator, was an expert in military and diplomatic affairs. The simple fact was that New France had enjoyed peace during Frontenac's governorship. Although one might discount what he had to say about the cabal (they were probably just merchants and the like who often panic at the merest suggestion of war), his military and diplomatic assessment of New France's position could be trusted.

Colbert had appointed as Frontenac's successor an easy-tempered nobleman of the robe who would both follow his instructions to the letter and be careful in his dealings with other officials in New France. Perhaps Sieur de La Barre could give to New France the internal tranquility that would complement the external peace preserved by Frontenac. Colbert did not think it important that La Barre had little relish for military matters; Frontenac's reports showed that he would need none, so secure were France's relations with its barbarian neighbors.

Unfortunately for Colbert and La Barre (and numerous French settlers), Frontenac had completely misrepresented the situation in New France. Exactly when Frontenac himself realized that relations with the Iroquois were collapsing is not clear. Certainly from the very beginning he knew they were more than unruly children. In his very first negotiation with them on Lake Ontario, he realized that, despite their compliant pose, they were formidable, even at the diplomatic level. He wrote back to France that if it did not sound too ridiculous he had to admit "the eloquence, the shrewdness and the finesse with which all their deputies addressed me . . . reminded me of the Venetian Senate." The reference to Venice was an apt one, for of all the governments of Christendom Venice was most likely to do business with the infidel Turks to further its own ends. The diplomatic stance of both Venetian and Iroquois combined eloquence, shrewdness, finesse, and the lack of scruples.

Frontenac returned to Fort Frontenac each year to talk to these North American Venetians (and also perhaps to see at firsthand how the furs were coming). Through his reception by the Iroquois representatives, and particularly the tone of their speeches, he could gauge how the treaty stood, how much longer these Venetians would profess friendship for this Turk. In 1681 the signs were so bad that Frontenac allowed to slip into his dispatch an admission that he certainly must have hoped had been forgotten after his recall. "The Indians are becoming hostile despite everything that I say to hold them in check; the journeys that I make nearly every year to Fort Frontenac no longer impress them as they did in the beginning."

Perhaps the novelty of his Lake Ontario appearances was wearing off, but the problem went far deeper than that. As there had been factors beyond Frontenac's control that had earlier pushed the Iroquois toward peace, so there were now factors beyond his control that were inclining them to war. Most notably, the Andastes who had so harried the Iroquois to their south had themselves, after suffering unexpected raids from the English, sued the

Iroquois for peace, and by some accounts had been absorbed into the Iroquois entirely, increasing even more a warrior population that was already recovering from the earlier smallpox epidemics. The Iroquois were now strong, and their corn caches large. They no longer had so much reason to humble themselves before Onontio.

Over all these circumstances Frontenac had no control whatsoever, but this is not to say that he bore no significant responsibility for the coming war with the Iroquois. He did indeed bear responsibility, because he had effectively subverted Colbert's policy against the western expansion of New France. Frontenac had come to New France to do something glorious and also to repair his own finances. Western expansion could meet both of these needs; Frontenac could at once be the founder of an empire and the skimmer of fur profits.

To do this he had to circumvent no less a man than Colbert, but Colbert was thousands of miles away. Frontenac had only to read Colbert's dispatches in search of an opening, a justification that Colbert would have to accept, the bureaucratic equivalent of a northwest passage. He had to find a way to make Colbert approve of western expansion in spite of himself, as he did of the founding of Fort Frontenac. Colbert's response to Frontenac's glowing report on the fort had been cool, almost scolding, but it had provided acceptable rationalizations for further action:

"His Majesty's intent is that you should not make long voyages up the Saint Lawrence River, nor even that in the future the colonists should spread out as much as they have done in the past. On the contrary he wishes you to strive persistently, during all your stay in that country, to crowd them together, and to group them and settle them in towns and villages, and so to give them the greater possibility of protecting themselves well. . . . You should apply yourself to have cleared and settled those vast fertile places, that are nearest the sea coasts and the communications with France, rather than that you should think of discoveries in the interior of the country, so remote that they can never be inhabited or possessed by Frenchmen. This general rule may have its exceptions in two cases. One if the lands of which you take possession are necessary to the commerce and trade of the French, and if they can be explored and possessed by some other country which can trouble French trade and commerce. But as there is no place of such a kind, His Majesty is always of the opinion that you can and must leave the Indians free to bring their furs without putting yourself to the trouble of going so far to seek them."

In circumventing Colbert's intentions Frontenac had one chief agent, René-Robert Cavelier. Cavelier, from a wealthy merchant family in France, had originally joined the Society of Jesus there, but had left when his superiors repeatedly refused to assign the unprepared novice to the order's most prestigious mission, China. He came to New France, and established a seigneury to the west of Montreal, on the way to China—hence the name he gave it, La Chine. The mundane realities of homesteading did not hold Cavelier long, but long enough for him to feel justified in knighting himself La Salle. Both as Cavelier and as La Salle, he seldom troubled with facts when something grander might serve. René-Robert Cavelier was one of those through whom the gale of life blew very high.

By the time Frontenac arrived to assume his governorship, La Salle had become an accomplished forest ranger, but his ill-defined yearning for great achievement was still unfulfilled. Frontenac and La Salle quickly realized that they were meant for one another. La Salle was the forest ranger whom Frontenac sent ahead to scout the site for Fort Frontenac, and whom he left behind in charge of it. La Salle tattled to Frontenac about Fénelon's sermon on civil disobedience, and also produced a series of backwoods testimonials on the harmlessness of brandy. Through all this La Salle made an important discovery: Governor Frontenac was one of those divinities for whom flattery is never disobliging. (La Salle's underlings would discover the same about him.) About the founding of Fort Frontenac, La Salle wrote to his lord, "It is impossible to put into words the praises that all the Iroquois nations sing of your person." For Frontenac's sake, nonetheless, La Salle tried the impossible repeatedly.

Fort Frontenac was the making of La Salle, in more ways than one. Frontenac had funded it out of his own pocket in the full expectation that Colbert would reward such a glorious exploit with government reimbursement. Colbert agreed to the fort, but punished his governor by refusing financial support and any permission for fur trading there. Frontenac, little more than two years in the New World, could see his new creditors already beginning to circle. Then La Salle made a clever proposal.

Why not suggest to Colbert that La Salle himself take over the fort as a seigneury? La Salle could raise the money from his family in France to pay all of Frontenac's debts and expenses. Colbert would be saved from the embarrassing situation of a bankrupt governor. And the fur trading could resume because La Salle would then just be doing business from his homestead. (And Frontenac, presumably, could still count on his percentage.) Frontenac put all his influence at court behind the scheme, and somehow it was approved. Indeed, La Salle not only got Fort Frontenac but was ennobled as well; he was now legally La Salle.

The annual expenses of the fort were roughly 20,000 livres. The net profits were estimated between 60,000 and 120,000 livres. Even after giving Frontenac (and perhaps Perrot) a cut, La Salle was clearly becoming a rich man. By 1677 he had completely rebuilt the fort, with much of its eight hundred yards of walls in masonry. La Salle and Frontenac had the beginnings of their empire.

Nonetheless, their empire was far from secure. About the time La Salle was rebuilding Fort Frontenac in grand style, Louis Joliet—the same Joliet who thought brandy traders should be hanged—was exploring with the Jesuit Marquette the greatest river of North America, the Mississippi. La Salle had earlier sought such a river as a passage to the west, to the Orient and the fabled wealth of China. Joliet hoped for such a western passage too, and explored the Mississippi far enough to realize in disappointment that it drained into the Gulf of Mexico. In 1676 Joliet petitioned the king for permission to settle the Illinois Valley, which ran from the southern tip of Lake Michigan to the Mississippi. If he was granted this, La Salle and Frontenac would find their fort flanked by another Frenchman. They could see the supply of furs perhaps being lessened; most certainly their hopes for expansion would be dimmed.

They had one advantage, however, apart from Frontenac's influence at court. Joliet was an honest man; he represented what he wished to do truthfully. His request, therefore, contradicted Colbert's plan to concentrate the population of New France. The petition was denied. "His Majesty is unwilling to grant the leave asked by Sieur Joliet to go to the Illinois country. . . . The number of settlers in Canada should be increased before thinking of settlement elsewhere."

La Salle and Frontenac now had their chance. Obviously they could not say that another country was about to take the Mississippi. They settled on a complaint Colbert had written to Frontenac a few years before: "the worst thing about Canada is the entrance to the river which, being so far to the north, allows ships to enter only during four, five, or six months of the year." One can sympathize with Colbert's frustration, especially when he had a governor in New France who would do you knew not what. Frontenac and La Salle chose to play on Colbert's desire for centralization of government and his desire for frequent communication with his provinces—to play that against his plan for a compact colony that would not be militarily overextended.

La Salle applied for permission to continue the exploration of Joliet to the mouth of the Mississippi in the hope of finding a suitable site for a cold weather port. He would establish forts along the way to keep communication open with Fort Frontenac (communication—one must suspect—that would chiefly be conducted in converted beaver).

Colbert and his subordinates, to their credit, were far more suspicious of this scheme than they were of La Salle's last. La Salle had to return to France to prosecute his case personally, and also to be sure that sufficient bribes were placed in influential hands. La Salle was finally granted his petition, but with conditions designed to assure that his was to be the kind of expedition he represented it as. In particular, he had to complete his work within five years, and he was forbidden to trade with Indians who already traded with the French. (As for the latter condition, they might as well have wished that the heavens be adorned with another sun.)

Over the next four years La Salle did establish his series of forts from the Great Lakes down to the Mississippi. After four years he had, however, yet to reach the mouth of the Mississippi. Why rush when there were so many Indians to trade with along the way? Those who had traded happily with the French before found it especially convenient to have Frenchmen save them the trip by coming to their villages. La Salle blithely acted as if Colbert had given him a monopoly on the whole western fur trade. Only in 1682, after Colbert complained, "I have seen little success attend the enterprise of Sieur de La Salle," did he finally get around to descending beyond the area already explored by Joliet, and then only to fulfill at the last moment the terms of his grant. By this time, the French and the Iroquois were in a virtual state of war.

Look at these developments from the Iroquois perspective. Onontio and his agents, while professing peace and paternalistic concern, had first placed a fort between the Iroquois and the Ottawa, and had then established a whole series of forts to their west. It was bad enough having hundreds of French forest rangers seeking out furs the Iroquois wanted for themselves. Now there were permanent forts to assure that the French received most of the trade without the Iroquois so much as having the chance to act as middlemen. And the Iroquois knew at firsthand that these were posts for trade, not exploration; they did not have to base their conclusions on what La Salle and Frontenac said in dispatches. They could see for themselves, as Colbert could not.

But now the Iroquois were strong again, and allied with the Andastes. The Dutch and English traders with whom they usually did business were urging them on. Yet they did not want to commit themselves prematurely. In particular, they wished to avoid a two-front war, against the French to their north, and to the west against the Indian trading allies of the French, such as the Miamis and the Illinois.

The Iroquois strategy, although eloquently dissembled by their diplomats in their meetings with the French, was obvious to almost everyone. Lull the French into thinking themselves safe, the beloved parents of their compliant Iroquois children; then strike to neutralize the western allies, under the cover of some pretext or other, with fulsome diplomatic assurances to the French that only limited objectives were involved. Then force these western tribes into an alliance with the Iroquois. (Once they realized the unreliability of the French and the strength of the Iroquois themselves, what choice would they have?) Finally, turn the collective strength of the Iroquois nations against New France until once again a Frenchman would be afraid to cross his own door to piss.

When the Iroquois began to paw against the western tribes tentatively, even they must have been surprised at the inactivity of Frontenac. Frontenac chose to take their explanations uncritically, and chose to ignore the pleas of those Indians in the west who could see a catastrophe in the making. Frontenac would write to the king that to settle the trouble it would be necessary only to let the Iroquois see a few hundred French troops. Frontenac at this point knew that his own days as governor were numbered—and at times he seemed himself to be acting to ensure that this number was small. As to the Iroquois threat, he did nothing. He took no military action; he tried no negotiations, even failing to go to Fort Frontenac for the usual meetings; he did not even improve the defenses of New France, woefully decayed after a decade of peace. He did nothing about the Iroquois menace, except to convince Colbert that it did not exist.

So Colbert appointed as Frontenac's successor a meek civil servant who would follow his instructions and offend no one on the Sovereign Council. When La Barre arrived in New France and was apprised of the true situation, he was horrified. "I have found this colony on the verge of being forced into war by the Iroquois and in a condition to succumb." But Frontenac, not his inexperienced successor, was believed. Any trouble with the Iroquois, Frontenac could assure his superiors, was due to the ineptitude of La Barre—a firm paternal hand was all that was needed. La Barre was reduced to pleading with Colbert: "The situation in the country is not understood either by you or by my lord . . . it has been depicted to you in a fashion far removed from the truth." Frontenac could laugh disdainfully that this was the voice of inexperience and fear, a man whose sword was worn as a sartorial accoutrement.

La Barre knew he was faced with an all-out war against the Iroquois. When they sent a delegation protesting their peaceful intentions, as of course they would, La Barre observed, "Past experience indicates that they have never discussed or treated for peace except when they wished to perpetrate a great deception and launch a surprise." Incisive as were his observations, La Barre still did nothing. He knew but could not act. His intendant remarked in disgust, "I can find no disposition whatsoever in the mind of M. le General to wage war with the Iroquois."

Finally La Barre assembled an army to invade the Iroquois country, and then waited some more, for an angel of mercy, perhaps, to snatch him out of his predicament. The Iroquois began to boast that if the French ever did get around to invading their country the Five Nations would finally have the opportunity to test the rumor that French flesh tasted salty. Then La Barre sent to the Iroquois a plan for a negotiated settlement, and the intendant was furious: "You must understand that if we do not destroy them they will destroy us."

La Barre might have understood, but he still could not bring himself to act. By the time the negotiations began he did not have to. By then his army was being routed, as the Iroquois representatives could well see, by an influenza epidemic. The French could not possibly fight now, and the Iroquois dictated the terms. The Iroquois were to be left to do as they willed with the Illinois. In return, the Iroquois promised not to harm the other tribes. (Of course, the Iroquois knew they would not have to. The others, once they realized what the cowardly French had allowed to happen, would almost certainly follow the Andastes into an Iroquois alliance.) As for future negotiations between the French and the Iroquois, the chief Iroquois negotiator asserted that these would now take place on Iroquois soil. No longer would the Iroquois be willing to make the long trip to Montreal. As for Fort Frontenac, the Iroquois diplomats would not come there either; the crickets were too noisy at night, and disturbed their sleep.

The signed treaty was sent back to France, where it was met with astonishment. The Master of Versailles was not accustomed to having peace terms dictated to his representatives by savages and crickets. "I have no cause to be satisfied with the treaty made between Sieur de La Barre and the Iroquois; his abandoning of the Illinois has displeased me greatly." La Barre was recalled in 1685 and returned to France a broken man, his earlier years of effective service to the crown largely forgotten. One would like to think that he and Duchesnau had the opportunity to get together at least once, to compare bitter notes.

Louis might not have been satisfied with La Barre, but Frontenac had much cause to be. La Barre had demonstrated what happened when this most demanding position in the French empire was entrusted to an ordinary man. The greatness of Frontenac's governorship could now be seen in relief. As far as Frontenac was concerned, virtue need no more blush, nor merit sigh.

"Frontenac has at last obtained, by his perseverance and through the good office of his friends, his return to Canada." So an informant at court wrote associates in Montreal in 1689, adding: "Take good care to forewarn everyone so that no one will appear distressed at the return of M. de Frontenac, or it could be reported to him and have evil consequences. It is essential to retain his friendship. As he is supported at the Court, his conduct will be upheld there and complaints will not be listened to readily."

Frontenac was almost seventy years old now, but still ravenous for further honors and glory. He was also still opening his wings too wide at court; after only a few years there he was once again on the edge of bankruptcy. And in his campaign for reappointment he had one pivotal advantage: Colbert had worked himself into an early grave. There was now no one in high government who could effectively contradict his own account of his governorship.

Colbert himself had appointed the successor to La Barre in 1686. Governor Denonville had achieved much in his three years, but at the expense of his own health. He had launched a campaign into the Iroquois territory. To his frustration the Iroquois would not stand and fight, but the Indian allies were at least reassured that the treaty of La Barre was an aberration. Denonville had also significantly improved the French defenses, but he himself warned that this was futile, given the French pattern of settlement. He saw at firsthand the wisdom of Colbert's insistence that the French should cluster together in villages, rather than spread out along the river, each homestead ribboning back from its own river frontage. Colbert had been ignored, and so now the Iroquois could massacre a settlement piecemeal and dissolve into the woods before any counterattack could be mounted. Denonville's own assessment was that only Iroquois ignorance of French vulnerability prevented them from gradually sweeping away the whole colony. Then, in 1689, at the very end of his governorship, Denonville learned that one should never underestimate the knowledge of the Iroquois about matters that concerned them.

In that year the Iroquois destroyed the westernmost settlement of the French, La Chine. The Iroquois had approached La Chine unobserved during a storm, and had divided up into killing squads, one to a house. Of the seventy-seven houses, fifty were destroyed. Perhaps twenty-four settlers were killed outright, and at least three times that number were taken prisoner. The governor sent two detachments of troops to reinforce the local fort. The second of these was ambushed, only a handful making it to the fort at all. That night the Iroquois celebrated, it was reported, by roasting to death and eating five captive children.

There was a brutal justice in this massacre. La Chine had been founded by La Salle, and La Salle had threatened the well-being of the Iroquois. But La Salle by that time was himself dead. He had spent so much of life disguising his true motives from others that after Frontenac's recall he began to disguise his true motives from himself. La Salle ended his life trying—with permission from Paris—to establish a colony on the Gulf of Mexico. The expedition was conceived in folly and endured in madness. The colonists eventually realized the insanity. Then, amidst the suffering, despair, and fury that attended this realization, La Salle was murdered.

The massacre at La Chine marked a change in attitude in New France. There always had been the risk of a settler or family being killed by Indians, but now the risk seemed immediate and wholesale. A complete seigneury had been destroyed in a single day. It was too late to change the pattern of settlement to the pattern Colbert had recommended. The colonists, especially those around Montreal, simply felt pure terror and the need for revenge.

Shortly after the La Chine massacre some forest rangers arrived in Montreal after a successful trading run along the Ottawa. They brought with them two Iroquois captives who had been taken on the way. These captives were brought to the central square, and there turned over to some local mission Indians who slowly tortured them to death before a large and appreciative crowd.

Denonville had already requested his own recall before the La Chine massacres, and it had already been decided to grant this loyal and effective servant of the crown his wish. He would return to France for a distinguished semi-retirement. Of course, that did not prevent Frontenac from slandering his administration.

Frontenac's initial report after returning to New France later that year shows him up to his old trick of misrepresenting things to his own advantage. The massacre at La Chine he made even worse than it was, his estimate of the dead being two hundred. He also denigrated Denonville's achievement in keeping the fur trade open and allowing poorer families to participate in it; Frontenac, the old champion of the fur trade, wrote, "The abundance delights only a few merchants and a small number of individuals who have a share in it, but the colony as a whole is thereby neither richer nor more content." (An accurate assessment, but of the fur trade in his own administration, not Denonville's.) In general, Frontenac tried to present the situation of New France as so desperate that only heroic leadership of the most extraordinary kind would save it. The aged Frontenac had returned from his own comfortable retirement to redeem his beleaguered people.

Actually the situation was grave enough without Frontenac's exaggerations. There was now no longer any question in the colony about the relative importance of the intendant and the governor. The military leader was supreme over all; Frontenac's position within the colony was now unquestionable. He also had as large a charter as the wind, to blow on whom he pleased. Once he realized this, Frontenac decided to settle his old score with the Sovereign Council, which had many of the same members who had reduced him to paroxysms of impotent rage.

Frontenac did not need to attack the council or even to make demands of it. He simply declined to attend its meetings without saying why. But they needed him there, since in this time of crisis his decisions were those on which the welfare of the colony most depended. They sent him a delegation to ask why he was not attending; he replied they knew well enough. They did not, but they could guess. Frontenac wanted some symbolic act of submission. They settled on the ceremony by which the parliament of Paris received the king himself. From now on, whenever the governor arrived in the anteroom of the council chamber, he was to be announced immediately by the captain of guards, business was to cease, and the chamber to be cleared of spectators; two councillors were to be selected to have the honor of escorting his High and Mighty Lord to his seat.

Frontenac, on being informed of this plan, professed pleasure that his subjects still regarded him in that high esteem they had formerly, and assured them that he would not have permitted them in their gratifying enthusiasm for his person to have honored him more profusely than was fitting to one of his station. Needless to say, Frontenac now attended the meetings of the Sovereign Council assiduously, undoubtedly timing his entrances for maximum effect.[5]

Nonetheless, the torture deaths of the captives in Montreal more than Frontenac's ceremonial triumph in Quebec suggested the direction of his immediate plans for New France. There was a will among the French to do unto their enemies as their enemies had done unto them. The problem was that the Iroquois could not be surprised as had been the residents of La Chine. They would know the French were coming, and they would refuse to stand

---

[5]Frontenac not only had humbled the Sovereign Council, he also no longer had to worry about his other adversary, the formidable Bishop Laval. Laval, unlike Frontenac, had never sought power for its own sake. So, in 1688 (the year before Frontenac's return), he had retired to a seminary he had founded in New France. There he would spend the twenty years remaining for him in a life of prayer, penance, and charitable acts.

and fight. They had nothing worth a pitched battle against superior forces. They would simply abandon their villages.

Here Frontenac had a piece of good luck, the kind of luck that seemed to follow him throughout his career. In 1689 the English Parliament had deposed the Catholic James II in favor of the Protestant Dutch monarch William of Orange. Louis XIV would not accept this action that was at once dishonorable and against French interests. Parliaments did not make kings, kings made parliaments—and anyway, William of Orange was perhaps Louis's most annoying enemy among the sovereigns of Europe, certainly the most effective in aligning them against him. In 1689 Louis declared war against the Dutch and English in the name of the true English king.

The French might not be able to massacre Iroquois, but they could launch similar surprise attacks against British settlements, particularly frontier settlements that were engaged in the fur trade and were therefore supplying and encouraging the Iroquois. If the French could destroy such settlements, the Iroquois would have to turn to the French for their required European goods and to do this they would first have to sue for peace.

Frontenac now was in his element. Famine, sword, and fire crouched at his heels like hounds waiting for his word of release. To send them against the British had much to recommend it. The French did not want to destroy the Iroquois as a force on the North American continent. Only the strength of the Iroquois kept the British on the far side of the Alleghenies. A submissive, not a destroyed, Iroquois Confederacy was what France needed. To strike at their British sources of supply was a way to achieve this.

In 1690 three war parties left to raid English settlements. The party from Montreal left in January with 210 men, half French, half Indian. Their objective was Schenectady, a small English village to the west of Albany. As had happened in La Chine, the war party slipped into the settlement, late at night, unobserved. Not even the usual defensive precautions were being taken in this part of New York because of differences within the community between those newly loyal to William and those still to James. Quietly the raiders placed a small group at each house, then all at once they attacked. About sixty persons were massacred. The mayor of Albany would write, "The cruelties committed at said place no pen can write nor tongue express; women big with child ripped up and the children alive thrown into the flames, and their heads dashed in pieces against the doors and windows."

The two other parties sent out by Frontenac at the same time, these against settlements in New England, met with similar success. A Frenchman wrote of one of these attacks, "This strike is of great advantage because it breaks off all the talk of peace between our Indians and the English. The English are in despair, for not even infants in the cradle were spared." In all three attacks neither infancy nor age found any safety in helplessness. Yet the slaughter was not indiscriminate. Forest rangers and Indian allies might have been the executioners, but Frontenac had prepared the blow—and he ordered that any Iroquois found in the settlements were themselves to be spared. He intended to drive a wedge between the Iroquois and the terrorized English to get the Iroquois to negotiations. He did not want any unnecessary Iroquois deaths to have to explain.

In Schenectady the thirty Iroquois who were found were released unharmed. They, however, did not appreciate the nuances in Frontenac's policy. They immediately formed a war party to avenge their fallen allies, ambushed the raiders on the way back to Montreal, and took nineteen of them prisoner. This was the only serious loss in the expeditions.

Frontenac had returned to his people, and in less than a year they were celebrating a great victory, and it *was* a great victory for French morale after the horror of La Chine. Nonetheless, whatever its effects on morale, not everyone was happy about the way Frontenac had planned the raids. Some of the Indians who had taken part in them were much distressed that they were directed against the English who had done these Indians no harm. Why kill them and spare the Iroquois? Moreover, Frontenac's intendant thought that all the forces should have been concentrated on Albany, the most important center of Iroquois trade; this latter point was significant.

Frontenac, a true creature of the highly centralized French system, did not understand the relative autonomy of the English colonies. He saw the northern colonies as a unified whole, acting in concert against French interests. This they were not—until, that is, Frontenac terrorized them indiscriminately. Now these same colonies sought to form a concerted plan to conquer New France.

It was in October 1690 that a fleet from Boston appeared before Quebec. The commander, William Phips, had earlier distinguished himself in a raid against another French settlement; he made a huge profit out of this raid by ignoring the terms of the surrender to which he had earlier agreed. (Phips, like Frontenac, was one of those for whom the Ten Commandments were not law, but a series of suggestions, and rather unrealistic ones at that.) Now this same William Phips was demanding, under white flag through a messenger, that Quebec surrender itself to his tender mercies.

The messenger was led, blindfolded, into the presence of Frontenac, who had been preparing himself for such a scene all his life. The blindfold was removed, and the blinking messenger saw Frontenac in his full splendor. Frontenac gazed down upon him with the look of Jove, high and stern and dominating, full of menace and angry pride. The British representative delivered Phips' message, demanded an answer in writing within the hour, and even had the cheek to offer the governor his watch if he needed one.

At this impudence Frontenac unleashed his thunder. He denounced the English king as a usurper, defended his own raids as glorious, praised the bravery of his men, and reminded the messenger that Phips had already proven himself a dishonorable man. ("The divine justice which your general invokes in his letter will not fail to punish such acts severely.") When the messenger, now meek, asked for the answer in writing, the thunder rolled again. "No, I have no reply to make to your general other than from the mouths of my cannon and muskets. He must learn that it is not in this fashion that one summons a man such as I. Let him do his best; I will do mine."

Phips must have soon realized that he had no chance to take the formidable fortress that was Quebec. His expedition was supposed to have been coordinated with a diversionary land attack from Albany on Montreal. With the French troops pinned down defending Montreal, Phips might have been able to mount a dangerous assault on Quebec. However, the land forces had to turn back in disarray before reaching Montreal, the British colonies exhibiting once again their inability to act together effectively. Phips was left to try his best against Quebec, with all the French troops concentrated against his. He temporized, fought a few indecisive skirmishes, cannonaded the city (while the city returned the compliment), and finally sailed off, lest his ships be trapped by the freezing of the Saint Lawrence. Albany would attempt another assault on New France the next year, but by then the French were ready for it. After an ambush and some savage fighting, much of it hand-to-hand, the Albany troops retired once again. And Frontenac once again was a hero, nodding to the universal applause.

Frontenac, greedy as he was for this applause, was parsimonious in his acknowledgment of those who had won it for him. Yet the true heroes (if any) of the raids on the British settlements and the repulse of the counterattacks by land were not Frontenac and his fellow officials in Quebec. The true heroes were the forest rangers, that generation of French settlers who had grown up gliding through the wilderness in search of game and furs. Earlier Colbert and his intendants might have disdained them as a threat to the compactness and prosperity of the colony. And Frontenac might have sought to curtail their activity to bring it under the control of his own agents like La Salle. And the bishop and his missionaries would denounce them as without morals and scruples, no better than the savages among whom they lived (if not worse, for they had freely abandoned the civilized state). But all this was now of the past. With the massacre at La Chine, and the incinerations at Montreal, their time had come: Their unseemly vices had become manly virtues.

The forest ranger might regard his farm as hearth and home, but the woods were his element. He was as at home in it as any Iroquois. Now the colony needed his skills for its survival, those very skills that earlier had been taken as a sign of a Frenchman turned savage. The forest ranger had become the knight errant of New France—and on his strange chivalry depended the survival of civilization, of French civilization, in this New World. The forest ranger tomahawking the sleeping Schenectady settler was the ironic fulfill-ment of Champlain's prophecy decades before that there would come a mar-riage of the French and Indian peoples. As Frontenac had become a servant to remain a nobleman, so the ranger would become an Iroquois to remain French.

After the repulse of the second Albany expedition, the British no longer directly attacked the French, to the great displeasure of the Iroquois allies. Frontenac now had to bring the Iroquois to negotiations for peace, no mean task. The French Indian allies and the forest rangers he encouraged to do their work. They should, in particular, hunt the forest to harvest Iroquois scalps for which the governor would pay well, so well that he would have to argue peri-odically with economizers at Versailles.

Throughout this war of attrition, Frontenac endeavored to preserve his pose as the good father who wished only the best for his Iroquois children: "The great Onontio, whom you all know, has come back again. He does not blame you for what you have done; for he looks upon you as foolish children, blames only the English, who are the cause of your folly, and have made you forget your obedience to a father who has always loved and never deceived you."

Frontenac knew as well as anyone that the Iroquois were not foolish chil-dren, any more than the great Onontio was above deception. His successful tactics were an imitation of theirs. And if going to war to protect your position in a lucrative trade was the act of a child, then among the foolish children of the world could be numbered a Colbert. Nonetheless, Frontenac would per-sist in treating them so, and finally the day came when they, like the members of the Sovereign Council, had to treat him as he wished them to. Smallpox was once again ravaging the human beings of eastern North America, Euro-pean and Indian alike; the Europeans, unlike the Indians, could replenish their population by immigration. With the attrition of war and the death by epidemics, together with the passivity of the British colonies, Frontenac could afford to wait the Iroquois out in what had become a strange, aloof sort of siege.

Periodically Frontenac would attempt to begin negotiations, sometimes with embarrassing results. One delegation from Frontenac was given a reception that must have severely tried Onontio's Olympian patience. Two of the delegation were roasted alive and eaten; the third was made to run the gauntlet. Yet Frontenac still waited, and in this policy there was but one danger.

This danger was more serious than losing a few delegates to Iroquois stomachs, as distasteful as that might be. Frontenac's waiting policy, with its conciliatory tone to the Iroquois, was particularly worrisome to the Indian allies of the French. The savages seemed to have the memory of a Colbert, and without memoranda and reports. They distinctly remembered that Frontenac in his first governorship had claimed the Iroquois as his friends and had done nothing against them while they attacked at their leisure the Ottawas, the Miamis, and the Illinois. Denonville had won back their loyalty by his decisive invasions of the Iroquois territory, but now Frontenac had returned and they remembered how he had betrayed them before. Their confidence in their own recollections could not be shaken by even the most adroit misrepresentations of Onontio.

This provided the Iroquois with their only realistic chance. If they could form an alliance against the French with these, their age-old enemies, then they could hope to push the French out of the Mississippi Valley and back up the Saint Lawrence. Their earlier successes had resulted from peace with the Andastes; now they needed peace with these other tribes. If they could get just one to enter into an alliance, the others would be almost forced to follow. To overcome their great reluctance, the Iroquois had to convince these tribes that Frontenac and the French were about to betray them again.

Frontenac in his support of an ever-growing fur trade was giving the Iroquois strong arguments. The French were now trading weapons for hides with the Sioux, traditional enemies to the west for some of these tribes. Did they wish to fight a two-front war, Sioux to the west and Iroquois to the east, with the cowardly French as usual doing nothing? Did they wish to be exterminated as a people as had the once-great Hurons who had also relied upon the French?

Every time Frontenac sent a peace initiative to the Iroquois they would send off their own diplomats to the other tribes to inform them that once again Onontio was trying to betray them. He was not only arming one enemy; he was professing fatherly love for the other. Once such diplomats seemed to have succeeded with the Ottawas, and had left for their own country assured that Ottawa leaders would soon follow them to conclude a treaty. The terms had already been agreed upon. As the Ottawa leaders themselves were leaving, some French happened into the village. They could not dissuade the Ottawas from their foolishness, but they did have an Iroquois with them that they had captured on their trip. They wished to torture him to death, but they had not fully mastered the intricacies, their own culture being so backward in these matters. Would the Ottawas be so good as to postpone their departure to assist? During the torture the Iroquois broke, and begged for a merciful death. This Iroquois was no true warrior, but a dog. The French now began to chant, "To the pot! To the pot!" A fine meal was had by all, and the French alliance preserved.

Of course, this would not have happened if there had not already been extreme reluctance to conclude the treaty. Traditional fear, distrust, and hatred of the Iroquois by their neighbors weighed heavily against any such treaty even when the Iroquois could present mutual advantages with extreme plausibility. The children of Deganawida would be the true friends of no one.

This was Frontenac's great advantage in his policy, however foolish his permission of Sioux trade. He would assure his Indian allies he would make no treaty with the Iroquois that did not include "all my children both white and red, for I am the father of both alike." And Onontio continued to pay thirty-two livres for each Iroquois scalp, despite complaints that some allies were learning how to divide a scalp into two or three.

Between 1690 and 1698 the number of Iroquois warriors, it is estimated, had declined from 2,800 to 1,320. The Iroquois made one last effort to form an alliance against the French, and seemed to have it within their grasp when Frontenac with a perfect sense of timing played his trump card: He invaded the Iroquois territory. He attacked the central nation of the Onondaga, the capital of the Great Tree of Peace. As was to be expected, they fled without a conclusive engagement. Only one Iroquois was killed, a decrepit old man left behind who, as he was being tortured to death, lectured his captors on how they should conduct themselves when they were captured by the Iroquois, as surely they would be one day. This was no dog. Large caches of Iroquois corn were destroyed, and the Onondaga would face a winter of hardship. More important, by this invasion the western allies were convinced of French loyalty, and the Iroquois diplomats were now rebuffed. The futility of any further attempts at alliances against the French was now obvious—and the Iroquois finally sued for peace.

The actual negotiations were extremely difficult. They lasted three years, and at times seemed very close to collapse. And this should be taken as a sign of their difficulty, not of insincerity on the part of either the Iroquois or the French. The Iroquois would have preferred a peace between themselves and the French alone, which would have left them free to duel with the western tribes, but also would have left the French alliance in tatters. The French negotiators would not consider such an exclusive peace. Louis XIV, through his representatives, was going to bring peace to all his children in North America. He was going to end their fighting not just with their father, but also among themselves.

Because of this insistence, the negotiations involved, by one estimate, thirty-three different tribes. Thirty-three independent headmen, eminences so long at one another's throats, had to work toward a stable peace that would reduce their opportunities to prove themselves worthy of honor above their peers. Throughout the negotiations, the British did their best to cause difficulties. Most fundamentally, they claimed that they had to be a party in the negotiations because the Iroquois were their subjects. But the French knew that in the end the Iroquois could not admit to being British dogs.

Perhaps the most difficult issue in the negotiations, after it was settled that the peace was to be general and the Iroquois did not belong to the British, was the exchange of prisoners of war. The French insisted that all French prisoners be returned, even those who had been so long captive they no longer wished to return. (Captive children who survived an Iroquois victory celebration were likely to be raised as Iroquois, and might no longer be familiar with either the language or the customs of their original people.) The Iroquois countered by asking for the return of all Iroquois as well, even those who had converted to Christianity and now lived at mission settlements. These too should be returned to their native villages, whether or not they wished. The French replied that these cases were not equivalent, and if the Iroquois did not start negotiating in good faith the French would immediately launch another invasion. This left Tegannissorens, then the greatest of the Iroquois diplomats, exasperated: "You come and speak of peace and have scarce sat down to smoke a pipe, but talk of coming and knocking us on the head, and therefore I say, nobody knows your heart."

The exchange of prisoners was particularly difficult because the number of captives still alive would always be considerably less than those known taken. The exchanges required trust on both sides, which was at times sorely tested. The headman of one tribe known to have taken many Iroquois prisoners brought to the exchange only one, but saved the day by explaining with candid good humor, "I have brought you only one prisoner because if you have showed a liking for my flesh, I have also liked yours, and I have eaten my prisoners just as you have eaten yours." Dignified laughter spread throughout the assembly, and the negotiations once again proceeded.

Frontenac himself did not live to see the completion of this treaty that was the greatest achievement of his governorship. In 1696 Frontenac had led the invasion that had brought the Iroquois to the peace talks. Seventy-six years old, he had had himself carried on this expedition in a chaise. If we are to believe his account, the expedition succeeded because the Iroquois were "so terrified to see me march against them in person." Frontenac thought that after so notable a personal success His Majesty might "hold me worthy of some mark of honor that may enable me to pass the short remainder of my life in some little distinction." Seventy-six years old, and still ravenous for honors. Louis responded with the Military Order of Saint Louis, not altogether satisfactory to Frontenac because someone else in the colony had already received it. Seventy-six years old, and still jostling with others for pre-eminence. In Quebec in 1697 Frontenac had begun the negotiations for the peace, and had the greatest pleasure of rejecting the New York governor's claim to sovereignty over the Iroquois: "He claims the Iroquois, but they are none of his. They call me father, and they call him brother."

Even the conventional pieties of Frontenac's will did not lack touches of his eternal arrogance; to one person he left his reliquary "filled with the most rare and precious relics that could be found." He was not a man given to regrets, but as he was dying he must have regretted that he would not participate consciously in the pomp of his own funeral. And he would have very much regretted not hearing the eulogy preached on that occasion, a eulogy that not even Frontenac would have found understated, as the beginning shows:

"This funeral pageantry, this temple draped in mourning, these dim lights, this sad and solemn music, this great assembly bowed in sorrow, and all this pomp and circumstance may well penetrate your hearts. I will not seek to dry your tears for I cannot contain my own. After all, this is a time to weep, and never did a people weep for a better governor."

In the margin of one surviving copy someone has written: "The eulogist did not know the old fox."

Chapter IX

A SOCIETY OF FRIENDS

HILE NEW FRANCE was developing, a new colony was being established in British territory, a colony that seemed to many heaven-sent, a sacred valley with promise beyond human prayers. It was an enterprise Frontenac would have found utterly incomprehensible. Either the world was a different place from the one the French governor knew or someone on the British side had taken leave of his senses.

To be sure, Frontenac would have understood well the military, political, even economic pragmatics involved in the founding of Pennsylvania. He certainly would have envied the charter William Penn had gained for his colony: It gave the proprietor almost monarchical control over his inhabitants, just what Frontenac had always thought his own due. Frontenac could also have sympathized with Penn's original financial plight; the son of a powerful nobleman, Penn had fallen on hard times, and had had to use his connections at court to get a colonial position through which he could repair his fortune. Frontenac knew that role by heart. So there was much about the founding of Pennsylvania that Frontenac would have understood—almost everything, in fact, except the vision that lay at its heart.

The vision was that of George Fox, "that new and heavenly minded man," as Penn called him. In 1647 Fox had undergone a religious crisis. Still in his early twenties and before he had settled on a profession, he had experienced the doubts that many were feeling in the seventeenth century. But Fox could not seem to quiet his; they swarmed over him, and conventional doctrines and consolations helped him not at all. And the worldliness of a Frontenac attracted him not at all; it mistook the mirth of a moment for happiness. Finally he reached the verge of despair. He lost all faith in religion and in his fellow man. Then, O then he heard a voice, and when he heard it his heart did leap for joy.

He realized the meaning of a verse from Scripture which he had often mouthed: "The kingdom of God is within you." Finally he realized what this meant. God is within us all, and therefore every human being is as prone to love as the sun to shine—then, of a sudden, for Fox "all things were new, and all the creation gave another smell unto me than before, beyond what words can utter. I knew nothing but pureness and innocency and righteousness. I was come up to the state of Adam before he fell." (We cannot even imagine how Frontenac would have responded to such words, although he almost certainly would have racked his memory for an experience to top it.)

Fox then realized that no matter what Calvin and the petrified physiognomies of Puritanism claimed, we are not slaves to sin, only a few of us to be redeemed at God's caprice. Rather, within every crusted human shell the sanctifying pearl of light can be found. We need only look for it to find it. Each person need only look within himself to find it. And then, afterward, when he looks outward again upon the world, it will be new and a pure joy, as on the first day of creation when all the choirs of angels sang in joyful harmony at the light. In such words George Fox, wandering from place to place like the apostles of old, proclaimed the light to all who would listen.

Yet whenever he professed his vision, he was set upon with the dry bones of theology, tradition, ritual, and convention. He had little patience for those who would dissect his new world with Jewish or Greek distinctions, would submit it to old systems of ancient prejudice. "Do you not see the blood of Christ?" he had once shouted to a collection of such Pharisees and Philistines. "See it in your hearts, sprinkling on your hearts and consciences?" Without the light to see the salvational blood, red and bubbling with life, we are left with the empty categories of law and reason. Law and reason can only teach us what we must not do, the letter that killeth. In all things that which is good and sublime is revealed to us only by the spirit of divinity within our own hearts. This divinity should be our joyful sustenance. We should willingly leave our parents and earn our bread in a foreign land rather than act against our inner light. No matter how overwhelming opinion and evidence against us, our inner conviction should be a sweet and sufficient guarantee of our innocence. We must only fear sins against the Holy Spirit, compromises with powers of this world, compromises that besmirch the inner splendor of our being. Worldliness remains to us a foreign tongue; no matter how long we try to speak it, we retain the accents of our true vocation.

Few could see this inner splendor as intensely as did George Fox. But all could see him trembling as he described it, "shaking like an aspen leaf in his paroxysms of fanatical excitement" (one contemptuous critic wrote). To certain susceptible souls he could communicate this excitement almost before he spoke; his enthusiasm would spread like a tongue of fire leaping from person to person, until a whole crowd would pulse with a divine radiance, fused into a single living organism of light.

Of course, there were those who refused to see. One who refused gave the movement its common name. George Fox had been hauled before Justice Bennet in Derby in 1650, who began to question Fox closely on theological matters. Or rather he tried, only to be exhorted by Fox to shake himself free from the dead husks of dogma and tremble before the Lord. The dignified justice was not amused; he owned as how he was "a Christian and no Quaker." The name stuck. And so did the hostility. Anglican and Puritan could agree on few things, but one was that Quakers should be extirpated. A Puritan would cite Scripture; a Quaker would blithely assert that the Bible was a declaration of the fountain but not the fountain itself; the Puritan would cover his ears or reach for a weapon. Quakers who insisted on preaching the inner light in Massachusetts were beaten and imprisoned and in the last eventuality executed. How else was a godly person to respond to enthusiasts who on occasion would shed their clothes to testify in the sight of the Lord?

Persecution, however, only seemed to confirm followers of George Fox in their convictions. They seemed to esteem persecution as a divine call to the post of honor. Nonetheless, their true vocation was not to suffer or to repent, but to rejoice. And also to bear witness to the light, not primarily as individuals but rather as members of a single living community. Even those who did not initially see the light within themselves should be able to recognize its consequences for those who lived according to it. Dwelling in the light would remove the occasion for war and even violence; hearts would be gathered together and transported back to a time before war and strife had entered this world. Together they could show that heaven is not a fortified city thronged with angelic hosts but rather a flower of perpetual gladness, a glistening white rose of bliss, its endless petals already open, its soft nectarous perfume suffused everywhere, suffusing everything.

In a sense the test of the inner light was its capacity to animate a group. In the meetings that the followers of Fox organized in place of traditional rituals or services, all were equals. The Apostle John had written that this was the "true light which lighteth every man that cometh into the world." And so the Quakers would wait in silence until someone felt called upon to speak, and then they would listen while others spoke until a sense of the meeting was developed on any controversial point. Not a vote, mind you, in which one side would win and the other lose. But a consensus in which all agreed. Then the Meeting could be assured that the Inner Light that is in us all was being served. One of Fox's most articulate disciples described the ideal as follows: "As many candles lighted and put in one place do greatly augment the light, and make it shine forth, so when many are gathered together into the same life, there is more of the glory of God, and His power appears to the refreshment of each individual; for he partakes not only of the light and life raised in himself, but in all the rest."

That such an ideal should have quickly made the Quakers the most vilified group in all Christendom (except for the Jesuits, with whom they were frequently linked in attacks) was evidence of how far into the darkness mankind had descended. And the Society of Friends (unlike the Society of Jesus) seemed singularly ill-equipped to play a significant role in the broader world. Yet, as George Fox might remind us, there is more to this world than is imagined by our cynicism and shrewdness.

What could scarcely be imagined was that young William Penn should become a leader of this despised and disreputable group and that the king should approve his leading a new colony into the New World.

A key to this was Penn's father, a man after Frontenac's own heart. Admiral William Penn had played the difficult game of seventeenth-century British politics with something approaching consummate skill. Not a Puritan, he had still served Cromwell ably, especially during his punitive campaign against the Irish papists; fittingly, Penn would be awarded extensive Irish estates that would be the early basis for the family fortune (although occasionally requiring harsh punitive action and always requiring an indifference to the suffering of the abjectly poor). Then in the declining days of the Puritan dictatorship Penn dexterously changed sides; so ardent an advocate of the Restoration did he become that he was among the group that escorted Charles from the continent back to Britain and his kingship. The admiral was soon knighted, and was the highest ranking officer under James, Duke of York, Charles's brother, heir and titular commander of the British navy. Penn once again made himself discreetly useful. He was apparently the ghostwriter of the treatise on naval tactics that was supposed to lay to rest any doubts of James's competence as a naval commander. Then, in actions against the Dutch, James would get credit for successes, and Admiral Penn would take the blame for any failures. (In this instance, there was much credit and little blame.) The admiral, as always, knew how to be obliging to his superiors, be they Puritan, royal, or whatever.

He also had made one permanent contribution to the growing British empire. In his greatest victory he had taken Jamaica from the Spanish in 1654. This was of far more importance to the empire than the mere addition of an island. With the island came its sugar plantations, and with these came a slave-based economy. Britain now had reason to engage in the African slave trade to a degree it never had before.

The Duke of York found this to be a strategically crucial opportunity. Eager to hurt the Dutch whatever way he could, he judged the slave trade a most promising way. Just as he would take New Netherlands from the despicable Dutch, so he would challenge their dominance in the slave trade. The heroism of Admiral Penn had provided him with a market for this black gold. (One day, not too far off, Virginia planters would provide him with another.)

In 1663 the Duke of York established, with the approval of his brother, a joint stock company, the Royal Adventurers to Africa (eventually to be succeeded by the Royal African Company) to exploit this opportunity. Exploit it they did, first with thousands of slaves a year, then tens of thousands—until the British had outstripped the Dutch and even the Portuguese in the trade, creating immense wealth in Britain and its New World colonies. And every slave brought to the New World by the British during the latter part of the seventeenth century would be permanently branded with a DY, for Duke of York.

So in taking Jamaica Admiral Penn had provided an essential impetus to what became a glorious opportunity for James to prove his worthiness of eventually being a king to his people.[1] Contributions like Penn's could assure permanent preferment at court for a son, especially as beautiful a young man as young William was, especially at a court as worldly and corrupt as that of Charles.

Imagine the admiral's annoyance then when he discovered that young William had fallen in with the wrong crowd at university—with earnest youths who spouted radical religious views that seemed to have Cromwellian political implications. William apparently had forgotten to check his calendar. The year was 1660, not 1640—and the political tide of Puritanism was in

---

[1]From Jamaica Admiral Penn apparently got his own first slaves. There would always be a few around the Penn estate—one was particularly prized for his entertaining performances at the admiral's lavish parties. Not everyone was pleased by the British excursion into the business of slavery. George Fox himself traveled to Jamaica and was appalled at the treatment of the slaves. He urged the planters (to their fury) that they should treat slaves like indentured servants, with definite terms of service—or at least they should be treated as human beings and not worked to death "in that Christ died for us all." Fox preaching against the established order in the admiral's Jamaica epitomizes the double parentage of William Penn.

irretrievable ebb, at least for the time being. Nonetheless, the admiral knew how to handle a youthful indiscretion.

He had William packed off to France, to cultivate a taste for the pleasures of this world. He even had him presented at the court of Louis XIV, which on occasion made Charles's court look like a nunnery. So the younger Penn mixed with the likes of Frontenac. (Could they ever have actually met?) Penn even fought a duel over some trivial slight. The education seemed to have had its desired effect, as the admiral was sure it would.

Samuel Pepys, who worked under Admiral Penn and also lived near him, recorded in his diary that William returned from France with many of the affectations of a French fop. Pepys, it must be said, was far from a neutral witness. Although he pretended to befriend the admiral "out of great necessity and discretion," he admitted to his diary, "I hate him with all my heart." Moreover, he was not altogether comfortable watching young Penn, all decked out with laces and embroideries, high-heeled shoes and elegant pantaloons, chattering in French with Pepys' wife so fast that Pepys could not follow it and so playfully that he worried he himself was being fitted for horns. The admiral, one would like to think, also noticed the flirtation, and with much self-congratulation.

So the admiral judged it safe to send his son to study law in London, especially at Lincoln's Inn where he could mix with, among others, the Duke of Monmouth, the bastard son of Charles. The admiral judged wrong.

In 1665 William Penn witnessed the fourth horseman of the Apocalypse visit London. ("And I looked," wrote the Apostle John, "and, behold, a pale horse; and his name that sat on him was Death, and Hell followed with him.") The Great Plague, the worst since the Black Death, struck London, and seemed destined to spread throughout Britain. Nothing, it seemed, or no one save God could help London. There alone almost one hundred thousand were counted dead; and few would have thought that any number could measure the evil marked by the mass trench graves. Some said this was as nothing compared to what would be coming the very next year, the year when the beast of the Apocalypse would appear, the beast with the mark 666 branded on his forehead.

For the admiral the plague was danger enough. Once again he swept his son away, this time to Ireland where Penn could learn how to run the family estates, and also to put down rebellions of wild and desperately poor Irishmen. Penn, as usual, did as he was told; but he also heard the news from London. Just as the plague seemed to be abating, a fire raged through the largely deserted city, destroying generations of human effort in a single great conflagration. (Was this the hell to accompany the pale rider of death?)

The London Plague and Fire was a catastrophe so complete and meaningless that the surviving strong could take additional strength from it. Faced with the ruins of London, Christopher Wren committed himself to architecture to help rebuild shattered London, a commitment that culminated in his design of St. Paul's Cathedral. Sifting through the memoirs of the awful time, Daniel Defoe could find the materials for his first, perhaps *the* first realistic novel, *The Journal of a Plague Year*. Amidst the ruins of the plague and fire there seemed to be something for everyone who survived. Blind John Milton could find in it a confirmation of his recently completed epic theodicy, *Paradise Lost*, which justified the ways of God to man and explained how death and discord had come to rule the world. The desire for knowledge, the desire for what his Satan called the "God-like fruit," Milton insisted, was the source of all human suffering. What better instance of that suffering was there than the Great Plague, what better instance of that desire than Isaac Newton? For Newton is said to have discovered gravity while home from Cambridge waiting out this very plague. And if Newton's discovery of gravity was but a ritual repetition of man's first disobedience, then it had an appropriate setting—Newton in a garden, temporarily preserved from the death all around; Newton in a garden staring at an apple.

So the geniuses of England turned this plague that was the death of so many to their own advantage. The towering achievements of Newton and Milton and Wren and even Defoe might make us forget the effects this disaster may have had on a young man who had been trying to learn the law, and trying too, perhaps, to forget his earlier religious indiscretions.

Penn himself admitted that this was the moment in his life when he was almost lost: "The glory of the world was with me and I was ever ready to give myself unto it." He had had his portrait painted as the young gallant in his armor. But this vaunted armor could be pierced by simple words. While still in Ireland, he heard a Quaker preach.

There is a faith that overcomes the world and a faith that is overcome by the world. The doomed faith is to be found out there; its highest songs are of slaughter and death, its histories little more than scrolls of war, its emblems the eagle and the wolf, its highest wisdom mournful resignation. We can believe we are only barnacles on a dead universe, or we can seek the kingdom of God within, and find the faith that will overcome all.

When Admiral Penn heard the incredible news that William had converted to the Quaker faith, he ordered his son home forthwith. He then confronted his son, who looked the same but claimed to be transformed. He could hear for himself his son proclaim the new gospel in terms that must have made the old man cringe.

We get some sense of what it was like to be around William in the first flush of his conversion from his correspondence during this period. What he said in his letters he must also have imparted to his worldly father. He would, for instance, proclaim the complete transformation of his own vision of the world:

"In this State of the New Man all is new: Behold new Heavens, and a new Earth! Old Things come to be done away; the old Man with his Deeds put off." He would, of course, describe the old man and his deeds in rather wearisome detail: "O what Tremendous Oaths and Lies! What Revenge and Murders, with Drunkenness and Gluttony! What Pride and Luxury! Chamberings and Wantonness! What Fornications, Rapes, and Adulteries! What Masques and Revels! What Lustful Ornaments and Enchanting Attires! What Proud Customs and Vain Compliments! What Sports and Pleasures! Again, What Falseness and . . ." With the "Again" we can imagine the admiral's eyes glazing over and his face assuming a blankly wearied expression.

To have a son behaving like a religious buffoon who brings down the house in a Restoration comedy was not a laughing matter. Yet even the admiral must have had a hard time suppressing a guffaw if he ever read young William's earnest sermon to the Dutch. The Dutch should pray that God would wither their great commercial empire; this would be a wonderful grace for them, for it was the only way the Dutch would be saved from their covetousness. The admiral had never realized that he himself was a missionary to the Dutch; he was actually saving Dutch souls by sending their ships to the bottom.

But pity the poor admiral. He must have made inquiries into Fox and the Quakers to discreet sources at once informed and respectable. What would he have been told? To try to imagine, we can turn to that historian of informed respectability, Thomas Babington Macaulay, who in his *History of England* would distill for us the judgments of the respectable classes, judgments with which Macaulay himself fully concurred.

George Fox had a mind "in the most unhappy of all states, that is to say, too much disordered for liberty, and not sufficiently disordered for Bedlam." He insisted upon teaching his strange theology, all a-tremble in his famous leather breeches. We can commend him for this—he after all always kept his breeches on, which was more than could be said for some of his followers when they felt compelled to give public witness to the Lord of their pubic witlessness. What was the intelligible message of this great seer? That it was wrong to defend yourself against assassins and pirates? That a Christian was bound to face death itself rather than touch his hat to the greatest of mankind? Macaulay sympathized with the "jolly Anglican divine" who recommended to Fox that he just smoke a little tobacco and sing a few psalms. What Macaulay lamented was that Fox had managed to make a few converts to whom he was "immeasurably inferior in everything except the energy of his convictions." Then Fox would spout his usual incomprehensible rhapsodies, and they would shape it into something vaguely resembling sense.

Admiral Penn lamented too, since his son was one of those who transformed Fox's gibberish into immaculate inanities. Joining this band of crazy heretics was going to ruin his son's prospects unless the admiral could do something. Threats, including disinheritance, did not work—in fact, seemed to confirm William in his divine mission. Ridicule and wheedling were out of the question, for even implicit appeals to good sense were irrelevant to his son's thoughts (if they could still be called thoughts) on religion. So, coolly analyzing the situation, the admiral admitted that the frontal assault had failed and a flanking maneuver was futile. All that was left was the tactical retreat. The admiral reconciled with his son, and did his best to keep his temper when William thee'd and thou'd his betters, and refused to take off his hat at the most inopportune times. When his son wrote a tract, "No Cross, No Crown" (on the couplet: "The way to bliss lies not on beds of down/and he that hath no cross deserves no crown"), the admiral joked to his son, "If you are ordained to be a cross to me, God's will be done and I shall arm myself as best I can against it."

Admiral Penn still had ambitions for his son, whatever God's will in the matter. He remained a very obliging young man. Moreover, anyone who had seen the portrait of him in his Irish armor, just before his conversion, could not help but be struck by his beauty, his wonderful dark eyes and flowing hair, feminine mouth, and cheeks seemingly still unshaved, as if adorned only by the first down of youth.

The admiral succeeded well in getting his son accepted at court, better than he could reasonably have expected. Charles and James found William a most charming young man. James even seemed to have sympathy for William's despised Quakerism; for he, unlike his brother, made no secret of his own Catholicism. Catholic and Quaker might be worlds apart theologically, but they did share many enemies. So the admiral succeeded well, probably beyond his own expectations. By the time he went to his rest in 1670, he could go content that his son had great prospects for a prominent place in Britain, worthy of the admiral himself.

Let us hope that the ghost of the admiral departed this earth with his death; for, if it had lingered, the 1670s would have been an anxious time for it. Not content to be a prominent spokesman for the Quakers, William then also developed political ideas not uncommon among his sect. With extravagant religions, it seemed, there came in tow extravagant politics. Young Penn believed, for instance, that governments were instituted for the sake of the governed and, worse, that legitimacy somehow required their consent. Some of his other positions seemed for many people indistinguishable from those of Jesuits suspected of plotting the overthrow of the established British government—nonsense, of course, but in the excitable 1670s dangerous nonsense. But not nearly as dangerous as his outspoken and imprudent support for some of the most outspoken and impudent republicans in the realm: he actually campaigned with Algernon Sidney, whom the king would execute in 1682.

Clearly in the mid-1670s that charming, good-hearted, and well-connected William Penn was walking down a path that could lead to a gibbet. In the memory of the honorable service of Admiral Penn, and out of genuine affection for his well-meaning but remarkably stubborn son, something had to be done to anticipate this disaster-in-the-making. Then Penn himself amazingly came up with an idea. He wanted to found a colony in the New World.

The admiral apparently had left his finances in a great tangle, and his son was casting about for a way to untangle them. Nothing like money to get idealists to think about practicalities. (Who was it who said that he never met a Platonist who did not have an independent source of income?) Among Penn's assets was an outstanding loan from his father to the king worth more than ten thousand pounds. Penn knew better than to expect Charles to pay; the king only paid the debts he chose, and he chose very few.

So Penn asked for land. James, Duke of York, had more than enough to do to control the region from the mouth of the Hudson north. Penn asked for land on the Delaware. This land was really an appendix to New York, and had up to this point been ineffectively settled by a variety of nationalities. Penn proposed that he try to make this a prosperous colony, and in selling rights to the land make the Penn family once again solvent.

The request was granted in due course over the strenuous objections of those in the government who urged the king not to "encourage Penn's pretensions." But in a sense the king and his brother may have meant precisely to encourage his pretensions. It was as if they were sending Rasselas out into the world. Despite the fact that the king just at this time was trying to centralize his control over other colonies such as Massachusetts and Virginia, he nonetheless made Penn virtually king over this new colony—"True and Absolute Proprietor" read the charter. There may even have been a little mischief in rejecting Penn's suggested name—New Wales—and calling it instead Pennsylvania, for Penn was soon nervously writing to a fellow Quaker to explain that despite appearances the colony had not been named after him, rather "Pennsylvania" meant in Welsh "head woodlands." Had Charles and James known of this letter, it would likely have been the source of much mirth. Let Admiral Penn's son try to be both humble and a king at once. (He apparently had already learned how hard it was to be both holy and insolvent.)

William Penn for his part thought that Charles and James and any number of other worldly gentlemen were in for a big surprise that might instruct them profitably on the kingdom of God that is within all of us. They might think him an Icarus, but he would fly his own way. Pennsylvania was going to be, in the phrase he often repeated, "a holy experiment." The very kind of experiment for which, Penn had concluded sadly, there was no room in Restoration England. He added, "The deaf adder cannot be charmed." Charles, had he known of this letter, would certainly have been left uncharmed by that sentence.

Penn, of course, knew perfectly well how to be charming to kings and princes when he chose. He certainly was not going to bring to the attention of Charles that he meant for Pennsylvania to serve as a reproach to England. As he wrote to fellow Quakers, "For matters of liberty and privilege, I propose that which is extraordinary, and to leave myself and successors no power for doing mischief, that the will of one man may not hinder the good of a whole country; but to publish those things now and here, as matters stand, would not be wise, and I was advised to reserve that till I came there."

Penn clearly thought that if Charles and James knew what he really intended to do they would have his charter revoked. Perhaps so; certainly those at court who opposed the original generous charter would have used this new intelligence to try to open the issue up again. On the other hand, Penn's views on government, and on just about everything else, were well known. He was not one to hide his inner light under a bushel. More likely, the king and his brother would have been surprised not at all; Penn's plans would have made them relish even more the prospect of watching little Billy Penn, still childish at the age of thirty-five, learn lessons of the world Charles and James had each imbibed at their mother's bosom (or that of some other estimable lady).

Pennsylvania was going to be a holy experiment, all right—an experiment in which James and Charles could watch power and responsibility act on Penn's vaunted holiness. It would be an experiment that might lead to an education. In the wilderness of Pennsylvania the exquisitely indulged soul of William Penn was going to be faced with a choice. He could retreat into an impotence that would preserve the empty integrity of his conscience. Or else he could strive to meet the concrete needs of his struggling colony, only then one day to realize that his exquisite soul had faded like a shapeless vapor into nothingness. Charles and James could congratulate themselves that they had done well by their valued servant, the admiral. And the ghost of the admiral, if it still haunted the court, could depart in peace and thanksgiving. William Penn was going to gain the glory of the world, whether he professed to want it or not.

Young Penn himself, of course, showed no signs of apprehension. He was immediately publicizing his new colony, especially among Quakers both in Britain and on the Continent. At times his confidence was almost airy: "God will plant America and it shall have its day in the Kingdom." He turned out no less than eight tracts promoting his colony. From the peopling of Smith's Virginia on, such promotional tracts had repeatedly set whole new standards for hyperbolic prevarication. Penn, in contrast, engaged in honest understatement.

In one of his tracts he included a section in which he detailed the unavoidable hardships of colonial life. He urged prospective colonists to recognize "how much people are apt to fancy things beyond what they are, and that imaginations are great flatterers of the minds of men." He was most concerned that "none may delude themselves with an expectation of an immediate amendment of their conditions." When a young Quaker acquaintance wrote to him obviously seeking encouragement for becoming a colonist, Penn rather reminded her of her obligations to her mother and father: "It is most clear to me to counsel thee to sink down into the seasoning, settling gift of God, and wait to distinguish between thy own desires and the Lord's requirings."

Penn was, on the other hand, quite clear in his own mind that Pennsylvania was to be a seasoning, settling gift of God for him, one the Lord required that he grab with both hands. (Charles and James would have agreed with the seasoning, settling part.) Penn was particularly concerned about the Indians, who he thought had been treated so unfairly, with unnecessary harshness, by other colonies. He did not regard the charter of King Charles as giving him title to Pennsylvania except in the eyes of Caesar. In the eyes of God the Delaware Indians owned the Delaware Valley. He would have to purchase the land from them, and at a generous price, if the two peoples were to live with one another in friendship as Penn fully intended that they would. A Quaker colony, unlike a Puritan one, could not drive Indians from their traditional lands by force of arms.

Penn was unworried about this task, which literally entailed a peacemaker inheriting the earth. He believed that all men approached in friendship would respond as friends, sooner or later. He was also aware that the Delaware Indians, like so many natives who lived near European colonies, had been devastated by disease. Their population had been so reduced that they only needed a fraction of their traditional land to support themselves. So Penn wrote through an agent to the king of the Delawares the following letter, which he hoped would be the beginning of many productive exchanges:

London, 18 October 1681

My Friends

There is one great God and power that has made the world and all things therein, to whom you and I and all people owe their being and well-being, and to whom you and I must one day give an account for all that we do in this world. This great God has written his law in our hearts, by which we are taught and commanded to love and help and do good to one another, and not to do harm and mischief one unto another. Now this great God has been pleased to make me concerned in your parts of the world, and the king of the country where I live has given unto me a great province therein, but I desire to enjoy it with your love and consent, that we may always live together as neighbors and friends, else what would the great God say to us, who has made us not to devour and destroy one another, but live soberly and kindly together in the world.

Now I would have you well observe, that I am very sensible of the unkindness and injustice that has been too much exercised towards you by the people of these parts of the world, who have sought themselves, and to make great advantages by you, rather than be examples of justice and goodness unto you; which I hear has been matter of trouble to you and caused great grudgings and animosities, sometimes to the shedding of blood, which has made the great God angry. But I am not such a man, as is well known in my own country. I have great love and regard toward you, and I desire to win and gain your love and friendship by a kind, just, and peaceable life; and the people I send are of the same mind, and shall in all things behave themselves accordingly. And if in anything any shall offend you or your people, you shall have a full and speedy satisfaction for the same by an equal number of honest men on both sides, that by no means you may have just occasion of being offended against them. I shall shortly come to you myself, at what time we may more largely and freely confer and discourse of these matters. In the meantime, I have sent my commissioners to treat with you about land and a firm league of peace. Let me desire you to be kind to them and the people, and receive these presents and tokens which I have sent to you as a testimony of my good will to you and my resolution to live justly, peaceably, and friendly with you. I am your friend.

WM PENN

He also made plans to assure that the Indians would be treated fairly by his colonists. He was going to outlaw trade with them except at public market-places where the Indians would have the opportunity to compare goods and rates. Offenses against the Indians would be punished the same as offenses against settlers. Disputes between Indians and settlers would be adjudicated by juries of six colonists and six Indians. Any improvements that colonists could make on their grounds, the Indians could make on theirs.

Pennsylvania was to be a land of friendship between Indians and colonists, and friendship had to be based on equality. To the amazement of those who knew the histories of Virginia and New England, Indian affairs in early Pennsylvania worked out just about as Penn had planned. It was also just about the only thing that did.

The problems started almost immediately. While he was recruiting the first settlers and investors, Penn also had to establish a frame of government for his new colony. Penn soon discovered to his surprise that these two enterprises were at odds.

In his initial draft of the Pennsylvania constitution he plainly expressed his radical views on politics, and he established institutions that reflected them. People will only love and obey a government to the extent to which they participate in its decisions. Leaders tend to have the powers of government serve their own ends, whereas these powers should be used for the sake of the governed. Human beings have so ignored the voice of light and truth spoken in their own hearts that they use the law to effect unprofitable revenge on the less fortunate, or even to enforce their preferences upon the society at large.

In his "Fundamental Constitution of Pennsylvania" Penn sought to take care of his people as other framers of government had not. "In reverence to God the Father of lights and spirits," he declared that everyone should be able to worship God in whatever way each believed most acceptable to God.

Debtors prison was outlawed, and capital punishment restricted only to murder and treason. Ballots would be secret, and the rich would not be allowed to
serve on juries that were judging the poor. The lower house of the legislature
would be the most powerful instrument of government, since it was the closest to the people. He made it large (almost four hundred members) and suf-
frage for it broad (all male citizens). All legislation would originate there, and
even there no law or tax would be passed unless the legislators had already
consulted their constituents on the issue. (Penn added this last provision so
that "they may always remember they are but deputies and men entrusted to
the good of others and responsible for that trust.") This was a government
that would prevent everyone, even Penn and his descendants, from doing mischief.

As soon as he started to recruit large investors into his colony, however,
Penn found that they did not share his egalitarianism. Penn wanted to sell
large, five-thousand-acre tracts; to make such purchases attractive, he was also
prepared to include, as a bonus, choice lots in his new city, Philadelphia. His
prospective first citizens of Philadelphia, most of them well-to-do Quaker
merchants, may have loved their poorer brothers as much as William Penn
did, but they did not trust them. More precisely, they did not find an investment attractive that would soon be at the mercy of the rabble—or, rather, of
the demagogues by which the rabble would soon be led. It was the Inner Light
versus the Outer Pocketbook.

So Penn was faced with his first hard choice. He could preserve the purity
of his intentions, but that would mean fleeing from the actual world. His
purity would then be theoretical, the purity of a monastery, walling oneself up
into a self-willed impotence. Or he could, and did, with some reluctance but
with little hesitation, quickly recast his constitution into a form of which
Governor Berkeley would have approved. The power was placed in the hands
of the governor and the great landowners of the colony. The governor and
especially the upper house had all the powers of initiative. The lower house
had only modest opportunities to review and check the decisions made by the
mighty.

Penn could console himself that many of his cherished measures had
remained untouched—freedom of conscience, for instance, and the limitations on capital punishment. The changes themselves were not so bad. The
men who were insisting upon them were of the highest moral character. Who
was he to question their intentions? In fact, he could be far more careful in
selecting the great landowners of his colony as to their character than he ever
could for the smaller freeholders. As he revised his Frame of Government

again and again and again (through at least twenty complete drafts), he seems to have begun to question his own belief that this frame of government was important except as a recruiting device. Perhaps to think it was crucial was a vanity in the man responsible for writing it. So he seems to be arguing near the conclusion of the preface to his final draft: "But lastly, when all is said, there is hardly one frame of government in the world so ill designed by its first founders, that in good hands would not do well enough; and history tells us, the best ones in ill ones can do nothing that is great or good." This contention, if believed, would provide a justification for Penn's compromises. The framer of a government should consent to any ill designs to assure that the government ends up in the best possible hands.

If Penn thought such curly reasoning would persuade his idealistic friends, he was bitterly disappointed. These friends were not hesitant about expressing to him their disapproval of his compromises. The changes, one said, were "unsavory and unjust." The government as described, another wrote, was "the basest on earth, not to be endured or lived under." What characteristics of a tyranny did it lack? As for Penn's assurances that in practice the government would be just, did his friends have to remind him of the inevitable deformity of any government that does not grow out of the character and will of the people?

He seemed prepared for these objections, but not quite prepared for the vehemence with which they were expressed. This touched him to the quick. He began one letter, "There are many things make a man's life uneasy in the world which are great abatements to the pleasure of living; but scarcely one equal to that of the unkindness or injustice of friends." He knew that a Quaker must be willing to throw himself on the thorns of this world and bleed. But must he also be forsaken by friends? Still, Penn found himself able to persevere. He had not been, he insisted, diminished by the unexpected betrayals. "A steady virtue will make sufficient comfort and sanctuary," he concludes his most aggrieved letter of this period, and then signs it: "Thy real friend, Wm Penn." One of Penn's closest associates in this period would later say in Penn's defense, "I know very well it was forced from him by friends who unless they received all that they demanded would not have settled the country."

Penn left for the New World in the summer of 1682. He had organized the most effective colonizing expedition since Winthrop and the Puritans had left for Massachusetts more than half a century before. During the early 1680s thousands of new colonizers sailed up the Delaware to the new colony of Pennsylvania. Penn had done his recruiting well, thanks in part to the network of Quakers that had spread throughout Britain and was now spreading throughout Europe as well. He drew heavily from Wales and northern England; whole settlements were organized from the Netherlands and Germany. (One of the earliest towns of Pennsylvania would be Germantown.)

Since the Quakers generally were recruited from the lower classes, Penn's settlers were workers, farmers, and craftsmen, just the kind of hardworking people to set up a colony. Moreover, there was a small group of prosperous Quaker merchants who committed to Pennsylvania as well. In order to conduct their trade with a minimum of government persecution and fines, many of these merchants had already established their businesses in other colonies along the Atlantic coast; now they could transfer their operations to the new Quaker colony and bring with them decades of experience in colonial trade.

Penn's own voyage to the New World was harrowing. He had clearly been apprehensive about the dangers. His letter to his wife on his departure made that clear. (She was pregnant and had to stay behind.) It began: "My love, that sea, nor land, nor death itself can extinguish or lessen toward you, most endearedly visits you with eternal embraces and will abide with you forever." He added separate notes to each of his three children, including one-year-old William Jr., as mementos of a father whom they might never get to know.

Penn apparently had premonitions of death on this voyage, and then a smallpox epidemic broke out on board, killing thirty-one during the voyage. When he arrived finally on the Delaware alive and healthy, he was ebullient. Standing on board, he exclaimed to a friend next to him while they both looked out at a settlement site: "Providence has brought us here safe. Thou has been the companion of my perils. What wilt thou that I call this place?" The friend suggested Chester after his hometown in England, and William Penn with a sweep of his hand dubbed it so.

"O how sweet is the quiet of these parts, freed from the anxious and troublesome solicitations, hurries, and perplexities of woeful Europe!" He would in time find troublesome solicitations, hurries, and perplexities aplenty in woeful Pennsylvania, but Penn's early letters back to Europe present an Eden. All the concerns about his colony and its survival were projections of the "fear of our friends and the scarecrows of our enemies." The country of Pennsylvania was like "the best vales of England watered by brooks; the air sweet; the heavens serene like the south of France; the seasons mild and temperate; vegetable productions abundant, chestnut, walnut, plums, muscatel grapes, wheat and other grain; a variety of animals, elk, deer, squirrel and turkeys weighing forty or fifty pounds, water-birds and fish of divers kinds, no want of horses; and flowers lovely for colour, greatness, figure, variety." Penn is intoxicated with his good providence. Even when he admits a flaw in his new

Eden, he still jokingly puts the best face on it: "The weather often changeth without notice, and is constant almost in its inconstancy."

Penn had every reason to be pleased. He had decided to establish his major city on the confluence of the Delaware and Schuylkill rivers; Philadelphia, it would be called, the City of Brotherly Love. The love, however, that the plans for this city most obviously expressed was the love of order. This order was not one discovered in nature, but imposed upon nature by man's own inner light. The prophet Isaiah had said, "the crooked shall be straight and the rough places smooth." That surely was going to be the case in Penn's city, a city that as much as possible would lie foursquare.

His plan for the city was clearly derived from those put forward for the rebuilding of London after the Great Fire of 1666, themselves so typical of the seventeenth-century rationalism that made mathematics the measure of all things. The streets were to be arranged in a strict gridiron interrupted only by four symmetrically placed parks and a large central square. The land Penn selected allowed him to work this out on a rectangle, one mile long and two miles deep. It was, the nineteenth-century historian John Fiske observed, "the squarest and levelest city, no doubt, that our planet had ever seen." Yet there would be plenty of others aspiring to this regular perfection, for the Philadelphia model would be the norm as the American colonies spread in the nineteenth century to the south and west, until there would be dozens, even hundreds of little Philadelphias, all with their predictable arrangement of streets and their central square, all unknowingly reflecting the reassertion of order after the horrors of the London Plague and Fire.

Such rationalism was obviously far from the spontaneous enthusiasms of George Fox; one can hardly imagine him in a flat city of squares. The wooden and brick houses of Philadelphia went up so fast, it was said, and were so uniform that owners had to put chalk marks on the walls to distinguish one from another. Yet even the building, fast as it was, could not keep up with the demand that new settlers were making upon housing. Thus along the banks of the river newcomers lived in natural caves in the limestone cliffs. Penn himself was much disturbed to learn that some of these caves had quickly degenerated into dens of iniquity, serving the primitive and vicious desires of some citizens of his orderly city of love. So Penn could bemoan the rank weeds that spontaneously spring up about the most orderly of human habitations.

The cave dwellers were not the only aliens in his colony. Shortly before he had left England Penn had persuaded James, Duke of York, to include the old Swedish and Dutch settlements along the Delaware in his colony. Since the conquest of New Netherlands, these settlements had been officially in James's province of New York. They could scarcely be governed effectively from New York, any more than they could from New Amsterdam during the days of Stuyvesant. James gave them to his friend Penn, for they meant little to New York and a great deal to Pennsylvania. With this grant Penn controlled the whole of the Delaware valley to its mouth; Pennsylvania had access to the sea without traveling through the waters of any other colony.

Before his arrival in the New World, Penn had sent ahead an open letter to the settlers along the Delaware, informing them of this change and trying to ease any misgivings: "I hope you will not be troubled at your change or the king's choice, for you are now fixed at the mercy of no governor that comes to make his fortune great; you shall be governed by laws of your own making, and live a free and, if you will, a sober and industrious people."

Penn first landed in the New World at one of these settlements, Newcastle, and must have been encouraged by the enthusiastic welcome that greeted him. He went through the formal ceremony of the transfer of power, and then spoke to assure them personally of his intentions. It all went very smoothly. His only unease seemed to be the name of one settlement. He really would prefer that Whorekill be called instead New Deal. Actually, these three lower counties should have been renamed Pennkill, for the inhabitants of this region more than any other would present a persistent challenge to Penn's leadership and thereby threaten his Holy Experiment.

Once the building of Philadelphia was well underway, Penn arranged to meet also with the Delaware Indians to conclude a treaty with them personally. Tradition has it that the meeting occurred at a place called Shackamaxon, under a great elm tree which still stood into the nineteenth century when it was felled by windstorm not too long after the Louisiana Purchase. By all accounts, the meeting was all that Penn could have hoped for. The treaty concluded under that great tree of peace remained in force through the colonial period. Voltaire would say that it was the only treaty between the colonists and the Indians "that was never sworn to and never broken."

Yet there was something strange about this meeting. Important as it was, and as well-documented as Penn's other activities of the period were, no sources remain that describe this particular meeting. It clearly took place; it was not a myth. Yet no documents of it survive, as if in this triumphant negotiation there was something unseemly, something damaging to the memory of William Penn and the founding of Pennsylvania.

There survives only the general oral tradition about the great elm, and the specific memories of an old woman who claimed to have witnessed the event as a young girl. She remembered it vividly not because she understood at the time its historical significance; parleys with the Indians were common occurrences on the frontier in those days. She remembered it vividly because Penn was the handsomest man she had ever seen, before or since. She also told of the celebration after the treaty formalities concluded. The handsome Penn was joyous, his spirits overflowing. He ate the Indian dishes with relish, and resolved to learn their language so he could communicate with his new friends directly. (It was much like Hebrew, he later concluded; perhaps these native Americans really were the ten lost tribes.)

Then something extraordinary happened that made the evening even more memorable to the young girl. The Indians began to dance in celebration, to jump and hop with the throb of the drums, and to whoop and chant their weird songs. Finally Penn could contain himself no more. This was no time for gloomy sternness. Then there he was, unbelievably, there was Governor William Penn, proprietor of all Pennsylvania, friend of King Charles, William Penn up dancing with the Indians, leaping and shouting and shaking as if trying to be more Indian than the Indians.

Turning from the wonder of the girl at this handsome man dancing with abandon, we can only imagine the shock of Penn's party at this breach of decorum. Had Penn entirely taken leave of his senses? For a fleeting moment some must have worried that Penn would strip off his clothes to free his limbs.

And what would Penn have said if his friends on the way back to Philadelphia had gently admonished him for succumbing to carnal frivolity? Since they had not been fully moved by the moment, he would have to cite authorities they respected. They did remember—didn't they?—that on the great judgment day we will all dance and take hands. Had his friends forgotten Psalm 149? It bids us *now* to sing a new song unto the Lord, and to praise His name in dance. Penn was only praising the Lord of the Dance, for He surely must take pleasure in His people, as with every step they are delivered further into heavenly purity and bliss. Let everything that breathes, let every breath be full of praises of the Lord. There was a time for dignity, and a time for ecstasy. So he could warmly exhort his dear friends not to be like haughty Michal looking down from her high window in disdain.

And what could these dear friends say in rebuttal? Perhaps they could remind him that they were now returning to a careful quadrille of streets called Philadelphia. Now was a time for dignity, and also discreet silence. No one should have to explain to King Charles and Whitehall what happened under the great elm. Let the event be forgotten, or at least unrecorded. So they all agreed, not realizing that this event would never be forgotten by one impressionable young girl.

In his first months in Pennsylvania Penn traveled to the neighboring colonies, to meet his new friends and to describe the new song, or at least the new deal that was Pennsylvania. His visit to New York gave him pause, like some latter-day Jogues. The colony had fallen into its old habit of self-destructive bickering. Charges of treason were being leveled against high councillors. Citizens were refusing to pay taxes. In the midst of crisis, Long Island, eternally loyal Long Island, moved to declare independence from the rest of New York. Some things never changed. Penn felt called to preach earnestly to all factions that they should love one another, be kind and forgiving and generous. Anger would always find occasion to grow in communities that hated. One can imagine the New Yorkers listening attentively, trying to figure out the catch.

Penn returned to Pennsylvania perhaps a little shaken by his glimpse of how a colony could go wrong. New York seemed a mixture of equal parts vinegar, wormwood, and bile. He was more convinced than ever of the absolute importance of good intentions. He wrote to the new justices of the peace in the lower counties, "I cannot but in conscience endeavor to promote justice and righteousness among the inhabitants . . . , knowing He who is the judge of the quick and the dead will remember us for good, if we forget not Him, and that a government laid and begun by the line of equity and true judgment will not fail of prosperity."

Nonetheless, it was precisely his intentions that some of his old Quaker friends in England were starting to question, as a result of his ebullient letters. Penn was making himself a great man in the New World, but at what price? He was now laying out his fine city of Philadelphia with hundreds doing his bidding. But what was all this doing to his own soul?

In April 1683 James Claypoole, a Quaker merchant in England himself involved in trade with Pennsylvania, wrote him a delicate letter in which he insinuated the dangers he thought Penn was exposed to. He did so in good Quaker fashion, not by accusing Penn of weakness, but by confessing such weakness himself:

"Oh, I have found it a great hindrance and hurt, when I have had precious gifts and openings, and an utterance has been given for the service of the Lord. Looking a little at self, I have been shut up and sorrow has come over me, and I have travailed in spirit and cried to the Lord many a time that I might be removed out of the way that would exalt self and this hinders the work of the Lord. And truly my fervent desire still is that I may be kept in the simplicity, in tenderness, in fear and true humility, and be nothing but what the Lord will, that I may be as low as the dust of the earth as to His truth and service, and empty unless the Lord fills me. I know it is always best with us when we are kept low, for the Lord beautifies the meek with salvation . . . and the beauty of humility shines most and is most amiable in persons that are set in high places."

Lest Penn think too quickly that Claypoole meant by "high places" the powerful of this world, Claypoole then describes some time he had spent with the now-aged George Fox, and marvels at the "innocent, pure, heavenly seasoning, savory life that appears always in him as a continual meeting." The implicit question was obvious. Would William Penn, if he continued in his present enterprise, have a life as pleasing to God?

If Claypoole or others who wrote him in this spirit thought that they might get from Penn some humbling expression of doubt, Penn's early responses must have been a sore source of worry. In these letters Penn is full of praise for God; he is also, quite clearly, full of himself:

"Oh! That I may be kept in my place, for that end the Lord has called me, in this unexpected thing. His ways are unsearchable and past finding out; for He it is that in His own time reveals them. He has placed His name in some measure upon me. I pray that He may be glorified by me, that in the end I may reap an everlasting inheritance. I know my weakness, but also I know His strength, and He is able to glorify Himself, and serve His poor people by me, in which I would not that any should be offended, for that will not be for their good."

Penn is also exuberant about the New World. His critics in England do not realize what this place is. The very quantity of nature is overwhelming, and leads to a simplicity in men so to be preferred to European cunning. He is so attached to this land that England retains no charms for him. Who would not prefer his green country town of Philadelphia to that dismal cramped city on the grimy banks of the Thames? "If no other thing occur, I am like to be an adopted American." But from England came a warning voice from George Fox himself. He wrote an open letter to Penn and the other colonists: "My friends that are gone, and are going over to plant, and make outward plantations in America, keep your own plantations in your hearts, with the spirit and power of God, that your own vines and lilies be not hurt."

Penn would have much occasion in the early years of Pennsylvania to reflect on the distance between his inward and outward plantations. His first occasion was the debate over confirmation of his Frame of Government. He had set out a form of government as he thought best after wide consultation. He naively thought that his grateful colonists, or rather their representatives, would accept this frame with hardly any discussion, except for the sake of clarification. The confirmation he thought was going to be more a celebration of his wisdom and goodheartedness than it was to be a political transaction.

He had each of the six counties select seven representatives to what was in effect a constitutional convention. Once they convened, they made it pointedly clear that they, both collectively and individually, thought they knew much better how to frame a government than did Proprietor William Penn. For one thing, they thought the size of the assembly and council was much too large, and he agreed that each could be reduced by two-thirds. But then he must have gulped when they reasoned that the triple vote he had given himself in the council should be reduced to a single one. Of course, the reasoning was obvious enough: One vote in the new council was worth three in the old. However, this meant also that the vote of William Penn, founder of the colony, would count for no more than anyone else's. This kind of egalitarianism was a shoe that pinched in a tender place.

When the assembly and council then first met, things got little better. The assembly began to get unruly against the interests of the council. Why should the assembly lack the right to introduce legislation, and be lorded over by the council? Penn could not say simply that this was the way he preferred it, or this was the way to get more investment into the colony. So he hid behind a legality. This was the Frame of Government on which his charter depended. To make so fundamental a change would risk having the charter revoked. It is hard to think Penn himself believed this *ad hoc* argument.

However, once he saw his assembly in action, he had reason to distrust its judgment—or, more importantly, its loyalty to his ideals. The three southern counties on the Delaware were a powerful faction in the assembly, and balanced the three Quaker counties around Philadelphia. Pennsylvania was, in effect, being divided between Quaker and non-Quaker districts. The Quaker colonists might be loyal to his work to establish a place for them, but those older settlements owed him nothing, except what the law demanded. Their representatives quickly made it clear that they were going to be looking out for their own interests. They banded together and almost elected a non-Quaker as the very first speaker of the assembly. This sent a shudder through the Quaker communities in Pennsylvania and England. Penn found himself having to explain away this close call, for apparently his enemies had quickly seized on this as another scarecrow.

Penn, in his vain ambition to expand his colony at all costs, now put at risk the Quakers who had trusted him. Soon Quakers would be aliens in their own colony. Penn responded to these charges without really refuting them. He agreed that "in the event that they outnumber us in a vote we are gone." He also admitted that this had already almost happened in the election of the speaker. Nonetheless, he still repudiated the suggestion that any acceptable alternative existed to this risk. "If you Quakers had the power, none should have a part in the government but those of your own way." The implication was clear, and had a polemical bite characteristic of Penn: "you Quakers" are not "true Quakers." Such a letter is sad to read. Penn had not been long in the New World, and he had had many successes; nonetheless, already he was starting to sound beleaguered.

Part of the problem was economic. His colony was obviously becoming a thriving success. Anyone who witnessed its rapid growth would scarcely have been surprised to learn that in a very few years it would surpass Virginia in population, or that in only twenty years Philadelphia would be the largest city in the colonies after Boston. Yet the man who had made this prosperity possible was himself from the very beginning not participating in it.

Penn did not expect a large return on his investment. But he did expect some reasonable return; and it did not occur to him that his own income from the colony would not cover his expenses. But that was what happened. Far from compensating him for the old debt of his father, the colony was consuming more and more of his sustenance—10,000 pounds alone in the first two or three years. Naively, Penn actually sent out an agent in November 1683 to collect his 1684 quitrents early. He was sure his "Loving Friends and Tenants" would cooperate because he had a temporary shortage of funds. The loving friends and tenants, if they did understand, didn't seem to care, for the agent returned almost empty handed. Penn would, moreover, find the quitrents extremely difficult to collect even when they were in arrears. There was friendship, and then there was business. Brotherly love, even in its own city, apparently paid no bills. The more prosperous the Pennsylvanians, the less inclined they were to give Penn his due. If the Holy Experiment continued succeeding like this, the Holy Experimenter was going to end up bankrupt.

What made all this the more painful was that Penn's very honesty was being questioned, and in public too, by some of the leading citizens of his colony. To encourage large land purchases, Penn had promised a bonus of one acre in the new town of Philadelphia for every fifty purchased in the colony. As Philadelphia was being laid out, these lots had to be distributed.

Many problems started right here. Not everyone was satisfied with the location of his lot. Penn clearly had given preference to those who he thought would become solid citizens in his new colony; and there were so many details to attend to that some purchasers got their lots only as an afterthought, and ended far from the docks that would be the commercial center of the town.

Penn found himself offering lame explanations and making petty deals. To one offended purchaser he explained that he had put him far from the docks because he thought he would prefer the quiet. When the purchaser responded that he did not mind noise (especially that of two coins a clinking), Penn decreed that a fair be established right next to the property of this disgruntled Philadelphian, and the value of his land multiplied immediately.

What increased tensions and suspicion was that Philadelphia simply did not have enough land to meet the promises Penn had made in England. A purchaser who had the right to fifty city acres might find himself given one acre near the center of Philadelphia, and the other forty-nine far in the outskirts, so far that only a visionary might see them as part of Philadelphia rather than its countryside.

Matters were not helped when it was realized that much of the best land in Philadelphia was not being distributed at all, but kept by Penn himself, to sell at his own pleasure and for his own profit. This became crucial to Penn when he realized that the rest of Pennsylvania was not going to pay him his due; he had his own family to worry about. Then Penn tried to collect quitrents on all Philadelphia property, despite the fact that he had given many purchasers the distinct impression that these lands would be free from these obligations. Finally, a group of settlers presented Penn with a "Remonstrance from the Inhabitants of Philadelphia."

Not since his motives for changing his Frame of Government were questioned had Penn faced anything so painful and exasperating. The Remonstrance said plainly, all too plainly, that the purchasers had made a mistake in "reposing confidence in the justice of the proprietary." Penn had cheated, if not swindled, them. They asked only that Penn in the future act toward them "with the same favor and tenderness he has ever expressed to us." From now on he should live up to his word.

This questioning of his integrity would have been bearable if it had been made by strangers—the citizens of the three lower counties, for instance. One could understand how they, worldly men that they were, might suspect Penn of motives unworthy of a Quaker. But those questioning him now were Quakers, and among his closest associates in the planning of this colony. To their "Remonstrance" he could not bear to write a full reply, but still he had to respond.

So he went through the Remonstrance, responding in writing paragraph by paragraph. He offers at one point to take back the land that he gave them.

But only once does he positively lose his temper; the charge that Penn has not freed the land from Indian title he dismisses as "disingenuous." His critics will not even give him credit for his unquestionable achievements. "This is beyond modesty and justice."

Penn still did retain some unqualified supporters. Among them was Francis Daniel Pastorius, a German Quaker who led one of the colonizing efforts to bring Germans and Dutch to establish their own town under Penn's tolerant rule. Pastorius wrote: "William Penn is loved and praised by the people. Even the old vicious inhabitants must recognize they have never seen so wise a ruler." Pastorius, of course, knew he was overstating; among the vicious "should" does not lead to "must." Pastorius sadly reported how beleaguered Penn had become by 1684, the year of the Remonstrance. Penn in that year had risen in a Quaker meeting and lamented that "brotherly love is not yet so abundantly to be found in this our Philadelphia as he on his part desires."

Penn must have gained some respite from the trials of Pennsylvania in the company of men like Pastorius who, even when Penn made mistakes, would not question his motives. In one of his letters Pastorius refers to a visit Penn made to Pastorius's humble Philadelphia house, where he still was using oilpaper for windows until he could get glass. Penn noticed with approval a Latin sentence Pastorius had written on the oilpaper window over his front door: *Parva domus sed amica bonis, procul este profani.*

The sentence could have been the motto for Penn's colony, at least now that the ecstasy had passed and the limitations of the enterprise were evident. "A small home but friend to the good; profane, be far away." But how do you keep the profane away? You close the walls, only then to realize in horror that you have locked the enemy within the gates. Even the Latin itself implied the futility of this wish. "Profane, be far away" is a phrase from the sixth book of Virgil's *Aeneid.* This is what Hecate howls like a dog when she separates Aeneas from his friends and starts to lead him into the fiery confusion of the underworld to see horrors unfit for living eyes. Virgil himself hesitated before trying to describe them.

We, more unworthy still, can do no better than let John Dryden, Penn's contemporary, translate Virgil's words for us—a reflection of a reflection of a reflection of the chaos at the heart of our earth.

Just in the gate, and in the jaws of hell,
Revengeful Cares and sullen Sorrows dwell;
And pale Diseases, and repining Age,
Want, Fear, and Famine's unresisted rage;

Here Toils, and Death, and Death's half-brother Sleep
(Forms terrible to view), their sentry keep;
With anxious Pleasures of a guilty mind;
Deep Frauds before, and open Force behind;
The Furies iron beds; and Strife, that shakes
Her hissing tresses, and unfolds her snakes.
Full in the midst of this infernal road,
An elm displays her dusky arms abroad:
The god of sleep there hides his heavy head,
And empty dreams on every leaf are spread.

Whatever the revengeful cares and sullen sorrows with which Penn had to dwell, whatever the hissing tresses he had to face, he had no intention of permitting his Pennsylvania to become an elm of empty dreams. Nonetheless, that was precisely what Pennsylvania threatened to become, and not because of selfish land squabbles in Philadelphia or scrambles for power and preference in the colonial government. Pennsylvania was most threatened by its own charter.

Penn had been granted as his southern boundary the fortieth parallel. He thought this boundary generous for a colony that lacked a coastline. The fortieth parallel, together with the grant of the lower three counties, gave him dominance over the Delaware waterway. Moreover, he thought he was also assured of northern access to the great Chesapeake Bay. This latter was crucial for the long-term development of the colony. The major river of western Pennsylvania was the Susquehanna, which emptied into Chesapeake Bay. This river should be the eventual site for a second great city of Pennsylvania, as long as access to the bay was not at the pleasure of Maryland, the colony to the south. The fortieth parallel seemed to give Pennsylvania exactly what it needed, both the Delaware and the Susquehanna.

However, all this careful reasoning was based on bad mapping, as Penn came to realize to his horror in 1682. The fortieth parallel did not even give Pennsylvania Philadelphia. If the charter was enforced to the letter, Pennsylvania would be a land-locked parcel of land that was essentially worthless. Penn had to insist that the letter killeth but the spirit giveth life. In a series of missives to Lord Baltimore, his representatives, and British government officials, Penn argued, cajoled, pleaded, and occasionally came close to whining that when his documents said forty, they really meant thirty-nine.

Lord Baltimore demurred. The letter might killeth Pennsylvania, but it gaveth much life to Maryland. Proprietor Penn could see to his colony's interest; Proprietor Baltimore would see to his. Baltimore had no interest in sharing the Chesapeake with anyone else; Virginia was enough.

Penn tried to negotiate: "I have declined the rigor of my plea, and both proposed and pressed some of the mildest and most healing expedients." He offered to exchange his two lowest counties to Baltimore for an opening onto the Chesapeake.

Baltimore, however, did not think he was going to have to give away anything to have these counties drop into his lap. He simply publicized the fact that Penn was bargaining them away. He added that if these counties were part of Maryland the quitrents would be a fraction of those that had been assessed by Penn.

A pro-Maryland faction quickly came to life on the Delaware. When Penn supporters opposed them, Baltimore played his trump card. He, unlike the Quakers, was quite comfortable with armed force, and had a militia to do his bidding. If Penn did not like the letter of the law, he could learn about the real world from the wrong side of a gun. Baltimore had his forces march into the lower counties and build a fort to cut off contact from Philadelphia to the rest of Delaware.

Finally Penn reached the unavoidable conclusion that this dispute could not be settled by negotiations between him and Baltimore. Why had he been made a neighbor to such as him? Nothing was left but for Penn to appeal to his friends, the king and his brother, and in person. In August 1684 Penn sailed for England. He obviously expected to return to the colony soon, immediately after the matter was settled at court. In fact, he would be gone from his colony fifteen years, three of which he would spend in hiding, in fear of his life.

From on board ship, before leaving, he wrote one last letter to the colonists, "dear Friends and people." Penn had become increasingly exasperated with them for meddling in what he believed to be primarily his affairs. Nonetheless, in his "Farewell to Pennsylvania," as it came to be called, there is little sign of this, only fulsome affection and good wishes. It begins: "My love and my life is to you and with you, and no waters can quench it nor distance wear it out or bring it to an end. I have been with you, cared over you, served you with unfeigned love, and you are beloved of me and near to me beyond utterance."

Penn's own mind, as he waited to be carried back to England, was far more mixed than he allowed himself to show in this farewell. Penn was weary, not in years but in experience. Pennsylvania had never quite become the kind of society he had hoped for, and now even what he had achieved was at risk, unless he was to play the fawning courtier once again. This weariness came through in the last letter he wrote before he left, to his wife. He asked her to remember him to his children, and ended the letter by saying simply, "I am theirs and thine in that which is not of this dying world."

So we can imagine Penn standing on the deck of the *Enterprise*, waiting for the tide to change, lost in thought. Penn had much to brood about. As a worldly experiment, his colony was a success. Yet it was only a city of man he had created. He had thought that as a Quaker his task was to bring the Reformation to its fruition. To the Quakers had been left the task of burning the last ships of the old Adam, the last ties to the ancient city of man. Who had not seen Rome, stood among its ancient ruins, and read how this most mighty of worldly cities had sunk into flames again and again, whenever its people lacked the ferocity to defend its walls? All was determined by Vulcanic arms and Martial skills. Yet such had no place in a kingdom of light, a community of love. Penn had thought a city of God would be exempt from such necessities.

He had said that his colony needed many talents, but in every colonist only one thing was truly necessary: an open heart. Puritans might be able to whip cursed nations with a sword, but what did they achieve? A Christian, they forgot, never wars by right, but only by perversion. Of course Pennsylvania had not fought with swords—but all the other fighting, all the envies and spites, were there aplenty. He looked at his own Philadelphians, and sometimes he saw only individuals idolizing their own arrogant restlessness. Why else wouldn't they do their daily tasks and enjoy simple friendship in peace, like Pastorius? Pastorius and his people were to his mind like the fireflies that rose from the grass in the hazy blue of a summer evening, a quietly joyous festival of lights.

Of course, Penn's own soul had yearned for some mighty act—not of battle, of course, but of reconciliation. He too could not rest content. He loaded the air with prayers, and the winds took and scattered them as empty offerings to the clouds. The winds? Had he himself not written, "The tallest trees are most in the power of the winds, and ambitious men in the blasts of fortune"? Here he was, against his will, being blown back to Britain, and away from the colony and people who most needed his presence. His aphorisms about human nature, he was discovering to his surprise, also applied to himself.

And what are we who are still living in this dying world to say to such brooding? Perhaps we should pause here to offer the faltering Penn our praise. He may not need it, but we should give it anyway. He was a most fortunate man, even in his defeats. His convictions gave him strength to act, the Old

World an opportunity, the New World a place. His dance with the Indians was colonization as it should have been; his principle of religious tolerance an ideal of the republic that would be. In the future, nation will follow nation as tribe once followed tribe, like waves of the sea; such succession is the order of nature, and regret is useless. But if history has any power, the name of Penn and what he tried to achieve on the Delaware will never be taken from human memory—if history has any power.

Penn had thought that once in England he could quickly resolve the issue of the Maryland boundary and then return almost immediately to Pennsylvania. He was half right. He did reach a compromise with Maryland that gave him all the Delaware but no entrance on the Chesapeake. But in fact that did not finally resolve the problem. The final resolution would not be reached until long after Penn and Baltimore had gone to their eternal rewards, and really not even then. The dispute was apparently settled when the Mason-Dixon Line was drawn in the late eighteenth century. But then this became a boundary line for a still greater altercation, the greatest in American history.

Still, he seemed to have accomplished his purpose as far as anyone could know. However, he also became centrally involved in issues at court that seemed to dwarf the parochial concerns of Pennsylvania, purely political issues that would keep him from Pennsylvania for more than a decade. He would try to continue to lead the colony from afar. In practice, that meant he had great responsibilities in theory and little power in practice. He had the ring and not the stone, he said.

The most apt classical allusion was an obvious one. The heroic Aeneas had to absent himself from his troops for a while, and they seemed determined to destroy themselves in the interim. The defenses Penn had carefully constructed in his Frame of Government were collapsing; and the only interested parties were those involved in the destruction.

In Penn's absence the Pennsylvania government virtually ceased to function. Its officers were more interested in pursuing their private objectives, so the government met infrequently, and even then the interests of the commonwealth were ignored in the spate of private wrangling. The council and assembly were at such loggerheads that no law was passed in the colony for two years. Quakers who had so successfully resisted authority in England with such sweet temper now showed themselves capable of resisting their own authorities with a temper far from sweet. One of Penn's letters during this period is unintentionally funny to a degree that might have caused the good Quaker to blush; he is writing to the leaders of his colony as if trying to

explain to squabbling kindergartners how to behave on the playground during recess:

"The noise of some differences that have been in the province have
reached these parts, with no advantage to the reputations of the country. Not
entering into the merits of the matter; quietness is that which in so troubled
an age of the world has great invitation in it. If anything be amiss let it be by
more hidden and gentle ways be remedied. An infancy of government can
hardly bear the shakes a riper age may and sometimes as a last remedy must
endure. . . . If faults are committed, let them be mended without noise and
animosity. The pomp and clatter of complaint is oftentimes a greater grievance to the public than the thing complained of."

Why did the people he trusted choose to behave like children? At times he
consoled himself that the colony only required his firm parental hand, or perhaps the back of his hand, to regain its senses. Still, why God had permitted
the situation to deteriorate so quickly was inexplicable to Penn. Writing about
it, he had to catch himself from questioning Providence: "The reproaches that
I hear daily of the conduct of things bears hard upon my Spirit too. The Lord
orders things for his glory."

Things did not seem to be ordered for William Penn's glory. The only item
on which all the factions could heartily agree, it seemed, was that William
Penn had outlived his usefulness to the colony, if he ever had any. Even when
no private motive could be imputed to Penn's recommendations, they still
ignored him.

Let us take just one instance. In 1688, four years into his stay in England,
Penn panicked upon learning that the laws of Pennsylvania were going to be
reviewed by the British government. Many of Penn's laws would not be
looked upon with kindness by the British monarchy—and who knew what
the consequences would be when it was realized that Penn had actually implemented his radical ideas? So worried was Penn that he recommended outright
deception. All the laws of Pennsylvania should be set aside, and a new set
passed that would be acceptable to the central government. When danger was
passed, then the old laws could be reinstituted. The Pennsylvania officials,
however, rather than acting upon the secret advice, in fact recorded the
incriminating letter and then did nothing more. Whatever the proprietor was
for, they were instinctively against—anyway, if there was a crisis, then all the
blame could be placed (thanks to the letter of warning) on the head of the
jesuitical Penn.

Penn finally admitted what had been obvious to all: His friends in Pennsylvania were not acting in good faith. Since he could not trust them, he had

to find someone outside the colony, indeed outside the Society of Friends, to reassert order in his colony, lest it degenerate into the chaos that had been the ruin of the New Netherlands.

It was a measure of his desperation that he decided he needed to have the reins of government held by the rigid hands of a Puritan soldier. John Blackwell, who had served under Cromwell and now lived in Massachusetts, was Penn's choice to serve as governor in his place, with his full authority and his full confidence. He wrote to Blackwell, "Rule the meek meekly; and those that will not be ruled, rule with authority." What Penn had forgotten was that Quakers were past masters of meekly refusing to be ruled with authority.

When Penn wrote to Pennsylvania to inform the council of his decision, he seemed to lose his nerve. The appointment of Blackwell was so obviously a rebuke to those who professed to be his friends that he had to soften it. He therefore presented Blackwell as someone who was going to help them to do what they already wished to do. He added the fatal concession, "If he does not please you, he shall be layed aside." It was a foregone conclusion that Black-well was going to please them about as much as the meddling of William Penn. Under these circumstances Solomon himself would not have pleased. So into the valley of Pennsylvania rode John Blackwell.

Expecting an escort suitable to his new honorable station, Blackwell wrote the officials in Philadelphia telling them when he would arrive in New York. They could meet him there, and escort him to his colony. They could have, but they did not. After waiting for a few days to make certain the snub was no accident, Blackwell made his own way to Philadelphia. When he got within a day of arrival, he sent a messenger ahead to inform the council that he would meet with them at three the next afternoon. The messenger got through, but somehow the message did not. Needless to say, when Blackwell arrived at Penn's house, the site for the meeting, the council was not there. The council seemed entirely oblivious to his existence. Yet not everyone in Philadelphia seemed so ignorant of his person; his arrival was greeted by a crowd of boys who taunted him. Did he really hear jeers about vile Puritans martyring inno-cent Quakers?

Blackwell had been in battle before, but never one like this, where the enemy tried to win by pretending that the opposing force did not exist. Finally the council met, and Blackwell presented his credentials, not failing in the process to mention his disappointment at his reception or lack thereof. Thomas Lloyd was the member of the council who then had to inform Blackwell in all sadness that his credentials were not in order because they lacked the Great Seal of Pennsylvania; Mr. Lloyd happened to be the keeper of that seal. Mr. Blackwell owned as how he would publish his commission and act upon it, with or without the seal. Mr. Lloyd asked if he might have a few moments to discuss the matter in private with the rest of the council. These few moments lengthened into a full hour before a somewhat impatient Mr. Blackwell was called back into the meeting room. The council was happy to inform him that his credentials had been judged legitimate, but would Mr. Blackwell mind if they waited until tomorrow before transferring to him power? Mr. Lloyd then in all candor had to admonish Mr. Blackwell for his disrespect; this was much too serious a matter for Mr. Blackwell to spring on the council as a surprise. The business of the day completed, Lloyd then took the almost governor to a tavern where everyone had a mirthful time, perhaps a little too mirthful to the suspicious Puritan's mind. Blackwell had come to be governor, but on this first day had been played with, like a mouse. This day was the first of many.

Blackwell quickly realized that Pennsylvania had become a society in which a small group of merchants and large landowners was running the government for their own selfish ends. Yet he, as a non-Quaker, was prevented from doing anything. In his exasperation he began to make bitter witticisms, the last refuge of impotent rage. The Quakers pray with each other on the Sabbath and prey on each other during the week. The mosquitoes in Philadelphia are worse than armed men, but worse than the mosquitoes are the unarmed men. Blackwell did not know anything about inner light, but he had inferred the existence of a "whistling air" in some men's heads that prevents them from hearing reason. As for Penn's sweet treatment of his colony, Blackwell had to point out that you can give a stomach more honey than it can bear.

For his part, Blackwell was being administered more gall than his stomach could bear. Lloyd was using his possession of the seal to exercise *liberum veto* over every measure he did not like. When Blackwell tried to move against him through impeachment, everyone was up in arms—at least figuratively—in defense of Lloyd; good Quakers, after all, did not commit impeachable acts, unlike (say) papist kings or Puritan autocrats. The assembly had become—as Blackwell in his calmer moments called it—"a monkey house."

Blackwell exhorted his council, "Be not led aside . . . by cunning craftiness, specious and smooth-tongued delusions of any man or men of unstable minds, unsteady principles in Government, unexperienced proud and ambitious spirits, assuming more than is meet to themselves." He almost sounded like Penn. The usual discussions between Blackwell and his council were so filled with intemperate outbursts that the clerk decided they were "fit to be had in oblivion." So he left unrecorded exchanges that might bear comparison to the best scenes from Restoration comedy. Or so one might conclude when reading the fragments of what does survive—such as the exchange that ends with Blackwell asking if he wore his sword in vain when there were about him so many tongues in need of being lopped off. Actually the image of rich Quakers wagging their tongues at a raging Puritan general captures well the spirit of brotherly love reigning in Pennsylvania five years after Penn's departure.

Take, for instance, Frontenac's 1696 invasion of the Iroquois that eventually brought them to the peace table. Upon learning of the invasion, the governor of New York promised military support for the Iroquois. In fact, the king had ordered the colonies to provide protection of these allies. New York, of course, would bear the brunt of this task; Massachusetts, however, was also sending six hundred troops. What did Pennsylvania intend to contribute?

Blackwell presented the request for help with his strong endorsement. One of the Quakers responded that he saw no danger to Pennsylvania "but from the bears and wolves"; all this talk of papists and Indians could serve only to "scare the women and children." End of discussion, with smug smiles all around, except for one dark glare that had not a little in common with that characteristic of rampaging wolves and bears.

By January 1690 Blackwell fully understood his situation. He wrote to Penn, "I have to do with a people whom neither God nor man can prevail with, who despise all dominion and dignity that is not in themselves." He added, in case Penn had missed the chief implication, "Alas! Alas! Poor governor of Pennsylvania." In only a year, Blackwell had been reduced to "woe is me."

During the year in which Blackwell was being defied in deed, Penn was being mollified in words. Penn, more than a little distracted by tumultuous events in England, finally decided that he had no choice but to side with the Quaker merchants and landowners. He wrote to Blackwell chastising him for his unchristian behavior and suggesting he rule in a more Evangelical spirit. Blackwell, however, did not see the point of turning the other cheek when you are being pummeled on all sides. He resigned as governor, but not before giving the well-intentioned Quaker a little Puritan wisdom on the ways of the world. "When a fire is kindled in a city, we do not say, coldly, Yonder is a great fire. Pray God it do no harm. And in times of public defection, we are not to read a tame lecture of contemplative divinity, but to oppose growing evils with all earnestness."

Penn left Blackwell in Pennsylvania with the authority to collect his quitrents, whether as a consolation or further punishment is hard to say. This he earnestly attempted to do, and for his trouble was given little money but entertained to many lectures on contemplative divinity. As one observer put it, the wealthy of Pennsylvania professed the purest love for Friend Penn but "they stagger when he comes near their purses."

How different things were from what Penn had hoped, and how similar to what Charles and James had probably expected. One of the first ships that had arrived in Philadelphia after Penn left had been a slaver. Its cargo of one hundred fifty was quickly snapped up by wealthy Philadelphian Quakers.

Slavery was another of the increasingly typical compromises that Penn made. He seems to have wanted the slaves in Pennsylvania to have limited terms, much as Fox had recommended for Jamaica. That recommendation was set aside. In his scramble for money, Penn himself had engaged in the trade through intermediaries. Fox's clear opposition to slavery had become muddied by Pennsylvanian rationalization. These Africans, after all, were going to be slaves. Wasn't it better that they be sold and owned by kindly Quakers, true children of the light? In such an instance slavery would not change the godly master, but rather he would modify and soften this perennial human institution.

So now the slavers regularly stopped at bustling Philadelphia, and sold the portions of their cargoes that had survived the brutal crossing. Not everyone viewed this development with worldly equanimity. Among the few who did not were Pastorius and the Dutch and German Quakers who had founded settlements like Germantown. They were a people who greatly resembled the original Pilgrims. They had worked as craftsmen in the commercial centers of the continent. They had suffered both persecution and quiet exploitation— and had feared assimilation into a society that valued money over human beings. On the long voyage to the New World and freedom they had one last great fear that they still remembered, the fear of being captured by Turkish pirates and sold into slavery, a degradation far worse than anything they had yet suffered at the hands of those who worshipped this dying world.

In a meeting in Germantown in 1688, at about the same time that Blackwell was resigning, these Quakers asked a question of their fellow Pennsylvanians in a public petition to the general meeting of Quakers in Philadelphia. Weren't Christian slavers worse than Turkish, for they professed to believe in the Golden Rule? Pennsylvania was founded for liberty of the spirit. How could that be reconciled with the treatment here of human beings as if they were cattle? They asked "lovingly" for answers to these and similar questions. They in good conscience could not satisfy those "to whom it is a terror and fearful thing that men should be handled so in Pennsylvania." Among the four leaders who signed the document was Francis Pastorius, who in this instance likely had another opportunity to quote his favorite line from Virgil: *procul este profani.*

So the Friends from Germantown bid their fellow Quakers to travel in spirit away from their cozy homes to where slaves toiled and suffered nearby. Then they too could experience the shame and wrath and anguish and despair that was slavery. Did they not now hear the voice within them saying, "As ye have done to these, ye have done to me"?

The petition was sent, and those receiving it acknowledged it, only to set it aside as a "thing of too great a weight." Too great a weight. Weighing was done in the counting house, not the meeting house. One does not weigh the light. So the heartfelt gesture of Pastorius and his friends only served immediately to make the enveloping darkness of Pennsylvania more visible to them (and to us). Yet it did show that the spirit of Fox was still alive in this colony—and that indeed one small group most concerned with remaining true to this spirit could take it further than either Fox or Penn ever did (for neither had condemned slavery outright). And that itself was ground for hope.

Or so it was taken in the nineteenth century when this petition was recovered and this voice crying in the wilderness made itself heard once again. The Quaker poet and abolitionist John Greenleaf Whittier said that it was like a seed which after laying dormant for years had finally sprouted, grown up, bloomed, and borne fruit. But he did not add, good Quaker that he was, that this seed came to fruition only after fields like Pennsylvania's Gettysburg had been well watered with blood.

The civil wars that gripped Pennsylvania in the early 1690s were of a milder, more humorous sort. William Penn played the straight man in the sketch, writing earnestly sententious letters worthy of Polonius. With the resignation of Blackwell he tells the council that he has decided to "throw all in your hands" and recommends to them "the diligent pursuit of peace and virtue." He exhorts them to "avoid factions and parties, whisperings and reportings, and all animosities." The last piece of advice was like asking the beaver to avoid forests and streams.

The trouble began almost immediately. The lower counties were not pleased about Quaker high-mindedness concerning military defenses. They were content with a policy of pacifism as long as they could be sure that any attack by the French would come by land; then the residents of the lower counties would have time to repent that policy while the French looted Philadelphia.

Unfortunately, there was the possibility of an attack by sea. Then the lower counties would be on the front line, to hold out until Quaker regiments materialized out of thin air. The older colonists had seen too much not to want to make a Delaware invasion—by the French or anyone else—as unattractive as possible. That meant military preparations.

At first the colonial government in Philadelphia seemed willing to permit the lower counties to take whatever defensive measures their fears dictated. However, on reflection—that is, when they began to calculate the costs and consult the light—the council decided against "raising men and money and housing a constant militia which in all likelihood, in considering our principles and poverty, might have caused us to leave our half-made plantations, our unfinished houses and return poor and with grief to our native country."

Principles and poverty. That was a laugh. The members of the council were not poor, unless never thinking you have enough wealth is counted as being poor. They were not going to return to England poor and in grief—they were going to stay in Philadelphia poor-mouthing and being driven in carriages. The Quakers had principles that led to other people's poverty. Well, they could penny-pinch at someone else's expense.

The leaders of the lower counties now advocated secession from the Quaker oligarchy to the north. They appealed to fellow Delawareans to help them "assert our right before it is quite lost." The council in Philadelphia, in response, decided that the uprising showed the degraded morals of the lower counties, how much they were in need of Quaker leadership. Penn was reduced to offering such bromides as "O my friends put an end to these jarrs and heats, and let humility and wisdom rule all passions and interests." But the lower counties were threatening to take their passions and interests directly to the king, who if he looked into this hot jarr might well decide that Penn was no longer fit to be proprietor of Pennsylvania. Penn once again gave in, this time against the interests of his council. He provided the lower counties with their own deputy governor, a concession that made them *de facto* independent from Philadelphia; the colony of Delaware had been born, belated grandchild of New Sweden. Of course, this gave the council occasion to complain once again, as it had been doing throughout the crisis, that Penn was choosing to believe slanders against those who most had his true interests at heart.

While all this was going on, fighting between the council and assembly continued apace. The wealthy Quakers on the council tried to run the government as they saw fit—namely, in their own interests. In the process they managed to offend a wide range of colonists—non-Quakers, the lower and middle classes, and those still loyal to Penn. They had used the fall of Blackwell, for instance, to conduct a systematic purge of all those officehold-ers who had shown any sympathy for the proprietor's rights. The council was so insensitive to these other interests that a conflagration seemed inevitable. The only uncertainty was what issue was going to occasion it.

It might have been the tax proposed in 1692 by the council. A petition against it was circulated, and quickly had 250 signatures denouncing the imposition as an act of "bondage and slavery." But the assembly was up to the challenge, and rejected the bill.

Then there was the case of Peter Babbit. He and his cronies stole a ship, but rather than putting to sea he decided to become a riverine buccaneer, the Captain Kidd of the upper Delaware. He would prey on ships and settle-ments, and the poor pacifists in Philadelphia would have to suffer his dep-redations with suitable Christian meekness. Now, if Quaker leaders only interpreted their principles strictly, it would be "Yo ho ho" for Captain Babbit and for them a bottle of glum. The Quaker pacifists did not hesitate for long, however, before sending out an armed force to take care of the matter. No one was killed, but a number were wounded. There must have been some derisive laughter from the lower counties, and at least one mock epic was written, this with the title "The Fighting Quakers' Expedition in Pennsylvania."

This embarrassing episode might have disappeared without much further comment. But there was a catalyst who would use it to put the whole of the Quaker community to the test. The catalyst was named George Keith.

Once Penn had left Pennsylvania, George Keith may well have been intel-lectually the most distinguished Quaker in the colony—or at least he would not have blushed to hear that said about him. He had preached with Penn in the Old World before coming to the New. And he had been called to Philadelphia to found a school. Keith, unlike most Quakers, prided himself on his intellectual accomplishments. He had named one of his houses "Well-spring." To those who knew Scripture this would evoke the verse, "Under-standing is the wellspring of life unto him that hath it; but the instruction of the fool is folly." ·

To Keith's disappointment, very few Quakers would have gotten the allu-sion. Very few knew their Bible well enough, to say nothing of theology. So he would have to sit through Quaker meetings in which well-intentioned bump-kins would be moved by the Spirit to babble errant nonsense. He founded his school to educate the young, but what good was that when the society as a whole was satisfied with its ignorance. Barclay and others in England had pro-vided intellectual teeth for Fox's intuitive Christianity, but that dimension was nowhere to be found in Pennsylvania, except for George Keith. This gave him his mission.

How could he have an impact on the contented imbecility of Pennsylvanians? The affair of Babbit gave him one occasion. The leaders of the Quaker colony had obviously violated the principles of Quakerism. They did so because these principles had not been clearly enough promulgated. If certain beliefs made one a Quaker, then certain other beliefs made one a non-Quaker, by whatever name one went. And the meeting had to have the power to exclude from itself aspiring members who were not really Quakers.

Was a leader who authorized an armed expedition against other human beings a Quaker? Since such expeditions seem throughout history to have been an essential part of all human governments, could a true Quaker be a government leader? And what about slaves? Could a true Quaker buy and sell human beings? Did not Christ redeem all from bondage?

These were difficult questions, difficult and unavoidable, Keith thought. But they were not the kinds of questions that could be effectively addressed by people whom Keith called "raw and unseasoned." The meeting would do well to encourage such folks to serve the light by holding their tongues.

This suggestion was not taken kindly, especially by those who thought that it might possibly be meant to refer to themselves. This was a challenge to the very spiritual egalitarianism that was the heart of Fox's vision of Christianity. It implied the need of a hired, specially trained clergy—and that would lead to a hierarchy and that would lead . . . why, Keith was advocating "downright popery."

Keith's response to this charge was to the effect that the instruction of fools is folly. And then the folly really began. Keith denounced his critics as "fools, idiots, silly souls, hypocrites, hereticks, heathens, rotten ranters, tyrants, popes, cardinals." A veritable college of Quaker cardinals then rose to respond in kind to this brat of Babylon, this aspiring pope primate of Pennsylvania, this reviler of his brethren. Then one Quaker leader decided to hoist Keith on his own petard. He agreed with Keith that a Quaker orthodoxy ought to be established; the best way to begin was by excluding that notorious Quaker heretic George Keith. Keith responded eagerly; let the meeting decide who was the heretic and who the true Quaker. By this time the secretary of the monthly Quaker meeting in Philadelphia sadly recorded that true Quaker worship had long since ceased "by reason of a turbulent and unsubdued spirit, which has much disquieted us." Even Francis Pastorius was losing patience; he wrote a poem denouncing Keith as a bull of Blasham full of boastful bel-

lowing. The voice of God could not be heard amidst such noise. Penn waded
in from afar; Keith had, he wrote, "stomach enough to lick up vomit."

The Keithian controversy is better understood when it is realized that all of
his followers—and they may have been half the Quakers in Philadelphia—
were outsiders to the governing elite on the council. Keith's own preoccupation may have been theological, but the tumult his charges caused within
Pennsylvania was partly due to the challenge that they posed to this less and
less popular elite. One bemused observer has written that Keith intended to
be the Calvin of the Quakers but he ended up their Servetus. This little
Switzerland had no need for such a heretical challenge to the established
authority. Keith eventually left Pennsylvania, returned to England, and after a
while entered the Church of England (which presumably also contained fools
but fools taught to listen politely to their betters). So ended, it seemed, the
Keithian controversy, another one of what Penn had called the "scurvy quar-
rels that break out to the disgrace of the Province."

This was not the time, however, for Pennsylvania to call attention to herself. Part of the problem was the position of Penn in Britain itself. When he
had returned, he found the government quite different from what he had left.
He was received well by the king, his ministers, and the Duke of York. Even so
he would write, "Yet I found things in general with another face than I left
them: sour and stern and resolved to hold the reins of power with a stiffer
hand than heretofore, especially over those that were observed to be State or
Church Dissenters, conceiving that the opposition which made the government uneasy came from that sort of people, and therefore should either bow
or break." Things became sourer still after Charles died and James became
king.

Penn, ever hopeful, saw an important role for himself in this new frame of
things, perhaps of more significance than the role he had played in Pennsylvania. He would use his position as friend to James to woo him away from this
destructive rigidity. Or so he seems to have rationalized to himself and to others his new stint as courtier. Let Thomas Babington Macaulay describe how
he looked to others, in particular to those who wanted to believe the worst (as
Macaulay, a nineteenth-century Whig historian, himself most assuredly did):

"The Quaker now became a courtier, and almost a favorite. He was every
day summoned from the gallery into the closet, and sometimes had long audiences while peers were kept waiting in the antechambers. It was noised abroad
that he had more real power to help or hurt than many nobles who filled high
offices. He was soon surrounded by flatterers and suppliants. His house at
Kensington was sometimes thronged, at his hour of rising, by more than two

hundred suitors. . . . He afterwards solemnly protested that his hands were pure from illicit gain, and that he never received any gratuity from those whom he had obliged, though he might easily, while his influence at court lasted, have made a hundred and twenty thousand pounds. To this assertion full credit is due. But bribes may be offered to vanity as well as to cupidity; and it is impossible to deny that Penn was cajoled into bearing a part in some unjustifiable transactions of which others enjoyed the profits."

A bribe offered to vanity—this was the way to bring down a beautiful soul: Appeal to its own sense of intrinsic worth, praise its beauty while leading it into the dirt. What beautiful soul could deny a king his friendship? What beautiful soul would not be diminished by such a friendship? There was something unseemly about trying to exercise your chief influence over mankind as a backstairs intriguer.

But perhaps the beauty of a soul is transient, like all other human possessions. On what better project should Penn spend his than on helping his people, and promoting toleration and peace? He certainly could point to concrete results. In 1686 James released more than one thousand Quakers who were in prison. Subsequently James would decree two Acts of Indulgence that would extend religious liberty, although do little to lessen suspicions that he meant to reestablish Catholicism as the state religion. Penn's pride in his role in these events verged on vanity. He would brag to a friend that his persuasion "works much among all sorts and are much spoke of." They were much spoke of, but not always favorably. The best historical memoir of the period gives a stinging portrait of Penn: "A talking vain man . . . he had such an opinion of his own faculty of persuading that he thought none could stand before it, tho' he was singular in that opinion. For he had a tedious luscious way, that was not apt to overcome a man's reason, tho' it might tire his patience."

Then came the Glorious Revolution of 1688. James fled to France and was replaced by William and Mary. This was scarcely a glorious revolution for Penn. Now, far from being an honest courtier at the heart of a splendid but corrupt court, he was an ordinary citizen on the edge of treasonous circles plotting the restoration of James. Penn protested that his only crime was to love too well a hapless friend. He was not believed. Repeatedly he was accused of treason, but never quite enough evidence was found to convict him. He professed his innocence without repudiating his friendship with James. For instance: "I should be glad to do him any service in his private affairs: but I owe a sacred duty to my country; and therefore I was never so wicked as even to think of endeavoring to bring him back."

In this his most difficult period it is hard not to think of Penn in military terms, however much that might have appalled him. He is like an ancient warrior who Zeus himself has decided will neither succumb nor succeed; he retreats slowly, bold and glaring, attacked on all sides, his helmet clanging with numerous blows, his shield rent, his limbs exhausted, until finally he relents and retires to the safety of the shadows.

After attempting to clear his name without complete success and now fearing (correctly) that he would be arrested a fourth time, Penn went into hiding, remaining there for three years. While in hiding, Penn began to refer to himself as a "man of sorrows." George Fox had just died. His beloved wife was ill and would soon die. Stories that he was a Jesuit and plotting a Jacobite invasion persisted. His finances were in a shambles, and an old agreement he had made while promoting Pennsylvania now threatened him with debtors' prison.

He did try during his forced retirement from public life to regain his earlier sense of spiritual wholeness by writing. He wrote a book of aphorisms, *Fruits of Solitude;* but some of the aphorisms betrayed the bitterness he had tasted in the world. For instance, "Let the people think they govern and they will be governed." He also indulged his utopian imagination on the broadest scale by trying to envision a unification of Europe that would mean the end of all war. So he wrote and reflected and waited.

It was during this dark period that the colonial leaders of Pennsylvania first stymied Blackwell and then stymied each other. Not surprisingly the new king, William of Orange, had little patience with this Holy Experiment gone awry. The charter of the colony was revoked, and the king sent his own governor to take it over. Penn could do nothing, but the colonial leaders were up to the challenge.

The new Governor Fletcher was given the Blackwell treatment. He immediately established a council with a majority of non-Quakers and was hailed as a liberator by the lower counties. However, he was soon writing back to England complaining that the Quakers were doing their utmost to baffle everything he tried, even things obviously to their benefit. "My door was never shut, but it was avoided, as if it were treason for the speaker, or any other representative to be seen in my company during your sessions." Their utmost turned out to be quite sufficient.

The situation with defenses was increasingly serious now. James was in the court of Louis XIV. War between France and England, even in the colonies, was in a sense over legitimate succession to the English throne. Fletcher pleaded with the Pennsylvanians for defense money. He promised that the Quaker money would only be spent for humanitarian aide to Indian allies, and hence "shall not be dipt in blood." He began to suspect that the principle objection was not the blood but the money. The Quakers wanted to keep all they had. In stalemating the new governor, Penn's old enemies were doing him a good turn. Fletcher's letters, laden only with ill news, followed like Job's servants, one upon the heels of another.

The king and his ministers finally decided that the Quaker colony needed at least in principle to be governed by a Quaker proprietor. They also chose to believe that Penn was no longer, if he ever had been, involved in Jacobin plots. Penn could come out of hiding and petition for the restoration of his colony. He was eager to comply with any conditions. He specifically promised that his Pennsylvania would do its military duty by "supplying such quotas of men or the defraying of their part of such charges as their majesties shall think necessary for the safety and preservation of their majesties' dominions in that part of America."

So William Penn finally returned to his colony in 1699. As the colony had changed much in the fifteen years of his absence, so had Penn himself. He was not a broken man, but a much diminished one. He now fully appreciated the limits of what he could do in this world, and appreciated the price that had to be paid even to do that.

Some things had not changed. The colonists were still wrangling over the Frame of Government for Pennsylvania. Recently franchise had been extended for rural dwellers and restricted for city dwellers, apparently to try to preserve Quaker power against the increasing number of non-Quaker immigrants in the cities. Of course, this was unfair; of course, it could only delay the inevitable. During his second stay in the colony Penn would have to negotiate yet another constitution, which in turn would settle absolutely nothing. Nonetheless, most changes in the government did serve to lessen the importance of the proprietor; nothing new there.

Yet this persistent bickering had had its effect on Pennsylvania, for the colony had become in certain respects a lawless place. This lawlessness has to be understood in the context of the reforms instituted by Charles after his Restoration. The government had intended to exercise a much tighter control over colonial trade so that custom duties could be collected. However, imperial officials soon discovered to their collective disgust that American colonists, in Pennsylvania and elsewhere, had developed a deep conviction that they were not bound by laws passed by any other than their local assemblies. Or, as colonials of another generation would put it, no taxation without representation. However, the Quaker merchants of Philadelphia did not really want representation in Parliament. They simply wanted to buy cheap and sell dear.

And if they had a chance to buy goods sufficiently cheap, they proved to be singularly uninterested in inquiring as to the origins of those goods. Since most colonial officials were essentially amateurs who supported themselves by other business, even they, when it came to smuggling, almost invariably winked and looked the other way. On some prosperous Philadelphia wharves, smuggled goods were as common as scales on a fish—or so the wits said.

The few devoted servants of king and empire in the colonies, such as chief of customs Edward Randolph, faced an impossible task. Even when on rare occasions malefactors were captured, they had to be tried in local courts by a jury of their peers. "Peers" in such cases usually meant a collection of twelve individuals likely guilty of the same high crimes and misdemeanors. As a result, "beyond a reasonable doubt" in such cases took on the proportions for the prosecution of an epistemological Everest.

Government officials did their best to level Everest by changing the rules. Shortly after the Restoration Charles, at the behest of Admiral Penn and others, had had the maritime courts reformed into efficient units of monarchical administration. Now the government decided that rivers such as the Delaware were really not part of Pennsylvania but rather waters under the direct jurisdiction of the monarchy and its admiralty courts, where common law did not apply. The long and the short of it was that smugglers would no longer have the right to trial by jury. Smugglers were not going to sit in judgment of smugglers.

Or rather that was just the short of the law, its intention. The long of the law, as with laws always, was its interpretation and implementation. This required a minimum of good faith on the colonists' part that did not seem to exist in Pennsylvania. The long of it, if the Quakers had anything to say about it, was going to be very long indeed, something to bequeath to the ingenuity of their grandchildren.

Of course, everything was to be done in the spirit of devout patriotism. The devout patriots in this instance, however, also happened to be Philadelphia lawyers. Under the guise of implementing the act, they impishly reshaped it so that juries would still be required. Of course, everyone understood the game the Pennsylvanians were playing, a game that was likely soon to become popular throughout the assemblies of British North America. Edward Randolph denounced it as a "sham law [that] had utterly destroyed the design and intent" of the British act. A colleague put it more succinctly: the colonials were just growing "grass to hide their snake." Parliament had to admit in embarrassment that the loophole was really there in the original legislation. So it all would have to be rewritten to preclude its willful misinterpretation in this way. This did not mean that Philadelphia lawyers could not find other ways to willfully misinterpret.

While that battle of wits was progressing, Penn was still in England making plans to return to Pennsylvania. He had to spend time solemnly sympathizing with the fulminations of royal officials and assuring them that they must be mistaking the motives of his officials. What else was a newly restored proprietor to do? Yet privately he must, at least occasionally, have given in to a little smile. He had experienced at firsthand the resourcefulness of his colonists when money was at stake; he himself had yet to find an effective way to collect his quitrents, and he had been at it for more than a decade.

Or rather he might have given in to a smile, had not smuggling and illegal trading been connected with something far more grave. With studied myopia, colonial merchants bought goods very cheap. But the cheap goods could have been smuggled *or* they could have been simply stolen. Once you have thwarted the legitimate efforts of government to regulate maritime commerce, you were halfway to placing the high seas outside the law, a place where men were free to do their worst, with impunity. Sadly, failure to enforce laws against smuggling effectively was connected with a failure to enforce laws against outright piracy. And piracy was a crime against humanity, against the very moral order of creation, an attempt to return this world to its primordial chaos. Piracy was not a matter for knowing smiles or winks or shrugs.

Yet so piracy seemed to have become in the American colonies. If a pirate tried to despoil their own settlements, as Peter Babbit had tried on the upper Delaware, then colonists could be counted upon to take concerted action against him, even Quaker colonists. But if he was preying on other people, especially if he had been successful preying on shipping far away—if he had, for instance, taken ships in the Indian Ocean—then what matter that he had stolen and destroyed and murdered and enslaved? It had all happened so far away. He was an estimable person, to be feared a little, but to be admired much, for his swashbuckling daring as well as for the gold he had to spend.

Such seemed to be a pervasive attitude among the colonists, especially those of the wealthier classes. The British colonies, after all, would produce the greatest of these pirates, Captain Kidd, who would turn to piracy after getting the British government to outfit his ship, ostensibly as a weapon against the pirates (a nice touch, that)—and who would only be caught and executed because he returned to his home port of New York to resume his place in society as if he had done nothing wrong.

New Yorkers may have been able to boast of Captain Kidd—and boast some of them did—but if imperial officials in Northern America were to be believed, no colony was more guilty of harboring pirates than Pennsylvania. Pennsylvania had this reputation even among the other colonies. One governor wrote concerning some notorious pirates, "I hear several of them are in Pennsylvania, where the government, owing to the falling out among the Quakers themselves, is very loose." There were many reports of pirates deporting themselves in Pennsylvania trading centers—to quote from one— "with as much confidence and assurance as the most honest men in the world, without any molestation whatever." And to hear customs chief Edward Randolph describe Pennsylvania, you'd think half the Quaker meeting houses in Pennsylvania were flying the Jolly Roger.

Penn tried to disagree. What little truth there was in the reports, Penn would insist, represented only temporary and local lapses. The officials at Whitehall were unconvinced, however. They believed that Pennsylvania leaders were actively conniving with the pirates.

Take, for example, the man Penn had chosen to be his governor until he returned, his cousin William Markham. William Markham's own son-in-law was a notorious pirate, who had once been arrested for piracy off the Carolinas but now preferred to ply his trade in the Indian Ocean—when he wasn't resting in Pennsylvania between excursions. When a justice of the peace issued a warrant for three men wanted in England for piracy, Markham's wife and daughter accused the justice of being an "informer" after they had warned the men of his intention to arrest them; the men were finally captured, but they then escaped from Markham's jail under suspicious circumstances, never to be recaptured. When Captain Kidd himself showed up in Pennsylvania waters with reportedly thirty tons of gold aboard as ballast, he was feted as a celebrity by residents. The judge of the local admiralty court then organized a surprise for him that resulted in the capture of a few of his men; if he had had the support of Markham, he insisted, they could have brought Kidd himself to justice. (Markham, of course, denied everything; had anyone made such charges to his face, he declared, "I would have been after him and taught him what wood my cudgel was made of.")

The government official who claimed that Pennsylvania had become "the only receptacle for pirates and illegal traders" was certainly exaggerating. But Penn would insist, "we have never had a spot on our garments." That was obviously false. Penn knew perfectly well that the colony had become a chief receptacle. One of his loyal Quaker supporters in Pennsylvania had apprised him that Pennsylvania had become the chief haven for the "murdering bloody crew of privateers." He added, "It's better the Government were out of our hands and in the hands of others that they might bear their own shame and reproach which we must expect to bear while we called Quakers bear the name of Government."

Penn believed rather that it was better to fib to Whitehall than to let his enemies harm his colony. The critics of Pennsylvania, he assured the government, were charging Pennsylvania with the very crimes of which they were guilty. That "one-eyed gentleman" Edward Randolph sold pardons to pirates; he wished them arrested only to increase business. Another of the critics, Francis Nicholson, was a notorious seducer of innocent maidens. And Reverend Edward Portlock of Philadelphia, the Anglican divine who preached against Quaker inactivity on the piracy front, actually himself used his church as a bank for piratical gold. William Penn, in his days as courtier to James, had obviously learned that verbal dueling required both parries and thrusts. Nonetheless, he left for Pennsylvania knowing full well that his Holy Experiment had produced a den for thieves.

So Penn left for Pennsylvania in 1699, with a new young wife and a daughter of marriageable age. He was now in his fifties, a corpulent gentleman with little remaining trace of the beauty so striking in the younger man. Life had taken its toll. He was also bringing with him a secretary to ease the burden of the work. By all rights this should have been his son, known as Billy, now just on the edge of manhood. However, among his many sorrows was the growing recognition that he had failed as a father; none of his sons would be worthy of his name. Billy Penn, in particular, had shown himself already to be a rakehell. Penn could delude himself that this was a phase he would outgrow (he would no more outgrow it than Penn outgrew his youthful religiosity), but he did not delude himself that he could rely on his son now for important responsibilities. Accompanying him, therefore, was a learned young Quaker, James Logan. Logan, whose library would eventually provide the foundation for the American Philosophical Society, would decades later as an old man tell the story of that voyage to another aspiring young man, Benjamin Franklin.

During the crossing piracy was a common worry. When the captain sighted an armed ship on the horizon, he cleared the deck for action. All noncombatants went below—and that included Penn and his frightened entourage—except for James Logan, who presented himself for duty and was given a gun to man. The ship turned out to be without malevolent intent. When Penn returned to the deck, he rebuked the young Logan for compromising his Quaker principles; but Logan was not without a reply. "I being thy servant, why didst thou not order me to come down? Thou was willing enough that I should stay and fight the ship when thou thought there was danger."

It is hard to believe that the story is true in all its particulars. Logan the

young man could scarcely be expected to have challenged his patron so directly; and Logan the old man could scarcely be expected to resist rounding out a
good story; and Benjamin Franklin, young or old, could always be counted
upon to lend the truth a witty hand.

Let it suffice to say that young Logan probably thought what he claimed to
have said. Penn rebuked Logan for violating his Quaker principles. And
Logan thought how hypocritically the old man was behaving. This was a measure of how far Penn had diminished in stature, even to those closest to him
and most sincerely committed to his service. Penn's motives were no longer
sacred to anyone.

The arrival in Pennsylvania was far from triumphant. Penn stopped first in
the lower counties, and found the population in no celebratory mood. They
had just suffered through a fever epidemic that had killed two hundred or
more. When Penn looked out over the populace he saw "only pale faces and
sunken countenances" that might have brought back memories of the London of 1665. Some young men tried to enliven the proceedings by firing off
the old cannons, perhaps relics of New Sweden or Pete Stuyvesant. But a cannon exploded, mangling an arm of the boy in charge so badly that it had to be
amputated, an amputation that saved the boy only for a lingering death from
blood poisoning.

Penn reached Philadelphia on a Sunday, when the Quakers were at their
meeting; so the party that met him at the dock was largely composed of enemies and opponents. Penn was none too pleased by this. According to Logan,
he quickly surveyed the crowd to find a friend, and then showered his attention on him, ignoring the rest as much as possible.

Nonetheless, Penn was received as a hero in the Quaker community. He
set up his temporary residence with Edward Shippen, a Quaker merchant
reputed to be the wealthiest man in Pennsylvania. (The front lawn of
Shippen's mansion was so large, it was said, that he had a herd of pet deer to
graze it.)

Despite Penn's obvious preference for his own people, and particularly for
the wealthiest among them, he soon had won over even the most suspicious
imperial officials by the energy with which he pursued the policies of the king.
One wrote: "He regrets and abhors what has been done and assures the King's
officers of his favor and encouragement. He is very zealous in promoting all
things that doth in any way promote the King's interest."

He quickly sacked William Markham, whose son-in-law rather than taking his seat in the assembly would soon be traveling back to England to stand
trial for piracy. The Philadelphia lawyers could only frown when Penn had

their clever little circumvention of the admiralty courts rescinded. Penn and the council, moreover, voted a ten-pound bounty on pirates. He even pushed through a bill outlawing trade between Madagascar and Pennsylvania; some members of the assembly had never heard of Madagascar before, but Whitehall would recognize it as a chief haven for pirates in the Indian Ocean. Pennsylvania, so recently considered the Madagascar of North America, also passed pious proclamations of opposition to piracy: "We have and always had a just abhorrence of them and hope we shall upon all occasions use our utmost diligence and endeavours to discountenance them and suppress them."

All this read very well in England. Perhaps it was not noticed then that Penn on other matters had proceeded very slowly—indeed not at all in fulfilling his promise to establish a Pennsylvania militia. He did establish a lookout for the lower colonies. Delawareans might wonder what good a warning would be if you had not the means for defense. Perhaps the pious Penn merely wanted to give them time to make a final act of contrition.

Repairing relations between his colony and the central government was one of Penn's chief objectives in returning to Pennsylvania. But he did have others. The author of the original Frame of Government for this colony wanted a permanent frame of government finally established; and the son of Admiral Penn wanted his investment in this colonial enterprise to start paying an ample return. If Penn's missives back to England seemed to be doing their work, the problem of a constitution seemed as intractable as ever. His good will got him little there. His exhortations against factions would be applauded and then ignored. He tried to pressure Pennsylvanians by declaring that he would rule on his own until they provided an adequate frame.

In frustration he settled on a secondary project. He would codify the laws of Pennsylvania. Many laws had been passed helter-skelter in the rapid succession of administrations, but they were as irregular and uncertain as the streets of a medieval city. Penn and his advisers set about turning them into a Philadelphia. The final code of approximately a hundred laws began with one assuring religious freedom and ended with one designed to assure fair treatment of the Indians. There must have been times when he was shaping this code that Penn could think he was still back in the 1680s, spinning ideals out of his head and projecting them upon the wilderness.

Of course, Pennsylvania was now wilderness only in part. The lack of an effective government had not prevented Philadelphia, in particular, from becoming a bustling little commercial center, now the second largest city of the colonies after Boston. Visitors could not believe that it was scarcely twenty years old. Philadelphia was irrefutable proof that Penn's enterprise was a great success. Yet, to be honest, Penn did not much like Philadelphia as it had turned out.

He had hoped for a green country town, with plenty of space and all the buildings on ample lots. Philadelphians, however, seemed to prefer the energy produced by having people live one on top of another. It had to be preference, for there was ample room. Yet here they lived in ever closer quarters, as if they were trying to imitate a prosperous English port like Bristol. The trajectory of the city, although in Penn's eyes needless and lamentable, was too far advanced to change. Today it would aspire to be another Bristol, tomorrow to be another London—and so it would replicate all that Penn had left the Old World to avoid.

Penn, despite the fact that much of his business required him in Philadelphia, preferred to avoid the city as much as possible. He set up his permanent residence on his country property, Pennsbury, about twenty miles farther up the Delaware. During the dark days when he was friend and advisor of the doomed James, Penn had tried to direct the development of this property from afar. As for the numerous laborers required on the estate, he wrote, "It was better they were blacks, for then a man has them while they live."

So Penn repaired to his estate, now run by two white overseers and an ample labor force of slaves. He seems to have provided each of his family with his or her own body servant, although he was much displeased with the one chosen for his daughter Letitia—"a most impudent slut," he wrote.

In Pennsbury he lived very well, as befitted the successful son of an admiral. (Presumably the income supporting this came from British sources, for Penn was still having trouble collecting Pennsylvania quitrents.) He loved to show off Tamerlane, the stallion he had brought with him from England. The table he kept was magnificent; a visiting governor said he had not seen the like in all the colonies. And then there was his barge. He confessed that "above all dead things I love my barge." With six slaves at the oars, he traveled the twenty miles between Pennsbury and Philadelphia like a potentate, a true colonial grandee.

While lavishly entertaining at Pennsbury, Penn had the chance to renew old friendships, such as that with Francis Pastorius. Pastorius had not changed. He was the same friend, Penn wrote, "sober, upright, wise, pious and of a reputation approved on all hands and unimpeached." Would that the same could be said about himself.

Penn renewed contacts with the various Indian groups. He negotiated an important treaty with the Susquehannas for land along their river to which they seem to have moved back after Bacon's rebellion; this would open up central Pennsylvania for settlement. He also met with the Delawares to renew the famous treaty of friendship. This was a poignant meeting for him and them, a reminder of older and simpler times for both. They did their best to recapture that long past moment, but the differences refused to be set aside. Penn had to use an interpreter, for he had forgotten what he had once known of the Delaware language. And then when the Delawares at the end of the meeting began to dance, Penn could only look on. He had bad gout, and he was no longer fit for dancing, only for being rowed in a barge.

In the second year after his return the situation began to deteriorate in all-too-familiar ways. Penn's effort to get the financial support from the assembly that he thought was his due as proprietor was thwarted. Finally he was given the proceeds for an excise tax on alcohol, but without any clear means of collecting it. Was Penn to go tavern to tavern with hand outstretched?

Absolutely no progress was being made on a constitution. The Delaware counties were once again complaining vociferously to London about their oppression and exclusion—and London, alas, seemed to be listening. Penn tried to make them feel more loyal by having the assembly meet there once, but all that did was to fan separatist sentiments further.

Quakers and non-Quakers were now bickering bitterly in Philadelphia. The center for the anti-Quaker sentiment was the growing Anglican community, who were also sending wild charges to England about religious and political suppression. A good Anglican, they complained, could not hope to get a fair trial before a Quaker judge, and all the judges were Quakers. These charges in particular outraged Penn, and he wrote numerous letters in rebuttal, charging the Anglicans with projecting onto Quakers the very injustices they intended to perpetrate themselves if they ever got the chance. He wrote for instance: "Yet no less than the outing of us and overturning the Government is the ambition and sedition of some violent tempers the chief of which have neither house nor land in the Province, and eat the Bread they get in it by the indulgence of those they would injure and destroy."

He did not quite deny that the Quakers were manipulating things to their own disproportionate advantage, with his approval. He rather argued that this was only just. "We cannot yet be so self-denying as to let those that had no part of the heat of the day, not one third of the number, and not one fourth of the estate, and not one tenth of the trouble and labour should give laws to us, and make us dissenters, and worse than that in our own country." The choice, it seemed to him, was between the *status quo* and allowing Quakers to be persecuted as they had been in New England.

Needless to say, in this atmosphere of distrust little progress could be made on a new frame of government, and not much further progress was being made against smuggling and piracy. London began to receive reports that the promising beginnings made by Penn in that regard had proven to be little more than feints intended to gull the loyal servants of the king. It was hard to avoid the judgment that in almost all important respects the return of Penn, despite its initial promise, was a simple failure. He was the ghost of Christmas past.

In 1701 Penn learned that a new plan to remove him as proprietor of Pennsylvania was already well advanced in the British government. Some thought its final implementation a foregone conclusion. By this point Penn's personal presence was doing little good in Pennsylvania. Penn decided that he had to return to Britain to present his case personally. He announced that he would be gone from Pennsylvania only briefly, until this minor matter was settled. His wife and daughter knew better, however. They insisted upon returning with him; remote Pennsbury held few charms for them, barge or no barge.

The council and assembly seem to have realized he might never return as well (which he never did). They finally hammered out a new frame of government; this they presented to Penn as a surprise while he waited to sail. The frame gave control of the colony essentially to the assembly, significantly reducing the power of both the proprietor and his council. (The council would now be no more than an advisory body to the governor.) It was the kind of constitution that the young Penn might have admired, and the elder Penn would have opposed. But this Penn to whom it was presented was not just older and more conservative, he was also very tired and very concerned about his personal investment in Pennsylvania. This was not the frame of government he wanted, but that he had a frame of government at all might show Whitehall that his colony was still governable. Penn sighed and signed and sailed off, leaving young James Logan as his representative in a colony that was no longer in any inner sense his.

He did manage to retain his proprietorship according to Whitehall, but barely. Then he almost lost it to debts. Before strokes finally sent him into the mental dusk of his last years, he described himself as a man crucified between the injustice and ingratitude of the New World and the extortion and oppression of the Old. He had wounds that water would not wash nor time heal. Here was a Friend in whom little gladness was left, embittered by disappointed hopes and empty dreams.

Little he heard from Pennsylvania could have cheered him. It too was clearly part of the dying world. Logan wrote that once he left all the powers broke loose from their center and "Hell itself is transplanted hither." But Logan was young and a newcomer, and Penn knew better. There never had been a center, and hell had always been there, just toying with him.

We should not remember Penn as he was when he read the letters from Logan, old and sad and spiritually wizened. We should remember him as he was before the glory of the Lord had fled from his limbs. We should remember him as he was that night when he danced with the Indians, leapt for joy around the fire in the midst of the darkness, under the great elm.

CHAPTER X

ACADIAN NEUTRALS

L OUIS XIV, AS HE AGED, persisted in his love for the splendid folly
of conquest. He was still determined to bestride the world like a colos-
sus, so he continued to fight war after war against coalitions of his
European neighbors. France at times seemed determined to fight alone
against all Europe. This was the only way Louis could unite Europe: against
him. But there were limits to what even he could do to make his enemies
tremble, to astonish the world.

At times Louis would be equipping as many as 200,000 troops who themselves would be collectively fighting on as many as four fronts. All this while
the building of Versailles proceeded apace, while Louis's opulent entourage
grew as well. Actually, the most marvelous edifice in all France was neither
Versailles nor the military establishment, but the system of taxation that year
after year managed to transubstantiate the sweat of poor laborers into the uniforms of soldiers, the fat of courtiers, the decorations of a room.

Even so, a Louis XIV, no less than a Louis de Buade, can overspend his
means. However much eternal glory Louis accumulated, glory paid few bills.
By the 1690s the policies of the Sun King had brought once-prosperous
France to the verge of economic collapse. One pamphlet of the period concluded: "Who does not realize that conquests, instead of increasing the
grandeur of the state, are burdensome and cause it ruin? . . . The Prince's
grandeur always brings misery to his subjects." Truly, in splendid Versailles as
much as in any Iroquois village, human limbs floated in the cooking pots and
children screamed as they were hung up to roast—but no Iroquois headman
would ever have been a cannibal to his own people.

"Your people, Sire, whom you should love as your children, and who up to
this time have been so devoted to you, are dying of hunger. The land is left

almost untended, towns and countryside are deserted, trade of all kinds falls off and can no longer support the workers: all commerce is at a standstill. . . . For the sake of getting and keeping vain conquests abroad, you have destroyed half the real strength of your own state. Rather than take money from your poor people you ought to feed and cherish them. All France is now no more than one great hospital, desolate and unprovided. . . . The very people believe you have no pity for their sufferings, that you care only for your own power and glory. They say that if the king had a father's heart for his people, he would surely think his glory lay rather in giving bread and a little respite after such tribulations than in keeping hold of a few border posts which are a cause of war."

Thus another pamphlet pleaded with Louis to realize that, although those who bore the brunt of his policies might themselves be mere human wretches, he was still accountable for their blood. One important group of the border posts maintained at great cost was the series of forts established along the Mississippi by La Salle. Since the European market for American furs had long been glutted (thanks in part to these very forts), they had largely outlived any economic purpose they ever had, and their abandonment had more than once been proposed.

Colbert in his opposition to their original founding had understood why, once they were established, they would prove virtually impossible to abandon, no matter how unprofitable. Once the king's honor was involved, money would be no object. To withdraw from these forts without a battle would be dishonorable in the extreme.

Colbert, as usual, was proven right, this time posthumously. The aging Louis insisted that the forts not only be maintained but be improved and expanded, whatever the cost. Colbert's plan for a compact colony of New France, a colony that would contribute to the economy of France rather than be a drain on it, had turned out to be like one of those pleasing dreams that leave you, upon waking, with only the regret of ever having believed in it. Defenders of Louis—the Prince of Versailles never lacked for apologists— could respond that these forts, while economically past their day, now had a crucial strategic position for the Bourbon dynasty. There was something to this justification.

By the early eighteenth century it was clear that Louis and his line would have a legal claim to the Spanish throne when it next became open. If Louis could make this claim good, then Bourbon possessions would range from South America to the Arctic Circle, to dominate the New World. The two parts of this one great empire would be connected over land by that very series of forts that La Salle had providentially established along the Mississippi.

But, of course, Louis had first to make good the Bourbon claim to the Spanish throne. Needless to say, his traditional opponents would be far from pleased to see his house gain such a predominant position in both western Europe and the New World. Grandeur is always opposed by the timid and mediocre. Alliances would be formed against him, probably led by Britain and the Dutch republic, those insect states that had so annoyed him before. Another war would have to be fought, undoubtedly another war to be paid for by more taxes and more starvation. But what could Louis do? The Bourbons had a clear legal right to the Spanish throne. To fail to exercise it would be to compromise their honor. What were innocent lives in the scale against an imperiled honor?

Voltaire once wondered who should be considered truly great, Louis XIV or his Dutch nemesis William of Orange. William had only defended his country, and ruled it without subjugating it; he never persecuted anyone for religion, was only simple and modest in his manners—some might call this greatness in a king. "But those who are more impressed by the pleasures and *éclat* of a brilliant court, by magnificence, by patronage of the arts, zeal for public welfare, passion for glory, and a gift for commanding; those who are more struck by that haughtiness with which ministers and generals annexed provinces to France, on the orders of their king; who are more astonished at seeing a single state resist so many powers; those who esteem a king of France who can give Spain to his grandson . . . will give preference to Louis XIV."

The War of the Spanish Succession, once it began, lasted more than ten weary years, the heroic butchery ending only in 1713 with the Treaty of Utrecht in which Louis formally renounced Bourbon claims to the Spanish throne. The group in New France most affected by this war was, ironically, a group of peasants who up to this time had managed to stand apart from the grand pretensions of Louis XIV. Indeed, no more striking contrast to the pretensions of a Bourbon or even a Frontenac could be imagined than the life led by the people of Acadia.

Acadia was the French name for a large, irregularly shaped peninsula that jutted out into the Atlantic below the mouth of the Saint Lawrence. Actually, it was not so much a peninsula as a large island still connected to the mainland by a slender isthmus called Chignecto. It was as if Acadia had tried to detach itself from the rest of the continent and had not quite succeeded. The sea, however, was still trying to receive it into its embrace; every day it would send huge tides swirling around Acadia, the largest tides in the world, sometimes more than sixteen feet. Sea fogs would pitch their moist tents over Acadia for weeks on end, giving everything a dreary grayness and the tang of salt.

After various French and British attempts to establish a permanent colony on Acadia (or Nova Scotia as the British called it), a French colony finally took hold at about the time of the Sun King's birth. It flourished in its own peculiar way, but this was not a flourishing that would have been recognized as such by anyone fresh from Versailles or Boston or even Quebec. Acadia seemed to hang suspended in an unrelated epoch of its own. That was its appeal to the sentimental imaginations of the nineteenth century, like Longfellow's: it was an escape from time, history, from the tohu-bohu of the modern world. Let us try to imagine an Acadian village as it would be conjured up in the mind of a Longfellow.

It is near the end of a day, during an Indian summer. The village reposes in the midst of cultivated fields, which are now fast ripening—and beyond these fields is untouched forest. It is a village of strongly built houses, with frames of oak and chestnut, such as the peasants of Normandy built in the reign of the Henrys, thatched roofs and dormer windows, gables protecting and shading the doorways.

The women are finishing their afternoon's work at the spinning wheel and loom, the children are playing near the pathways that pass for streets, and the men are straggling back from hunt or field, or from helping repair the distant dikes that keep the great sea tides temporarily at bay. Darkness is beginning to seep grayly from the forest, across the fields toward the village where a few of the weather vanes on the chimneys are gilded by the setting sun. The faint sounds of the Acadians themselves—gossiping, laughing, arguing—blend with the fragile chorus of summer insects, themselves accompanied by the percussive croaking of frogs. But then human sound and movement is suddenly stopped, although the insects and frogs continue, for from a building that looks little different from a barn has issued the single high note of the Angelus, floating above the whole scene. And as the twilight now deepens toward true darkness, from each house comes a single column of pale blue smoke like incense ascending into the night sky, and wolves in the woods begin their evening serenade. So Acadian life might picturesquely appear to a Longfellow or to us. But to those in the seventeenth or eighteenth centuries, it presented quite another aspect.

"To what a wilderness, O heaven, have I come! Nothing before my eyes but streams and forests, huts of mud and cottages; though well prepared for the condition of this place, how one can live here I don't know. O what a scene of poverty! Already I, with but a taste, have had enough of this new France.

And here what penance for the old I'll do." So one seventeenth-century visitor from France recorded his first impressions, impressions that were typical. For anyone who enjoyed social standing anywhere else, to arrive in Acadia was to want to go back home. Yet few visitors did any penance at mealtime. A large portion of many a contemporary account of Acadia is an awed catalogue of all these peasants had to eat.

Of domesticated animals the Acadians preferred pork, but they also raised beef and mutton, if simply letting these animals run loose and occasionally rounding them up can be called "raising." Game was abundant—and they hunted deer, elk, bear, moose, even seal. (Our visitor had to say that seal made "a very nasty stew, no matter how it is prepared.") Acadians also relished wild partridges and rabbits. Duck and geese were easily taken in season, as was an incredible variety of fish—trout, salmon, pike, smelt, flounder, sturgeon, shad, bass, and sardine. And Acadia was near the greatest cod fishing in the world.

As for vegetables, they had all kinds except artichokes and asparagus. They had so much cabbage they would eat only the hearts, and feed the rest to their pigs. Pigs, in fact, seemed to eat better in Acadia than peasants in France. The many inlets of Acadia, especially the huge Bay of Fundy, had extensive marsh-lands around them. By diking these the Acadians recovered extraordinarily fertile land on which they grew their staple crop of wheat with remarkable yields. As for fruits, apples and strawberries were so plentiful that it was hard to believe they were not weeds. (Food-bearing plants should not grow so easi-ly.) The Acadians produced their sugar from the sap of the sycamore, reddish and very good; beer they brewed from the tips of spruce trees, thin and not so good—which might explain why "the most common beverage is water." It was said that "the Acadians are always vigorous; and can stand hard work because they eat a great deal and do not have constant employment."

The Acadians were consistently and constantly religious to a degree that many French visitors found embarrassing. Scrupulous religious observance was at the very center of Acadian social life, but in these observances were none of the refinements that would suit genteel tastes. The churches them-selves were largely nondescript. One visitor told of having stumbled into what he took to be a poor farmer's one-room cottage. But it turned out that the farmer was also a priest who lived in one part of his cottage and said Mass in the other. What the priests lacked in aesthetic accoutrements, however, they made up for in moral authority. They enjoyed an almost superstitious defer-ence from the parishioners. A church where illiterate peasants sat in the front pews was a road to heaven that would have pleased few educated Frenchmen.

A lot to eat, little to do, and much religion—that was the essence of Acadian life; that and reproduction, and at reproduction the Acadians excelled. Immigration to Acadia had always been modest, even by the standards of New France. About sixty families had established the permanent colony in the 1630s. Sixty settlers joined them in 1671, and perhaps another sixty soldiers opted to stay in Acadia after their tour of duty ended during the late seventeenth century. That was about all the European breeding stock, and yet the population grew substantially throughout the seventeenth and early eighteenth centuries: The European population was 441 in 1671; 885 in 1686; 1,136 in 1701; and up to 1,773 in 1714.

All this was achieved without any effective centralized planning, by Colbert or anybody else. Acadians just married young and had lots of children. "In almost every family five or six children are to be found, and often many more; the swarming of brats is a sight to behold and one is amazed to see the numbers which are fed by the parents' labor." In the 1693 census there were no unmarried women in their thirties, and only four in their twenties. Any surplus of males, so common in such colonies, was absorbed by marriages with Indian women; and the children from such unions do not seem to have been discriminated against, marrying subsequently into the oldest families. Indeed, one of the missionaries to the local Indians, the Micmacs, would eventually predict concerning them, "I do not give more than fifty years to them . . . before one sees them so mixed with the French colonists that it will no longer be possible to tell them apart." The Acadians and Micmacs were starting to resemble two streams that in merging lose their individuality in each other.

The mission to the Micmacs had been one of the most successful in New France; Catholicism had supplanted the native religion, much as French hatchets, pots, and arrowheads had supplanted the products of traditional Micmac craftsmanship. And the primitive piety of the Micmacs and the Acadians were not that far apart, at least from the vantage of sophisticated France.

The Micmacs, now dependent upon European goods, much preferred to get them from the French. They knew—and their missionaries did not cease to remind them—how their neighbors to the south in Maine, the Abenakis, were continually fending off the incursions of English settlers. The English did not leave their Indians in peace; they expanded continually and took over the land.

The Acadians, in contrast, were friendly neighbors who provided trade goods for fur, food during the hard months of February and March when the hunting was bad, and the occasional groom for the odd daughter. With such people the Micmacs could live peaceably.

Of course, what the Micmacs found so agreeable about the Acadians the few European visitors usually found reprehensible. The Acadians were content with a merely passable way of life. They seemed to have no more desires than their rudimentary needs, and no more needs than satisfactions. They had little and seemed unaware of what was lacking. They were obviously content—and for most European visitors the Acadians' happiness was a symptom of their imbecility. Only an imbecile would prefer contentment to civilization.

The Acadians were consistently and roundly criticized for their laziness, their lack of ambition. As one Frenchman put it, they were "indifferent husbandmen, and do no more labor than what necessity urges them to." Another estimated that the average Acadian worked no more than one third of the time. How could they be so content when there was obviously so much to do? There were forests to be cleared, then large fields to be fertilized and planted, surpluses to be gathered and traded. Only then could Acadia take its place in the world. But what did the Acadians do? They sat back, content just to dike the lowland marshes. The forests they left to the game and the Indians, with whom they sometimes hunted. How unlike this colony was to the bustling British colonies to the south, or even to Quebec! Their lives glided over the land as lightly as a canoe that crosses a river leaving a wake little larger than a ripple.

When the Acadians did find themselves with surpluses either in food or furs, they traded with whoever was handy, often the Yankees. They were inclined to trade for gaudy things; the women were particularly fond of scarlet cloth, the kind of cloth Puritans would think appropriate only for harlots and adulteresses. When Acadians got money, they would simply squirrel it away like good peasants. One governor was instructed: "There is plenty of money in Acadia, but . . . the inhabitants do not put it in circulation; it is your business to discover the means of getting it in circulation"—he never did. The Acadians did not spend their money, nor did they have any tolerance for an Acadian who tried to get ahead through business.

"In such a vast country where trade should be open to all in order that it might be established, no one dares to do any business; if a settler attempts anything of the sort, even in the neighborhood, from one house to another, trouble is made for him on some fine but specious pretext, suggested by base interests; business is taken from him, and in this way districts which might have become productive, are rendered forever barren."

This visitor to Acadia might well have been mistaken in thinking that budding businessmen were being singled out for persecution. Other contemporary accounts report that the Acadians were always squabbling with one another on fine but specious pretexts. It was their chief recreation—and when a court system was established among them, it was used as a wonderful stage on which to act out their domestic dramas, and the Acadians became known as the most litigious people in the western world. If the land amply supplied their material needs and the Church took care of morals, legal disputes dispelled boredom. And so these disputes, despite the earnest efforts of peacemakers, were never really settled. Acadia retained the anarchic buzz of interminable wrangling. The Acadian adults, no less than their children, looked to the outsider like swarming brats. How unendurably shocking that they would neither work hard nor stop arguing!

To make matters worse, the Acadians did not seem to care a sou what outsiders thought of them. Pity the poor placeserver sent from France or Quebec to be their governor. They were ungovernable. One visitor of the 1680s observed to Versailles, "If all the settlers of Acadia were gathered together into one or two settlements, they would be more important and would be better off, for, scattered as they are, they are neither useful nor profitable."

The Acadians did not want to be important if that meant allowing other people to decide for them what was profitable, useful, or being better off. When a governor tried to govern them, they did not rebel—they just paid no attention. One seventeenth-century governor groaned, "They live like true republicans, not acknowledging royal or judicial authority." In the eighteenth century the litany of complaint continued: "All orders sent to them, if not suiting to their humors, are scoffed and laughed at, and they put themselves upon the footing of obeying no government." And again: "They are a litigious sort of people, and so ill-natured to one another as daily to encroach upon their neighbors' properties, which occasions continual complaints, yet they all unanimously agree in opposing every order of government." If Frontenac had been assigned here, he would have been dead of apoplexy within a few weeks—and no one would have noticed.

These were the Acadians: ill-natured, anarchic, smug; a people who would make minimal demands on the land, on the Indians, on themselves; a people content to spend their time on family affairs and local squabbles, who preferred leisure to labor, bright-colored cloth to true wealth; a people religious to the point of superstition; poor in most things and uncultured in all—not the kind from which one would expect greatness or even mediocrity. They only wished to be left alone, as much by their own government as by foreigners. And their military philosophy could be summarized by a sentence from Voltaire (of whom, of course, they'd never heard): "Let the heroes slaughter each other, and let us live at peace."

No one could have been further from the values shared by the Sun King and his minions than this querulous group of yeomen. And yet of all the French in the New World these were as a people destined to pay most dearly for the persistent Bourbon pursuit of glory. In the repeated wars between France and the alliance led by the British and the Dutch, that almost-island Acadia was assuming more and more strategic importance. The Acadians were to learn that modern history is a chaos from which no one can fully detach himself.

Acadia is separated from the mouth of the Saint Lawrence only by Cape Breton Island, and hence it provided ideal bases from which either to defend or attack the entrance to this crucial waterway of New France. Moreover, Acadia stretches into the Atlantic far to the east of Massachusetts; hence it also provided ideal bases from which to defend or harass the maritime commerce of New England. Whoever controlled Acadia began with a naval advantage in any New World test of strength between France and Great Britain. The Acadians might well have wanted to be left alone, but they were in the wrong place. As a result, they were assured of the very attention to which they did not aspire.

When the War of the Spanish Succession began, the French used Acadian ports to attack British ships. Moreover, the loyal Indians of the northeast, both the Micmacs of Acadia and their southern neighbors the Abenakis, were used by the French to terrorize British border settlements. When New England wanted to take reprisals, Acadia was the obvious target. In 1704 the first of these naval raids was sent out from Boston. The attackers could not quite overrun the French garrison, so they contented themselves with destroying the farms nearby. No wonder the Acadians resisted attempts to cluster them in large villages near French military fortifications. The Acadians were more interested in food than world politics. They did not care to understand why the British and French persisted in wanting to kill one another. They only knew that killing and being killed was a soldier's way of earning his bread—and that Acadians earned their bread otherwise. Hence, when British and French heroes fought, the Acadians preferred to be somewhere else.

Those Acadians who had the misfortune to have homesteads near where the French stationed troops had developed their own method of civil defense. When the British attacked they would simply pile as many of their valuables as they could into carts, and take off for the forest. One visitor to Acadia long before the war broke out said that as his ship approached, the Acadians were for a time uncertain of its nationality. "When we landed and they knew we were friends, we saw the carts coming back."

After the British attack of 1704 failed but barely, a new French governor was appointed; this appointment shows how important Acadia had become in French military planning. Governor Subercase was probably the most experienced military leader in New France. He had been a brigadier in Frontenac's decisive campaign against the Onondaga. In this new war he had already distinguished himself by leading a successful raid against British settlements in Newfoundland. He could preserve Acadia for France if anyone could.

What Subercase found in Acadia he did not like. He regarded the Acadians as so narrowly selfish as to be simply disloyal. "Nobody could suffer more than I do at seeing the English so coolly carry on their trade under our very noses." The French officials in Acadia were as a result completely demoralized. "I am as much in needs of a madhouse as of a barracks; and what is worse, I am afraid that the evil spirit of this country will drive me crazy too." In short, he concluded, "There is no country on earth I would not rather live than in this, by reason of the ill-disposed persons who inhabit." But Subercase also had to admit contrarily, "The more I consider these people the more I believe they are the happiest people in the world." This was the particular form of schizophrenia to which Acadia drove any ambitious person forced to live there. Looking at the smug Acadians, one might begin to think that being happy in this life is not difficult.

In 1707 Subercase repulsed two attacks on Acadia, only partly by his own skill. This skill would have been of little use had not the leaders of these attacks been both timid and incompetent. Subercase knew his luck could not continue indefinitely, and he pleaded with France for support. He no longer had money to pay his troops or buy provisions for them. "I have managed to borrow enough to maintain the garrison for the last two years, and have paid what I could by selling all my furniture." (The next time the British attacked he could watch his furniture being given safe conduct to the forest by Acadians.)

Subercase's pleas reached France when the fortunes of Louis in this particular war (and perhaps any of his wars) were at their nadir. Louis had suffered a series of defeats so disastrous that even some of his inner circle of sycophants were wondering if the War of the Spanish Succession was not being used by God to remind the Sun King that he was after all a mere creature. With France on the verge of having peace terms dictated to it, the troubles of Acadia were dismissed as a mere nuisance. Subercase found himself being informed that "the king would abandon the colony if it continues to be such a burden."

While France was understandably preoccupied with minimizing its losses in Europe, the British were planning to conquer the whole of New France. In this conquest Acadia was going to be the first stop for the invading sea forces. British colonials gathered their troops for the great invasion, and waited for the promised fleet to arrive from Britain. Then the very weakness of France, which had caused the military neglect of Acadia, temporarily came to its rescue.

The British fleet, poised for the invasion of New France, was at the last moment diverted to the European theater. Articles of peace, articles of French capitulation really, had been secretly drawn up that very year, and had just been approved by the French representatives. All that was required was Louis XIV's personal approval, which was thought inevitable. One article of the peace specified that all colonies taken during the war would be returned to their original owners. The invasion of New France was pointless. And it was postponed indefinitely.

But Louis could not bring himself to sign the treaty. He knew he should, but he could not sign something that even a modest monarch would have found humbling. So the war continued, and in 1710 a fleet of thirty-six British vessels with thousands of troops appeared off Acadia.

Subercase, his fort already a shambles without a shot having been fired, was outnumbered ten to one. He could skirmish with the British with his loyal Indians, but he did not dare even let his regular troops out of the fort lest they desert to the woods. The canoes had to be guarded, but the drafted Acadian militiamen managed to slip away still. Wonderful Acadia! Subercase returned British cannon fire just to keep up pretenses.

With almost no resources Subercase still did his best. He sent an officer to the British commander under a flag of peace. The French had women in the fort; would the British commander grant them safe passage? The commander gallantly replied that he had not come to make war on women. But he also noticed that the French emissary, while delivering his message, did not fail to look around. He suspected, rather ungallantly, that the messenger's errand was as much for intelligence as for mercy. The French emissary was therefore detained in the British camp, and the British reply was carried to Subercase by one of their own.

Subercase now was in earnest shock. In all his military service he had never heard of a mere messenger sent under a flag of truce being arrested—and, by the way, would the British commander please be so good as to send all future communiqués in French, for the French commander regrets that his English is not so good? The British commander, in response, wondered (in English) why Subercase was now more concerned about the return of his officer than the safety of his ladies—but he would certainly be happy to write Subercase in French, if Subercase would first do him the honor of writing him in English, for his own French, alas, was neither so good. Subercase had gotten nowhere, but at least it had taken him a week.

He inquired of the British emissary, now his hostage as well, where the British commander had his headquarters. If Subercase only knew, he could make certain that it was spared cannon fire. The French were going to win this contest, but they certainly wanted to win it fairly. Subercase would feel personally almost dishonored if a stray cannonball happened to wipe out the whole British general staff. The British emissary, to whom Subercase's chivalry did not seem altogether above suspicion, replied, "Sometimes in a bottom, sometimes in a hill, sometimes in a hedge, sometimes between two bear skins." (If the French officer had only been allowed to return, Subercase might have had an idea where those bear skins were hung.)

Subercase now had sudden concern about the health and morale of the British troops. How were they bearing up? The bitter Canadian cold was certainly difficult to endure. His British captive replied that it only served to remind them of home.

The British commander finally made it known that he was done negotiating with Subercase; the choice was surrender or fight. Well, somehow Subercase had not been able to find his honorable brother-in-arms with a cannonball—and, unfortunately, there was not a blizzard or plague in sight. He surrendered. His men with Subercase at their head were allowed to leave the fort with full military honors, colors flying—and they were guaranteed safe passage back to France. Subercase himself was allowed to take six cannon with him, but these in fact he quickly sold to the British to be able to pay off his remaining debts before leaving, and perhaps to buy back a few of his chairs.

Subercase had much praise for his distinguished adversary, and promised to pay him a return visit the next spring, with a few thousand friends. Actually, when Subercase returned to France, he retired almost immediately. He wished no more assignments to places like Acadia. And he did leave behind one piece of mischief for the French government. In his articles of surrender he had described his own region of command more than generously—indeed, he included under "Acadia" substantial portions of the Canadian mainland. This made the ceremonial surrender more grandiose, but this description would eventually be used by the British to document claims of sovereignty that extended far beyond the traditional boundaries of Acadia.

Even so, one must not be too hard on Subercase, although he did get a little carried away by the occasion. After all, if Louis XIV could claim the whole Spanish empire for his line, should not an able but ill-supported colonial governor be permitted a little exaggeration as well?

While Acadia was being occupied by the British, elsewhere things were going well for France. In Europe the series of unexpected defeats had been followed by a series of equally unexpected victories. France was far from winning the war, but she was now strong enough to negotiate a peace—and Louis could be reassured of God's continued commitment to his people and himself.

This divine commitment, however, was not sufficient to prevent the loss of some territory as a result of his Spanish adventure. In the New World his chief loss was to be Acadia. Actually, during the negotiations for the Treaty of Utrecht, Louis realized belatedly the geographical importance of Acadia. He no longer regarded it as a burden to be abandoned for its trouble. He wrote to his negotiators, "It is so important to prevent the breaking off of the negotiations that the King will give up both Acadia and Cape Breton, if necessary for peace; but the plenipotentiaries will yield this point only in the last extremity, for by this double cession Canada will become useless, the access to it will be closed, the fisheries will come to an end, and the French marine be utterly destroyed."

Louis offered for the restoration of Acadia three islands in the West Indies. When this was refused, he offered concessions in both Hudson Bay and Newfoundland, but the English rejected these as well. The best the negotiators could do was to retain Cape Breton, the island to the northeast of Acadia, between it and the mouth of the Saint Lawrence.

This island, all that stood between the British and the entrance to Saint Lawrence, all that stood between the British and control of contact between France and New France, had to be strengthened. First its name was strengthened. Now it was no longer a mere peasant, Cape Breton—now it was a true Isle Royale. Isle Royale was to be defended by a great fort, Louisbourg, to be built there. And this island was to be populated by loyal, courageous, steadfast, patriotic Frenchmen—namely, the Acadians.

The Treaty of Utrecht specified that Acadians were free "to remove themselves with all their movable effects." And the occupying British forces were responsible for providing transport. The French thought they could trust the English at least here, and so they could. In the four years that the British had occupied Acadia between its fall and the Treaty of Utrecht, they had had a taste of what it was like to try to govern these people. So the French officials could count on the British to provide the boats—the people on whom they could not count were the loyal, courageous, steadfast, patriotic Acadians.

At first everything seemed to be going according to plan. The British authorities permitted French officials to hold a series of meetings, one at each of the main settlement areas in Acadia. The many advantages of moving to Isle Royale were explained in scrupulous detail. The meetings were well attended and the crowds very appreciative. They seemed to be having such a good time. A delegation of Acadians was transported to inspect their new homeland. The French officials were so confident that they regarded this trip as a mere formality before the mass migration began. Everyone was stunned when the mass migration never materialized—everyone except anyone who had had any previous dealings with the Acadians. One of their priests diplomatically did try to explain their refusal:

"It would expose us manifestly (they say) to die of hunger, burdened as we are with large families, to quit dwelling places and clearances from which we derive our usual subsistence, without any other resource, to take rough, new lands, from which standing wood must be removed. . . . One-fourth of our population consists of aged persons, unfit for the labor of breaking up new lands, and who, with great exertion, are able to cultivate the cleared ground which supplies the subsistence for them and their families."

The reasoning can be put less diplomatically. Cape Breton was becoming an island royal, and settlements were to be placed in Louis's town. French government and military were going to dominate this artificially established colony to a degree that they had never dominated Acadia. Significantly, as the Acadian population had grown in the late seventeenth and early eighteenth centuries, it had moved proportionately away from wherever there were French garrisons. Everyone on Cape Breton was going to be in the shadow of a French garrison.

Moreover, while the Acadians were establishing themselves on Cape Breton, they were not going to be getting as much to eat as they would if they stayed—maybe enough, but not as much. And they were going to work a lot harder. Why do that? They were even going to have to clear forests, something they had managed to avoid for generations in Acadia. And the older people, these respected heads of extended families, preferred to remain where they had always lived, even if that meant some slight inconvenience to the king of France. On reflection, the Acadians decided they were birds that did not want the trouble of building a new nest in a strange tree.

But did the Acadians really want to be British subjects? Well, not quite—but then the Acadians had never really considered themselves French subjects either. Inevitably, there would always be some outsiders stationed in Acadia because that was the way the world was. Obviously the Acadians would prefer officials who were Catholic and spoke French—but most of all they would prefer officials who were weak, so weak they could not intrude into Acadian life even if they wanted to. In this sense British Protestants made much better officials than did French Catholics.

In addition, the Micmacs hated the British. The first British governor had sent out a woodcutting expedition from the fort at Port Royal (now called Annapolis). Only twelve miles from the fort it had been massacred; seventy men in all had been lost. The British governor was now buying his wood from Acadians, and the British troops were not inclined to take sightseeing trips in the countryside.

So the British were reduced to sitting in their garrisons, staring up toward Cape Breton, thinking deep geopolitical thoughts. And the Acadians would be left alone, to tend their dikes and fields, to hunt in the woods with the Micmacs, to squabble with one another (now in a British court, a wonderful novelty), and to watch their families grow.

The British, however, had this strange idea that since the Acadians had chosen to stay they should swear allegiance to the British crown. When in 1714 George I ascended to the throne, they even had a formal oath drawn up. With much pomp it was presented to the Acadians, who rejected it with no pomp at all.

Actually, a few dozen inhabitants of Port Royal (who presumably supplied things to the fort) did happily swear to an oath, but somehow it was not quite the one the British provided. They promised to be loyal if the British government promised to let them leave with their goods whenever they wanted. This was not an oath of allegiance, it was a deal. The Acadians promised to be temporarily loyal, if the British promised to let them go when they decided to become disloyal. This was not the kind of allegiance the British government had in mind.

In 1717 another try was made. Once again, the Acadians were supplied with an oath. Once again, some of them returned their own version. The British governor did not want to negotiate with his subjects; he wanted to be obeyed. But negotiations are what he got. The Acadian document respectfully observed that the British did not seem to be having very happy relations with the Micmacs, and that it would grieve the Acadians deeply if the Micmacs started to mistake them for British. Therefore, they could in good conscience only sign the oath if the British were to promise to protect them. "Unless we are protected from them, we cannot take the oath demanded without exposing ourselves to have our throats cut in our houses at any time."

The official who received this communiqué was infuriated by it. The Acadians were not obeying the law, and obedience to the law is the first principle of a good society. (The Acadians could reply, of course, that they were no nation of philosophers.) What actually seems to have infuriated the official most was not what the document said (which was bad enough) but its physical condition. It was filthy, and he found himself having to apologize to his superiors for sending themselves so dirty an item. (Alas, hygiene was another of the polite arts not highly developed in Acadia.)

The document might have been dirty, but it was shrewd in the extreme. It set as a condition something that, however reasonable it sounded, both sides knew could never be met. Shrewder still was the alternative condition the dirty document offered, an alternative condition under which the Acadians would happily pledge their allegiance. They would take an oath of allegiance if it specified that the Acadians "will take up arms neither against his Britannic Majesty nor against France nor against any of their subjects or allies." They would swear allegiance if they were given permanent status as noncombatants.

Time and again the British government tried to get the Acadians to swear allegiance—and time and again they added their own conditions. After a while the Acadians began to claim that the special status they were requesting as French neutrals under British rule was not unreasonable because the British themselves had failed to fulfill the stipulation of the Treaty of Utrecht to provide them with transportation for their emigration. The British responded that they had not supplied the transportation because the Acadians had decided to stay, and could never quite understand why the Acadians regarded this response as self-evidently irrelevant.

When George II ascended the throne, a British officer was so eager to get the Acadians finally to pledge their allegiance that he submitted to every concession they asked: "1) That they shall be exempt from taking up arms against any one, so long as they shall be under the rule of the King of England; 2) That they shall be free to withdraw whithersoever they will think fit, and that they shall be discharged from this signed agreement, as soon as they shall be outside the domination of the King of England; 3) That they shall have full and entire liberty to practice their religion and to have Catholic, Apostolic and Roman priests."

The functionaries in London were far from pleased with these unauthorized concessions, and did not regard the oath as legitimate. Nonetheless, the

British Empire had in fact capitulated, at least temporarily, to these dirty contentious farmers who had not a single plenipotentiary among them. The British in their official documents had begun to refer to the Acadians as the "French Neutrals."

And the Acadians went back to doing what they did best—farming, fishing and hunting, eating, bickering, praying, and making babies. Under the British they were particularly successful at making babies. A population that was under two thousand in 1710 when the British took over would become by 1740 close to ten thousand. By this time it had begun to dawn on the British that in these very numbers the Acadians were inflicting upon them another defeat.

In 1740 a governor wrote back to London, "The increase of Acadians calls for some fresh instruction how to dispose of them." A few years later the governor of Massachusetts, William Shirley, concluded that the original conquerors of Acadia should have "sent away the French inhabitants when they were not so numerous . . . in 1710, and have them replaced during times of peace with Protestant subjects." In 1749 a new governor of Nova Scotia on his arrival noted in disgust that Acadia "has been called an English province for thirty-four years and I don't believe that the King has one true subject without the fort of Annapolis. I cannot trace the least glimpse of an English government."

The new governor, however, was being unfair. The man he was succeeding, Paul Mascarene, was prepared to argue that the Acadians had proven quite true subjects, if one forgot about the formality of the oath. Mascarene was well satisfied with both the Acadians and his own handling of them. "I used our French inhabitants with so much mildness, administered justice so impartially and employed all the skill I was master of in managing them to so good purpose" that they now obviously preferred a continuing British rule to a return of the French. Mascarene was, of course, congratulating himself in this assessment—and yet the French agreed. They saw the policy of mildness as shrewd in the extreme, and ominous. Or as a governor of New France wrote: "The English, having in view the conquest of Canada, wished to give the French of that colony, in their conduct towards the Acadians, a striking example of the mildness of their government. . . . They have left them the appearance of liberty so excessive that they have not intervened in their disputes or even punished their crimes. They have allowed them to refuse with insolence certain moderate rents payable in grain and lawfully due. They have passed over in silence the contemptuous refusal of the Acadians to take titles from them for the new lands which they chose to occupy."

The Acadians seemed to have the kind of government they had always wanted. And they in turn had become British subjects who were, if not exemplary, at least acceptable. Mascarene had worked hard to convince both Governor Shirley of Massachusetts and the Board of Trade in London that the Acadians were passable subjects. He knew perfectly well that before the most recent war the British Board of Trade had declared: "It is absolutely necessary for Your Majesty's Service, that these French inhabitants should be removed; for it is not to be expected, that they will ever become good Subjects to Your Majesty; and there is all the reason in the world to apprehend, that upon any rupture between the two crowns, they may openly declare in favor of France."

All the reason in the world had turned out to be false, and Mascarene was not going to let anyone forget that. The Acadians had not sought an occasion for treachery. They had proven as good a group of subjects for the one crown as they had ever been for the other. Mascarene would take the Acadians' side against the slanders that had become commonplace in London, Boston, or even among the ignorant within the fort at Annapolis. Punish any Acadian that allowed himself to be gulled into treason, but do not punish the Acadians on the supposition that they might become traitorous.

Mascarene was a good advocate. Even William Shirley, who if he could have had his way would have patriotically removed all the French from the whole of North America (if not the world), was at least partly persuaded by Mascarene's arguments. He realized with some reluctance that the expulsion of the Acadians, although it could be justified legally, was probably both impractical and immoral. He conceded, "It may perhaps be deem'd too rigorous a punishment for their behavior grounded on such a mistake, to involve the innocent with the guilty in the loss of their estates and the expulsion of their families out of the country." Shirley, under the tutelage of Mascarene, had begun to feel some sympathy for this peace-loving people who were "continually plac'd between two fires."

The softening of Shirley was not entirely Mascarene's doing—part of it was pragmatism. During the War of the Austrian Succession, the British with the strong support of Shirley had attempted a conquest of New France, and had failed miserably. Their one great victory was the capture of Louisbourg; and then at the peace talks, to the utter horror of Shirley and his fellow colonials, the British had traded Louisbourg back to the French for other concessions. As much as Shirley wanted complete victory, the British had not even made any significant gains; nor, with Louisbourg back in French hands, were any substantial gains foreseeable. Under such circumstances the neutrality of the Acadians looked good.

Paul Mascarene had one final reason for hope as he left office in 1749. The Acadians would never be left in peace so long as the British and French disputed over the boundaries of Acadia. Although the Treaty of Aix-la-Chapelle did not specifically resolve such boundary disputes, its eighteenth article said that any remaining disputes between France and Britain "shall be amicably adjusted immediately by the commissionaries appointed for that purpose, on both sides, or otherwise, as shall be agreed on by the powers concerned." One such dispute was the meaning of the clause in the earlier Treaty of Utrecht where Louis XIV had ceded to Britain "Nova Scotia, otherwise called Acadia, in its entirety, conformable to its former limits; as also the town of Port Royal, now called Annapolis Royal, and generally all dependencies of the said lands."

What did the "former limits" and "all dependencies" mean in practice? "Nova Scotia," as it was long ago defined in a land grant to Sir William Alexander, included all land from the Acadian peninsula to the Saint Lawrence. By such a definition the British would be justified in establishing a fort across the river from Quebec. The French had their own definition of "Acadia." It was only the southern half of the peninsula. Each side could and did defend its particular interpretation with many reasonings very ingenious and very uncertain.

The military reality, however, was rather straightforward. The French could exercise their control over the northern half of the peninsula only through the raids of the Micmacs—that is, they had no real power on the peninsula beyond the ability to harass the British. The British, on the other hand, could occasionally show the flag on the mainland, but the moment they returned to the peninsula it went back to French control. The real boundary between Acadia and New France was the Chignecto isthmus. Indeed, the boundary could be drawn even more precisely.

The Missaguash River cut the peninsula roughly in half. In 1750 the French established Fort Beauséjour on its western banks; from this fort it hoped to direct French efforts in the northern peninsula. Almost simultaneously, the British had sent out troops to occupy the St. John River Valley on the mainland. Blocked by the new French fort, they built their own, Fort Lawrence, on the eastern bank of the Missaguash. There the two hostile forces sat, within clear sight of each other—like two nests of insects, threatening to devour each other over a piece of mud.

Everything seemed to be working toward a peaceful settlement of the Acadian question, however disappointing this might be for the heroic patriots of the forts. A boundary for Acadia had been established *de facto*. The Treaty of Aix-la-Chapelle provided the legal means for a formal resolution. When the

French proposed that a commission be established to settle North American boundary disputes, and the British quickly agreed, there was good reason to be optimistic. Indeed, the British in accepting the invitation even seemed to concede the French claim that the land beyond the isthmus was theirs. "It never was the King's intention in settling His province of Nova Scotia, either to infringe upon the right of His Most Christian Majesty, or to take forcible possession of a country (the right to which His Majesty had agreed should be referred to Commissionaries to be named by each court) before those Commissionaries could have possibly met to settle the boundaries of it." In short, the British insisted—in a spirit of almost repentance—that they "Neither yet made nor had any intention of making any establishment without the limits of the peninsula." This was untrue, but perhaps the British were lying to signal their good intentions for the future.

The commissioners who were appointed on each side also showed that both countries regarded this commission as crucial in keeping the peace within North America. Leading the French delegation was Roland-Michel Barrin, Comte de La Galissonière, who had just finished a term as governor of New France. On the British side was Governor William Shirley, probably the most knowledgeable colonial official on the question of northern boundaries. The commissioners were supposed to treat not only the Acadian boundaries, but also disputes about the western borders of the British colonies and a difference over the possession of certain islands in the West Indies. Nonetheless, Acadia, everyone recognized, was the pivotal issue. Indeed, the Duke of Newcastle put it even more forcefully: "I think it the most ticklish, and the most important point, that we have almost ever had, *singly*, to negotiate with France."

The Acadians undoubtedly had at the very best a faint idea what these very important persons were doing far away in Europe. Such matters were well beyond their field of vision. And if someone had taken the trouble to explain it all to them, he would likely have been met with an indifferent shrug. Nonetheless, Mascarene would have known the importance of these negotiations for the Acadians whom he now in a strange way respected. If the negotiations succeeded, the Acadians were likely to be left in peace for another generation.

In August 1750 the first meeting of the commissioners took place at the Paris home of La Galissonière, another promising sign. As their first official act, they exchanged instructions—and there and then promising signs stopped. The French had been empowered to discuss a much broader range of issues than the British. The governments had obviously not been in as close communication with each other in preparing the commission as would have been hoped. Still, this was a minor setback. The commissioners agreed to inform their respective governments of the discrepancy and ask for clarification.

They then proceeded to establish the order in which the various issues would be discussed. The British commissioners suggested that the Acadian issue be settled first, and then the West Indian disputes could be turned to. Obviously, the Acadian question was the most important. The French, however, preferred another arrangement. They preferred to discuss the two questions simultaneously. La Galissonière, moreover, suggested that the commissioners agree as to the principle on which they were going to settle the boundaries; both sides should express their willingness "to renounce anything that would give their respective colonists in America the temptation and the means to annoy, attack, or invade each other with ease and success."

Shirley now became suspicious. What was La Galissonière after? The French obviously thought that if the British could successfully attack Louisbourg again, they could control the entrance to the Saint Lawrence and hence invade New France with ease. Did the French want to discuss the two issues of Acadia and the West Indies together so that they would have the opportunity to tie French concessions in the West Indies to British concessions in Acadia? Were they going to try to get through negotiations what they could not get militarily? Were they trying to swindle these British negotiators out of northern Acadia much as they had swindled other British negotiators out of the Louisbourg fort that Shirley and his men had so gallantly taken in the last war?

In fact that seems to have been exactly what La Galissonière wanted. A few years earlier he had written a secret report in which he argued that New France was militarily indefensible if the French did not control the northern coast of the Acadian peninsula. New France needed to be able to keep in communication with France during the long winters when the Saint Lawrence was not navigable. An overland route to the Atlantic was a strategic necessity and Louisbourg plus the northern half of Acadia was a strategic necessity as well if the conquest of New France was not to be a persistent temptation for men like Shirley. The negotiators of the Treaty of Utrecht had given to La Galissonière half of what he needed. He was going to try to get the other half, and this principle of renouncing territories that might tempt colonists to conquest was a first step.

But the British were wary, and the French found their principle of renunciation—which seemed so innocuous on the surface—rejected forcefully.

British commissioners assured their French brothers that they had not come to Paris to compromise their Majesty's true rights.

In a subsequent meeting La Galissonière finally unveiled his arguments that "Acadia" did not include all of the peninsula—indeed, it did not even include Port Royal. The British incredulously asked him if he might help them by drawing these "true" boundaries, for the Acadia he imagined they could find nowhere on their maps. The French replied that this was not necessary. After all, the British were the "demanders" (read "invaders"). Whatever they could not prove to be within the ancient boundaries of Acadia was obviously without. The British should assume the burden of proof—and the French would then tell them which of their proofs, if any, were convincing.

The British, however, could never be persuaded that this was an equitable division of labor. At the end of this particular meeting, now that it was clear that the French commissioners would never accept the *de facto* boundary of Acadia, the negotiations were for all intents and purposes (except those of propaganda) over. The commissioners admitted as much when they agreed that all future communications between them would be in writing. Now that they both realized the particular diplomatic minuet they were dancing, they no longer felt the need to look each other in the face.

With the commissioners reduced to exchanging historical disquisitions on boundaries, the commission no longer had any reason to continue. Such exchanges could occur just as effectively through normal diplomatic channels. The British occasionally suggested the dissolution of the commission for this reason. But the French resolutely rejected this sensible suggestion, presumably because the British thought of it first. And so the minuet continued.

The earliest maps show that Acadia is only a small portion of land along the southeastern coast. How could the British explain that?

The earliest maps also show New France as a thin strip along the Saint Lawrence. Will the French be willing to accept that as a boundary as well?

Canada is not at issue here, Acadia is. And the Treaty of Utrecht specifies "ancient" boundaries.

"Ancient" does not mean "oldest," but "traditional" or "customary." And Governor Subercase himself delineated these in the very terms of his surrender.

What Subercase surrendered and what the negotiators at Utrecht agreed to are quite different things. "Ancient boundaries" in the latter context was a concession on the part of the British that restored much of the peninsula back to France.

And so it continued, month after month, resembling more and more one of those interminable wrangles that the Acadians so enjoyed. Actually the negotiations, if they can be called that, almost broke down at one point—appropriately not over a substantive issue but a purely verbal one. The French had objected to the intemperate language of the English. The English replied that the language in question was not intemperate. The French replied that the memorial was in French and they knew *gauche* French when they read it. The English vowed never to send another memorial to their counterparts except in English. The French complained that French was the language of diplomacy, the language of culture, the language of the world. How could they be expected to read things written in a barbarous and insular tongue? Finally a magnificent compromise was reached. The English would submit their communications in both English and French. Henceforth, if the French complained about the intemperate language, the English could reply the original was chaste. This linguistic phase of the negotiating took a whole year.

The negotiations were finally terminated in 1755. One would say "mercifully terminated," if this end had not been occasioned by the beginning of war between France and Britain. Subsequently the French published a collection of all the memorials of the French and British commissioners (in French), since these memorials as a whole obviously supported the French claims. The English responded by printing their edition of the same memorials, since these memorials (at least in English) obviously supported the British claims. The French responded the next year with a volume explaining why the facts supported the French contention that the memorials supported French rather than British claims. . . . After all this, war was a relief at least in its straightforwardness.

While the negotiations in Paris had been going nowhere slowly, the situation of the Acadians—which had seemed so promising in 1749—was deteriorating rapidly. The return of Louisbourg to the French meant that Acadia had to become New England's firmest rampart against the intrusions of the French. The British troops that had occupied Louisbourg were to be transferred to Acadia, but what were they to guard? George Dunk, the Earl of Halifax, had convinced the Board of Trade that "the only means of preserving this country is by a well regulated settlement of it. . . . I take the present consideration to be no other than whether we shall settle or we shall lose the province of Nova Scotia."

Protestant settlement of Nova Scotia had been proposed since the original conquest, but Halifax finally got the financial support of the government. The French Acadians, behaving completely in character, had left the best harbor on the Atlantic coast of Acadia, a harbor of extraordinary military and commercial potential, unoccupied. The British could develop it with a few thousand settlers and the garrison from Louisbourg. The British government agreed, and named the new town in honor of its proposer, Halifax. Other settlements, some of continental Protestants, were also proposed and given financial support.

Men were promised fifty acres (plus ten more for every additional family member), no taxes for ten years (and low taxes after that), free passage, and tools sufficient to establish the homestead. It sounded too good to be true, and soon ditties were being published in London about the promised land called Nova Scotia.

> Let's away to New Scotland, where Plenty sits as queen
> O'er as happy a country as ever was seen;
> And blesses her subjects, both little and great,
> With each a good house, and a pretty estate.

Although there was some grumbling about the quality of the people attracted—one official called it an "asylum for all vagabonds"—the town of Halifax survived and grew. By 1757 its population was three thousand.

This new settlement was obviously threatening to the Acadians. The British settlers did not displace any Acadians from land they already held, but they were still a disturbing presence. The Acadians, no less than the Indians, knew of the huge, ever-expanding population of New England. Who was to say where the settlement of Nova Scotia was going to stop? Would one day they have enough Protestant settlers to expel the native Acadians entirely?

When a new governor tried, like his predecessors, to order the Acadians to take an oath of loyalty to the British crown, the Acadians gave their tried-and-true reply. They would be happy to swear to an oath that guaranteed their status as neutrals.

To the new settlers Acadian behavior seemed incredible, or rather British toleration of it did. How could the Acadians get away with such impudence? For these despicable people disrespect and ingratitude seemed a hereditary trait. And their refusal to sign the legitimate oath was just a bluff, which the new settlers very much wanted to have called. As they struggled to survive their first few winters on these desolate northern bays, they looked with envy at the already-established Acadians. They found themselves surrounded by French barbarians and Indian savages living together in comfortable circumstances, at least far more comfortable than things were in Halifax for people unused to the hardships and isolation of frontier life. Knowing the Acadians hardly at all, the new settlers had little trouble passing judgment on them all.

One settler jotted down in his diary: "They sent a memorial sign'd by a thousand French as I thought somewhat insolent etc. The governor answer'd it—still refused taking oath—still pretend their fear of the Indians. Argued with but to no purpose—why all this?" Looking out at French Acadia from struggling Halifax, settlers saw a land of milk and honey, and butter and eggs, and treachery and sedition.

Why all this? Why take seriously the venerable humbug about their neutrality when they still could not even speak English? They had the reputation of being neutral only because they had not yet done anything openly treasonable. But everyone knew that they were as pro-French as the Indians. The Acadians were just shrewder. They were not only enemies of the British, they were bloody treacherous dissemblers so good at their game that they were hardly ever caught. Everyone knew they were intermarried with the Indians, and shared with them their priests and papist superstitions. The Acadians had nothing to fear from these Indians, and they knew it.

So suspicions could turn to certainties in embittered minds. And the activities of the Micmacs were additional cause for bitterness. The British had much to fear from them, and that made the Acadians' apparent duplicity even harder to tolerate.

The British had made the mistake of allowing some loyal Indian troops from New England, Mohawks, to go on a rampage against the Micmacs during which they spared neither women nor children. This ended what little hope there was of a peaceful coexistence between the Micmacs and the new British settlements. Any attempt to expand these settlements beyond a few well-protected enclaves like Halifax was met with severe reprisals.

For instance, a Major Gilman tried to establish a sawmill at a place called Dartmouth. That very year four of his workers were killed (two found scalped, two decapitated) and a fifth carried off. Gilman, however, persisted. By 1751 his sawmill was a small town in embryo when the Micmacs attacked again, and treated the British as the Mohawks had treated them. No one was spared.

"A little baby was found lying by its father and mother, all three scalped. The whole town was a scene of butchery, some having their hands cut off, some their bellies ripp'd open, and others their brains dash'd out." John Wilson's *A Genuine Narrative of the Transactions in Nova Scotia*, published in London in the early 1750s, could not have presented a more striking contrast with the whimsical ditties of a few years before. "These Indians chain the unfortunate prisoner to a large thick tree, and bind his hands and his feet, then beginning from the middle of the craneum, they cut quite round towards the neck; this being done, they then tear off skin, leaving the skull bare; an inflammation quickly follows, the patient fevers, and dies in the most exquisite torture." O let's away to Nova Scotia, where Plenty sits as queen over as happy a country as ever has been seen.

No one had any doubt that these attacks on the British were in fact being supplied and directed by the French. The British governor wrote, "What we call here an Indian war is no other than a pretence for the French to commit hostilities on His Majesty's subjects." And in this judgment the British were entirely right, as contemporary French documents make clear:

"It is to be desired that these savages should succeed in thwarting the designs of the English and even their settlement at Halifax. They are bent on doing so; and if they can carry out their plans, it is certain that they will give the English great trouble, and so harass them that they will be a great obstacle in their path. These savages are to act alone; neither soldier nor French inhabitant is to join them; everything will be done of their own motion, and without showing that I had any knowledge of the matter. This is very essential; I have written to the Sieur de Boishebert to observe great prudence in his measures, and to act very secretly, in order that the English may not perceive that we are providing for the needs of said savages."

So the Marquis de La Jonquière, the governor of New France, described his strategy. In Acadia he had found a way to improve on Frontenac's old tactics. Now Frenchmen would no longer have to fight beside Indians and like Indians; now they could privately employ Indians as their surrogates, and then publicly strike a high moral stance.

Of course, if the French were not going to fight beside their Indian allies, how could they still direct their operations? La Jonquière had thought of that too. "It will be the missionaries who will manage all the negotiation, and direct the movements of the savages, who are in excellent hands, as Reverend Father Germain and Monsieur Abbé Le Loutre are very capable of making the most of them, and using them to the greatest advantage for our interests. They will manage their intrigue in such a way as not to appear in it."

Monsieur Abbé Le Loutre was particularly capable of making the most of them. In August 1753 a French official wrote, "Last month the savages took eighteen hundred English scalps, and Monsieur Le Loutre was obliged to pay them . . . Acadian money, which I have reimbursed him."

When Le Loutre eventually wrote his autobiography—in the third person—he insisted that his own motives were entirely religious. "The loss of so many souls confided to his care, who would have been infallibly perverted if the English had been able to win them over, was what he alone considered; no other motive could be brought to bear on the Missionary." Nonetheless, he also admitted that he had been offered religious liberty and a huge bribe to stop his raids. "The Missionary replied that everything in the world could never cause him to commit the crime of unfaithfulness to his King, that he was a Frenchman and would die one." For Abbé Le Loutre the choice between dying as a Frenchman and living as a Christian was not hard. In his chapel a fresh scalp might be hung next to the crucifix, and without any sense of incongruous juxtaposition.

His Micmacs had been the ones who had suffered from the Mohawk raid led by the English. The English he hated and would continue to hate until doomsday. Should he not hate what was detestable? Were there not times when cruelty was right? He knew how to hate the British because he knew how to love his king, and also his God.

Le Loutre was a wonderfully effective agent. As one contemporary said in admiration, "Nobody was more fit than he to carry the discord and desolation into a country." So effective was he, so zealous in the service of discord and desolation, that he sometimes worried the French themselves. "Excite them to keep the Indians in our interest, but do not let them compromise us. Act always so as to make the English appear as aggressors."

Needless to say, the British were not fooled in the slightest. They knew perfectly well that the Indians were being directed by the French missionaries. While Le Loutre was paying out a hundred livres for any British scalp, the governor of Nova Scotia was offering a hundred pounds for his.

The British settlers waited anxiously for news of a final settlement of the Acadian boundaries. That diarist at Halifax wrote: "What I dislike most is that the French have not orders from Europe to draw off their Indians. If anything is settled about the boundaries by the Commissioners, the French might have news tho' we have not. Therefore, I fear they have not settled affairs as we hope for." The commissioners, of course, had not now solved the boundaries as was hoped nor would they ever. And as the French-directed terrorism continued, the British settlers of Halifax had less and less patience with Acadians.

This was an understandable response. Knowing that the Indians were being directed by some French priests, and knowing too that other French priests occupied the leading position in Acadian society, who would not conclude that the Acadians, like the French government, were giving covert aid to the Indians? This was not an unreasonable conclusion, but it happened to be essentially false. Much as earlier the French used the Treaty of Utrecht to try to induce the Acadians to move, now they secretly violated the Treaty of Aix-la-Chapelle to force them to.

The very dispatches that show that the Indian campaign against the British was being financed and directed by the French show also that the Acadians on the whole were trying as usual to remain neutral. "We must give up altogether the idea of an insurrection in Acadia. The Acadians cannot be trusted: they are controlled by fear of the Indians, which leads them to breathe French sentiments, even when their inclinations are English. They will yield to their interests; and the English will make it impossible that they should either hurt them or serve us, unless we take measures different from those we have hitherto pursued." The chief measure that this dispatch had in mind was to turn the Indian terrorism against the Acadians to force them to move into French-controlled territory. There actually survives a communication to the Acadians entitled "Orders by the Savages to the French Inhabitants," which was almost entirely written by Le Loutre.

"Sire, it is to your own interest and that of God that brings us to drive the English from these parts. You see your missionaries driven out, your churches abandoned, your religion snuffed out, it is God that sends you help." The Acadians had to abandon their homesteads and take up arms against the British. Of course, the claim about their religion being suppressed was not true. But Le Loutre was a good enough casuist to explain that lying was only a vice when it did harm—and this particular lie was serving the greater good. Le Loutre was himself praised in one French dispatch as follows: "One thing is sure that without this missionary who has made the Acadians believe whatever he would and has promised them much, they would be very tranquil and so would the English in Chibuctou and on very good terms with the Indians."

Actually the Acadians, in particular those who lived on the isthmus of Chibuctou, were not as gullible as they were presented in this dispatch. When the British had marched to establish Fort Lawrence on the eastern banks of Missaguash, Le Loutre was there first with his Indians. He forced the Acadians to abandon their village of Beaubassin to come to the French side of the river. The village was burned to the ground, all one hundred forty buildings including the village church, which Le Loutre is said to have lit personally.

Soon some of the displaced Acadians were secretly petitioning the English to be allowed to return to Acadia. But they had to be assured neutrality, or the Micmacs under Le Loutre's directions would surely kill them as traitors. At Fort Lawrence there was a Captain How, who was fluent in French and had developed particularly good relations with the Acadians. As such, he was dangerous to Le Loutre's cause. So he was lured into a rendezvous with the French under a white flag, and he was murdered by the Indians. A missionary later explained that the Indians were revenging the Blessed Virgin, a statue of whom How had supposedly mocked some years before.

Despite the efforts to encourage them to remain where they were, the Acadians still tried to find a way to return. In 1753 at Fort Lawrence, eighty swore an oath of loyalty to King George II and were repatriated. Reports were that many more would do so if only they did not have to swear this oath; if they did return and swear the oath, "they would every day run the risk of having their throats cut and their cattle destroyed." By 1754 the Acadians at Beauséjour were reported to be "little short of mutiny" against Le Loutre and the French commander.

Nonetheless, Le Loutre had had his effect. His ruthless tactics had managed to frighten two or three thousand Acadians into abandoning their homes. French officials realized that the Acadians had done so under dire compulsion. As one who had seen them put it, "they leave their homes with great regret, and they began to move their luggage only when the savages compelled them."

And the Acadians who resisted Le Loutre's blandishments, those who remained behind, felt themselves increasingly under siege. When Le Loutre paid for a scalp, could he tell if it was British or Acadian? Might he not reason that the slaughter of a few Acadians would encourage the others?

By 1754 Le Loutre's own religious superior, the Bishop of Quebec, was questioning his methods. The displaced Acadians were obviously becoming more and more bitter against Le Loutre, and against the Church and France. Le Loutre's treatment of those who remained in Acadia was questionable on even more fundamental grounds. "Is it right for you to refuse the sacraments, to threaten that they shall be deprived of the services of a priest, and that the savages shall treat them as enemies? I wish them conscientiously to abandon the lands they possessed under English rule; but is it well proved that they cannot in conscience return to them, *secluso perversionis periculo?*" This, unfortunately, was mere bluster. The present Bishop of Quebec was no Laval. He blusters and then quails. "I think the question too embarrassing to make it the subject of a charge; and I confess that I should have much trouble in deciding, even at the tribunal of penance." A murderous priest was indeed a difficult case—for applied moral theology, and for ecclesiastical public relations.

If the Bishop of Quebec would risk nothing, Thomas Pichon would risk all. Pichon was a minor French official who had become increasingly disillusioned by the French violations of the treaty, at least according to his own later account. He did not believe that "obedience to duty and necessity excuses everything." Obedience to necessity had led the French to conclude the Treaty of Aix-la-Chapelle without any intention of adhering to its conditions. Now French officials were expected to help France "to gain land without, however, admitting the design to do so and in protesting the candor of their intentions, and to continue this move without hesitation up to the moment that they are sufficiently strong to tear away the veil of constraint." A Le Loutre might be content with such a policy. Pichon would quote a Micmac leader and ask, "Is it possible to interpret these words so as to cleanse us of this blot?"

Pichon, a great admirer of Voltaire, would eventually write his own indictment of French policy in a series of letters, much as Voltaire had praised England at the expense of France in his own *Philosophical Letters Concerning the English Nation.* But Voltaire was merciless in exposing mixed motives, how high-sounding justifications often mask the basest selfishness. Thomas Pichon was an ambitious man who, whatever his qualms about French policy, had calculated—correctly—that his own quickest road to advancement was to betray his country. He was given his opportunity when he was appointed a civilian administrator at Fort Beauséjour. Pichon almost immediately offered to spy for the commander of Fort Lawrence, and was quickly accepted with many assurances.

So in 1755, when in Paris the commissioners' negotiations on Acadian boundaries were ending, and when general war between Britain and France seemed imminent, the British knew the strengths and weaknesses of Fort Beauséjour and could be assured of advance warning of any plans there. With such an advantage the British decided upon a preemptive strike against Beauséjour. To wait for a formal declaration of war—well, what place had legalisms in the real world?

The sudden appearance of substantial British reinforcements at Fort Lawrence caught the French commander, if not Thomas Pichon, entirely by surprise. Beauséjour would have to hold out until Louisbourg could be notified and send reinforcements. In the meantime Abbé Le Loutre and his Micmac irregulars had to be used to convince the neighboring Acadians to do their part for God and king.

The commander ordered the Acadians to come to the fort for militia service. They did not seem altogether enthusiastic. They explained to the commander that the British regarded them as British subjects; for them to serve at the French fort meant they would be regarded as traitors. They would come to the French fort, but only if the commander threatened them with death. The commander so threatened, and the Acadians entered into the French service in the strange category of neutral combatants.

The French hoped to stop, or at least delay, the British crossing of the Missaguash. When the British proved too numerous and well supplied, a siege of the fort was inevitable. Le Loutre and the French commander decided that the Acadian homesteads around Beauséjour would provide the sieging British with shelter and provisions; as many as possible were put to the torch by the retreating French.

These were the homesteads of many Acadians at Fort Beauséjour. Some of these Acadians had originally settled near what was now Fort Lawrence. They had already had one home destroyed by Le Loutre for the sake of military strategy. One was enough.

The French commander noted with shock that the Acadians now no longer found their role as neutral combatants to their taste. Those Acadians who could, deserted to the woods. Those who remained behind were less than eager workers preparing the fort for siege. They made it plain that they did not want to be trapped in the fort to die of fire or plague. Le Loutre did his best to quell their doubts, while Pichon secretly did his to fan them; Pichon found a more receptive audience.

Less than two weeks after the arrival of the British troops at Fort Lawrence, the British had progressed far enough to begin to cannonade the fort. That very day the French commander learned that the reinforcements he had requested from Louisbourg would not be sent. Only two days later, after a large explosion had killed a number of French officers, and despite the willingness of Le Loutre to fight to the last Acadian, the French commander, as outmatched as Subercase had been decades before, offered terms for surrender while Le Loutre himself slipped away into the forest. Among the conditions was that the Acadians in the fort not be punished since they had been compelled to serve. The British commander quickly agreed. The news of this victory was met with great joy at Halifax, except for the concession made to the Acadian traitors at the fort. The earlier exodus of those few Acadians who had yielded to Le Loutre's persuasion had already removed what little doubt remained in Halifax that all the professed "neutrals" were traitors waiting for their chance. The episode at Beauséjour showed exactly what they would do in a crisis—first fight for the French, and then if they lost try to hide once again behind their phony neutrality.

The new governor, Charles Lawrence, for one, was not going to let them play much longer at their dishonorable game. Lawrence had been involved in the founding of the fort he named after himself, Fort Lawrence. He had risen to lieutenant governor and then the governor had unexpectedly resigned because of eye trouble. Lawrence could not have been happy under the governorship of his predecessor; Governor Hobson seemed to sympathize with the predicament of the Acadians. For Lawrence this was just another example of his failing sight. Lawrence himself had no eye trouble; he saw everything as it was: black and white.

He saw clearly that he had been lucky to get the governorship so soon. This was his chance to rise high in His Majesty's service, and His Majesty's service was his only chance to rise high, and rising high was the sum of what he wanted. His predecessor's bad luck was his own good. You always rose at the expense of someone else. For you to command, others had to obey; for you to be higher, others had to be lower. A great man, when his chance comes, must be willing to squeeze the orange and throw away the rind.

His predecessors had failed to govern Nova Scotia effectively because they had only half-wills and used only half-measures. No one would ever criticize Governor Lawrence for that. He had used Pichon's reports about Beauséjour to convince Shirley to supply him with troops for a preemptive strike, a strike which had been so successful that for the first time in a generation Nova Scotia seemed secure against French harassment, at least by land.

Now he had to solve the other problem of Nova Scotia, the Acadians. As early as 1754, while still lieutenant governor, he had written to the Board of Trade to express his views of the Acadian problem (and perhaps also to undermine Governor Hobson, who consistently reported that mildness was proving a successful policy). "As it has been generally imagined here that the mildness of an English Government would by degrees have fixed them in our interest, no violent measures have ever been taken with them. But I must observe to your Lordships that this leniency has not had the least good effect; on the contrary, I believe that they have at present laid aside all thoughts of taking the oaths voluntarily . . . and, indeed, while they remain without taking the oaths to His Majesty . . . and have incendiary French priests among them there are no hopes of their amendment."

Lawrence saw the Acadians through the eyes of a Halifax settler. He was infuriated that Acadians prospered while loyal subjects suffered. People in the Protestant settlements often did not have enough food, and yet rumor had it that the Acadians preferred to trade their surplus crops with Louisbourg. The Protestant settlements had to become self-sufficient soon. How much longer would the British government be willing to spend forty thousand pounds a year just to keep these settlements in existence?

Lawrence knew how to ensure the survival—indeed, the prosperity—of these settlements. For the British to prosper, the government had only to remove the Acadians. About this Lawrence was clear, even in 1754: "As they possess the best and largest tracts of land in this province, it cannot be settled with any effect while they remain in this situation, and tho I would be very far from attempting such a step without Your Lordships' approbation, yet I cannot help being of the opinion that it would be much better, if they refuse the oaths, that they were away."

The problem was that their Lordships' approbation was not forthcoming to Lawrence, either as lieutenant governor or governor. There were awkward legalities—for instance, the Acadians seemed to have legitimate titles to their lands, titles guaranteed by treaty. Lawrence was referred to the chief justice to find out if what he wanted to do was actually possible under the law. Lawrence chose not to follow up this suggestion. He would follow another, surer path to his end. Governor Lawrence was determined to get their Lordships' tacit approval, whether they knew they were giving it or not—and certainly without questions of justice ever having been formally decided.

When Lawrence informed the Board of Trade about the fall of Beauséjour, he did tell them about the traitorous Acadians who had supported the French, but he failed to convey the article of surrender which guaranteed them no reprisals. Why should a conquering hero stoop to the servitude of keeping faith? He told the Board of Trade that he had ordered the British commander to use the captured Acadians for whatever labor he needed and then "to drive them out of the country." This is what he told the Board of Trade. What he actually told the commander was somewhat different.

After the fall of Beauséjour the British troops had extended their control far onto the mainland by taking two more forts. Not only was the Chibuctou isthmus secure, so was the route to it. Lawrence did write to the commander about "extirpating" the French who lived on the mainland route: "Unless we remain in possession, undoubtedly the French will return and re-establish; and we can never expect a lasting peace with the Indians, without first totally extirpating the French who incite them to make war, or support them whilst they make it. By the French, I mean both Acadians and Canadians; for it is a question with me, whether the former in those parts are not more our inveterate enemies than the latter."

Anyone who spoke French was for Lawrence the enemy. Certainly if he wanted to extirpate settlers who just happened to live on a militarily important route, he would have no qualms about removing those Acadians who had actively served at Beauséjour. However, he was careful not to bring up the matter directly with the British commander, who after all had himself agreed to the surrender terms. Rather, Lawrence nibbled around the edges of the issue. He admonished the commander not to make any specific promises about the land titles: "I am as yet far from being determined about the fate of your rebellious inhabitants." And he rejected out of hand reports that many of these Acadians were genuinely neutral: "I must have some very convincing proofs of their sorrow and repentance for what is past, before I can prevail with myself to think of their continuing in the possession of those valuable lands."

In truth, Lawrence did not want convincing proofs—he wanted the Acadians away, those who had served at Beauséjour, those who lived nearby, and all the rest. Since you could not tell the guilty from the innocent, all must go; only then could Lawrence be sure that he had a loyal population. This was what he wanted, but doing it was another matter. The Board of Trade was never going to order it, and Lawrence was never going to get caught being insubordinate. So he had to proceed very carefully.

He informed the Board of Trade that he had ordered the Beauséjour traitors to be driven from the country. But he did not so order; rather, he waited for the Board of Trade to respond, if at all. When they did not respond, then they had tacitly agreed that Lawrence could exile traitorous Acadians. This was a step in the right direction, but only a step. Lawrence still had to expand the definition of traitor so that it would cover not only those who bore arms against Britain but also those who refused to swear an oath to bear arms for Britain.

He was helped in taking the next step toward the general expulsion of Acadians by a commander of a lesser British fort in Acadia. Alexander Murray was a kindred spirit to Lawrence—he detested Acadians. Under his leadership, Fort Edwards was even more frequently at odds with the local Acadians than would have been usual. Murray had learned that complaints against his Acadians would never go unappreciated at Halifax. And he interpreted orders from Halifax in ways that were calculated to provoke the Acadians and thereby give him further cause to complain.

Early in his governorship Lawrence had outlawed the export of corn—the Acadians would either provision the Protestant settlements or their surplus food would rot. Murray seems to have reasoned that this order was unenforceable on a disloyal and deceitful population, at least directly. The only way the Acadians could be prevented from trading at Louisbourg would be to prevent them from traveling long distances at all. So Murray confiscated his Acadians' canoes and boats.

Later, when preparations for the assault of Beauséjour were underway, Halifax worried that the Acadians would serve the French side. Murray happily enforced the Halifax order that the Acadians give up their guns. Murray's

Acadians could now neither travel to Louisbourg nor shoot the British—nor could they effectively hunt or fish.

They complained in a sharp petition sent to Murray for the governor. Murray did not receive their petition kindly. The Acadians had the audacity to remind him of their legal neutrality and their traditional rights, and to complain of his arbitrary treatment. Murray in a happy rage sent the memorial on to Governor Lawrence, with his own comments. They had treated his person and his office "with great indecency and insolence." But Murray was not only indignant, he was also suspicious.

Why did they really need their canoes and guns *now?* Why did they feel strong enough to insult so important a person as Alexander Murray? Murray could only conclude that "they had obtained some intelligence, of which we were then ignorant of." His own guess was that they were in contact with an approaching French fleet.

The fleet, of course, was a figment of Murray's malignant imagination. But his confidence that in Halifax he would be believed over anything the Acadians said in their defense was firmly rooted in reality. The Acadians themselves realized this, and soon wrote an alternative report to the council at Halifax, a report that in effect apologized for the tone of the first while reasserting their neutrality and their rights to their guns and canoes. The change in tone made no difference. They had chosen their time most badly.

Fort Beauséjour had fallen the previous week, and they were called to Halifax to explain themselves. Fifteen of the petitioners came; ten others had fallen prudently ill. The council at Halifax, with Lawrence himself sitting on it, chose to regard their original petition as a piece of mutinous arrogance. They were lightly praised for their apology and their prompt coming to Halifax, but then the cross-examination began.

When did they ever provide intelligence to the British? Weren't they really helping the Indians secretly? The Acadians seemed to realize how ominous were the proceedings; there was something happening they did not understand. They tried to fend off the accusatory questions as best they could.

Finally, the matter of the oath was brought up. They assured the council they were willing to swear the traditional oath that guaranteed both their obedience to the British crown and their military neutrality. They were informed that the old oath was now no longer good enough, especially when war had been almost formally declared, especially for a group of people who had behaved so insolently to His Majesty's officials. According to the minutes from this meeting, "They were then informed that a very fair opportunity now presented itself to them to manifest the reality of their obedience to the government by immediately taking the oath of allegiance in the common form before the Council." The Acadians responded that they had not come prepared to swear to a new oath. The council was incredulous that after all this time they had not decided between France and England. Had not they sorted out their loyalties yet?

Now the Acadians only wanted to leave to join their fellows in their sick beds. They respectfully asked that they might go home to "consult the body of the people upon this subject as they could not do otherwise than the generality of the inhabitants should determine, for they were desirous of either refusing or accepting the oath in a body." This had always been an Acadian source of strength; they had usually acted in unison in thwarting efforts to rule them.

But the Halifax council would have none of it. The council was as determined to provoke a crisis as the Acadians were to try to avoid one. The Acadians were told to decide for themselves *now*, and as individuals. They asked if they might have a little time to talk the matter over among themselves. Permission granted. An hour later, the Acadians offered once again to swear the traditional oath. They were again informed that the old oath was no longer good enough. They were given till the next morning to reconsider.

The next morning they persisted in their contention that they could not swear the new oath as individuals without consulting their people. They were informed that they were henceforth to be regarded as French subjects. They were sent bewildered from the room, and were brought back only to hear the council's general determination of the matter. "The council after consideration, were of the opinion that directions should be given to Captain Murray to order the French inhabitants forthwith to choose and send to Halifax, new deputies with the general resolution of the said inhabitants in regard to taking the oath, and that none of them should for the future be admitted to take it after having once refused so to do, but that effectual measures ought to be taken to remove all such recusants out of the province."

Now they finally understood the choices and were thoroughly frightened. Deportation had never been mentioned before. Once it was, they were immediately ready to swear the oath in whatever form required. But Lawrence and the council did not want their oath, they wanted them gone. The Acadians had played into a well-prepared trap, as the legalistic response of the council showed. They were "informed that as there was no reason to hope their proposed compliance proceeded from an honest mind, and could be esteemed only the effect of compulsion and force, and is contrary to a clause in an Act of Parliament, I, Geo. 2. c. 13. whereby persons who have once refused to take the oaths cannot be afterwards permitted to take them, but are considered as popish recusants; therefore they would not now be indulged with such permission, and they were thereupon ordered into confinement."

What is particularly interesting about this legality is that under it Lawrence would have been already justified in considering all Acadians recusants, for they had all already refused the oath and more than once. Having them refuse once again was a mere formality for appearances' sake. But appearances had to be kept up, and the oath had to be proposed once again, in such a way as to assure that the Acadians would behave in character and refuse it. This was an easy enough matter for the impudent petitioners; they were simply not told the punishment until too late. The others would have to be told the threatened consequence. But how could Lawrence then be sure that they would refuse?

Only one thing could assure their refusal: religion. If the oath was presented in such a way that the Acadians suspected it would compromise their right to practice their religion, they would refuse no matter what the consequences. Note the legal precedent Lawrence and the council invoked (and would invoke at the other meetings) to justify only giving the Acadians a single opportunity to swear. It is not an act of Parliament about swearing allegiance to the British government. It is an act of Parliament about swearing allegiance to the Church of England. People who refused to swear were forever branded legally as popish recusants. Le Loutre had been repeatedly telling the Acadians that the moment the British felt militarily secure they would prevent the free exercise of the Catholic religion, much as that exercise had always been prohibited in Shirley's Massachusetts. (There, just to be a Catholic priest was a capital offense.) A series of treaties and governors had assured the Acadians otherwise, but here the worst predictions of Le Loutre seemed to be true. The British felt militarily secure, and now they were calling the Acadians popish recusants. How could the Acadians be expected to understand that Lawrence and Le Loutre were brothers under the skin, who needed one another to be themselves?

Lawrence continued to prepare his case for the general expulsion of Acadians. He wrote to London to inform his superiors that after the victory at Beauséjour he thought the time propitious to propose to the Acadians that they swear to the unqualified oath they had so long resisted. He had decided to begin with a group of deputies who "were attending in town upon a very insolent memorial they had delivered to the Council." These verbally traitorous Acadians refused to swear. They were warned that if they did not swear, they would be exiled. They persisted in their refusal and thereby tacitly chose exile.

This, of course, was a plain lie, but remember Lawrence was not so much interested in the truth as preparing his eventual case. He did not have to admit that these Acadians subsequently had, for some unmentioned reason, reconsidered. He informed the Board of Trade that he would not decide if he was going to allow them to swear "until we see how the rest of the inhabitants are disposed." Of course, he had made up his mind about them, just as he had made up his mind about those at Beauséjour and all the rest.

Lawrence also informed the Board of Trade, "I have ordered new deputies to be elected and sent hither immediately, and am determined to bring the inhabitants to a compliance or rid the province of such perfidious subjects." He checked with two British admirals who happened to be in Nova Scotia to help with the siege of Beauséjour—and they approved of his actions. He closed, "Your Lordships will see our proceedings in this case at large, as soon as it is possible to prepare the minutes of the Council."

The Lordships and their underlings who were reading Lawrence's dispatches would naturally have expected another one soon. This would tell them of the meetings with the deputies, how many swore the oath, how many refused, the general mood, and what Lawrence proposed now to do. The Lordships then could consult among themselves and give or withhold their approbation as they saw fit. They would naturally wait to see what happened before committing themselves one way or another. The Acadians had been a problem for a long time.

But Lawrence was determined that the Acadians would be a problem no longer. He was going to remove the problem on his own authority, without a direct order from his superiors. He had carefully suggested tentatively his preferred line of action; and his superiors, by saying nothing, had tacitly approved of it. Or at least he would say that he assumed they had, if it ever came to that.

On July 18, Lawrence had promised to write another dispatch "as soon as possible" with respect to "our proceedings in this case at large." "As soon as possible" turned out to be October 18. "Our proceedings in this case at large" turned out to be not the meetings of the new deputies, but the deportation of everyone whose deputies refused to swear the oath. On October 18, Lawrence wrote to the Lordships that the popish recusants of all Acadia had been deported *en masse*.

The assemblies had been held in due course. The Acadian representatives had been warned that they would be given only one opportunity to swear the unqualified oath, much as papists in Britain had been given only one chance to swear allegiance to the Church of England. These representatives were willing to give any assurance but that. They were then dismissed, apparently again having thwarted a British attempt to compromise their neutrality. Lawrence and his council, however, began at once to plan the wholesale removal of the Acadians.

Lawrence was now going to do what he had recommended in his report as lieutenant governor to the Board of Trade in 1754. In that report he had written: "The only ill consequence that can attend their going would be their taking arms and joining with the Indians to distress our settlements, as they are numerous and our troops much divided." If Lawrence and his troops drove the Acadians into French Canada, he certainly could expect the men to join any force that the French organized to retake Acadia. He would have forced them into active opposition to the British. He would have achieved exactly what Le Loutre had tried but failed to achieve during his years as a terrorist.

A year had passed since that report, and Lawrence and his associates had now figured out a way to avoid this only ill consequence. The Acadians were to be scattered like leaves in the first windstorm of autumn, seized, whirled aloft, and dispersed at random far afield. He would scatter the Acadians among the British colonies of North America. The Acadians would not only be exiled; they would be exiled thousands of miles away; they would be placed in climates and societies entirely alien from those in which they and their fathers and their grandfathers had prospered; and most importantly, they would be separated from one another. They would cease to exist as an identifiable group. Of course, this would be very expensive. Who was going to pay for it, especially since Lawrence was far from asking the support of the Board of Trade? Here again, the council came up with a clever stroke. The Acadians themselves should pay. Their lands, their crops, their livestock—these they had forfeited to the Crown, and these would buy their passage.

The success of the plan required that it be kept secret—from the Board of Trade, which might countermand it, and from the Acadians who could easily thwart it by slipping away to Canada. Captain Murray was instructed, for instance, that he was to allow his Acadians to complete bringing in the harvest as if nothing had changed. Why should the British have to bring it in for themselves? Only then was he to use some stratagem to get all the men, especially heads of households, in one place. Then he was to arrest them for deportation and to keep them under guard until the passage could be organized for them and their families. It was a wonderful time for Murray, knowing as he did that he finally had the upper hand, purring like a cat with a saucer of cream. With what amusement he learned that the Acadians, when the transport ships came to one port shortly before the men were arrested, had actually visited the ships for news and to inquire innocently of their errand here!

When the trap was sprung, Murray arrested 183 Acadian men. He wrote to one of the other British officers that he was "extremely pleased that things are so clever at Grand Pré and that the poor devils are so resigned. Here they are more patient than I could have expected for people in their circumstance and which still surprises me more is the indifference of the women who really are or seem quite unconcerned. When I think of those of Annapolis I applaud our thoughts of summoning them in. I am afraid there will be some lives lost before they can be got together, you know our soldiers hate them and if they can find a pretext to kill them, they will."

The very next day he was writing concerning the spoils. "I have seen several horses, but cannot find any that I think will please him, but am this day informed of a black horse belonging to one Aman Gros, of Grand Pré, which I am told will answer his purpose for his own riding. I therefore desire you to be so good as to order René LeBlanc's son or some other French man to catch him and the bearer will bring him to me, you will extremely oblige your most obedient servant." But yet even someone as insensitive to the Acadians as Murray, someone who had happily played his small role in provoking the crisis that led to the deportation, could not be consistently happy amidst so much human disaster. After the arrest he wrote, "I long much to see the poor wretches embarked and our affair a little settled and then I will do myself the pleasure of meeting you and drinking their good voyage."

The officer with whom Murray was going to drink the Acadians' voyage was John Winslow, a captain who had been second in command at the siege of Beauséjour and who now was responsible for the deportation at one of the most heavily populated areas in Acadia. For Winslow, who kept a diary, this deportation was the most wretched experience in his military career. Never had the duties of the public man more sharply conflicted with the sentiments of the private. His diary reveals a mind living through an antinomy without a mediating term.

Winslow's orders had been blunt. "If fair means will not do . . . you must proceed with the most vigorous measures possible not only in compelling them to embark but in depriving those who shall escape of all means of shelter or support by burning their houses, and by destroying everything that may afford them the means of subsistence in the country."

Lawrence told Winslow to threaten the Acadians about the Indians; if any British soldiers are killed by Indians, Winslow was to say, he would summarily execute an equal number of Acadians who lived closest to the scene, since they obviously would have been culpable. "An eye for an eye," Lawrence said. He also wanted Winslow to establish his headquarters in the village church, whatever discomfort that might cause the superstitions of the locals.

Winslow, as far as is known, never did make the threat. He did follow the order about the church, but in a way that would minimize the offense. Ahead of time, he advised the village elders of his order so that they might "remove all sacred things to prevent their being defiled by heretics." Anyone who could ironically refer to himself as a heretic was not an appropriate instrument of Governor Lawrence's administration.

He did not use a trick to get the Acadians to assemble. He simply announced that "his excellency the governor has instructed us of his last resolution respecting matters proposed lately to the inhabitants and has ordered me to communicate the same to the inhabitants in general and in person." And the announcement was firm that all males over ten must attend: "No excuse will be admitted of on any pretence whatsoever on pain of forfeiting goods and chattels on default."

Four hundred eighteen men and boys—in Winslow's phrase "their best men"—appeared at the meeting. Winslow began with a formal preamble that referred to the "indulgences" that the British crown had granted to the Acadians. "What use you have made of them you yourself best know." Having said that not in accusation but in sorrow, Winslow added: "The part of my duty I am now upon . . . is very disagreeable to my natural make and temper as I know it must be grievous to you who are of the same specie." The common bond of humanity having been acknowledged by Winslow the man, then Winslow the soldier recited his orders: "That your lands & tennements, cattle of all kinds and livestock of all sorts are forfeited to the Crown with all other your effects saving your money and household goods and you yourselves to be removed from this his Province . . . I shall do everything in my power that all those goods be secured to you and that you are not molested in carrying them off and also that whole families shall go in the same vessel and make this remove which I am sensible must give you a great deal of trouble as easy as his Majesty's Service will admit and hope that in whatever part of the world you may fall you may be faithful subjects, a peaceable & happy people. I must inform you that it is his Majesty's Pleasure that you remain in security under the inspection & direction of the troops."

Winslow was going to try to follow his orders with the maximum possible humanity, but this was a pretty feeble consolation. His now prisoners met his announcement with "incredulity and astonishment." The Acadians said "that it was a great grief to them that they had incurred his Majesty's displeasure and that they were fearful that the surprise of their detention . . . would quite overcome their families." Winslow allowed them to select representatives to inform the families the reason for their detention.

Winslow was responsible for the deportation of 2,743 Acadians who lived in his region, of whom 1,105 were children and 820 aged. In this task, fear of failure served him for zeal. He knew that for many of the Acadians, especially the young men, there would be but one wisdom left: escape who can. He had to make sure they were not able. He knew too that his troops, no less than Murray's, would welcome the opportunity to shoot an Acadian or two and pilfer goods that were to be the Acadians' not much longer (much as Murray was hunting out that fine black horse). Winslow handled these matters with a firm competence, but the central theme of his account is not competence but grief. "This troublesome affair . . . is more grievous to me than any service I was ever employed in."

He knew that many Acadians, especially the women, did not believe that the deportation was really going to occur. So, during the days, they waited for news in the churchyard, standing by the graves and hanging on the headstones. This was typical of the grim dilemmas that faced him daily. If many were not convinced, this would make them more docile until the deportation began. As a soldier, he should be delighted at this self-delusion prevalent among the enemy (or perhaps like Murray, convince himself that this meant they really did not care, being something less than fully human). But Winslow, as a fellow human being, desperately wanted to convince them so that they could prepare themselves for the terrible day.

After a while some Acadians became entirely convinced that the British were going to carry out the threat. Those under guard at the churchyard began to be restless, full of activity without any obvious purpose. Winslow ordered that the younger men be grouped together and placed on the transport ships as a precaution. They believed the deportations were beginning, and "answered they would not go without their fathers." Winslow ordered his soldiers to fix their bayonets and march toward them. Thus prodded, the young men marched off "praying, singing, and crying, being met by the women and children all the way (which is one and a half miles) with great lamentations upon their knees praying, etc."

Lawrence was not making things any easier. He had instructed Winslow to dismiss summarily all petitions on behalf of the Acadians. Eventually Winslow would defy these instructions and pass one along, one that "they so importune with me to send that I could not put them off." Moreover, Lawrence was starting to requisition Acadian herds for the loyal but struggling

Protestant settlements. Winslow tried to explain that the Acadians still regarded these herds as their own. He pleaded with Lawrence just to wait until the
Acadians were gone before redistributing their wealth. If Lawrence did not
care about the unnecessary pain this caused the Acadians, he might have some
sympathy for what it did to Winslow himself. "It hurts me to hear their weeping and wailing and gnashing of teeth." Winslow just wanted the nightmare
to be over; he wanted to be "rid of the worst piece of service yet ever I was in."
Murray wrote to him shortly thereafter to inform him that he had already gotten his portion of the cattle Lawrence wanted. Murray wanted to know when
Winslow was going to gather his. Winslow did not reply.

The closer he came to being rid of this piece of service, the more distressed
Winslow became. The day before the embarkation, he wrote in his diary:
"Even now could not persuade the people I was in earnest." The embarkation
began successfully on October 8, 1755. Winslow's diary entrance for the day:
"October 8th. began to embark the inhabitants who went off very solentarily
and unwillingly, the women in great distress carrying off their children in
their arms. Others carrying their decript parents in their carts and all their
goods moving in great confusion & appeared a scene of woe & distress."

Presumably, it was not the Acadians who felt "solentarily"—they were
being herded together in their misery. It was Winslow himself who was feeling
the empty solitude of command. And yet, as the rest of this entry in his diary
shows, Winslow, even on such a day of woe and distress, had to occupy himself with the soldier's business of cruelty.

"Filled up Church and Milburry, with about eighty families, and also
made the strictest inquiry I could how those young men made their escape
yesterday, and by every circumstance found one Francis Hebers was either the
contriver or abetter who was on board church & this day his effects shipt, who
I ordered ashore, carryd to his own house & then in his presence burnt both
his house and barn, and gave notice to all the French that in case these men
did not surrender themselves in two days, I should serve all their friends in the
same manner & not only so would confiscate their household goods and
whenever those men should fall into the English hands they would not be
admitted to quarter, as the whole French inhabitants in these districts became
obligated to me, that if their several friends might be admitted to carry them
provisions on board & to visit them they would be responsible for each other.
Orders of the Day. Paroll Landree."

Was this Landree an Acadian who was being paroled from the deportation
for his proven loyalty to the British crown? It seems unlikely, for René LeBlanc
was not paroled. LeBlanc had been notary public during the British regime,

and had suffered much for it. The Indians took him captive, pillaged his house, and turned him over to the French who held him—probably in Fort Beauséjour—for four years. From the beginning of the present crisis LeBlanc had worked with Winslow to try to prevent bloodshed. Even in the early days of the crisis when Winslow was so worried about the safety of his own position that he was feeling more than a little suspicious of everything Acadian, he singled out LeBlanc and his family for praise as trustworthy. So well known was their loyalty that when Murray wanted that black horse he suggested that LeBlanc's son ride it over to him. And René LeBlanc was the Acadian elder who persuaded the young men that nothing was to be gained by running off. Winslow had been able to persist in his relatively humane implementation of Lawrence's inhuman orders precisely because of LeBlanc. And yet he was not spared.

But would he have wanted parole if it had been offered? He was now an old man with twenty children and more than one hundred grandchildren. All of them certainly could not be spared. His only chance to keep his family together was to go into exile with them. This chance was not good. The six to seven thousand Acadians deported (an equal number may have escaped to New France) were deposited, sometimes without warning to local officials, in the British colonies along the Atlantic coast. Some would eventually be sent back to France and then replanted in Louisiana. But most became unwanted and unwilling residents in the British American cities, with little reliable information on the fates of family and friends.

Typical was what happened to LeBlanc. He did not succeed in keeping his family together in exile. During the deportation they were separated, and they subsequently spread throughout the British colonies. He himself was put on shore at New York with his wife and two youngest children. He eventually made his way to Philadelphia, where three more of his children were. That was as far as he got in reassembling the fragments of his life. The ordeal was too much for his health, and he died soon after.

This little bit of LeBlanc's later life has itself survived because the Acadians in Pennsylvania became organized, and wrote a petition to the British king, George III. This petition reviewed the history of Acadia, and emphasized the sufferings of the Acadians themselves, both before the deportation and especially after:

"Thus we, our ancient parents and grandparents (men of great integrity and approved fidelity to your Majesty), and our innocent wives and children became the unhappy victims to those groundless fears: we were transported into the English colonies, and this was done in so much haste, and with so little regard to our necessities and the tenderest ties of nature, that from the most social enjoyments and affluent circumstances, many found themselves destitute of the necessities of life: parents were separated from children, and husbands from wives, some of whom have not to this day met again; and we were so crowded in the transport vessels, that we had not room even for all our bodies to lay down at once, and consequently were prevented from carrying with us proper necessaries, especially for the support and comfort of the aged and weak, many of whom quickly ended their misery with their lives."

As an example of this undeserved misery, the petition told the story of René LeBlanc. Of course, justice for LeBlanc was now no longer possible. But justice was still possible for the many Acadians who continued to suffer in exile, including his descendants: "The miseries we have since endured are scarce sufficiently to be expressed, being reduced for a livelihood to toil and hard labour in a southern clime, so disagreeable to our constitutions, that most of us have been prevented, by sickness, from procuring the necessary subsistence for our families; and therefore are threatened with that which we esteem the greatest aggravation of all our sufferings, even of having our children forced from us, and bound out to strangers, and exposed to contagious distempers unknown in our native country."

They could only implore His Majesty to inquire into their treatment: "This, compared with the affluence and ease we enjoyed, shows our condition to be extremely wretched. We have already seen in this Province of Pennsylvania two hundred and fifty of our people, which is more than half the number that were landed here, perish through misery and various diseases. In this great distress and misery, we have, under God, none but your Majesty to look to with hopes of relief and redress: We therefore hereby implore your gracious protection, and request you may be pleased to let the justice of our complaints be truly and impartially inquired into, and that your Majesty would please to grant us such relief, as in your justice and clemency you will think our case requires, and we shall hold ourselves bound to pray."

This petition was never answered, unless sending sour informer Thomas Pichon to spy on the Pennsylvania Acadians can be considered an answer. His Majesty's government had already closed the matter of the Acadians. Governor Charles Lawrence, upon informing Lord Halifax and the Board of Trade of the deportation, had concluded his report somewhat defensively:

"If on this or any occasion either to your Lordship or the Board I have been guilty of any omission as to points that should have been wrote upon or the explanation of them, I promise myself your Lordship's goodness in consideration of the multiplicity of troublesome things I have lately on my hands will hold me in some measure excused."

A few months later the Board responded—in a letter dealing with other matters, there was an aside, included as if to finish a subject of little consequence, a minor distraction. "We have laid that part of your letter, which relates to the removal of the French inhabitants, and the steps you took in the execution of this measure, before His Majesty's Secretary of State; and as you represent it to have been indispensably necessary for the security and protection of the province in the present critical situation of our affairs, we doubt not but your conduct herein will meet with His Majesty's approbation."

Even Charles Lawrence must have been somewhat surprised it had all been so easy.

Chapter XI

A WORLDLY WAR

✣

I T WAS AT ROME, on the 15th of October 1764, as I sat musing amid
the ruins of the Capitol, while barefooted friars were singing vespers in the
Temple of Jupiter, that the idea of writing the decline and fall of the city
first started to my mind."

This is Edward Gibbon's own, famous account of the origins of his massive
Decline and Fall of the Roman Empire, which he began to publish about a
decade later, a work now regarded as the greatest historical narrative ever written in the English language. And an Olympian achievement it is, surveying
from afar the flow of centuries and the course of wars and empires, with a sublime detachment broken only occasionally by a bemused disdain, the perspective of a god.

Strangely, the humble Acadians played their own tiny role in the inspiration of the great author for his monumental enterprise. Gibbon had long nur-
tured literary ambitions. Throughout much of his early adulthood he had
searched for an historical subject worthy of his talent and industry, a subject
that would provide him with the material to fashion a literary immortality for
himself. He had almost settled on the history of the Swiss. He admired the
way this small, feisty people had managed to protect their liberty amidst the
great wars of Europe; they provided the best mercenaries for those wars, but
then defended their own mountainous country against all comers. This one
small and relatively unimportant place could provide him with the material
for a celebration of liberty. But now Gibbon knew better.

He could see that the Swiss were an anomaly who had survived the processes of time intact only because of their mountains and because they possessed little that the world wanted. Put them in the mainstream of history, and
they would follow the Acadians into oblivion. Gibbon had learned this lesson

from the recent war that had made the Acadians innocent victims. The war showed, as all great wars did really, that history was not made by such insignificant little chips of humanity. In the processes of history Acadians counted for nothing, except perhaps as kindling.

Gibbon had served in the militia during that great war, a home defense against a possible French invasion. His responsibilities consisted of a great deal of empty business that left him little opportunity to read or research but much time for reflection. Gibbon realized, as the reports came in, that he was living through a war unprecedented throughout history. It was a war on a worldwide scale, the very first world war.

The war had begun in the interior of North America where France and Britain vied for dominance. Soon French and British forces were fighting all over the world. Britain won decisive naval battles off the coasts of Portugal and of France itself. The British raided French outposts in Africa, attacked and took French islands in the Caribbean. At about the same time the British were trying to take Quebec, they were breaking French resistance in India. (Hence began a dominance in the subcontinent that would last until Gandhi.) When Spain tried to intervene on France's behalf, British forces attacked and took both Havana and the Philippines.

Long before this war it had become a patriotic commonplace to speak of the ocean as Britain's true empire.

> Rule, Britannia, rule the waves;
> Britons never will be slaves.

James Thomson wrote these lines in 1740 for his *Alfred: a Masque,* but Thomson saw more in the waves than just a line of defense against slavery. He saw the sea, and the commerce that moved across it, as tiny Britain's means to world dominance. Near the very end of *Alfred* he had a holy hermit prophesy:

> I see thy commerce, Britain, grasp the world:
> All nations serve thee. . . .
> Shores yet unfound, arise! in youthful prime,
> With towering forests, mighty rivers crowned:
> These stoop to Britain's thunder. This new world,
> Shook to its centre, trembles at her name:
> And there her sons, with aim exalted sow
> The seeds of rising empire, arts and arms.
> Britons, proceed, the subject deep command,
> Awe with the navies every hostile land.

It was during the war against France that patriots like Thomson began, in retrospect, to assume the mantle of prophet. A history of the war published in
London after it had ended offered an official interpretation in less grandiose
terms, yet liberally seasoned with moral outrage:

"The French and Spaniards were the aggressors in this war. Their motives
were ambition, envy, and hatred. The French perfidiously encroached upon
our American territories; and, in time of profound peace, formed a plan, and
began with its execution, to drive the English out of America, and thereby to
annihilate, or to reduce our trade and navigation to a dependence on their
naval power and commerce. The Spaniards, having enjoyed all the advantages
of peace, during a long and bloody war between England and France more
perfidiously joined our enemies, without provocation, or any visible motive,
than to force England to submit to such conditions of peace, as might best
favour the designs of the Bourbon family. Whereas, if we turn our thoughts to
the English, we may trace their real object throughout the whole war, to gain
an honourable, firm, and lasting peace. They did not take up arms, till necessity obliged them to defend their property, and to repel force by force: neither
did they prosecute the war with any other view, or upon any other plan, than
to compel the enemy to accept such conditions, as might leave no embers for
a new war."

Gibbon knew better, however. He could see the war as a final fruit of the
European dynamism that had begun in the Italian Renaissance and had burst
on the whole world when Philip the Prudent had failed to yoke it to traditional Catholicism and the Spanish crown. No single person or country or
group then could control it. It had spread helter-skelter, with now one country, now another gaining preeminence in a given region. But no one truly
comprehended the process. Such momentous events would not stoop to
explain themselves to mere mortals.

In an important strategy session during the recent war, George III had
inadvertently given evidence of how far events had outstripped the capacity of
individual leaders to keep abreast of them. Throughout that session George
had consistently confused the Mississippi with the Ganges. When his chief
minister, the Duke of Newcastle, was asked why he had not corrected the
monarch, he admitted that while he knew there was something wrong in the
king's geography, Newcastle himself was "far from knowing exactly the state
and limits of those countries."

Such blithe ignorance was no longer excusable. Every educated person had
to realize, as a result of this war, that the whole world was a European place,
and would be for the foreseeable future. The European powers were dividing

the world into empires for themselves. In this division St. George was to receive the dragon's share. Gibbon's fellow citizens now needed an imperial education; they had to have a vision of empire that would keep pace with their power.

The Romans could provide this. Europe and Britain now seemed as securely in control of the world as Rome had been of the Mediterranean basin. And Gibbon knew where to begin. He "meditated Tacitus," as he put it.

What Gibbon got from Tacitus, above all else, was an insider's analysis of the mortal flaws within Roman rule. It was understandably a bitter analysis, for by describing the mortal weaknesses of the Roman Empire Tacitus was, in effect, predicting the end of everything that he and his forebears had worked to build and preserve. The gloom of his analysis led his Renaissance admirers to nickname Tacitus "the prince of darkness."

But Gibbon was not looking for gloom, for a darkness visible. He needed to adapt Tacitus to his own situation, to show how what had happened to the old empire of Rome need not happen to the new empires of Europe. He wanted the new leaders of Europe to assume with self-confidence the burden of empire.

This burden entailed a hardness that the Romans eventually lost. The destruction of barbarians, Tacitus had said, should be "a sight to gladden Roman eyes." So, too, the destruction of the Acadians or the Hurons should be a sight to gladden British eyes. Gibbon would teach his readers to understand the necessities of civilization. No longer could they be squeamish about the imposition of order, nor about the preservation of the hierarchies and inequalities on which alone civilization could be based. All civilizations had their centers and their peripheries, the rulers and the ruled. An imperial people had to set aside all sentimentality, especially the sentimentality that instinctively reveres everything that time and circumstances have rendered useless.

Gibbon would publish the first volumes of his great history in 1775, and he intended to dedicate it to the contemporary British leader who personified in his imperial policies the Roman wisdom Gibbon was trying to teach: Lord North. This was as it should have been, for this great war did have two aspects. It laid the foundations for the British Empire that would dominate much of the world from the eighteenth to the twentieth centuries. Nonetheless, in the North American theater of this war, ironically the one theater in which the British were in the end completely successful, the war also laid the foundations for the first great defeat of that empire, for it gave American colonists an education in independence. While British like Gibbon concluded from the war that they were already citizens in a new Roman Empire, many leading

American colonists as a result of the same war began to think that they might well become the founders of a new Roman Republic.

After all, the war had removed the French as a threat to the colonies from the west and north; so if the colonists chose to stand against Britain, they could fight for independence without worrying about French treachery at their back. The war had also taught them the limits of vaunted British military prowess. The colonists realized that their way of fighting, learned in large part from the Indians, was far better suited to the wilderness than the discipline of British professionals. The war even led a few among the colonists to think that Americans had already become a new people, and would soon be strong enough to assert their independence, if need be by force.

An obscure schoolmaster at Worcester, Massachusetts, wrote in his diary near the beginning of the war: "All creation is liable to change; mighty states are not exempted. Soon after the reformation, a few people came over into this new world for conscience' sake. This apparently trivial incident may transfer the great seat of empire into America. If we can remove the turbulent Gallics, our people, according to the exactest calculations, will in another century become more numerous than England itself. All Europe will not be able to subdue us. The only way to keep us from setting up for ourselves is to disunite us."

By the end of the war many would think the calculations of the twenty-year-old John Adams too timid. The colonies, if they wished to set up for themselves, did not have to resist all Europe, only Britain—and perhaps not alone, perhaps with the support of Britain's European enemies so eager to check its power.

Of course, Adams's speculations would be empty daydreams if the British did not first achieve a complete victory over the French in North America. And in 1755 any victory, even a partial one, seemed most unlikely. In the early days of this war anyone who claimed that this was the dawn for a great British Empire was likely to be told that if it was a dawn, it was one so initially overcast the sun was scarcely in evidence.

The major advantages in a test of power in North America seemed largely on the French side. Nature herself apparently had set the boundaries for the two competing North American empires—and Nature in this instance seemed to speak the language of the turbulent Gallics.

France's was a riverine empire. From the Atlantic it extended down the Saint Lawrence to the Great Lakes, then across portages from the Great Lakes (obscure places like the one the Indians called Chicago) to rivers that emptied into the Mississippi, and then down the great Mississippi to the Gulf of

Mexico, and the growing southern city of New France, New Orleans. This was the French empire, first traversed by the doomed madman La Salle.

It had an impeccable logic, at least on a map. Or it did to Francis Parkman, the nineteenth-century American who spent his life writing the history of New France, and of the struggle with the British that doomed it. With Canada and Louisiana the French held, as Parkman puts it, "the keys of a boundless interior, rich with incalculable possibilities." Of course, the British also desired the incalculable possibilities that came with the possession of a boundless interior. However, as the rivers opened up the interior of North America to the French, so mountains seemed to close it to the British.

The British colonies were generally restricted to the coastal plains of eastern North America. British colonists, needless to say, would also follow their rivers into the interior; but these rivers would usually end within a hundred miles, in the coastal mountains. Nature seemed to have wanted any nation that developed on the coastal plain to remain a ribbon-shaped country, a shorter, flatter, North American version of Chile.

Of course, these North American mountain chains were no Andes. Gaps and passes were discovered among them that made the interior accessible to hardy frontiersmen, of whom Daniel Boone would eventually become the type. Those earlier pioneers who did push to the west usually found Indians eager for trade but murderously resistant to settlement, much as would Boone later in the century in the Dark and Bloody Ground called Kentucke.

The Indians generally preferred British trade goods to French ones, but they also seem to have learned that the French would befriend them and leave them largely autonomous whereas the British would befriend them and then dispossess them. This was a lesson, of course, that French soldiers, traders, and missionaries had been teaching for almost a century now, and that Indian refugees from the coastal plains had been confirming. As a result, British westward expansion faced, after the mountains, a human obstacle at least as formidable. In any test of strength with the French the British could expect to be fighting the Indians as well.

The British really had only one advantage, but that was a significant one: population. The French lacked the sheer numbers to establish permanent settlements along the vast stretch between Saint Lawrence and New Orleans. Forest rangers would regularly traverse the land, as would missionaries, but New France simply had not the numbers to settle so vast a country. Its total population in 1750 was little more than eighty thousand, with two-thirds of that being concentrated along the Saint Lawrence.

In contrast, the British colonies, as Adams's diary entry indicated, had ample numbers for a westward expansion that would swamp Indian and French alike. The total population of the British colonies exceeded one million, with even tiny Rhode Island having forty thousand. Nonetheless, the French, few as they were, at least had a central authority, whereas any unified action by the British seemed precluded by the rivalries among the colonies themselves. In fact, at times the colonies themselves seemed more inclined to go to war against one another than to fight the French. When schoolmaster Adams speculated in his diary about the future, he had concluded that the only way to prevent American independence was "to disunite us." Any contemporary who read that comment would probably have drawn the conclusion that we will therefore never be independent, for we always disunite ourselves.

This factiousness went far deeper than the differences, say, between Puritans of New England, Quakers of Pennsylvania, and Cavaliers of Virginia. The population of the British colonies, which Adams seems to equate with its strength, had been achieved only by opening immigration to almost all European nations, by absorbing foreign colonists who were already here, and by the forced immigration of slavery. The babel that Jogues had observed in the doomed New Netherlands had now spread throughout the British colonies—Stuyvesant's revenge. According to contemporary estimates, less than half of the colonists were British in origin. (And, one might add, less than half of that half had any good reason to think of Britain with affection.) Whole sections of some colonies had about as much connection to the British flag as the Acadians did. Under such circumstances, how could a difficult war against the French be waged for the sake of British Empire?

Governor Shirley of Massachusetts was all for war against the French, as were many of his merchants in Boston. Nonetheless, he saw clearly that the loyalty of British American subjects could scarcely be counted upon. His own people, he reasoned in January 1755, would stand firm; but in the other colonies he only saw trouble. The Dutch of Albany "would surrender to the French upon the first summons if they could preserve their trade." The Quakers who controlled Pennsylvania would as a matter of principle not attend to their own defense, let alone help with anyone else's. Moreover, large portions of their rural population were Germans or Dutch who did not even speak English; they would happily change flags if their land titles were assured and taxes lowered. The same, he could have observed, was true of the Swedes along the Delaware. And he did observe that there were many Catholics in colonies like Maryland who would be happy to be able to practice their religion without the penalties under which they now chafed, even in the colony founded by the Catholic Lord Baltimore. But this Catholic threat paled before a far more ominous prospect among the southern colonies. The simple fact was that Negro slaves were capable of bearing arms. In an open war with the French these slaves "would be in great danger of being seduced from their fidelity to their masters by promises of liberty and lands to settle upon." By offering emancipation the French could as effectively bind as many slaves to their cause as they had already bound so many Indians who wished to retain their autonomy. In short, a total war against the French could result in a complete collapse of the British colonies, except for New England.

This grim analysis by perhaps the shrewdest colonial governor of his generation only serves to emphasize what seems to have been a consensus in the early days of the war: While both sides of the conflict had obvious strengths and weaknesses, the overall strategic advantage was held by the French. There was also, surprisingly, a consensus on where this apparent advantage would first be tested: the Ohio Valley.

The Ohio River and its valley, French and British agreed, was among the most beautiful places in the world. There the earth had been fattened by the decayed vegetation of centuries, black with loam. Jefferson was expressing the common judgment when he wrote that the Ohio was simply the most beautiful river in God's creation; the French in fact did not call it the Ohio but rather La Belle Rivière. However, French and British subjects did not lust after the Ohio primarily for its aesthetics.

The Ohio was the most vulnerable link in the vast chain of French claims from Quebec to New Orleans; it also provided the most convenient base for possible raids against Virginia, Pennsylvania, and even western New York. Let one British officer summarize the common wisdom of the time: "This country, lying in the middle space between their settlements in Canada and Louisiana . . . and at the back also of our middle colonies, would give them an opportunity not only of joining their two very distant plantations . . . but also of preventing us from extending our settlements backward beyond the great mountains towards the Mississippi, and of attacking them on that side." In short, this was the kind of place generals should be willing to have armies die for.

However, the inhabitants of the Ohio in the mid-eighteenth century were neither French nor British but a jumble of tribes who disputed possession amongst themselves. There were the indigenous Wyandots and Miamis, as well as the Illinois just to the east. However, the disruption caused by the British colonies' persistent expansion had driven a number of other groups here as well. A group of Iroquois came here to escape the endless wars of their

Confederacy; for their desertion they were given the contemptuous name Mingoes (later popularized by James Fenimore Cooper). Large influxes of Scotch-Irish immigrants had displaced portions of the Delaware from their traditional lands in Pennsylvania; they drifted into the Ohio Valley, fondly cherishing the memory of Penn (or Miquon as they called him) and bitter at the hard treatment they had received since his departure. The Shawnees, in contrast, came to Ohio from the south, and they knew only the bitterness of an expanding plantation system that had no place above slave for them.

So the fertile, beautiful Ohio supported a large population of Indians, unusual in its diversity and volatility. Indian affairs along the Ohio were so complicated that no one of European origin claimed to understand them except in brag or bluff.

This concentration of population was a great attraction for traders who did not mind risking their scalps for profit. It was estimated that three hundred traders from the British colonies alone each year made their ways across the serrated ranges of coastal mountains to take their chances. They were, not surprisingly, about as bad a group of representatives as Virginia and Pennsylvania could offer. While the governors of Virginia and Pennsylvania would agree on little else about Ohio, they did agree that the traders both colonies sent to this place were, as one put it, "a set of abandoned wretches." But as a group they were successful in developing an appetite for British goods, including rum.

This was the slippery state of Ohio in the mid-eighteenth century. Its overwhelming beauty still intact, its aboriginal life jumbled and confused, its trade in the hands of gallows bait—and on every map of North America pointed to as the Strategic Pivot for the whole continent.

In 1749 the governor of New France, La Galissonière, decided to demonstrate French claims to the Ohio as well as to reconnoiter the region by mounting an expedition under the leadership of Céloron de Blainville. Twenty-three large canoes, carrying more than two hundred fifty men (soldiers, forest rangers, and loyal Indians) set off past the rapids of La Chine, near La Salle's ill-fated homestead, on June 15.

Céloron carried with him a paternalistic message from La Galissonière, first scolding his "children" for allowing the British traders to "seduce" them, and then assuring them that "I will not endure the English on my land. . . . Listen to me, children; mark well the word that I send you; follow my advice, and the sky will always be calm and clear over your villages."

Céloron also carried with him lead plates to be left at suitable intervals along the Ohio. Anyone discovering them—and a number were discovered in

the early nineteenth century by people who could not read the French—
would be informed that Céloron had passed by here in 1749 to "restore tran-
quillity in certain villages of these cantons" and to leave this plate as "a token
of renewal of possession heretofore taken of the aforesaid River Ohio, of all
streams that fall into it, and all lands on both sides to the source of the aforesaid streams."

Céloron returned to Montreal a few months later after a voyage conserva-
tively estimated at twelve hundred leagues, having performed a great feat for
the French empire but himself more impressed at its futility if not followed by
a permanent military force sufficient to assure the loyalty of La Galissonière's
seduced children. Numerous as were the Indian villages on the Ohio, he
wrote, "each, great or small, has one or more English traders, and each of these
has hired men to carry his furs. Behold, then, the English well advanced upon
our lands, and, what is worse, under the protection of a crowd of savages
whom they have drawn over to them, and whose number increases daily."

The British authorities felt little more secure in Ohio. However effective
the traders were in winning the Indians over from the French, abandoned
wretches could scarcely be expected to provide the foundation for adding
Ohio to the list of British provinces. These traders were in practice against any
authority, whether French or British. And, of course, the British colonial
authorities did not agree among themselves about how to treat these traders
any more then they could agree about what to do in Ohio more generally.

The governor of Pennsylvania had sent out his own reconnoitering expedition to the Ohio. It had returned strongly recommending a fortified trading
post at the crucial fork of the Ohio we now call Pittsburgh. For his trouble the
governor found himself being chastised by his assembly members; far from
being willing to appropriate money for the post, they questioned the governor
for wasting good money on the expedition. And when the governor of New
York, recognizing the importance of the initiative, tried to assist Pennsylvania
in its effort to win the Indians of the Ohio to the British cause, he was bluntly informed by his assembly, "We will take care of our Indians, and they may
take care of theirs."

The governor of Virginia was at once more cautious and more effective on
the Ohio question. He refused to appoint magistrates for the region until the
boundary disputes with Pennsylvania were settled. On the other hand, he
encouraged the organization of a company that might settle this matter once
and for all, and in Virginia's favor. The Ohio Company of Virginia was an
investment scheme for the cavalier elite of the Old Dominion, including two
brothers named Washington. The company had carefully worked through the

official channels in England to get a land grant of five hundred thousand acres on the Ohio; to gain title to this land, the company had only to fulfill the conditions of the grant within seven years: A fort had to be built, a garrison maintained, and one hundred families settled on the Ohio, all this at the expense of the investors in the company. The year after Céloron de Blainville returned from the Ohio, Christopher Gist was reconnoitering the region for the Virginia investors. His description of the Ohio itself, like all others of this period, was glowing; but his accounts of dodging both Indians still loyal to the French and Pennsylvania traders with murder on their minds were worrisome.

The muddled Ohio was obviously waiting for someone to make a decisive move, and the French were the ones who attempted it. The way was prepared by an Indian expedition of 1752 led by the Frenchman Charles de Langlade. Of all the Indian headmen of the region, the most outspokenly loyal to the British—and hostile to the French—was the leader of the major Miami village, Pickawillany. His policy toward the competing European intruders was reflected in the names by which they knew him. The British called him Old Britain; the French by the insulting "La Demoiselle" ("the Maiden"). Langlade, at the head of a raiding party of Ojibwas and Ottawas, destroyed Pickawillany village—and in the subsequent celebrations they used the corpse of La Demoiselle as a dainty dish for victorious warriors against Old Britain.

In 1753 the new governor of New France, Marquis Duquesne, ordered that the French make their decisive move into the Ohio valley. He did this despite a certain reluctance from the ministers in France, who seemed to have some residual affection for the antiquated Colbertian dream of a compact colony. They also, truth be told, had a firm conviction that most Canadians were larcenous rogues. So they warned Duquesne to be on his guard; the Canadians would recommend public projects only when there was a great potential for private profit.

When Duquesne insisted on the necessity of building a series of forts connecting the Great Lakes to the Ohio, Paris acquiesced with considerable grumpiness. Duquesne was scolded repeatedly like a gallant who had been swindled at a country fair. He was on every occasion reminded of the possibility of dishonesty, the general expense of the colony, and the great reluctance with which this project was approved. For instance: "Build on the Ohio such forts as are absolutely necessary, but no more. Remember that His Majesty suspects your advisers of interested views."

Duquesne thought that anyone who looked at an accurate map could see straightaway how many forts were absolutely necessary—and the only interest required was a devotion to the *fleur de lis*. The French already controlled Lake Erie with two forts—Fort Niagara between Erie and Lake Ontario, and Fort Detroit at the western end, on the passage up to Lake Huron or across to Chicago on Lake Michigan. All that was needed was a series of forts connecting Erie to the Mississippi. The first new fort would be at Presque Isle (near what is now the town of Erie), to protect the southern coast of Lake Erie. This would be the staging ground for the portage from the Great Lakes to the first of a series of rivers the French would follow to the Mississippi; at the end of this portage, at a small river called French Creek, there would be built the second fort, LeBoeuf. French Creek would then be followed until it emptied into La Belle Rivière (a portion of the river that the British insisted upon calling by a separate name, the Allegheny); here would be built Fort Verango. Then down the Beautiful River to its major fork, that with the Monongahela; here would be the major fort of the whole system, much as Fort Niagara was the major fort of the southern Great Lakes. This fort would be called, in honor of the man who advocated its building, Duquesne.

The plan was simple, obvious from a map, and could be sketched out in a few minutes. Its implementation, on the other hand, was sickeningly hard, a prodigious feat from which any sensible person would have shrunk. Almost everything to be used in the building of the forts, including the great Fort Duquesne, had to be transported across vast distances of unforgiving wilderness. The portage from Lake Erie to French Creek alone was twenty miles, across which two thousand men had to carry twenty thousand pieces of baggage. It was a portion of terrain with which each man became intimately acquainted, and along which almost all survivors left some friends.

The sixty-three-year-old commander of the expedition, Paul Marin, quickly worked himself to death managing the early stages, and was replaced by an equally dedicated and somewhat hardier second-in-command, Michel Péan. But their resourcefulness and example could not keep the expedition on schedule. By the time winter was setting in, the French had built only two of their forts and had also taken over a British trading post at Verango. Péan garrisoned these three outposts, and then sent the rest of his troops back on a winter's stroll to Montreal. Duquesne had only to look upon those who survived to know what they had gone through, and to realize what his superiors in the comfortable apartments in La Belle France could never imagine.

"I reviewed them, and could not help being touched by the pitiable condition to which fatigues and exposures had reduced them. Past all doubt, if these emaciated figures had gone down the Ohio as intended, the river would have been strewn with corpses, and the evilly-disposed savages would not have failed to attack the survivors, seeing that they were specters."

So massive a French advance did not pass unnoticed by British spies. Governor Dinwiddie of Virginia, in particular, had received detailed and alarmed reports from traders of this slow but formidable French advance into territory that the king of England had reserved for the Ohio Company of Virginia. He informed London that a wind was blowing in the American woods that, if unchecked, would soon become a bellowing storm, and all would tremble before its strength. In Europe the French might pretend a peace, but in America they were provoking war.

Even so, if the fates had decreed war between France and Britain over the Ohio, they would have to find their own way to begin it. Dinwiddie, a professed man of peace, would not anticipate their decision by foolhardiness. He assured the British minister that he wished to attempt a peaceful resolution of what might just be a misunderstanding or a tentative probe. He asked London only that he be allowed to challenge the French on the legitimacy of their advance into His Majesty's territory. In response to the provocation he wished only to send an envoy to demand immediate French withdrawal.

His request of London was quickly approved, as quickly as he knew his demand of France was going to be rejected. Nonetheless, this was a necessary diplomatic preliminary to open hostilities. And the envoy, if observant, might learn something useful about the strengths and weaknesses of the French position.

Who should the envoy be? Christopher Gist was the obvious choice, since he knew the Ohio better than anyone in the British colonies. But Gist was not a member of the planter class, and his word would carry little weight in tidewater Virginia. He lacked the breeding to be anything more than guide. Dinwiddie thought he knew just the man to be titular leader of this expedition; only twenty-one years old, inexperienced outside the Potomac valley, with some credentials as a surveyor, but of obvious ambition and a thirst for honor, and with an impeccable pedigree.

This was, of course, George Washington. Washington's older brother had been a central member of the Ohio Company, and Dinwiddie had known him well. After his premature death the family honor had fallen on George, who was still seeking a position worthy of himself in Virginia society. Many influential people within that society were eager to help him, including Dinwiddie and the Fairfax family. These old families stuck together, and the service of the Washingtons to the Old Dominion went all the way back to

grandfather John Washington who, true to his royalist convictions, had remained loyally behind Governor Berkeley during Bacon's Rebellion.

This little expedition might give young George an opportunity to show his
mettle. To be honest, he was to be little more than a glorified errand boy, and
the errand itself was intended to fail in its expressed intent. The French did
not drag thousands of pieces of luggage to La Belle Rivière in order to turn
around and carry them back because Governor Dinwiddie sent them the message that they should. Nonetheless, the task had to be performed, and to be
performed with a dignity that could not be expected from a frontiersman like
Christopher Gist. Young Washington, so sombered by his brother's death, was
nothing if not dignified in his bearing. Washington accepted the appointment
eagerly and the expedition can be followed through the jog-trot entries in his
journal.

After some difficult wilderness travel, Washington and Gist finally made
first contact with the French at Verango, the old British trading post now
occupied by a small French force. They were received graciously by Captain
Joncaire and his three sons, and Washington describes somewhat smugly his
dinner there. The French had "dosed themselves plentifully" with wine while
the young major from Virginia remained alert, taking mental notes. In particular, he remembered the exact words of Joncaire, somewhat in his cups, "It is
our absolute design to take possession of the Ohio—and by God, we will do
it!" To Dinwiddie and almost anyone else who knew about the recent French
expedition this would scarcely have been a lightning-bolt revelation, but to
the young man sitting stiffly in his blue and buff regimentals it seemed important enough to record.

Joncaire, whether in his cups or out, apparently had known exactly what
he was doing. While Washington was sipping his wine and drinking in intelligence, Joncaire had his sons extend ample French hospitality to Washington's Indian guard. As a result, Gist had all he could do to get them to continue when the time came to push on to Fort LeBoeuf. We can imagine Joncaire
enjoying this quite a bit, and a smile flickering across his lips when he insists
that Washington's party be accompanied to LeBoeuf. It would not do for so
charming a young man to get lost so far from home.

When Washington reached LeBoeuf, he was impressed, almost despite
himself. Here, in the remote wilderness, was a complete fort worthy of the
coast—not just a fortified trading post like Verango, but a proper fort, its
ramparts even bejeweled by a few cannon. A glance at it persuaded eloquently concerning the seriousness of the French advance; it persuaded without the
need of words or syllogisms. Still, Washington had to translate this impression

into words, lest those back in the relative comfort of tidewater Virginia underestimate what was happening here. So he described the fort in detail, the fort so many French had suffered and died to build:

"It is situated . . . near the water; and is almost surrounded by the creek, and a small branch of it which forms a kind of island. Four houses compose the sides. The bastions are made of piles driven into the ground, standing more than 12 feet above it, and sharp at top: with port holes cut for cannon, and loop holes for the small arms to fire through. There are eight 6 lb. pieces mounted, in each bastion; and one piece of four pound before the gate. In the bastions are a guard house, chapel, doctor's lodging, and commander's private store: round which are laid platforms for the cannon and men to stand on. There are several barracks without the fort, for the soldiers' dwelling; covered, some with bark and some with boards, made chiefly of logs. There are also several other houses, such as stables, smiths, shops etc."

The French, moreover, were obviously committed to push farther down the Ohio. Washington counted more than two hundred canoes ready for immediate use, and many others in the process of being added to this inland fleet.

Washington, of course, solemnly presented his letter from Dinwiddie to the French commander, whom he described in his diary as "an elderly gentleman with much the air of a soldier." The fifty-four-year old new commander, Jacques Legardeur, was old enough to be Washington's father but scarcely decrepit yet; the last year he had explored to within sight of the Rockies. The letter politely expressed surprise to find French establishments on the Ohio, which is "notoriously known to be the property of the Crown of Great Britain." It begged to be informed on what authority the French commander and his men violated the territorial integrity of the British Empire. It then earnestly exhorted them to repair their mistake and leave forthwith.

Legardeur realized that this was serious but also in its way wonderfully amusing. Sitting in his well-built fort, looking at a young Washington for whom the Ohio was the far west, Legardeur must have thought that this ultimatum (for that was what it was) was about as grounded in reality as the Virginian claim that their province had as its western boundary the California coast and the Pacific Ocean.

Legardeur decided to try to have a little fun with the earnest Washington. He complimented Major Washington on the importance of his mission. So important was it that Legardeur was not the man to whom it should be directed. Washington needed to go to Quebec to present this letter to the governor himself.

Had Washington proudly swallowed the bait, he would have spent a few months on a grand tour of French outposts before reaching Quebec, while the French continued to extend and to fortify their position on the Ohio—a grand tour that would have resulted only in a predestined refusal of Dinwiddie's demand of withdrawal. (As another British colonist who had tried to negotiate with the French over the Ohio put it, "The French give amusing or evasive answers, but still go on with their works . . . pursuing their grand design.") Washington may have been inexperienced but he was no fool (and perhaps was getting a little impatient at being politely treated as if he were one). He insisted upon a response from Legardeur himself.

So Legardeur composed the gracious and predictable letter that Dinwiddie could have written for him months before, except for the French. Legardeur praises the charming, young, the oh so young Major Washington. He regrets that Dinwiddie has misaddressed a request that should have been sent to Quebec (if not Paris). As for himself, he is but a poor soldier who must follow orders "with all the exactness and resolution which can be expected from the best of officers." His orders, unfortunately, are inconsistent with Dinwiddie's request. So he must remain where he is.

Having received the expected reply, Washington rushed back toward Virginia. Of course, as Legardeur could have told him, one does not rush in the wilderness without danger. Washington, all impatience, insisted that he and Gist push ahead of the main party in order to gain a few days. As a result, they were almost killed twice: once by a treacherous Indian guide they had had to use, once by falling into icy rapids.

He reached Williamsburg in January after a journey that Washington would only admit was as fatiguing as it was possible to conceive. He had done his duty well enough on an important enough mission, with enough danger and incident along the way, that he became a hero of a modest stature.

Dinwiddie, who was certain that the colonies would soon need many such dutiful heros, had Washington's journal for the expedition published and distributed throughout the colonies. Most importantly, he also sent a force to try to retard the French advance. A few dozen men, under the command of a Captain Trent, were sent off to occupy the crucial forks of the Monongahela and Allegheny until sufficient reinforcements could be raised. This, it turned out, was too little, too late.

At the very moment Trent and his men were putting up their walls at the forks, Duquesne was sending out a major French expedition from Quebec to complete his series of forts. When the French arrived in April after an arduous voyage, they were confronted by Captain Trent and a modest installation he called Fort Prince George.

The French commander exchanged with Trent almost the identical pleasantries that Washington had exchanged with Legardeur, only this time English and French roles were reversed. This time the French commander expresses surprise that the British troops have occupied land that everyone knows belongs to the French king, and bids them withdraw. This time the English commander responds he would be going against his orders if he did any such thing, and suggests that perhaps his gracious French counterpart would like to take this matter up with his superior in Virginia. The French commander does not think such a trip necessary or provident.

Here the difference in the two situations intrudes. The French commander has been accompanied to the forks with five hundred troops, perhaps fifteen times more than are now exchanging worried looks in Trent's hastily constructed fort. So, when Trent asks for a little time to consult his honor as to what is required of him in this situation, the French commander replies he will give Trent and his honor an hour to come to their senses; Trent and his men can give up the fort without incident, or the French will simply take it over their dead bodies. Trent's honor decides that he and his men should give up the fort peacefully and alive. So the French commander, in recognition of this good sense, invites his British counterpart to an elegant supper before he begins the long trek back to Virginia. The next day, as his men march off, they can hear the French tearing down their fort; Fort Duquesne is to be so large and elaborate that the modest British effort has to be simply razed before construction can begin. Fort Duquesne is built in the expectation that soon the British will throw as many as five thousand men against it.

If Dinwiddie had known that the French expected a force of thousands from him, he would have had a bitter laugh. While sending Trent ahead, he was also trying to raise a significant force to reinforce him. For instance, the newly promoted Colonel Washington was to concentrate on getting volunteers from the Virginia militia; but Washington soon found that almost no one shared his enthusiasm for a sojourn along La Belle Rivière. He said, "You might as easily raise the dead" as get the three hundred volunteers he was supposed to. Dinwiddie decided to send Washington and his 159 men on ahead, in April, to be followed, he hoped, by hundreds of troops each from North Carolina, Maryland, New York, and Virginia itself. Washington was to make his way to Ohio, collecting Indian auxiliaries and loyal frontiersmen like Gist. These troops, under Washington's command, would be the first of a series of reinforcements to secure a portion of the Ohio for Virginia and Britain.

Then news came of Trent's surrender. Now Washington was simply to establish a defensive position near Fort Duquesne, and wait for the reinforcements that would make an assault possible. Washington obeyed his orders. He reached the Ohio, and established himself on a low and oozy expanse of land called Great Meadows, probably far enough away from Fort Duquesne to be safe if his forces did not draw attention to themselves.

However, his movements had long been followed by Indians loyal to the French and reported to Fort Duquesne. A small force was sent out from Fort Duquesne to reconnoiter the situation. Its commander, Coulon de Jumonville, was instructed that if contact was made with the British force he was to read a message to the British commander, the standard expression of surprise at territorial violation followed by the standard bidding to withdraw.

Washington, thanks to Gist, had his own effective Indian scouts. From them he learned where Jumonville and his men had camped. He ambushed them, killed nine including Jumonville, and captured the rest except for one Canadian who somehow managed to escape. For Washington, this, his first engagement, left him almost giddy with pride. He wrote, "We obtained a signal victory. I heard the bullets whistle, and believe me, there is something charming in the sound."

The escaped Canadian, however, bore back to Fort Duquesne another version of the event that was far from charming in its sound. The English had surprised them, he said, and had sent two volleys into their position. Then Jumonville, through an interpreter, called upon the English to cease firing for he had something to say. The firing did cease. Then Jumonville began to express surprise to find British forces in a territory notoriously known to be French, and suddenly was shot dead through the head.

This was raw conduct, a shameful crime, an egregious violation of the civilized codes of war, made only worse when the beardless youth permitted the Indians under his command to scalp the French, including the young heroic Jumonville. This version of the event would make its way from Fort Duquesne to Quebec to Paris, and from there to all the great courts of Europe. The name Washington became the epitome of perfidious Albion. Young Washington had so disgraced himself that he should hide his face from darkness itself.

Let the conclusion of one account from the period convey the spirit of a number, which had Washington ordering the killing to embolden his Indians. "The murder produced on the minds of the savages an effect very different from that which cruel Washington had promised himself. They have a horror of crime; and they were so indignant at that which had just been perpetrated before their eyes, that they abandoned him, and offered themselves to us in order to take vengeance."

This is, not surprisingly, a half-truth. Washington's Indians had not been enthusiastic about his handling of this affair, but they were not repulsed by it, as their participation in the scalping shows. Nonetheless, they did soon after desert him, but the reason was much more mundane. They had concluded he was a bad commander.

Washington, having won his charming victory (whether by means fair or foul), now had his blood up. He insisted upon pressing forward toward Fort Duquesne rather than falling back to defend himself against the French attack that was likely to come, an attack that Washington was little better equipped to repel than Trent had been. This was all obvious, and yet not to Washington, still enthused about his first blood. The Indians tried to remonstrate with him, and when ignored they simply began to dissolve into the wilderness.

As one of their leaders later explained, Washington "was a good-natured man, but had no experience, and would by no means take advice from the Indians, but was always driving them on to fight by his direction; he lay at one place from one full moon to another, and made no fortifications at all, except that little thing upon the meadow."

The "little thing upon the meadow" was a fort that Washington did hastily throw up in Great Meadows after he had belatedly realized the stupidity of pressing an attack to Fort Duquesne and retreated back there. Fort Necessity he called it; it was scarcely a fort but necessity was soon all around it in the form of numerous French troops led by the brother of the dead Jumonville. At this moment it was clear to everyone, including Washington, that the absent-without-leave Indian allies had shown impeccable judgment. Which, of course, was more than could be said of the young commander.

For some reason he seems to have expected the French to come out and fight him on the open field around his fort. The French, however, preferred to sit in cover and submit the fort to a withering fire. The weather was bad—sheets of rain had quickly turned Washington's fort into a quagmire, while French fire punctuated the quagmire with bodies and colored it with blood. After about nine hours of this (through one night), about a third of Washington's troops had been killed or wounded. Another day or two of this, and the other two-thirds would join them.

Washington tried to inspire his men. This was their day; they need only dare, for fortune befriends the bold. Let them now fight a stubborn cruel fight. Such martial eloquence faded before a few facts. For instance, ignorantly advancing toward a superior enemy, Washington had left Great Meadows exposed, and now without an effective defense. His men, as a result, were now targets trapped inside their own stockade.

Undoubtedly, Washington could hear murmurs and discontents among the soldiers. Hopeless of flight, more hopeless of relief, his men a feeble, fainting, and dejected crew, Washington, however much he wanted to stand fast in the face of danger, could only—what? Surely not submit to unconditional surrender. Jumonville's brother could not be expected to treat prisoner Washington kindly, or his men.

Then something astonishing occurred, a *deus ex machina*. Jumonville offered to send a man to parley with Washington. This was too good to be true. It must be only a ploy to reconnoiter the fort, and see how truly wretched their condition. The offer to parley was but a preparation for a final assault. Washington refused the offer firmly. And one can imagine the looks of resignation and disgust that passed among his men. You might as well speak to the wind or chase a cloud as try to hold this position much longer. Yet Washington would not even talk about yielding. His exalted sense of duty and honor was going to get them all killed.

What neither Washington nor anyone in his fort realized was that Jumonville had received reports of a major British relief column marching toward Great Meadows. This phantom column was to arrive in a day or two. So Jumonville, as much as he wanted to avenge his brother's murder, had come to believe that his own position would soon be untenable. He might have questioned the intelligence, but no one on the French side could believe that the British had sent such a meager force as Washington's to retake the Ohio. Even perfidious Albion could not be so stupid.

So Jumonville reversed his offer to parley. This time he invited Washington to send an envoy to the French camp to negotiate a surrender. Now there was no longer a reason to refuse, although as Washington made up his mind a few of his men must have been holding their breaths or saying their prayers. Washington sent off to the French camp his interpreter, the same Dutch trader who had accompanied him to Fort LeBoeuf and now probably expected to die with him here in the mud of Great Meadows. In due time the Dutchman brought back the articles of surrender and translated them for Washington.

They were straightforward, and unobjectionable. Washington and his men could retire with full honors. The only special provision the French commander required was that Washington acknowledge responsibility for "the death of ensign Jumonville." This was no problem for Washington since Jumonville had obviously been killed in an engagement with Washington's troops. Why should he deny that? So Washington signed the articles, and his

surviving troops were permitted to withdraw without further hostilities. This
bitter withdrawal began on July 4, 1754.

Only much later did Washington and the officers he consulted realize that
their translator had, apparently in the interests of peace and his own skin,
indulged in an extraordinary euphemism. He had translated "*l'assasinat*" as
"the death." Washington had signed articles of capitulation in which he had
admitted assassinating Jumonville. Of course, he would have knowingly done
no such thing, even perhaps if that meant they all ended their days in the mud
of Great Meadows. The interpreter knew Washington well enough to know
that. Later when the true terms were learned he could always claim that bad
light, fatigue, and haste had led to this unfortunate oversight on his part; he
would be explaining, it should be added, with his scalp still on his head and air
still in his lungs.

When Washington and his troops straggled back into Williamsburg (and
the task of supporting, carrying, and encouraging the badly wounded had
made a difficult voyage truly horrific), Governor Dinwiddie had more important things to worry about than the reputation of one ambitious young man,
no matter how dutiful and willing that young man had proven to be. The
British colonies were about to lose the west, once and for all. Not a British
outpost remained beyond the Alleghenies. Dinwiddie seems to have expected
his own colony and all others to rise up as one at this outrage.

The actual response was more than disillusioning. He spoke his words of
outrage and warning and was considered a Cassandra for his trouble. His own
assembly taunted him by scoring debating points rather than giving him the
financial support that was needed. And the other colonies seemed to be determined to make the burgesses of the Virginia assembly look like farsighted,
magnanimous statesmen. Dinwiddie began to write about how much he
deserved to be pitied; as for those who thought the Ohio something of little
matter, he said with a certain weariness, "Truly I think they have given their
senses a long holiday." Did they not see that the sky to the west was so foul it
would not clear but by a great storm that would envelop them all?

One man, however, saw the crisis perhaps even more comprehensively
than did Dinwiddie. And he was, fortunately for the British colonies, the
most famous person they had, already as respected in Europe as young George
Washington was becoming reviled. His name was Benjamin Franklin.

By the time we first come across Ben Franklin, he is in his mid-forties, and
has already established himself as our American Jacob, a man in whom worldliness has been exalted to the proportions of a religion, our sublime meta-
physician of the main chance. He had quickly become a leading citizen in his

adopted city of Philadelphia (having migrated from his native Boston, which he found oppressive), and was full of schemes for its improvement. (Someone once said that the dark night of the soul Franklin would treat as a problem in street lighting, and the slough of despond as an instance of improper drainage.) He was a leader in the Pennsylvania Assembly, and was particularly adroit at working around Quaker scruples. Let the assembly vote funds for food relief for war victims, especially for "corn, wheat and other grains." And who can object when "other grains" is interpreted as including gunpowder? (Gunpowder is, after all, granular.) Let the assembly fail to provide for a militia, and Ben Franklin will quickly contrive to hold a lottery to raise funds for a volunteer force. Franklin knew how to make Pennsylvania politics work, in part through persuasion, in part through winks and nods. And as for the godly virtue the Quakers professed—well, it was a fine imaginary notion but could if unchecked by reason draw the raw and inexperienced into real mischief while they hunt a shadow. Franklin's own religion was fulfilled in social performance, and quite lacking in angels and visions. The sense of being useful might not be as gratifying as a sinless conscience, but it would do.

Franklin had initially made his way as a printer. Since 1731 he had been publishing *Poor Richard's Almanac*, with its half-spoofed conventional sayings that seemed to transform ironic sententiousness into an art form. His newspaper, the Pennsylvania *Gazette*, which he had been publishing for longer than the almanac, gave him the opportunity to write on whatever came his way or struck his fancy, from an unlucky lady wrestler to an unusual *aurora borealis*, from the need for a paper currency (to be printed perhaps by B. Franklin, at a small profit) to the "Providence of God in the Government of the World" (the world does run pretty well but God on occasion cannot resist a little tinkering with His invention). Franklin, of course, was himself an inveterate tinkerer, with everything from eyeglasses to stoves; he had well entitled an early series of essays "The Busy-Body." As Melville would put it, Franklin was "the Jack of all trades, master of each, mastered by none—the type and genius of his land."

Franklin was regarded as the type and genius of his land not only by his fellow Americans but by Europeans as well. Among his tinkerings he had repeated a number of the experiments on electricity that were causing a sensation in learned circles of Europe; repeating them, he could not resist improving upon them and upon the conclusions that the savants of Europe had drawn from them. Electricity could be explained by a single fluid, not the two then commonly thought. Moreover, water vapor seemed held in the sky as clouds by electricity that then was discharged as lightning bolts. Having confirmed this latter conclusion by an experiment with a kite (and somehow not having killed himself in the process), Franklin set about tinkering with God's providence by constructing lightning rods that would render harmless this, His most awesome means of expressing His displeasure. One gets the impression that this contrivance, and particularly the discomfort it caused preachers, gave Franklin more pleasure than his theory which was sweeping Europe. As he would later put it, "What signifies philosophy that does not apply to some use?" For Franklin all philosophy that would abstract mankind from practice and the present was no more than words.

Already in the mid-1750s his fame seemed to be taking on a life of its own, growing daily. Honorary degrees were starting to roll in, from Harvard, Yale, William and Mary, St. Andrews, and eventually Oxford. He had already won the Copley Medal and was a member of the Royal Society of London; eventually no learned society in Europe would feel complete unless Benjamin Franklin was included in its list of members. Franklin's work on electricity, it was said more then once, seemed to open a path into the realm of miracles.

All this attention, Franklin said, was a delicious pleasure in which he could take a secret pride, like a girl with a new pair of garters. Yet there was nothing secret about Franklin's pride in his fame. His fame, like everything else, he sought to put to good use; he would describe himself as someone who "hath eminently distinguished himself . . . in the literary world, and whose judgment, penetration and candor, as well as his readiness and ability to suggest, forward or carry into execution every scheme of public utility, hath most deservedly endeared him not only to our fellow subjects throughout the continent of North America but to his innumerable friends in Europe."

Modest old Ben was not, except when it served a purpose. Eventually some of his contemporaries would tire of the tendency to attribute everything good that happened in the colonies somehow back to Franklin. John Adams with characteristic sourness would, decades later, write that people talked as if the American Revolution had been made by Franklin and Washington alone—and as for Washington, he had been pulled down from the heavens by Franklin during one of his experiments.

In 1754, Franklin understood as well as Dinwiddie the dangers of what was happening in the Ohio Valley. And if Dinwiddie moaned that colonial leaders had given their senses a holiday, Franklin was just the man to figure out a way to call them back to work—or at least to try. He had already begun to use his newspaper to this purpose.

On May 9, 1754, Franklin had reported in his Pennsylvania *Gazette* the news "from Major Washington" that the French now possessed the Ohio Valley. The loyal Indians of the Ohio, Franklin insists, were calling upon the colonies of Pennsylvania and Virginia to help them repulse the invaders. Well should the colonial governments be willing to comply, for otherwise the lucrative fur trade would be lost. Nonetheless, Franklin has to admit, "The confidence of the French in this undertaking seems well-grounded on the present disunited state of the British colonies, and the extreme difficulty of bringing so much different governments and assemblies in any speedy and effectual measures for our common defence and security, while our enemies have the very great advantage of being under one direction, with one council and one purse." To emphasize his point, Franklin placed at the end of his report a cartoon, the first political cartoon (it has often been claimed) in the American tradition. It showed a snake divided into segments, and it bore the motto "Unite or Die." The cartoon was a great success, being reprinted in newspapers throughout the colonies.

This was but a first step in what Franklin intended to be a campaign for colonial union. The next was a conference called in Albany to negotiate a trade agreement with the Iroquois Confederacy. Here Franklin, the intellectual handyman, thought he might have the opportunity to achieve something far more important, actually to mend the divisions that had so weakened the British colonies. Franklin had long had in mind the means he thought would do the mending. The Iroquois, strange to say, were not only providing the opportunity for this; they had long been providing by their example the method—or so Franklin thought.

Among the many subjects on which Franklin had become expert were Indian treaty negotiations. This was not because he himself had had much experience. But he had discovered early that for some reason published accounts of these treaties and their attending negotiations were sure-fire sellers. So Franklin set about collecting, publishing, and re-publishing everything he could find on the subject and in its general vicinity.

In the process he had recognized a common complaint that ran like a thread through all the negotiations with the Iroquois. The Iroquois could not understand why the British colonies did not confederate the way the Iroquois nations had. For instance, on July 4, 1744 (exactly ten years to the day before Washington's retreat from Great Meadows), the Iroquois leader Canassatego had concluded a speech by exhorting his British friends: "Our wise forefathers established union and amity between the Five Nations. This has made us formidable. This has given us great weight and authority with our neighboring Nations. We are a powerful confederacy and by your observing the same methods our wise forefathers have taken you will acquire much strength and power; therefore, whatever befalls you, do not fall out with one another."

The truth of this was obvious to anyone with a brain in his head, especially now that the colonies faced an increased threat from a centralized and determined New France. Clearly the British colonies were risking the vine to snatch this or that sweet grape. The Iroquois recommendation was stunning in its simplicity, but also powerful in its aptness because it implicitly responded to the chief objection to any unification of the colonies—namely, that the individuality of the colonies would be destroyed by such a centralized authority, much as Massachusetts had swallowed Plymouth. The example of the Iroquois Confederacy showed that this need not happen.

Franklin had studied the classic book on the Iroquois by his old friend Cadwallader Colden, his *History of the Five Indian Nations*, first published in 1727 and reprinted in 1747. In Colden's estimate the Iroquois had outdone even the ancient Romans in achieving a balance between central authority and local autonomy. As Colden put it, "Each nation is an absolute republic by itself, governed in all public affairs of war and peace by the sachems of old men, whose authority and power is gained by and consists wholly in the opinions of the rest of the Nations in their wisdom and integrity." This was a system of government with which any European of reason should feel comfortable. It was stable, having lasted in its present form so long that its origins were shrouded in myth. Moreover, it preserved individual liberty to a degree that some British colonies did not: "The Five Nations have such absolute notions of liberty that they allow of no kind of superiority of one over another, and banish all servitude from their territories. They never make any prisoner slave."

Franklin was convinced by Colden's arguments and his own investigations and experience that the Iroquois did indeed possess what the British colonies desperately needed in their struggle against New France. As he put it in a letter of 1751, "It would be a very strange thing if Six Nations of ignorant savages should be capable of forming a scheme for such a union and be able to execute it in such a manner, as that it has subsisted ages, and appears indissoluble, and yet a like Union should be impracticable for ten or a dozen English colonies to whom it is more necessary and must be more advantageous; and who cannot be supposed to want an equal understanding of these interests."

This jibe was not in a private letter. Franklin had published James Parker's essay "Securing the Friendship of the Indians," and then—just to make sure that his readers responded to the essay as Franklin wished—he included with it his candid letter to the author. Therein he sketched what he took to be the logical implication of Parker's proposal for improving Indian trade. There must be, Franklin insisted, a voluntary union of the British colonies. Not one imposed by the British parliament. Not one improvised to meet some passing crisis. Not one proposed by some ambitious governor. But a general confederacy of the type already perfected by the Iroquois.

The colonists, the letter continued, may like to indulge in feelings of superiority over the poor benighted savages of North America. But if they are superior to them in all things, then these same colonists ought to be able to excel them on the simple matter of a political constitution to protect the commonwealth. And yet the Iroquois have long possessed a constitution that is far superior in many respects to anything the colonists have devised. In fact, nothing like it could be found in Europe either, except perhaps the confederacy of the Swiss cantons that has helped that small people to preserve their liberty.

Could the Iroquois outstrip the colonists on so basic a human contrivance as a constitution? The flexibility of their wise confederacy has recently been demonstrated for all to see. They have admitted a new nation, the Tuscaroras, within their confederacy; they are now the Six Nations, not the Five. If the British are so superior to these ignorant barbarians, then the British colonies ought to be able to manage a confederacy twice as large, with twelve separate groups incorporated under a single umbrella. Certainly they need to establish such an arrangement now; no one could seriously contend it is not in our collective interest.

"I imagine such an union might thereby be made and established; for reasonable, sensible men can always make a reasonable scheme appear such to other reasonable men, if they take pains, and have time and opportunity for it, unless from some circumstances their honesty and good intentions are suspect." Of course, Franklin well knew that reasonable, reasonable, reasonable was exactly what the colonial leaders had not, not, not been in dealing with one another, while suspicion and dishonesty and bad intentions had been an enduring source of pain.

Since 1751 Franklin had been looking for an occasion to present his eminently reasonable scheme for colonial union. The treaty conference at Albany was as if made to order. He got himself elected as one of two representatives from Pennsylvania. This was not hard because he had for years been a leading member of the assembly. But that also meant that some members were more than a little suspicious of him, knowing him always to be looking for an opening to promote one of his innumerable schemes for improvement. Therefore, while the assembly acquiesced to Franklin as an obvious choice for the most recent wrangle among the colonies over a common Indian policy, they did do their best to tie his hands. They stipulated that the representatives were empowered to negotiate on nothing except a treaty with the Indians. Just the sort of thing to make Franklin smile to himself. Did not the small-minded yokels realize that such an ill-intentioned stipulation no reasonable man would consider binding?

Even before arriving in Albany Franklin had begun to solicit both support and suggestions for the proposal of colonial unification that he most certainly was going to present to the assembled delegates. He had no doubt that his scheme for public utility and the common good would endear him to all other men of right reason—or, rather, that it should.

The proposal that Franklin finally presented at Albany was for the union of the colonies under a President General and a Grand Council. The president would be appointed directly by the Crown; the representatives on the council would be elected by the assemblies of each colony. A colony would have between two to seven representatives on the Grand Council, to be determined by population and taxes. Massachusetts, for instance, would have the full seven, New York four, and Rhode Island only two of the forty-eight total membership of the council. The president and his council would have exclusive control over Indian affairs—treaties, trade, and land purchases; they would also be responsible for new settlements, such as those both Virginia and Pennsylvania wanted to make on the Ohio. Since the purpose of the union was primarily defense, the president and his council should also have sole responsibility for raising troops, paying their salaries, building forts, and protecting commerce, as well as the power to impose duties and taxes to finance these activities. Franklin was very careful to impose limits on these broad powers; the government could not impress men in any colony without the express consent of its legislature, nor could it raise taxes for any purpose other than those listed in the articles of confederation.

Franklin's innovative plan was only a few pages in length. He also wrote the discursive "Reasons and Motives for the Albany Plan of Union." There he first justified the plan in general, and then each article in detail. In short he wrote both the precursor of the Constitution as well as its Federalist Papers. If there was a task that needed doing, Ben Franklin was willing to try his hand at it.

The response in Albany was more than even the usually sanguine Franklin could have hoped. It upstaged the treaty negotiations and passed unanimously, with scarcely any discussion. Its merits were accepted as virtually self-evident. Unite or die. Colonial union was required for simple self-preservation. Whatever euphoria Franklin felt at the reception of his plan by the delegates at Albany, he knew better—as Poor Richard might have admonished—than to count his chickens before they hatched. This particular chicken, as it turned out, was dead long before that. By the very fact that they had spent time together worrying over the common good, the representatives at Albany had been transformed into being completely unrepresentative of their squabbling provinces.

The Albany Plan of Union, although enthusiastically embraced at the Albany Congress, also needed the approval of the individual assemblies of the colonies. Then would be required an Act of Parliament to implement it. This eminently reasonable plan, after the endorsement in Albany, got exactly nowhere.

Franklin would write of the Albany Plan, "Its fate was singular. The Assemblies did not adopt it, as they all thought there was too much prerogative in it, and in England it was judged to have too much of the Democratic." Melville said of Franklin that he was everything an American might be except a poet. But in regard to this bitter occasion he could even find the right poetry, albeit someone else's. He quoted a couplet from the Roman satirist Juvenal (in Dryden's translation):

Look round the habitable world, how few
Know their own Good, or knowing it pursue.

Nonetheless, Franklin was ever chipper, at least when he faced the world, everything grist for the old optimist's mill. Eventually he would explain even this defeat in more or less positive terms; in failing here he had contributed to the coming of the American Revolution. "The different and contrary reasons of dislike to my Plan makes me suspect that it was really the true medium; and I am still of the opinion it would have been happy for both sides of the water if it had been adopted. The colonies so united would have been sufficiently strong to have defended themselves; there would have been no need of troops from England; of course, the subsequent pretense for taxing America, and the bloody contest it occasioned, would have been avoided." If only people had been a little more reasonable, if only poor Benjamin had been king.

And Franklin was right, up to a point. (Franklin was almost always right, up to a point; it was just that his point often was fairly low on the range of human possibilities.) This episode, at least viewed from after the American Revolution, does seem pregnant with future happenings. And the American Revolution, let us admit, is for us so momentous an event as to cast its shadow long before its occurrence.

After the rejection of the Albany Plan, Governor Shirley tried to revive it in what might be called a Tory version. Since the provincial assemblies had not the good sense to support the union, Shirley thought they were obviously incompetent to consider it, or to be part of the plan once implemented. Let them be excluded from any say in the union whatsoever. That certainly would overcome London's objection that the plan was too democratic. Let the king and Parliament unilaterally decree a union of the colonies and let its Grand Council be composed of the most farsighted leaders in the colonies—namely, the governors like Shirley himself.

To this self-serving proposal Franklin responded with a series of blistering letters to Shirley, which he published in Britain (since they were not really intended for Shirley but for British policy makers). These embodied the republican response to Tory loyalists, and thereby anticipated many arguments that would later be framed during the Stamp Act crisis that immediately preceded the revolution.

Franklin pointed out that Shirley's plans in the name of effectiveness would simply exclude the American people from any role in selecting the Grand Council that would nonetheless have the power to tax them. This showed a sovereign contempt for the sovereign people. And who would be the farsighted statesmen deciding the fiscal and military matters for the colonists without consulting them? Did Franklin have to remind Shirley of the unpleasant fact that governors, appointees of the British government, frequently come to the New World to make—or worse, to repair—their fortunes, and to return to England as soon as possible, like pearl divers rising for air? Such governors, in contrast to the able Shirley, have little interest in and less knowledge of the American people. They are, in effect, foreigners imposed upon them by the will—one will not say caprice—of the king and his ministers. They do represent the king; but the assemblies, for better or worse, represent the people. In Shirley's scheme the king would be all, the people nothing, in the decisions of the government; there was a word for that: tyranny. Such taxation without representation, Franklin should not have to tell Shirley, would be met with "extreme dissatisfaction." (Franklin was choosing his words carefully here.) And so it should, for such a system would put the British subjects "on a footing with the subjects of France in Canada that now groan under such oppression."

Franklin was too discreet to draw the corollary from this proposition— namely, much of the American population would decide that whether they were French or English subjects was all the same to them, not the attitude to foster at the beginning of a great war. There are moments in these letters when Franklin's litany of objections sound very much like Jefferson's litany of charges in the Declaration of Independence.

Shirley's plan, like Franklin's, went nowhere. And the French were still on the Ohio, consolidating their position and chasing out any British traders that they found in the region. Clearly the disunited colonies had shown themselves incapable of dealing with this threat. The British decided to handle it directly. It was too important a matter to be left to mere colonials.

A professional force of two regiments, thirteen hundred men, was to be transferred from its Irish garrisons to America. These hardened soldiers would provide the core for a decisive assault to make the Ohio as truly British as Ireland was. They would be under the command of Major General Sir Edward Braddock.

Braddock had risen through the ranks in the prestigious Coldstream Guards during a career of more than forty years. His contemporary, Horace Walpole, a gossip of genius, gave the contemporary, somewhat mixed assessment of the general: "Desperate in fortune, brutal in behavior, obstinate in his sentiments, he was still intrepid and capable." For Walpole, it must be said, this was somewhere near high praise. (Walpole on Dante: "Extravagant, absurd, disgusting, in short a Methodist parson in Bedlam.")

William Thackeray, a century later, tried a fuller sketch of Braddock, with a few strokes of an abler pen, of this "stout chief, exemplar of English elegance . . . his face as scarlet as his coat—swearing at every word; ignorant of every point off parade, except the merits of a bottle and the looks of a woman; not of high birth, yet absurdly proud of his no-ancestry; brave as a bull-dog; savage, lustful, prodigal, generous; gentle in soft moods; easy of love and laughter; dull of wit; utterly unread; believing his country the first in the world, and he as good a gentleman as any in it."

He was the king's choice to re-take the Beautiful River, a general who, it was said, would not retreat from table until he was outnumbered by the empty bottles at least five to one.

Braddock made a varied impression on those colonials whose bacon he thought he had been sent to save. Dinwiddie quickly judged him to be just what the colonies needed—"a very fine officer, and a sensible, considerate gentleman." Dinwiddie's enthusiasm, of course, was partly an expression of relief that London had not only seen the seriousness of the situation on the Ohio but also had sent someone else to be responsible for it. (No one among Braddock's many associates had ever called him considerate, but for Dinwiddie his mere presence with regiments was consideration enough.)

Other colonials gave less glowing reports. Shirley had quickly used his influence to get his son the prestigious position of secretary to Braddock; if Braddock became president of the united colonies, Shirley's son would have his career made. But soon Secretary William Shirley Junior was writing some very unflattering accounts of his new mentor. He did not doubt Braddock's bravery or honesty. He did soon doubt most emphatically Braddock's suitability for the task at hand. He wrote, "We have a general most judiciously chosen for being disqualified for the service he is employed in almost every respect." And you, young Shirley, you shall die by Braddock's side, a sacrifice to his mistakes and your father's hasty ambition for you.

Not surprisingly, it was Benjamin Franklin who gave the most judiciously lukewarm assessment. He thought Braddock would have done well in a European war. Braddock, however, refused to recognize that this was not a European war. As a consequence, Franklin thought, "he had too much self-confidence; too high an opinion of the validity of regular troops; too mean a one of both American and Indian."

Even as Virginians watched deep-drawing British ships disgorge their freight of war, they thought the British high command had made an obvious strategic misjudgment. The troops and materiel should not have been landed in Virginia but in Pennsylvania. From Virginia to the Ohio was pure wilderness; through Pennsylvania, in contrast, there were miles of prosperous farms before the mountains, farms where supplies could be commandeered along the way.

Braddock's superiors knew America as little as he did—and they had been hoodwinked, it was rumored, by a shrewd Quaker merchant who also happened to be a major investor in the Ohio Company of Virginia. Braddock was going to have to cut the road that would assure Virginia dominance along the Ohio. The mistake, it was said, cost Braddock about six weeks and about forty thousand pounds, some of which undoubtedly found its way into the good Quaker's ample pocket.

Braddock's own strategy for the campaign seemed to some as ill-chosen as his staging area. He was committed to a direct assault on Fort Duquesne, clearly now one of the strongest points in the French defense. Colonials suggested an alternative. Why risk everything on such an engagement? Braddock could easily overwhelm the smaller force that guarded Fort Niagara, thereby cutting off all supplies for Fort Duquesne, which would eventually fall into Braddock's lap like a ripe apple.

"Eventually," however, was not an adverb in General Braddock's military vocabulary. Such well-intentioned advice from amateurs was just another example of the colonials' inflated sense of their own importance, an unwitting attempt to make a straightforward operation complicated. He had only to transport his big guns to Fort Duquesne, which would then "hardly detain me about three or four days." Duquesne secure, he would then sweep up to the

Great Lakes, taking all the forts along the way, until in the last action of his campaign he would forcibly pluck Niagara from the French tree. It was May now; he intended to celebrate Christmas in Philadelphia, his work in the New World completed.

When Braddock sketched out his plans to a quizzical Benjamin Franklin, Franklin gently raised the problem of Indian ambushes on so long and toilsome a march. Braddock responded with bemused condescension concerning mosquitoes and other minor nuisances. "These savages may indeed be a formidable enemy to your raw American militia. Upon the King's regular and disciplined troops, it is impossible they should make any impression."

Friendly Indians certainly made no impression upon Braddock and his fellow officers. He had little use for fickle, painted savages. He treated their offers of assistance with such obvious condescension that most of the volunteers left indignant. As one headman said angrily, "He looks upon us as dogs." When eighty scouts were finally recruited for him, he seemed pleased to allow them to come along with his great army. Then he discovered that they had brought women with them, women whose loose habits were disrupting the discipline of the king's regular troops. Such auxiliaries he did not need, so he sent the whole bunch of them packing. By the time his army began to make its way through the wilderness, the number of his Indian scouts was less than ten.

The three hundred colonial troops assigned to General Braddock made almost as little impression as the Indian scouts. His dispatches back to Britain portrayed them as close to more trouble than they were worth. As he put it in one, they were "very indifferent men, the country affording no better; it has cost infinite pain and labor to bring them to any sort of regularity and discipline; their officers very little better." These men were not used to obeying commands, and did not take kindly to them. And yet they backed one another against British authority as if they were all sworn members of a secret confederacy.

The colonial troops were bad enough, but the civilians were worse. Braddock needed supplies and the wagons to carry them. The colonials pretended they had none to give, or little at outrageous prices. Braddock's exasperation at dealing with impudent profiteers, or those he took to be such, at times approached murderous rage, especially against the Quakers, who usually responded to his requests with a serene obstinacy. Occasionally one gets the impression that Braddock would have liked to march on Fort Duquesne by way of Philadelphia, just to have had the pleasure of conducting a long and destructive siege on those who had most vexed him. But when he threatened to get his supplies by what he called "unpleasant methods," he was met with only shrugs and smiles.

Braddock did not need unpleasant methods; he needed only Benjamin Franklin. Franklin took charge of the matter, and within two weeks had raised everything Braddock wanted, and at reasonable prices. Braddock would write of Franklin as "almost the only instance of ability and honesty I have known in these provinces."

There was at least one other exception to Braddock's condemnation of those he encountered in these colonies, a young colonel in the Virginia militia who seemed eager to learn and follow regular army ways. George Washington, along with the doomed young Shirley, was among Braddock's inner circle of advisors. Washington tried to stand up to Braddock when he contended with characteristic warmth that the American colonies were "devoid of honor or honesty." But Washington admitted he made little headway.

So the British forces began their march, cutting Braddock's road from Virginia to the Ohio. Writers from that day to this have tried to evoke the slow advance of this great army fated to destruction. Francis Parkman, not surprisingly, has done it best: "Thus, foot by foot, they advanced into the waste of lonely mountains that divided the streams flowing to the Atlantic from those flowing to the Gulf of Mexico—a realm of forests ancient as the world. The road was but twelve feet wide, and the line of march often extended four miles. It was like a thin, long party-colored snake, red, blue, and brown, trailing slowly through the depth of leaves, creeping around inaccessible heights, crawling over ridges, moving always in dampness and shadow, by rivulets and waterfalls, crags and chasms, gorges and shaggy steeps. In glimpses only, through snagged boughs and flickering leaves, did the wild primeval world reveal itself, with its dark green mountains, flecked with the morning mist, and its distant summits pencilled in dreamy blue."

The king's regular and disciplined troops, unlike Parkman, were scarcely enjoying the picturesque views; they were far from the bright fair green of Ireland, and knew it. And the American troops to whom they had condescended for months while near the coast now began to have some fun as they saw uncertainty and perhaps even the flicker of fear cross British faces. They could happily explain to their superior British brethren the ways of the wilderness, especially the ways of the indigenous inhabitants hereabouts, all about scalping parties and torture deaths and massacres in which the adversary is never seen until too late. Perhaps the British troops laughed all this off as horror fiction as they marched past places such as the Great Savage Mountain and through a dismal little wood called the Shades of Death. Then Indian markings began to be seen on trees, and were liberally interpreted by the colonial militiamen. Then the occasional soldier was found scalped and mutilated, although no one had seen an Indian or heard a thing. Braddock's army now became a snake each segment of which suddenly looked over its shoulder from time to time, as if half expecting to see the shades of death—which they soon would.

If anyone was ebullient in the march, it was Colonel Washington, despite a debilitating fever. He could not wait to reverse the stinging surrender at Great Meadows. He was impatient at Braddock's methodical, by-the-book advance, the steady march that was supposed to be like the progress of a machine. To his impetuous eyes it seemed that Braddock was halting to level every molehill and bridge every brook. Some days they made only three miles, a snail's pace to someone brimming with gallant rashness.

The problem, as Washington saw it, was Braddock's cherished baggage, including the artillery. As soon as the main force got within striking distance of Fort Duquesne, Washington urged Braddock to let the wagons and artillery lag behind. In what he called "the warmest possible terms I was master of," he argued that advance forces should be sent out to prevent any reinforcements reaching the fort. The siege could be begun sooner, and continued until the artillery was brought up to give the French a choice between surrender and obliteration.

Somehow Washington convinced Braddock. He took the rash advice, and made the fatal order for a vanguard to march out at full speed. And march they did toward unforeseen destruction, a field of slaughter. Washington, one suspects, was worried that his fever, which left him barely able to sit a horse, might not allow him to participate in the great reversal of his earlier defeat. He needed the battle to come soon, or he might be watching it at a distance from a litter.

When the advance army finally reached the Monongahela, the regular troops were by all reports in the highest spirits. The laborious march was almost over; they had left behind the unfamiliar, unnerving terrain; they were about to perform the maneuvers for which they had spent years training. The spectacle of the final fording was unforgettable to all those there who survived the day. As one who did put it, "A finer sight could not have been beheld, the shining barrels of the muskets, the excellent order of the men, the cleanliness of their appearance, the joy depicted on every face at being near Fort Duquesne, the highest object of their wishes—the music re-echoes through the mountains." Washington said simply that it was the most thrilling sight he had ever seen; he was soon to see one of the most horrible.

Colonel Gage, the commander of this advance force, was more relieved than thrilled at the successful fording. This was the moment for the French to ambush, and the moment had passed without incident. So they were not going to dispute the British advance. They were apparently reconciled to a British siege—that is, to defeat. He had only to get his troops to Duquesne as quickly as possible. This was going to be even easier than Braddock had predicted.

So Gage ordered his troops to advance at full speed. This meant leaving behind the small pieces of artillery, but no matter. There would be plenty of time for the artillery to catch up as his men were digging in. He undoubtedly observed the high ground to his right, ground that he would have been careful to secure if he were going to meet an enemy soon. But he was not careful: he and his men were done with leveling molehills or securing ridges. Gage's decisions were made in the spirit of Washington's advice and Braddock's decision to follow it.

The French in fact had intended to ambush the British force at the Monongahela, for the French commander, Contrecoeur, had realized that this was the only chance to save his fort. He knew, as the British did not, that he was to expect no reinforcements from Quebec: oblivious to the imminent danger and pleased with his recent work, Quebec had only sent him his replacement, Captain Beaujeu.

Beaujeu was a perfect choice to take over the fort. A man of aristocratic lineage, he had already served with distinction at Niagara and Detroit and was a wonderfully effective leader of Indian allies, who generally revered him. In short, he was precisely the kind of European soldier whom Braddock could never understand, someone for whom the embracing of the new did not entail the repudiation of the old.

Quite naturally, Contrecoeur had selected Beaujeu to lead a force of Indians and Canadians to ambush Braddock. Beaujeu relished the task, but his Indians most decidedly did not. They knew the size of Braddock's force, and did not relish encounters with artillery of the type he had with him. To die nobly in battle was one thing, to be blown to pieces another. One asked Beaujeu, "Do you want to die, my father, and sacrifice us too?" Beaujeu responded, "What! Will you let your father go alone?" He finally convinced them that he was going to go whether they accompanied him or not. Their affection for him finally overcame their prudence, and they reluctantly agreed. So he led out his force, himself barechested and dressed in buckskins, an elegant silver gorget around his neck. Thirty-six French officers, seventy-two regulars, forty-six Canadian militia men, and more than six hundred

Indians marched out behind him, to meet a British army of about three thousand.

Beaujeu was hurrying his men the final mile to the Monongahela when his advance scouts told him they were too late. The negotiations with the Indians had robbed him of his chance for an ambush. The British army had already forded the river.

The sensible thing at this point might have been to retreat to the safety of the fort. So small a force had little chance against Braddock's army in an open fight. Nonetheless, Beaujeu, true to his name, decided to try his luck. The front line of the English suddenly saw before them Beaujeu calmly waving to the right and then to the left, directing his Indians to take cover in the trees on both sides of the advancing British column.

The British, ignoring the movement which they likely took to be a panic in the face of superior numbers, fired directly ahead into the remaining men, the small force of Canadians and French regulars. On the third volley Beaujeu himself fell, killed instantly by a bullet through his brain. The French began a retreat, and the British filled the sky with a victory huzzah, and began the advance they expected would turn a skirmish into a complete rout. This tiny battle was going according to the book, just an ordinary maneuver. This delusion, however, did not last.

The soldiers in the British force, professionals long inured to bloody combat, only slowly realized that something was going strangely wrong. Men were falling, too many for the small force in front of them, and the bullets whizzing past seemed to be coming from all directions. Finally they realized that the enemy who was killing and wounding so many was not the enemy in front of them but an enemy they could not see, hidden in the trees along their sides. Puffs of smoke were seen from the rise on the right that Gage had disdained to occupy. Amidst the pops of rifles, the whoops of Indians were heard but no Indians were seen, except an occasional one darting from tree to tree so quickly that there was no time to aim at him. And all the while more men were falling, sometimes two or three at a time.

A strange anxiety started to lay hold even of the bravest of them. The men were becoming confused, disoriented. Rather than concentrating their fire ahead as they knew they should, they began to fire in all directions. Trees and puffs of smoke became their chosen targets, not the French soldiers in front of them, who now were standing firm.

Only the American militiamen responded with a sense of purpose. They immediately, almost instinctively, began to head for the trees themselves, to fight the Indians on American, not European, terms. But the British officers did not understand, and cursed them for cowardice, and risked their own lives to herd them back into what had become a shooting gallery. As one American put it, "It greatly surprised me that I must stand still to be shot." The Americans who did make it to the trees found themselves in a withering crossfire between the Indians before them and the British regulars on their side, for the British were firing at anything that moved among the trees.

Washington saw this with disgust, and could do nothing about it. "Our poor Virginians behaved like men and died like soldiers, for I believe that out of three companies that were there that day, scarce thirty were left alive. . . . It is imagined (I believe with great justice, too) that two-thirds of both killed and wounded received their shots from our own cowardly dogs of soldiers."

The advance force became completely demoralized. Only years of discipline retarded the panic that was spreading palpably from man to man in glances and shudders and moans. The officers did not panic. As a group they behaved heroically among the quavering men; but that only meant they were falling in larger numbers, easy targets for Indian sharpshooters. Gage estimated that within the first fifteen minutes of the engagement, fifteen of his eighteen officers had been killed or wounded seriously, as well as half of his three hundred men.

Gage tried to have the force retreat fifty paces and regroup. They did so in a last collective spasm of habitual obedience, and for their effort they found themselves no better off. Braddock had known of the engagement almost immediately. Once he realized its seriousness, he had ordered reinforcements marched to the front. Like most of the reasonable decisions made by British command that day, this one was a disaster.

The reinforcements rushing forward in good order collided with Gage's retreating force in bare order, and the result was all order lost, and all hope. The troops now huddled together as timid as children. Braddock himself rushed to the front and performed what courage could, seeking by his own example to cheer the fight. But still pale horror sat on almost every British face. He cursed them, beat them with the flat of his sword. These base, grovelling, worthless wretches, he'd pluck the tongue of anyone who showed cowardice. As one mount after another was shot out from under him (at least four), he seemed entirely undeterred and unflinching, commandeering another one and continuing to try to bring his troops to order.

Gage himself remembered that Braddock at one point tried to organize assaults on the high ground to the right from which was coming the most galling fire. He would prevail on a small group to do so. They began to make their way up the slope, but only until their officer or perhaps a couple of men at the forefront fell, and then the rest immediately gave way. After two hours of disastrous battle, Braddock tried a final assault on the high ground. This time he had one hundred fifty men, but the officers leading were picked off one after another until the men lost their nerve and tumbled back down in what one observer called "the utmost panic and confusion."

This was, however, not the utmost panic and confusion of the day. This occurred shortly after, when Braddock himself fell, grievously wounded. Now nothing was left but flight. The wagoneers, seeing the men at the front break, simply cut the harnesses and rode the horses off bareback to safety. (One of the wagoneers was Daniel Boone, another Daniel Morgan; both lived to demonstrate their bravery on other days.) And the British troops ran as fast as they could. Washington could barely believe his eyes; vaunted British regulars had "broke and run as sheep before hounds, leaving the artillery, provisions and everything we have with us a prey to the enemy." When he and others tried to rally the troops just to retake some of the invaluable materiel, "it was with as much success as if we had attempted to have stopped the wild bears of the mountain." Washington's estimate of regular forces had undergone severe correction in a short time.

All this loot, including the scalps of the dead and dying, probably saved the lives of those remaining, for the Indians had no inclination to follow up the rout with so much plunder readily at hand. The retreat, nonetheless, was a scene on which only Horror itself could smile—the dead, the dying, the groans, lamentations, and cries along the road of the wounded for help.

Of the eighty-six officers, sixty-three had been killed or seriously wounded; of the remaining men, fully two-thirds were casualties. Braddock's own wound was mortal; the bullet had passed through an arm into his lungs. He died a lingering death, knowing both the nature of his wound and the extent of his defeat. According to a popular account, he at one point asked for a pistol that he might "die like an old Roman." According to another, with dying eyes he praised the colonial troops, having learned too late their superiority to his own regulars. Braddock died amidst the still-retreating tramp of the troops. He was buried on the road itself, so that any evidence of the grave would be obliterated by the passing feet and wagons lest his corpse be disinterred and submitted to indignities by his villainous savage foes, who did not abide by the rules of war—who did not know there were any.

As far as we know, no wanton hand ever did disturb his remains; the exact location of the grave has never been found. The site of the battle itself became known as Braddock's Field. Three years later, there still could be seen bones lying there one on top of the other, thick as the leaves that cover a forest floor after an early frost, mingled memorials of violent death. For about half a mile in length and about one hundred yards in breadth was a plain bleached field of white, broken only occasionally by a faded fragment of a British redcoat or colonial blue being played with by the breeze.

The response in the colonies to the dire news of Braddock's defeat was shock and fear, but also disgust and a little pride. Shock because the defeat was so entirely unexpected. Fear because the whole frontier now lay open to French and Indian raids; this was the kind of defeat that would send all wavering Indians to the French side. Disgust because of the apparent stupidity of the British troops, who did not seem to know enough to put a tree between themselves and an Indian rifle. Disgust as well at the stupidity of Braddock; he and his vaunted Regulars were being compared to many things now by colonial wits, mostly to various animals, mostly to one or another breed of dog. But this disgust was related to a small pride that would grow as the story of Braddock's defeat was told and re-told and amplified.

In this ignominious defeat the Americans alone had distinguished themselves. The American leaders had warned Braddock about the foolishness of his plans. American soldiers had fought gallantly, while the British cowered like the dogs they were. One patriotic vignette has Braddock cursing his own men for cowardice while praising the Virginians. Another has him with his dying breath expressing regret to Washington, "Oh, my dear colonel, had I been governed by your advice, we never should have come to this."

Of course, Braddock might well have been brooding regretfully on his deathbed about Washington's advice—not quite for the reason the vignette suggests. Nonetheless, it is fitting that Braddock did confess to Washington, at least in story, for Braddock quickly became transformed into the personification of what was wrong with the British Empire, and Washington into what was right with America.

Washington had not just survived the debacle of Braddock's defeat; he emerged from it invigorated, like a young god. He had rushed to the front with Braddock, and had been in much of the worst of the fighting. Like Braddock, he had horses shot out from under him. But he alone of Braddock's staff emerged without a scratch, although he did later notice bullet holes in his clothes and one through his hat. In retrospect, Washington himself could scarcely believe his good fortune; it defied reason, and so he attributed it to "the miraculous care of Providence that protected me beyond all human explanation." An Indian opponent agreed; he said that after a while he urged his warriors, "Fire at him no more; see ye not that the Great Spirit protects that chief; he cannot die in battle." Less than a month after the battle,

Washington's name had become an exemplum for a divinely ordained America of limitless possibilities. So the Reverend Samuel Davies asked his Virginia congregation to consider "that heroic youth, Colonel Washington, whom I cannot but hope Providence has hitherto preserved in so signal a manner for some important service to his country." It is not too much to say that the Washington Monument first began to rise from the hideous bone-yard of Braddock's defeat.

Washington's monument was begun, and so was the first world war, the whole of the wilderness between New France and the British colonies becoming a demonic theater of cruelty, the woods bursting with war whoops, innumerable bayonets glittering between the boughs. British forces thrust up the defile toward Lake Champlain, only to be ambushed by the French and Indians. At first it seemed like Braddock's defeat *redux;* but after suffering heavy losses, the British managed to regroup and counterattack. The French commander (himself left a permanent invalid by wounds he got that day) said that the British fought like good boys in the morning, true men at noontime, and very devils in the afternoon. The French withdrew, having taken comparable losses; but the British became human again, and found themselves too exhausted to follow up the advantage. With this the campaign ended, a campaign that Parkman aptly described as a "failure disguised as an incidental success."

There were a few inconsequential consequences of this engagement. The British officially changed the name of a lake nearby from that given it by Isaac Jogues, Holy Sacrament, to Lake George. A small body of water where, according to one account, the British deposited bodies to prevent the Indians from taking scalps became forever Bloody Pond. Also a new fort was built, to be named after the king's grandson William Henry; Fort William Henry itself soon to be the scene for further bloody havoc.

During the summer the grieving Governor Shirley tried to lead an assault on Fort Niagara, to cut off the Ohio as Braddock should have. The campaign fizzled without so much as a significant engagement. All Shirley succeeded in doing was to lose a second son, this one ingloriously to dysentery. So the first year of the war came to a close, and the only action taken against the French that patriots could point to as an unqualified success was Lawrence's deportation of Acadian Neutrals. That lone hostile act had been carried out properly. Judged by this year, the British empire in North America looked like another tottering Troy waiting to be shaken off its foundations of sand.

The French themselves realized they did not have to think of conquests or sieges. They had only to unleash their dogs of war, and soon all the British frontier would smell of human carrion. Within a year the new commander of Fort Duquesne could brag, "I have succeeded in ruining the three adjacent provinces, Pennsylvania, Maryland and Virginia, driving off the inhabitants and totally destroying the settlements over a tract of country thirty leagues wide." These raids had only cost him two officers and a few other men, whereas Indian villages near Fort Duquesne were filled with British goods and prisoners to do with as they pleased. Braddock's defeat had only been the beginning of the carnage. "The enemy," he wrote by way of conclusion, "has lost far more since the battle than on the day of his defeat."

What the French commander claimed the other side confirmed. To Washington had fallen the impossible task of protecting the three hundred fifty miles of the Virginian frontier. He wrote despairingly about the situation: "Every day we have accounts of such cruelties and barbarities as are shocking to human nature. It is not possible to conceive the situation and danger of this miserable country. Such numbers of French and Indians are all around that no road is safe."

This is Washington the man not the monument, without any glib reference to being charmed by Providence. At times he sounds almost like Brébeuf pleading with God for his doomed Hurons. He sees the destruction happening all about him, and yet sees nothing for himself to do. The pleas from the victims "melt me" into a "deadly sorrow." He only wishes he could somehow offer himself as a "willing sacrifice" to stop the dreadful butchery.

But it did not stop, and nowhere was it worse than in Pennsylvania. The Delawares, after Braddock's defeat, had gone over to the French in large numbers, and now showed themselves to be among the most skillful raiders. Benjamin Franklin went to see at firsthand the panic that drove families from their homesteads to the nearest fortified towns, like Bethlehem, where there was no more room at the inns, or the shops, or even in the cellars. Every available space was being used to shelter refugees, who were fed on empty hopes, deluded by empty terrors, inflamed by empty words, and shedding many useless tears.

These border towns, teeming with war and bitterness, sent pleas for help to Philadelphia, at times addressing its leaders as if they were inhabitants of a different planet. One, for instance, tried to persuade the governor that "it is really very shocking for a husband to see the wife of his bosom her head cut off, and the children's blood drunk like water, by these bloody and cruel savages."

The governor himself, and many other citizens, thought they knew whom to blame for having left Pennsylvania at the mercy of the Indians. The British were partly to blame, of course; but the true villains were the sanctimonious Quakers who dominated the assembly. The governor berated them for taking satisfaction in Braddock's defeat. (He who lives by the sword . . .) The Quakers did not seem to want to understand that the sword was the only way to survive in this world. So they had left the province inadequately defended in order to increase their Mammon in the name of Christ.

Even Franklin, who had been frequently allied with the Quakers in the assembly against the governor, now partially turned against them. He proposed a militia bill in the assembly, one that would be distasteful to strict Quakers but still allowed them special status as conscientious objectors. In support of the measure he wrote a dialogue for his *Gazette*. One exchange gives a sense of the feeling at the time. One speaker says, "For my part, I am no coward; but hang me if I'll fight to save the Quakers." Another responds, "That is to say, you won't pump out the ship because 'twill save the rats as well as yourself."

Franklin, ever adaptable, now became a military man, Colonel Franklin, with many of the same frontier responsibilities as the younger, more experienced Colonel Washington had in Virginia. He continued to speculate and tinker. He tried to come up with better weapons against the Indians; one plan was to train packs of large, fierce dogs to hunt them down. If Mars was the god of the times, then Franklin would try to be a serviceable devotee.

The Quakers found it less easy to adapt to the brutality of the present crisis. They were now being taxed for war, without any possibility of Franklinesque verbal circumlocutions for conscience's sake. By April 1756 Governor Morris had established a bounty "for the scalp of every male Indian enemy above the age of 12 years old, produced as evidence of their being killed, the sum of one hundred and thirty pieces of eight." The bounty would soon be extended, at reduced rates, to women and children. During one notable meeting of Friends in Philadelphia, a wagon was being paraded outside through the streets, a wagon full of scalped and mutilated bodies, to raise the fighting spirit of Philadelphians.

The time had obviously come for the Society of Friends to clarify its relationship to the City of Man—in particular, that city of man called Pennsylvania. And that clarification would occur largely due to the small, still voice of one man, John Woolman. Woolman was not the kind of man likely to make it into a history written by an Edward Gibbon, except perhaps briefly as the easy target for sophisticated irony of a kind that Woolman would himself never use or understand. There was much goodness in John Woolman, but no shrewdness or humor. His autobiographical *Journal* makes for dull reading, and yet the sweet, soft simplicity of his temper lingers long after the book has been set aside unfinished, lingers like a pleasing fragrance in the air, an invisible benedictive presence.

Why, Gibbon would ask us, waste time on a simpleton like Woolman when important events are occurring? The British now have a dynamic young leader, William Pitt, that darling of fate. He alone comprehends the vast chessboard of war that events have laid out before him. He comprehends, and knows how to act. He is already organizing a new army under an able general to bring the British colors back to the Ohio and to retake Fort Duquesne (henceforth to be known as Pittsburgh) and to begin to push into the heart of New France.

Gibbon is right. All this is happening, and it is important. But we have had enough for the time being of carnage and stinking corpses, of the darlings and victims of fate, of the shrewd and the ironic, of a base, degenerate world that forever courts the yoke of war and bows its neck to Caesars. We need a brief respite from all that. So let us listen for a while to the voice of Woolman. There will be plenty of time, there is always plenty of time, to return to the joyless deserts of war.

Woolman had grown up in New Jersey, a southern portion of New Netherlands that had been detached after the British conquest. Quakers prospered there, in a Southern manner, with many slaves. In 1734, when Woolman was still a teenager, a plot of insurrection by the slaves was discovered, or projected, and the purported leader—a young man—burned alive.

Woolman, sincere and inarticulate, responded to the Quaker call to an inward life, and made Quaker teachings distinctively his own. God was a being invisible and incomprehensible in Himself, the ways of His Providence dark and intricate; our understanding tries to trace them in vain. Yet as we cultivate our inward sense of Him, we can love Him in all His visible manifestations, and find therein an earnest of eternal peace. Since by His breath the flame of life was kindled in all sentient creatures, we should countenance no cruelty even to the least of them. The train of thought seemed self-evident to Woolman, but where it led he was not altogether certain. It did seem to entail a kindness to animals that was uncommon.

One day he was being employed as a scrivener, and was writing out a will. He came to the passage in which the slaves were bequeathed, and he found he could not write it. He tried but he could not; it was as simple as that. Simple too was understanding why, although that came a little later.

How could anyone who would not countenance cruelty against the least of God's creatures countenance slavery? Yet Quakers owned slaves. This just

showed how hard it was, even for Quakers, to accept the happiness of humility. The root of the problem is avarice. To have more than one needs, one must
live off the labor of others, usually unwilling labor of which slavery was the
extreme form. Yet, as near as Woolman could determine, the increase of
wealth led to only one thing: the desire for still more wealth.

Woolman tried to avoid this slippery slope by becoming a simple tailor.
Whenever he began to accumulate wealth despite himself, he would close up
shop and travel among the Quaker communities scattered about the colonies.
He loved the Quakers of the backwoods, with all the rudeness and hardships
of their life. As he put it, "It becomes a disciple of Christ to be therewith content." He grieved for the Quakers of the coast who he thought lived off the
poor and the weak. The wealthier a Quaker magnate, the worse he treated his
servants. And as for slavery, it was "a dark gloominess hanging over the land,"
a gloominess that portended a day of judgment; a dark cloud on which he
could see the glint of the red horse.

Although Woolman in his life labored for an inward stillness, he found
himself less and less able to keep his peace about the betrayal of the light that
was occurring daily all about him, especially within the Society of Friends. In
1754 he published in Philadelphia (now his home) "Some Considerations on
the Keeping of Negroes." It was typical of Woolman, full of kind, consoling
care and friendly sorrow. It began with the mild observation that wisdom dic-
tates we should not uncritically accept generally approved customs or popu-
larly received opinions; we must rather judge them by the treasures of our
soul, the standard of truth. So we must never dissemble and speak a language
foreign to our hearts. The main body of the essay begins by quoting the
Gospel of Matthew, "Forasmuch ye did it to the least of these my brethren ye
did it unto me."

Woolman would spend much of the rest of his life working against slavery;
abolitionism may well begin its continuous history in North America with
him and like-minded Quakers of his generation. But the 1750s presented
him, as it did most others living in the British colonies, with more immediate
challenges.

On February 7, 1754, Woolman had a vision. He was looking out over an
orchard but there were two suns in the sky, as if competing to dominate it.
Out of the west came streams of fire until they spread directly overhead. And
he saw a house—his house?—full of people whose faces were all sadness and
deep torment. And then across the green field, under the red sky, marched a
great multitude of men, military men. And as they passed some looked at him
with contempt. Their captain, a militiaman, broke ranks to come up to

Woolman to explain to him that they had been assembled to improve the discipline of war. Then the strange vision ended.

When the war prophesied by the vision actually began—the vision had somehow known the news before the event—Woolman realized what the treasures of the soul, the language of the heart required of him. He should have nothing to do with helping improve the discipline of war. Should Friends solicit hell for aid or arm fiends?

We must bear witness to the peaceable kingdom. Charity is never ill-timed. However loud fear and grief and rage and pain, charity still must speak the language of compassion. Against the lords and sovereigns of this world we have only our conscience. Whatever happens to us, we know we will meet again in happier climes and on a safer shore. And this also we know: When violence prevails and vicious men bear sway, the post of honor is a private station.

By 1756 the Quakers had relinquished their control over the government of Pennsylvania, members of the assembly resigning their seats or refusing to stand for reelection. They reluctantly concluded they could not conduct a war and remain Friends. Woolman had convinced them, as much by the living witness of his life as by his words, that to be true to the Inner Light they had to end voluntarily Penn's Holy Experiment. Penn's woods had to be left to those more fit to rule its dark recesses.

Chapter XII

MONTCALM AT QUEBEC

N EVER WAS A GENERAL in a more critical position than I was; God has delivered me; His be the praise! He gives me health, although I am worn out with labor, fatigue, and miserable dissensions that have determined me to ask for my recall. Heaven grant that I may get it!"

Thus the Marquis de Montcalm wrote to his mother in 1758. This is not the kind of letter one expects to read from a general who knew he was at that very moment being celebrated in Paris as the saviour of New France. Montcalm had just decisively won the greatest battle of his career, and he is praying to heaven to be recalled. He prays to be recalled while knowing that he probably will not. This prayer is really an expression of something close to despair. How had he come to this sorrowful pass?

Montcalm had had every reason to rejoice at his original appointment to New France. He was formally "Louis-Joseph de Montcalm-Gozon, lord of Saint-Véran, Candiac, Tornemire, Vestric, Saint-Julien d'Arpam, and baron of Gabriac." A most distinguished lineage it was, a string of names rich with the history of France, a glittering web that stretched across the whole *ancien régime*. "Gozon" was, for instance, added after the marriage in 1438 between a Montcalm and the daughter of Deodat de Gozon, then grand master of the Order of Saint-John of Jerusalem.

Montcalm's blood was, at least in part, the blood of a crusader. And this blood demanded he serve in arms wherever his Majesty sought to send him. Indeed, honor and duty required that he seek for himself the most arduous and important tasks. Before his appointment to New France he had already distinguished himself. In the disastrous battle the French lost before Piacenza he had been in the forefront of the fighting, and his men had been cut down around him. When he himself was finally taken prisoner, he had already received five wounds, two of them saber wounds to his head. More than just brave, Montcalm was a thoroughly trained professional soldier and his appointment as major general in charge of all troops in North America at the age of forty-four was a triumph for himself and his family, something in which they all had ample reason to rejoice.

And yet as one looks through his earlier correspondence, one finds another Montcalm sometimes breaking through the disciplined front of the professional soldier. One senses a man, although professionally competent and justly proud of that competence, who was personally unsuited for the career his lineage and his society had set for him, a man oppressed by his station however well he might wear his chains. This Montcalm wanted only to be amongst his family—reading his books, improving his lands, attending to his children. Even in one of his earliest campaigns, long before he was married, at a time when in his inexperience he might still be charmed by the sound of bullets, he wrote to his father wanly, "I am learning German, and read more Greek, thanks to my loneliness, than I had done for three or four years." This loneliness, this dissatisfaction became a more and more persistent theme in letters after he married and his family grew. The life of the camp and the supposed glories of fighting were to him no compensation for his absence from the simple pleasures of his home, that tissue of small things that alone gave life charm for him. He realized all the more how fragile was the happiness he found within his family, how easily it might be destroyed by things he could not control. In 1752 he wrote concerning his six children: "May God preserve them all and make them prosper for this world and the next! Perhaps it will be thought that the number is large for so moderate a fortune, especially as four of them are girls; but does God ever abandon his children in their need?

> *Aux petits des oiseaux il donne la pâture*
> *Et sa bonté s'etend sur toute la nature."*

An Acadian would not have caught this allusion to Racine, but he otherwise would have been entirely at home with Montcalm's sentiments. Yet Montcalm was no simple farmer who could rest content in his family and their concerns. He accepted the demands the greater society made upon him—and so he had aspired to the command of New France, and eagerly accepted it when it was offered.

But this was the public Montcalm who sought and eagerly accepted command. The private Montcalm began to lament his promotion almost as soon as he reached Quebec. Again and again he wrote of how much he missed his family and hoped the war would end soon. He yearned for peace and his own return.

"Think of me affectionately; give love to my girls. I hope next year I may be with you all." "There is not an hour in the day I do not think of you, my mother and my children." "Love to my daughters, and all respect and affection to my mother. I live only in the hope of joining you all again." At one point he apologizes to his wife Angelique for not being able to gossip with her about military plans, as he was when a lower-ranking officer not privy to military secrets. He does gossip with her about the parties and balls he attends in Quebec and Montreal, always emphasizing how pretentious and tedious they were. (Letters to other correspondents seem to suggest that he did not find all the parties altogether unendurable nor all the ladies there altogether tedious.) He is eager for Angelique to tell him news, any news, the more trivial the better, especially about his children—a new dress for a daughter, for instance. "The new gown with blond trimmings must be becoming, for she is pretty." There was especially his little daughter Mirète. Her smile to him was a deep truth wordlessly understood, a spark in his life from some central sun.

When he is given a new decoration from the king himself, Montcalm writes to Angelique that he is of course proud to have brought honor to the name Montcalm, but personally and just between them, "I think I am better pleased with what you tell me of the success of my oil mill." This was an oil mill Montcalm had set up before leaving, but had never seen in operation.

Oil mills or royal decorations—Montcalm privately wanted to think that he preferred the oil mills, but decorations and brittle glory were what the public Montcalm was seeking in New France. One looks in vain in Montcalm for any sense of the coming catastrophe for the Old Regime in France. But this is not surprising. The splendor of the expiring monarchy was somehow at its most impressive as it calmly rolled like a great, smug river toward its sudden abyss. Old France was secure for Montcalm; in New France he was going to have the opportunity to excel, and then he would return to the happiness of his family, content with having done his duty, with having fulfilled his higher calling.

Almost from the first, however, Montcalm had sensed difficulties. He knew perfectly well that he was to be officially under the command of Governor Pierre Vaudreuil, a native Canadian from a distinguished French family who himself had much experience in colonial administration but almost none in military command. Montcalm would naturally have expected that once there he would have a free hand in conducting military affairs as he saw fit. This expectation received a rude shock when Montcalm read his own official instructions. They did not just mention his subordination to Vaudreuil; they mentioned it again and again and again.

"Marquis de Montcalm is to command only under this Governor's authority and be his subordinate in all matters . . . M. de Montcalm shall have only to execute and see that the troops under his command execute all the Governor's orders . . . M. de Montcalm shall always submit to the orders and instructions of this Governor . . . In a word, the Governor General shall rule and decide all military operations. And M. le Marquis de Montcalm shall have to execute them as prescribed."

Montcalm could not have known that Vaudreuil had urged, indeed almost insisted, that no European commander be appointed as commander of the forces defending New France: "I must, my Lord, have the honour to represent to you that it is not necessary to have a general officer at the head of these four battalions; they can be disciplined and exercised without that. War in this country is very different from the wars in Europe. We are obliged to act with great circumspection so as not to leave anything to chance; we have few men, and however small the number we may lose, we feel its effect. However brave the commander of those troops may be, he could not be acquainted with the country, nor perhaps, be willing to receive the advice subalterns may offer; would rely on himself or on ill enlightened counsels, and would not succeed, though he should sacrifice himself . . . I must not conceal from you, my Lord, that the Canadians and Indians would not march with the same confidence under the order of a commander of the troops from France as they would under the officers of this colony. I flatter myself that you will approve my representations, the object of which is the good of the service and of this country."

Montcalm's instructions were the result of the ministers' effort to mollify Vaudreuil now that the governor's strongly expressed advice was being ignored. The ministers were going to allow Vaudreuil to use his legal position as fully as he chose. And Montcalm was not long in New France before he realized that Vaudreuil intended to exercise his power of command fully. More than that, Vaudreuil was intent on demonstrating that Montcalm simply was not needed—and Montcalm was not long in feeling that his own presence was being treated as superfluous. Montcalm, as soon as he realized this, decided that his honor required him to fight a two-front war—in the field against the British, and on paper against Vaudreuil. If Montcalm was ever to exercise his command fully, Vaudreuil had to be put in his place.

He wrote back to his superior about Vaudreuil in glowing terms. "The Governor-General overwhelms me with politeness; I believe him to be satisfied with my conduct towards him, and I think it convinced him that general officers can be found in France who will study the public good under his orders, without pretension or finesse. He is acquainted with the country; possesses in his hands both authority and means; is at the head of business; he it is who must prescribe it; it is mine to relieve him of the details relative to our troops, in what regards discipline and the execution of his plans."

This is only Montcalm showing his superior (who, after all, had drafted his instructions) what a good soldier he is, cheerfully following his orders with the best possible grace. But at the very time he is writing this, Montcalm is also writing in cipher to his patron within the French government (the man responsible for getting him his appointment) a somewhat different portrait of Governor Vaudreuil: "M. de Vaudreuil particularly respects the Indians, loves the Canadians, is acquainted with the country, has good sense, but is somewhat weak, and I stand very well with him."

The somewhat weak governor loves Indians and Canadians, but what of the French? A week later Montcalm is more explicit with the same correspondent: "I am on good terms with him, but not in his confidence, which he never gives to anybody from France. His intentions are good, but he is slow and irresolute." Montcalm's tactics are clear. He intends slowly, resolutely to put more and more material damaging to Vaudreuil in his reports. He wants Paris and Versailles to conclude that Vaudreuil is an incompetent who places the interests of his colony over the interests of France. Montcalm wants to achieve this without compromising himself. He does not want to appear a disloyal subordinate, a nobleman who cannot work with local officials. He wants to appear the innocent party. But in this respect Montcalm was about as innocent as Vaudreuil, at the best.

However attractive Montcalm appears when discussing his daughter's new dress, his loneliness in the field, his oil mill, and his struggles with Greek, he is a different person when he feels his dignity is challenged. Then it is *Marquis* de Montcalm. Those who forget that do so at their peril. Nonetheless, even when Montcalm behaves like a vain courtier (as he will in this campaign against Vaudreuil), his human side keeps breaking through.

He finds it impossible to keep his own counsel. He has to unburden himself to others, as if he were back in the bosom of his family. He knows that to be effective he has to keep up the pretence of a loyal subordinate, and therefore to get Vaudreuil off his guard. He knows his whole campaign depends upon it—and yet he cannot. He will bare his frustrations to his French subordinates, at times shocking them with the frankness of his language. Sometimes his language, at least in letters, will shock even himself, and he will urge correspondents to burn the letter immediately after reading it (which frequently they do not).

Montcalm is simply incapable of persistent duplicity, although he realizes his position as military commander demands of him such duplicity. Inevitably he talks too much. He loses his temper too often, or in the wrong place. Someone he thinks loyal is really not, or someone he thinks not in earshot really is. Inevitably Vaudreuil always seems to know of Montcalm's verbal indiscretions. And Montcalm is left upset with himself, and sadly suspicious of those closest to him.

At times, usually in a letter to his family, he will step back from his role in New France, from all the facades he must assume, and all the responses he must try to evolve—step back and view it from the outside, with a detached disgust. He would write to his mother, "The part I have to play is unique: I am general-in-chief subordinate; passing on orders, meddling with nothing or on certain occasions everything; esteemed, respected, loved, envied, hated, haughty, amenable, difficult, friendly, polished, pious, gallant—and deeply desirous of peace." He had in New France the opportunity to be everything except satisfied. He could look at his life here and say sincerely that nothing was so unlike him as himself. At times he seemed a vast problem to himself.

Still, there was important business at hand. His self-respect required that he do well at his appointed task, or as well as possible in the circumstances. What he needed first was a trustworthy evaluation of the military situation—not one from the governor and his Canadian cronies, but one from a fellow professional experienced at war. The natural place to seek such was from the officers who had served under his predecessor as general, Baron Dieskau. The same day that Montcalm was sending back to France his own first dispatches, one of these very officers was writing back concerning his first conversation with the new commander:

"I am very well satisfied with M. Montcalm. I shall accomplish impossibilities to deserve his confidence. I have spoken to him in the same terms that I did to M. Dieskau, namely: Rely only on Regulars in an expedition, but on the Canadians and Indians to harass the enemy; and me to points of danger with your orders; do not expose yourself. M. de Vaudreuil is prejudiced against M. Doreil, the Commissary ordonnateur, and me, because he suspects we report to the Court what passes. I always continue my course, adopting every possible precaution; I continually pay my court to him. The Colonial officers do not like those of the regular army. It is incredible to what a degree luxury prevails in this country, and to what an extent the King is robbed in consequence of the bad administration of affairs. All the French who arrive here are shocked at the waste that is made. The Governor and Intendant are too easy and too remiss in a country where greater strictness is required than in any other. There is no police. The Canadian is independent, wicked, lying, braggart, well adapted for skirmishing, very brave behind a tree and very timid when not covered. I believe a defensive course will be adopted on both sides. M. Montcalm appears to me not to have any desire to attack the enemy. I believe he is right. In these countries a thousand of us would keep three thousand of them in check. The enemy are, at least, three thousand stronger than we."

Montcalm, true to his temperament, had made up his mind quickly as to what he thought should be done. But Vaudreuil had supreme command, and Vaudreuil thought differently. Moreover, as Montcalm would soon learn to his chagrin, it was Vaudreuil, not Montcalm, who understood the situation. Vaudreuil understood in particular that the very strategic weakness of New France required that it keep the offensive. The British troops vastly outnumbered the French, as the general population of the British colonies dwarfed the population of New France. Moreover, the French had a frontier that stretched all the way from Louisbourg to the Ohio Valley. A substantial proportion of the French resources, both in men and wealth, had to be used simply to keep its remote forts adequately supplied. And if this were not enough, the relative severity of the Canadian winters (compared, say, with those of Pennsylvania) meant that New France, unlike the British colonies, was frequently going to be dependent on food from France—and yet the British largely controlled the sea. In short, Vaudreuil realized that in a simple test of strength with the British colonies, New France would be conquered. Vaudreuil's job was to keep things complex, and his chief means of doing so were the Indians and the Canadian forest rangers.

The kind of terrorist campaign that the Delawares were waging in Pennsylvania was in fact occurring all along the frontier. Vaudreuil boasted that in this campaign his allies were killing one hundred British for every casualty suffered. Of course, among this hundred were many women and children, and the way his Indians chose to dispatch their victims was often grisly. But these were not unfortunate incidental aspects of the campaign for Vaudreuil; rather, they were essential. He was not seeking military victory for New France—that was impossible. He was rather seeking to demoralize his enemy; to make them sickened of the war; so sickened that, despite their objective superiority, they would sue for peace.

The New York *Gazette* a week before Montcalm arrived in Quebec reported that a Lieutenant Brooks of Connecticut had been taken by the Indians only two miles from his fort, Fort Edwards; when he was later discovered, he had had "his mouth cut open and tongue cut out, his entrails taken out of his body and afterwards crammed into his mouth." This was, from the Canadian point of view, a good death well reported. In such a campaign, both regular troops from France and generals like Montcalm (with their regular ideas) were in fact the true auxiliaries. Their importance was only to assist the Indians and Canadian militiamen who would range in the forest and keep the British at bay.

On the other hand, a French general, however well trained, however courageous, could not be expected to understand Vaudreuil's strategy, any more than Braddock had understood what was happening to him until it was too late. New France was better off without a French general, who would only get in the way. And now that unfortunately it did have a French general, Vaudreuil did not want his advice because he knew ahead of time that the advice would be precisely wrong. Montcalm's advice would be wrong, and his sense of honor out of place. Vaudreuil could only hope that Montcalm would realize this quickly and then just follow orders meekly. He hoped it but did not expect it.

Montcalm's French officers did learn rather quickly, and to their own disgust, about the Indians. Louis-Antoine de Bougainville, one of the subordinates who arrived with Montcalm and with whom he was particularly close, at first perceived the Indians as noble savages, with Bougainville playing the role of aesthetic connoisseur of native dancing: "Extraordinary spectacle, more suited to terrify than to please; curious, however, to the eye of a philosopher who seeks to study man in conditions nearest to nature. These men were naked save for a piece of cloth in front and behind, the face and body painted, feathers on their heads, symbol and signal of war, tomahawk and spear in their hand. In general these are brawny men, large and of good appearance; almost all are very fat. One could not have better hearing than those people. All the movements of their body mark the cadence with great exactness."

By the end of his first summer in New France, however, Bougainville had seen his noble savages in action. Now he writes not out of philosophical curiosity but out of fear of moral contagion: "The cruelties and the insolence of these barbarians is horrible, their souls are as black as pitch. It is an abominable way to make war; the retaliation is frightening, and the air one breathes here is contagious of making one accustomed to callousness."

Bougainville by this time had realized that he could not interfere too much with these cruelties, nor take too great an offense at Indian insolence, because Indian cooperation was essential to Montcalm's errand in the wilderness.

Montcalm wrote home that he and Bougainville talked hours on end about his olive press.

Vaudreuil, in the meantime, was thinking about Lake Ontario. New France still maintained two forts on Lake Ontario: Fort Frontenac at the northeast of the lake, where it drains into the Saint Lawrence, and Fort Niagara at the southwest, where Lake Erie drains into it. The British had, however, established their own fort—actually a cluster of three—at the southeast corner of the lake. Vaudreuil saw these British forts as a grave threat, for these forts could easily harass the fur trade that flowed along these great lakes to Montreal and Quebec. Indeed, they represented the British attempt to divert that trade to Albany and thereby sever the economic tie between New France and its western allies. The British had only to convince the Indians that neutrality in the struggle between France and Britain was in their own best interests. Vaudreuil knew that the neutrality of the Indians in this struggle would doom New France.

The destruction of these British forts was to be Montcalm's first major task in the New World—or rather, Montcalm, in destroying these forts, would be finishing a task already largely done by Vaudreuil. The last winter Vaudreuil had used the Canadians and Indians to isolate these forts (called by the British Oswego and by the French Chouagnen) from the nearest British settlements. Their main supply depot had been destroyed and then the captives massacred when the Canadian commander, during the victory celebration, became, in Vaudreuil's cool phrase, "no longer master of his men." The forts had spent the rest of the winter under siege from an unseen enemy. Those from them who ventured out were killed, as slowly as possible, preferably within hearing of the fort.

At the end of the winter a messenger from the fort announced in Albany, "Oswego is still a part of the British Empire." But no one was betting that it would remain so for long. One British colonial expressed the general opinion when he wrote, "If we hold it, it is only because of the enemy's lack of skill and capacity." But it was not going to be because of Vaudreuil's lack of skill or capacity. The autumn before he had already provisioned Fort Frontenac for the thousands of troops he intended to send there this very spring. Vaudreuil was going to allow Montcalm to reap the fruits of a year's preparation; Montcalm could command the forces, assisted by Rigaud de Vaudreuil, the governor's brother, who would be in charge of the Canadian and Indian auxiliaries.

The orders were given to Montcalm suddenly, with little warning and no adequate explanation. Montcalm had not even been consulted on the plan, and now he was ordered off to a siege that made no sense in European terms. For Montcalm the objective seemed sufficiently military (unlike the objectives of so many Canadian raids), but he did not see sufficient preparations for the undertaking. He was unaware of any serious planning. He clearly did not have enough artillery, nor enough troops. He could not be sure that Vaudreuil's estimates of British forces were themselves accurate. He certainly could not be expected to take three important forts under such circumstances. Perhaps he could salvage something from Vaudreuil's foolishness by at least harassing the enemy. He would follow orders, but he could not refrain from pointing out that this was what happened when you allowed amateurs to command professionals.

He wrote at length to Paris to make sure that everyone realized Vaudreuil was responsible for this action, not Montcalm. "In order to be successful, we would require secrecy and swiftness, which are not the virtues of the Colony. You may be assured, my Lord, that I readily devote myself to this project, and that I count myself as nothing on an occasion of so much interest and which has appeared to me quite pregnant with obstacles to be surmounted. Increased diligence on the part of the enemy may oblige me, on my arrival at Frontenac to renounce this grand project, but we shall have made a diversion."

By the time Montcalm had reached Fort Frontenac he was no more optimistic. He wrote to one of his French subordinates, listing his options and adding, "If I do nothing of which I write here, do not be surprised. One has to be rash, or a good citizen, to risk such an undertaking with less artillery and less troops than the besieged, and horrible distress as regards victuals." Montcalm added, "What I write you is for you only." On re-reading his letter, he must have worried that its tone would shock his subordinate and assured him in a postscript that he would welcome letters from him equally candid. A few days later Montcalm wrote again: "I do not want it to be said that I embarked on a siege only to raise it later or that I exposed my artillery to unnecessary risks. I am leaving the day after tomorrow in the evening or early the following day with four field pieces, ammunition for two thousand men, and less king than pirate."

Canadians like Rigaud might feel comfortable playing the pirate in the name of good citizenship. The Marquis de Montcalm did not. As the campaign slowly progressed, he repeatedly looked for reasons to delay the advance, all the while hoping that he could find a justification for turning back. He never found that justification. Montcalm was continually being prodded by his officers and by the adventuresome actions of the Canadians and their Indians. He responded with pessimism and procrastination.

When Montcalm had reached within a league of the first fort, Rigaud offered to go on ahead with a few hundred Canadians to begin the siege. A day after Rigaud began this siege, and while Montcalm was just completing the road for the rest of the army, the British retreated from the fort. So Rigaud could boast that his troops by themselves had taken the first fort. Let him boast, for the next two would not be so easy—or so Montcalm could console himself.

A river separated the first fort from the other two. Montcalm decided to establish his artillery in the first fort, and from there to cannonade the others. He also ordered Rigaud with his Indians and Canadians to cross the river while this was going on and then to try to cut off communication between the two forts still held by the British. But Montcalm failed to set up his artillery properly, and the British began to win the artillery duel. The British, now realizing their advantage, were preparing to come out of their fort to engage the French directly when their inspirational commander, a Colonel Mercer, was killed—cut in two by a cannonball in the sight of his men, according to one account. The counterattack was postponed, but the British advantage in the artillery exchange persisted. Later, one of the French there wrote: "The English, one must agree, have very little understanding of war; they surrendered at the very moment when we were being knocked out by their artillery."

Why did they suddenly surrender? The death of Mercer was one factor. But the captives who returned to New France told of another, as is recorded in a letter of the time: "They would have held out longer in Chouagnen, so they assured me, if Canadians and Indians had not crossed the river; they saw them advancing with such ardour, although they were in water up to their chests, that they feared they might be caught and killed in their entrenchments, which were being bombarded from behind by our artillery."

The British had surrendered not out of deficient understanding of war, but rather because Vaudreuil had over the past winter provided them with a vivid education in war Canadian style. These were soldiers who had seen the remains of incautious compatriots who had been caught by the Indians. If they did not surrender to the French at the earliest moment, they might come to envy Colonel Mercer his quick if shocking death. They could not face the Indians and Canadians in their murderous ardor. The new commander simply panicked out of fear of falling into the hands of the Indians.

Montcalm, at least initially, was well satisfied with his victory. He thought his earlier reports of the difficulties involved would only increase the estimate of his achievement. Or so he wrote to a patron back in France. "I had left, my dear chevalier, with ten belts and one hundred strings of wampum, few troops, even less artillery, militia men badly armed; but I had a supply of strings. Therefore I am master of the three forts of Chouagnen, which I demolish, of sixteen hundred prisoners, five flags, one hundred guns, three military chests, victuals for two years, six armed sloops, two hundred bateaux, and an astonishing booty made by our Canadians and Indians. All this costs only thirty men killed and wounded. The expedition will be deemed useful and brilliant by any one who reviews the detail of my operations, and appreciates justly the courage and good will of our French troops. I have never seen such exertions at works accompanied with so much cheerfulness."

He even offered a mock apology for the tactics: "My operations are so strongly against general rules that the audacity of this enterprise would be deemed rashness in Europe: therefore, the only favor I beg from you, my Lord, is to assure His Majesty that, if he ever gives me some command in his armies, as I hope he will, I shall follow very different principles."

But this was all bluff, for he knew perfectly well the interpretation being placed on the victory by Quebec, that envious beehive distilling gall instead of honey. The victory was Vaudreuil's, not his. Vaudreuil had prepared for the siege, and had ordered it. Montcalm had only objected to the order and procrastinated in its implementation. Who of the two knew military operations better? Vaudreuil had said the forts would fall, while General Montcalm said all that could be done was a little diversion. And the forts fell, almost without a fight. Moreover, to whom did they fall? Not to Montcalm and his French regulars, but to Rigaud, the Canadians, and the Indians.

Vaudreuil and those around him were merciless in making this point. While Montcalm was praising the French regulars for their courage and good will, Vaudreuil was praising the Canadians and Indians for their courage and ill will—he said that the British surrendered because of "the cries, threats, and hideous howlings of our Canadians and Indians." Moreover, Vaudreuil was far from modest about his own role in the campaign: "The measures I took assured our victory, in spite of opposition. If I had been less vigilant and firm, Oswego would still be in the hands of the British." And his Intendant François Bigot agreed, "If M. De Vaudreuil had not been firm in the order he had given to lay siege to it, the English would still be in possession." Montcalm was reduced to a struggle merely to save face. He wrote to his patron: "The greatest joy I experience at having succeeded in this expedition, emanates from the circumstance that such success is due to a general officer, whose selection you alone have determined." Perhaps if Montcalm could just appeal to the vanity of his French superiors, they might at least believe a little of his version.

Whether or not he was believed in Paris, Montcalm still had to live in New France. And there he was given no rest. Even the Bishop of Quebec issued a victory statement in which he praised everyone's contribution to the victory, everyone except those "weak minds" who judged the campaign as "too great for our strength." Montcalm wrote to a French subordinate, "Our friend the Bishop has just issued the most ridiculous statement in the world, but don't mention it for it draws forth the admiration of the whole of Canada. It is much to be regretted that such an intelligent man, such a noble character, should have been so suspicious."

The man in New France to whom this last sentence best applies is not the bishop. In his public writings Montcalm might still be able to sustain a veil of politeness, but privately he seethes. He has been humiliated, and he will not admit it—even to himself. Yet he can never get away from it, he is never allowed to forget it, and so he becomes increasingly defensive and bitter.

Over this winter he takes almost everything personally. When Vaudreuil becomes seriously ill, he thinks people are using it as another occasion to insult him: "People who are uninformed have been very uneasy and disturbed as to what would become of the Colony, in the event of M. Vaudreuil's death." When this event (for which Montcalm obviously hopes) fails to occur, he writes, "The Marquis de Vaudreuil is arrived well enough and able to work as much as before, that is to say little."

There is a fierce wretchedness about him now. He seeks any occasion for his venom, and this attitude seems to infect his subordinates. Bougainville on Chouagnen: "The Indians and Canadians have taken Chouagnen unaided . . . an easy operation in the opinion of the Canadian people, the Marquis de Vaudreuil, and the Bishop, who, so he said, could have captured it with his clergy; doubtless in the same way that Joshua took Jericho, by marching twice around the walls."

Montcalm would not endure his French subordinates to say a single good word for Vaudreuil, and one who tried he derided as suffering from the "Canadian disease." He wrote back to Paris about the "self-flattering talk of the Canadians who consider themselves on every point the first nation in the world." His predecessor Dieskau, he contended, had come to grief precisely because he had taken the Canadians at their word. This statement was intemperate enough. Worse still, Montcalm began to lie. Not the clever lies of a Frontenac that would be hard to catch out—but plain lies that any informed person could see. Montcalm claimed that since the Canadians could not be depended upon, he was careful never to expose them to fire. (Was sending Rigaud and his Canadians ahead of the main body of troops to begin the siege not exposing them to fire? And did not they show themselves more than reliable?) Montcalm eventually even worked himself up to denying his opposition to the campaign. More than that, he reversed his and Vaudreuil's roles. "You may, my Lord, assure his Majesty that diversity of opinions will never injure his service, so far as I am concerned. It is to this diverseness of opinions and to the respectful firmness I always infuse into it, that the Chouagnen expedition is due. The Marquis de Vaudreuil, after having desired it, was ready to renounce it, and I encouraged him by memoirs." By this time Montcalm probably believed what he was saying himself.

Montcalm was now becoming suspicious of everyone. In one of his dispatches he condemns a subordinate for following the governor's orders "too literally." These orders, after all, had been "issued eighty leagues off, by a Governor who knows not how to speak of war." Montcalm adds that when he is away from Quebec, the governor makes changes there "either through ignorance or to cause me disgust." Moreover, the orders and even the letter Vaudreuil sends to Montcalm and his loyal officers are diabolically clever; they are written with "inexcusable duplicity" so that Vaudreuil will get all the credit for any victory (as he did for Oswego) and yet Montcalm and his French troops will be exposed to blame in case of defeat.

Over the winter of 1757 Vaudreuil had ordered a similar raid against another of the British frontier forts. Once again, Montcalm was not consulted in the decision. Once again, when he was informed, he did not approve the plan. Nor did he approve that Canadian forces were going to be used without the French, nor that Rigaud was in command. "This detachment seems to have been decided upon," Montcalm wrote in his personal journal, "in a spirit of prejudice, of intrigue and jealousy against the army." Montcalm was convinced he was right about this raid, and Vaudreuil wrong, both professionally and morally. But the raid was a success, and Montcalm was left to nurse his ever-multiplying suspicions.

The next spring Montcalm was ordered to lead his troops on the path already blazed by Rigaud (once again). The objective was the valley surrounding Lake Champlain, the corridor extending from Montreal to the Hudson Valley. If either the French or the British controlled the valley of Lake Champlain, then they would be able to make quick thrusts into the heartland of the enemy. In 1757 neither side did; control of the valley was balanced, much as control of Lake Ontario had been in 1756. As the campaign of 1756 had given the French complete control of Ontario, so the campaign of 1757 was to do the same for Champlain. This Vaudreuil had decided without consulting his nominal military commander, Montcalm.

Actually Montcalm had reason to be pleased with Vaudreuil's decision. The advanced French position was Fort Carillon (called by the British Ticonderoga); the advanced British position was Fort William Henry. Montcalm was instructed to move his eight thousand troops from Carillon to William Henry, and reduce it by siege. He was going to be able to conduct a traditional siege, and for such a siege he had sufficient men and supplies (although barely enough victuals). He would happily bear the harsh necessities imposed by war, especially to escape temporarily the malicious caprices of Vaudreuil.

Even so, Vaudreuil still caused him difficulty, if only indirectly and at a distance. Vaudreuil had managed to convince an unusually diverse collection of Indian groups to join the French in this campaign, with profuse promises of plunder. The sixteen to eighteen hundred warriors thereby added to Montcalm's army included not only traditional allies such as Micmacs and Abenakis, sometime allies such as the Iroquois, but even the far western Indians such as the Sioux and Chippewas. This was for Vaudreuil a triumph of native diplomacy, worthy of a Frontenac. Montcalm, however, was left to deal with these allies on a day-to-day basis, a task for which he was neither experienced nor suited. Moreover, he could only communicate with them through a panoply of interpreters who, when they were not missionaries, were the very kind of Canadians whom he most despised.

No matter how much experience one had had with Indian affairs, the variety of the groups now assembled was a daunting spectacle. One Jesuit, who traveled with his Abenakis from Acadia, himself tried to evoke the indescribable by cataloguing the ornaments worn by the various groups: "Imagine a great assembly of savages adorned with every ornament most suited to disfigure them in European eyes, painted with vermilion, white, green, yellow, and black made of soot and the scrapings of pots. A single savage face combines all these different colors, methodically laid on with the help of a little tallow, which serves for pomatum. The head is shaved except at the top, where there is a small tuft, to which are fastened feathers, a few beads of wampum, or some such trinket. Every part of the head has its ornament. Pendants hang from the nose and also from the ears, which are split in infancy and drawn down by weights till they flap at last against the shoulders. The rest of the equipment answers to this fantastic decoration: a shirt bedaubed with vermilion, wampum collars, silver bracelets, a large knife hanging on the breast, mooseskin moccasins, and a belt of various colors always absurdly combined. The sachems and war-chiefs are distinguished from the rest: the latter by a gorget, and the former by a medal, with the King's portrait on one side, and on the other Mars and Bellona joining hands, with the device, *Virtus et Honor.*"

Virtue and honor were precisely what the missionary did not see in evidence. He worried that his Christian Indians were going to revert to the savage practices of the various pagan groups, some of which had traveled fifteen hundred miles to join this expedition. They had come, as (to tell the truth) had the Abenakis, in the hope of prisoners, scalps, plunder—any material evidence of successful bravery that could be transported back to their villages. He did not think these other allies would be restrained by European morality. He had already seen the body of an English prisoner being consumed by some savages near where he celebrated Mass, and in sight of other terrified prisoners; when he tried to rebuke the cannibals, the response was, in French no less, "You have French taste; I have Indian. This is good meat for me." The missionary was then genially bid to overcome his cultural chauvinism and try a bite.

Montcalm did his best to address his irregular troops on their own terms. To a collection of them he spoke as follows: "Children, I am delighted to see you all joined together in this good work. So long as you remain one, the English cannot resist you. The great King has sent me to protect and defend you; but above all he has charged me to make you happy and unconquerable, by establishing among you the union which ought to prevail among brothers, children of one father, the great Onontio."

So Montcalm slowly spoke and the translators chattered away, each to his own group, the various languages mixing together in the midst of this united nations of the American wilderness. Montcalm then lifted a huge belt of wampum and continued, "Take this sacred pledge of his word. The union of beads of which it is made is the sign of your united strength. By it I bind you all together, so that none of you can separate from the rest till the English are defeated and their fort destroyed."

Of course, Montcalm knew better. These tribes may be allies of the French, but they were rivals of one another. And as soon as one of them got what it had sought, it was likely to leave for home, taunting the rest with its trophies of manhood. For instance, one war party intercepted a large English scouting party, killing many and taking many more captives. After allowing the French to interrogate the prisoners, the Indians deserted, prisoners in tow. These Indians knew well that eventually the French would give generous ransoms for British captives.

As far as Bougainville was concerned, Montcalm and his command were almost as much captives of the Indians as these unfortunate soldiers: "I shall say once and for all that irrespective of the obligation which one has of being a slave to these Indians, of hearing them night and day in council and in private, when caprice takes hold of them, when a dream, or an excess of vapors and the constant objective of begging brandy or wine leads them on, they are always lacking something from their equipment, their arms, or their toilet, and it is up to the general of the army to issue requisitions for the smallest of these distributions, an eternity of little details, petty and one of which Europe has no idea."

Bougainville went on to describe some of those things of which Europe had no idea. An Indian raiding party kills by reliable count eleven British, but brings back thirty-two scalps—it seems the braves had mastered the art of dividing scalps to increase their rewards from the French. Or a British corpse comes floating by an Indian camp—"they crowded around with loud cries, drank its blood, and put its pieces into the kettle." The Iroquois (who had now come over to the French side in significant numbers) want to conclude meetings of the allies by singing their songs, but the western tribes object because those songs traditionally have been sung against them. Would the Iroquois please stop singing their war songs at the end of the meetings? And would the Delaware braves please stop saying that Iroquois men wear skirts? Bougainville adds, "These are the comrades who are our shadows day and night, I shudder at the ghastly spectacles which they are preparing for us." Bougainville does his part, nonetheless. At one parley he dances the war dance, chanting over and over "Let us trample the English under our feet." And he does it well enough to be adopted into the tribe.

The Indians did provide an important service to Montcalm as he prepared to advance against Fort William Henry. They prevented British scouts from gaining accurate intelligence concerning Montcalm's preparations, and also made difficult any communication between William Henry and Fort Edward, the major British fort to its south where General Daniel Webb sat with the main body of British forces. Montcalm, on the other hand, wanted to have the Indians play as unimportant a role as he could, once the siege of William Henry began.

This was to be a siege in the European style, progressing with the proscribed inevitability of a hanging. Montcalm established batteries within range of the fort, intending to cannonade its defenses until weakened. All the while, his troops would be digging trenches close enough to its walls to be the base for a final assault. The British commander Colonel Monro could see what was happening, and sent a message to Webb asking for the reinforcements that alone could break the noose slowly tightening about his neck.

Montcalm himself announced his presence by a polite note suggesting surrender: "I owe it to humanity to summon you to surrender. At present I can restrain the savages, and make them observe the terms of a capitulation, as I might not have power to do under other circumstances; and an obstinate defense on your part could only retard the capture of the place a few days, and endanger an unfortunate garrison which cannot be relieved in consequence of the dispositions I have made. I demand a decisive answer within an hour."

An obstinate defense was exactly what Monro intended, until his outnumbered troops were relieved; and then to the attack. He responded to Montcalm with a cannonade. So a duel of artillery ensued, in which the French got the better. At one point, a French cannonball took out the British flagpole—and when a British soldier tried to repair it, another cannonball took off his head. Monro issued an order that any British soldier heard suggesting surrender should be hung from the walls of the fort, an order that spoke eloquently if obliquely about declining British morale.

Everything was going according to Montcalm's plan, but that meant he had his own problem with morale. The Indians complained against the plan they did not understand. They were unhappy about their inactivity and Montcalm's failure to consult them. Montcalm profusely if insincerely apologized—and also remonstrated them that braves had been taking unnecessary risks by exposing themselves to fire before the fort; of course, they might pick off the occasional, unwary sentry, but why risk themselves when it would have no influence on the outcome of the siege? Montcalm, it seemed, understood Indian objectives little better than Champlain had a century and a half before.

Actually, the Indians had already made an important contribution. They had killed a British messenger sent to William Henry from Fort Edward, the British fort nearest to it. The now-bloodstained letter begged to inform Monro that Webb had decided against sending reinforcements. William Henry was going to have to hold out as best it could with what it had. And so Montcalm could go about his business methodically, without hurrying—however much that might exasperate the lounging braves. The fort was going to fall; his task was to make sure it was taken with the minimum loss of life. That meant he had to do his best to have the fort surrender without an assault, however much this might disappoint the bloodthirsty.

Montcalm waited until the siege was well enough advanced that an assault seemed imminent. Then he sent Bougainville under a flag of truce to pay his respects to the commander of William Henry—and to deliver, a bit tardily to be sure, the intercepted message concerning reinforcements. Montcalm had waited until this message would have its maximum effect.

A few days later the fort formally surrendered. The surrender may have been hastened by the lenient terms that Montcalm offered. Montcalm would allow the British forces, after surrendering their arms, to march out of the fort back to British lines to the south; all Montcalm demanded in return was the British commander's promise that none of these troops would take the field against the French for the next eighteen months. However barbaric his allies and the surroundings, Montcalm meant to fight this war as a civilized war between civilized men.

Montcalm knew that he could probably have forced an unconditional capitulation on the British. However, such a surrender would have been, for Montcalm at least, morally irresponsible, whatever its immediate military advantages. The war had disrupted both the fragile Canadian agriculture and also the supplementary supplies from France. Montcalm, although adequately supplied otherwise, had barely enough food for his own men—and the situation in Quebec was not much better. To take the British as prisoners, he knew (although the British commander could not have), would be to sentence them to extreme deprivation, if not simple death by starvation. These might be the enemy, but they were also human beings.

Then there were his allies, to whom a feeling of common humanity was an inexcusable weakness. As frustrated as they were by the inactive role he had consigned them, they would be utterly infuriated when they learned that his maneuvering had made a bloody assault unnecessary. He simply did not know how long he could control them (or for that matter their Canadian friends so beloved of Vaudreuil). Let the British surrender the fort one day, and march south the next. He should be able to restrain them that long. As Bougainville explained, "It is never permitted to sacrifice humanity for only the shadow of glory."

Vaudreuil, for his part, wanted to make sure that Montcalm's victory— and this victory was Montcalm's—would give him only the shadow of glory. Taking Fort William Henry was not enough. The British commander for the whole region, the very one who had refused to aid William Henry, now was holed up at Fort Edward, the only fort between Montcalm and the Hudson Valley. Now was the time for a decisive strike. (And the British commander in chief for all of North America, James Campbell, Earl of Loudoun, was at this time afraid that Montcalm might do just that: "Fort Edward, if attacked . . . must fall and Montcalm would have the way open to Albany and New York itself.")

But Montcalm refused to attack. His suspicions of Vaudreuil once again came to the fore: Vaudreuil's order was just another of his duplicitous traps. If Montcalm succeeded in a second siege, then Vaudreuil would take all the credit, and perhaps even claim that Montcalm had opposed this further action. If Montcalm failed, then his successful siege of William Henry would be forgotten, and he would be left with all the blame. He was not going to be tricked by Vaudreuil; he was not going to risk overextending himself.

Montcalm was not thinking very clearly after the fall of William Henry because of a shameful thing that happened then. He had been unable to protect effectively his prisoners, whose safety he had guaranteed on his word. He thought he had done everything in his power. He had met with his Indian headmen before he had signed the articles of capitulation. He explained to them the terms of the surrender. He explained how their honor and his were at stake. The articles had to be followed to the letter. The chiefs agreed to the surrender terms. Then Montcalm told them they would have to control their young men. They said they understood, but Montcalm was mistaking politeness for acquiescence.

What Montcalm had agreed to itself made no sense in traditional Indian terms. They had come to fight alongside the French. They had won a great victory, and now were being told to return home without compensation. They deserved booty, scalps, slaves; but now the French were protecting the British from the Indians, their enemies from their friends. This made no sense at all.

Discipline began to break down almost immediately. The British troops who were not seriously wounded had no sooner evacuated the fort than Indians and Canadians swooped in, looking for booty. They took whatever they could, including the scalps of those left behind in the infirmary. The missionary to the Abenakis saw one warrior running from the fort carrying "a human head, from which trickled streams of blood, and which he displayed as the most splendid prize that he could have secured."

Now the rivalry between Indian groups began to do its ugly work. Those who had broken the terms of the peace had been rewarded for their service, whereas those who had respected it were to go home empty-handed. As this festered, Montcalm thought it was becoming too dangerous to have the British wait until the next morning to leave. They should sneak away at midnight. But the Indians got wind of their preparations, and surrounded them. Montcalm then changed his mind; now any movement of the British might precipitate a massacre. They should wait until morning. As one of the surrendered remembered, the night was the longest of his life: "All the remainder of this night the Indians were in great numbers round our lines and seemed to show more than the usual malice in their looks which made us suspect they intended us mischief."

Bougainville wrote in his journal: "Everything was done to stop them, consultation with the chiefs, wheedling on our part, authority that the officers and interpreters attached to them possessed. We will be most fortunate if we can avoid a massacre. Detestable position of which those who are not here can have no idea, and one which makes the victory painful to the conquerors." And a few days later Bougainville wrote, "A great misfortune which we dreaded has happened . . . the capitulation has been violated and all Europe will oblige us to justify ourselves."

The French could explain that the British prisoners bore at least a little responsibility for this great misfortune. The prisoners were so frightened of the Indians they started to give them rum to make friends. And then after witnessing a night of Indian debauch, seeing how frenzied the Indians had become with drink, the British panicked, and tried to march out of camp before Montcalm could arrange for an armed escort. Montcalm and Bougainville could explain all this, but who would listen? Prisoners, for whose safety Montcalm had pledged his word, had been massacred. Ripped-open bellies, torn-out bowels, half-eaten flesh dangling from legs, trunkless and scalpless and lipless heads were being held high in a pageant of blood. Such sights had been seen many times before in this ghoulish New World war of terror, but this massacre was different. This jubilee of death had occurred after a formal capitulation.

Montcalm could try to explain. It had not been a general massacre, as the British press claimed. The indiscriminate killing had occurred only for a few minutes. The Indians had tried to take possessions away from the British, and when resisted by some then began to respond with violence, which quickly became a homicidal frenzy. For a few minutes the shouts and whoops of those that killed mingled with the screams and groans of those dying, mingled until at a certain distance they were all but indistinguishable, evoking neither pity nor relief. But soon the killing subsided, with perhaps seventy-five, perhaps a hundred fifty, certainly not more than two hundred, lying dead. And then the Indians began in earnest to seize captives, one per man, to carry back home as trophies, eventually to ransom. The British became meek, now knowing full well what any resistance would mean.

The French soldiers were frightened too, although some officers did risk their lives to attempt to restore order. Frequently their efforts to help only made matters worse. Montcalm, for instance, arrived at the scene after the indiscriminate killing had stopped. In a rage he seized a young man from his Indian captor—and then watched in horror as all the warriors nearby dispatched their own captives—better to take back a scalp than nothing at all. So Montcalm's courageous anger cost a few more innocents their lives.

Montcalm could try to explain all this, and how the French will eventually try to ransom all the Indian prisoners from Fort William Henry. But what good would it do? Bougainville asks, "Will they in Europe believe that the Indians alone have been guilty of this horrible violation of the capitulation?" And Montcalm, knowing the answer, can only respond, "What would be an infraction in Europe, cannot be so regarded in America."

Bougainville writes in his journal, "My soul has several times shuddered at spectacles my eyes have witnessed." He tries to describe one such spectacle and then suddenly stops. "That is enough of the horror, the memory of which I would hope could be effaced from the minds of men." But, of course, for Bougainville and Montcalm these memories are ineffaceable. In seeking some meaning in these meaningless horrors, Bougainville's mind turns to that saddest of epic heroes, Aeneas, and the advice he was once given: "*Heu fuge, crudelis terras, terras fuge littus iniquum.*" After Priam's guiltless race had been massacred, Aeneas with a remnant escaped first to Thrace, and reaching there he intended piously to offer sacrifices to the gods. He sought to provide a covering for his altar by tearing some branches from dogwood nearby, but then saw an "awful omen, terrible to relate."

> For from the first tree's severed roots
> drops of black blood drip down. They stain the ground
> with gore. My body shudders cold. My blood
> is frozen now with terror. I try again
> and tear a tenacious stem of a second root.
> And from that second bark black blood flows down.

Finally a moan rises from the earth.

> Why are you mangling me, Aeneas? Spare me.
> I am buried here. Do spare
> the profanation of your pious hands.

There is only one way to spare himself from profanation:

> Oh, flee these lands of cruelty, this shore of avarice.

Bougainville, like Aeneas unable to decide if he should tell of the horrors he has seen or remain silent, adapts this advice that issued from the bloody ground of Thrace, adapts it to the bloody ground of Canada:

Oh, flee these lands of cruelty, this shore of iniquity.

But, of course, there was no immediate escape possible for Bougainville or Montcalm. Their duty, unlike that of Aeneas, was to remain in a land where blood and bark mingled. They had to winter in Quebec, chained to their roles within a society they detested. Vaudreuil naturally was doing his best to use the events of the last campaign to weaken further Montcalm's support at court. He had his own explanation of the massacre: "The Marquis de Montcalm took precautions he alone considered proper; he consulted only his own judgment, and perhaps the occurrence would not have been had he condescended to devolve on M. de Rigaud, the Missionaries, Officers and Interpreters the care of restraining the Indians; but he was so prejudiced that he placed confidence in himself alone."

While the massacre demonstrated once again Montcalm's incompetence in peculiarly Canadian matters, his failure to pursue his advantage with an attack on Fort Edward demonstrated an incompetence of a more general kind. Vaudreuil could only assure the court that he had done everything in his power to impress upon Montcalm the importance of a second campaign. Vaudreuil at least still retained a "zeal . . . for his Majesty's service and the glory of his arms."

Montcalm, for his part, wanted to lose his memory, for his memory brought him regrets; to lose too his imagination, for his imagination painted only horrors. But, of course, that was not true. He could still remember his chateau, his wife, his wonderful daughters—he could imagine what they all were doing now. But these images were now so faint as to seem almost a lost innocence. He sighed for earlier days, loathed his present, and trembled at the unhappy future.

Montcalm responded to Vaudreuil with an unaccustomed mildness. He only wants from Paris two things, one for his office, the other for his person. As for his office, he does not dispute the need for a "strict subordination" of the military commander to the governor, but could Paris not see fit just "to manifest some esteem for me, and to desire that my opinions as regards military operations, may be somewhat listened to?" The request is plaintive—and the other request, the request for himself personally is more plaintive still: "As for me, my lord, I ask no other favor than my recall at the earliest possible moment."

His lord, however, was granting Montcalm no favors. The dispatches from Paris showed that Vaudreuil's version of events was believed, not Montcalm's. "The experience won in the last campaign, has undoubtedly shown you how useful the Canadians and Indians can be in all military moves that you may be called upon to make. It is safe to rely upon the valor and even the good will and zeal of the Canadians if they are not treated in a manner that will disgust them."

As if this were not pointed enough, another minister wrote, "His Majesty has directed me to make known his desire that you should busy yourself as much as you can to foster between the troops under your command and the residents of Canada those feelings of friendship and good understanding without which it cannot be hoped that they will work together and manifest their zeal for the success of your undertakings. As your own example would be, no doubt, most instrumental in teaching them their duty, you cannot show too much moderation and affability on every occasion towards Canadians and Indians."

Affability? He is supposed to show affability to Indians when they massacre helpless captives who have surrendered under a pledge of safety? And to the Canadians who encourage them and even participate in their gruesome horrors? Or to Governor Vaudreuil, their friend and advocate, whose every action is shrewdly, successfully calculated to excite Montcalm's disgust? Is Montcalm supposed to be moderate in his disgust, affable while being betrayed?

Montcalm tried to control himself. First he composed one letter where he sustains throughout the oily tone of a courtier justifying himself. "The wise counsel you give me proves to my mind how much you are pleased to interest yourself for the success of my mission. You can assure the King that what you so strictly recommend on his part is exactly followed on mine; therefore, have I acquired to the highest degree the confidence of the Canadians and Indians. With the former when I am on the march or in camp, I have the air of a Tribune of the people; my success, which any other might have had, and the intimate acquaintance with the manners of the Indians, the attention I pay them, has won for me their affection. This is so strong that there are moments perhaps, when my Governor is astonished at it."

Montcalm tried to control himself, but then he feels compelled to write a second letter. And in this all his bitterness and resentment burst forth, bitterness and resentment that were quickly becoming his daily bread. "You want the valor of the Canadians, you read me some lessons respecting the conduct to be observed towards them and the Indians. You kindly add, that it is not in regard to myself, but that private accounts make mention of the harshness with which some of our officers treat the one and the other. I have taken very good care not to show that letter; it would have afflicted our officers who are but too well persuaded, and not without cause, that people in the Colony are, through a spirit of low jealousy, occupied only in running them down; those imputations are false. Those accounts which you mention to me, have been written, my Lord, by persons as ill-instructed as they are ill-intentioned."

Then Montcalm adds something that is a true measure of his desperation. He claims that he had shown the minister's criticism of him to both Governor Vaudreuil and Intendant Bigot. He claims that they were both shocked by it, and that they had both promised to write on Montcalm's behalf to disabuse the minister of his misapprehensions concerning Montcalm's conduct.

Would Montcalm have really shown the minister's rebuke of him to Vaudreuil and Bigot, to the very well-instructed and ill-intentioned people who were undoubtedly the source of the criticism? Or was he rather trying to dramatize, to dramatize through a fiction, the duplicity with which he constantly had to live? If the minister believed Montcalm, he would have to conclude that Vaudreuil and Bigot were misrepresenting themselves to Montcalm—they were not only excluding him from the military councils and criticizing him to Paris, they were even misleading him as to their assessment of his performance.

That winter was hellish for Montcalm—indeed, Montcalm's hell took on a new dimension of torment. He had long suspected financial corruption in Vaudreuil's administration, not entirely without justification. Vaudreuil did not himself personally benefit from the corruption; rather, Vaudreuil had learned to use financial gain as a resource of his rule. He had repeatedly protested, to no avail, that loyal colonials were not rewarded sufficiently by the administration in France. The best administrative posts routinely went to well-connected French, while qualified Canadians were passed over; a Montcalm would be made military commander, while Vaudreuil's brother Rigaud would be ignored even for the governorship of Montreal. To remedy the injustice, Vaudreuil used his financial power. He tried to reward those families who were contributing their lives to New France.

Montcalm could not be expected to understand this, any more than he could have been expected to have truly understood the tactics of Indian fighting. All he knew was that even to repair a Canadian fortification took much, much longer than it should. The reason? Well, in one of his first attempts to repair some fortifications, Montcalm discovered that the Canadian who was the engineer in charge also happened to have the wine concession. The slower the fort progressed, the larger his profits as barkeep. And, of course, this engineer/barkeep turned out to be a relative of Vaudreuil. (The Canadians were all related to one another, he would say with disgust.)

These Canadians might be at times brave soldiers and at others competent administrators, but they were always bad citizens, for their loyalty was always to their small group and not to the general good. The corruption that was only annoying in 1756 had become intolerable by 1758. The crops had failed again, and New France was going to suffer a persistent famine until the war was over. The ordinary people were going to have to survive on starvation rations: two ounces of bread per person a day. People who wanted meat would have to kill their horses. The suffering during this winter dwarfed anything directly caused by the war during the rest of the year.

And yet Vaudreuil, Bigot, and their cronies continued conspicuously to consume their ill-gotten gains. Montcalm thought that government officials ought to set an example by refraining from all parties, formal dinners, receptions, and the like. As Bougainville put it, "There are times when magnificence is a crime against the state." As usual, the Canadian officials did the opposite of what Montcalm thought right. He wrote to his wife Angelique, "In spite of public distress we have balls and furious gambling."

According to Montcalm, frenzied gambling at extremely high stakes became the rage. One could not help but ask where Bigot had gotten the tens of thousands he was throwing away at gaming tables nightly. And Montcalm, who believed his office demanded that he at least attend these functions, could watch while his own younger officers got caught up in the gambling and risked ruining themselves.

Although historians can find no evidence for Montcalm's wild charges, the ever-loyal Bougainville shared Montcalm's despair. He had concluded from his Canadian experience that the "spirit of greed, of gain, of commerce, will always destroy the spirit of honor, of glory, and military spirit." Such was the way of the world; but if this was so, then Montcalm and Bougainville were absurdly wasting their lives. And Bougainville could see what Canada was doing to Montcalm. He was being destroyed before Bougainville's eyes. Bougainville had begun to compare Montcalm to Cassandra, crazed by the world's indifference to his good advice. How easy was it for moralists to say, "Be just and you will be happy."

The prospects for the campaign of 1758 were far from good. The French were inevitably going to get a late start for lack of provisions. In mid-May Bougainville wrote, "What can we do, we who are dying of hunger? The expression is literal. Many people keep alive only by fish and fast when they catch none." The well-provisioned British, in contrast, were preparing to attack at all points. They would attack both at Fort Duquesne and Lake Ontario to cut off the French from the west. They would attack Louisbourg, then occupy the entrance to the Saint Lawrence, and perhaps even attempt a siege of Quebec. Finally, they would strike at the heart of New France by taking control of Lake Champlain and thence be able to drive right to Montreal. Of all these the most crucial was Lake Champlain. If this fell, New France was doomed—on this Vaudreuil and Montcalm agreed. They also agreed that Montcalm should lead the troops at Carillon, the southernmost French fort on Lake Champlain. They agreed on this, and little else.

Vaudreuil decided that Rigaud, his Canadians, and Indian allies should be detached from Montcalm and sent on a raid into the Mohawk Valley of New York. Vaudreuil believed that this would create a diversion and also assure the loyalty of the Iroquois. Montcalm was convinced that this diversion would only assure his own defeat at Carillon, for even with Rigaud he was likely to be dangerously outnumbered. But Montcalm knew Vaudreuil would risk ruining the whole colony just to ruin Montcalm—that was the kind of patriotism and loyalty Montcalm had come to expect in this land of iniquity from which he could not flee.

If Montcalm had any doubts that Vaudreuil intended his destruction, the orders that Vaudreuil sent him removed them. Montcalm was confronted with pages and pages of instruction, such as you might give a child with no mind of his own. And then at the end Vaudreuil had the audacity to add, "We regard as useless entering into any fuller details with the Marquis de Montcalm on whatever may concern the objects of his mission or tend to the glory of his Majesty's arms and the good of the colony; we refer them to his knowledge, his experience and his zeal, in which we have always reposed our confidence."

Montcalm's fury at the orders was virtually uncontrollable. Here he was going off to almost certain defeat (and perhaps to his death)—and Vaudreuil would not give him all the troops at his disposal, would load him with orders that made no sense, and would then mock him with a sarcastic assurance of his confidence. Montcalm wrote in his journal: "The Marquis de Vaudreuil has delivered to me, at ten o'clock this evening, his ridiculous, unintelligible and captious instruction. If I had accepted, it was framed in such a manner, that any unlucky event could be imputed to me, whatever measures I would have taken." He sent the orders back to Vaudreuil with a note dated "Montreal, the 23rd, at night!":

"Sir, I have the honor to beg of you to read again the Instructions with which you have honored me this evening, and the annexed Memoir, and I expect from your equity that you will think it sufficient that I take upon myself, under circumstances which may be critical, to defend as much as it will be possible for me, the frontier of Lake St. Sacrament with 4000 men, against very superior forces, without burdening me with instructions, the obscurities and contradictions whereof appear to render me responsible for events which may happen and I must anticipate. I render justice to the uprightness of your intentions, but I cannot leave until you have furnished me an instruction with all the changes as necessary as they are indispensable to preserve the reputation of a General officer who has served with so much zeal for your own glory and the defense of this Colony."

However bitter Montcalm was upon leaving Quebec, the situation at Carillon should not have improved his mood. An aide who arrived with him wrote later, "There was enough to make me shudder. Fort Carillon was not finished. It was capable of containing only a garrison of 400 men; provisions only for 10 or 12 days; no Indians, no retreat." As for the relative size of the two armies, Montcalm's worst fears were exceeded—by reliable report, the British army outnumbered his own five to one.

Montcalm's dark mood should have been even further darkened by these circumstances—and yet a certain buoyancy returns to his writing, for the first time in months. At least he is far away from Quebec and Vaudreuil. At least he can now do something, something he understands. He can select a site for the impending battle. He can fortify it as well as possible, and be content to let the British do their best, for he surely will do his. He was almost certainly going to be defeated, and perhaps even killed. (In a difficult battle he would never shield his person from the fighting.) But whatever happened, he would have the satisfaction of having fought honorably. And if the worst happened, at least he would be finished with this awful business.

The atmosphere was bracing. He even began to convince himself he could win. "I have victuals for eight days only, no Canadians and not one Indian. They have not come yet. I have to deal with a formidable army. Nevertheless, I do not despair. My troops are good. From the enemy's movements I can see that he wavers; if, thanks to his slowness, he gives me time to establish myself on the ground I have selected on the heights of Carillon and to entrench myself there, *I shall beat them.*"

Anyone who watched the massive British army approach would have given him little chance. Let Parkman describe for us, with characteristic brightness, the movement of the British army across Lake George, as if it were a pageant of pleasure rather than the prelude to the dangers and toil of a bloody battle of a vicious war:

"On the evening of the fourth of July, baggage, stores, and ammunition were all on board the boats, and the whole army embarked on the morning of the fifth. The arrangements were perfect. Each corps marched without confusion to its appointed station on the beach, and the sun was scarcely above the ridge of French Mountain when all were afloat. A spectator watching them from the shore says that when the fleet was three miles on its way, the surface of the lake at that distance was completely hidden from sight. There were nine hundred bateaux, a hundred and thirty-five whaleboats, and a large number of heavy flatboats carrying the artillery. The whole advanced in three divisions, the regulars in the centre, and the provincials on the flanks. Each corps had its flags and its music. The day was fair and men and officers were in the highest spirits. Before ten o'clock they began to enter the Narrows; and the boats of the three divisions extended themselves into long files as the mountains closed on either hand upon the contracted lake. From front to rear the line was six miles long. The spectacle was superb: the brightness of the summer day; the romantic beauty of the scenery; the sheen and sparkle of those crystal waters; the countless islets, tufted with pine, birch, and fir; the bordering mountains, with their green summits and sunny crags; the flash of oars and glitter of weapons; the banners, the varied uniforms, and the notes of bugle, trumpet, bagpipe, and drum, answered and prolonged by a hundred woodland echoes. 'I never beheld so delightful a prospect,' wrote a wounded officer at Albany a fortnight after."

Of course, the beautiful smile of the lake crossing was but a preparation for the sickening grimace of battle. Meanwhile, Montcalm had been making his own preparations. He was having built breastworks and an extensive abatis in front of his fort. The abatis, one British soldier later said, looked like a forest felled by a hurricane. And now the British hurricane was going to have to cross it to reach the fort. Or would it?

Belatedly Montcalm seemed to realize how indefensible his position was. His giddiness and confidence passed before the reality he knew to be approaching. All the British had to do was flank his position and attack him from the rear. Even a frontal attack would overwhelm his position if supported by the British artillery. So Montcalm made preparations to give up the battle before it began. He had boats made ready for a retreat he would order at the first sight of the main British artillery. But this sight didn't come. Unbeknownst to Montcalm, he was already well along on a roll of extraordinary luck.

The British army was commanded by General James Abercrombie, but really led by the thirty-four-year-old General George Howe. Howe was to British generalship what Pitt was to its politics. Pitt himself described him as "a character of ancient times; a complete model of military virtue." Everyone who encountered him was awed by his promise, and charmed by his person.

As it happened, an advance column of the British encountered some French, whom they badly mauled. As it happened, Howe was with the column. As it happened, on the first exchange of fire, a bullet burst a gaping hole in Howe's head. And, it was said, the soul of Abercrombie's army expired with him.

Certainly Abercrombie's own generalship seemed to, as well. He had now to make decisions on his own. Abercrombie chose to believe intelligence obtained from French captives. These captives doubled Montcalm's forces for him, and also invented massive reinforcements expected momentarily. Abercrombie made his decisions accordingly. He decided he must attempt a frontal assault because attempting to flank so large a force was pointless. Moreover, he had to attack immediately, before the French reinforcements arrived; that meant he would attack before his own artillery arrived. By such reasoning Abercrombie decided to attack the French position in perhaps the only way he could have and still lose: a frontal assault without artillery support. Even then his men almost overran the French position.

Time and again the British forces attacked across the abatis; time and again they were stopped before reaching the breastworks. Montcalm estimated that over a six-hour period they attacked his position six times. The closer the attacking forces got to the breastworks, the heavier the casualties. The few berserkers who were able to leap over the breastworks, Highlanders mostly, were dispatched quickly within.

Then suddenly it was over: Abercrombie had had enough. His forces began a withdrawal, and the French could look out over the flattened forest of their abatis, now gaily festooned with bright ribbons of British dead. It was as breathtaking in its way as the grand sight on Lake George had been that morning.

Abercrombie was soon to return to England to disgrace, Howe's corpse to a niche in Westminster Abbey. The British had lost almost two thousand, the French less than four hundred, men. Montcalm wrote to Angelique, "Without Indians, almost without Canadians or colony troops—I had only four hundred,—alone with Levis and Bourlamaque and the troops of the line, thirty-one hundred fighting men, I have beaten an army of twenty-five thousand. They passed the lake precipitately with the loss of at least five thousand. This glorious day does infinite honor to the valor of our battalions. I have no time to write more. I am well, my dearest, and I embrace you."

His letters to France are forgivably boastful and exaggerated. His discus-

sions of the battle with Bougainville were of a cooler sort. The more they ana-
lyzed it, the more incredible it seemed. Bougainville was speaking for them
both when he wrote, "Never has a victory been more especially due to the finger of Providence." How the French had won God only knew.

Vaudreuil, once again, tried to minimize Montcalm's achievements. Once
again, he complained that Montcalm had not followed up his victory with a
further thrust south. And, having failed to give Montcalm sufficient Canadian and Indian troops for the battle, now he made great show of bringing
them up as reserves, at a time when they would only consume Montcalm's
meager supplies. Montcalm dismissed Vaudreuil's pretensions with open contempt. "It is always astonishing that the Marquis de Vaudreuil considers himself qualified at a distance of fifty leagues to determine operations of war in a
country he has never seen, and where the best Generals, after having seen it,
would have been embarrassed. The Marquis de Vaudreuil forgets that the
British army was at least 20,000 strong, and according to several prisoners
25,000. Supposing that it had lost in killed and wounded 5,000 men, that a
portion of the Provincials had returned, they would still have 12 or 14,000
men, and consequently the superiority in the field, and would be at liberty to
do what they pleased in their country. . . . Were I so fortunate, Sir, as that
your important occupations would permit you to be at the head of the army,
you would see everything yourself, and I should have the satisfaction to
receive clearer and less embarrassing orders, and you would have judged that I
have combined boldness, prudence and some activity." In the midst of this
letter—which can only be called a tirade—Montcalm writes, "The Marquis
de Vaudreuil will find in my observations some distrust of him."

But for all the harshness of this response, Montcalm, as soon as the campaign of 1758 was over, began to take another tone. Montcalm had luckily
and unexpectedly held at Lake Champlain, but the French had lost everywhere else. Fort Duquesne had to be abandoned. Fort Frontenac had been
destroyed. Louisbourg had been taken by the British, and only stiff resistance
there had prevented the British troops from continuing on to siege Quebec.
Now was the time Montcalm wrote his mother: "Never was a general in a
more critical position than I was; God has delivered me; His be the praise! He
gives me health, although I am worn out with labor, fatigue, and miserable
dissensions that have determined me to ask for my recall. Heaven grant that I
may get it!"

All he now wanted was to leave, to go home, to see his family. To this end
he would try to make his peace even with Vaudreuil—they could at least agree
that Montcalm should return to France. He promised never again to respond

to Vaudreuil's orders in anger, nor to criticize him. He thought they both should admit that they both were in part responsible for the difficulties between them. Montcalm sensed he had the upper hand in his war with Vaudreuil, but he was going to be a humane victor, if only to achieve his own ends. Bougainville had been prescient when after the victory at Carillon he quoted Julius Caesar: "Up to the present I fought for glory, but today for my life." Montcalm, having avoided complete ruin at Carillon, was done with ambition. Assured of Vaudreuil's support, he wrote to France once again requesting his own recall. "The trouble and contradictions I experience, the impossibility in which I am placed of doing good and preventing evil, determine me earnestly to pray His Majesty to grant me this favor, the only one for which I am ambitious."

True to his words, Montcalm was careful not to use his request as an occasion to complain against Vaudreuil. But Vaudreuil, in supporting the request, obeyed the letter but not the spirit of their truce: "I pass over in silence all the infamous conduct and indecent talk he has held or countenanced; but I should be wanting in my duty to the King if I did not beg you to ask for his recall."

As Montcalm waited for the reply to his request, he expressed often his concern, "I should like as well as anybody to be Marshal of France; but to buy the honor with the life I am leading here would be too much." More poignantly: "I shall always say, Happy he who is free from the proud yoke to which I am bound. When shall I see my chateau of Candiac, my plantations, my chestnut grove, my oil mill, my mulberry trees? Oh good God! Good night; burn my letter."

Montcalm had sent his most trusted colleague, Bougainville, back to France to present his views at court, both of the desperate situation of New France, and of his own need for recall. Unfortunately, these two missions were, in the end, at cross-purposes. Bougainville soon learned that the weakening situation of France in the European theater of the war precluded any reinforcements for Canada. When one minister explained to Bougainville that you do not try to save the stables when the house is on fire, Bougainville made a reply worthy of Montcalm: "At least, Monsieur, no one will say that you talk like a horse."

With no new troops for New France and the situation as desperate as Bougainville and Montcalm claimed, a true miracle worker would be required to preserve New France for another year. And Bougainville's descriptions of Carillon could only have helped confirm the impression that Montcalm himself was a man capable of military miracles. Across the document that was to

grant Montcalm's request for recall is written in hand, "On mature consideration this arrangement is not to be made, M. de Montcalm being necessary in
present circumstances." Perhaps the ministers reconsidered; more likely the
king himself intervened. As the minister of war put it to Montcalm, "The
memory of what you did last year leads his Majesty to hope that once again
you will find means to foil their plans." Montcalm the man had been defeated
by the victory of Montcalm the general.

In fact, Bougainville apparently had his own agenda during his stay in
France. He wanted Montcalm recognized for the great man he was, even if
that meant Montcalm would have to stay in New France. Indeed, Bougainville now thought New France was a place in which Montcalm could flourish;
he had written in his journal after Carillon: "Now war is established here on
the European basis. Projects for the campaign, for armies, for artillery, for
sieges, for battles. It no longer is a matter of making a raid, but of conquering
or being conquered. What a revolution! What a change!" The time for
Canadian guerilla fighting was over. Even before he left, Bougainville could
see that the Canadians were trying to talk of the war in European terms:
"Everyone is a Turenne or a Folard. Great misfortune for this country; it will
perish, victim of its prejudices, of its blind confidence, of the stupidity or of
the roguery of its chiefs."

The only way for New France to survive was to have Montcalm firmly in
charge of its military operations. That meant Vaudreuil had to be put in his
place. Bougainville, on his own authority and for the good of France, was
going to continue the war against Vaudreuil although his own general had
already signed a truce. In this war Bougainville showed far more shrewdness
than Montcalm had. When he returned to New France, he told a shocked
Montcalm that on his behalf Bougainville recommended Governor Vaudreuil
for the order of St. Louis. Bougainville explained that this recommendation
supposedly from Montcalm had "gained credit for you; moderation, you
know." Montcalm could not have been too annoyed at this sly misrepresenta-
tion of his true sentiments, for while Vaudreuil got his pretty award
Montcalm was given *de facto* military command. France had endorsed
Montcalm's strategy for the final defense of New France.

Vaudreuil, persistent in his faith in the Indians and forest rangers, had
wanted to resist the British advance everywhere possible; Montcalm rather
wanted to withdraw from the distant forts that so drained manpower and supplies. He wanted to consolidate his forces in the Saint Lawrence Valley, in particular at Quebec. All the French had to do was hold out at one point. If the
French could just hold out in Quebec until the war ended (as it might soon),

they should be able to regain much of New France at the peace table. The ministers in Paris agreed with Montcalm, hero of Carillon.

"As we must expect the English to turn all their forces against Canada, and attack you on several sides at once, it is necessary that you limit your plans of defense to the most essential points and those most closely connected, so that being concentrated within a smaller space, each part may be within reach of support and succor from the rest. However small may be the space you are able to hold, it is indispensable to keep a footing in North America; for if we once lose the country entirely, its recovery will be almost impossible." The grim response of Montcalm was, "We will save this unhappy colony or perish."

Vaudreuil, no longer a real threat to Montcalm's power, was treated by Montcalm and his French officers as comic relief from their task of preparing for the inevitable siege. Even an officer who was shocked at Montcalm's bluntness about Vaudreuil in front of the servants would still himself write of the governor as if he were a character out of a low comedy: "M. le Marquis de Vaudreuil, Governor General and in this capacity general of the army, made his first tour [of the new defenses]; after all, youth must be instructed. As he had never seen either a camp or work of defense, everything seemed to him as new as it was amusing. He asked singular questions. It was like a man born blind who has been given sight."

Satisfied as Montcalm must have been at having finally achieved full command, and busy as he was in preparing Quebec and his men for what was coming, Montcalm did have occasion to think of home. He had asked Bougainville, while in France, to arrange the marriage of a daughter. When he received a letter from him announcing the engagement, Montcalm wrote immediately to Angelique: "I think I should have given up all my honours to be back with you, but the king must be obeyed; the moment when I shall see you again will be the finest of my life. Good-bye, my heart, I believe I love you more than ever." These were the last words he would ever write her.

Apparently Montcalm had a premonition of his end when Bougainville finally did return from France. Montcalm must have expected joyful details of the wedding and his new son-in-law. Instead, Bougainville had shattering news. One of his daughters was dead. Bougainville had been informed shortly before he sailed. He did not know how she died; he could not even find out which of the daughters had died. The ship could not wait. Which of his daughters? Montcalm thought about this much. He finally decided that it was probably little Mirète. She was "most like me." The sorrow was like a heavy bell that once struck rang on and on by its own weight. This was grief enough to make a strong man stoop.

The next month the siege of Quebec began. The British plan was to send one army under the command of General James Wolfe up the Saint Lawrence to cut off Quebec. This army would eventually be joined by an army under the command of General Jeffrey Amherst, which would make its way up through Lake Champlain. Montcalm had no doubt that if these two forces joined at Quebec the city would be lost. So he sent half of his forces to Champlain to impede Amherst's advance. Montcalm was not hoping for another miraculous victory like Carillon. He only hoped to lose slowly, slowly enough that by the end of this year's campaign he would still be in control of Quebec—or, failing that, his army would still be intact somewhere in New France.

One portion of his forces would retreat slowly before Amherst, avoiding at all costs a decisive battle. Montcalm would stay in Quebec, hoping to stalemate Wolfe's troops there. But he could not count on being able to hold Quebec, so he refused to have the bulk of his provisions brought into the city. He had them at some distance, where they would be safe from British cannons, and where they would be on a natural route of retreat for his army should Quebec become untenable. He would retreat across the plain that Abraham Martin had cleared more than a century before, with money left him by Champlain.

The British fleet carrying Wolfe's troops arrived before Quebec on June 26—and their anchoring itself was a great shock for Montcalm. They had managed to get their ships much farther up the Saint Lawrence than the Canadian pilots had assured Montcalm was possible. Vaudreuil on this score wrote one of his rare admissions of Canadian inadequacy: "The enemy passed sixty ships of war where we had hardly dared to risk a vessel of a hundred tons." And one of the British masters passed off the feat, "Damn me, if there are not a thousand places in the Thames fifty times more hazardous than this." Montcalm could feel betrayed once again by Canadian claims of competence.

He, nonetheless, had his own plan for making the Saint Lawrence more hazardous for British ships too close to Quebec. He had some fire ships prepared, at the expense of a million livres. With these he hoped to destroy the British ships and with them most of the British supplies. This was his chance for a quick victory, a chance he could take with little risk.

The fire ships seem to have caught the British by surprise, but the head ship was ignited by its captain prematurely. The other captains followed his lead, allowing the British ships time to cut cable and outrace the floating infernos. Only one French captain realized what was happening, and he refused either to ignite or abandon his ship until he was within striking distance of the British. Trying to maneuver his way through to the British, Captain Dubois de la Multière (his name deserves to be recorded) was, with his crew, finally trapped amidst the other exploding French ships, the only deaths from the million-livre fireworks display.

Weeks later, after there had been much skirmishing between both sides, Montcalm tried another fire attack, this time with barges. The British, however, were no longer surprised and received little damage. But the attack had been sufficiently dangerous that General Wolfe did not want another. He sent a message to Montcalm and Vaudreuil under a flag of truce. "If you presume to send down any more fire rafts, they shall be made fast to the two transports in which the Canadian prisoners are confined, in order that they may perish by your own base inventions."

This was in character. Wolfe, a man of poor health and great ambition, had been promoted over many more senior officers precisely because of his impetuousness. No one could have been temperamentally less suited for countering the patient strategy that Montcalm had chosen. Earlier in this same war Wolfe had listed for a confidante the military lessons he had already learned. Among them was "that, in particular circumstances and times the loss of 1,000 men is rather an advantage to a nation than otherwise, seeing that gallant attempts raise its reputation and make it respectable; whereas the contrary appearances sink the credit of a country, ruin the troops, and create infinite uneasiness and discontent at home."

After receiving his command of the attacking forces for Quebec, Wolfe was equally candid in his assessment of his opportunities there. He did not think that he could successfully besiege Quebec unless he was reinforced by Amherst. But he would still find ways to create infinite uneasiness and discontent in New France. "If, by accident in the river, by the enemy's resistance, by sickness, or slaughter in the army, or, from any other cause, we find, that Quebec is not likely to fall into our hands (persevering however to the last moment), I propose to set the town on fire with shells, to destroy the harvest, houses, & cattle, both above & below, to send off as many Canadians as possible to Europe, & to leave famine and desolation behind me; *belle resolution, & tres chrétienne!* but we must teach these scoundrels to make war in a more gentlemanlike manner." Wolfe was a man who fully enjoyed the elemental pleasures of making war.

Montcalm, however, was not going to oblige him. To Wolfe's surprise,

Montcalm did not even oppose the landing and positioning of the British troops. Apart from the fireships and continual Indian harassment (both of which Wolfe regarded as ungentlemanly tactics), Wolfe was left to himself. For lack of something better to do, he divided his forces into three. Vaudreuil and Bigot thought that with the British forces divided, the French should sally forth to do battle. Montcalm, despite the urgings of his officers to attack, would have none of this, for it was exactly what Wolfe was trying to invite.

When the British erected a battery that troubled the major French camp, Montcalm simply moved the troops out of range. One of his subordinates had urged Montcalm to attack the battery, but Montcalm simply replied: "Drive them thence and they will give us more trouble; while they are there they cannot hurt us; let them amuse themselves." Montcalm was going to do as little as possible, for he had to be very careful about expending his resources. As he wrote in his journal, "We have an immense number of cannon, enough mortars, four thousand bombs, many bullets, but powder is lacking. On that subject many things could be said." Earlier he would have vituperated against Bigot and Canadian corruption—but now he said nothing more. His tactics had begun to influence his personality, and Montcalm was serenely playing for a draw.

Montcalm might be able to move his troops out of range, but he could not move Quebec—and so Wolfe decided to take out his frustration against the city. He had his cannon aimed no longer at the French batteries (which at any rate could fire very little because of the lack of powder) or on other military targets; he had them aimed at the buildings of Quebec. The French understood perfectly well what Wolfe was doing. He simply wanted to terrorize the noncombatants and cause as much destruction as possible. One French journal of the siege reports that after the first serious bombardment, "The people all fled their homes and sought refuge upon the ramparts, on the side next to the country. When day appeared, and the gate was opened, women and children were seen flying in crowds along the fields; and the damage done to the town during the first night was very considerable." This was on the night of July 12.

The fact that all the inhabitants who could had fled did not deter Wolfe from his bombardment—he still had a detested city to destroy. He had by this time realized that incendiary bombs were especially effective against deserted, nonmilitary targets. Three times fires got completely out of control. On August 8 to 9 alone, Quebec lost 152 buildings and one of its major churches. (The cathedral had burned to the ground two weeks before.) One observer on the British side complained in a letter (to Charles Lawrence, of all people),

"We frequently set their town on fire, have burnt down a large church and many other buildings, but I can't learn that we hurt their batteries, and therefore individuals suffer more than the common cause, and indeed I fear the campaign will end so." According to one account, more than five hundred houses had burned, and of those left standing there was "not a single house without a hole in it." Wolfe might not be any closer to taking Quebec, but he was at least teaching the French how to make war in a gentlemanly manner.

When his men captured some obviously well-born ladies who were fleeing Quebec, Wolfe treated them gallantly before returning them to the city. It was subsequently reported back to Montcalm that, "Several of them even supped with General Wolfe, who joked considerably about the circumspection of our Generals; he told these ladies that he had afforded very favorable opportunities for an attack and had been surprised that no advantage had been taken of them." But Montcalm was not going to be moved by the jokes Wolfe was telling at his expense. And Wolfe himself was coming to appreciate Montcalm's shrewdness, as he wrote to his own mother. "My antagonist has wisely shut himself up in inaccessible entrenchments, so that I can't get at him without spilling a torrent of blood, and that perhaps to little purpose. . . . The wary old fellow avoids an action, doubtful of the behavior of his army. People must be of the profession to understand the disadvantages and difficulties we labour under arising from the uncommon natural strength of the country."

While Wolfe was taking what satisfaction he could in lighting up Quebec each night, he was making no progress in formulating a plan to assault the city. Or rather, he made one plan after another, rejecting each in turn. Finally, he decided the time had come to act. Plan six was not any better than the previous five, but he was not going to leave without trying an assault.

A British assault was duly mounted and rebuffed with discouraging ease. Wolfe at least had his torrent of blood, to little purpose. For twenty minutes French riflemen poured heavy fire into eight hundred British troops as they tried to make their way up a sandy slope toward a French defensive position. A sandy slope, no traction, twenty minutes, much bravery, and more than four hundred casualties. Wolfe's impetuosity had cost his army a man every three seconds—and all he could do was complain about their "strange behavior." It is not strange behavior to fall down after having been shot fair in the chest.

Needless to say, the professional reputation of General Wolfe was no longer in the ascent among the men he commanded. One of those who participated in the assault wrote as follows in his journal: "The very situation of the breast work, which is on the verge of a quick and long ascent, wou'd have been a barrier against any assailant; but when lin'd crowded with an un-number'd host of troops, the attempt was, I had almost said, impracticable; which some Genl Officers scarcely hesitate to say. One of them of knowledge, fortune and interest I have heard has declar'd the attack then and there, was contrary to the advice and opinion of every officer; and when things are come to this, you'll judge what the event may be!"

Montcalm's reputation among his people, in contrast, had never been better. Story had it that his special providence had saved the French in this battle as well: the French troops, although winning the battle, were just about run out of ammunition when a sudden thunderstorm made the incline the British were working up completely impassable.

Things continued to go poorly for General Wolfe. Amherst was no longer expected. There was talk among the men about how he was being "out-generall'd," and he was having difficulties even with his brigadiers. He had, after all, now been before Quebec for more than two months—and all he had was six plans and one defeat to show for his efforts. Being no closer to victory, Wolfe consoled himself with spreading more desolation and famine. Now the Canadian countryside became the special object of his ministrations. Before his appointment to Quebec, Wolfe had written to a superior, "Tho' I am neither inhuman nor rapacious, yet I own it would give me pleasure to see the Canadian vermin sacked and pillaged and justly repaid for their unheard-of cruelty." Wolfe was now going to take his pleasures where he could find them. So he began the systematic destruction of the Canadian settlements along the Saint Lawrence. The slightest provocation (or less), and a whole community would be completely destroyed, perhaps the inhabitants massacred as well. One of Wolfe's brigadiers, against whom he was apparently considering charges of insubordination, wrote to his wife, "I never served in so disagreeable a campaign as this." It was, he wrote, "a scene of ambition, confusion, and misery." It was "a scene of skirmishing, cruelty and devastation." It was "war of the worst shape." It was "a scene I ought not to be in. For the future, believe me, my dear, I will seek the reverse of it."

So Brigadier General Townsend expressed sentiments similar to those Samuel de Champlain probably had during the wars of religion a century and a half before. Champlain in his future had sought the reverse, had sought to build a colony in what was then the desolate Saint Lawrence Valley. Now that same valley was being returned to its former state of desolation. It was being visited with the very destruction that Champlain more than a century before had come to the New World to escape. How many homesteads were destroyed by Wolfe is impossible to say, so enthusiastically were his orders car-

ried out by the general soldiery. Contemporary estimates of 1400 are, if anything, conservative. The Saint Lawrence Valley had become an infernal world,
with smoke and fire on all sides and bombed-out Quebec its capital. Such
horrid deeds as the British were committing should make the planets themselves stop and listen.

The Canadians, to Wolfe's surprise, only became more defiant; Wolfe did
not understand why old people of seventy or children of fifteen were firing on
large British detachments from the edge of woods. Vaudreuil, looking down
on the scene from the heights of ruined Quebec, lamented that the British
seemed determined to destroy everything Canadian, which was everything
Vaudreuil himself valued.

Montcalm looked down too, and all he could do was look. What more
could he do? He also knew that most of the militia down there were, in his
own phrase, "old men or children." And he knew if he gave battle Wolfe
would stop. Yet his training, his sense of higher duty, all his careful strategic
planning told him that whatever his personal feelings about the destruction
he saw all about him in Quebec, and the desolation he saw spreading below,
he could do nothing more than watch. He had to remain a calm mountain
before the baying of this rapacious wolf.

Suddenly Montcalm was informed of a major movement in the British
troops. One of their main camps was being abandoned, and Wolfe's forces
consolidated. Many in Quebec thought that Montcalm ought to attack the
rear guard of the moving troops. Montcalm refused. Of course, Wolfe's largely abandoned camp did invite attack—but Montcalm could not be sure that
Wolfe intended this in order to ambush the French and force them into a
major battle. (Indeed, Wolfe had left behind under cover two thousand troops
just for this purpose.) Anyway, Montcalm did not need a victory; he had only
to wait for the coming of winter, and it was already September. To win the
siege of Quebec, Montcalm needed only to observe the British movements,
and simply be certain the French defenses were in place wherever Wolfe decided to spill his soldiers' blood.

Montcalm thought he knew where any such attack would have to take
place. Wolfe would have to come across onto the shores northeast of Quebec,
as he had attempted and failed to do earlier. The French defenses were strong
there, but nothing compared to the natural barriers that would face Wolfe on
the shores above Quebec. Sentries were posted along these steep cliffs, and a
small number of troops could massacre the British army before it made the
ascent. Along these cliffs was also the route to the supplies for Quebec. And,

just to be completely safe, there he placed his most trustworthy subordinate, Bougainville, with ample troops to protect this route.

On the night of September 12, 1759, the sentries were expecting supply ships to attempt a secret run past the British positions on the opposite bank. Late that night they heard the boats approaching, shouted a challenge, and were appropriately answered in French. The sentries then passed on the word that the boats were theirs. Later, people in Quebec heard a certain amount of gunfire in the general direction of the heights. They were saddened because obviously the supply boats had been seen by the British, and perhaps would not make it through—the famine in Quebec was going to get worse. Then, on the morning of September 13, 1759, Montcalm was told that the British army had somehow made it to the heights and were marching on Quebec, across the Plains of Abraham.

Montcalm went out to reconnoiter. His wit, his charm, his anger, sarcasm, bitterness, and especially his hope all seemed drained from him. On the ride out he did not speak. One soldier with him wrote, "It seemed as if he felt his fate upon him." There was a livid deadness in his cheeks.

The British troops were now between Montcalm and the provisions for Quebec. This could not be denied as the dawn strengthened and gave substance to the scene. And Bougainville, his trusted Bougainville, who had under his command many of Montcalm's best troops, was nowhere to be seen. The army that Montcalm could array against Wolfe was approximately the same size, but there similarities ceased. Wolfe's soldiers were almost all professionals ("of the profession," as Wolfe would put it). Montcalm's army was only partly professional. Montcalm had tried to spread the militia throughout his army, but he knew as well as anyone that in the kind of battle he was going to have to fight, amateurs had little chance against properly disciplined professionals, especially when the amateurs were going to have to charge the professionals. He would need another miracle. Courage might still conspire with chance, but the loss of a battle here would be irreparable, long past the cure of patience. He said vacantly to a subordinate, "We cannot avoid action; the enemy is entrenching, he already has two pieces of cannon. If we give him time to establish himself, we shall never be able to attack him with the sort of troops we have." He added with a shiver, "Is it possible that Bougainville doesn't hear all that noise?" Then walked away.

One of the British professionals later gave an admirably concise account of the battle, which itself took only minutes. "The French line began the charge about nine advancing briskly and for some little time in good order, a part of their line began to fire too soon, which immediately catch'd throughout the whole, then they began to waver but kept advancing with a scattering fire—When they had got within about a hundred yards of us our line mov'd up regularly with a steady fire, and when within twenty or thirty yards of closing gave a general one; upon which a total rout of the enemy immediately ensued."

Montcalm had led the French advance, a prominent target on his white charger, as if his own safety were a careless trifle. During the rout he allowed himself to be led from the field only after he had been severely wounded in the stomach. The next morning, somewhere amongst the empty, stark ruins of Quebec, he died. They found for his body a shell crater for a grave, in the cracked foundation of a church. (Notre Dame de la Recouverance, one would like to think, although contemporary sources specify it as the church of a convent .) There the body could still rest as dust.

But his spirit, we must believe, did not long linger. Rather, with an indignant moan he should have soon fled this our earth, eagerly in search of another shore—a foaming, glistening strand from which to look back upon the human struggle, his own and others', suddenly to see what it all had been for, and then to rejoice. Yes, to rejoice.

SOURCES AND
ACKNOWLEDGMENTS

✤

THIS NARRATIVE, of course, would have been impossible without the work of many scholars, most of whom will probably be appalled at the uses to which I have put their labors. Before
listing a few of the most important of these (some of them now undoubtedly turning in their
graves, and others reaching for their poison pens), I should acknowledge more personal debts,
although after ten years they are too many to be all remembered.

Barney Roddy Quinn and our children have been my sustenance for this book and all the
rest. Czeslaw Milosz has been its inspiration, as he has for so much of my work. A few friends
have done their part, all the more valued since others did not: Thomas Brady, Carol and
Leonard Nathan, Robert Middlekauff, and Thomas Hall. Many other people, some of whom I
knew not at all or only a little, went out of their way to offer help or encouragement, sometimes
without seeming to realize how important it was to me: Thomas Barnes, Christie Jones,
Howard Junker of *Zyzzyva*, Carol Thigpen, George Economu, Carl Brandt, Alain Henon,
Tom Mathews, Shifra Sharlin, Heiko Oberman, Charles Gillispie, Honore Grassi, Hayden
White, Norman Austin, Gregory Wolfe of *Image*, Thomas Sloane, and Tiziano Villa. To them
also my thanks. Some who helped me with the preparation of the manuscript over the years
actually at times did much more by serving as perceptive readers: Margaret Rebhan, Rebecca
Kidd, Kirsten Anderson, Gretchen von Duering, and especially Debra Fitzgerald. At a time
when my own university had apparently given up on this project (and when it had long been
clear that no American foundation would ever give a dime of support), the Humanities
Research Centre of the Australian National University provided me with an ideal intellectual
environment in which to do the final revisions and polishing while talking comparative history
constantly. Finally, my gratitude to my editor Betsy Uhrig and my agent Thomas D'Evelyn can
be guessed when I say that I had come to regard this unconventional work as entirely unpub-
lishable (except out of my garage), a conclusion emphatically shared by numerous other editors
and agents—but not these two.

Preface

M. H. Abrams, *Natural Supernaturalism* (New York, 1971). Wendell Clausen, "An Inter-
pretation of the Aeneid," *Harvard Studies in Classical Philology* 68 (1964): 139–47. W. R.
Johnson, *Darkness Visible* (Berkeley, 1976). Leonard Nathan and Arthur Quinn, *The Poet's
Work* (Harvard, 1991). Arthur Quinn, "On Reading Newton Apocalyptically," *Messianism*

and Millenarianism, ed. R. Popkin (Leyden, 1988); "The Color of Rhetoric," *Rhetorik zwischen den Wissenschaften*, ed. G. Ueding, (Tubingen, 1991); "The Moving Image of Eternity," *The New Oxford Review*, June 1991; "Selling History Short," *Bostonia*, Fall 1992.

Chapter 1

Kenneth Andrews, *Trade, Plunder and Settlement* (Cambridge, 1984). Philip Barbour, *The Three Worlds of Captain John Smith* (Boston, 1964). Warren Billings (ed.), *The Old Dominion in the Seventeenth Century* (Chapel Hill, 1975). Carl Bridenbaugh, *Jamestown* (New York, 1980). Nicholas Canny, "The Ideology of English Colonization: From Ireland to America," *W&MQ* 30 (1973): 575–98. Wesley Craven, *The Southern Colonies in the Seventeenth Century* (Baton Rouge,1949). John Fiske, *Old Virginia and Her Neighbors* (Boston, 1897). Edmund Morgan, *American Slavery, American Freedom* (New York, 1975). Helen Rountree, *The Powhatan Indians* (Norman, 1989). Bernard Sheehan, *Savagism and Civility* (Cambridge, 1980). John Smith, *Complete Works,* ed. Philip Barbour (Chapel Hill, 1986), 3 v. Lynn Tyler (ed.), *Narratives of Early Virginia* (New York, 1907). Alden Vaughan, *American Genesis* (Boston, 1975); "John Smith Satirized," *W&MQ* 45(1988):712–32.

Chapter 2

E. R. Adair, "France and the Beginning of New France," *Canadian Historical Review* 25 (1944): 246–78. Alfred Bailey, "The Significance of . . . the Laurentian Iroquois," *Trans. of the Royal Society of Canada* 27 (1933): 97–108. Morris Bishop, *Champlain:The Life of Fortitude* (Toronto, 1963). Samuel de Champlain, *Works of Samuel Champlain,* ed. H. P. Biggar, (Toronto, 1922–36), 6 v. Pierre F. X. de Charlevoix, *History . . . of New France,* trans. J. G. Shea (New York, 1870), 6 v. "Documents Relating to Negotiations with England 1629–33," *Canadian Archives for 1912*, pp.18–53. John Fiske, *New France and New England* (Boston, 1902). R. LeBlant and R. Baudry, *Nouveaux Documents sur Champlain et Son Temps* (Ottowa, 1967). Samuel E. Morrison, *Samuel de Champlain* (Boston, 1972). K. F. Otterbein, "Why the Iroquois Won," *Ethnohistory* 11 (1964):56–63. Francis Parkman, *Pioneers of France in the New World* (Boston, 1865). Bruce Trigger, "Champlain Judged by his Indian Policy," *Anthropologica* 13 (1971): 85–114. Marcel Trudel, *Histoire de la Nouvelle-France* (Montreal, 1963-6), 2 v.

Chapter 3

E. Arber, *The Story of the Pilgrim Fathers* (London, 1897). William Bradford, *Of the Plymouth Plantation,* ed. S. E. Morrison (New York, 1959). Walter Burgess, *The Pastor of the Pilgrims* (New York, 1920). Kate Caffrey, *The Mayflower* (New York, 1974). William Davis, *Ancient Landmarks of Plymouth* (Boston, 1899). Peter Gay, *The Loss of Mastery* (Berkeley, 1966). George Langdon, *Pilgrim Colony* (New Haven, 1966). D. Plooj, *Pilgrim Fathers from a Dutch Point of View* (New York, 1932). Jesper Rosenmeir, "With My Own Eyes," *The American Puritan Imagination,* ed. S. Bercovitch (Cambridge, 1974), pp. 77–104. Simon Schama, *Embarrassment of Riches* (New York, 1987). Bradford Smith, *Bradford of Plymouth* (Philadelphia, 1951). George Willison, *Saints and Strangers* (New York, 1945). Alexander Young (ed.), *Chronicles of the Pilgrim Fathers* (Boston, 1844).

Chapter 4

T. H. Breen, *The Character of the Good Ruler* (New Haven, 1970); *Puritans and Adventurers* (Oxford, 1980). John Fiske, *The Beginnings of New England* (Boston, 1889). Stephen Foster, "New England and the Challenge of Heresy," *W&MQ* 38(1981):624–60. David Hall, *The Antinomian Controversy* (Middletown, 1968). Francis Jennings, *The Invasion of America* (Chapel Hill, 1975). Massachusetts Historical Society, *Winthrop Papers* (Boston, 1929), 6 v. Perry Miller, *Orthodoxy in Massachusetts* (Cambridge, Mass., 1933); *The New England Mind: The Seventeenth Century* (New York, 1939); *Errand into the Wilderness* (Cambridge, Mass., 1956), chs.1–3. Edmund Morgan, *The Puritan Dilemma* (Boston, 1958). Darrett Rutman, *Winthrop's Boston* (Chapel Hill, 1965). William Simmons, "Cultural Bias in New England Puritan's Perception of Indians," *W&MQ* 38(1981)56–72. Alden Vaughan, *New England Frontier* (New York, 1979). Robert Winthrop, *Life and Letters of John Winthrop* (Boston, 1869), 2 v. Larzer Ziff, *Puritanism in America* (New York, 1973).

Chapter 5

James Axtell, *The Invasion Within* (Oxford, 1985). Lucien Campeau, *La Mission des Jesuites chez les Hurons* (Rome, 1987). Joseph Donnelly, *Jean de Brébeuf* (Chicago, 1975). T. Grassman, "Thérèse Oionhaton," *DCB* 1:523–4. George Hunt, *The Wars of the Iroquois* (Madison, 1960). Marie de l'Incarnation, *Word from New France*, tr. J. Marshall (Toronto, 1967). Wilfrid and Elsie Jury, *Sainte Marie among the Hurons* (Toronto, 1949). Nathan Knowles, "The Torture of Captives . . . ," *PASP* 82(1940):151–225. James Moore, *Indian and Jesuit* (Chicago, 1982). Francis Parkman, *The Jesuits in North America* (Boston, 1867). Gabriel Sagard, *The Long Voyage to the . . . Hurons*, ed. G. Wrong (Toronto, 1939). Francois Talbot, *Saint among Hurons* (New York, 1949). Reuben Thwaites (ed.), *The Jesuit Relations* (Cleveland, 1896–1901), 73 v. Bruce Trigger, *The Children of Aataentsic* (Montreal, 1976), 2 v.

Chapter 6

Van Cleaf Bachman, *Peltries or Plantations* (Baltimore, 1969). Stellan Dahlgren and Hans Norman, *The Rise and Fall of New Sweden* (Uppsala, 1988). Richard Dunn, *Puritans and Yankees* (Princeton, 1962). John Fiske, *The Dutch and Quaker Colonies in America* (Boston, 1899). Washington Irving, *History of New York* (New York, 1809). J. F. Jameson (ed.), *Narratives of New Netherlands* (New York, 1909). Albert Myers (ed.), *Narratives of . . . Delaware* (New York, 1909). E. B. O'Callahan and B. Fernow (eds.), *Documents Relative to the Colonial History . . . of New York* (Albany, 1856–87), 15 v. Oliver Rink, *Holland on the Hudson* (Ithaca, 1986). J. T. Scharf, *History of Delaware* (Philadelphia,1888), 2 v. Francois Talbot, *Saint among Savages* (New York, 1935). Allen Trealease, *Indian Affairs in Colonial New York* (Ithaca, 1960). Henri and Barbara Van Der Zee, *A Sweet and Alien Land* (New York, 1978).

Chapter 7

Charles Andrews (ed.), *Narratives of Insurrections* (New York, 1915). Bernard Bailyn, "Politics and Social Structure in Virginia," *Seventeenth Century America*, ed. J. M. Smith (Chapel Hill, 1969). Philip Bruce, *The Virginia Plutarch* (Chapel Hill, 1929), 2 v. Wesley Craven, *The Colonies in Transition* (New York, 1968). John Fiske, *Old Virginia and Her Neighbors* (Boston,

1897). Thomas Henry, *Wilderness Messiah* (New York, 1955). Robert Middlekauff, *Bacon's Rebellion* (Chicago, 1964). Edmund Morgan, *American Slavery, American Freedom* (New York, 1975). Richard Slotkin, *Regeneration Through Violence* (Middletown, 1973). P. A. W. Wallace, "Dekanawideh," *DCB* 1:253–55. Wilcomb Washburn, *The Governor and the Rebel* (Chapel Hill, 1957). Stephen Webb, *1676: The End of American Independence* (Cambridge, Mass., 1985). Thomas Wertenbaker, *Torchbearer of the Revolution* (Princeton, 1940).

Chapter 8

Alfred Bailey, *The Conflict of European and Eastern Algonkian Cultures* (Toronto, 1969). Jean Delanglez, *Some La Salle Journeys* (Chicago, 1938); *Frontenac and the Jesuits* (Chicago, 1939). Sylvie Dépatie et al., *Contributions à l'Étude du Régime Seigneurial Canadien* (Quebec, 1987). Sigmund Diamond, "Experiment in 'Feudalism,'" *W&MQ* 18(1961):3–34. W. J. Eccles, *Frontenac: Courtier Governor* (Toronto, 1959); *Canada Under Louis XIV* (Toronto, 1964). Pierre Goubert, *Louis XIV and Twenty Million Frenchmen* (New York, 1970). Richard Harris, *The Seigneurial System* (Madison, 1966). Francis Jennings, *The Ambiguous Iroquois Empire* (New York, 1984). Peter Moogk, "Reluctant Exiles: Emigrants from France in Canada before 1760," *W&MQ* 46(1989):463–505. Francis Parkman, *Count Frontenac and New France under Louis XIV* (Boston, 1877); *The Discovery of the Great West* (Boston, 1869). Jack Sosin, *English America and the Revolution of 1688* (Lincoln, 1982).

Chapter 9

Edwin Bronner, *William Penn's Holy Experiment* (New York, 1962). Mary Dunn, *William Penn* (Princeton, 1967). Mary and Richard Dunn (eds.), *The Papers of William Penn* (Philadelphia, 1981–7), 5 v; *The World of William Penn* (Philadelphia, 1986). Melvin Endy, *William Penn and the Early Quakers* (Princeton, 1973). Ronald Knox, *Enthusiasm* (Oxford, 1959). Albert Myers (ed.), *Narratives of Early Pennsylvania* (New York, 1912). Gary Nash, *Quakers and Politics* (Princeton, 1968). Catherine Peare, *William Penn* (Philadelphia, 1956). Jean Soderland, *William Penn and the Founding of Pennsylvania* (Philadelphia, 1983). Douglas Steere (ed.), *Quaker Spirituality* (New York, 1984). Frederick Tolles, *Meeting House and Counting House* (Chapel Hill, 1948). Michael Zuckerman (ed.), *Friends and Neighbors* (Philadelphia, 1982).

Chapter 10

J. B. Brebner, *New England's Outpost* (New York, 1927). A. H. Clark, *Acadia: the Geography of Early Nova Scotia* (Madison, 1968). James Hannay, *The History of Acadia* (St. John, 1879). Emile Lauvrière, *La Tragédie d'un Peuple* (Paris, 1924), 2 v. Max Lavelle, *The Diplomatic History of the Canadian Border, 1749–1763* (New Haven, 1940). Robert Pumilly, *L'Acadie Française* (Montreal, 1981); *L'Acadie Anglaise* (Montreal, 1983). George Rawlyk, *Nova Scotia's Massachusetts* (Montreal, 1978). John Reid, *Acadia, Maine and Nova Scotia* (Toronto, 1981). Robert Sauvageau, *Acadie: la Guerre de Cent Ans* (Paris, 1987). John Webster, *The Forts of Chignecto* (Shediae, 1930); *Acadia at the End of the Seventeenth Century* (Saint John, 1934). John Winslow, "Journal," *Nova Scotia Historical Society Collections* 3(1883):71–96.

Chapter 11

Harrison Bird, *Battle for a Continent* (New York, 1965). Randolphe Downes, *Council Fires on the Upper Ohio* (Pittsburgh, 1969). Allan Eckert, *Wilderness Empire* (Boston, 1969). John Fiske, *New France and New England* (New York, 1902). Lawrence Gipson, *British Empire Before the American Revolution* (New York, 1939–46), v. 4–6. Richard Hofstadter, *America at 1750* (New York, 1971). Francis Jennings, *Empire of Fortune* (New York, 1988). Donald Kent, *The French Invasion of Western Pennsylvania* (Harrisburg, 1954). Francis Parkman, *A Half Century of Conflict* (Boston, 1892). Arthur Quinn, "Meditating Tacitus," *Quarterly Journal Speech* 70 (1984): 53–68. Dale Van Evry, *Forth to the Wilderness* (New York, 1961). Justin Winsor, "The Struggle for the Great Valleys of North America," *Narrative and Critical History of America*, v. 5 (Boston, 1887), 483–622. John Woolman, *The Journal*, intro. by John G. Whittier (Boston 1872).

Chapter 12

E. R. Adair, "The Military Reputation of . . . Wolfe," *Annual Report Canadian Historical Association 1936.* Henri Casgrain, *Wolfe and Montcalm* (Toronto, 1905). Arthur Doughty and G. W. Parmelee (eds.), *The Siege of Quebec . . .* (Quebec, 1901), 6 v. Guy Frégault, *Canada: The War of Conquest*, M. Cameron trans. (Toronto, 1969). Lawrence Gipson, *British Empire before the American Revolution* (New York, 1949–54) v. 7–9. Edward Hamilton, *Adventure in the Wilderness* (Norman, 1964). Gustave Lanctot, *Histoire du Canada . . . 1713–63* (Montreal, 1964). André Lichtenberger, *Montcalm et la Tragédie Canadienne* (Paris, 1934). Francis Parkman, *Montcalm and Wolfe* (Boston, 1888). C. P. Stacey, *Quebec 1759* (Toronto, 1959). George Stanley, *New France: The Last Phase* (Toronto, 1968). Ian Steele, *Betrayals: Fort William Henry and the "Massacre"* (New York, 1990).

Abbreviations

DCB	Dictionary of Canadian Biography
PAPS	Proceedings of the American Philosophical Society
W&MQ	The William and Mary Quarterly

INDEX

✣

About the Author

Arthur Quinn was born and received his early education in northern California. After further studies at Princeton and Cambridge universities, he joined in 1970 the faculty of the University of California at Berkeley, where he still teaches. He is the author of six previous books, including *Audiences and Intentions,* a textbook, and *Figures of Speech,* which was a selection of the Book-of-the-Month Club. He is currently at work on a narrative about Gold Rush California and the coming of the American Civil War, and a collection of his essays.